Kent L. Steckmesser
Associate Professor of History
California State College at Los Angeles

McGraw-Hill Book Company
New York St. Louis San Francisco
London Toronto Sydney

The Westward Movement: A Short History

The Westward Movement:

A Short History

*Frontispiece: Governor Leland Stanford's
"special train" meeting a westbound wagon
train at the Great Salt Lake, May 8, 1869 -
two days before the Last Spike Ceremony.
(Courtesy of the Southern Pacific Railroad.)*

*The maps on pages 37, 61, 140, 238, 352,
and 361 are reproduced with some adaptation
from Plates 38, 40, 62, 114, 115, 141, 142,
and 143 of Atlas of American History
by permission of Charles Scribner's Sons.
Copyright 1943 Charles Scribner's Sons.*

The Westward Movement: A Short History

Printed in the United States of America.

Library of Congress catalog card number: 68-55275

1234567890   PEPE   754321069

60915

Preface

This book is a concise history of the Westward movement in America from 1607 to 1890. It is designed as a basic text for an undergraduate course in westward movement, and as supplementary reading in social history, American studies, and the Western aspects of general American history. The interests of the general or nonacademic reader have also been kept in mind throughout. Since the history is written from a humanistic point of view, emphasis has been placed on biography, social institutions, and folkways rather than on strictly economic and political developments. Important ideas, such as the "Northwest Passage" to the Orient or "Manifest Destiny," have also been carefully examined. Much effort has been made to record all the essential facts of those great internal migrations that shaped the course of American civilization.

The space limitations of a short narrative have not permitted any extended discussion of the Frederick Jackson Turner thesis concerning the significance of the American frontier. The author's point of view is neo-Turnerian; the basic thesis is accepted along with many of the major modifications suggested by scholars in recent years. Some of the important critical literature on Turner is listed in the bibliography for the last chapter, and these works should be consulted for a thorough study of frontier theory. The text itself is based upon the most recent research in Western history, and the bibliographies for each chapter list the most current key books and articles available at the time of publication.

Most of the work on the manuscript was done at the Henry E. Huntington Library in San Marino, California. The author is deeply indebted to the staff members there, particularly Mary Isabel Fry and Ann Hyder. A considerable amount of research was also done at Stanford University and Yale University, and the author wishes to thank the librarians at those institutions for making their facilities available to an inquisitive stranger. Professor Bayrd Still of

New York University not only made invaluable comments on portions of the manuscript, but also extended every courtesy to the writer, who was a visiting faculty member at the university.

The author has been influenced and inspired by the work of other historians of the American West, a field which has yielded some excellent writing. It is hoped that this narrative, too, captures some of the drama of an important phase of our national history.

Kent Ladd Steckmesser

Table of Contents

Maps

The Westward Movement: A Short History

I. The Seaboard Frontier

The English gentlemen who founded Jamestown in the spring of 1607 were woefully unprepared for the North American wilderness. Their knowledge of Shakespearean drama was of little use in solving the gritty problems of survival in an alien land. Though they planted the first permanent English colony in the New World, and thus started an American pioneering tradition, their history is a catalog of classic errors.

Jamestown The town itself was located some 30 miles up the James River, which was thought to be an eastern outlet of the Northwest Passage to the Orient. The site was low and swampy, an islandlike peninsula picked for defense against attack. It was also a fit breeding ground for the diseases which took the lives of sixty-seven of the original one hundred and five colonists during the first year. Yet so fertile was the soil that attempts to grow wheat yielded only towering stalks with no grain. This meant that the settlers were dangerously dependent upon the supply ships from England, and when these failed to arrive on schedule the result was a "starving time." Even at that, the men spent most of their time looking for gold rather than food. The joint-stock company which financed the original three-ship expedition, the Virginia Company of London, was a profit-seeking enterprise. They expected their colonists to discover gold and silver mines that would rival those of the Spanish in Central America. This was an unwise expectation, considering the Englishmen's ignorance of wilderness techniques. The home office also saddled the hapless colonists with a thirteen-man governing council whose constant bickerings imperiled the whole experiment.

One of the councilors was Captain John Smith, whose middle-class origins made him an inferior in the eyes of the aristocrats. Yet Smith played important roles in frontier history, literature, and legend. He saved the infant

3

settlement from extinction by seizing virtually dictatorial power as president of the council in 1608. He forced the dwindling band to dig wells for pure water, to erect a stockade, and to trade for corn with the Indians. He also led exploring expeditions up the nearby rivers and around the shores of "Chisapeack" Bay. Though these efforts led to his recall, they establish him as America's first frontier hero.

Smith's book about his experiences, published in England as *A True Relation* (1608), is the first piece of native American historical writing. He later published several other volumes, all of which made clear that as a lover he had no equal. The most familiar story is the legend of a romance with Pocahontas. The Indian princess allegedly saved Captain John from her father's chopping block, and "so prevailed upon him that I was safely conducted to Jamestown." Actually, Pocahontas was an uninhibited lass of twelve, who liked to perform handstands and cartwheels before the astonished Englishmen at the stockade. Years after Smith's departure she did in fact marry an Englishman, the tobacco planter John Rolfe. But though Smith lied, no one can really blame him for introducing the charming Indian heroine and the popular girl-saves-boy theme to American literature.

Fortunately for the English, the 5,000 local Indians under Powhatan were generally friendly. There were occasional armed clashes, but coexistence was the order of the day. Indian corn kept the emaciated pioneers alive during the horrors of the starving time (1608 to 1611), when some of the "poorer sort" turned to cannibalism. Indian cloaks of animal skins kept them warm. And that standard opiate, Indian tobacco, became the economic foundation of the Virginia frontier.

John Rolfe set out the first carefully nurtured tobacco plants in 1612. So luxuriant was the crop that the "Jamestown Weed" soon became the pre-ferred smoke in England. King James detested tobacco, describing it as "loath-some to the eye and hatefull to the Nose," but the need for customs revenue proved stronger than his conscience. And its proponents claimed that smoking would heal gout, cure hangovers, and reduce hunger. It was a medicine which "purgeth superfluous fleame and other grosse humors . . . whereby their bodies are notably preserved in health, and know not many greevous diseases where-withall wee in England are oftentimes afflicted." So the Virginians had an export crop, and the tobacco frontier began to move up those broad, pine-bordered rivers which bore names symbolic of both the familiar (James and York) and the strange (Rappahannock and Potomac).

The Virginia Company scrapped the committee system in 1611 and sent over stern-visaged Sir Thomas Dale as deputy governor. Dale administered the expansion of the colony under its 1609 charter from the King, which prom-ised Virginia all land "two hundred miles north and south of Point Comfort, and lying from the Sea Coast . . . up into the land throughout from Sea to Sea, west and northwest." Such sea-to-sea grants were customary in the seventeenth century, although the monarchs who gave them knew little of North American geography. When Charles II granted Connecticut a charter in 1662 for "all land west to the South Seas," he ignored the fact that this claim overlapped Virginia's.

Dale enforced discipline in the colony, including daily attendance at Anglican church services, with such penalties as flogging and branding. "Complaints were repaied with stripes." Yet even he was unable to curb the democratizing effect of the New World environment. The commoners who were brought over to grow food and tobacco for the company soon demanded land of their own. Millions of acres of virgin soil lay to the west; it was not right that the company possess it all. Dale began to grant 100-acre tracts, known as the "Old Hundreds," to the more energetic colonists. Additional grants were made as a bonus for successful cultivation. Landownership promised to turn hangdog Englishmen into proud Americans.

As the colonists moved up the rivers, they pressed more heavily upon the Indian lands. The close proximity of the two races presented a volatile situation throughout the history of the frontier. A script at this point would call for a "massacre" (if the Indians win) or a "war" (if the white men win). Sure enough, the explosion came shortly after the death of old Powhatan. The war leaders who replaced him struck with the usual Indian suddenness on a rainy March day in 1622. So swift was the onslaught that 357 settlers fell under clubs and arrows before they could reach the forts at Jamestown or Henrico. The seesaw battles that raged for 2 years following the Massacre of 1622 gave the English their first real taste of Indian fighting. This was a strange warfare, fought not by disciplined professionals during the daylight hours but by civilians at all hours of the day or night. European military techniques, like European customs generally, had to change in the American wilderness.

Punishment of the savages, by means of "marches" which destroyed their villages and crops, cleared the way for further progress up the tidewater rivers. The ocean tides surged inland as far as 80 miles, and seagoing ships could follow them to the wharves of the tobacco plantations. The steady movement west halted only at the "fall line," where tumbling cataracts stopped navigation. Access to the land was made easier by the purchase of "headrights." These were warrants which originated as a 50-acre bonus to wealthy planters for each servant and member of family that they brought to America. Although Virginia authorities tried to control all land purchases, headrights were freely sold by ship captains and thus became the unofficial medium for land sales.

By midcentury, then, Virginia was firmly anchored in the New World. Her 9,000 inhabitants were fairly well fed, clothed, and governed. The King had revoked the Virginia Company charter in 1625 and made Virginia a royal or crown colony, thus guaranteeing to the settlers all the sacred "rights of Englishmen." The trial-and-error lessons of the pioneer period were useful to settlers in Virginia's sister tobacco colony of Maryland, planted on the east side of Chesapeake Bay in 1634 by Lord Baltimore as a refuge for Catholics. A firm foundation had now been built for the further westward expansion of English civilization.

Pilgrims and Puritans

Even as the Virginians braved Indian attack to establish "particular plantations" along the Tidewater, another English frontier was forming some 400 miles to the north. The Pilgrims who landed at Plymouth in 1620 came not for gold and silver but for religious salvation. They were dissenters from the established Church of England (which was Anglican or Episcopal), claiming that its elaborate rituals and luxury-loving bishops made it "impure." They demanded that the church be purified by a return to the original purpose of God as found in the Bible. For their effrontery in pressing such demands, they were persecuted in England and then exiled to Holland. When tales of the New World reached them at Leyden, they decided to migrate to Virginia.

When the *Mayflower* rounded Cape Cod in late November after one of the most famous voyages in American history, the migrants found themselves far north of Virginia. Their maps told them that they were in a region which John Smith, who had explored there in 1614, had labeled "New England." Since they were beyond established government, the little band of one hundred Pilgrims drew up a typical "squatters'" agreement: the Mayflower Compact. They promised "for the glorie of God and the advancement of the Christian faith" to "covenant and combine ourselves into a civil body politick." Frontiersmen for hundreds of years would resort to similar compacts in such situations.

Faith in God was needed in that savage land. Between the alternating conceptions of America as Earthly Paradise or Howling Wilderness, the Pilgrims chose the latter. "What could they see but a hideous and desolate wilderness, full of wilde beasts and wilde men?" asked Governor William Bradford. Fortunately one of the wild men turned out to be the half-tame Squanto, whom Captain Smith had taken back to England as a slave but who had been returned by a trading ship the year before. Squanto gave the settlers some corn and taught them how to grow more, but even so, hunger and disease took half the original party that first winter. Yet none of the survivors wanted to give up. The Pilgrims' courage explains one reason why so many Americans have been eager to trace their ancestry back to Plymouth, and why the *Mayflower* has become the most crowded ship in American history.

The rocky coast and frigid climate of Massachusetts were fully as formidable as the Pilgrim records indicate. There was some hardscrabble farming about Plymouth, but the colonists soon found that their best hope lay in fishing and furs. Trading for the latter (corn and wampum for beaver pelts) took the Pilgrims as far north as the Kennebec River in Maine. Within a few years, cattle were imported to be pastured on the marshes, private landownership replaced the archaic communal system, and the hardy pioneers began "planting" new towns to the north and west.

In the north the Pilgrims were soon joined by those iron-willed Puritans of the Massachusetts Bay Company. Like their brethren at Plymouth, the Puritans criticized the Church of England and desired to establish their own Congregational system. Because it was a much larger and better-educated group, it was inevitable that the Boston colony would absorb the smaller towns to the south.

The Bay Colony was ostensibly a trading enterprise, but actually the company charter was a facade masking the religious plans of the Puritans. The Puritan leaders, such as the Oxford-educated governor, John Winthrop, were determined to establish a Bible commonwealth. If plays, dancing, and hilarious jokes were not sanctioned by Scripture, then the state must root them out. These leaders were known as saints or "the elect," since under Calvinist doctrine their unblemished conduct was evidence that they would be spared the torments of hell in the afterlife. The saints and the Congregational ministers together administered all laws, civil and religious. The American tradition of separation of church and state has few roots in Massachusetts Bay.

The first contingent of 200 settlers landed at Salem in 1629. But the "great migration" which began the next year was directed at the more commodious Boston Bay to the south. Here natural selection operated among the unseasoned Englishmen. Two hundred out of two thousand were carried away by sickness and starvation the first winter. Yet some praised the rigorous climate. Said Francis Higginson: "Many that have been weak and sickly in old England, by coming hither have been thoroughly healed and grown healthful and strong. For here is an extraordinary clear and dry air that is of a most healing nature to all such as are of a cold, melancholy, phlegmatic, rheumatic temper of the body." Higginson died within a year after penning these lines.

Despite the hardships, the Puritan migration continued, bringing over more than 20,000 people in the years up to 1643. Only one-fifth of these were church members ("freemen") entitled to vote and hold office. The rest were refugees from high land rents, the restrictive guild system, and a multiplicity of other oppressions. The combined population flowed westward to found Cambridge, Watertown, and Concord. Soon the human tide spilled over the boundary lines laid down in the King's charter: 3 miles north of the Merrimac River to 3 miles south of the Charles, from sea to sea. But by ingenious manipulation of geography, the ambitious Bay authorities stretched these boundaries to include most of New England from Connecticut to Maine.

The Puritan oligarchy was determined to control this westward movement. They did so through the system of "town planting." The Legislature (General Court) granted townsites to proprietors whose religious and political views were judged to be sufficiently orthodox. The proprietors agreed to build roads, divide the lands, hire a minister, and bring in new families. Their reward would be complete control of the undivided land in the township until it was all sold. Settlers who moved to the new town would be assigned a home lot, farming strips in the "upland," and use of the community woodlot and pasture.

This paternalistic system was well adapted to conditions in New England. It promised a close-knit community life, protection from the Indians, and security of land titles. This last feature made the Puritan frontier sharply different from the South, where indiscriminate location led to overlapping claims (shingling) and years of court litigation. Also, the family-size farms of New England were more congenial to village life than were the extensive and widely separated plantations of Virginia.

The strong individualism of the Puritans was thus balanced by a sense of community responsibility. All men shared in military drill, work of the roads, and maintenance of that patch of green in the center of the town known as the common. The town meeting became a familiar institution, and though dominated by proprietors in the early years, it later became the foundation of grass-roots democracy in New England. The whole system worked well through several generations, until the proprietors became absentee landholders in Boston. Their grip on the undivided lands and their lack of concern for the individual towns spelled trouble. When the General Court began selling whole townsites to absentee speculators in the 1720s, many dissatisfied farmers joined the westward migration.

The ironhanded control of the Boston saints was displeasing to many even during the earliest years of the town-planting system. One of these was Roger Williams, a Congregational minister who agreed with 90 percent of the Puritan doctrine. His unique views of the Puritan destiny and of biblical interpretation, however, were regarded as subversive by the orthodox clergy. Although his devotion to freedom has been overstated, Williams did feel that civil matters (the "weeds") should be kept separate from religious life (the "garden"), and that the civil magistrate should not coerce religious dissenters. He also maintained that the Indians' consent should be obtained before the English—whose King really had no authentic title to it—moved onto their lands. For these heresies he was threatened with a forced return to England, where the lightest penalty for treason in denying the King's authority would be the loss of both ears. Valuing his conscience as well as his ears, Williams fled south in the winter of 1636 to the snow-burdened forests at the head of Narragansett Bay. Friendly Indians under Massasoit permitted Williams, and those who followed him in the next few years, to buy land and establish the little settlement of Providence. "Rogue's Island" was what the discomfited Bay Colony leaders called it, but the official name became "Rhode Island and the Providence Plantations."

Thomas Hooker was another minister who led pioneers west in 1636. His 100 followers, driving their cattle before them in typical frontier fashion, founded Hartford on the banks of the Connecticut River. Within a year 800 people were living in several towns along the river, governed by an unauthorized constitution called the Fundamental Orders of Connecticut. The document was based upon Hooker's belief that the "foundation of authority is laid in the free consent of the people." Such were the startling and dangerous doctrines that seemed to spring from the frontier environment and experience.

English Expansion

By 1650 English fur traders had started exploring the back country along the great arc from Connecticut to the Carolina border. The professional fur trader looms large in American colonial history. He is the vanguard in the cycle of frontier exploration and settlement, a cycle which usually reads: fur trader–cattleman–pioneer farmer–townsman. The traders made the initial contacts with the Indians, contributed valuable geographical information, and advanced the territorial claims of their nation.

William Pynchon was an early example of the type. He began trading along the streams of far-western Massachusetts in the 1630s. Isolated from Boston by hundreds of miles of wilderness, he founded a town and a profitable trading post at Springfield on the Connecticut. But westward expansion of the Puritans' fur-trading frontier was restricted by the limited supply of beaver in the region, the north-south direction of the principal rivers, and Dutch control of the Hudson Valley. Fortunately, the pioneer farmers followed the traders so closely that territorial gains were soon consolidated, and prosperity could be based on small farming and handicrafts.

Further south the Virginia traders began probing the Piedmont, that region of rolling foothills which lay beyond the "fall line." In 1650 Captain Abraham Wood, under the patronage of the royal governor-cum-land speculator Sir William Berkeley, led a seven-man party southwestward to the falls of the Roanoke. Other explorers followed in the same direction, and by the 1660s there was a lively trade in furs with the Indians along the eastern slopes of the Blue Ridge Mountains. Some of the explorers suffered from various combinations of optical illusion, wishful thinking, and outright prevarication. German-born John Lederer in 1669 went all the way to the top of the Blue Ridge, where with typical frontier exaggeration he claimed to have looked back and seen the Atlantic Ocean. He also told of savages with silver tomahawks and a fondness for peacock feathers. More reliable adventurers made up the 1671 party under Thomas Batts and Robert Fallam, whom Captain Wood commissioned to find those rivers on the other side of the mountains which might lead to the South Sea. Passing over the formidable Appalachian barrier, they found a river (and named it the New) whose slight westward-flowing current convinced them that it led to the Northwest Passage.

In these same years another English colony was planted south of Virginia. The promoter-politician Lord Ashley and seven other proprietors received a King's grant in 1663 to colonize between the 31st and 36th parallels, from sea to sea. Included within this patent for "Carolina" was a tiny community at Albemarle Sound, established in 1653 as a buffer against Spaniards and Indians. But Ashley planned a larger settlement even further south. His ambitions were finally realized in 1670, when 150 colonists were landed at the mouth of the Ashley River to found Charles Town. The outpost was only 250 miles from St. Augustine, "in the very chops of the Spaniards." Menaced by these European rivals and their Indian allies, the Carolina frontier advanced with glacial slowness during the next 30 years. But the very existence of the colony was a measure of English ambitions in North America.

Until 1664 the only obstacle to an unbroken English frontier from the Kennebec to the Ashley was the presence of the Dutch along the Hudson River. The New Netherland colony had originated in 1609. In that year, Henry Hudson, an English sea captain employed by the Dutch East India Company, had sailed up the great river which bears his name. Encountering some Iroquois chieftains, he entertained them so generously with wine and liquor "that they were all merrie and in the end one of them was drunke." Following up this contact in 1614, the company established a post at Fort Nassau (Albany), where Iroquois furs were exchanged for the usual knives, mirrors, guns, and "firewater."

Beginning in 1621 the Netherlands government attempted to encourage settlement in the region. Homes began to rise on the lower tip of "Mannahata" Island, which had been purchased from the Wappinger Indians for trinkets worth $24—"the greatest real estate bargain in American history." The principal community, New Amsterdam, was soon surrounded by such satellites as "Breukelyn" and "Haerlem." But colonization went slowly. New Netherland remained a trading colony, despite attempts to encourage agriculture through the offer of large estates known as "patroonships" and smaller ones called "bouweries." The sparse population spelled weakness in the face of the growing New England colony to the north.

A succession of hard-headed governors attempted to protect the Dutch fur-trading posts, which were spotted all the way from the Connecticut to the Delaware. They were successful on the latter river, where a miniscule Swedish community at Fort Christina (Wilmington) was overwhelmed in 1655. On the Connecticut they could not hold their ground, for Fort Good Hope (1633) was soon isolated from below by Fort Saybrook (1635), at the mouth of the river, and from above by Hartford and Springfield. Persistent English attempts to cut in on the Dutch-Iroquois trade along the Hudson also had to be blocked. All these efforts were in vain, however, for in 1664 Charles II sent an English fleet under Col. Richard Nicolls to annex New Netherland. The outmatched Hollanders were forced to surrender the colony, which Nicolls renamed in honor of the Duke of York. The bloodless conquest gave England control of the center of the eastern seaboard, as well as an alliance with the most powerful Indian confederation in North America.

The fur trade was the basis of the English-Iroquois alliance. The Iroquois served as middlemen between Albany and the "Far Indians" of the Great Lakes. This position enabled them to maintain their superiority over the other tribes in the eastern region. They were continually trying to extend their influence into the interior, since their survival depended upon so doing. The English for their part valued the alliance not only for the economic benefits of the fur trade but also because the Five Nations were, as Governor Thomas Dongan of New York put it, "the bulwark between us and the French and all other Indians." But as the beaver supply in their own area became depleted, the Iroquois started poaching on the hunting grounds of tribes to the west, and intertribal wars followed.

The Crisis Year: 1676

Before the English colonies could turn to further expansion of their New World domain, they were wracked by internal convulsions. Insolent Indians and unruly frontiersmen almost shattered the still-fragile colonial structures of both New England and Virginia in the crisis year of 1676. Puritan hostility toward the Indians caused trouble in the north. The New Englanders' initial fascination with the savages turned to contempt as the Indians' sloth and immorality became apparent. Attempts at Christianizing them, exemplified by John Eliot's translation of the Bible into Algonquin, met with only moderate success or encouragement. But political and territorial pressures as well as racial hostility lay at the root of the conflict. In the 1637 Pequot War the tribe of that name was virtually exterminated because it stood in the path of English expansion along the Mystic River in Connecticut. The horrible lesson was not lost upon the adjacent tribes, and it was a full generation before the next bloodbath.

In the early 70s the stiff-necked proprietors at Plymouth began to harass the neighboring Narragansett and Wampanoag tribes. Indians were fined for hunting on Sunday, and sentenced to hard labor for drinking the rum offered them by sly farmers. Leader of the Wampanoags was King Philip (Metacomet), whose pride was viewed by the English as insolence toward his betters. He was forced to pay an annual tribute and to acknowledge his subservience to the Plymouth government. Such humiliations were practically an invitation to war.

The execution of three Wampanoags convicted of murder by an English court drove the young warriors of the tribe beyond the breaking point. Their initial assaults were directed at Swansea (Rhode Island) late in June of 1675. The hastily assembled English militia blundered through swamp and forest, "their feet continually shackled with the Roots spreading every way in those boggy Woods," while Philip feverishly built up his alliances. The failure of an attempt to trap Philip and his forces at Pocasset Swamp southeast of Providence meant that a long war was in the offing.

The militia were brave enough, but they were hampered by lack of experience in forest warfare and by intercolonial rivalries (particularly between Massachusetts and Rhode Island) that prevented any coordinated military effort. So town after town along the Connecticut River, in Massachusetts, and in Rhode Island went up in smoke, their citizens dead or captured. Deerfield, Northfield, and Lancaster were wiped out by what the colonists considered to be the "howling agents of Satan." They attacked Lancaster on a frosty February morning in 1676, firing the houses and forcing the hapless residents outside. "No sooner were we out of the House but my Brother in Law fell down dead . . . the bulletts flying thick, one went through my side, and the same (as would seem) through the bowels and hand of my dear Child in arms. One of my elder Sisters Children, named William, had then his leg broken, which the Indians perceiving, they knockt him on head. Thus were we butchered by those merciless Heathen, standing amazed, with the blood running down to our heels." The author of these lines was Mrs. Mary Rowlandson, who was taken prisoner by the heathen but who returned safely to publish one of the earliest specimens of the "Indian Captivity" narrative.

At its height the Indian offensive was carried to the very gates of Boston. In April 500 painted warriors attacked Sudbury, only 17 miles west of the Puritan metropolis. But then the Indian tide suddenly ebbed. The New Englanders had a 2 to 1 edge in population, as well as the material benefits of a more technically advanced civilization. Their ignorance of Indian fighting techniques was soon corrected by the employment of friendly Mohegan scouts under Uncas, long-time tribal enemy of King Philip. Destruction of the enemy food supplies seemed to have been a more decisive factor than military victories, however, although the English did win important battles like the Great Swamp Fight in 1675. Finally in August of 1676 "that monster" King Philip was himself slain. His head was displayed in Boston as a gruesome reminder of Satan's plot against the English Israel.

King Philip's War shook the foundations of the United Colonies of New England, and also weakened their attempts to remain independent of the Crown. Two-thirds of the towns were damaged or totally destroyed in the holocaust. One-tenth of the adult males in Massachusetts were killed or captured, and the toll was equally heavy in Rhode Island and Connecticut. The widows of the towns found little consolation in the fact that the conflict had cleared the way for white settlement of all of southern New England.

Indian troubles also caused a crisis in Virginia in 1676. As the plantations moved further up the rivers draining into Chesapeake Bay, conflict with the Susquehannocks and other tribes was inevitable. When a series of assassinations on both sides finally brought war, the upriver planters demanded an aggressive campaign of extermination. Sir William Berkeley, seventy-year-old royal Governor of Virginia, favored a more conservative policy. He recommended that "fforts or houses of defense should be built att the heads of Rivers for resort of the souldiers." This fort-building solution was bitterly criticized by the frontiersmen, who insisted that a large mobile force was better than these "useless fabricks." The planters believed that Berkeley was protecting the "Darling Indians" to safeguard his monopoly of the beaver trade. Other complaints about the Governor's administration were soon being voiced, and by May 1, 1676, local resistence to the Governor's policies—"Bacon's Rebellion"—was under way.

Nathaniel Bacon was a twenty-nine-year-old Cambridge graduate and tobacco planter from Henrico County. Though fairly well-to-do and a member of the Governor's Council, he had the kind of personal magic that attracts men from all classes. Indeed, Berkeley charged that he had "none about him but the lowest of the people." Bacon quickly became the leader of back-country farmers who were feeling the effects of a 15-year decline in tobacco prices. His supporters also had a number of specific political grievances: Taxes (paid in tobacco) were too high, and were laid in a discriminatory fashion which favored the Governor's pets; sheriffs and other officials were kept in office year after year, and held plural offices; only property holders could elect the Assembly, but this was a right which should belong to all freemen.

In solving the Indian problem, the young rebel took matters into his own hands. With 300 volunteers he marched north, attacking both friendly and hostile Indians in the approved frontier manner. One hundred fifty Susquehannocks and Occaneechee fell before the militia's muskets. As a result, Berkeley on May 10 branded Bacon a traitor and a rebel for usurping the Governor's prerogatives. Bacon and his "rabble" thereupon marched to Jamestown, forcing Berkeley to flee across Chesapeake Bay to the Accomac Peninsula. The Assembly was then packed with Bacon's supporters, who passed the "June Laws." These laws lightened the tax burden, limited terms of office, and introduced a more militant Indian policy. Bacon tramped west to attack some more friendly Indians, but returned to Jamestown in September when he learned that Berkeley was raising an army to suppress him. He drove Berkeley out of the capital city, and then burned it to the ground in retaliation for the Governor's resistance.

The rebellion fell apart after Bacon died of the "Bloody Flux" in October, for none of his associates had a comparable talent for leadership. As soon as Berkeley was returned to power he relentlessly pursued his enemies. Twenty-three rebels were tried and hanged until a royal investigating commission relieved the old Governor early in 1677. But the Baconist doctrines had an influence outside Virginia. The leaders and frontier followers of Coode's Rebellion in neighboring Maryland during the 1680s were called "rank Baconists." Such movements were the earliest of many sectional conflicts that would mark the westward movement for the next hundred years and more. Men who lived close to the green wall of the wilderness and all its hidden terrors quickly developed attitudes strikingly different from those of the politically powerful aristocrats who lived in the coastal towns. These differences would become greater as the frontier moved further west.

Even as the English colonists struggled to quiet domestic crises along the seaboard, their European rivals were marking gains along other New World frontiers. The English envisioned themselves as playing the leading role in North America. But other actors kept rushing in to disrupt the play, shouting in their strange tongues that they had the major role. France and Spain were competing with England for control of the continent. The prizes were land, precious metals, religious converts, a Northwest Passage, and national prestige. The dominant philosophy in the European courts was "mercantilism," which proclaimed that colonies were both source and symbol of national power. They would yield the raw materials and the gold bullion that were essential to ultimate victory in the international competition.

The Spanish Frontier

Spain got off to a head start in the race. The West Indian islands which Columbus had discovered in 1492 became the jumping off point for exploration to the west. From them Cortez the *conquistador* launched the epical campaign which took him to the Aztec capital and the heartland of Mexico in 1519. And from Puerto Rico in 1513 sailed Juan Ponce de Leon, seeking profits and fame. He discovered a great low-lying peninsula, whose rich vegetation and profusion of flowers suggested the name "Florída." Ponce de Leon never found the Fountain of Youth, sad to tell, which the Indians had told him lay in the interior. But he did explore both coasts of the peninsula from the St. John's River around to Tampa Bay.

In 1528 an elaborate 300-man expedition under one-eyed Panfilio de Narvaez landed at Tampa, eager for gold and silver. Second in command was Cabeza de Vaca, whose *Relacion* (1542) is the journal of an incredible odyssey across 6,000 miles of land and sea from Florida to Arizona. We see through his eyes the fruitless march to the Apalachen Indian villages, Narvaez' cowardice and desertion of his troops, and the terrors of Indian attack and shipwreck. De Vaca and a handful of survivors drifted across the Gulf of Mexico on homemade barges, eventually landing at Galveston Bay. They lived as slaves among the Texas Indians, subsisting on roots and prickly pear. Finally de Vaca gained the reputation of a medicine man, his chief cure being the pronouncement of an "Ave Maria" over his patients, and in this guise made his way west to the native villages along the upper Rio Grande and the headwaters of the Gila. In 1536, as one of only four survivors of the original expedition, he reached the Spanish settlements in Sinaloa. "The hardships I endured in this journeying business were long to tell—peril and privation, storms and frost, which often took me alone in the wilderness. By the unfailing grace of God our Lord I came forth from them all."

The report which de Vaca filed with the King belied his own experience. The tale was all of gold and emeralds rather than of the flea-infested Indian villages which he had actually seen. Perhaps his monarch's insistence that gold mines on the Mexican scale must exist in the North American interior warped de Vaca's own memories. In any case the King commissioned young Hernando de Soto to lead the next Florida expedition. A well-equipped party of 600 Spaniards left Cuba in the spring of 1539, and began their journey of conquest at Charlotte Bay. For 4 years the expedition wandered through the interior, using the Narvaez techniques of enslaving local Indian chiefs to act as guides. De Soto went north to the headwaters of the Savannah River in Carolina, and westward through Alabama to the great Mississippi River, which he was the first European to explore. The party traveled up the Arkansas River and then south into Texas, before coasting down to the Gulf and then back to Mexico. Half of the men, including de Soto himself, perished from disease and Indian attack. This castastrophe halted Spanish exploration of the interior for many years.

Yet Spain had to protect her sea lanes along the east coast of Florida from English and French marauders. The great walled city-fort of St. Augustine (1565) was the answer. It became the first permanent white settlement in North America, and the center of Spanish political and military power in the southeast. Other forts (presidios) were then planted as far north as Port Royal Sound in present-day South Carolina, but they were not successful. Vicious Indians, inadequate food supplies, and tropical disease plagued the outposts. The word "mosquito" is of Spanish origin, and the luckless *soldados* became all too familiar with the disease-carrying pests.

Pacification of the hostile Indians seemed to be a job ready-made for the Catholic missionaries. The missionary's basic function was to convert and civilize the savage. If the job was well done, the Christianized Indians would become valuable allies of Spain. They would, in fact, people the frontiers of this small European nation which lacked the population to stock colonies with its own citizens. Thus while the mission was primarily a religious institution, it also served important political purposes.

In Florida the missionary assignment went to the Franciscans—disciples of St. Francis of Assissi—who built their stations on the Georgia coastal islands and among the Apalachen villages on the Gulf of Mexico. They learned to gulp down the Indians' favorite food of alligator meat, and patiently taught farming as well as Christianity. Indian uprisings near the turn of the century wiped out many of the missions and brought sudden death to the friars. But the persistent Franciscans plunged back into the wilderness. By 1650 they had tamed 30,000 savages on the Florida-Georgia frontier, and had given Spain a buffer against the aggressive Englishmen to the north.

French Expansion

Meanwhile another Catholic power was making a determined bid for control of the North American heartland. The story of French exploration properly begins with Jacques Cartier, who in 1534 and again in 1535 sailed up the only large river which flows from the interior to the Atlantic Ocean: the St. Lawrence. Control of this waterway gave the French direct access to the interior lakes and the Mississippi. Cartier navigated his slender craft as far as the site of Montreal, where fearsome rapids (saults) barred the way to the South Sea. He wrote enthusiastic reports about "Canada," urging Francis I to start colonies there for the greater glory of the kingdom. But it was almost three-quarters of a century before France, torn by religious wars at home, could turn to New World colonization.

In 1603 a towering figure of French exploration appeared on the St. Lawrence. Samuel de Champlain was a fur trader, explorer, and military captain. The trading post which he founded at the mouth of the Saguenay River, Tadoussac, was at a spot well known to French fishermen. Since the early years of the sixteenth century, cod fishermen from most of the European nations had been working off the coasts of "new-founde-land." As they went ashore to clean and salt their catch for shipment home, they began to acquire beaver skins from the Indians in return for knives and trinkets. The French soon saw the potential in this profitable business, and by the 1580s they were trading as far as the Saguenay. For better or for worse, fur trading was to become the economic basis of New France. Thin soil, a short growing season, and the feudal system of seigniorial land grants all discouraged extensive agriculture along the St. Lawrence.

Champlain got the King's permission to found a colony in Canada. In 1608 he picked a beautiful spot backed up against high bluffs overlooking the river, and Quebec was born. The tiny settlement became the center of the French fur trade and the base for Champlain's far-ranging explorations of the interior.

The tribes with whom the French originally traded for furs were the Algonquin-Huron-Montagnais bands which were scattered along the north bank of the river. Champlain, like the Frenchmen who followed him, was a sympathetic student of the Indian. He recorded their customs and folklore in his journals and in such books as *Des Sauvages* (1605). He also made effective use in his explorations of the Indians' birchbark canoe and of their intimate knowledge of the inland waterways. The price he had to pay for these benefits was military assistance to his allies in their eternal wars with the hated Iroquois. Thus on one trip, in 1609, he fired a shot that echoed through the American forests for the next century and a half.

In the summer of 1609 Champlain accompanied a Huron war party south to the shores of a long lake to which he gave his own name. There he encountered an Iroquois band—the Mohawks—upon whom he demonstrated the superiority of the white man's weapons. "Our Indians . . . put me ahead some twenty yards, and I marched on until I was within thirty yards of the enemy, who as soon as they caught sight of me halted and gazed at me and I at them. When I saw them make a move to draw their bows upon us, I took aim with my arquebus and shot straight at one of the three chiefs, and with this shot two fell to the ground and one of their companions was wounded who died thereof a little later. I had put four bullets into my arquebus." As the terrified Iroquois fled, the triumphant Hurons harvested scalps and prisoners. The captives were subjected to all the customary tortures, which gave them a splendid opportunity to display their contempt for pain. Firebrands were applied to all parts of the body, fingernails were torn off, and sinews were ripped out by main force until the victim passed to the Happy Hunting Ground. But the fleeing Mohawks had long memories. They took back to their fellow tribesmen of the Five Nations (Seneca, Cayuga, Onondaga, Oneida) the news of French treachery. Iroquois hatred prevented the French from ever advancing south of the Mohawk River Valley, and may have cost them victory in the struggle for North America.

Champlain also led several trips to the west, seeking the rumored route to the Western Sea. In 1615, piloted by Huron guides, he paddled up the Ottawa River, portaged to Lake Nipissing, and made the discovery of Lake Huron at Georgian Bay. This was his last major trip, but until his death in 1635 he continued to send young protégés out from Quebec on similar probes. In 1634 Jean Nicolet went up the Ottawa and as far west as Green Bay on Lake Michigan, where he put on a damask robe in anticipation of his meeting with the expected Chinese. The Winnebago Indians who greeted him did not look like Chinese, however, nor did they know of any "Northwest Passage." Nonetheless, the French *voyageurs* would keep on searching for that fabled route.

From 1625 on, the "black robes" of the Society of Jesus became important agents of French expansion. With their customary zeal, they started planting missions along the interior lakes, naming them for the revered Catholic saints. St. Ignace at the strategic straits of Mackinac, and St. Joseph at the foot of Lake Michigan, were key stations. To the Indians whom they attempted to Christianize, the Jesuits were alternately gods or devils. The particular status depended upon the accidents of famine, pestilence, and warfare. When Indian fortunes declined, the strange foreigners with their crucifix and magic writing became scapegoats and targets for the tribesmen's fury. They were cast into the fires, and often eaten for supper. The *Jesuit Relations,* a 60-volume recitation of missionary accomplishments, is sprinkled with accounts of these martyrdoms.

The Jesuits were also victims when the Iroquois War broke out in 1648. Thousands of Mohawk and Seneca warriors crossed the St. Lawrence to invade Huron lands as far north as Georgian Bay. Armed with Dutch guns, they smashed the Huron Confederacy and sent the terrified survivors fleeing to northern Wisconsin. The resident Fathers in the Huron villages were tortured and burned. The vulnerable French lifeline to the interior, along the Ottawa River-Lake Nipissing route, was severed. If New France was to survive, it would have to be restored and then protected. Jean Talon finally secured the route upon becoming the King's Intendant (personal representative) in 1665. He sent into New York a thousand-man army, which burned enemy towns and crops with such efficiency that the Iroquois pleaded for peace. Talon then licensed twenty-five fur traders a year to go to the Great Lakes, and he encouraged the Jesuits to establish new stations in Wisconsin. He also sent Louis Joliet and Jacques Marquette out in 1673 to explore a great river which the Indians called the Messipi, a river which might possibly be the passageway to the Western Sea.

The two explorers, priest and fur trader, were fit symbols of French exploration. Marquette was a thirty-five-year-old Jesuit Father, and Joliet a Canadian-born woodsman with extensive wilderness experience. They set out from St. Ignace with five companions in birchbark canoes on May 16. At the head of Green Bay, they went up the Fox River and through the land of the "wild rice Indians." From the Fox they portaged to a westward-flowing river called the "Ouisconsing," and descended this until they reached the Mississippi in the middle of June. Then as they paddled southward they gave some memorable names to their discoveries. A muddy torrent which boiled into the Mississippi from the west was named for the Missouri tribe encountered there. Other tribes further down the river were the Kansa and then the Arkansa. At the Arkansas River, the weary Frenchmen decided to turn back. They knew now that the great river emptied into the Gulf of Mexico, and they feared capture by the Spanish. On the return trip they took the Illinois River, crossed the Chicago portage to Lake Michigan, and were back in Green Bay by the end of September.

This expedition aroused much interest in France, and it inspired one energetic young schemer with dreams of empire building. Robert Cavelier, Sieur de La Salle, had first come to New France in 1666. He obtained a seigniory near the outpost of Montreal, and soon became active in fur trading. In 1678 he secured a royal commission to explore and to build forts in the interior. With his chief aid, Henri de Tonty, he pushed west and erected Fort Crevecoeur on the Illinois and Fort Miami at the mouth of the St. Joseph. On the Niagara River he built the *Griffin,* the first trading vessel to sail the Great Lakes. The ship was lost, however, and a series of other trading reverses and Indian wars delayed his plan to explore the Mississippi. By the fall of 1681 he was again ready.

La Salle's party of forty-one Frenchmen and Indians left from Fort Miami, descended the Illinois River on sleds drawn across the ice, and after an uneventful journey reached the Mississippi delta in April of 1682. There La Salle took formal possession of the land, naming it Louis-iana in honor of his king. This trip gave France a claim to the entire Mississippi watershed. If they could make good on their pretensions, the French would be able to block the westward expansion of the English colonies.

La Salle attempted to expedite this plan. He returned to France and persuaded the King to let him build an outpost at the mouth of the Mississippi. But bad luck dogged the four-ship expedition which sailed in 1684. La Salle missed the mouth of the river, and landed instead at Matagorda Bay in Texas. For 2 years he searched the Texas coast for the Father of Waters, his party being whittled away by disease and Indian fights. Early in 1687 the survivors set out on a desperate journey to reach Canada. On the way La Salle was murdered by his own men, many of whom were ex-convicts, and with him died the first French bid for domination of the Mississippi and Gulf Coast region.

Yet the French were in fact well on their way to control of the St. Lawrence-Great Lakes-Mississippi waterway. Their forts, missions, and fur-trading posts dotted the interior. By the turn of the century French farmers, living with and often marrying into the local Indian tribes, were scratching away with primitive plows at the rich bottomlands around Kaskaskia and Cahokia in Illinois. The English would have to move fast if they were not to be hemmed in on the west.

Note: For brevity's sake, publisher's names have been omitted throughout the bibliographies. As for the place-names of prominent publishers in the Western field, "Norman" refers to the University of Oklahoma Press at Norman, Oklahoma; "New Haven" refers to the Yale University Press at New Haven, Connecticut; "Berkeley" refers to the University of California Press at Berkeley, California; "Cambridge" refers to the Harvard University Press at Cambridge, Massachusetts; and "Glendale" refers to the Arthur H. Clark Company of Glendale, California.

Selected Readings   North American geography is described in Ralph H. Brown's *Historical Geography of the United States* (New York, 1948); detailed maps are in Charles Paullin, *Atlas of the Historical Geography of the United States* (New York, 1932). An older work on the Indians is Clark Wissler, *The Indians of the United States* (New York, 1940). More recent surveys are William Brandon, *The American Heritage Book of Indians* (New York, 1961), and Alvin Josephy, *The Patriot Chiefs* (New York, 1961). For detailed references consult Frederick W. Hodge (ed.), *Handbook of American Indians North of Mexico*, 2 vols. (Washington, 1912), or John R. Swanton, *The Indian Tribes of North America* (Washington, 1952).

The best modern study of John Smith is by Bradford Smith: *John Smith: His Life and Legend* (Philadelphia, 1953). Documents of Jamestown are in Lyon G. Tyler (ed.), *Narratives of Early Virginia, 1606-1625* (New York, 1907). For Pilgrims and Puritans see Douglas Leach, *The Northern Colonial Frontier, 1607-1763* (New York, 1966), a well-written survey. Alden Vaughan, *The New England Frontier: Puritans and Indians, 1621-1675* (Boston, 1965), is a revisionist work which emphasizes the "justice and humanity" of the Puritans' Indian policy. Roderick Nash, *Wilderness and the American Mind* (New Haven, 1967), has an informative chapter on the Puritans. The journals of two leaders have been reprinted in William Bradford, *History of Plymouth Plantation* (New York, 1908) and other editions, and James K. Hosmer (ed.), *Winthrop's Journal*, 2 vols. (New York, 1908). Perry Miller's *Roger Williams* (Indianapolis, 1953) revises a traditional picture.

Lyman Carrier, 'The Veracity of John Lederer," *William and Mary Quarterly*, vol. 19 (October, 1939), is a defense of the explorer's reputation. Documents for King Philip's War, including Mary Rowlandson's account, are in Charles M. Lincoln (ed.), *Narratives of the Indian Wars, 1675-1699* (New York, 1913), while the definitive history of the conflict is Douglas Leach, *Flintlock and Tomahawk* (New York,

1958). Documents for Bacon's Rebellion are in Robert Middlekauff (ed.), *Bacon's Rebellion* (*Berkeley Series in American History*, Chicago, 1964), and in Charles M. Andrews (ed.), *Narratives of the Insurrections, 1675-1690* (New York, 1915). C. H. McIlwain's introduction to Peter Wraxhall's *An Abridgement of the Indian Affairs* (Cambridge, 1915) is a classic on the Iroquois. George T. Hunt, *The Wars of the Iroquois* (Madison, Wis., 1940), corrects many misconceptions. Allen W. Trelease, "The Iroquois in the Western Fur Trade," *Mississippi Valley Historical Review*, vol. 49 (June, 1962), revises the McIlwain-Hunt thesis that the Iroquois were fur-trade middlemen.

Documents of Spanish explorers are in Frederick W. Hodge and Theodore H. Lewis (eds.), *Spanish Explorers in the Eastern United States, 1528-1543* (New York, 1907). Cabeza de Vaca's *Journal* was published in paperback by Collier Books in 1962, and is worth reading in this or other editions. Herbert E. Bolton, "The Mission as A Frontier Institution in the Spanish American Colonies," *American Historical Review*, vol. 23 (October, 1917), is a key article. Champlain documents are in H. P. Biggar (ed.), *The Works of Samuel de Champlain*, 6 vols. (Toronto, 1922-1936). An excellent biography is Morris Bishop, *Champlain, The Life of Fortitude* (New York, 1948). Francis Parkman, *Pioneers of France in the New World* (Boston, 1885), deals with the missionary role. Perceptive comments on the same subject are in Frank R. Kramer, *Voices in the Valley* (Madison, Wis., 1964). Francis B. Steck, *The Jolliet-Marquette Expedition, 1673* (Washington, 1927), is reliable. Parkman's *LaSalle and the Great West* (Boston, 1879) is still standard, though it idealizes the subject.

II. The Old West

Frontiersmen of the English seaboard colonies began their exploration of the Old West at about the time the French Wars broke out in 1689. This region included the upland meadows and mountain valleys which lay along the Piedmont for 1,300 miles, from the Carolina back country through the Shenandoah Valley of Virginia, the Great Valley of Pennsylvania, and along the Allegheny front to the White Mountains of New Hampshire. It was a Promised Land of fertile limestone soil, towering forests, and salubrious climate. The Appalachian Mountains, whose peaks marked the western limits of this region, were a natural barrier between the Tidewater and the interior. While not especially high, their twisted ridges ran parallel to each other across hundreds of miles, and in the colonial period they were blanketed by a dense forest. Pioneers assaulting this mountain wall directly westward from Virginia had to chop their way up and over these formidable hogbacks. But the Great Valley was a natural trough running southwestward out of Pennsylvania, and thus it became the avenue for the new migration.

Non-English Frontiersmen The men who settled this frontier province were not only pure-blooded Englishmen, but also a motley mixture of Scotch-Irish, Germans, Irish, French Protestants, Dutch, and other assortments. They were a conglomerate horde, dumped unceremoniously into the social melting pot. Some of them were sponsored by religious or colonizing groups, others were released convicts, and many came as indentured or bonded servants. The indent was a contract under which an immigrant agreed to work as a laborer for several years in exchange for his passage. These bondsmen often went to the frontier after their period of service. As they built their log cabins, fought the Indians, and wrestled an arduous living from the land, they became more "American."

The Germans, who with the Scotch-Irish were the largest group of these migrants, were known variously as Palatinates, Salzburgers, and Pennsylvania Dutch. They were driven from their homeland by high taxes, military conscription, and religious persecution. Pennsylvania welcomed them from the very beginning of that colony in 1681, for the Quaker proprietor, William Penn, had a policy of toleration for all religions including German Dunkers, Moravians, and Mennonites. The British government also encouraged their settlement in New York after 1709, hoping to use them for producing pitch and other "naval stores." The manufacturing experiment failed, but the Germans stayed. They scattered far up the Mohawk Valley to establish exposed towns like Palatine and Herkimer. But Pennsylvania was always the mecca for German settlers; by 1775 they were one-third of the total population there. As land prices rose, many Germans started drifting south and west. Most of them followed the Great Philadelphia Wagon Road, or more accurately, "the bad road," which was laid down on an old Indian trail. This ran west from Philadelphia through Lancaster to Harris' Ferry on the Susquehanna, down through York to the Potomac, along the Shenandoah Valley, across the James to the site of Roanoke, and then southward along the Blue Ridge to Wachovia in North Carolina. The 1720s saw the beginning of a heavy German migration into the Shenandoah Valley, a 140-mile strip of rich limestone soil nestled beneath the Blue Ridge Mountains. Germans were also prominent in the North Carolina piedmont after 1740, particularly along the Yadkin River.

These settlers always went to heavily wooded areas, where the soil was known to be thick and where inherited practices could be applied in a new environment. The trees were cut down, rolled into huge piles, and burned. Then with characteristic thoroughness the work of planting grain and pasturing cattle went on. Their philosophy seemed to be *werke* and then more *werke*. Such people were ideally suited for pioneer farming. And they served other purposes as well. Governor Alexander Spotswood of Virginia settled a colony of them at Germanna, above the falls of the Rappahannock, in 1714, "to serve as a Barrier to the Inhabitants of that part of the Country against the Incursions of the Indians."

Though the Germans began to change their ways in the face of frontier conditions, they held on to their language and their Old World habits with remarkable tenacity. They (and the Swedes) brought with them the log cabin, which was unfamiliar to the English colonists, and made it the actual as well as the symbolic structure of the American frontier. They had a way with wood, and their skill could be put to immediate use in the splitting and notching of logs for the rude shelters. The typical log cabin had air conditioning of a sort, for the breezes swept through the mud chinking between the logs and filtered under the ill-fitting doors. There was also a form of central heating; the Germans built chimneys in the center of the cabin (and sometimes at the ends), and at night the children would scramble to get places closest to the fire. The Germans' talent

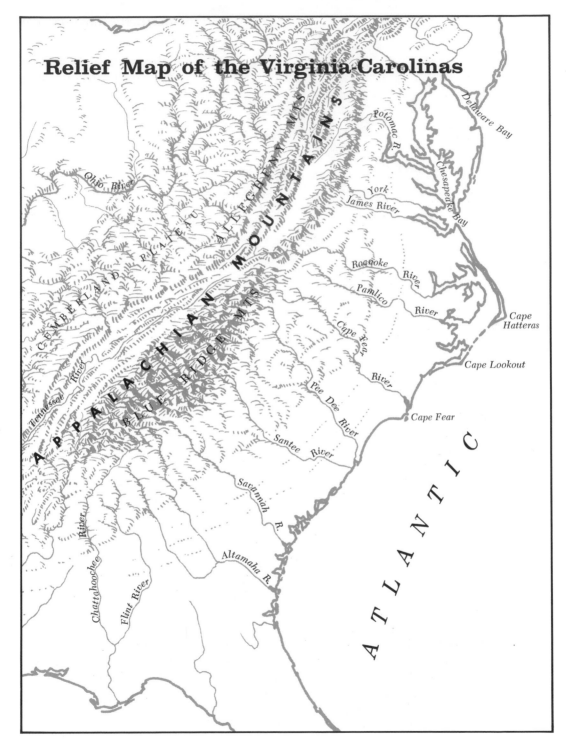

Relief Map of the Virginia-Carolinas

Conestoga Wagon. Source: Smithsonian Institution.

for carpentry was also revealed in such diverse products as the great "Palatine Barns" which dotted the Pennsylvania back country, the sweet-toned dulcimer with which they made music, and the famous Conestoga wagon which carried settlers west. The latter were huge canvas-topped vehicles which required six horses to pull them.

The Germans also had a talent for gunsmithing, and out of their small forges in Pennsylvania came fine frontier weapons. The supreme example was the Kentucky, or more properly, the Pennsylvania-Kentucky Rifle. The heavy, short-barreled Yaegers of the Old Country were modified to meet wilderness conditions. The barrel was lengthened (to 50 inches) for greater accuracy, the grease patch replaced the iron ramrod for easier loading, and refinements were made in the flintlock firing mechanism. The result was a weapon which was rugged and phenomenally accurate, and which from the 1720s on was the premier firearm of the American frontier.*

The Scotch-Irish were originally Scotchmen who had been settled in northern Ireland (Ulster) by the British government as part of the wildly optimistic plan to civilize the Irish. But famine, economic harassment, and religious persecution drove large numbers of these staunch Presbyterians out of the British Isles. The Woolens Act of 1699, engineered through Parliament by British sheep raisers, struck at their livelihood by prohibiting the export of this basic commodity. In the Test Act of 1709, Parliament proclaimed that applicants for civil service jobs or university educations had to be willing to take the sacraments of the Church of England. The result of these actions was that

---

*However, the musket remained the basic military weapon. Though it had less range and accuracy than the rifle, it could be loaded more quickly and could be fitted with a bayonet.

the Scotch-Irish crowded aboard ships bound for Pennsylvania, and thus names like Jackson, Robertson, and Rogers started appearing in American frontier annals.

Most of these migrants went directly to the frontiers of Pennsylvania, Virginia, and North Carolina, following on the heels of the Germans. A few went further north, where they served as a living barrier against the Indians. Worcester in Massachusetts, Londonderry in New Hampshire, and Cherry Valley on the New York frontier were all settled by Scotch-Irish. But the Puritan Congregationalists of New England did not welcome Presbyterian competition. So the major settlements were along the Susquehanna in the 1720s, and then in succession along the Juniata, the Shenandoah, and the Yadkin Rivers throughout the 1730s and 1740s.

Since most of these people were penniless, they became squatters, caring little for land titles or quitrents. One harried official complained that "both they and the Palatines pretend that they will pay, but not one in twenty has anything to pay with." Their right to the land was based upon occupancy and a "tomahawk claim," a boundary line of notched or initialed trees. When confronted with demands for payment of rent, they asserted that "it was against the laws of God and nature that so much land should be idle while so many christians wanted it to work on and to raise their bread." Less industrious than the Germans, they scotched or girdled their trees rather than chopping them down. A notch was cut around the bark of the tree, causing it to wither and die. Seed corn was then scattered among the stumps, hogs were let loose to feed on the acorns, and the gaunt woodsman's numerous progeny could live on johnnycake and sowbelly. Actually the abundance of wild turkey, deer, bear, and other game meant that the woodsman's table fare could be just as varied as his energy and the shooting accuracy of his Old Betsy would allow.

The settler's rifle was also essential when the Scotch-Irish fought the Indians, which they often did. The two antagonists understood each other quite well. Both were merciless in battle, knowing that survival for the one meant extermination for the other. "The essential American soul is hard, isolate, stoic, and a killer," remarked D. H. Lawrence, and the proposition might seem to apply to the Scotch-Irish of the frontier period. They were always aggressive fighters, to whom the pacifist statements of Quakers and other softhearted humanitarians made little sense. Their whole history had conditioned them to a flinty indifference to the sufferings of those outside the clan.

But there was friendship and a sense of equality among the settlers themselves. All "men" above the age of twelve contributed their share to harvesting, houseraisings, and defense. Frontier conditions tended to breed that political and social democracy praised by historian Frederick Jackson Turner. Every one was expected to do his share, and those who did not were "hated out" of the community. There was no basis for social distinctions. Neither wealth nor family standing seemed to confer any special status in the formative years of a

By His EXCELLENCY

By His *EXCELLENCY*

Joseph Reed, Esq. *President,*

And the SUPREME EXECUTIVE COUNCIL, *of the Commonwealth of* Pennsylvania.

A PROCLAMATION.

WHEREAS the Savages in Alliance with the King of *Great-Britain*, have attacked several of the Frontier Counties, and, according to the Custom of barbarous Nations, have cruelly murdered divers of the defenceless Inhabitants of this State: AND WHEREAS it has been found, by Experience, that the most effectual Mode of making War upon and repelling the Savage Tribes has been by Parties, consisting of small Numbers of vigorous, active Volunteers, making sudden irruptions into their Country, and surprising them in their Marches: WHEREFORE, for the Encouragement of those who may be disposed to chastise the Insolence and Cruelty of those Barbarians, and revenge the Loss of their Friends and Relations, WE HAVE thought fit, and do hereby offer a Reward of THREE THOUSAND DOLLARS for every *Indian* Prisoner, or Tory acting in Arms with them, and a Reward of TWO THOUSAND AND FIVE HUNDRED DOLLARS for every *Indian* Scalp, to be paid on an Order of the President or Vice-President in Council, to be granted on Certificate signed by the Lieutenant, or any two Sub-Lieutenants of the County, in Conjunction with any two Freeholders, of the Service performed. Such Reward to be in Lieu of all other Rewards or Emoluments to be claimed from the State.

GIVEN, by Order of the Council, under the Hand of His Excellency JOSEPH REED, *Esquire, President, and the Seal of the State, at Philadelphia, this Twenty-second Day of* April, *in the Year of our Lord One Thousand Seven Hundred and Eighty.*

JOSEPH REED, PRESIDENT.

Attest. T. MATLACK, *Secretary.*

GOD Save the PEOPLE

Typical frontier document: a Pennsylvania scalp bounty, 1780. Source: Library Company of Philadelphia.

frontier settlement. Such conditions horrified conservatives like Timothy Dwight, one-time president of Yale University: "A considerable part of all those who begin the cultivation of the wilderness may be denominated foresters, or Pioneers. The business of these persons is no other than to cut down trees, build log-houses, lay open forested grounds to cultivation, and prepare the way for those who come after them. These men cannot live in regular society. They are too idle, too talkative, too passionate, too prodigal, and too shiftless to acquire either property or character."

No one claimed that such pioneers would make ideal students at Yale. They were not bookish; the ability to wield an ax or follow a game trail was more valued than a knowledge of French verbs or Flemish painting. While there were literate individuals in a number of frontier communities, particularly among the ministry and the occasional "Irish" schoolmasters, the atmosphere was of necessity practical and unintellectual. And the Scotch-Irish shared the lustiness of all frontier people. Marriages, for example, were celebrated with enormous feasts which saw the roughhewn tables groaning under proteins and starches: venison, bear meat, potatoes. Rye whiskey flowed freely, adding to the hilarity. Dancing then lasted all night, with reels, jigs, and square sets following in exhausting succession. Physical rather than cerebral activity was the keynote of their lives.

The material as well as the cultural level was quite primitive on the farther frontiers. One ate off wooden plates, slept under bearskins, and wore homemade linsey-woolsey (flax and wool) or buckskin. The skins were fashioned into shirts which reached almost to the knees. Fringes were left on the sleeves to drain off water and to serve as thongs in an emergency. Deerskins were also used to make leggings and moccasins. The latter were far from being ideal footwear; they were not particularly stylish, and in wet weather they were simply "a decent way of going barefooted." Yet a man with furs enough to buy only salt and iron from the eastern settlements had to make his own clothing and utensils.

The do-it-yourself habit extended to all areas of daily life, including medicine. Rabid wolves occasionally burst from the forest and bit settlers. The treatment was a huge pill made of pitch and bitter herbs, and containing a strip of paper with various charms written on it. If hydrophobia did not kill the patient, the pill certainly would. For rattlesnake bites, bullet wounds, and bear clawing there was no cure. Poultices of native plants would be applied to the wound, but the main reliance was upon prayer.

In some areas the movement of German or Scotch-Irish farmers was blocked by huge speculative holdings. Along the Hudson River in New York, favorites of the royal governor had secured enormous manorial estates. Many of these patents belonged to old Dutch families like the Van Rensselaers. Whether English or Dutch, though, the owners followed restrictive policies. Quitrents were high, and land was leased rather than sold. Thus the small farmer was locked out. The Albany fur traders also opposed farming along the Hudson-Mohawk axis. They knew that when farmers moved in, the Indians moved out.

The Southern Frontier

In Virginia, too, the typical frontier farmer felt the pressure of unfavorable social and economic developments. Huge tracts in the Old Dominion were

reserved for "gentlemen." Lord Fairfax, who became George Washington's pa-
tron, was granted 6 million acres along the Rappahannock and in the Shenandoah
Valley. Tidewater speculators carved out other grants of similarly hoggish proportions along the Piedmont and in the valley. Some farmers were willing to
pay quitrents to such landlords; many were not. They became squatters, or else
moved on toward the Blue Ridge to escape rent collectors. The rise of Negro
slavery also propelled many commoners toward the west. Slaves had been
brought into the colonies as early as 1619, but they did not become a significant
percentage of the labor force until the turn of the century. Then they were put
to work on the plantations in preference to the mulish European immigrants.
The plantation frontier moved inexorably west, since tobacco was an acid crop
which rapidly exhausted the soil and American planters cared little about conservation. The rise of plantations worked by black labor created a class of
wealthy aristocrat-planters, and caused a steady exodus of the unpropertied.

Slaves were also introduced into South Carolina to work on the rice
plantations. Expansion west from Charleston had been slow until the 1690s.
Then rice had become the agricultural staple and deerskins the commercial
salvation of the languishing province. The Charleston traders led pack trains up
to the headwaters of the Savannah River, there to barter for skins with the
Cherokee. Soon they were trekking west from their depot at "Savannah Town,"
halfway up the river, to trade with the powerful Creek tribes in the interior of
present-day Georgia and Alabama. The rapid commercial expansion westward
was aided by geography and by skillful manipulation of the Indians. There
were gloomy pine forests to the west, but no mountain barrier comparable to
that facing the English frontiersmen further north. The route to the Mississippi
was fairly level, the chief obstacles being a series of north-south rivers with
improbable names like the Chattahoochee and the Tallapossa. The Carolina
traders also won over the tribes by marrying into them. Creek and Cherokee
chieftains named McGillivray or Ross are testimony to the zeal with which the
polygamous traders (most of whom had wives back home) implemented their
objectives.

Farmers lagged behind the traders in both North and South Caro-
lina. In these colonies a belt of "pine barrens," 80 miles wide, lay along the fall
line and made land unattractive to settlers. Treacherous Indians hovered along
the flanks of the colony, and they had to be stamped out in the Yamassee War
(1715). Much of the land along the lower Savannah was malaria-ridden, and the
disease decimated the bands of Swiss and Scotch-Irish who attempted settlement there. By 1730 the farming frontier had advanced only 80 miles from the
coast.

However, cattlemen preceded farmers along both the Carolina and
Virginia frontiers. Herds of runty cows were pastured on the upland meadows.
In the fall of the year the "Cow Men" would round them up and drive the fatter
ones to market in Charleston or Williamsburg. The meat was tough to chew,

but then only the French Huguenots who had settled in Charleston demanded filet mignon.

The British southern frontier was further extended by the colonization of Georgia in 1732. Humanitarian and military purposes were behind the project. Reform groups in England planned the colony as a refuge for debtors and other "miserable wretches." Few debtors actually came, but the Georgia Trustees did finance the settlement of hundreds of "charity colonists," most of whom were unemployed tradesmen. Military and imperialistic motives, however, were uppermost in the mind of Sir James Oglethorpe, the one Trustee who actually came to America. Fully conscious of the French and Spanish threat to the southern border, he established the town of Savannah and several other military outposts, after securing the Creeks' consent to settle land between the Savannah and Altamaha Rivers. A group of hardy Scotch Highlanders, equipped with the inevitable bagpipes, were posted at Darien near the mouth of the Altamaha. Two hundred German Salzburgers were stationed at Frederica on St. Simon's Island, below the Altamaha, to guard the inland waterway against attack from St. Augustine.

The King had given the Georgia Trustees a charter to govern the colony on a nonprofit basis for 20 years. Though they were well-intentioned, the Trustees committed blunders which illustrate the disparity between Old World preconceptions and the actual conditions in America. Many of the immigrants from the rigorous climate of northern Europe sickened and died when they were suddenly thrust into the malarial lowlands along the Savannah. The Trustees blamed the deaths on Demon Rum, and prohibited the drinking of rum punch. But Georgians continued to guzzle bootlegged liquor despite the regulation, and many of them lived to a ripe old age. Landownership was restricted to 50 acres for each colonist, since the Trustees hoped to avoid the consolidation of land into great estates such as had occurred in Virginia. It was to be a democratic society, with each peasant living under his own mulberry tree. (The mulberry leaves were to feed silkworms, since silk production was another part of the great plan which never materialized.) The 50-acre unit proved to be poorly adapted to cattle raising or woodcutting, which were more suitable occupations in Georgia than conventional farming. And finally, Negro slaves could not be brought in, since it was felt that the poor would not work diligently if they had slaves. All these various prohibitions were repealed before the King took over the colony in 1751, but by that time Georgia had clearly fulfilled its twin objectives.

By the end of the French and Indian War in 1763, the Old West frontier had been extended until it was close up against the Appalachian Mountain barrier in both Pennsylvania and Virginia. The "backwoodsmen" who lived along this frontier were in process of forming a new society. It was not English, or German, or Scotch-Irish, but some of each. The interaction of Old World inheritance and New World environment was also creating a distinctive national character, one which would in time be called American. The visible evidences of the frontier way of life—the log cabin, the long rifle, and the buckskin hunting shirt—were well on their way to becoming familiar American symbols. And they instantly suggested a whole constellation of individual traits and values.

In New England during the same period, settlement had edged into far-western Connecticut and Massachusetts despite a succession of border wars with the French and Indians. By 1750 movement up the Housatonic and west from the Connecticut Valley into the Berkshires had resulted in the establishment of such hill-country towns as Litchfield (1720), Great Barrington (1730), and Pittsfield (1743). There had also been a "northward movement" up the Connecticut and Merrimac Valleys into southern Vermont and New Hampshire, although the full torrent of settlers did not engulf those colonies until after the end of the last French war. In its social composition, this whole movement was less cosmopolitan than that of the southern frontier. The Scotch-Irish founded a number of frontier towns, but the vast bulk of the migrants were native sons of New England. However, in both regions the result was the same: the creation of an interior or "western" society that was quite different from that of the seaboard. In New England the contrast was less marked because the settlers preserved the old traditions through church and school. The differences that did exist were highlighted by the transition from the old religious-oriented system of town planting to one of dollars-and-cents land speculation. By 1715 the General Courts in both Massachusetts and Connecticut were auctioning off townsites to the highest bidders, ignoring the time-honored traditions of compact settlement and proprietary paternalism. It wasn't long before the Westerners were ranting about high land prices and about the general neglect which their communities suffered at the hands of gimlet-eyed Boston speculators.

Tidewater—Frontier Contrasts

The theme is thus counterpoint, for the frontier people everywhere were different from those in the Tidewater regions. The contrast between the two cultural patterns was most obvious in the southern colonies. Here the seaboard was English and Episcopal, a land of large plantations worked by slaves or bonded labor. The back country had many non-English stocks, and a wild variety of dissenting religious sects. There were numerous small landholders engaged in diversified farming, and few slaves or indentured servants. The Tidewater aristocrats still had a derivative culture. They sent their children to English schools, copied London fashions in dress and furniture, and regarded the backwoodsmen as uncouth oafs.

The frontiersmen for their part were a rambunctious lot who resented outside control, be it political, religous, or economic. Even the faint symbols of such control were unwelcome. When the Rev. Charles Woodmason tried to start an Episcopal congregation on the South Carolina frontier, the

Scotch-Irish Presbyterians set fifty-seven dogs to fighting outside his church, forcing him to call off services. An official state religion had little chance of survival among the contentious folk of the back country, who quarreled as much among themselves as they did with the seaboard officials. The key trait seemed to be a sense of freedom, which at its extreme became lawlessness.

All settlers seemed to experience this liberating effect. Even the Germans, who held most tenaciously to the old ways, went through many changes on the frontier. Their language began to reflect American influences, as when they spoke of "zaplings" and "seyder presses." Though their agricultural techniques never descended to the characteristically wasteful practices of the American planters, the Germans' farming standards fell below those of the mother country. With millions of acres to spare, why husband the soil as carefully as before? But the chief change was the sense of dignity and the sense of liberty which accompanied the change from German peasant to American farmer. The frontier generated equalitarian tendencies.

The supreme embodiment of the democratizing influence of the Old West frontier was not a German or a Scotch-Irishman, however, but Thomas Jefferson. Of English and Welsh descent, Jefferson was born in 1743 at a frontier community on the Rivanna River in western Virginia. He got many of his democratic ideas from European philosophers, particularly John Locke. But he also grew up among pioneer farmers, Scotch-Irish and Welsh, Quakers and Baptists. From them he absorbed a belief in self-reliance, an antipathy for an "established" church, and a general faith in democratic political practices. These ideas, certainly characteristic of the frontier, were reflected throughout Jefferson's later career.

With the political boundaries still running east and west, the Tidewater politicians dominated the quite different societies that were forming west of the fall line. The practical results of this situation differed from one colony to another. In Virginia, the colonial government gave early recognition to the west, and thus averted serious trouble. In South Carolina, Charleston ignored the Westerners, who then solved their own problems through extra-legal "Regulator" organizations. The textbook case has always been North Carolina, where a clique of eastern politicians ignored frontier demands and thus provoked the most memorable of the Regulator movements.

The Carolina Regulators

In this province the royal Governor, William Tryon, appointed all the county justices, militia officers, and sheriffs. Many of these officials were constituent members of the "courthouse gangs" which reigned supreme in Carolina politics. In addition, they often held seats in the colonial Assembly, in which the Tidewater was overrepresented by virtue of having smaller counties. Corrupt sheriffs pocketed many of the fees and taxes; even the Governor was unable to get a full accounting of these embezzled funds. The taxes in the colony were heavy, the main form being a poll tax under which a man who was worth "10,000 pounds . . . [paid] no more than a poor back country settler that has nothing but the labour of his hands to depend upon for his daily support." Specie was scarce; like a magnet attracting nails, the seaboard always drew hard money out of the back country in taxes and payments for manufactured goods. Yet if a farmer could not pay his taxes in specie, the sheriff speedily sold his property from under him.

A movement to "regulate" these abuses arose in Orange County in 1766. The farmers demanded paper money, property rather than poll taxes, publication of all laws, and a prohibition on multiple officeholding. When these demands were not met, the Regulators issued a manifesto in 1768 which has the characteristic ring of the American frontier: "We, the subscribers, do voluntarily agree to form ourselves into an association, to assemble ourselves for conference for regulating public grievances and abuses of power, in the following particulars." Taxes and exorbitant fees were among the particulars mentioned. Such insolence could not be tolerated by the ruling caste. Col. Edmund Fanning, a multiple officeholder at the county seat in Hillsborough, called the movement "insurrection." With the simplicity and directness of frontiersmen everywhere, a band of Regulators rode by the colonel's house and fired a fusillade which left his roof looking like a pepper shaker.

The Regulators were mostly Scotch-Irish, with a sprinkling of Germans. The agitators who egged them on were of English descent. Herman Husband was a Quaker propagandist whose pamphlets had such impertinent titles as *A Fan for Fanning and a Touchstone to Tryon*. Another who was "outlawed not for his fighting, but for his songs" was a schoolteacher with the intriguing name of Redknap Howell. His native American ballads attacked the officials sharply:

> From Hillsborough Town the first day in May
> Marched those murdering traitors.
> They went to oppose the honest men
> That were called the Regulators.

Husband and Howell helped to win for the Regulators the war of words that followed the collapse of the movement itself.

Governor Tryon decided that his political career was endangered, and that the Regulators must be crushed. He rounded up some of their leaders in 1769 and had them tried. Only three were convicted, and Tryon in a sudden about-face pardoned them. The Regulators then decided to elect their own partisans to the colonial assembly. They were completely successful in the four counties involved in the movement, but unfortunately Governor Tryon dissolved the assembly on an unrelated issue after only 10 days in session.

As a result, the Regulators turned to violence in the fall of 1770.

A raging mob clubbed the luckless Colonel Fanning so badly that it almost caused his "immediate dissolution." He was run out of Hillsborough and his house burned to the ground. The homes of other officials, including that of Judge Richard Henderson of the superior court, were also burned down. Moderate elements, including Presbyterian ministers in the western counties, denounced this violence and lent their support to the Governor. With this encouragement, Tryon organized a military expedition to march against Orange County.

In May of 1771 he led his thousand-man army out of Hillsborough to disperse the 2,000 Regulators gathered at nearby Alamance Creek. The farmers who opposed him were "the Mob"—in fact as well as in name. They had no military organization, their tactics being the usual frontier style of every man for himself. Tryon's militia crushed the rebels within 2 hours, at a cost of nine killed on each side. Seven prisoners were executed after this "Battle of Alamance Creek," but Tryon pardoned all Regulators who would take an oath of allegiance to the government. Over 6,000 eventually did so, and the western counties were at peace. However, the whole episode left a legacy of bitterness in the Carolina back country. Some ex-Regulators became Tories when the Tidewater gentry supported the Revolution in 1776. Many of them simply saddled their horses and moved west into the valleys of the Appalachian Mountains. There the land was untouched, and a man could be free of sheriffs, courts, and too much government.

Selected Readings   The key essay is Frederick Jackson Turner's "The Old West," in *The Frontier in American History* (New York, 1920). Theodore Roosevelt's *Winning of the West*, 6 vols. (New York, 1889), also remains a classic, though a number of his statements have been revised. Oliver P. Chitwood, *A History of Colonial America* (New York, 1960), has an excellent chapter on "The Old West."

Jesse L. Rosenberger, *The Pennsylvania Germans* (Chicago, 1923), is satisfactory. Henry J. Ford, *The Scotch-Irish in America* (Princeton, 1915), is standard; John Dillin, *The Kentucky Rifle* (Washington, 1924), is useful; but Carl P. Russell, *Guns on the Early Frontiers* (Berkeley, 1957), is indispensable. Frontier weapons are also discussed in John K. Mahon, "Anglo-American Methods of Indian Warfare, 1676-1794," *Mississippi Valley Historical Review*, vol. 45 (September, 1958). George Shumway, Edward Durell, and Howard C. Frey, *Conestoga Wagon, 1750-1850* (York, Pa., 1964), has an informative text and many photos. Joseph Doddridge, *Notes on the Settlement and Indian Wars of the Western Parts of Virginia and Pennsylvania* (Pittsburgh, 1912), is entertaining reading and a valuable primary source.

New York is covered in Ruth L. Higgins, *Expansion in New York* (Columbus, Ohio, 1931). Lois K. Mathews, *The Expansion of New England* (Boston, 1909), is still quite useful. Carl Bridenbaugh, *Myths and Realities: Societies of the Colonial South* (Baton Rouge, 1952), is a brilliant series of essays. Verner W. Crane, *The Southern Frontier, 1670-1732* (Durham, 1928), is essential. Sarah B. Gober-Temple and Kenneth Coleman (eds.), *Georgia Journeys* (Athens, Ga., 1961), has many revealing documents.

Documents bearing on the Regulator movement are in William L. Saunders (ed.), *The Colonial Records of North Carolina*, vols. VII and VIII (Raleigh, N.C., 1890). See also John S. Bassett, "The Regulators of North Carolina," *American Historical Association Annual Report for 1894* (Washington, 1895), and Richard W. Brown, *The South Carolina Regulators* (Cambridge, 1963). The traditional view that the Regulators became Tories in the Revolution, expressed in Robert DeMond's *The Loyalists in North Carolina During the Revolution* (Durham, 1940), is challenged in John Alden's *The South in the Revolution* (Baton Rouge, 1957).

III. The French Wars

England and France fought a series of wilderness wars between 1689 and 1763 which affected frontier settlement, shaped the American military tradition, and determined the destiny of the continent. The first three of these conflicts began in Europe over dynastic rivalries, and the American colonists became pawns for their distant monarchs. The European orientation of the wars is indicated by their American titles: King William's War, Queen Anne's War, and King George's War. The last of the sequence began in America as the French and Indian War, then spread to Europe where it was known as the Seven Years War. These wars found their Thucydides in Francis Parkman, whose multivolume *France and England in North America* remains the standard formulation of the struggle as one of Anglo-Saxon Protestant liberty versus French Catholic absolutism.

The Rivals   On paper the English had such a decisive edge in wealth and population that they should have crushed the obstreperous Frenchmen as easily as one swats a fly. In 1690 there were 205,000 English colonists compared with 13,000 Frenchmen, and the gap widened to a 16 to 1 ratio by 1755. The English were solidly in control of their settled territory, while the French posts in the interior were insecurely anchored to agricultural communities and were subject to the razor-edge balances of Indian diplomacy. However, in war as in love, appearances are often deceptive. The English colonists or "Americans" (the term was becoming common in the 1740s) were amateur soldiers. They had few experienced commanders, no regular military organization, and a revulsion for military service. They were impeded by intercolonial rivalries that were almost as bitter as the wars with the common enemy. While the mother country gave the Americans little assistance, the Lords of Trade could still complain that: "His Majesty has subjects enough in those parts of America to drive out the French from Canada; but they are so *crumbled into little governments*, and so disunited, that they have hitherto afforded little assistance to each other, and now seem in a much worse disposition to do it for the future." On the other hand, that very absolutism which was the disgrace of the French political system was a decided advantage in war. The Governor (who ruled in conjunction with a Bishop and an Intendant) could call out his Regulars and his provincial militia at a moment's notice. He also had the use of bushrangers or *coureurs de bois*, those tough and experienced foresters who worked well with New France's Indian allies. Thus it was, in Parkman's words, "union confronting division, energy confronting apathy, military centralization opposed to industrial democracy; and for a time, the advantage was all on one side."

King William's War

King William's War began in 1689 when Louis XIV refused to recognize the accession of the Protestant William and Mary to the English throne following the overthrow of Catholic James II. As soon as word reached America, both sides marshaled their Indian friends for an attack on the enemy's frontier. The French-allied tribes were the Abenaki in Maine, Catholicized Iroquois from Caughnawaga (near Montreal), and "Western Indians" such as the Huron and Ottawa. The Five Nations of the Iroquois were generally behind the British, but they maneuvered between the two sides in an attempt to preserve their independent position. The Iroquois actually initiated the war in America when a 1,500-man force attacked the settlement of Lachine, only 8 miles from Montreal, in August of 1689. The screams of 120 men, women, and children captives being burned or mangled at the Iroquois torture stakes were to be the characteristic sound of this woodland warfare.

The French were quick to retaliate. The offensive was directed from Quebec by Count Frontenac, a fiery old professional soldier whom the King had called out of retirement to resume the Governorship of New France. Frontenac sent wolf packs of *coureurs de bois* and Indians, usually under French officers, to slash at the English frontiers in New York, New Hampshire, and Maine. On February 8, 1690, the Dutch farmers of Schenectady found to their sorrow that making snowmen was not an appropriate wartime diversion. The town was surrounded by a wooden stockade, but on the night of the attack the gates had been left open, and only two snowmen were on guard. The Frenchmen and Indians rushed in and tomahawked sixty sleeping inhabitants *sans merci*, taking the survivors into captivity. Other parties hit Salmon Falls in New Hampshire and Casco in Maine. "The popish design against the Protestant interest in New England," to quote the contemporary words of Capt. Sylvanus Davis, was well launched.

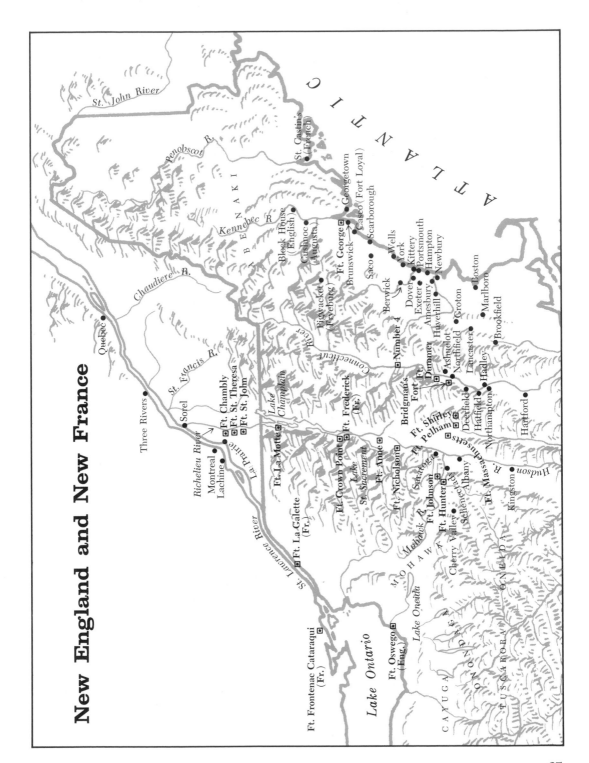

New England and New France

ATLANTIC

St. John River

Penobscot R.

Kennebec R.

ABENAKI

St. Castin's (French)

Georgetown
Casco (Fort Loyal)
Scarborough

Block House (English)
Cushnoc (Augusta)
Ft. George
Brunswick
Saco

Wells
York
Kittery
Portsmouth
Hampton
Newbury

Pigwacket (Fryeburg)

Berwick
Dover
Exeter
Amesbury
Haverhill
Groton

Boston
Marlboro
Brookfield

Chaudiere R.

Number 4
Ashuelot
Northfield
Lancaster
Hadley
Northampton

Connecticut River

Quebec

St. Francis R.

Three Rivers

Sorel

Bridgman's Fort
Ft. Dummer
Ft. Shirley
Pelham
Deerfield
Hatfield

Hartford

Richelieu River

Montreal
Lachine

Ft. Chambly
Ft. St. Theresa
Ft. St. John

Lake Champlain

Ft. Frederick (Fr.)

MASSACHUSETTS R.

Hudson

La Prairie

Ft. La Motte

Ft. Crown Point
Lake St. Sacrement
Ft. Anne
Ft. Nicholson
Saratoga
Ft. Johnson
Ft. Hunter
Cherry Valley
Albany
Schenectady
Ft. Massachusetts

Kingston

St. Lawrence River

Ft. La Galette (Fr.)

Mohawk R.

MOHAWK

ONEIDA

Ft. Frontenac Cataraqui (Fr.)

Lake Ontario

Ft. Oswego (Eng.)

Lake Oneitta

CAYUGA

ONONDAGA

TUSCARORA

37

New England had just begun mending the fabric of settlement—torn by King Philip's War—when the French and Indians struck. Massachusetts had a militia system, and the settler-soldiers were once again called upon to defend the borders. During the war the General Court designated certain towns, such as Lancaster and Deerfield, as "Frontier Towns" which the inhabitants were forbidden to leave upon forfeit of their lands. Many of these towns built stockades of sharpened logs, with "flankers" or blockhouses at the corners from which defenders could fire along the walls. More common were the garrison houses, built of heavy timber, with loopholes, and having a projecting upper story like a blockhouse. Refugees would gather in these fortified houses at the first news of the enemy's approach.

The classic problem in this frontier war, as in most such wars, was that the best defense was a vigorous offense. Small bands of French-Indians could spring upon the exposed farms before the surprised settlers had a chance to flee to the garrisons. Connecticut tried to organize companies of rangers to scout beyond the frontier line, and Massachusetts offered scalp bounties to encourage aggressive patrolling. But frontiersmen were unwilling to enlist for long periods of military service; they were farmers rather than soldiers. And numbers of them deserted the official Frontier Towns despite the consequent loss of their land.

The New Englanders realized quite correctly that the best way to stop the French attacks was to launch a seaborne assault and take Quebec. An attempt was made under Sir William Phips, an energetic Boston merchant. On August 21, 1690, a fleet of 34 ships left Massachusetts and anchored off the enemy citadel in October. The commander and his citizen-soldiers hemmed and hawed aboard their ships—just long enough to permit Frontenac to bring in reinforcements and thus guarantee the failure of the invasion.

In New York the Iroquois paid a heavy price for their alliance with England. In the winter of 1693 Frontenac sent a mixed force of Regulars and mission Indians into the Mohawk country west of Schenectady. They burned the villages, destroyed food supplies, and took 300 captives. The English militia pursued, and in a series of battles that were fought in a blinding snowstorm, recovered most of the prisoners. Both sides suffered from famine during this countermarching; the French boiled their moccasins for food, and the Iroquois friends of the English commander offered him the partly cooked hand of a dead Frenchman for breakfast. (He declined, with thanks.) In the summer of 1696 Frontenac himself led another large force into the Onondaga territory, again burning towns and foodstores. This time no Yorker militia pursued the invaders, for the New York defense fund had been exhausted and the armed forces depleted. The Iroquois learned that the colony could not protect them and in the next war they would make their peace with the French.

The Treaty of Ryswick, signed on September 30, 1697, brought the inconclusive war to an end. France recognized William as King of England, and in America the prewar boundaries and conquests were restored. The colonial leaders vaguely understood the need for intercolonial cooperation to prevent a repetition of their blunders, but they were still groping for a method to that end.

One offshoot of the war was a rich deposit of folklore in New England. The terrors of the war itself were real enough, but they were multiplied in minds capable of the Salem witchcraft delusion of 1692. There were tales of phantom warriors (near Gloucester), and of Indians seen conversing with the Devil. Cotton Mather, Boston's famous clergyman-author, had an answer for everything. In his view, "this inexplicable war might have some of its original among the Indians, whose chief sagamores are well known unto some of our captives, to have been horrid sorcerers, and hellish conjurors, such as conversed with Demons."

Some of the lore had a basis in fact. Such was the story of Hannah Dustin, a frontier Amazon. At the tail end of the war, in March of 1697, a band of Abenakis raided Haverhill in northern Massachusetts. Mrs. Dustin, her week-old baby, and a nurse were carried off. The warriors killed the baby by dashing its head against a tree. As they made their way north, the Indians taunted the women by telling them that they would be stripped and tortured before being sold to the French. In desperation the two women and a young boy captive decided to attempt an escape. Late at night, as the Indians slept, the three whites silently stole tomahawks and swiftly caved in the heads of ten of the twelve savages. For the ten scalps (two warriors, three squaws, seven children) which Hannah and her companions dutifully collected, the commonwealth of Massachusetts paid a bounty of 50 pounds. This story, told for many years around New England fireplaces and memorialized in John Greenleaf Whittier's "A Mother's Revenge," well represents the ferocity of frontier warfare.

The French used the truce between wars to build up their chain of posts in the interior. The oddly named La Mothe Cadillac, a colonial captain who had an eye on the profits of the fur trade as well as on the glory of France, suggested that a new fort be built at the *etroit* or narrows connecting Lake Huron with Lake Erie. This post would block the English from the upper lakes, and indeed from the whole northwest. Cadillac's plan was approved in 1701, and a picket fort went up on the west bank of the Detroit River to mark the origin of a famous city. Mission towns were also established at Cahokia (1699) and Kaskaskia (1700) in Illinois to strengthen French claims to the Mississippi.

Further south, French fears of English expansion led to the revival of LaSalle's great plan. "If the English once render themselves master of the Colbert [Mississippi]," wrote LaSalle's brother Jean in 1690, "they will also gain the Illinois, the Ottawa, and all the nations with whom the French of New France carry on trade." In response to these warnings, the King dispatched Pierre Lemoyne, Sieur d'Iberville in 1698 to secure the mouth of the Mississippi. Iberville found the great river, but decided to build his fort at Biloxi. He and his brother Jean Baptiste, Sieur de Bienville, explored the Gulf Coast rivers, and painfully built up alliances with the Natchez and Choctaw tribes. In 1701 he built a new post at Mobile Bay, so close to the Spanish fort at Pensacola that the Spanish King protested. Louis XIV hoped that Louisiana would become a profitable colony, with pearls and buffalo skins as the main products, but these hopes were never realized. It became a dumping ground for convicts and prostitutes, and a favorite political football for the French court. Eventually Iberville and later Bienville had to exert all their skill in forest diplomacy to protect the outpost at Mobile and to keep Louisiana in French hands.

Queen Anne's War

In 1702, shifting European alliances brought on Queen Anne's War. When the King of Spain died childless, Louis XIV wanted to place his own grandson on the throne. The Grand Alliance, which included England, supported another claimant, and Queen Anne declared war over the "Spanish Succession" in May of 1702. Spain became a French ally in this as in the next two wars, with the result that the Florida-Carolina border was a war theater. The aggressive Carolinians under Governor James Moore launched a quick attack against St. Augustine in the fall. A combined force of militia and Indians burnt the town, but the great stone fort withstood a 7-week siege. The next year Moore led another mixed contingent against the Apalache missions in northwestern Florida. A thousand Christianized Indians were herded off to become slaves on the Carolina plantations. The Spanish soldiers cowered behind the walls of Fort San Luis (Tallahassee) while the mission system crashed around their ears. A French and Spanish counterattack on Charleston in 1706 was beaten off with heavy losses for the Spaniards.

The main battleground, however, was once again New England. The Iroquois agreed to a peace with the French, much to the delight of the Albany fur traders, and thus New York was spared the afflictions of Maine and Massachusetts. The French-Indian scythe swept through Maine from Wells to Casco Bay, cutting down "one, two, three or more men, women or children, waylaid in fields, woods and lonely roads or surprised in solitary cabins," as Parkman put it. These assaults lasted the course of the war, and prevented any frontier expansion in that direction. Enemy raiders also traveled the forest on snowshoes to attack the northwestern frontier of Massachusetts.

Deerfield, the Connecticut River settlement which described itself as "the most Utmost Frontere Town in the County of West Hampshire," was again the victim of Indian warfare. The town's 300 inhabitants were protected by an 8-foot palisade, and several of the houses were fortified. However, Hertel de Rouville and his 250 Canadians and Abenakis scaled the walls before dawn on February 29, 1704, "the watch being unfaithful," and battered their way into the houses with hatchets. In the nightmare scene that followed, half-clad villagers were tomahawked in their beds or out on the red-stained snow. A few of the garrison houses withstood the onslaught, but the triumphant raiders carried off 111 prisoners. Among them was the Reverend John Williams, whose Harvard education had not weakened his faith in weapons. When the savages broke through his door he reached for his pistol, "uttering a short petition to God for everlasting mercies for me and mine." Fortunately for him the weapon misfired, and so he was seized instead of killed. His family was also taken to Canada, his seven-year-old daughter Eunice eventually becoming the squaw of a Caughnawaga brave. Upon his release Williams published *The Redeemed Captive Returning to Zion*, which kept the Deerfield massacre alive in the memory of subsequent generations as the representative episode of this war.

Massachusetts appealed to the other colonies for men and money, but the old attitudes of intercolonial suspicion (and indifference) persisted. An expedition to invade Montreal in 1709 did enlist soldiers from all the New England colonies, but the project died for lack of support from England. The Massachusetts people continually appealed to London for troops and ships with which to launch an attack on Quebec. The Court responded with all the alacrity of a tortoise. It did lend the New Englanders 500 Royal Marines, who helped take Port Royal (renamed Annapolis Royal), Nova Scotia, in 1710. But when it finally approved of the Quebec scheme in 1711, it sent as commander of the army a hanger-on whose chief qualification was that his handsome face appealed to the Queen, and as admiral of the naval force, an officer who knew nothing at all about the North American seacoast. It is anticlimatic to report that the grand expedition (seventy-one ships in all) crashed into the rocks at the mouth of the St. Lawrence without even approaching Quebec.

All in all it was a lackadaisical war. The American colonists fought in the usual happy-go-lucky fashion, with the customary inefficiency. A sigh of relief greeted the Treaty of Utrecht in 1713, in which England got the better of the bargain. France surrendered Acadia (Nova Scotia) and Newfoundland; Spain gave up Gibraltar and agreed to the Asiento, a contract which permitted the British to sell African slaves and to send one trading ship a year to Spain's Caribbean colonies. The question of who owned the major prize—the vast interior of the continent—was left undecided.

No sooner was the treaty signed than both England and France began maneuvering their chessmen across the board of the American wilderness. The French raced to occupy all the chief waterways into the west. In 1720 Louis Joncaire browbeat the Seneca, and so got their grudging consent to construct Fort Niagara at the mouth of the Niagara River. The English countered with Fort Oswego, a loopholed stone trading house built in 1725 on the site of the modern city of Oswego. Traders from the two powers competed for both furs and political influence along this lakeland frontier. The French were also brazen enough to establish a fort on Lake Champlain, the historic invasion route from Canada. Fort Crown Point was built in 1731 on the west side of the lake at a spot commanding all water traffic. They also strengthened their grip on the interior by fortifying the passes between the Great Lakes and the Mississippi. Fort Miami guarded the Miami-Wabash portage, Vincennes became a post on the Wabash itself, and Fort de Chartres went up on the Mississippi between Cahokia and Kaskaskia in 1720. At the mouth of the river, Governor Bienville, the "Father of Louisiana," established in 1718 a permanent station named New Orleans.

French Canadians also explored the trans-Mississippi West in the interim between wars. Juchereau de St. Denis was sent out from Natchitoches in 1715 to explore the Red River; the next year he went all the way to the Mexican border at the Rio Grande. In 1739 the Mallet brothers, Paul and Pierre, traveled up the Platte and then went south through Colorado to Santa Fe, where they remained for almost a year. Better known are the explorations of the northern prairies by Pierre de la Vérendrye and his sons. This intrepid fur trader had built a chain of posts northwest of Lake Superior, and from one of them, Fort La Reine on the Assiniboine, he set out in 1738 to find "La Mer de l'Ouest" or Western Sea. He reached the Minataree villages at the Great Bend of the Missouri, but the desertion of his interpreter prevented further exploration. Vérendrye sent his two sons Louis-Joseph and François out to make another attempt in 1742. They set out across the endless prairie for the land of the Horse Indians (probably Cheyenne), who allegedly could guide them to the sea. In Wyoming the brothers reached the Rocky Mountains—62 years ahead of Lewis and Clark. On their return along the Missouri they planted a lead plate (rediscovered in 1913) near Pierre, South Dakota, as a symbol of French possession. Lead bullets, however, were to prove more effective than lead plates in the winning of the West.

King George's War

King George's War broke out between England and France in 1744. It was preceded by a seriocomic Anglo-Spanish encounter called the War of Jenkin's Ear. Capt. Robert Jenkins was an Asiento smuggler whom the Spanish caught red-handed, and whom with unusual mercy they punished by lopping off his ear rather than by putting him to death. Spain's searching of British ships in the Caribbean was causing heated debate in Parliament by 1739, with Jenkins' pickled ear the symbol of national humiliation. England declared war in October of that year, and in America the new colony of Georgia was the main scene of action. 1740 saw General James Edward Oglethorpe making another of the perennial British attempts to take St. Augustine, this time with a force of 1,800 Indians, Carolina militia, and Scotch Highlanders. The siege was unsuccessful, and 2 years later the Georgians had to repulse a Spanish attack at St. Simon's Island. Since Spain and France were allies under the Family Compact, the war broadened into another Anglo-French contest in March of 1744.

In New England the main interest centered on an expedition to capture Louisbourg. This massive fort, the "Gibraltar of the New World," was on Cape Breton Island. It guarded the main entrance to the St. Lawrence, and was a base for French privateers who constantly menaced the American fishing fleets. Governor William Shirley of Massachusetts rounded up volunteer soldiers from the four New England colonies, and put a prosperous merchant named William Pepperell in command of the expedition. The rank and file were lacking in military experience. In their corduroy coats, leather jackets, and coarse linens they made a raggle-taggle picture. Observers at the time, and historians since, have pointed out that this army had a typically American composition: a lawyer for a contriver; a merchant for a general; and farmers, fishermen, and mechanics for soldiers. Such a crowd would seem to have little likelihood of success. But thanks to good luck and the cooperation of a British fleet under Adm. Peter Warren, Louisbourg was taken in June of 1745 after a 6-week siege. "It was an enterprise," said a French contemporary, "less of the English nation and its King than of the inhabitants of New England alone. . . . Nobody would have said that their sea and land forces were of the same nation and under the same prince."

There was also border warfare in the summer of 1745. The Canadians and Indians followed the timeworn pattern by attacking Vermont (Putney), New Hampshire (Keene), and Massachusetts. And this time New York was pulled back into the fighting. Saratoga felt the knife in November, and the following spring raiders appeared at the very doorstep of Albany. New York's own plans to attack Crown Point in 1746 went awry for lack of funds, so the colony left the fighting to her Iroquois allies. New York's agent to the Five Nations was William Johnson, who was to become one of America's best-known frontier traders and diplomats.

Sir William Johnson. From a painting by Thomas McIlworth. Source: Courtesy of the New-York Historical Society, New York City.

Johnson was a rough and jovial Irishman who came to America in 1738 to manage the Mohawk Valley lands of his uncle, Admiral Warren. He immediately made a hit with the Iroquois, to whom he was known as Warraghiyagey or "He-Who-Does-Much." Johnson gave them fair prices for their furs, learned their languages, and took Mohawk wives. (Legend, if not history, says that he fathered a hundred half-breed children.) He had a sharp eye for land values, and was constantly adding to his estates around Johnson Hall. At one council the Mohawk chief Hendrick reported having had a dream in which Johnson gave him a fancy dress coat. Johnson immediately stripped off his coat and gave it to the delighted chief. At the next council, Johnson said he had dreamt that the chief had given him a choice 5,000-acre tract along the river. Hendrick gave him the land, remarking: "Now, Sir William, I will never dream with you again; you dream too hard for me." Johnson finally persuaded the Iroquois to take the warpath in the spring of 1747, but they made only a few ineffectual raids to the north.

George Croghan was another bluff Irishman who became a famous frontier trader, speculator, and Indian agent. In 1741 his base of operations was at Croghan's Gap near the site of modern Harrisburg, Pennsylvania. From here he took pack trains loaded with powder and rum across the mountains to the Indian towns near the forks of the Ohio. He prospered because, like Johnson and unlike most traders, he made fair trades and he took the trouble to learn Indian languages. During the war British naval supremacy on the Atlantic cut off the flow of French trading goods to America, so Croghan and others of the "Pennsylvania traders" pushed further west along the Ohio. Croghan's post at Logstown, 17 miles south of the forks, became the base for trade with the Wyandot and Miami tribes which lived up the Muskingum, the Scioto, and other tributaries of the Ohio. By 1748 Croghan had enough influence to order the construction of a palisaded fort at the Miami village of Pickawillany (Piqua, Ohio). He also called leaders of the Shawnee, Delaware, and Wyandot tribes together in August to sign the Treaty of Logstown, by which they pledged eternal allegiance to England. Such audacity would be punished by the French as soon as they were able to do so.

The Ohio Country

The Treaty of Aix-la-Chapelle ended King George's War in October of 1748. Louisbourg was handed back to Louis XV, a concession which caused little amusement in New England. Otherwise there was no change in America. Both sides seemed to understand that they had been practicing for the decisive conflict. And immediately all eyes turned toward that river which the British called the Ohio, and the French "La Belle Riviere."

The French sprang into action first, by sending Capt. Céleron de Blainville and 200 soldiers to claim the Ohio watershed and to drive out the

English traders. From Lake Erie Blainville went down the Allegheny, then west along the Ohio as far as the Great Miami. In practically every village he found Scotch-Irish traders from Virginia or Pennsylvania, and playing the comedy with a straight face, ordered them to leave French soil. He also buried some of those lead plates so beloved by the French, their chief value being that they could be rediscovered years later by delighted schoolchildren. Blainville was particularly concerned to see the pro-British atmosphere at Pickawillany, but he did not have enough men to secure the alliance of Indians in an area to which both the French and English had definite claims.

English claims to the Ohio country were based upon various sea-to-sea grants and upon the Treaty of Lancaster (1744), in which the Iroquois had transferred their supposed sovereignty over the valley to the British. The principal British effort in the region, however, was not made by the Crown but by a private land company. The Ohio Company of Virginia was an early-day "realty" firm. It was organized, as were most speculating companies, by influential men in both England and the colonies. Among the important Virginians involved were Thomas Lee, George Mason, Robert Dinwiddie, and George Washington. In 1749 the Crown granted the company 200,000 acres of land along the Ohio on condition that it build a fort and settle 200 families there within 7 years. Colonel Lee sent out a grizzled frontiersman named Christopher Gist to explore the region of the grant. In company with George Croghan, whom he found trading on the Muskingum, Gist passed as far west as Pickawillany. He was enthusiastic about the region, reporting to his employers: "it is fine, rich, level land, well timbered with a great number of little streams and rivulets, and full of beautiful natural meadows, covered with wild rye, blue-grass, and clover, and abounding with turkeys, deer, elks, and most sorts of game, particularly buffaloes, thirty or forty of which are frequently seen in one meadow."

But before the company could do more than lick their chops over this paradise, the French moved in. A new Governor, Marquis Duquesne, directed an aggressive campaign to seize the whole valley. His first step was to send a French-Ottawa raiding party under Charles Langlade to burn down that nest of wicked Englishmen and anglicized Indians at Pickawillany. This accomplished, his next move was to build in 1753 a string of log forts between Lake Erie and the forks: Presqu' Ile, LeBoeuf, and Venango. These posts effectively intimidated the Indians and barred English traders from the West.

Lieutenant Governor Robert Dinwiddie of Virginia, acting on orders from the Crown, sent a letter to the French garrisons ordering them off of "English soil." Dinwiddie's messenger was George Washington, twenty-one years old but already a major in the Virginia militia. Accompanied by Christopher Gist and interpreters, Washington slogged up the Monongahela in December, 1753. At its confluence with the Allegheny he noted in his journal that the forks were the key to the whole region, and the ideal site for an English fort. The French commanders were quite hospitable to the young visitors, but after a polite exchange of pomposities, they vigorously denied the English claim to any part of the Ohio.

Battle of Great Meadows

Dinwiddie finally convinced the Virginia Legislature to vote funds for a fort, and Washington was placed in command of 400 ill-equipped militia who were to protect the building crew. He left in April of 1754, but at Wills Creek he learned that a large French force was already at the forks, building Fort Duquesne. In fact, Washington had a fire fight with an enemy scouting party near his camp at Great Meadows. Expecting a counterattack, he ordered his men to dig trenches and build a stockade. The slapdash fortification was christened "Fort Necessity." Five hundred French and Indians appeared in the surrounding forest on the 4th of July, and a 9-hour shooting match followed. George Washington's first battle was no more glamorous than any of his others; fought in a steady rain, it was the usual tale of blood and mud. The French proposed a truce, following which Washington signed a capitulation which permitted him to withdraw his troops, but in which he took the blame for the whole affair. In fact, a number of contemporaries criticized the novice commander for his actions at Great Meadows. William Johnson wrote: "The Unlucky defeat of our Troops Commanded by Major Washington gave me the utmost concern . . . this will not only animate the French, and their Indians, but stagger the resolution of those inclined to Us, if not effectually draw them from our Interest. . . . I wish Washington had acted with prudence and circumspection requisite in an officer of his Rank . . . he should rather have avoided an Engagement until our Troops were all Assembled." Perhaps Johnson was too severe; Washington was only twenty-two years old, and he learned from his experience. However, the defeat did threaten to expose the whole western frontier to Indian attack.

The French and Indian War

Great Meadows opened the French and Indian War in America. The two mother countries technically remained at peace until 1756, but the British government decided that the enemy must be driven from the Ohio Valley immediately. This was clearly a job for Regulars, and the capture of Fort Duquesne was entrusted to Maj. Gen. Edward Braddock, a burly professional from England's famed Coldstream Guards regiment. "The general was, I think, a brave man, and might probably have made a good figure in some European war," commented Ben Franklin, "but he had too much self-confidence; too high an opinion of the validity of regular troops; too mean a one of both Americans and Indians." Braddock brought two regiments from Ireland with him, and beefed up his force with Virginia militia and a handful of sailors and Indian scouts to make a total force of 2,500 men. Among the famous American alumni of the

"Braddock's Defeat." From a painting by W. E. Deming. Braddock is in the center, about to fall from his horse. Source: State Historical Society of Wisconsin.

expedition were George Washington, serving as Braddock's aide, and a wagon driver named Daniel Boone.

Starting from Fort Cumberland on the Potomac, Braddock finally got his unwieldy column moving on June 9, 1755. The terrain was dense forest, through which axmen had to chop a 12-foot-wide corridor, known thereafter as "Braddock's Road." Nine miles from Fort Duquesne, the French and Indians opened fire upon the advancing Englishmen from a hidden ravine made to order for ambush. The blue-coated American militia took cover, but the red-coated Regulars were ideal targets for the invisible marksmen. This was a moment of truth for soldiers trained in the European military tradition, who found in the few moments before they died that the old lessons no longer applied. Actually, Braddock did not even follow the old rulebook. He did not have enough scouts out to keep him informed of the enemy's whereabouts, and he positioned his baggage train so that it blocked troop movements. Braddock tried to rally his bewildered platoons for a counterattack, but fell mortally wounded. The rear regiment then barged into the forward column, creating more confusion and giving the enemy additional targets. In the holocaust that followed, Washington had two horses shot from under him, and several bullets ripped through his clothes. The troops became a panic-stricken mob, racing back down the Monongahela "as sheep pursued by dogs," and leaving the wounded to be burned by the victorious savages. It was a costly defeat for British arms, with sixty-three of the eighty-six officers killed or wounded. And it left the Pennsylvania and Virginia frontiers wide open to French war parties.

Washington commanded the 1,500 Virginia militiamen who were now called upon to defend 350 miles of frontier. He acted with his usual fortitude, but the task was well-nigh impossible. Turncoat Shawnee and Delaware warriors poured over Braddock's Road and fanned out to attack settlements everywhere west of Fort Cumberland. Washington finally put together a string of forts and organized a patrol system, but desertions and the built-in deficiencies of a strictly defensive policy hampered his efforts. In Pennsylvania the situation was even worse. The Quakers were pacifists, and many of the Germans detested the very idea of military service. In addition, a bitter struggle between the Governor and the Assembly over taxes blocked funds for troops and supplies. So the unprotected Scotch-Irish and German farmers along the Susquehanna went down by the hundreds. "We are in as bad circumstances as ever any poor Christians were ever in," wrote one of them, "for the cries of widowers, widows, fatherless and motherless children are enough to pierce the most hardest of hearts." In desperation a group of frontiersmen brought a wagonload of mangled corpses to the Assembly house in Philadelphia, cursing all Quakers and demanding funds for an all-out war. A gift of 5,000 pounds from the proprietors finally spurred the Assembly into adopting defense measures, including a ring of forts west of the Susquehanna, which held the Indians in check.

Governor William Shirley of Massachusetts became commander of the British army in America following Braddock's death. He conceived several ambitious campaigns, including an assault upon Crown Point to be led by William Johnson. Johnson's Yankee militia and Mohawks defeated a French army under Baron Dieskau on September 8, but Sir William failed to press on and take Crown Point. His farmer-soldiers drifted back home while he built Fort William Henry on Lake George. The French not only reinforced Crown Point, but also started a new fort 12 miles further south at Ticonderoga.

Among Johnson's soldiers was a towering, granite-hard New Hampshireman named Capt. Robert Rogers. Rogers organized a company of Rangers who dressed in green uniforms and fought Indian-style. Indeed, he wrote a report on frontier tactics which is virtually a manual of guerrilla warfare. Included were such principles as surprise, mobility, and camouflage. The Rangers were adept at tracking, animal calls, and marksmanship, and Rogers himself knew the dense thickets and rocky gorges around Lake Champlain as well as his own farm. He became a celebrity because of his daring raids around the French forts, which were often conducted by use of such picturesque devices as snowshoes and ice-skates. His reports were often witty, as when he captured a French sentry near Ticonderoga: "I took five of my party, and marched directly down the road in the middle of the day, till we were challenged by the sentry. I answered in French, signifying that we were friends; the sentinel was thereby deceived, till I came close to him, when perceiving his mistake in great surprize he called, Qui etes vous? I answered, Rogers, and led him from his post in great haste, cutting his breeches and coat from him, that he might march with greater ease and expedition." It wasn't long before Rogers had ascended into pure folklore. In one story concerning his escape from Indians near Lake George, he was pursued to the sheer precipice of Rogers' Rock. There he reversed his snowshoes and then retreated, leaving the redskins convinced that he had actually plunged over the brink.*

After all this scrimmaging in America, England and France formally declared war on May 18, 1756. It became a world war, with battles in Africa and India as well as in Europe and America. The ponderous British war machine got off to a creaky start, being burdened in America with incompetent "political" generals and by an undisguised hostility between the Regulars and the Colonials. Consequently, 1756 and 1757 were years of accomplishment for the French and Indians. Their talented commander, the Marquis de Montcalm, led them to the capture of Oswego in August of 1756. In the same lucky month the next year he forced the surrender of Fort William Henry. Here Montcalm could not control his brandy-soaked Indians, and they butchered 200 prisoners before he could restore order. That winter the New York settlements experienced the same horrors that Virginia and Pennsylvania had known.

*Rogers' reputation in America was blighted by his Tory activities during the Revolution. But Kenneth Roberts rescued it in his novel, *Northwest Passage* (1937), and Rogers has subsequently become a popular figure on television and in motion pictures.

A change in fortune occurred when William Pitt became Secretary of State in 1757. He revitalized the English war efforts by replacing the old military incompetents with younger leaders like Jeffrey Amherst and James Wolfe. He brought the American colonies more fully into the war by offering them a million pounds worth of "compensation," or more realistically, bribes, to raise troops. This huge debt would affect the course of American history, but the results soon justified the effort. The fall of Louisbourg to Amherst and Wolfe in the summer of 1758 marked a turning point in the war. At the same time Col. John Bradstreet captured Fort Frontenac, thus giving the British control of Lake Ontario and severing the French lifeline to the Ohio. In the fall Gen. John Forbes cut a new wagon road across the laurel-choked ridges between Carlisle and Fort Duquesne. When the vanguard of his army under Colonel Washington approached the fort, they found it razed and abandoned. Forbes renamed it Fort Pitt, and the surrounding settlement was called Pittsburgh.

In 1759 the British delivered other sledgehammer blows at the staggering Frenchmen. Amherst advanced upon Ticonderoga and Crown Point, finding them both abandoned by the retreating enemy. Wolfe's army of 9,000 Regulars captured Quebec in September after an epic battle on the nearby Plains of Abraham, in which both Wolfe and Montcalm were killed. Montreal was forced to surrender a year later, and the French signed a capitulation. Only mopping-up operations were necessary in 1761. In the west these were conducted by Major Rogers, who accepted the surrender of Detroit and other French posts before the end of the year.

Treaty of Paris

The Treaty of Paris officially ended the Seven Years War on February 10, 1763. It made Great Britain the strongest nation in the world. France was eliminated from North America, with all her territory east of the Mississippi except New Orleans and two small islands at the mouth of the St. Lawrence being ceded to England. Spain had belatedly joined the war in 1762, and among the penalties for her numerous defeats was the surrender of Florida. For consolation France gave her the town of New Orleans and the vast Louisiana territory lying west of the Mississippi. A strong and vigorous England, a feeble and declining Spain thus became the contending powers on the continent.

The defeat of France meant that the English language and culture would be carried into the American West. But there was danger for England in the victory. The Americans had learned the lessons of frontier fighting, while the hidebound British generals had not. When the Virginians crouched behind trees rather than traditionally facing enemy fire in massed columns, General Braddock struck them with the flat of his sword and called them cowards. Major Rogers' recommendation that troops squat on the ground to allow the enemy's first volley to pass overhead was good advice, but to the European professionals it was unmanly and unsoldierly behavior. General Wolfe's famous statement that "the Americans are in general the dirtiest, most contemptible cowardly dogs that you can conceive" reflected a misunderstanding of the new tactical requirements.

So the victory was not an unmixed blessing for England, because it created as many problems as it solved. The English-held area was doubled, and the problems of administration and defense became that much more complex. The London government felt that since it had saved the colonists from French tyranny, it had a right to regulate the fur trade, land policy, and westward expansion in general. These efforts at closer control were regarded in the colonies as a new brand of tyranny, and a spirit of resistance began to grow. Peter Kalm, a Swedish university professor who toured America in 1749, predicted even then that the defeat of the French might lead to separatism, since "in times of war these dangerous neighbors are sufficient to prevent the connection of the colonies with their mother country from being quite broken off. The English government has therefore sufficient reason to consider the French in North America as the best means of keeping their colonies in due submission." Now that the "dangerous neighbors" had been subdued, His Majesty's American subjects began to think that they could also dispense with His Majesty.

Selected Readings   Any study of the Anglo-French conflicts must begin with Francis Parkman. *Count Frontenac and New France under Louis XIV* (Boston, 1898) deals with King William's War; *A Half-Century of Conflict*, 2 vols. (Boston, 1898), covers Queen Anne's War and King George's War. *Montcalm and Wolfe*, 2 vols. (Boston, 1898), describes the French and Indian War. A critique of Parkman's work is W. J. Eccles, "History of New France According to Francis Parkman," *William and Mary Quarterly*, 3d ser., vol. 18 (April, 1961). An excellent short history is Howard H. Peckham, *The Colonial Wars* (Chicago, 1964). Details of the Anglo-Spanish struggle in the South are covered in Verner W. Crane, *The Southern Frontier*, and in an illuminating article by Albert Harkness, Jr., "Americanism and Jenkin's Ear," *Mississippi Valley Historical Review*, vol. 37 (June, 1950).

The northern frontier is described in Frederick Jackson Turner, "The First Official Frontier of the Massachusetts Bay," in *The Frontier in American History* (New York, 1920). See also Douglas Leach, *The Northern Colonial Frontier, 1607-1763* (New York, 1966). John Williams, *The Redeemed Captive Returning to Zion* (Boston, 1707), is an excellent primary source. Cotton Mather's views of the Indians are in *Magnalia Christi Americana*, vol. VI (Boston, 1702). Nellis M. Crouse has studied two important Frenchmen of the period in *LeMoyne d'Iberville, Soldier of New France* (Ithaca, 1954) and *La Verendrye: Fur Trader and Explorer* (Ithaca, 1965). The latter work is more helpful than the former, and contains a summary of the scholarly debate over the extent of the Verendrye family's travels.

Aspects of the northern frontier are also considered in Arthur H. Buffinton, "The Policy of Albany and English Westward Expansion," *Mississippi Valley Historical Review*, vol. 8 (March, 1922); also Anthony F. C. Wallace, "Origins of Iroquois

Neutrality: The Grand Settlement of 1701," *Pennsylvania History*, vol. 24 (July, 1957). James T. Flexner's *Mohawk Baronet: Sir William Johnson of New York* (New York, 1959) is a key biography. Nicholas B. Wainwright, *George Groghan, Wilderness Diplomat* (Chapel Hill, 1959), is well researched. Kenneth P. Bailey's *The Ohio Company of Virginia and the Westward Movement, 1748-1792* (Glendale, 1939) remains the definitive work on an important subject. George Washington's role in the French and Indian War is thoroughly traced in volumes I and II of Douglas Southall Freeman's *George Washington*, 7 vols. (New York, 1948-1957). Lee McCardell's *Ill-Starred General: Braddock of the Coldstream Guards* (Pittsburgh, 1958) should be read only in conjunction with the important article by Stanley Pargellis, "Braddock's Defeat," *American Historical Review*, vol. 41 (January, 1936). John R. Cuneo, *Robert Rogers of the Rangers* (New York, 1959), is excellent. Rogers' own *Journals* (Albany, 1883) are worth reading.

IV. The Trans-Appalachian Frontier

The British government's western policy started with a bang and ended with a whimper. George III cast covetous eyes on the American West, eagerly anticipating a huge income from the sale of land and the taxes on furs. His ministers accordingly groped for an administrative policy that would satisfy these hopes—but without success. The land was vast, the colonists recalcitrant, and the problems surprisingly complex. To begin with, the officials' geographical knowledge was at a child's level, being gleaned largely from old French books. During the war when his generals advised the Duke of Newcastle that Annapolis should be defended, he replied: "Annapolis, Annapolis! Oh, yes, Annapolis must be defended; to be sure, Annapolis should be defended,—where is Annapolis?" More than sound geographical information was needed before the ministers could solve the swarm of problems that faced them: the claims of various colonies to Western territory; the demands of private land companies; the efficient administration of the fur trade; the successful handling of the Indians. The government had little success in any of these areas during 12 trying years. British ineptitude in the conduct of Indian relations, for example, was immediately demonstrated by the outbreak of an Indian war known as Pontiac's Conspiracy.

Pontiac's War Sir Jeffrey Amherst, hero of the last French war and now commander of all British forces in North America, regarded Indians as "pernicious vermin." The extent of his contempt was clearly indicated by the policies which he instituted. His soldiers were ordered to cease all fraternization with the savages. The customary free ammunition was no longer to be given away at the forts, rum rations were to be stopped, and the practice of giving presents to the Indians was

53

to be ended as a useless expense for the Crown. Experienced frontiersmen, including William Johnson and George Croghan, warned that these steps would bring disaster. But Amherst, "cold and reserved," remained convinced that the savages could be ignored now that their military usefulness was at an end.

This abrupt about-face in policy was practically made to order for various anti-British agitators in the West. Many French traders were still hostile toward their recent enemies, and they inflamed the Indians by telling them that a French army would soon return to "drive the red-coated dogs into the sea." The Delaware Prophet, a half-mad medicine man, went through the villages preaching expulsion of all white men from the continent. Such exhortations inspired Pontiac, a noted war chief among the Ottawas, to organize a loose confederation of tribes for an armed attack upon the British forts in the West. The Ottawas were traditional allies of the French, and were feared by even the most warlike of the eastern tribes. One of their customs was to drink the blood of slain enemies in the belief that their power would be thus transferred to the victors.

Pontiac's immediate target was Fort Detroit. He had planned to have Ottawas carrying concealed weapons infiltrate the walls and thus surprise the garrison. However, an informer told the British commandant, Major George Gladwin, about the plot and he was able to frustrate it. Pontiac finally unleashed his warriors on May 9, 1763, but though they successfully attacked a number of parties outside the walls, they were unable to take the fort itself. In fact, Gladwin held on with bulldog tenacity through a siege which lasted until the end of October.

On other fronts Pontiac's tribal allies scored impressive victories. The Potawatomies surprised Fort St. Joseph on May 25, and the Chippewas overran Fort Michilimackinac by the ruse of a lacrosse game. As the ball bounced into the stockade, the braves rushed in after it and then fell upon the unsuspecting defenders. Further east, the Shawnee, Delaware, and Seneca also took up the hatchet. Forts and frontier settlements everywhere in western Pennsylvania were destroyed with heavy loss of life. These attacks do not seem to have been the result of a carefully planned operation directed by Pontiac, as Parkman's term "conspiracy" would suggest, but were rather a spontaneous explosion of pent-up rage at the supposed British maltreatment. Pontiac may have been a born leader, but neither he nor any other Indian chieftain had the political organization which could guarantee coordinated action. Be that as it may, the uprising was so effective that by July 1, Forts Pitt, Niagara, and Detroit were the only white islands remaining in a red sea.

Back in New York an enraged Amherst, his smugness suddenly punctured, suggested that smallpox be spread among the enemy. In fact the commandant at Fort Pitt had already initiated "germ warfare" by giving infected blankets to several visiting Delawares, who thereby carried an epidemic to their own villages as well as those of the Shawnee. Amherst acted more convention-ally by sending Colonel Henry Bouquet and his Highlanders to relieve the be-sieged Fort Pitt, and other troops were ordered to Detroit. By November Pontiac knew that no French army would ever come to his assistance. He arranged a truce and then slipped away to the Illinois country, there to be murdered by an Indian assassin in 1769. Thus ended the last genuine Indian opportunity to drive the white invaders back across the mountains.

Pontiac's uprising added to the internal difficulties of the colonies. As the Indians smashed eastward into Pennsylvania, they took a heavy toll in lives and property. The frontiersmen were helpless, since they were shackled by an irresolute and tight-fisted Quaker Assembly which refused to vote funds for defense. In desperation the Westerners struck blindly at the nearest targets. These happened to be peaceful Conestoga Indians living near Lancaster. Fifty armed men from Paxton township killed six of these Indians in December, 1763, and then advanced upon Philadelphia intending to attack Moravian Indians who had been taken to the city for protection. Regular troops were ordered out to meet these "Paxton Boys," who soon appeared in blanket coats and moc-casins, brandishing tomahawks and "uttering hideous outcries." Ben Franklin headed a team of negotiators which persuaded the Boys to submit a *Declaration and Remonstrance* instead of fighting. In this document the frontiersmen de-manded a more aggressive Indian policy, and a greater representation for the western counties in the colonial Legislature.

The Proclamation Line of 1763

The Indian war also forced the British ministry to act on the "western prob-lem." Their solution, embodied in the Royal Proclamation of October 7, 1763, was to run a boundary line between the white and Indian lands. The crest of the Appalachians, the most obvious landmark, became the boundary. All whites living west of this line were to "remove themselves." Fur traders wishing to go across the line had to obtain licenses from the British military, which was to rule the area. No private persons (read speculators) could purchase land from the Indians. The Crown was thus reasserting its control over westward migra-tion by declaring the trans-Appalachian region to be a big Indian reservation. It was also attempting to buy time; the line presumably would force settlement north (to Nova Scotia) and south (to Florida), thus giving the ministers a chance to work out a long-range policy for the West.

Certain groups in both America and England supported the so-called Proclamation Line. Fur traders applauded any plan that would keep the West in a primitive condition. Some landowners and employers along the seaboard feared that westward migration would cut into their profits or draw away their workers. British manufacturers of the "mercantilist" persuasion believed that rapid settlement of the interior would have the undesirable effect of encouraging manufacturing in America. And various reform or religious groups, such as the Quakers, felt that the Indians should be protected for humanitarian reasons. On the other hand, American land speculators generally opposed the line. They had obtained grants in the transmountain region from the colonial governments, but these were now canceled under the proclamation. And the frontier farmer,—that usually penniless squatter who represented "the people"—went west despite the King's edict. In fact, 30,000 of these hardy souls crossed the line between 1765 and 1768. The British government was thus defying history. Of more immediate significance was the fact that when laws are passed which cannot be enforced, people are tempted to evade the law.

George Washington's reaction to the Proclamation Line reflected the views of the speculators. Land warrants had been issued in lieu of pay to many veterans of the French war, and through purchase of these warrants Washington had acquired title to more than 30,000 acres on the Ohio and Great Kanawha Rivers. He advised his agent, William Crawford, that he was interested in securing more land despite the Proclamation Line: "I offered in my last to join you in attempting to secure some of the most valuable lands in the King's part, which I think may be accomplished after a while, notwithstanding the proclamation, that restrains it at present, and prohibits the settling of them at all; for I can never look upon that proclamation in any other light (but this I say between ourselves), than as a temporary expedient to quiet the minds of the Indians." He went on to suggest that land surveys could be carried out under pretense of hunting game, the usual "cover" for speculators.

Land Companies

The many land companies that blossomed after the war all scrambled to get Crown recognition of their now-illegal claims in the West. Washington was involved in the Mississippi Company, which asked for 2½ million acres at the junction of the Ohio and the Mississippi. George Croghan in 1766 joined a Philadelphia trading firm with the resounding title of Baynton, Wharton, and Morgan to form the Illinois Company. The Baynton group was one of several known as "Suffering Traders" because of their heavy losses in Pontiac's War; and to help them forget their financial miseries they begged the King for a 1.2-million-acre grant bounded by the Mississippi, the Wisconsin, and the Wabash. The most ambitious scheme was hatched by the Indiana Company. Formed in 1765 by Croghan, Ben Franklin, the Baynton firm, and other prominent colonials, the company started out reasonably enough by petitioning for 3½ million acres between the Monongahela and the Ohio just west of the Proclamation Line. By 1769 this group had become the octopus among American land companies. It bought off competitors (such as the old Ohio Company) and distributed stock to influential politicians in London.* In that year it petitioned for 20 million acres between Pittsburgh and the Scioto (nothing modest about them!). It also proposed a new colony in this region, to be named Vandalia in honor of the Queen's supposed descent from the ancient Vandals. Only the approach of the Revolution caused the Privy Council to defer final approval of the grandiose project.

The power of the land speculators was clearly revealed in the negotiation of Indian treaties, by which the Proclamation Line was moved westward and more of the West opened to settlement. General Braddock had appointed two Superintendents of Indian Affairs, and these officers were retained after the war. Sir William Johnson, who administered the region north of the Ohio River while John Stuart handled the south, suggested in his 1764 "plan for management of Indian Affairs" that the two officials be made independent of both the military and the colonial governments. In this way they would be able to supervise trading more effectively and see to it that the Indians were not cheated by unscrupulous whites. Johnson also recommended that all trade be confined to government posts, where interpreters could make sure that fair prices were offered and where gunsmiths could keep the savages happy by repairing their firearms. This plan was tried out for 4 years, but it failed because the Indians did not like to travel long distances to the government stations. In fact, French traders from St. Louis (founded in 1763) and New Orleans went to the Indian villages and came away with all the best pelts. Consequently, in the Hillsborough Plan of 1768, regulation of the fur trade was returned to the colonial governments. The superintendents, however, were to be responsible for negotiating new boundary lines with the Indians. By 1768 the pressure from American speculators was so great that the ministry ordered Johnson and Stuart to readjust the Proclamation Line by running new boundaries west of the Appalachians. And the speculators appeared in person at the treaty conferences to make sure that their desires were satisfied.

In the conference at Fort Stanwix, New York, in the fall of 1768, Johnson had specific instructions to run a new line from Owege in New York to the mouth of the Great Kanawha on the Ohio. Under pressure from speculators he violated these instructions by extending the line north from Owege to Fort Stanwix, and west from the Kanawha all the way to the mouth of the Tennessee, thus opening vast tracts in western New York and south of the Ohio River to lawful occupation. Sir William even managed to keep from laughing as he reported with assumed innocence that the Iroquois had simply *insisted* on surrendering their claims to the Kentucky region. But the evidence indicates that the Indiana Company, which had Samuel Wharton at the conference, offered the Superintendent a sizable cut of the profits to be made from exploita-

---

*One of these was the banker Thomas Walpole, so the project was also known as the Walpole Company.

tion of the newly opened land. So for £10,000 worth of trade goods, the Five Nations magnanimously gave away southwestern New York, western Pennsylvania, West Virginia, and then threw in Tennessee and Kentucky for good measure!*

Dr. Thomas Walker was also at Fort Stanwix representing the Loyal Land Company, a Virginia firm which had claims to the territory south of the Ohio in which the Indiana Company was interested. The good doctor apparently agreed to concessions made to the Indiana Company because this would force Superintendent Stuart to redraw the southern boundary line farther west, thus opening up the Loyal Company's lands in the Kentucky country. And this was exactly the way it worked out. Stuart had already in 1768 signed the Treaty of Hard Labor with the Cherokees, which ran the boundary from the Great Kanawha down to Chiswell's mine in the southwestern corner of Virginia. But the Fort Stanwix treaty forced him to move the line once again. In the Treaty of Lochaber (1770) it was run from the Kanawha to the Long Island of the Holston. To add insult to injury, when John Donelson surveyed this line the next year, he ran it along the Kentucky rather than the Kanawha by "mistake," thus opening up even more territory to the west. As the speculators chortled over these ill-gotten gains, the Shawnee and Delaware warriors whose hunting grounds had been taken away gathered in their smoke-filled lodges and talked of war.

Trans-Appalachian Settlement

While the British ministry struggled unsuccessfully to find a satisfactory western policy, restless pioneers pushed across the mountain barrier to establish the familiar buckskin and log-cabin culture on the west side of the Appalachians. Some followed the Kittanning Path, which ran from the upper Susquehanna to Fort Pitt. Most came over Braddock's Road and Forbes' Road. Even before the end of the French and Indian War, cabins and cornfields were appearing around Fort Pitt and along such tributaries of the Monongahela as the Cheat, the Redstone, and the Youghiogheny. Colonel Bouquet viewed the invasion of these "vagabonds" with justifiable apprehension. Their presence threatened to ignite another Indian war, particularly since the region had been guaranteed to the savages in the Treaty of Easton (1758). Bouquet accordingly ordered the "scoundrels" to go back East, and when the orders were ignored, he burned cabins and forcibly removed as many of the squatters as he could catch. Pontiac's Rebellion had a more stimulating effect upon the intruders, but as soon as that threat receded they came back across the mountains in droves. Governor Dunmore of Virginia explained why they did so: "But My Lord I have learnt from experience that the established Authority of any government in America

*The British government refused to accept the cession west of the Kanawha, but this was a technicality which the Americans ignored.

and the policy of Government at home, are both insufficient to restrain the Americans; and that they do and will remove as their avidity and restlessness incite them. They acquire no attachment to Place: But wandering about Seems engrafted in their Nature; and it is a weakness incident to it, that they Should forever immagine the Lands further off are Still better than those upon which they are already Settled." The immediate result of this land lure was the rapid settlement of western Pennsylvania, particularly after the Fort Stanwix treaty in 1768 had legalized land purchases between the Appalachians and the Ohio.

In the same period other pioneers began moving out of Virginia and North Carolina to plant settlements in Tennessee and Kentucky. Northeastern Tennessee was a land of beautiful mountains clad in primeval forest. Through the valleys ran a number of sparkling rivers which all drained westward to form the great Tennessee: the Clinch, the Holston, the Watauga, and—name of names —the French Broad. The superabundance of game in the region had early attracted roving hunters, among the first of whom (1746) was the Stephen Holston who gave his name to the river. However the Cherokees, a proud and independent mountain tribe, were a constant threat to these early intruders. Not until 1770 did migration begin in earnest. Then James Robertson came to the Watauga from North Carolina. A typical Scotch-Irish frontiersman in his courage and tenacity, Robertson also had qualities which made him a leader in the community. He persuaded a number of his friends to cross the mountains, and these were soon joined by hundreds of ex-Regulators who fled North Carolina after the defeat of their movement by Governor Tryon in 1771. The sense of independence which these migrants brought with them was reflected in the political history of eastern Tennessee.

The Wataugans soon had an opportunity to prove their adaptability. Surveys for the Lochaber Treaty line revealed that the settlements were west of the boundary. There was also uncertainty as to whether the region belonged to Virginia or North Carolina. The pioneers met the test by forming their own government, the Watauga Association. Representatives of the fortified hamlets from the Holston to the Nolichucky met in convention and drew up the Articles of Association. This document created an elective five-man committee, which ran the government with full executive, legislative, and judicial powers. Among the commissioners were Robertson and John Sevier, the latter a dashing and ambitious frontiersman who was destined to play a leading role in southwestern politics over the next few decades. One of the first acts of these commissioners was to sign a treaty with the Cherokee for the leasing of land. They also administered rough justice to the lawless individuals who appeared in Watauga as they did on every frontier. Little time was spent pondering abstract theories of law; a horse thief was arrested on Monday, tried on Wednesday, and hanged on Friday. The Wataugans continued to practice self-government until 1778, when they officially became a part of North Carolina. The whole experiment has often been cited as a model of frontier democracy.

Kentucky

Northwest of the Watauga settlements lay America's original Garden of Eden, Kentucky. If any region approached the Earthly Paradise dreamed of by the first settlers in America, this one did. Here there were parklike savannahs, broken by clusters of live oak trees and carpeted with the world-famous blue-grass. The limestone soil was as rich as any in the country. There were numerous streams and rivers, and the canebrakes along their banks were choked with game. Buffalo, which in the eighteenth century roamed as far east as the Appalachians, and deer were especially plentiful. Lazy hunters had merely to lie in wait by the salt licks, and they could bag enough meat for a fortnight. But there were obstacles to immediate settlement: the land was rimmed on the east by the main range of the Appalachians, and to the north the easier route of the Ohio River was dominated by fierce Indian tribes which used Kentucky as a battleground.

The first well-known explorer of the region was not typical of the frontiersmen who followed. Dr. Thomas Walker was a well-educated Virginia physician who had at one time tutored Thomas Jefferson. Walker's record of his trip through eastern Kentucky in 1750 is therefore meticulous and informative. The journey was undertaken to examine the 800,000 acres which the Crown had just granted to the doctor's Loyal Land Company. Starting from the east side of the Blue Ridge, Walker and five companions crossed the upper reaches of the Holston and the Clinch, following buffalo trails over one ridge after another. In April they passed through a wide gap in the mountains, which Walker named Cumberland Gap, and which subsequently became an important gateway to the West. Walker explored the upper reaches of several of the principal rivers, including the Cumberland, the Kentucky, and the Big Sandy. But he and his rain-soaked crew stumbled eastward, like blind men feeling an elephant, without ever having reached the heart of the bluegrass country.

Other explorers of "Kaintuck" were closer to the conventional mold for such types. John Finley was an irrepressible Irishman who loaded some trade goods in a canoe and paddled down the Ohio in 1752. He encountered Shawnee warriors, who for some inexplicable reason did not roast him over a slow fire. Instead they invited him to build a trading post on the Kentucky River, which he did. In 1753 Finley's camp was attacked by an Ottawa raiding party, but he managed to escape across the mountains. After the voluble frontiersman got back to Pennsylvania all he could talk about were the beauties of the bluegrass country. When Finley served as a wagoner with Braddock's army in 1755, one of the fellow teamsters with whom he talked was a young North Carolinian named Daniel Boone.

The names of most participants in the westward movement are unknown. On occasion, however, a hero emerges from the crowd and his name and exploits are preserved in history. The prime requisite for heroes along the frontier

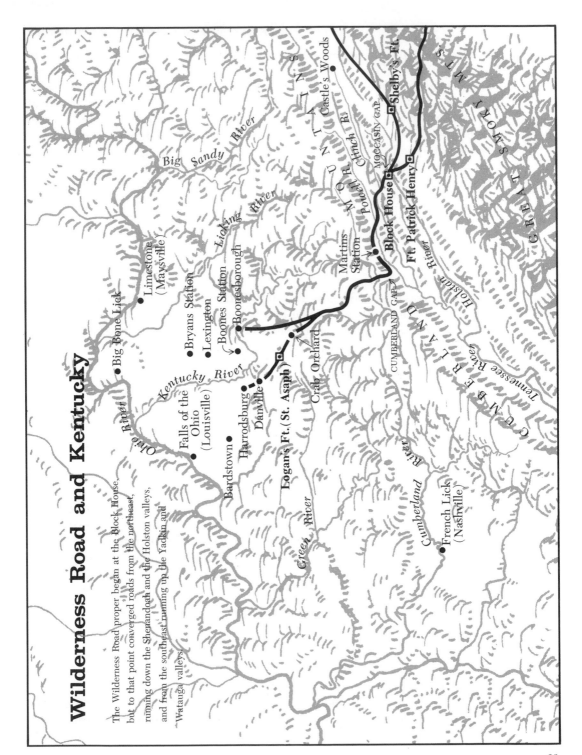

Wilderness Road and Kentucky

The Wilderness Road proper began at the Block House, but to that point converged roads from the northeast, running down the Shenandoah and the Holston valleys, and from the southeast running up the Yadkin and Watauga valleys.

Castle's Woods

Shelby's Ft.

GREAT SMOKY MTS.

MOCCASIN GAP

Block House

Ft. Patrick Henry

Clinch R.

Powell Clinch R.

Big Sandy River

Licking River

Limestone (Maysville)

Martins Station

Big Bone Lick

Bryans Station

Lexington

Boones Station

Boonesborough

CUMBERLAND GAP

Holston River

Ohio River

Kentucky River

Crab Orchard

Falls of the Ohio (Louisville)

Harrodsburg

Danville

Logan's Ft. (St. Asaph)

Bardstown

Cumberland River

Tennessee River

Green River

C U M B E R L A N D

French Lick (Nashville)

was proven ability in combat against the Indians. And the hero not only had to outshoot the redskins, he also had to outsmart them. Traditions about local heroes emphasize their cleverness. One of the standard stories has the frontiersman splitting logs near his cabin, when a half dozen Indians rush up and exult over their capture of a noted enemy. The cool woodsman asks the red men to help him hold open the last log while he removes the wedge. They agree, and are then trapped when the green wood snaps shut, pinning their fingers. This feat is attributed to John Lovel of Washington, New Hampshire; David Malcolm of Brunswick, Maine; Tom Quick of Milford, Pennsylvania; and Daniel Boone of Kentucky. But Boone alone became a nationally known symbol of America's Heroic Age, which lasted for a little more than a century until it ended with Buffalo Bill Cody.

Daniel Boone

Boone was born in 1734 near Reading, Pennsylvania, but the family shortly moved to North Carolina's Yadkin River. There Daniel grew to his mature size of 5 feet 8 inches and 175 pounds—a far cry from the giant of popular imagination. He had a natural aptitude for those skills most valued on the old frontier, including tracking and marksmanship. Boone was alternately farmer and hunter; by 1767 his hunting trips were taking him across the Blue Ridge and as far as the Big Sandy in Kentucky. His trip of 1769 became the most famous in the history of the Old Southwest. John Finley, now a peddler of needles and pins, appeared at Boone's cabin in 1768 and the two men spent the winter talking of nothing but "Kentucke." In the spring of 1769 they led four companions and a pack train westward toward the mountains and the Promised Land beyond. Romantic legend insists that this trip was undertaken because of Boone's love of adventure. He did enjoy long trips in the wilderness, but there were more prosaic reasons for the journey. Daniel had the usual large family (five sons and two daughters), and he was more often in debt than out of it. The expedition was financed by Judge Richard Henderson, who had elaborate plans for land speculation in Kentucky, and who employed Boone to scout out the most desirable tracts. The men would also have a chance to collect some frontier "cash": deerskins.

The little cavalcade passed through Cumberland Gap and then went north along an Indian trail known as the Warriors' Path. Camp was made on a tributary of the Kentucky known ever since as Station Camp Creek. The men spread out to hunt for skins and to explore the country. On one occasion Boone was captured by Shawnees, who warned him that if he stayed in the country he would be killed. They called Kentucky the Dark and Bloody Ground, because it was the traditional battlefield for many warring tribes. Boone escaped, but the Indian warning had a dampening effect on his companions. Even Finley, the eternal optimist, decided that maybe Kentucky wasn't quite ready for white occupancy. So all went back East except Daniel and his brother Squire, who had come out a few months after the others. In the spring of 1770, Squire too went back to the Yadkin for supplies, leaving Daniel alone in the wilderness. He thoroughly enjoyed his solitary rambles through the heart of Kentucky. While European philosophers like Rousseau were idolizing the "natural man," here he was in fact rather than theory. In the fall of 1770, the story goes, a squad of hunters under Casper Mansker heard strange sounds coming from a nearby thicket. Upon investigating, they found Daniel Boone stretched before the campfire singing an old English folksong.

Boone returned home in the spring of 1771. His encounter with the "Long Hunters" (so called because of their extensive trips in the wilderness) indicated that Kentucky was now well known to a number of adventurous frontiersmen. Yet Boone was subsequently credited with the discovery of the region. One nineteenth century biography called him "The First White Man of the West," ignoring Walker, Finley, and a host of other less well-known explorers. James Smith of Pennsylvania had in 1766 gone through Cumberland Gap and hunted the upper reaches of the Cumberland and the entire length of the Tennessee. Casper Mansker belonged to a party under James Knox, which roamed all over western Kentucky in 1770 and 1771. But who remembers a name like James Smith?

Most of Boone's renown can be traced to a brief sketch about him published in 1784 by one John Filson, a Pennsylvania schoolteacher. Filson wrote in a flowery style, and made his hero into a polished gentleman and a coonskin-capped philosopher. (Boone actually wore an old felt hat, since skin caps were too hot and attracted fleas.) At one point he has Boone saying that the Cumberland Mountains "are so wild and horrid, that it is impossible to behold them without terror. The spectator is apt to imagine that nature had formerly suffered some violent convulsion; and that these are the ruins, not of Persopolis or Palmyra, but of the world!" Boone was an accomplished scout and had admirable personal qualities, but it was simply happenstance that he became the representative hero of the trans-Appalachian frontier.

By the spring of 1774 land speculators were practically bumping into each other as they staked out claims in the bluegrass region. Among them was James Harrod, a fearless Pennsylvanian who laid out the little stockade village of Harrodsburg on a hill 8 miles west of the Kentucky River. Another was John Floyd, an unacademic schoolteacher from Virginia, who was making surveys for influential friends back East. Virginia had several parties of surveyors in the area that year. She claimed all land east of the Kentucky, on the basis of the 1609 charter, and organized it as "Fincastle County." However, all the claims made in Kentucky were illegal, since the Proclamation Line was still in effect and the Crown had not accepted the Fort Stanwix cession west of the Great Kanawha. This made little difference to the frontiersmen. Of more immediate concern was the threatening attitude of the Shawnees.

Lord Dunmore's War

The tribesmen, embittered by the Fort Stanwix treaty and by the increase of white invaders in Kentucky, finally exploded in a frontier conflict known as Lord Dunmore's War. Dunmore, the last royal Governor of Virginia, helped provoke the clash himself. He was a penniless Scottish peer, and like most royal governors he was determined to improve his financial situation through land speculation. Embroiled in a bitter dispute with Pennsylvania over ownership of the Ohio River region, he shouldered his way into Pittsburgh and then appointed Indian-hating Dr. John Connolly as commander there. The Shawnees had learned that the "Long Knives" from Virginia were more dangerous enemies than the Pennsylvanians. Dr. Connolly did not disappoint them, for his troops attacked a Shawnee peace delegation. This was too much for the long-suffering savages, who fell upon the outlying settlements in June of 1774. Dunmore now had what he wanted, an opportunity to drive the Indians from Kentucky and thus open up that desirable land for profit-seeking Virginians like himself.

The Governor immediately sent Daniel Boone and Michael Stoner out to Kentucky to warn the surveyors of their danger. The two men raced across 800 miles of wilderness in 60 days, ranging as far north as the falls of the Ohio. Boone even paused at Harrodsburg to build a small cabin for himself, a display of equanimity which none of his companions was tempted to emulate. Most of the surveyors got back across the mountains safely. A number of them enlisted in the militia under Col. Andrew Lewis, who was ordered to march straight up the Great Kanawha to the heart of the Shawnee territory. His volunteers assembled on the Greenbriar, dressed in the usual buckskin-linsy combinations, and equipped with the long flintlock rifle, bullet pouch, powder horn, tomahawk, and knife. Such future fighting men of the Revolution as James Robertson, James Harrod, Benjamin Logan, and John Floyd were there—learning the basic lessons of frontier warfare. On October 10, the backwoodsmen met Chief Cornstalk's Shawnees in a bloody battle at Point Pleasant, near the mouth of the Kanawha. It was a classic frontier engagement, tree-to-tree and hand-to-hand, with the Shawnees finally withdrawing across the Ohio. To save their villages, they agreed in the subsequent Treaty of Camp Charlotte to permit white occupation of Kentucky.

The Transylvania Company

The Shawnee defeat encouraged the plans of Judge Richard Henderson of North Carolina to establish a princely and profitable domain in the new country. He and some influential friends formed the Transylvania Company for purposes of land speculation in Kentucky. The company first planned to lease the area between the Kentucky and Cumberland Rivers from the Cherokee Indians, but by 1775 they had decided to buy it—despite British policy. In March of 1775 he assembled the savages at Sycamore Shoals on the Watauga, and there traded £10,000 worth of guns, rum, and other commodities for two-thirds of modern Kentucky.

For a judge, Henderson was amazingly indifferent to the law. In buying Kentucky lands he violated the Proclamation Line of 1763, the various governmental prohibitions on private treaties with the Indians, and the claims of both North Carolina and Virginia to the area of the purchase. Henderson might have justified his purchase by citing quasi-legal precedents such as the Camden-Yorke decision. This was an unofficial British judicial opinion which had sanctioned private purchases from the "Indian princes"—of India. Speculators from the Illinois-Wabash Company used this decision as a pretext to buy Indian lands north of the Ohio in 1774. But the judge never even bothered to invoke this flimsy authority. He simply went ahead with his illegal operations, apparently hoping that someone, somewhere, would eventually give him post facto approval for what he was doing. He attempted to get such approval from the newly assembled Continental Congress by sending to that body an agent with the unfortunately suggestive name of James Hogg. Congress simply referred him back to Virginia. The immediate reaction of the colonial governors was not too encouraging. Dunmore of Virginia blasted Henderson and his associates as "disorderly persons," while Martin of North Carolina denounced them as "an infamous Company of land Pyrates." But Henderson had a thick hide, for he ignored the insults and went right ahead with plans for a colony in the purchased area.

Daniel Boone was hired to lay out a road to the company's lands on the Kentucky River. The veteran woodsman left Sycamore Shoals before the treaty conference had ended, and with thirty skilled axmen he carved out a pack trail subsequently known as Boone's Trace, or more popularly as the Wilderness Road. This "road" was often no more than a series of blazed tree trunks. It ran for 225 miles from the Long Island of the Holston to the Kentucky River, crossing swollen rivers, steep mountains, and dense cane thickets. Prowling Shawnees attacked Boone's party near the end of the trail and killed two men, certain proof that Lord Dunmore's War had not really cleared the savages from the bluegrass. Once on the banks of the Kentucky, Boone began building log cabins around a bubbling spring, and thus laid the foundations for a settlement which came to be called Boonesborough. Meanwhile Henderson himself was leading forty emigrants up the road. His arrival on April 20 was greeted with a twenty-gun salute, and the Transylvania experiment was under way.

Henderson's ambitious schemes soon brought him into conflict with the other Kentucky settlers. Transylvania was to be a proprietary colony, with the proprietors controlling all land sales and collecting annual quitrents of 2 shillings per hundred acres. The quitrent was of feudal origin, being originally a cash payment by which a tenant "quit" himself of actual service to his lord by paying a rent instead. Such an archaic device was ill-suited to frontier America, and proprietors had had considerable difficulty in collecting such rents on earlier frontiers. The company also gave every indication that it would claim the most desirable lands for itself. Thus it threatened the interests of men like James Harrod, who had returned to Harrodsburg with his followers in March and was now rebuilding that settlement. Benjamin Logan had accompanied Henderson part way up the Wilderness Road, but had split off to found St. Asaph's (or Logan's) Station, south of Harrodsburg. Such independent frontiersmen were almost certain to clash with a feudalistic land company.

The judge attempted to conciliate his fellow settlers by holding a conference to frame a government and iron out the problems of land titles. Delegates from the various settlements met under a giant elm tree at Boonesborough in May of 1775. Befuddled by legalistic jargon, the representatives approved a constitution which called for perpetual quitrents and a veto power by the proprietors. They also established court and militia systems, and then in a burst of hopeless idealism passed an act "to prevent profane swearing and Sabbath breaking." However, the honeymoon ended later in the year; when the company announced a large increase in land prices, the settlers defied them.

The Kentucky settlements flourished despite the proprietor-settler dispute. Symbolic of the future growth was the arrival at Boonesborough in September of the first white women in Kentucky—Daniel's wife Rebecca and daughter Jemima. Their presence was a mortgage to the future, a guarantee that the frontiersmen were now committed to permanent settlement in the bluegrass region. Items long unfamiliar to male eyes appeared at the stations: soap kettles, washboards, hickory brooms, spinning wheels—and looking glasses. Daniel Boone displayed great courage in bringing his womenfolk to the Dark and Bloody Ground. The forests around the fort were infested with bloodthirsty savages, and the outpost was over 200 miles from so-called civilization. It is thus understandable why Boonesborough has been cited as a classic example of the pioneer spirit.

The problem of a satisfactory government for Kentucky soon became acute. There were rumblings of a possible war from the east, where the Continental Congress was making impertinent demands of the Crown, and a rebellion there would mean Indian attacks in the West. The settlers needed powder and bullets for self-protection, and they decided that Virginia would be most receptive to their pleas. Petitions were carried over the mountains to Williamsburg in 1775 and again in 1776, asking that Kentucky be made a part of the Old Dominion. The bearer of the second of these documents was George Rogers Clark, who was to play a leading role on the northwestern frontier during the Revolution. Indeed, the Rogers-Clark clan of Albemarle County, Virginia, made abundant contributions to western expansion, with George's younger brother William serving as co-commander of the famous Lewis and Clark expedition.

Fifteen-year-old James Ray was roasting a duck near Harrodsburg in the spring of 1776, when the 6-foot Clark strode from the forest and introduced himself. Ray invited the visitor to take a few slices of meat, then watched in open-mouthed amazement as Clark devoured the whole bird. The young Virginian became a popular figure at Harrodsburg despite his gargantuan appetite, and the settlers there sent him East along with John Gabriel Jones in June to plead their case against the Transylvania proprietors. The petition capitalized upon the democratic "spirit of '76" by arguing that the Transylvania grant, if permitted, "will afford a safe asylum to those whose principles are Inimical to American Freedom." The settlers also pointed out that Fincastle County stretched for 300 miles from east to west, an area much too large for effective protection or administration. Clark found that Governor Patrick Henry and Assemblyman Thomas Jefferson were sympathetic to the settlers' point of view. The eventual outcome was that in December of 1776, Kentucky was made a new county of the state of Virginia.

Judge Henderson had lost his gamble to make Kentucky a propri-etary empire. But though he failed in his immediate ambitions, the judge had made a contribution to the settlement of the West by opening a trail across the mountains and by giving Kentucky at least a temporary system of government. In recognition of these services, Virginia in 1778 granted him 200,000 acres along the Ohio River. But by that time the Kentuckians' arguments with the Transylvania Company had been forgotten in the greater struggle against the British-allied Indians that was part of the Revolutionary War.

Selected Readings   Dale Van Every, *Forth to the Wilderness, 1754-1774* (New York, 1961) is good, although his interpretation of the Proclamation Line is debatable. Clarence W. Alvord, *The Mississippi Valley in British Politics*, 2 vols. (Cleveland, 1917), is a classic. Francis Parkman's title, *The Conspiracy of Pontiac*, 2 vols. (Boston, 1910), influenced historical interpretation for many years. More recent views are in Howard H. Peckham, *Pontiac and the Indian Uprising* (Princeton, 1947). Donald H. Kent, "A Note on Germ Warfare," *Mississippi Valley Historical Review,* vol. 41 (March, 1955), documents an unpleasant subject. Brooke Hindle, "The March of the Paxton Boys," *William and Mary Quarterly*, 3d ser., vol. 3 (October, 1946), is im-portant. Abstracts of contemporary documents may be found in Wilbur R. Jacobs (ed.), *The Paxton Riots and the Frontier Theory* (Berkeley Series in American His-tory, Chicago, 1967).

Land speculation is covered in Kenneth P. Bailey's *The Ohio Company* (Glendale, 1939) and in George E. Lewis, *The Indiana Company* (Glendale, 1941). Ray Allen Billington, "The Ft. Stanwix Treaty of 1768," *New York History*, vol. 25 (April, 1944), is excellent. Thomas P. Abernethy, *Western Lands and the American Revolution* (New York, 1937), is a standard treatment. Beverly Bond, Jr., *The Quit-Rent System in the American Colonies* (New Haven, 1919), is a solid monograph. Washington's role as frontier soldier and speculator is detailed in Freeman's *Washing-ton*, vol. II, and in James T. Flexner's *George Washington: The Forge of Experience* (Boston, 1965), a satisfactory popular account covering 1732-1775. The text of the Proclamation of 1763 is in *Wisconsin Historical Collections*, vol. 11 (1888). John R.

Alden, *John Stuart and the Southern Colonial Frontier* (Ann Arbor, 1944), is a highly detailed monograph.

Dr. Thomas Walker's *Journal* was published by the Filson Club (Louisville, 1898). Lucien Beckner, "John Findley: The First Pathfinder of Kentucky," is in *Filson Club History Quarterly*, vol. 1 (April, 1927). The best biography of Boone is John Bakeless, *Daniel Boone* (New York, 1939), based upon the Draper Manuscripts at Wisconsin. Other books important for Kentucky history are Robert L. Kincaid, *The Wilderness Road* (Indianapolis, 1947), and Thomas D. Clark, *A History of Kentucky* (New York, 1937). Kathryn Harrod Mason, *James Harrod of Kentucky* (Baton Rouge, 1951) is excellent. Carl S. Driver, *John Sevier, Pioneer of the Old Southwest* (Chapel Hill, N.C., 1932), is standard, but does not seem to capture Sevier's personality.

V. The Frontier in the Revolution

His Majesty George III had spent vast sums of money defending the American colonies in the French war, and he wanted some return on his investment. To help pay the continuing costs of administration, including the support of a 10,000-man army still in America, the King's ministers devised a tax program through which the Americans could contribute their fair share. But the ungrateful wretches met every new tax proposal, from the Stamp Act of 1765 to the Tea Act of 1773, with the shrill cry of "no taxation without representation." New Englanders and Virginians ordinarily had little love for each other, but they could agree that the home government had no right to tax them without their consent. So the road to revolution was littered with the debris of discarded British tax laws.

Quebec Act   In Western policy, too, the government seemingly could no nothing right. It had started to drive nails into its own coffin with the Proclamation Line of 1763, and the process was continued with the Quebec Act of 1774. This act was motivated by the best intentions. It was designed to give civil government to the French Catholics living in the Great Lakes-Illinois country. These people had been subjected to military government ever since 1763, and no provision had been made for the practice of their religion. The act partially established French civil law in the area, extended toleration to all Catholics, and set the southern boundary of Quebec Province at the Ohio River. This last provision threatened Western interests, since land speculation and fur trading north of the Ohio would now be controlled by Montreal. It is significant that in the peace negotiations at the end of the Revolutionary War, the Americans insisted that the Canadian boundary be placed where it had been before the Quebec Act. But the most violent reaction to the act came not from frontiersmen but from

New Englanders, whose fear of Papists bordered on the psychotic. They saw the law as part of a government plot to force Catholicism upon the colonies, and in their propaganda it was cited as another of the dangers to American liberty.

The Indian Menace

When the war began after the skirmishes at Lexington and Concord, the main threat to the western frontiers of the would-be nation was not the British army. Indeed, by 1775 all the western garrisons had been withdrawn except those at Mackinac, Detroit, and Niagara; the troops were posted in the eastern cities where they were attempting to control the turbulent "Sons of Liberty." The main threat, as always, came from the "tawny serpents" of the forest, those scalp-hunting tribesmen who paced the frontier line like zoo animals before feeding time. The settlers were to shoulder most of the responsibility for their own defense against these dangerous neighbors. George Washington, commander-in-chief of the new Continental Army, was sympathetic to the Westerners since he had known the horrors of frontier warfare at first hand. But he could not spare desperately needed troops for a frontier campaign. Consequently, the frontiersmen had to depend upon the state governments for what little aid they did receive.

The Continental Congress tried to help. In July of 1775 it created three Indian departments and appointed commissioners for each. These commissioners met with the Ohio River tribes at Pittsburgh in October and signed a treaty recognizing the river as the boundary; no raids were to be carried out on either side. The most that Congress could hope for was that the Indians would remain neutral, which was like asking the leopard to change its spots. And unfortunately the British held all the trump cards when it came to Indian alliances. Their trade goods were better in quality and cheaper in price than those of the Americans, whose manufacturing system was scarcely above the handicraft stage. England also had Indian superintendents like Sir John Johnson (son of the late Sir William) and Col. John Stuart, whom the savages regarded as their friends. The American hunters or Long Knives, on the other hand, were known as landgrabbers whose relentless invasion of hunting grounds had to be stopped if the Indians were to survive. The Americans could expect that the savages would strike hard all around the frontier, treaty or no treaty.

Ticonderoga

In the north the Americans wanted Canada. The first step to this goal was to secure the natural invasion route by seizing Fort Ticonderoga on Lake Champlain. Ethan Allen and his Green Mountain Boys surprised the fort on May 17, 1775, forcing it to surrender (according to Allen's account) "in the name of the great Jehovah and the Continental Congress." Ethan Allen was a 6-foot-2-inch

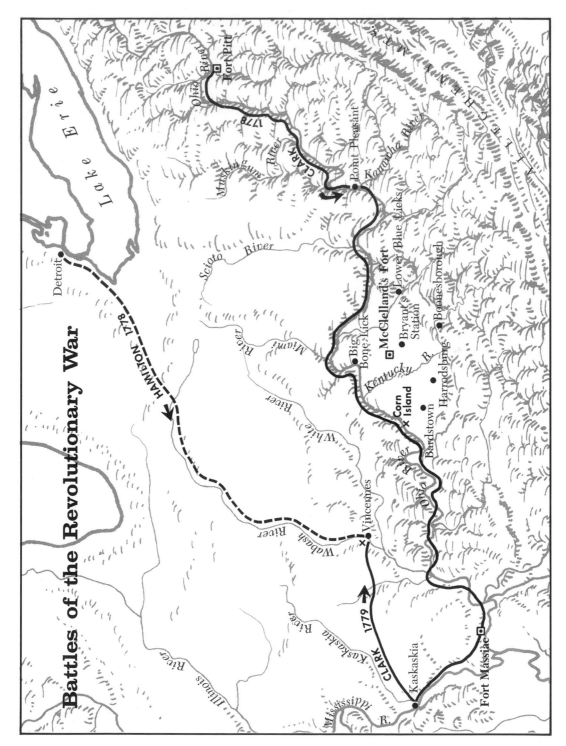

Battles of the Revolutionary War

Lake Erie

ALLEGHENY MTS.

Detroit

HAMILTON 1778

CLARK 1778

Ohio River

Fort Pitt

Muskingum River

Scioto River

Point Pleasant

Kanawha River

Miami River

White River

Wabash River

Vincennes

Kaskaskia River

CLARK 1779

Kaskaskia

Mississippi R.

Illinois River

Big Bone Lick

McClelland's Fort

Bryant's Station

Lower Blue Licks

Boonesborough

Harrodsburg

Kentucky R.

Corn Island

Bardstown

Ohio River

Fort Massiac

muscle man whose bombastic political oratory matched his reputed feats of strength. It was said that he could bite nails in two, and that he could lift up a bushel bag of salt with his teeth and hurl it over his back. Allen's Green Mountain Boys were a vigilante or Regulator group formed in 1770 to protect land claims against New York. Governor Benning Wentworth of New Hampshire had begun granting tracts of land on both sides of the Green Mountains as early as 1749. These "New Hampshire Grants" were all located on lands claimed by New York State, and out of the long-lasting border dispute that followed there eventually emerged an independent Vermont.

Ticonderoga became the base for Gen. Richard Montgomery's invasion of Canada that summer. Montgomery took Montreal, temporarily cutting the British supply route to the interior, but he and Gen. Benedict Arnold failed to capture Quebec. Their withdrawal marked the end of American efforts at conquest to the north. New England exerted constant pressure throughout the war for a second attempt, and Washington subsequently gave much thought to another invasion. But he could not spare the troops, and the French-Canadians were indifferent to the patriot cause.

The Americans also hoped to annex the Floridas. But here again their attempts were abortive. Troops could not be spared to capture Mobile, Pensacola, and St. Augustine, posts from which the British supplied their Indian allies in the southwest. Hence the conquest of the Floridas was left to Spain, as part of the Spanish-American alliance of 1779. Blocked on the north and on the south, the Americans saw that the West offered the greatest opportunity for expansion. And it was in the central colonies facing the Great Lakes and the Ohio that the epic frontier battles were fought.

Action in the South

The Watauga settlements in eastern Tennessee were the first to be bloodied. July of 1776 was a momentous month back in Philadelphia, where the new nation was officially being born, but in Watauga it was remembered as the time of the first Cherokee attack. The tribesmen, armed with British muskets, decided that to save their lands they must strike hard at the Americans. Though he supplied them, Colonel Stuart tried to dissuade the Cherokees from attacking. In most respects the British officials on the frontier had more in common with their American enemies than with their savage allies. Among the practical difficulties involved in British sponsorship of raids was the fact that Indians could not distinguish Tories from patriots. A white man's scalp was a white man's scalp. But the British cabinet decided to make full use of the Indians, and Stuart had no choice but to obey. He and the other officers of the Crown were out to win a war.

The Cherokees were an intelligent tribe, but they always had bad luck with the Americans. The Wataugans were waiting for them, having been alerted to the attack by an informer. Log forts had been built at two historic locations: Eaton's Station on the Long Island of the Holston, and Sycamore Shoals on the Watauga. Squads of hard-faced riflemen led by James Robertson and John Sevier gathered at these stockades. At Eaton's Station on July 20 the outnumbered frontiersmen smashed the war party under Chief Dragging Canoe and sent the invaders reeling westward. In the next 2 months militia armies from the Carolinas and Virginia threaded their way over tortuous mountain trails to attack and burn the most distant Cherokee villages. The humiliated tribesmen had to sign treaties in 1777 conceding American rights to land north of the Nolichucky.

Victory in the first of the Cherokee wars meant security for Kentucky's vulnerable lifeline along the Wilderness Road. The Kentuckians sorely needed whatever help they could get. Lieutenant Governor Henry "Hair Buyer" Hamilton at Detroit was rousing the trans-Ohio tribes for a concerted drive against the Kentucky frontier. It is doubtful that Hamilton offered money for American scalps, but supplying the red men with shiny new muskets, tomahawks, and scalping knives was in effect inviting them to wage all-out war. The Shawnee, Wyandot, and Mingo warriors needed little urging to attack the hated Americans. Only General Montgomery's closure of the St. Lawrence supply route for 9 months prevented heavy raids in 1776.

Defense of Kentucky

Even so, there were premonitory episodes that summer. On July 14, Jemima Boone and the two Calloway sisters were boating on the river near Boonesborough when Shawnee warriors seized them and carried them north. The girls acted like the heroines of fiction and films by dropping strips of clothing along the trail, so that Daniel Boone and his friends were able to follow and rescue them. But other encounters did not have such Hollywood endings, and those who traveled the forest trails did so in peril of their lives. When George Rogers Clark returned from Virginia in December with 500 pounds of gunpowder, he had to bury the kegs near the mouth of Limestone Creek, since the path to Harrodsburg was swarming with war parties. His wisdom became evident when a band of renegade Indians under "Captain Pluggy" attacked little McClelland's Station and forced its abandonment. But the powder was recovered and distributed to the three stations, Boonesborough, Harrodsburg, and Logan's, where the residents looked forward to 1777 with apprehension.

These forts were in a direct line of descent from the stockades and garrison houses of New England. Boonesborough was built in the form of a hollow square approximately 260 feet long by 160 feet wide. There were twenty-six one-story cabins whose back walls formed a palisade of sharpened logs. At each corner of the fort there was (by 1778) a two-story blockhouse, with projecting second story and loopholes cut to provide enfilading fire along the length of the walls. The cabins had in-slanting roofs so that fires could be quickly extinguished. The chief drawbacks of these log forts was of course the danger from enemy fire arrows and their complete vulnerability to cannon. Of the three stations, Harrodsburg was the only one with a spring or supply of drinking water inside the walls.

The frontiersmen used native materials, and the furnishings at Boonesborough indicate their characteristic ingenuity in this respect. Tables, rain barrels, and chairs were fashioned out of local hardwoods like walnut and hickory. Deerskins were used as seats for chairs, and elk or deer antlers held rifles and fishing poles. Gourds were used for water dippers and egg baskets. On a shelf over the fireplace were the whiskey jug, tinderbox, quill pen, and one imported item—a Bible. The settlers were dependent upon the East for powder, iron, and lead, but eight-tenths of the items used in their daily lives were of local origin.

The men entrusted with the defense of the Kentucky frontier were good examples of the citizen-soldier tradition. The frontiersmen's contributions

Boonesborough in 1778. From George Ranck, Boonesboro. *(1901) Source: Yale University Library.*

to the Continental Army were overstated by nineteenth century historians. A regiment of Virginia riflemen under Daniel Morgan did serve with Washington's army. They were good sharpshooters and skirmishers, but they did not learn massed fire and their individual style of fighting was not suited to Washington's conventional block-infantry line. On their own ground, however, the backwoodsmen developed a reputation for competence in the kind of fighting which their environment required. George Rogers Clark, whom Virginia had commissioned a major and placed in charge of the Kentucky militia, was the most famous of these frontier fighters. His captains were Daniel Boone, Benjamin Logan, and James Harrod, men who could command the loyalty of their fellows at the respective stations. Serving with them were less-celebrated comrades whose feats were just as remarkable. Perhaps the best example of this type of genus *Americanus* was Simon Kenton, acknowledged as one of the outstanding scouts and Indian fighters of the Ohio-Kentucky frontier.

Kenton had assumed the alias of "Butler" and fled to the frontier after supposedly killing another youth in a brawl. He was a Long Hunter in Kentucky for 2 years beginning in 1771. After serving as a scout in Dunmore's War, he returned to the Limestone Creek area and staked out his own clearing. When the Revolutionary War began, the Boonesborough settlement hired him as a "spy" or scout to range the woods and watch for war parties. Kenton loved to snoop around the Indian villages and to steal horses from under the noses of the red men. In the fall of 1778 he was, inevitably, captured by the Shawnees on one of these rustling expeditions. "The Condemned Man" was put to unspeakable tortures, including the running of the gauntlet, and had two near-miraculous escapes from death at the stake. On one of these occasions he was saved by an old scouting companion from Dunmore's War, the Tory renegade Simon Girty. Kenton eventually escaped from captivity at Detroit and made his way back to Kentucky. He lived to a ripe old age there and in Ohio. Like James Harrod and many of the other pioneers, Kenton could neither read nor write, but in the frontier period, physical stamina and a lust for combat were more useful attributes than literacy.

The Indians struck Kentucky in waves throughout the "Year of the Three Sevens." On April 24 Boonesborough was attacked by several hundred raiders who ambushed a party of defenders outside the fort. Boone was shot through the ankle in this engagement, but was carried to safety by Kenton. The Indians raged all around the three stations, destroying cattle and crops. At Harrodsburg only the turnip patch was left untouched, since the savages apparently did not know this vegetable. Thus the settlers could at least have boiled turnips for breakfast, fried turnips for lunch, and baked turnips for dinner. Skilled woodsmen like Harrod and Kenton managed to keep the fort dwellers from starvation by slipping out at night for hunting trips which took them 20 miles or more from the forts. But the settlers' situation was grim, and many brave men became statistics.

Clark in Illinois

The way to stop the terror was to capture Detroit, where the savages received encouragement and supplies. This fact of life was apparent to George Rogers Clark, who started to do something about it early in April. Two volunteer spies, Benjamin Linn and Samuel Moore, were sent to reconnoiter the defenses at Kaskaskia and Vincennes. Kaskaskia was a Mississippi River village with a largely French population of 500 whites and a militia garrison commanded by one Rocheblave. Vincennes, located 180 miles northeast of Kaskaskia on the Wabash River, had a smaller population and a solidly built log fort with the uninspiring name of Fort Sackville. The two spies reported that Kaskaskia was off guard, and that the French residents at both places were lukewarm toward the British. Clark decided to lead an expedition against the two villages as a preliminary step to the seizure of Detroit.

He got the consent of Governor Henry and the Virginia Assembly for this campaign. It seems clear that Virginia land-company interests were perfectly willing to support military efforts in the Northwest, since the Illinois country would probably belong to Virginia after the war. At any rate, Clark went to Fort Pitt and recruited a vest-pocket army of 175 frontiersmen. He flatboated the men down to the falls of the Ohio, his future base of operations. From here he set out, on June 26, 1778, on his journey of conquest.

The boats were beached near the mouth of the Tennessee, since to avoid discovery Clark chose to follow the 120-mile overland route rather than taking the Mississippi. Kaskaskia was surprised and captured without a shot being fired. Clark was then careful to win over the French residents, utilizing for this purpose the news of the recent Franco-American alliance. Through the good offices of the Kaskaskia priest, Father Gibault, the French at Vincennes were also well-disposed toward the Americans, and a token force occupied that town without difficulty. On the other hand, Clark displayed bluster and bravado in dealing with the northwestern Indian tribes. In conferences held that fall with the Potawatomie, Winnebago, and other tribes, he largely destroyed the British influence among them.

Governor Hamilton decided to strike back. He led his army, composed largely of French-Canadians and Indians, down the Maumee-Wabash route and recaptured Vincennes on December 17. A shortage of supplies and the flooded condition of the country caused him to postpone an advance to Kaskaskia. Thus the initiative passed back to Clark, who decided to gamble everything upon an attempt to retake the post.

Clark's army of 170 men left Kaskaskia on February 6, 1779. There was a decidedly Gallic flavor to the American forces in the Revolution, and here about half of Clark's men were French volunteers. The 180 miles to Vincennes was a vast flood plain. The men had to wade from one wooded island to another through slush and ice water that was often chest-high. Some amusement was occasioned by the little drummer boy who had to float along on his instrument. Clark proved his great leadership qualities on this march, keeping his nearly starved men going by jokes, songs, and sheer will power. Vincennes was finally reached on February 23, and the attack on Fort Sackville began.

The backwoodsmen advanced to within 30 yards of the fort, and used their Kentucky rifles to good effect. The defenders were picked off behind the embrasures as they tried to man the artillery pieces. During a lull in the siege Clark's men captured a band of Frenchmen and Indians returning from a scalp raid in Kentucky. Four of the Indian captives were seated on the ground in full view of the garrison and tomahawked to death. Clark, his buckskins splattered with blood, made quite a picture as he held a conference which the shocked Governor Hamilton later reported: "Colonel Clarke yet reeking with the blood of these unhappy Victims came to the Esplanade before the Fort Gate, where I had agreed to meet him and treat of the surrender of the Garrison—He spoke with rapture of his late achievement, while he washed off the blood from his hands stained in this inhuman sacrifice." But Hamilton felt he had no choice but to surrender to his barbarous antagonist. He was outnumbered, and only 33 of his 79 men were British Regulars. After the surrender Clark sent the unfortunate governor on a humiliating journey back through Kentucky, where he was jeered as the "Hairbuyer." In Virginia Governor Thomas Jefferson put him in irons in the Williamsburg jail.

Clark had won an important victory for the young United States. One may acknowledge as much without having to agree with Lafayette's famous judgment that he was second only to Washington among American commanders. His territorial conquests were known to the American negotiators in Paris, and undoubtedly affected the final peace treaty. Clark neutralized many of the potentially dangerous Indian tribes, and he upset the British timetable in the Northwest. He posed a threat to Detroit which kept the enemy off balance. Clark made good use of psychological warfare, but his actual situation was quite precarious. He was 1,000 miles from Virginia, and he received no reinforcements. Only the supplies sent upriver by Oliver Pollock, an American agent in New Orleans, enabled Clark to hold the Illinois country. Even at that he spent much of his own money, leading to personal bankruptcy after the war. But Clark kept up a brave front, writing on March 16 to Captain Lernoult, the commander at Detroit: "I learn by your letter to Gov. Hamilton, that you were very busy making new works, I am glad to hear it, as it saves the Americans some expences in building. My compts. to the Gentlemen of yr. Garrison, I am yours, etc. G.R. Clark." The victor of Vincennes never had the men to take Detroit, but the bluff worked for a precious length of time.

Failure to capture Detroit meant more misery for Kentucky and the upper Ohio frontier. The successive American commanders at Fort Pitt—Edward Hand, Lachlan McIntosh, and Daniel Brodhead—all devised ambitious schemes to seize the enemy citadel. But the lack of material support from Congress and the continuing Virginia-Pennsylvania border dispute brought all these plans to nothing. Fort Pitt was also plagued by the defections of Tories. Simon Girty went over to the British in March of 1778, and his leadership of Indian raids along the Ohio made his the most hated name in frontier annals. Even more serious at the same time was the escape from house arrest of Alexander McKee, former deputy Indian agent at the fort. His great influence among the trans-Ohio tribes was put to immediate use by the British, who commissioned him a colonel and placed him in charge of the Indian effort against the frontier. His success in the assignment was to be measured by many buckets of American blood.

New York Warfare

New York also had a monumental Tory problem, as became evident in the same years that Clark was fighting in the west. Nearly one-half the population was judged to be loyal to the King, and more Yorkers served in the Tory than in the patriot forces. In the Mohawk River Valley Sir William Johnson's heirs and friends could rouse the Iroquois and the Tory farmers for raids on that frontier. Sir William's son John Johnson, his son-in-law Guy Johnson, his brother-in-law Joseph Brant, and the father-and-son team of John and Walter Butler became the leaders of these mixed contingents. In this area even the German and Scotch-Irish tenant farmers, who ordinarily had little cause for loyalty to the Crown, were initially Tory because of their devotion to Sir William. The Highland Scots who had settled west of Schenectady were also Loyalists. They served in John Butler's "Tory Rangers" and John Johnson's "Loyal Greens." The patriot countermeasures included confiscation of Tory property together with floggings, imprisonment, and executions of suspected Loyalists.

The Iroquois initially attempted to remain neutral. But through the efforts of Tories like Brant all of the Six Nations* except the Oneida and Tuscarora took up the hatchet. The latter were persuaded to remain neutral by Samuel Kirkland, a dissenting minister who like many of his profession supported the Revolution. Joseph Brant was himself a student of the Bible, one of his hobbies being the translation of the Scriptures into Mohawk. Brant was a strange figure, who appeared one day in the silks and wig of an English gentleman, and the next day with the shaved head and war paint of a Mohawk chief. His steady purpose was to protect the Indian world against the white race, and in 1776 the main threat to Mohawk lands came from the Americans. Laudable as Brant's intentions may have been, Iroquois participation in the war resulted in the final destruction of their political and military power.

In the summer of 1777 Gen. John Burgoyne led a British army

*The Five Nations became the Six Nations after the Tuscaroras joined the league in 1722.

down the Lake Champlain route from Canada. His defeat at Saratoga on October 17 was one of the most momentous of the war, for it led to the French-American alliance. Cooperating with Burgoyne was an army under Gen. Barry St. Leger, which was to move east from Lake Ontario along the Mohawk. St. Leger had 875 men, most of whom were Tories, and 1,000 Indians led by Brant. But at the battle of Oriskany, a few miles east of Fort Stanwix, Gen. Nicholas Herkimer's Palatine farmers stopped the British advance. The enraged Senecas did an about-face and proceeded to "dash out the brains of the Tories." St. Leger found himself retreating from his own "allies" as well as from the patriots.

There followed in 1778 a dirty little war marked by such Tory attacks as those on the Wyoming and Cherry Valley settlements. The overall British strategy was to break up the frontier communities, destroy food supplies that might go to Washington's army, and rescue Tory families. Many of the latter lived in the lush Wyoming Valley of north-central Pennsylvania, so John Butler led his Rangers and several hundred Senecas there in July. Over 200 scalps were gathered in the methodical attack, and the valley was left a burned-out wasteland. Hysterical accounts of refugees gave this episode the title of "Wyoming Massacre," but actually Butler kept a pretty tight rein on his Indians. More deserving of condemnation was Walter Butler's attack of November 11 on the Cherry Valley, a little settlement 50 miles west of Albany. Butler lost control of his Senecas, who cut down unarmed men, women, and children by the dozens. But it was that kind of a war, and the Americans were not innocent of atrocities.

Washington finally sent a major army to the New York-Pennsylvania frontier in 1779. He planned the campaign himself, and gave Generals John Sullivan and James Clinton 4,000 men to do the job. "Civilization or death to all American savages," was the grim Fourth of July toast given by Sullivan's officers. Moving north from Tioga, Pennsylvania, the Americans fought a thousand-man Tory and Indian force under Brant and Walter Butler at the battle of Newton on August 29. The British were routed, and now it was the Americans' turn to lay waste to the Iroquois towns of western New York. The Sullivan-Clinton campaign did not end Indian attacks in New York. In fact, Joseph Brant mounted devastating raids along the Mohawk in the later stages of the war. But by that time the outcome of the conflict had been decided.

Attack on Boonesborough

Kentucky and Tennessee also suffered from heavy attacks until the end of the Revolution. In January of 1778 Daniel Boone and thirty men from Boonesborough went north to the Blue Licks on a saltmaking expedition. Salt was indispensable to the settlers, since it was used to preserve meat. Water at the licks was boiled in big kettles until the salt was precipitated. On this trip a large Shawnee war party captured Boone, and knowing that resistance was suicidal he persuaded his companions to surrender. The captives were taken to the Ohio villages, and Boone himself became the adopted son of the Shawnee Chief Blackfish. "Big Turtle," as he was called, spent 4 months with his savage hosts, but in June he decided to escape after learning of a planned attack on Boonesborough. He plunged into the forest and outdistanced his pursuers in a 160-mile chase to the fort, where his warnings about the attack caused a sudden burst of preparation.

Chief Blackfish with a dusky horde of 400 Indians and a party of eight British officers under Lieutenant De Quindre finally appeared on September 7. Inside the stockade were fifty men and boys who in Boone's words "had determined to defend the fort while a man was living." The Indians besieged the little outpost for 9 days, an unusually long period of time for the restless warriors. During the siege there were long-range rifle duels, in one of which Boone picked off a Negro renegade at 175 yards. The besiegers attempted to dig a tunnel under the fort walls, but a providential rainstorm collapsed the diggings. This siege is a classic in frontier defense, and has been the historical prototype for many similar episodes in Western novels and films.

The lemminglike rush of settlers to the frontier continued despite the war peril. Clark decided to establish his base of operations near the falls of the Ohio, and brought out twenty families who founded Louisville in 1778. Throughout 1779 and 1780 swarms of would-be Kentuckians poured over the Wilderness Road. Others piled their spinning wheels, cooking pots, butter churns, scythes, and axes into Conestoga wagons and took the old Forbes' Road to Fort Pitt. There they transferred to flatboats which took them down the Ohio to the mouth of the Limestone, the Licking, or the Kentucky. A number of these migrants were Tories who had found the eastern settlements to be too hot for comfort. But most were simply responding to some unreasoning instinct to move west.

The Virginia Land Law

There was no certainty that such people would be rewarded for their pioneering. In fact the Virginia land law of 1779 bade fair to deprive them of their hard-won claims. The law granted 400 acres at the nominal price of $4 an acre to those who had settled in Kentucky prior to January of 1778. After these claims were validated, the remaining land was to be sold at £40 the hundred acres, with no limitation on the amount that one man might purchase. This was an open invitation to speculators, as the Kentuckians immediately recognized. Petitions from these "Destressed Inhabitants of the county of Kentucky" in the fall of 1779 complained that 400 acres was too small a preemption claim, and that many settlers had been unable to mark off their land because of constant Indian fighting. Thus they faced "the disagreeable necessity of becoming tenants to private gentlemen who have men employed at this junction in this county at one hundred pounds per Thousand for running round the land, which is too rough a medicine even to be dejested by any set of people that have suffered as we have." The "private gentlemen" were Tidewater speculators and magnates like Robert Morris, who bought up 1½ million acres of Virginia's western lands with depreciated Continental currency. Eight other men had a quarter million acres each of Kentucky land.

The law required that a settler identify his claim "specially and precisely." In most cases it was impossible to satisfy this vague requirement. Surveys were inaccurate, and the best tracts had been surveyed by a half dozen different claimants. This "shingling" of land claims led to years of court appeals, some of which involved the earliest pioneers. For example, Daniel Boone's suit against James Harrod in 1788 went through twenty-five continuations until its dismissal in 1893. Usually the large speculators rather than the pioneers were victorious in these suits. They had the money to employ lawyers, such as young Henry Clay, who flocked to Kentucky after the frontier period. Heroic Indian fighters like Boone and Kenton had to leave the state because of their "imperfect" land titles.

The Tennesseeans living along the Holston and Watauga also had trials and tribulations. The Chickamaugas, an offshoot of the Cherokee, took to the warpath in the spring of 1779. Led by such inveterate foes of the white man as Dragging Canoe and Bloody Fellow, they attacked the Holston settlements and the Wilderness Road. A counterexpedition of 600 volunteers under the famous Welsh-born frontiersman, Evan Shelby, went down the Tennessee in canoes and destroyed all the Chickamauga towns. Chief Dragging Canoe remained a constant threat, however, for he soon rebuilt his towns and got fresh war supplies from the British at Pensacola. But even the menace from these Indians did not stop the settlement of central Tennessee.

The Cumberland Settlements

In February of 1779, James Robertson, the doughty defender of the Watauga frontier, explored the "French Lick" country around the southern bend of the Cumberland River. His sponsor was Judge Richard Henderson, once again up to his ears in western speculation and promotion. Henderson felt that the French Lick region would be below the Virginia state boundary, and thus that his Sycamore Shoals purchase from the Cherokee would be valid there. So in the winter of 1779-1780 he sent Robertson on a second trip, this time with a party of colonists overland through Cumberland Gap and across Kentucky. This was a heroic achievement in itself, for during the hard winter of '79 numbers of settlers in Kentucky died from starvation and cold. Robertson got through, however, and began building cabins at the site of Nashborough (later Nashville).

Meanwhile, Henderson sent another group of settlers to Nashborough under Capt. John Donelson, by boat down the Tennessee to the Ohio, and then up the Cumberland. Some 200 men, women, and children were in the flotilla, which took 4 months to cover some 900 miles of water. The expedition was attacked at the rebuilt Chickamauga towns on the Tennessee, and one boat carrying smallpox victims was cut off and annihilated. When the settlers passed through the canyons of the Cumberland Mountains, the Indians appeared on the heights above and fired down on them. In April the exhausted survivors, having lived for the last few days on "Shawnee salad" of green herbs, finally struggled into the settlement.

In May of 1780, 256 colonists signed the Nashborough Compact, a typical frontier constitution. The government was to be administered by twelve elected judges, called the Committee of Notables, of whom Robertson was the chairman. Provision was also made for land sales, for the support of widows and orphans, and for the indispensable militia system. The settlers also petitioned Congress for an exemption from taxes because of their "remote and exposed" situation. Indeed, life here was as dangerous as at any settlement in frontier history, with continual depredations by Chickamauga and Creek war parties up until 1794. Only a strong religious faith and the inborn tenacity of men like Robertson kept the Cumberland stations going.

The Tennesseeans also had to meet another danger from across the mountains to the east. Lord Cornwallis had captured Charleston in May of 1780, and was now marching northward. His subcommanders, Lt. Col. Banastre Tarleton and Maj. Patrick Ferguson, were raising Tory guerrilla bands and attacking patriot strongholds throughout the Carolinas. As Ferguson, in command of the left flank of the advancing army, moved through North Carolina he threatened to cross the mountains and lay waste to the Holston settlements. The reaction of the Westerners was to organize a force of 1,500 men under such leaders as John Sevier and Isaac Shelby to stop the invaders.

King's Mountain

Ferguson was a hard-bitten professional among whose accomplishments was the invention of a breech-loading rifle. He was contemptuous of the mountaineers, describing them as "a set of mongrels." This attitude may explain why, after retreating before their advance, he decided to make a stand at King's Mountain. This was a heavily wooded ridge rising about 60 feet above the surrounding countryside. It was in South Carolina, a mile and a half below the North Carolina boundary. Ferguson's 1,100 men were mostly well-trained Tory volunteers from the Carolinas, New York, and New Jersey. The battle was fought on the afternoon of October 7, 1780, and it matched British bayonet charges against the patriots' rifle marksmanship. The latter won the day, partly because the terrain was suited to Indian-style tactics. As Ferguson's men charged down the slope, the mountaineers would fall back and pick them off from behind trees and boulders. After Ferguson was killed, his second in command arranged a surrender, and the short but fierce battle was ended. The victors celebrated by hanging nine prisoners in retaliation for the execution of some patriots the year before. As the historian of the British army remarked: "The victims were of course Americans, for it was not Mother Country and Colonies, but two Colonial factions that fought so savagely in Carolina."

Though it was a minor engagement, the victory at King's Mountain discouraged the southern Tories and ended the immediate threat to the western country. It delayed Cornwallis' advance into Virginia, and thus may have led indirectly to his defeat at Yorktown the next year. The battle also gave a needed boost to the Revolutionary cause at a time when the American military effort in the Northwest was sputtering to an inglorious conclusion.

Clark on the Ohio

Along the Ohio frontier George Rogers Clark had to rush from one threatened point to another, hastily improvising defenses against massive British-Indian expeditionary forces. One of these under Capt. Emanuel Hesse came down from Mackinac in May. Its object was the seizure of St. Louis and of the Illinois towns as a necessary prelude to British control of the Mississippi. Fortunately Captain Fernando de Leyba at St. Louis and Clark at Cahokia led such spirited defenses that the invaders were driven back. Clark immediately had to race back across 300 miles of wilderness, dodging Indian patrols along the way, to help defend Kentucky against Capt. Henry Bird's expedition from Detroit. Bird commanded a thousand fight-hungry Indians under Alexander McKee and the Girty brothers. He also had terror weapons: two cannon which could reduce wooden forts to kindling. Ruddle's Station surrendered on June 20 after only two shots from the cannon. The Indians then butchered 200 captives in spite of Bird's attempts to stop them. News of this massacre brought plenty of vengeful Kentuckians to Clark's headquarters at Harrodsburg, and in August he marched them up the Miami and attacked the two principal Shawnee towns at Chillicothe and Piqua. These were hardly decisive blows, but the 72 scalps which the Americans brought back proved that the old Mosaic law of an eye for an eye and a tooth for a tooth was one which the frontiersmen understood above all others.

The next year, 1781, was a nightmare for Clark. His dream of an expedition to Detroit was shattered once and for all. The depreciation of the Continental currency wrecked the American supply system, and the reluctance of men to enlist for distant military ventures was widespread. Governor Jefferson fully supported Clark's plan to take Detroit, writing that "if that Post be reduced we shall be quiet in future on our frontier, and thereby immense Treasure of blood and money be saved." But he could not give Clark the men he needed, since Virginia was even then being invaded by Cornwallis. Clark, with little more success in getting men at Pittsburgh, wrote that "the inhabitants cry out for an Expedition, but too few I doubt will turn out, affraid I believe

that they will be led on to something too desperate for their Delicate stomacks."
He then went down to Kentucky where the militia colonels advised him that
they too were unable to raise a large enough force to attempt Detroit. The
despondent commander thus had to be content with the usual defensive policy.
The Kentuckians were cooped up in forts that were short of ammunition, and
as John Floyd reported, "the most distressed Widows and Orphans perhaps in
the world make up a great part of our Inhabitants."

The final year of the Revolution saw no improvement in the West.
American troops had been withdrawn from the Illinois towns, and Fort Nelson
at the falls of the Ohio (Louisville) was the westernmost bastion on the Ohio
River frontier. Clark constructed (partly at his own expense) several gunboats
to patrol the river and the trails from the north. But this was a holding action,
and the American offensive operations during 1782 ended in disaster. Col.
William Crawford, friend and land agent of George Washington, led 480 men
from Fort Pitt to attack the Sandusky villages. After a battle on June 5 the
Americans were forced to retreat, with Crawford being captured and tortured
to death. The archfiend Simon Girty watched with amusement (according to an
eyewitness) as the colonel's ears were cut off, powder charges fired into his body,
and red-hot coals heaped on his scalped head. Crawford's horrible demise was
related to the butchering 2 months earlier of 90 peaceful Moravian Indians
(mostly Delaware) at Gnadenhutten, a missionary settlement 100 miles west of
Fort Pitt. It was Crawford's misfortune that his captors were Delawares.

The Kentuckians also suffered a needless defeat that summer. On
August 15 a war party under Alexander McKee appeared before Bryan's Station.
They played a cat-and-mouse game with the defenders, who proved to be equal
to the occasion by thwarting all of McKee's strategems. A relief column of 180
men under such famous frontier colonels as John Todd and Daniel Boone
arrived, and then pressed on after the enemy. At Blue Licks, scene of Boone's
capture 3 years before, the frontiersmen fell into a trap. Boone advised waiting
for reinforcements, but hotheads led by Hugh McGary rushed across the
Licking River and the rest of the men followed. Seventy-seven men were killed
in the Indian crossfire, including John Todd and Boone's son Israel. The defeat
caused despair in Kentucky. "The Ballance stands upon an equilibrium," wrote
Andrew Steele, "and one stroke more will cause it to preponderate to our
irretrievable wo, and terminate in the Intire Breach of our country." Fortunately
for the Americans, the preliminary articles of peace were signed at Paris on
November 30, and the war began to grind to a halt.

Peace Negotiations

There seem to have been many reasons for the British defeat in the Revolution.
The troops were at a long distance from the home base, their leaders misjudged
the stubbornness of the Americans and the physical obstacles in the colonies,

and there were various strategic mistakes. The failure of British diplomacy to prevent a Franco-American alliance was also of key importance. France had entered the war in 1778 for the purpose of humiliating Great Britain. She did not want to create a strong United States. As the French foreign minister Charles de Vergennes wrote: "We do not desire that a new republic shall arise which shall become the exclusive mistress of this immense continent." To this end, the treaty of alliance specified that America get French approval for any peace treaty with England.

Spain had very reluctantly joined the war in 1779. She had given underhanded aid to the Americans since 1776, and supplies from her warehouses at New Orleans had helped to support George Rogers Clark in Illinois. But she feared that an independent America would be aggressive, and would threaten her control of the lands bordering the Gulf of Mexico and the Mississippi. In fact, Spain took steps during the war to seize the key points in this region. Bernardo de Galvez, the energetic Governor at New Orleans, captured the British posts at Natchez and Mobile in 1780. The next year he realized his greatest ambition by taking Pensacola, thus giving his nation a solid claim to Florida. At the end of the war the Spanish were in a position to deny American pretensions to navigation of the Mississippi. Vergennes supported his European ally on this matter, as well as on the desirability of keeping the Americans penned up east of the Tenneessee River. The Americans would have to do some fancy diplomatic juggling if they were to get the most favorable boundaries for their new nation.

Fortunately the British were willing to cooperate with their American cousins in this game. British policy under the Earl of Shelburne was to draw America away from France and Spain by granting not only independence but also a generous peace. Shelburne's agent in Paris, Richard Oswald, accordingly offered the American envoys many concessions, including a boundary as far west as the Mississippi River. These envoys, John Jay, John Adams, and Benjamin Franklin, decided to forget about Vergennes and the French alliance and get the best terms they could on their own. After all, hadn't the French foreign minister sent his secretary to London for secret talks with Shelburne?

In the preliminary articles signed in November of 1782, the American boundary began at the St. Croix River and ran west through the "highlands" and the middle of the Great Lakes to the Mississippi. The line went down that river to the 31st parallel, then east to the Chattahoochee, Flint, and St. Mary's Rivers, and on to the Atlantic coast. Spain was given the region between this line and the Gulf. The treaty stated further that American and English citizens would have full rights to navigation of the Mississippi, that the Americans would put no obstacles in the way of Loyalists attempting to recover their confiscated property, and that the British would evacuate the northwestern posts at Detroit and elsewhere "with all convenient speed." The final treaty embodying these points was signed on September 3, 1783.

The Americans had won a great diplomatic victory by forgetting about their pledge to France. Vergennes, in fact, applauded them for having gained much more than he had thought possible. The great area south of the Lakes and west of the Appalachians was acknowledged to be American, and the Indian tribes of Ohio now became American subjects. Spain was pushed to the west bank of the Mississippi in this area. In short, the British had helped to create a veritable American empire. The question that now had to be answered was whether or not the United States government could administer these vast western lands any more effectively than the British had done.

Selected Readings   Dale Van Every, *A Company of Heroes, 1775-1783* (New York, 1962), is the best general account of frontier military activity. Jack M. Sosin, *The Revolutionary Frontier, 1763-1783* (New York, 1967), emphasizes land speculation. John Alden, *The South in the Revolution* (Baton Rouge, 1957), is an excellent survey. Charles H. Metzger, *The Quebec Act, a Primary Cause of the American Revolution* (New York, 1936), emphasizes the religious prejudices aroused by the act. Charles H. McIlwain's *Introduction* to Peter Wraxall, *An Abridgement of the Indian Affairs . . . of New York* (Cambridge, 1915), is a good analysis of the Iroquois. Thomas P. Abernethy, *Western Lands and the American Revolution* (New York, 1937), is indispensable.

Frederic F. Van de Water, *The Reluctant Republic: Vermont, 1724-1791* (New York, 1941), is the best survey. Ethan Allen, *The Narrative of Colonel Ethan Allen* (Philadelphia, 1779), also issued in paperback (New York, 1961), is a primary source with the author's famous "Great Jehovah" claim. John Bakeless, *Daniel Boone* (New York, 1939), has much on the Kentucky warfare. George W. Ranck, *Boonesborough* (Louisville, 1901), is a classic. Patricia Jahns, *The Violent Years: Simon Kenton and the Ohio-Kentucky Frontier* (New York, 1962), is a well-researched popular biography. James A. James, *The Life of George Rogers Clark* (Chicago, 1928), is the best of the biographies. Milo M. Quaife (ed.), *The Capture of Old Vincennes* (Indianapolis, 1927), contains the journals of Clark and Hamilton. John D. Barnhart, "A New Evaluation of Henry Hamilton and George Rogers Clark," *Mississippi Valley Historical Review*, vol. 37 (March, 1951) revises a traditional picture.

William H. Nelson, *The American Tory* (Oxford, 1961), is thorough. North Callahan, *Royal Raiders* (New York, 1962), deals with Loyalist military efforts. Alexander C. Flick, *The Sullivan-Clinton Campaign in 1779* (Albany, N.Y., 1929), is standard.

Albigence W. Putnam, *History of Middle Tennessee* (Nashville, 1859), deals with the Cumberland settlements and reprints the Nashborough Compact. Lyman C. Draper, *King's Mountain and Its Heroes* (Cincinnati, 1881), is scarce but valuable. See also Carl S. Driver, *John Sevier*, and J. W. Fortescue, *History of the British Army*, vol. III (New York, 1902). John W. Caughey, *Bernardo de Galvez in Louisiana, 1776-1783* (Berkeley, 1934), and James A. James, *Oliver Pollock: The Life and Times of an Unknown Patriot* (New York, 1937), deal with key figures in the Southwest. Paul C. Phillips, *The West in the Diplomacy of the Revolution* (Urbana, 1913), is old but highly informative. Samuel F. Bemis, *The Diplomacy of the American Revolution* (New York, 1935) also discusses the West.

VI. West by Northwest

Who owned the western lands, the nation or the states? The question was not merely academic, as was proven by Maryland's refusal to ratify the Articles of Confederation until Congress accepted her resolution: "That the United States in Congress assembled shall have the sole and exclusive power to ascertain and fix the western boundary of such states as claim to the Mississippi or the South Sea, and to lay out the land beyond the boundary so ascertained into separate and independent states, from time to time, as the numbers and circumstances of the people thereof may require." The debate over cession of the western lands to Congress pitted the six "landless" states, led by Maryland and New Jersey, against the seven landowning states headed by Virginia. The former argued with considerable justice that the West had been "wrested from the common enemy by the blood and treasure of the thirteen states." They emphasized further that these lands would serve as a bond of national union, and that they could be used both for veterans' bounties and as a source of revenue for Congress. The landed states stood firmly upon their ancient "sea-to-sea" grants from the Crown.

Creation of the Public Domain   Maryland's arguments for cession were cast in nationalistic and patriotic terms, but economic self-interest also loomed in the background. The landless states would probably have higher taxes, since they had no revenue from land sales, and thus they might be stripped of population. More importantly, land speculators from these states thought they would have a better chance of gaining concessions in the area if they could deal with Congress rather than with individual states. The Illinois-Wabash Company had been formed in 1780 from two separate firms which had both purchased Illinois land from the Indians under the dubious Camden-Yorke decision. The members

87

of this company, mostly prominent Maryland and New Jersey politicians including Robert Morris and Maryland's Governor Thomas Johnson, knew that Virginia would never recognize these purchases. With congressional ownership, however, they were confident of getting a proviso confirming the claims. Through their influence Maryland withheld ratification of the Articles of Confederation from 1778 until 1781, when Virginia finally ceded her lands north of the Ohio.

The pressure on Virginia had increased after New York had ceded its shadowy claims to Ohio, supposedly based upon Iroquois conquests, early in 1780. There also was a spirit of compromise among leading Virginians on this issue. But to her act of cession, January 2, 1781, Virginia attached several conditions. Two chunks of land north of the river were held out for state veterans' bounties. One was a "Virginia Military Reserve" located between the Scioto and Little Miami Rivers, and the other was a 150,000-acre tract opposite Louisville for George Rogers Clark and his men. Another provision was for nullification of the prewar land company purchases from the Indians: a direct smash at the Illinois-Wabash Company. The Maryland government had no choice but to ratify the articles (on February 2), but her speculators fought a 3-year battle in Congress to have the obnoxious Virginia requirement removed. They lost, and on March 1, 1784, Congress finally accepted the Virginia cession, thus making the "Old Northwest" national property.

Between 1784 and 1802 the other five landed states also ceded their western claims. Connecticut did so in 1786, but withheld 3½ million acres along Lake Erie as a Western Reserve. The southern states moved much more slowly. They had heavy war debts, and thus wished to sell the land before turning it over to the national government. When Georgia finally ceded her lands in 1802 they had all been sold; thus the United States government got only political sovereignty over them. But in the region northwest of the Ohio, the state cessions created a vast public domain.

The government had to devise some system for the sale of these lands, for squatters were already settling on them. They drifted down the Ohio on rafts and built their ramshackle lean-tos on the north bank opposite Wheeling, at the mouth of the Muskingum, and along other rivers as far west as the Great Miami. Col. Josiah Harmar sent an army detail to post "No Trespassing" signs along the river and to warn the intruders to leave. Some cabins were burned, but at larger settlements the squatters stolidly chewed tobacco and fingered their rifles while a gaudily attired young officer read the orders for their removal. After vague promises to depart as soon as possible, they went right back to work on their "tomahawk claims." In 1785 Fort Harmar was built at the mouth of the Muskingum—to turn back squatters rather than Indians.

The Land Ordinance of 1785

A desperate need for revenue forced the government to act on the land problem in the spring of 1785. Under the Articles of Confederation the Congress had no taxing power; it could only request contributions from the individual states. Thus the northwestern lands had to be sold to help retire the Revolutionary debt as well as to meet current expenses. The two models for land legislation were the New England system of survey before settlement, and the Southern method of indiscriminate location. The first method offered security for land titles; the second appealed more to frontiersmen because it rewarded initiative. The New England influence prevailed, and on May 20 the famous Land Ordinance of 1785 was signed into law.

The public domain was to be marked off in townships 6 miles square. Each township would be subdivided into thirty-six sections, with 640 acres to the section. Half of the townships would be sold as a whole, and the others by sections. The minimum price was $1 an acre, though the government hoped that at the public auctions the prices would go considerably higher. Congress reserved four sections of each township for later sale, and set aside section 16 for public schools.* The surveys were to begin at the "Seven Ranges," located along the River in southeastern Ohio. The rectangular survey system thus devised was used all the way to the Pacific.

The ordinance favored speculators rather than settlers. The minimum purchasable unit of 640 acres was too much land for the kind of agriculture carried on in the Old Northwest, and $640 was much too high a price for a pioneer farmer. Consequently speculators bought up sections and townships at the auctions, and resold smaller parcels to settlers at much higher prices (up to $5 an acre). These prices drove many disgruntled frontiersmen into the ranks of the squatters. Another drawback was the slowness of the surveys. Thomas Hutchins, newly appointed Geographer of the United States, took his surveyors to Ohio in September. His reports praise the beauty and fertility of the soil. But negatives are also noted: sand flies and mosquitoes, poison ivy, briars, Indians, but particularly the difficulty of surveying a tangled and ravine-slashed wilderness. Only four of the ranges had been laid out by the spring of 1787. Although the ordinance established a land system which helped tie the West to the national government, Congress evidently had to find some speedier method of selling the public domain.

Private Land Company Contracts

So it happened that speculators gained the initial advantage from the land law. "Land jobbers and speculators are prowling about like wolves in many shapes," wrote George Washington to a friend in 1785. And when the "wolves" scented a big kill they converged on the National Capital. Many private companies offered to take over the job of carving up and selling the public lands, and Congress eventually signed contracts with three of them. These were the Ohio Company of Associates, the Scioto Company, and a firm headed by John

*Unfortunately, the states of the Old Northwest often sold the lands and put the proceeds in unwise investments rather than in schools.

Cleves Symmes. The basic idea was that Congress could fill its empty treasury by permitting the speculators to turn over a quick profit.

The Ohio Company was a Massachusetts organization started by two former Revolutionary generals, Rufus Putnam and Benjamin Tupper. Their scheme was to buy a large tract of Ohio land from the government with depreciated certificates of indebtedness which they and their associates had been given in lieu of Army pay. The company had little success in its negotiations with Congress until it sent the Rev. Manasseh Cutler to New York as a lobbyist. Cutler was a one-time Congregational minister of Ipswich, Massachusetts, an amateur scientist of the Ben Franklin type, and a lover of fine wines. He also had the born salesman's gift for exaggeration, as evidenced by a promotional pamphlet he later wrote in which he predicted that the national capital would be moved to the Ohio. In the course of his wining and dining, Cutler established cordial relations with Col. William Duer, secretary of the congressional Board of Treasury which conducted land sales. The two men concocted a typical American get-rich-quick scheme. The Ohio Company was to be given a contract for 1½ million acres, which were to be paid for on the installment plan at prices averaging 8 cents an acre. It was also to serve as a front for the Scioto Company, organized by Duer and other public officials whose speculating activities had to be kept a "profound secret." The Scioto Company would purchase another 5 million acres along the Scioto River, to be paid for in six installments at varying prices ranging downward from 66⅔ cents an acre. After making the down payment, the Scioto promoters planned to sell their shares at a fat profit to other speculators at home and in Europe.

On July 27, 1787, Congress approved the deal. In so doing it abandoned the Ordinance of 1785 and attempted to sell the public domain to private speculators at prices far below the minimum. In general, and for various reasons, the policy failed. The companies were unable to meet their payments even at the bargain prices, and so the land reverted back to the government. But one important bonus did come from Manasseh Cutler's dealings with Congress. This was the Northwest Ordinance of 1787.

Cutler knew that settlers with money would be reluctant to buy Ohio land unless they were assured of an orderly system of government. But Congress had formulated no policy regarding her western "colonies." Back in 1784 Thomas Jefferson had drawn up an ordinance suggesting that ten states be formed in the Old Northwest. They were to have rectangular boundaries, and outlandish names like Metropotamia and Assenisipia. As soon as a district had 20,000 white inhabitants it was to be admitted to Congress on an equal footing with the original states. Jefferson's ordinance was adopted, but it never became operative. Westerners objected to boundaries which did not follow the rivers, and Easterners thought the plan was too democratic. They felt that there should be a longer period of paternal control, and thus that the population requirement for statehood should be raised.

The Northwest Ordinance of 1787

On July 9 a congressional committee began drafting a plan of government for the region northwest of the Ohio. Cutler's exact role in the deliberations is uncertain, but he apparently made a number of suggestions and acted as an adviser. In any case the legislative package was whipped through Congress and became law on July 13, 1787. The first major section of the ordinance created a Northwest Territory and decreed that between three and five states should be established there. (Five were eventually formed: Ohio, Indiana, Illinois, Michigan, and Wisconsin.) The second section defined the evolutionary stages from territory to state. Initially there would be a governor, a secretary, and three judges, all appointed by Congress. When the population reached 5,000 adult men, the settlers could elect a general assembly (whose laws would be subject to the governor's absolute veto) and could send a nonvoting delegate to Congress. When the territory reached 60,000 population, it could write a constitution and apply for statehood. The third section of the ordinance contained a bill of rights. This guaranteed freedom of religion and many of the other rights later spelled out in the first ten amendments to the United States Constitution. The bill also prohibited slavery north of the Ohio. This suggestion came from certain slaveowning Virginians (the phraseology being borrowed from a similar section in Jefferson's 1784 ordinance) who believed that the statement in the Declaration of Independence that "all men are created equal" should be put into effect.

The Northwest Ordinance was not a perfect document as far as the frontiersmen were concerned. They objected to the property qualification of 50 acres for voting and of 200 acres for sitting in the assembly. The governor's absolute veto in the second territorial stage was also a bone of contention. But the ordinance instituted democratic political procedures which protected the West against permanent colonial status. Settlers could now go to the Ohio knowing that they or their sons would become citizens of a new state fully equal to the original thirteen. National political sovereignty would automatically be carried west with the tides of emigration.

Ohio Settlements

Under the influence of this beneficent legislation, optimistic settlers began chopping away at that solid green forest on the north bank of the Beautiful River. The Ohio Company's 1½ million acres included the mouth of the Muskingum, whose fertile valley (along with the protection offered by Fort Harmar) convinced Rufus Putnam that it would make an ideal townsite. In the spring of 1788 the general brought forty-eight sturdy sons of New England down the Ohio on a boat christened *The Mayflower*. The town, named Marietta in honor of Marie Antoniette of France, was a model of careful planning. It soon had the familiar Congregational church, a school, and a village green—all symbols of the New England tradition that was to have a marked influence in Ohio.

Marietta was the exception rather than the rule among the early north-of-Ohio settlements. Judge John Cleves Symmes headed a group of New Jersey speculators who asked Congress to sell them 1 million acres between the Great Miami and Little Miami Rivers. The judge went west in 1788 and proceeded to sell tracts all along these rivers before learning that Congress had finally approved only one-third of the required acreage. There followed years of court suits over the illegal titles, and many settlers had to pay the government for lands which they had already purchased from Symmes. The judge lost all his own lands, and acquired the unenviable reputation of being "the greatest land-jobber on the face of the earth." One positive result of the Symmes Purchase, however, was the founding of a little settlement opposite the mouth of the Licking River. The future city was soon named Cincinnati, in honor of an organization of Revolutionary officers called the Order of Cincinnatus. By the turn of the century Cincinnati had 750 residents, and was being called "the metropolis of the north-western territory."

The Scioto Company was responsible for another catastrophe in the wilderness. Colonel Duer planned on the sale of enough company shares in Europe to pay the first installment on the government contract. For reasons beyond the mind of man, he entrusted this job to a poet, Joel Barlow. Barlow was not a particularly distinguished poet, in fact his *Vision of Columbus* is a windy extravaganza, but he was even less accomplished as a salesman. At Paris in 1789 Barlow met an Englishman with the deceptive name of William Playfair, who persuaded him to sell land rather than shares. Playfair established the *Compagnie de Scioto*, and wrote an imaginative pamphlet entitled *Prospectus pour L'establissement sur les rivieres d'Ohio et de Scioto en Amerique.* This described a beautiful and "much frequented" city of Gallipolis, located in "the garden of the universe" where "frost in winter is almost entirely unknown." No wonder 500 Frenchmen bought 150,000 acres in this never-never land!

The Barlow-Playfair capers in Paris are a source of comedy, but for the French Five Hundred who came to America in 1790, life on the Ohio frontier was no joke. Colonel Duer practically exploded when he learned that the Frenchmen were coming. He was in the business of speculation rather than settlement, and besides that, his company had been unable to make the first payment to the government, and thus it owned no land at all. Hastily buying a tract opposite the mouth of the Great Kanawha from the Ohio Company, he sent axmen to clear away some of the forest and build log barracks. The Frenchmen who arrived at "Gallipolis" in October could not cope with the harsh demands of the wilderness. They were mostly middle-class artisans, jewelers, and wigmakers, whose soft white hands had never held an ax or a gun. Contrary to Playfair's pamphlet, the winter of 1790-1791 was bitterly cold, and so sickness was added to the food-supply problem. The next year the settlers began to drift back East, although some went out to the former French villages in Illinois. Gallipolis survived as a town, but by 1805 only twenty French families remained there. In the meantime, William Playfair had absconded with the funds collected in Paris, the Scioto Company lands had reverted to the government, and William Duer had been placed in a debtors' prison.

The Indian Threat

While the settlers had their problems with landjobbers, the Indians continued to be the greatest menace on the northwestern frontier. The Congress of the Confederation did little to help its citizens in this respect, other than issuing pretentious proclamations scarcely worth the paper on which they were written. On October 15, 1783, for example, Congress repudiated the Ohio River boundary which it had guaranteed to the Indians in 1775, and called upon the savages to withdraw beyond the Great Miami. But there was no military force to put teeth into such impressive edicts. The great citizen-army of the Revolution had been disbanded, and proposals to create a regular force raised fears of a "standing army." A multistate militia force of 700 men under Col. Josiah Harmar was "loaned" to Congress, but it was hardly capable of sustained operations.

The Indians' natural determination to defend their ancestral lands was stiffened by British encouragement. Guns and other trade goods continued to flow into the Ohio villages from the posts at Niagara, Detroit, and Mackinac. These posts were on American soil, according to the peace treaty, but the British army continued to occupy them for over a decade. The official pretext for their retention was American failure to fulfill other provisions of the treaty, particularly that involving restitution of the Loyalists' confiscated property. But the not-so-hidden purpose was to perpetuate the British fur-trade monopoly in the region. The bundles of glossy beaver pelts which went back to England each year sustained a number of powerful mercantile houses, and these merchants had no intention of handing their profits over to the Americans without a fight. The Northwest Company, for example, demanded government protection of its vast trading operations in the Great Lakes and on the Mississippi. This meant maintenance of the army garrisons at the northwest posts, and use of the Indians as a buffer against the greedy Americans.

Joseph Brant worked untiringly to hammer together an Indian confederation in the Northwest. His purpose was not only to serve British policy, it was also to save the Indians. With his educated mind Brant could see that the Indians' survival depended upon their learning the white man's ways. But this would take time, and meanwhile the Americans were coming on at their usual breakneck pace. Brant held a number of conferences at various Indian villages in 1785 and succeeding years, but each time that the confederation seemed on the verge of realization, it would splinter apart. Such tribes as the Delaware and Wyandot were willing to give up certain lands north of the Ohio, whereas a war faction of Shawnee and Miami insisted that the Old Boundary be fought for to the last man. The result of such differences was that Brant was no more successful than Pontiac had been in putting together a grand Indian alliance.

The Americans took advantage of Indian confusion to extract land cessions in a series of treaties. At the second Treaty of Fort Stanwix in 1784, the war-humbled Iroquois surrendered their claim to lands north and west of the Ohio. At Fort McIntosh in January of 1785 the Delawares and Wyandots signed away 30 million acres in central Ohio. But the hostile Shawnee refused to attend this conference. So one year later they had to be rounded up under threat of war and forced to sign the Treaty of Fort Finney, in which they ceded their lands east of the Great Miami. However, the Shawnee and allied tribes held a conference in the winter of 1786-1787 at which they repudiated all three treaties. This defiance was followed by increased raids from both sides of the border, which indicated that the war had never really ended.

Arthur St. Clair had been appointed first Governor of the Northwest Territory, and in the summer of 1788 he took up residence at Fort Harmar. He also held the office of northern Indian superintendent, and one of his principal assignments from Congress was to conclude a definitive Indian treaty that would open up Ohio. A motley collection of chiefs was finally gathered at the fort, and in January of 1789 they put their marks on a treaty surrendering most of modern Ohio. But once again a treaty signed by a handful of chiefs was ignored by rank-and-file warriors and by the more hostile tribes. Raids into Kentucky and on the river traffic continued. It was painfully apparent that only a thorough drubbing would teach the savages to recognize their masters.

Military Defeats

The American attempt to coerce the Indians yielded two military catastrophes known as "Harmar's Defeat" and "St. Clair's Disaster." The hard-drinking General Harmar now had about 600 Regular troops stationed at the various forts along the Ohio. President Washington also authorized him to employ Kentucky and Pennsylvania militia for the campaign. Harmar gathered his mixed force of 1,500 men at Fort Washington, on the site of Cincinnati, and from there started up the Miami River on September 30, 1790. His target was the cluster of Miami villages at the strategic Maumee-Wabash portage. Five towns and their food stores were burned, but two of Harmar's reconnaissance patrols were cut to ribbons with a loss of 183 men. His swift retreat back to the Ohio convinced the Indians that they could handle any American army sent against them.

The next year Governor (and Major General) St. Clair tried to succeed where Harmar had failed. Again a combined force of Regulars and militia was gathered—1,400 men in all. But on his march north from Fort Washington he was plagued by supply difficulties and desertions. St. Clair had had an indifferent military record during the Revolution. On this expedition he became ill, so the normal scouting procedures were not observed. This was unfortunate, to say the least, for soon to be pitted against them were 1,500 enemy warriors who had joined the Miamis under Little Turtle, one of the most renowned war chiefs in frontier annals. Also in this war party were a number of English advisers, including such old foes of the Americans as Alexander McKee, the King's western Indian agent, and Simon Girty, who dressed like a savage and even wore a large quill through his pierced nose. At dawn on November 4, 1791, the warriors attacked St. Clair's camp near the headwaters of the Wabash and achieved a complete surprise. There was a rout comparable to Braddock's defeat, though losses were much heavier. In fact, St. Clair's loss of 913 men killed and wounded out of 1,400 engaged was the greatest loss ever incurred in Indian warfare. It was a time for tears in the American settlements.

"The success of the Indians in their late engagement with General St. Clair will no doubt render them more daring and bold in their future incursions and attacks upon our defenceless inhabitants," reads a petition from Kentucky settlers to the Virginia government. The words were prophetic, for raiding parties hit the Ohio settlements and struck as far south as Harrodsburg and Lexington. Frontier history and folklore are filled with stories of heroic battles at isolated cabins during these raids. The floating anecdote of a mother slamming the cabin door against some of her children in order to save those already inside parallels the old Russian folktale of a family throwing one child from the sleigh to divert a pursuing wolf pack. But most frontier women defended all their brood with ax and gun if the men had been killed. South of Louisville, Mrs. John Merrill killed four Indians with an ax as they attempted to crawl through a hole in the front door. When they met such determined resistance, the Indians would usually break off the attack.

President Washington reacted to the crisis by persuading Congress to approve a new 5,000-man federal army for duty in the West. As commander of this "American Legion" he chose Gen. Anthony Wayne, hero of the Revolutionary battle at Stony Point. Wayne proved to be the man for the job. A stern disciplinarian, he spent 2 years drilling his lackluster recruits at Fort Washington until they became Regulars in habits as well as in name. Among Wayne's officers were the future explorers Meriwether Lewis and William Clark, and a tall young Virginian named William Henry Harrison. Harrison managed to avoid the twin vices of the typical officer, drinking and dueling, and instead spent his spare time reading military history and Cicero's *Orations*. His sobriety led to a lieutenant's commission and a post as Wayne's aide-de-camp.

By the summer of 1794 Wayne was ready to lock horns with the enemy. Peace negotiations had broken down over Indian insistence upon the Old Boundary, "which is the Ohio from its source." During the fall and winter of 1793-1794 Wayne had marched north to build two advanced posts, Fort Greeneville and Fort Recovery, the latter located at the site of St. Clair's defeat. Unlike Braddock or St. Clair, he kept scouts out at all times to avoid surprise. The British officials meanwhile had assured the Indians of support, and to prove the point had constructed Fort Miami on American soil at the Maumee Rapids. Wayne had every reason to expect that he might have to fight the British as well as the Indians.

Wayne at Fallen Timbers

By August 17 Wayne had advanced down the Maumee to the "Fallen Timbers," where a tornado had created a natural fortress of downed tree trunks. Instead of attacking immediately, he waited for 2 days while the Indians grew weaker because of their habit of fasting before a battle. But on August 20 he ordered his 1,500 Regulars and 1,500 Kentucky militia to charge through the timbers with fixed bayonets. Little Turtle's warriors broke under the relentless advance, and fled for the safety of Fort Miami. But there the British soldiers closed the gates on them. This was a bitter moment for the red men, who discovered once again that their "Father" the King had spoken with a forked tongue.

The victorious general moved back to the head of the Maumee, where he built Fort Wayne to control the strategic Maumee-Wabash and Maumee-Miami portages. The next year he called the humiliated tribes to Fort Greeneville, where on August 3, 1795, they signed away two-thirds of modern Ohio. The boundary line began on the Ohio opposite the mouth of the Kentucky, ran north to Fort Recovery, cut sharply northeast to the head of the Cuyahoga, and then went down that river to Lake Erie. Key points north and west of the line, including the mouth of the Maumee and the future Chicago area, were also surrendered. The Americans now controlled lands which had been theirs in name only.

Jay's Treaty

Wayne's triumph was followed by a negotiated surrender of the "northwest posts." Washington had sent John Jay to London in the summer of 1794 in an attempt to win by diplomacy what could not be secured through force. The British perceived that "almost every man has a weak and assailable quarter, and Mr. Jay's weak side is *Mr. Jay*." Hence Jay's Treaty, signed on November 14, is not one of the resounding triumphs in American diplomacy. It permitted the Canadian traders to continue operating south of the border, and guaranteed that no taxes would be levied on the furs which they carried back to Montreal. But

the posts were to be surrendered by June 1, 1796, and in July and October of
that year Detroit and Mackinac were finally occupied by American forces.

Expansion in the Northwest

With the British-Indian menace removed, settlers streamed into the Northwest
Territory. They were a cosmopolitan crowd: New Englanders, Virginians, and
Middle States men. Many Virginians followed the traditional route of the
Wilderness Road, which had been cleared for wagons by 1796. Since many of
them were veterans or had purchased veterans' land warrants, they settled on
the Virginia Military Reserve between the Little Miami and the Scioto. The
reserve was exempt from the Land Ordinance of 1785, so the tracts were laid
out according to the Southern method of indiscriminate location. Speculators
were also quite active in this area. Nathaniel Massie, for example, was an
experienced woodsman who pyramided military warrants and used them to lay
out the townsite of Chillicothe in 1796. Many settlers did not wish to pay the
speculators' prices, however, and they moved further north where they could
buy government land.

More and more of the Ohio settlers tended to come by way of
Pittsburgh. The town became an outfitting center for the western migrants,
13,000 of whom stopped there in the year 1794. They bought tools, foodstuffs,
and a specially made flatboat to carry them down the river. These boats were
made of oak, and were about 40 feet long and around 12 feet wide. Their hulls
were 3 or 4 feet above the water, and they generally had a cabin in the center
for protection against weather and Indian bullets. "It is no uncommon spectacle,"
wrote Timothy Flint, "to see a large family, old and young, servants, cattle,
hogs, horses, sheep, fowls, and animals of all kinds, bringing to recollection the
cargo of an ancient ark, all embarked, and floating down on the same bottom."
The clumsy craft were kept in the current by means of long oars or "sweeps."
At the end of the journey they would be abandoned, or else broken up and used
in the construction of a cabin. From 1792 the keelboat was also used. It was
longer and narrower than the flatboat, and had a shallow keel for greater
maneuverability. It could also be poled back upstream.

A number of New Englanders came west by way of New York and
settled in northern Ohio. The "Genesee lands" of western New York were being
developed by a variety of land companies which offered quite favorable terms.
But the more adventurous farmers preferred to press on through the wilderness
to Connecticut's Western Reserve. The state had allotted 500,000 acres at the
west end of the reserve, the "Firelands," for its citizens whose homes had been
burned by British troops during the Revolution. The remaining 3 million acres
in the reserve were sold to the Connecticut Land Company for private development. A burly Revolutionary veteran named Moses Cleaveland came west as
the company's surveyor in 1796, and began laying out a townsite at the mouth

of the Cuyahoga River. Cleveland (the misspelling became standard) grew slowly, having only fifty residents by 1806, and the same was true of the rest of the reserve. It was the old story of the speculators' high prices driving people to cheaper government lands.

Ohio as a whole boomed in population, going from 45,000 in 1800 to 230,000 in 1810. Fabulous stories about bumper crops reached the East by means of speculators' pamphlets and emigrant's guidebooks. The corn at Marietta was 14 feet high; potatoes grown along Lake Erie were as large as Connecticut pumpkins; 12-pound mushrooms were a commonplace. Easterners tried to counter these tales with propaganda of their own. Sarcastic letters described settlers suffering from fever and ague, or commented on the primitive life of uncouth settlers who all drank whiskey from the same bottle. In *Western Emigration*, Henry Trumbull warned his fellow Bostonians about "the idle tales of the peskit Ohio speculators, who with great parade tell us that that land is a perfect Paradise—that provisions abound in such profusion that geese, turkeys, oppossums, bears, raccoons and rabbits may be seen running around in the woods in droves, ready cooked, with knives and forks stuck in their flanks, crying out to the newly arrived emigrant, 'come eat me.' The reverse of this is the case, as you may perceive by my account of the mishaps and disasters that I met with." Yet nothing could stem the tide. Ohio was a fairly level land with rich black soil that made it a natural breadbasket. Connecticut and Massachusetts offered rocky hillsides, high taxes, and a conformist social order. Indeed, so many New Englanders chose the West that Connecticut's Assembly even considered a bill to prohibit emigration.

Ohio's Political Struggle

As Ohio grew, it developed political problems. Governor St. Clair was a staunch Federalist, and an autocrat in every fiber of his being. He probably would have made a good administrator in one of the settled areas east of the mountains, but he lacked the flexibility needed to govern a turbulent frontier. In addition, he had committed the one unpardonable sin in a frontier community: he had lost a fight with the Indians. The popular opposition to the Governor was centered in the Virginia Military Reserve. The settlers there were not from the more conservative Tidewater; they were Piedmont Virginians who supported Thomas Jefferson in national politics. The two forces clashed during the first sessison of the territorial Legislature in 1799, when St. Clair vetoed a bill to take a census in the region east of the Miami. He feared that a state formed along the line of this river would favor the Jeffersonian Republicans, and to secure a Federalist majority he wanted a dividing line at the Scioto.

The Republicans decided to back William Henry Harrison as their candidate for delegate to Congress. Harrison had resigned from the Army and was engaged in business at Cincinnati. He agreed to work for the Miami line and for "an amelioration of the laws for the sale of Public Land." After defeating St. Clair's son by an 11 to 10 vote of the legislative council, delegate Harrison persuaded Congress to pass both measures. On May 7, 1800, the Northwest Territory was divided along a line running northward from the mouth of the Kentucky River (2 years later it was reset along the Great Miami). The region west of the line was denominated as Indiana Territory, and Harrison was appointed its first governor. Before assuming this office he was able to pilot through Congress a significant revision of the land laws.

Harrison Land Law

The Harrison Land Act of 1800 reflected that grand old American custom of buying on credit. In this case the terms were one-fourth down, with 4 years to pay the balance. Administrative machinery was set up to help the settler, specifically the establishment of government land offices at Steubenville, Chillicothe, Marietta, and Cincinnati. The price was set at $2 an acre, but most important, the minimum purchase was reduced from 640 to 320 acres. This provision marks the beginning of a change toward the view that settlement of the federal lands was more important than revenue. Concern for the small farmer was reflected also in the subsequent reduction to 160 acres in the 1804 land law, and to 80 acres in 1820. The 1820 law, however, abolished the credit feature. It was found that too many settlers were claiming more land than they could pay for, and hence the government had a backlog of unpaid bills. But Harrison's law did prove to be, as he himself predicted, "the foundation of a great increase of population and wealth to our country." Under it, the small farmer had a chance against the speculator.

Statehood for Ohio

Meanwhile, the enabling act for statehood passed the Congress in April of 1802 despite St. Clair's violent opposition. In fact, the old Governor's bitter attacks on Republican officials over the statehood issue led to his dismissal from office. The Ohio convention went on to draw up a constitution modeled after that of another frontier state, Tennessee. But there were important modifications reflecting the democratic views of Ohio's small farmers. There was no property qualification for the Assembly, and all male taxpayers could vote. The governor was limited to a 2-year term, and his veto power was taken away. Congress accepted these and other provisions, and Ohio entered the Union as the first public-land state on February 19, 1803. The Northwest Ordinance had proved its value.

In the early years of the new century other settlers began filtering into Governor Harrison's Indiana Territory. They mingled with the French inhabitants at Vincennes and at the Illinois villages on the Mississippi, or moved to Clark's grant across from Louisville. Population grew so rapidly—from 5,600 in 1800 to almost 25,000 by 1812—that the administrative difficulties led Congress to create a separate Illinois Territory in 1809. The farmer-frontiersmen of the two territories took up public land under the new laws, and continued the old job of clearing the wilderness. They also served as a base for the next thrust into the West.

Selected Readings   Dale Van Every, *The Ark of Empire, 1784-1803* (New York, 1963), is good on the Northwest. Beverly W. Bond, Jr., *The Civilization of the Old Northwest* (New York, 1934), is an excellent scholarly study. Roy M. Robbins, *Our Landed Heritage* (Princeton, 1942), is a standard history of the public domain. A key article is Merrill Jensen, "The Creation of the National Domain, 1781-1784," *Mississippi Valley Historical Review,* vol. 23 (December, 1939). Walter Havighurst, *Wilderness for Sale* (New York, 1956), is a recommended popular narrative. Archer B. Hulbert, "The Methods and Operations of the Scioto Group of Speculators," *Mississippi Valley Historical Review,* vols. 1 and 2 (March and June ,1915), is highly informative. Theodore C. Pease, "The Ordinance of 1787," *Mississippi Valley Historical Review,* vol. 25 (September, 1938), lauds the document. Text of the Ordinance is in vol. 2 of Francis N. Thorpe, *The Federal and State Constitutions,* 7 vols. (Washington, 1907). Richard C. Wade, *The Urban Frontier* (Cambridge, 1959), details the rise of five Western cities between 1790 and 1830.

        Relations with the British and Indians is the subject of Louise P. Kellogg, *The British Regime in Wisconsin and the Northwest* (Madison, Wis., 1935); Randolph C. Downes, *Council Fires on the Upper Ohio* (Pittsburgh, 1940); and Marjorie W. Campbell, *The North West Company* (New York, 1957). Samuel F. Bemis, *Jay's Treaty* (New York, 1924), is standard. Harry E. Wildes, *Anthony Wayne* (New York, 1941), and Freeman Cleaves, *Old Tippecanoe: William Henry Harrison and His Times* (New York, 1939), are the top-rated biographies. Beverly W. Bond, Jr., *The Foundations of Ohio* (Columbus, 1941). is good. Payson J. Treat, *The National Land System, 1785-1820* (New York, 1920), describes the Harrison Land Law.

VII. West by Southwest

The history of the Old Southwest in the postwar period is a complicated tale of plots, Indian wars, land speculations, and filibustering expeditions. The principal characters are restless and ambitious American frontiersmen from the three settlements west of the mountains: Kentucky, Cumberland, and Holston. They opposed the Spanish governors of Louisiana and the chiefs of the southern Indian tribes in a great contest for ownership of the Mississippi Valley. During the course of this struggle their impatience with a feeble national government bred separatist movements that threatened the existence of the Union. But the story has the traditional happy ending.

American-Spanish Relations The two sources of American-Spanish conflict on the southwestern border were navigation of the Mississippi and ownership of the Yazoo country. Geography dictated that the American frontiersmen ship their crops down to the Ohio-Mississippi waterway. The shorter land route directly east had to cross mountains which made wagon freighting costs virtually prohibitive. Navigation of the Mississippi was thus a matter of economic survival for these western farmers. They had to get their wheat, corn, and pork down to New Orleans where it could be transferred to oceangoing vessels for shipment to the Atlantic coast. Furthermore, they felt that they had a "natural right" to travel the great river. But Spain brushed aside these claims, and closed the Mississippi to American trade in 1784. Her policy, maintained largely through inertia and tradition, was to severely limit all foreign trade with the empire. New Orleans was to be a Spanish port for Spaniards only.

A second dispute concerned the overlapping claims to the Yazoo strip. The Anglo-American treaty had given the Americans this strip of land, which included Natchez-on-the-Mississippi, as far south as the 31st parallel.

A secret article in the treaty, however, specified that if England retained possession of the Floridas in the Anglo-Spanish treaty, the boundary should be at 32°30', a line which ran east from the mouth of the Yazoo River. But Spain did get Florida in the Anglo-Spanish treaty, and her officials claimed with considerable justice that West Florida's northern boundary had always been the 32°30' line. She was enraged after learning of the secret article in the American treaty, and demanded unconditional surrender of the territory involved. It has been suggested that England deliberately played a two-faced game in the treaty making to keep Spain and America at each other's throats. But there is no conclusive evidence to support this supposition, and in any case it seems likely that the two nations would have collided over other issues.

There were constant rumors at the Spanish posts that an American expeditionary force was being organized to seize Natchez and the Yazoo country. In fact, the Spanish governors at New Orleans had recurrent nightmares of this sort. They imagined that boatloads of lantern-jawed riflemen were descending the Mississippi, as the Goths had descended on Rome, to capture not only the Yazoo strip but New Orleans itself. The governors' fears were compounded by doubts about the loyalty of their own citizens. The great majority of the Louisianans were French, while Florida's population was mostly British Loyalists and escaped Negro slaves. The only Spaniards in either province were the colonial officials and members of the army, and their great concern was that Louisiana would be a pushover for any American invasion force.

Though the frontiersmen issued many blasts of hot air about their intention to take Louisiana, they were actually a negligible military threat. Even if a large enough army could have been assembled on the Ohio, the Spanish fleet still controlled the Gulf of Mexico. Any Americans who reached New Orleans would have been sealed off from above and below by this superior naval force. Yet there were constant threats and enough actual episodes to cause alarm on both sides of the border. For example, land speculators were continually planning new colonies in the Southwest. These included one at Muscle Shoals on the Tennessee (William Blount and John Sevier) and another at Chickasaw Bluffs on the Mississippi (James Robertson). The most threatening to Spain was a project at the Walnut Hills near the mouth of the Yazoo. In 1785 the Georgia Legislature organized the area as "Bourbon County" to help get the land scheme going. Spain was horrified by this threatened invasion of her territory, and the Spanish commander at Natchez promptly expelled the Georgia commissioners sent to organize the new county.

Negotiation of the two key issues seemed to be a logical step. The Congress in 1786 did authorize John Jay to conduct talks at Philadelphia with the Spaniards' Don Diego De Gardoqui. The proposed treaty which Jay submitted to Congress reflected the interests of the northeastern commercial states. It included an official renunciation of all American claims to navigation of the

Mississippi for a period of 25 years. In return, Spanish ports would be opened to American trading ships. The northeastern states were enthusiastic about this provision, for England was punishing her former colonials by prohibiting them from trading with the empire. Spain represented an alternative opportunity for the merchant class of whom Jay was a leading example. The treaty did not pass, however, since under the Articles of Confederation nine votes were required to approve important legislation. The seven northern states voted for it, but the five southern states were opposed. The frontier regarded the treaty as a sellout and as a betrayal of its "inalienable right" to navigation of the Mississippi. A dangerous sectional pattern had made its appearance, and the national government had lost credit in the West.

Indian Relations

The inability of Congress to protect them against the Indians also alienated the Westerners. There were about 45,000 individuals in the four Civilized Tribes of the Southwest (the Chickasaw, Choctaw, Creek, and Cherokee). The Chickasaw were a small tribe who mustered 500 warriors and who lived along the Mississippi in western Tennessee. They became friendly with the Americans, a friendship which was never to be rewarded. The Choctaw, living in southern Mississippi under the strong influence of the Spanish, were the least important tribe in the politics of the period. The Creeks were the largest and strongest of these Indian nations, being able to raise 5,000 "gunmen." They merited the title "civilized" since they occupied permanent towns in Alabama and Georgia. Here they raised livestock and cultivated tobacco, beans, and corn. They owned a few Negro slaves, and they had a rudimentary political system. Each of the thirty-four towns sent delegates to tribal councils, although the warriors were so individualistic that decisions of the councils were not always carried out. Under a skilled leader in the 1780s, however, the Creeks did have a rough approximation of a political confederation. This leader was not called "Standing Bear" or "Iron Hawk," but had the unlikely name of Alexander McGillivray.

McGillivray was the son of a Scotch Loyalist trader and a Creek princess of the powerful Wind clan. He was raised among this tribe, but his father sent him to Charleston for several years of education just prior to the Revolution. There Alexander acquired a mastery of the English language which he employed to good advantage when he became principal chief of the Creek nation after the war. He was not a warrior; in fact he always left the fighting to others. Although he suffered from wracking headaches and an impressive variety of other physical ailments, these did not prevent him from protecting the interests of his mother's people. Foremost among these interests was seeing to it that the Americans did not advance from Georgia or Cumberland and swallow the tribal lands. This meant seeking the protection of Spain, but also playing off one power against another when the opportunity arose.

McGillivray worked closely with another Scotch Loyalist, William Panton, whose trading firm of Panton & Leslie operated out of St. Augustine. With grudging Spanish permission, Panton supplied the Creeks and other southwestern tribes with arms which were used to good effect against the Americans.

Though McGillivray sought Spanish protection, he often acted quite independently. For example, in 1786 he sent his warriors against the Georgia and Cumberland settlements. The attacks were quite successful, but they were contrary to Spanish policy in Louisiana and Florida which, as on other frontiers, was basically defensive. Governor Esteban Miró's orders were to avoid conflicts, a policy which was based partly upon the belief that American frontiersmen were ready to separate from their own government and seek Spanish protection. The prospects for such a development seemed to be quite favorable throughout the 1780s.

McGillivray wrote to Miró in 1784 that "the protection of a great Monarch is to be preferred to that of a distracted Republic." And there is little doubt that the United States government was "distracted" during the so-called Critical Period of the 1780s. The central government had no taxing authority, no executive leadership, and no effective military force. As far as the frontier was concerned, it offered no protection against the Indians, no system of territorial government, and no prospects of an eventual opening of the Mississippi. In fact, the Jay-Gardoqui negotiations had indicated that the Eastern states were hostile to the West and were prepared to sacrifice its interests. This situation led to various proposals to separate the West from the United States. It also encouraged several new-state movements, the most significant of which occurred in the Holston settlements.

The State of Franklin

In the spring of 1784 North Carolina ceded the Tennessee country to the United States. The settlers of the Holston-Watauga region were a nuisance to the state government. They were always complaining about the Indians and were demanding expensive services for which they could not pay. In the debates over cession, the Westerners were described as "off-scourings of the earth" and "fugitives from justice." The fact that some Tennesseans *were* fugitives did not diminish their resentment at such slings and arrows. Thus they were quite ready to break with the parent state. Yet there was no machinery for forming a territorial government under Congressional authority at that time. The only recourse was to form a separate state government, and hope for eventual admission to the Union.

The Westerners proceeded to frame a temporary constitution during a convention at Jonesboro in December of 1784. The document was based largely upon the North Carolina constitution, but with a few embellishments lifted from the Declaration of Independence and a long list of the Rights of

Man. They called the new state Franklin in honor of Benjamin Franklin. Perhaps this was a tactical error; if they had chosen "'Jefferson" they might have gotten greater support from the national government through the good offices of that energetic statesman. Col. Arthur Campbell of Virginia took a leading role in encouraging the formation of the new state, whose borders were to include parts of southwest Virginia as well as all of Tennessee west to the Cumberland mountains and south to the Cherokee country. The first General Assembly of the new state met at Jonesboro in March of 1785, and it elected John Sevier as Governor.

Sevier was a tall, handsome, graceful man who had settled on the Watauga in the early 70s. He was popular with women, and he loved to dance the old country reels like "The Flower of Edinburgh." He was a capable writer who had corresponded with Franklin, John Adams, and other national leaders. Yet he was also a man of action, and an eminently successful Indian fighter. A monument to him in Knoxville reads: "Thirty five battles, thirty five victories." These victories and his natural leadership qualities made him the most popular man among the east Tennesseans, to whom he was known as "Chucky Jack" after his move to the Nolichucky Valley at the end of the Revolution. As far as the state of Franklin was concerned, Sevier followed rather than led public opinion. He was at the time involved in a land-speculating venture at Muscle Shoals, and was reluctant to turn from that to a new-state movement. But once his friends had chosen him, he devoted himself to the governorship.

Meanwhile, in October of 1784, North Carolina had repealed her act of cession. The state's land speculators were behind the move. They had acquired title to most of the unappropriated land in Tennessee, and they now realized that it would be easier to complete their titles under the authority of North Carolina than to take risks with a new state. But the Franklinites refused to return to the fold. The letter which they sent to Governor Josiah Martin, dated March 22, 1785, is a classic statement of East-West differences. There is a reference to the geographical conditions which led to separation: "the high and almost impassable mountains which naturally divide us from the eastern parts of the state." There are complaints about the inequitable tax situation. The Westerners objected to the fact that their land taxes were as high as those in the East, and yet they "are taxed to support a government while they are deprived of all the blessings of it." The Indian troubles are blamed upon North Carolina's "mismanagement," a charge with some validity since the state had sold land to speculators without first clearing the Indian titles. Attention was also called to the Assembly's statements about "fugitives" and "off-scourings." Governor Martin's response was to call the movement a "revolt."

Franklin operated to all intents and purposes as a new state. It had a constitution, first drawn up in 1784 and permanently adopted in November of 1785. It had a governor, legislature, court system, tax collectors, and militia.

It signed treaties with the Indians, the most important of which, bearing the folksy title of the Treaty of Dumplin Creek (July, 1785), bought up Cherokee claims to a sizable tract of land south of the French Broad River. Such a brash assumption of sovereignty brought trouble with the United States government, which claimed authority over all the Indians. In fact the congressional Indian commissioners signed the Treaty of Hopewell in November, which ignored the Franklinites and ran the treaty line north of the French Broad. The episode added to the coolness between the Westerners and the Congress, which had previously indicated its unwillingness to assume the expensive burden of a new state at that time.

North Carolina was the state's principal opponent. Col. John Tipton was a North Carolina "loyalist" and a personal rival of John Sevier. He organized a Tennessee government that was committed to destroying the Franklin movement and returning the West to North Carolina's control. Thus through 1786 and 1787 there were two separate state governments with their own judges and sheriffs, a situation causing the residents no end of trouble. Young couples were caught in a dilemma: if they were married by Franklin officials they might find that they had lived in sin if such marriages were later declared illegal. The two sides engaged in a series of raids and skirmishes. Sevier and Tipton at one point engaged in fisticuffs: "Each exchanged blows for some time in the same way with great violence and in a convulsion of rage." The climax of the mock war came in February of 1788, when two men were killed during a siege and gun battle at Tipton's home.

The "lost state" of Franklin finally came to an end after Sevier's term of office expired on March 1, 1788. The combined opposition of Congress and North Carolina was too much for the infant state to withstand, and it faded into history as a quaint example of frontier self-government. Tipton arrested Sevier in October and took him East for trial, but the ex-Governor escaped and was eventually pardoned. He remained popular despite the collapse of Franklin. North Carolina again ceded the transmontane lands in 1789, and when Tennessee became a state in 1796, it elected "Chucky Jack" as its first governor.

Frontier Intrigue

Sevier was one of four frontier leaders who engaged in intrigues with Spain during 1788. In all cases there appears to have been less interest in serving Spanish policy than in advancing some favorite land speculation or colonizing scheme. Sevier wrote two letters to Governor Miró asking for money and munitions, the basic objective of these overtures being to protect the Muscle Shoals speculation from Indian or Spanish harassment. James Robertson wrote to Miró from Nashville, also seeking an alliance and a bargain which would save his settlement from the pounding of Creek and Chickamauga war parties

which were being armed if not encouraged by the Spanish. George Rogers
Clark was among those proposing to found a colony within Spanish territory.
These various proposals all came to nought. The most serious western separatist
movement was in Kentucky, and its chief advocate was an American Machiavelli
named James Wilkinson.

Wilkinson was a native of Maryland who had been a boy wonder
in the Revolution, being commissioned a brigadier general at the age of twenty-
one. He had been an incompetent clothier-general, and had engaged in the
Conway Cabal against Washington and in backstairs intrigues against Gen.
Horatio Gates, who was the first on a long list of Wilkinson's enemies which
eventually included Generals Wayne, Clark, Jackson, and others too numerous
to mention. In 1783 the retired general went to Kentucky where he became a
land speculator and politician. That territory offered heaven-sent opportunities
for a man of Wilkinson's peculiar talents. In 1784 Spain closed the Mississippi
to American trade. Westerners could no longer take their tobacco, flour, and
hams down to be traded for Spanish silver at New Orleans, where they had
also been accustomed to enjoying the twin delights of French wine and Creole
women. Wilkinson saw that he could profit from this explosive situation, but
first of all he had to destroy the reputation of his chief rival and Kentucky's
preeminent hero, George Rogers Clark. Throughout 1786 and 1787 he worked to
this end. Letters to influential Virginians from Wilkinson's friends declared
that "Clarke is eternally drunk." The program of vilification, aided by
Clark's failure in a Wabash Valley Indian campaign, was successful. Congress
fired Clark as Indian Commissioner and appointed Wilkinson in his place.
Having thus moved toward political leadership in Kentucky, Wilkinson was
now ready to carry on his intrigue with Spain.

In July of 1787 he went down to New Orleans with a boatload of
tobacco. Governor Miró permitted him to sell the cargo at a handsome profit,
and then listened eagerly as Wilkinson unfolded his schemes for the West. The
core of the plan was to have Kentucky secede from the United States and
set itself up as an independent republic under Spanish protection. This was
the famous "Spanish Conspiracy," which should perhaps be retitled the "Wilkinson Conspiracy" since he rather than the Spanish officials suggested it.
Wilkinson saw himself as the "Washington of the West," and this scheme would
presumably bring him not only political fame but also bags of money. The
would-be liberator prepared a memorial to Madrid outlining his plan, and then
took the oath of allegiance to the King of Spain. He got a private trading concession to sell tobacco free of duty at New Orleans, and was given a government
pension. By the end of 1796, he had received $26,000 for his alleged services
to the Crown.

Wilkinson returned to Kentucky in 1788 and began his behind-the-
scenes plotting for separation. Such friends as Benjamin Sebastian and Harry
Innes aided him in these machinations. Indeed, there was considerable senti-

ment for separation at this time. Kentuckians were dissatisfied with the national government, and they were particularly incensed by the "betrayal" of the Jay-Gardoqui negotiations. For that matter they were also exasperated with the Virginia government. There had been a strong movement for separation of Kentucky from Virginia in 1781 to 1784, backed principally by the non-Virginian element. By the late 80s even many ex-Virginians were convinced that Kentucky must separate itself. Four statehood conventions had submitted proposed constitutions to Virginia and to Congress, but each time, those august Assemblies had found reasons for delaying the measure. (Nine were eventually held before statehood was granted in 1792.) If Wilkinson could get concessions from Spain, particularly a reopening of the Mississippi, maybe his entire secession plan should be adopted.

Kentucky did not leave the Union. Dissatisfied as they were with Congress, the American frontiersmen still balked at a Spanish connection. Spain was an autocracy whose political traditions were alien to men accustomed to large measures of self-government. Theoretically, all land in the colonies belonged to the King. His orders passed down an elaborate chain of command: the Council of the Indies (which had supreme legislative and administrative powers), the various viceroys, the provincial governors, the alcaldes of the towns, and the local military commanders. The result was that a Spanish subject could not even post notice of a stray horse unless he got prior consent from the military commander of his district. There were government monopolies in many potentially profitable fields, and no private land speculation. Furthermore, Spain was a Catholic nation and it did not tolerate Protestants.

Few Westerners were affiliated with any religious denomination. This fact did not so much reflect widespread irreligion as it did the physical difficulties of building churches and finding ministers. The Methodists, Baptists, and Presbyterians were the three major denominations in the West at this time, the last of these being strong among the Scotch and Scotch-Irish. The Methodists and Baptists emphasized free-will doctrines and an emotional form of preaching which appealed to frontiersmen. The Methodist "circuit-rider" took the Gospel into pioneer communities which could not afford a resident minister. But whether they were practicing Christians or not, Westerners thought of America as a Protestant nation. They shared with their eastern brethren a suspicion of Catholicism that was engrained in American thinking for many generations.

The incompatibility between Catholic Louisiana and Protestant Kentucky was revealed by a sudden change in Spanish policy. In 1788 the King decided to open Louisiana and West Florida to American immigrants. They would be permitted to use the Mississippi as far south as New Orleans, their goods being subject to a 15-percent duty. Favorable land grants would be made to all those who took the conventional oath of allegiance. Religious toleration was to be granted to Protestants, a striking concession in view of Spanish history to this point. The new policy was aimed at building up a colonial population which Spain herself had been unable to supply. Inviting Americans into a territory was suicidal, as the subsequent history of Texas was to prove. But the thinking seemed to be that they could be more closely watched if they were Spanish subjects.

The new policy did not attract many Americans to Louisiana, for the reasons cited above. It did pull the props out from under Wilkinson's conspiracy. If anyone could trade down to New Orleans, of what use was a private concession? The archplotter continued to receive his Spanish pension, but he was soon forced to seek employment with the American army. Another reason leading to the collapse of the separatist movement was the adoption of the new United States Constitution. Most of the western leaders were dubious if not opposed to the new frame of government, since they regarded it as a grab for power by the Easterners. But after it was ratified they were willing to give it a try. The national government was given greatly enlarged powers in the areas of taxation, executive leadership, and foreign relations. If it used these powers wisely it could placate the West.

Washington's Policies

George Washington, elected President in March of 1789, played his cards well. The appointment of Thomas Jefferson rather than John Jay as Secretary of State was well received west of the mountains. Washington also followed a policy of appointing the disgruntled western leaders to key positions in the federal service. On May 20, 1790, Congress had created a government for the "Territory of the United States of America, South of the River Ohio." William Blount, a Tennessee land speculator suspected of separatist sentiments, was appointed to the double job of governor of this Southwest Territory and superintendent of its Indian affairs. Picked to serve under him as brigadier generals of militia were James Robertson and John Sevier. James Wilkinson was commissioned a lieutenant colonel in the regular American army, a post which he accepted "for Bread and Fame." His coplotters Benjamin Sebastian and Harry Innes were appointed to the offices of U.S. attorney general and federal judge for the district of Kentucky. It seemed that every man who gave evidence of participation in a separatist movement was rewarded with a federal job of some sort.

President Washington also added to the prestige of the federal government by signing a treaty with the Creeks. In the summer of 1789 the Spanish had seized several British ships at Nootka Sound in the Pacific Northwest. The episode ballooned into an international crisis that threatened to bring on another of the periodic Anglo-Spanish wars. The crisis placed Alexander McGillivray in a precarious position, since a war would cut off his supplies and leave him at the mercy of the Americans. Hence he was ready to accept Washington's invitation to visit New York and iron out the differences between the United States and the Creek nation.

The Treaty of New York, signed on August 7, 1790, did not yield particularly large territorial gains. McGillivray surrendered a strip of land between the Oconee and Ogeechee Rivers that was already occupied by the Georgians. Of more significance was his agreement to recognize American sovereignty over the Creek towns lying within the United States border. This formed a legal basis for future penetration of the tribal lands. In return, McGillivray was given a secret pension of $1,800 a year, and Washington promised to oppose land-company schemes in the Yazoo area. Of the several allied companies operating in the disputed territory, the most aggressive was the South Carolina Yazoo Company. The firm's general agent, Dr. James O'Fallon, attempted to exploit the Nootka Sound crisis by threatening to march a frontier army to the Walnut Hills if Spain did not permit a peaceful occupation. But the national administration opposed the project since it might bring on a war with the Indians, the Spaniards, or both. Hence Washington was quite willing to cooperate with McGillivray in crushing these speculators.

Spanish Policy

Despite his skillful handling of several major problems, the President still faced monumental difficulties on the southwestern border. These were caused both by changes in Spanish policy and by continuing dissatisfaction among the Westerners. The Spanish government decided that its open-door policy had been a failure. Americans had not settled in Louisiana despite the liberal land grants and the promise of religious toleration. The conspiracies with frontier leaders had not resulted in the separation of Kentucky from the Union. Hence the Spanish Court reversed itself once again and adopted an aggressive anti-American policy. Symbolic of the change was the recall of Governor Miró at the end of 1791 and his replacement by Hector, Baron de Carondelet. The baron's knowledge of French was apparently considered to be an asset in Louisiana, but he was in other respects unsuited to the job at hand. A bellicose individual, he attempted to use the Indians as military allies. He stirred up trouble between them and the Americans, whom he recognized as dangerous enemies: "Their method of spreading themselves and their policy are so much to be feared by Spain as are their arms. . . . Their wandering spirit and the ease with which those people procure their sustenance and shelter quickly form new settlements. A carbine and a little maize in a sack are enough for an American to wander about in the forests alone for a whole month." These nomads had to be stopped before they crossed the Mississippi in large numbers.

Carondelet tried to form a military confederation among the four Civilized Tribes by supplying them with money, guns, and advice. The prospects seemed particularly bright after the crushing defeats administered to Harmar and St. Clair in the north had proved the weakness of American arms. The spring of 1792 saw Chickamauga and Creek war parties again battering the

Nashville stations. In September a massive Chickamauga-Creek-Cherokee invasion of the Tennessee frontier resulted in some minor victories, but also revealed the fatal flaw of the confederation. This was the inadequacy of the Indian political system for the kind of centralized operations that Carondelet had in mind. Disputes among the chiefs, the individualism of the warriors, and traditional tribal enmities proved to be insurmountable obstacles to coordinated action. In fact, a Creek-Choctaw war broke out even as Carondelet was attempting to form his confederation. The death of Alexander McGillivray in 1793 also deprived him of the one Indian leader who might have been able to put together some type of intertribal political system.

The new aggressiveness of both the Spanish and the Indians enraged American frontiersmen and drove them almost to the point of insurrection. Fuel was added to the fire by virtue of the fact that in the trans-Appalachian region there was great enthusiasm for the French Revolution of 1791. Praise for the principles of "liberty" and "equality" was expressed through political clubs known as the "democratic societies." In national politics these clubs supported a pro-French faction headed by Thomas Jefferson. However, President Washington followed a policy of neutrality, officially stated in the proclamation of 1793, while Secretary of the Treasury Alexander Hamilton was decidedly pro-British. Into this tense situation came Citizen Edmond Genet, new French minister to the United States. Failing to get Washington's support for active assistance to the Republic, Genet decided to appeal directly to the American people. In the West this took the form of a projected filibustering expedition to be led by George Rogers Clark.

Clark was like a retired athlete, whose career reaches its peak in his early twenties. In 1792 he was forty years old, an unemployed hero who had received little recognition or compensation from his own nation. He had been involved in several abortive plans to attack Louisiana, and was ready for a new venture of this sort. In February of 1793 he wrote Genet, offering to raise an army of 800 men and seize New Orleans. Genet approved the plan and appointed Clark a major general in the "Independent and Revolutionary Legion of the Mississippi." The objective was to make Louisiana an independent state, with commercial ties to both the United States and France. There was popular support for such an expedition in Kentucky, since the national government had done nothing to help open the Mississippi to navigation. It was also expected that the French residents of Louisiana would rise up against their Spanish overlords. Clark began collecting men and supplies at the mouth of the Cumberland River, despite Washington's attempts to break up the expedition. The President was committed to a peace policy which would be doomed if Clark were permitted to attack Spanish territory.

The collapse of the filibuster came when Genet was dismissed and ordered to return to France. The new regime there wanted to put him under the guillotine. The ex-minister quickly decided that he would rather stay in the United States. He married a New York heiress and became an American citizen. The withdrawal of French financial support forced Clark to abandon his plan. In fact, his subsequent efforts to get payment for the supplies he had already purchased are another chapter in a long hard-luck story. But the enthusiasm which Clark's project aroused indicated something of the temper of the Western people.

Whiskey Rebellion

Western resentment at the national government's policies also flared up into armed rebellion. Farmers living along the Monongahela River in western Pennsylvania were no longer on the frontier, which had moved on down the Ohio. But they still retained a fierce independence, and their equalitarian spirit had been heightened by the French Revolution. Their anger was aroused by a federal whiskey tax of 7 cents a gallon, passed in March of 1791 at the urging of Secretary of the Treasury Hamilton. The tax was regarded as discriminatory by the Pennsylvanians, since it was levied on one of their principal sources of income. Rye and corn were too bulky to be packed across the mountains, but the whiskey distilled from these crops could be shipped at handsome profits. The farmers complained that the Easterners and Federalists who passed the law drank imported wine that was taxed at a lower rate. Hamilton's hard-hearted reply was that "of this class of taxes it is not easy to conceive one which can operate with greater equality than a tax on distilled spirits. There appears to be no article, as far as the information of the Secretary goes, which is an object of more equal consumption throughout the United States."

The law had been loosely enforced until 1794, but then the government tightened up its inspection and collection activities. This led to armed resistance by the radical element, and the so-called Whiskey Rebellion of 1794 was the result. Mobs ranged over four counties attacking the federal revenue officers in the name of the mythical "Tom the Tinker." The luckier inspectors merely had their heads shaved; the more unfortunate ones were tarred and feathered. This violence was too much for President Washington and Secretary Hamilton, who decided that the insurrection offered an opportunity to prove that federal law could be enforced west of the mountains. A militia army of 13,000 men was raised in eastern Pennsylvania, and it marched west in October to crush the rebellion and arrest its leaders.

Pinckney's Treaty

Even as Washington grappled with the rebellious Monongahelans, Baron Carondelet was extending Spain's military frontier further northward. One fort (Confederation) was built on the Tombigbee to block the Georgians, and another (San Fernando) went up at Chickasaw Bluffs to control the upper

Mississippi. The Baron sent optimistic reports to Madrid, claiming that his departure from the traditional defensive policy would stop the American advance. He was also responding to another overture from James Wilkinson, who proposed to raise an army of Kentuckians who would throw off the American yoke. Carondelet swallowed the bait with hook, line, and sinker. He sent the foxy brigadier general $16,000 to launch the second "Spanish Conspiracy." But Wilkinson had no real intention of undertaking a dangerous operation of this sort. He was perfectly willing to extract money from his gullible clients as he led them down the primrose path, but when it came to acting on his proposals he was always careful to back out.

Spain's Council of State was also preparing to disappoint the aggressive Governor. It is a commonplace that America benefited from strife in Europe. When war threatened, the European powers usually reduced their commitments in North America and sought the neutrality if not the friendship of the United States. In 1795 Spain faced the prospect of still another war with England. In this eventuality her colonies in Louisiana and the Floridas would be vulnerable, and thus their northern borders had to be made secure by winning American friendship. Thomas Pinckney, American minister to Great Britain, was sent to Madrid in the spring of 1795 to negotiate a treaty with the now-conciliatory Spaniards. The resultant Treaty of San Lorenzo, known in American history as Pinckney's Treaty, was signed on October 27, 1795. Spain surrendered the Yazoo Strip and agreed to abandon her forts north of the 31st parallel within 6 months. The Americans were granted free navigation of the Mississippi, and were permitted to deposit their goods at New Orleans. These concessions were a major triumph for Thomas Pinckney, the United States, and the western frontiersmen.

Pinckney's Treaty did not immediately solve all the problems of the southwestern frontier. A delay in the evacuation of the northern forts provoked more plots to seize the Spanish colonies by force. Carondelet had started to pull out his garrisons at the end of 1796, but he suddenly received orders warning him of the danger of an English attack from Canada. (Spain had declared war on England in October of 1796.) Hence the Chickasaw Bluffs fort was occupied until the middle of 1797, and the garrison at Natchez was not removed until the spring of 1798. Among three or four projects to invade the Spanish domain the most serious was the Blount Conspiracy. William Blount had been Governor of the Southwest Territory until his election to the United States Senate from Tennessee. His prime interests were in land speculation, both at Muscle Shoals and in the Yazoo country. But land values at these locations would not rise until commercial outlets, such as Mobile and Pensacola, were made available on the Gulf of Mexico. The conspiracy involved an attack upon both New Orleans and Pensacola by Tennessee frontiersmen and former Tories, the whole operation to be supported by a British fleet. But one of the Senator's confederates indiscreetly revealed the story during a drinking spree.

Blount was immediately expelled from the Senate to avoid an embarrassing inquiry, and President John Adams moved to seal off the conspiracy.

Speculators of the Blount type were also active in Georgia's second attempt to exploit the Yazoo lands. At the beginning of 1795 the state legislature, packed with speculators, sold most of Alabama and Mississippi to four Yazoo companies at prices averaging 1 cent an acre. This outrageous sale was rescinded by the subsequent "anti-Yazoo" legislature, but the validity of the contract had to be decided by the Supreme Court. In *Fletcher v. Peck* (1810) the justices said that the sanctity of contract was protected by the Constitution, and thus that the original sale was legal. Though the speculators added to the political turmoil along the southwestern border, they did attract some settlers through their organization of land sales.

Congress also aided settlement by organizing the former Spanish lands as Mississippi Territory on April 4, 1798. The border of the new political unit ran east from the Mississippi along the 31st parallel to the Chattahoochee-Appalachicola River line. The creation of a first-grade territorial government convinced many skeptics that it was safe to settle in the region. Large numbers of Americans also began moving into Spanish territory. Some, including Moses Austin and Daniel Boone, went to upper Louisiana and settled along the Missouri River. Most of the migrants settled in lower Louisiana, along the Red and Ouachita Rivers, or in West Florida around Baton Rouge and Mobile. Though they took the oath of allegiance to Spain, there was considerable doubt about the depth of their loyalty.

Kentucky

Kentucky, the kingpin of the Old Southwest, began to take on a settled look as thousands of migrants swarmed into what they called "the land of milk and honey." In 1783 the territory had an estimated 30,000 people, most of them battle-scarred veterans of the Indian wars. The census of 1790 pegged the population at 73,677, of whom 20 percent were Negro slaves. By 1800 the figure had more than tripled to 220,995. The "urban frontier" was represented by Louisville and Lexington. The latter was the largest town in the West, its population of 1,795 people outstripping Cincinnati or Pittsburgh. Lexington was a great trading center, the funnel through which eastern goods went to western Kentucky and Tennessee. It even had a weekly newspaper, the *Kentucky Gazette*, first published in 1787. And a brave attempt at education in a pioneer environment was the Transylvania University, founded in 1799.

The existence of a "university" did not signify a high educational level. There were only a few log schools at the old stations, and teachers, like ministers, were as scarce as hen's teeth. A class of "gentlemen" was in process of formation during the 90s. Such Virginia emigrés as John Breckinridge and Henry Clay were familiar with the English literary classics, and looked back to the Tidewater for their political and social ideals. Yet most Kentuckians lived a primitive agricultural life that left little time for "book larnin'." Crops had to be planted and harvested by hand, and the indispensable "Indian corn" was usually ground in handmills. Much time had to be spent repairing the tools, such as the wooden moldboard plows, which were easily broken. Although the Kentuckians were a rough lot, Easterners had an exaggerated idea of their barbarity. Harry Toulmin reported in 1793 that "the land speculators of Philadelphia and others, who know nothing of Kentucky, tell you that half the people, through the practice of gouging, have no eyes." These impressions may have arisen from the wrestling matches that were held during the two most popular holidays: the Fourth of July and May Day. Both were celebrated by the firing of guns, horseraces, and the drinking of that exhilarating beverage that was soon to make the name of "Kentucky Bourbon" world famous.

Kentuckians lived much the same kind of life as Tennesseans and Ohioans. In 1800 the frontier was still undifferentiated, and men of the Old Southwest were basically similar to those of the Old Northwest. Negro slavery was legal in both Tennessee and Kentucky, but it was not yet the basic form of labor or a sectional political issue. Frontiersmen on both sides of the Ohio had the same concerns: Indians, land policy, and navigation of the Mississippi. They felt that their interests were not being served by the Federalist administration east of the mountains. Delay in the execution of Pinckney's Treaty, for example, was blamed on this administration, whose negotiation of the treaty itself was overlooked. Thomas Jefferson's Republican party, on the other hand, had many supporters in the West, and they helped elect him President in the "Revolution of 1800." As it turned out, Jefferson exceeded their wildest expectations when he consummated the Louisiana Purchase in 1803.

Sale of Louisiana to France

Spain had offered to sell Louisiana to France as early as 1795, but the price had been too high. It was a pauper province on which Spain lost about $500,000 a year. Revenue through customs duties amounted to only one-fifth the cost of administration. There was no market in Spain for the rice, furs, and tobacco of Louisiana, and an archaic colonial policy prevented their export to suitable markets. Governors Miró and Carondelet both urged free trade with European and American ports to start the province toward solvency, but the Court ignored their advice.

By 1800 the Spanish-French negotiations were resumed. Charles IV wanted an Italian kingdom for his son-in-law, and he was willing to trade Louisiana for it. Napoleon on his part had ambitions for reviving the old French empire in North America. Hence the retrocession of Louisiana to France was made in a treaty signed at San Ildefonso on October 1, 1800. The treaty was kept secret, because Spain did not want to risk an American invasion of New

Orleans before Napoleon could take possession. Napoleon reneged on the Italian kingdom, but he demanded Louisiana anyway and there was nothing the Spaniards could do but turn it over to him.

When news of the treaty leaked out it caused a domestic and diplomatic crisis in the United States. The American people were doubly enraged by Spain's sudden ending of the right of deposit at New Orleans on October 18, 1802. This provocative act was believed to have been engineered by Napoleon, and to be a foretaste of the kind of policy that he would follow in Louisiana. The western legislatures drew up memorials asking the national government to take some action in response to these two developments, and there was again much talk of an armed seizure of the province. In Washington the Federalists thought they had an issue with which they could topple President Jefferson. They demanded that he order out a frontier army to take New Orleans before Napoleon's troops arrived. The sage of Monticello was in the tightest jam of his political career.

Jefferson had never been worried about Spanish possession of Louisiana. He knew that in course of time the Americans would take the province from this weak and aging nation. But Napoleonic France would be a strong and dangerous neighbor. Thus news of the retrocession inspired Jefferson's famous letter of April 18, 1802, to Robert Livingston, the American minister in Paris. "There is on the globe one single spot the possessor of which is our natural and habitual enemy. It is New Orleans, through which the produce of three-eights of our territory must pass to market. . . . The day that France takes possession of it . . . we must marry ourselves to the British fleet and nation." This letter, a minor classic in geopolitics, was handled in careless fashion so that the French spies would have a chance to see it. The strategy was to lead Napoleon into believing that the Americans would form an alliance with England unless he abandoned his plans. The President took more direct action in the spring of 1803 by sending James Monroe to Paris as a special envoy to try and purchase New Orleans and an adjacent strip of West Florida. Monroe was an excellent choice, since he was identified with the "Mississippi interest" through his ownership of western lands.

The Louisiana Purchase

On April 11, 1803, Livingston had been asked by the French minister Talleyrand if he "wished to have the whole of Louisiana." Napoleon had suddenly decided to sell the entire territory. His army in Santo Domingo had been virtually destroyed by a yellow fever epidemic and a slave insurrection, and he was on the brink of another war with England. The ex-corporal needed money for the war, and he also reasoned that selling Louisiana would help build the United States into a strong nation which would "humble" England. When Monroe arrived on the 12th he and Livingston began haggling with the finance minister

Barbé-Marbois over the exact price to be paid for the province. On April 30 it was finally agreed that the United States would pay 15 million dollars, one-quarter of which was for the settlement of various American claims against France. Thus two American envoys who had been sent to buy the town of New Orleans came home instead with title to some 800 million acres of land which they had purchased at around 3.6 cents an acre. No one knew the exact limits of the purchase, the treaty merely stating that the cession was of Louisiana "with the same extent that it now has in the hands of Spain and that it had when France possessed it." The obscurity surrounding the boundaries was exploited by the Americans, who eventually claimed that West Florida, Texas, and even Oregon were included.

The treaty caused complete surprise and astonishment in the United States. But soon the Westerners were smacking their lips over the grand opportunities for trading, land speculation, and government patronage that the new territory could offer. Jefferson himself had doubts about the constitutionality of the purchase, and the New England Federalists were quick to oppose it on this score. But they could hardly fault Jefferson for having peacefully purchased a territory for which they had been willing to fight a war only one year before. The President finally decided that "metaphysical subtleties" should not stand in the way of so important an acquisition. Fortunately for posterity he forgot about his strict-constructionist philosophy long enough to sign the treaty, and his friends even persuaded him to forego the constitutional amendment which he had thought necessary.

The Louisiana Purchase was indeed one of the most important events in American and world history. It doubled the area of the United States, and added natural resources of untold value to the national domain. It cleared the Mississippi of foreign nations and of the attendant intrigues, and thus acted as a great unifying force in the country at large. In this connection it should be remembered that on December 20, 1803, the province of Louisiana was officially transferred from France to the United States in a public ceremony at New Orleans. And the man who ran up the American colors on this momentous occasion was General James Wilkinson, of all people!

Selected Readings Two books by Arthur P. Whitaker, *The Spanish-American Frontier, 1783-1795* (Boston, 1927) and *The Mississippi Question, 1795-1803* (New York, 1935), are the starting point for reading in this area. Dale Van Every's *The Ark of Empire* (New York, 1963) has a brief general description of the period. Samuel F. Bemis, *Pinckney's Treaty* (Baltimore, 1926) and E. Wilson Lyon, *Louisiana in French Diplomacy, 1795-1804* (Norman, 1934), cover international aspects.

John W. Caughey, *McGillivray of the Creeks* (Norman, 1938), contains a short biography and a collection of letters. Angie Debo, *The Road to Disappearance* (Norman, 1941), has more on the Creeks. Samuel C. Williams, *History of the Lost State of Franklin* (Johnson City, Tenn., 1924), is not exciting, but remains the best account. Thomas P. Abernethy, *From Frontier to Planation in Tennessee* (Chapel

Hill, N.C., 1932), is also important. Carl S. Driver, *John Sevier* (Chapel Hill, N.C., 1932), is a generally satisfactory biography of Franklin's governor. James R. Jacobs, *Tarnished Warrior: Major-General James Wilkinson* (New York, 1938), is recommended. Thomas R. Hay, "Some Reflections on the Career of General James Wilkinson," *Mississippi Valley Historical Review*, vol. 21 (March, 1935), should also be consulted.

Leland D. Baldwin, *The Whiskey Rebels* (Pittsburgh, 1939), is good, while H. M. Brackenridge, *History of the Western Insurrection in Western Pennsylvania* (Pittsburgh, 1859), is a primary account. William H. Masterson, *William Blount* (Baton Rouge, 1954) is good. C. Peter MacGrath, *Yazoo: Law and Politics in the New Republic* (Providence, R.I., 1966), is a study of the political aspects of the giant speculation. Eugene P. Link, *Democratic-Republican Societies, 1790-1800* (New York, 1942), sheds light on political history in the West. A starting point for study of the Louisiana Purchase is W. Edwin Hemphill, "The Jeffersonian Background of the Louisiana Purchase," *Mississippi Valley Historical Review*, vol. 22 (September, 1935). An older work that is still relevant is J. K. Hosmer, *The Louisiana Purchase* (New York, 1902).

VIII. The West in the War of 1812

Historians have had a difficult time explaining the War of 1812. Woodrow Wilson, for one, declared that "the grounds of the war were singularly uncertain." Among the possible causes of the conflict one might mention maritime rights; the agricultural depression of 1808 to 1812; hunger for land in Canada and Florida; British manipulation of the Indians; and the defense of national honor. Many contemporaries seemed to think that the first and last of these were the key issues. Writing in 1816, Robert B. McAfee declared that it had been "a war to vindicate our honor and our rights." Attempts by diplomacy to get the British to stop the impressment of American seamen and to modify the commercial restrictions imposed by their Orders in Council had gotten nowhere, and the resultant sense of humiliation and frustration could only be washed away by war. Americans were supremely confident of their military prowess, Henry Clay going so far as to tell the Congress in 1810: "I verily believe that the militia of Kentucky are alone competent to place Montreal and Upper Canada at your feet." Not only did the militia fail to take Canada, but the whole American army had a hard time beating off the invading British armies, one of which burned the national capital in 1814. Yet a "second war of American independence" did seem to be necessary to those who supported it.

Harrison and Tecumseh   In 1800 William Henry Harrison had assumed the governorship of Indiana Territory, which then included all the lands in the Old Northwest beyond Ohio. He took up residence at Vincennes, a village of some 400 log and clapboard houses which looked out on the Wabash River to the west and on fields of wildflowers and strawberries to the east. In this idyllic setting Harrison worked hard at maintaining good relations with both French and American settlers, and spent his spare time "making war upon the partridges,

119

grouse, and fish." His principal task was carrying out President Jefferson's instructions to acquire the maximum amount of land from the Indians. The President hoped to encourage the natives to turn from hunting to farming, thus reducing their territorial requirements. But if this vocational rehabilitation failed, the only alternative would be to ship them to reservations west of the Mississippi. Jefferson was sympathetic with the Indians, but he fully intended that the Northwest should be occupied by those American farmers who were the backbone of the Republic.

The Jefferson-Harrison policy resulted in fifteen big land cessions by various Indian tribes up to the outbreak of the war. In exchange for annuities and presents the chiefs surrendered tracts throughout southern Indiana and Illinois. The most important cession was made at the Treaty of Fort Wayne in September of 1809. This treaty resulted partly from changes in the territorial structure. In 1805, Michigan Territory had been split off from Indiana, with William Hull being appointed Governor of the largely French and British population clustered around Detroit. Then in March of 1809, Indiana had been cut down to the approximate limits of the present state by the creation of Illinois Territory to the west. Thus Governor Harrison had to find room for his expanding population by taking more land from the Indians to the north. At Fort Wayne he got the heart of Indiana, 3 million acres of fine timber and prairie land along the Wabash and White Rivers. The treaty was signed with chiefs from the Delaware, Miami, and Potawatomie tribes which hunted in the area. Unfortunately there were no Shawnee at the conference, for the most bitter resistance to Harrison's plans came from two Shawnee brothers: Tecumseh and Tenkswatawa.

Tenkswatawa was the first to come to the attention of the Americans, to whom he was known as the Prophet. After a dissolute youth, he saw the light and became the leader of a messianic movement which attracted tribesmen from all over the Northwest. Such movements frequently arose among the Indians when they were being hard pressed by the advancing whites. The Messiah, claiming to have talked with the Great Spirit, promised his listeners salvation if they would only return to their old habits. Thus the Prophet said they must stop using whiskey, and must wear skins instead of blankets. Harrison scoffed at such goings-on, writing to the Delawares: "If he really is a prophet, ask him to cause the sun to stand still." This turned out to be a mistake, because the Prophet learned from a British trader that there was to be an eclipse on June 16, 1806. He stated that he would cause the sky to darken on that day, and when it did so, his reputation was secure.

It soon became apparent, however, that Tecumseh was the real leader of Indian resistance. In a face-to-face meeting with Harrison at Vincennes on August 20, 1810, he repudiated the Fort Wayne treaty on the basis that the ceded lands were the common property of all the tribes. "Sell a country! Why not sell the air, the clouds, and the great sea, as well as the earth?" Harrison described his rival as "one of those uncommon geniuses which spring up occasionally to produce revolutions, and overturn the established order of things." Born in 1768 to a Shawnee father and a Creek mother, Tecumseh had fought against Wayne at Fallen Timbers and in other skirmishes which had hardened his anti-American sentiments. His plan was to establish an Indian confederacy modeled on Pontiac's. Only a strong alliance of all the tribes from the Lakes to the Gulf would be able to hurl the invaders back across the Ohio. Governor Harrison always claimed that the British were spurring Tecumseh on, but the truth appears to have been the reverse. The chief kept pleading with the commander at Fort Malden to join him in fighting the Yankees.

By the middle of 1811 the Governor had decided that he must make war on the Indians rather than on the partridges and grouse. The brothers had established headquarters at Prophet's Town, where Tippecanoe Creek flows into the Wabash from the north. A military demonstration there would convince the plotters that resistance to the land treaties was hopeless. Harrison got his chance when Tecumseh went south to try and talk the Creeks into joining his alliance. The Governor wrote the War Department on August 6: "His absence affords a most favorable opportunity for breaking up his confederacy." To do the job, Harrison gathered an army of about 900 men at Vincennes. There were 500 deerskin-clad militiamen from Kentucky and Indiana together with some 400 Regulars of the 4th Infantry, attired in tailcoats and stovepipe hats. The little army arrived near Prophet's Town on November 6, and camped on high ground above the marshy prairie. Just before dawn on the 7th the Indians attacked to a signal of rattling deer hoofs. In the bitter 2-hour battle that followed they were beaten off with a loss of thirty-eight warriors killed. Fifty of Harrison's own men were killed and some one hundred wounded. But the next day he burned the abandoned town and then marched back down the Wabash. Tippecanoe was a minor engagement from the military standpoint, and the battle could be called a standoff, but it made Harrison the prime hero of the West. It helped him win the Presidency in 1840 on the campaign slogan of "Tippecanoe and Tyler Too." And it opened the northwestern phase of the War of 1812.

Declaration of War

The declaration of war was the work of a group of young Western and Southern congressmen whom a rival called "the buckskin boys." They are better known in the shorthand of American history as the War Hawks. Their leader was Henry Clay of Kentucky, and other prominent members of the pack were Felix Grundy of Tennessee and John C. Calhoun of South Carolina. They and their supporters had triumphed over the so-called "submission men" in the fall elections of 1811. They then elected Clay as Speaker of the House, and he proceeded to fill the important committees with prowar men. They worked

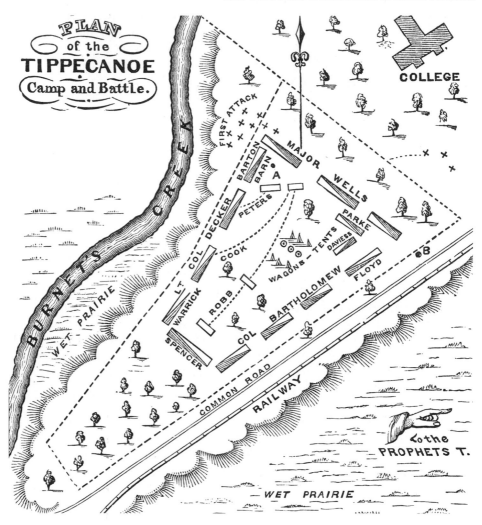

Plan of the battle of Tippecanoe. From Benson J. Lossing, Pictorial Field Book of the War of 1812. *(1869) Source: Huntington Library.*

steadily to convince a reluctant Congress and President that war was the only way to salvage our national honor.

The exact objectives of the Hawks were rather mixed. John Randolph complained that "'we have heard but one word—like the whip-poor-will, but one eternal monotonous tone—Canada! Canada! Canada!" A desire to conquer that province seems to have been less a matter of land hunger than a strategic move designed to force concessions from England on the maritime issues. Certainly the Westerners talked a great deal about the rights of neutrals and the impressment of American sailors. As disgusted New Englanders pointed out, this was strange talk indeed from men whose own naval force consisted of a few birchbark canoes. Yet one underlying point was that prices for the West's agricultural products had been sliding downward since 1808. Jefferson's attempts to coerce England by means of an economic embargo contributed to this effect, but prices kept falling after the embargo was ended. The resultant depression was blamed upon Britain's commercial restrictions, which included prohibition on direct trade with the Continent and heavy duties upon American exports to England itself. The western farmers argued with considerable justice that England was enforcing these restrictions to protect her own commercial system against American competition. War seemed to be the only way to relieve this intolerable situation.

The trans-Appalachian West did not have the votes to declare war by itself. But it got support from the South Atlantic states, where "honor" (both personal and national) had to be defended by force of arms if necessary. Senators and Representatives from Virginia, the Carolinas, and Georgia voted overwhelmingly for war. The combined votes of the West and South were enough to overcome the opposition of Federalist New England. The final tally for a declaration of war was 79 to 49 in the House and 19 to 13 in the Senate. President James Madison signed the document on June 18, 1812, with four of his five points being devoted to maritime rights. The fifth grievance cited the "warfare just resumed on our frontier by the savages," a reference to the supposed British encouragement of Tecumseh. As far as the frontier was concerned, both the Indians and the British who were suspected of encouraging them had to be removed in the interests of western expansion.

The Northwestern Campaigns

American military operations during most of the War of 1812 are a matter for either tears or laughter. The bellicose congressmen who prodded their colleagues into declaring war seriously overestimated the ability of the armed forces and underestimated the problems to be faced. Heavy reliance had to be placed upon the militia, but these troops volunteered only for 3- or 6-month terms. Often, as in General Dearborn's attempt to invade Canada in the fall, they refused to leave their own borders. The New England states opposed "Mr. Madison's War," and so the Governors withheld their crack militia companies from the federal service. The distances were vast, which made the supply and communications problems correspondingly severe. And to the chagrin of Clay and the other Hawks, the British proved to be competent soldiers.

Governor William Hull of Michigan, an elderly veteran of the Revolution, was given the job of chasing the British out of Fort Malden. This post was located across the river from Detroit, and was the main supply point for Tecumseh and the other Indians of the region. Hull did not want the job,

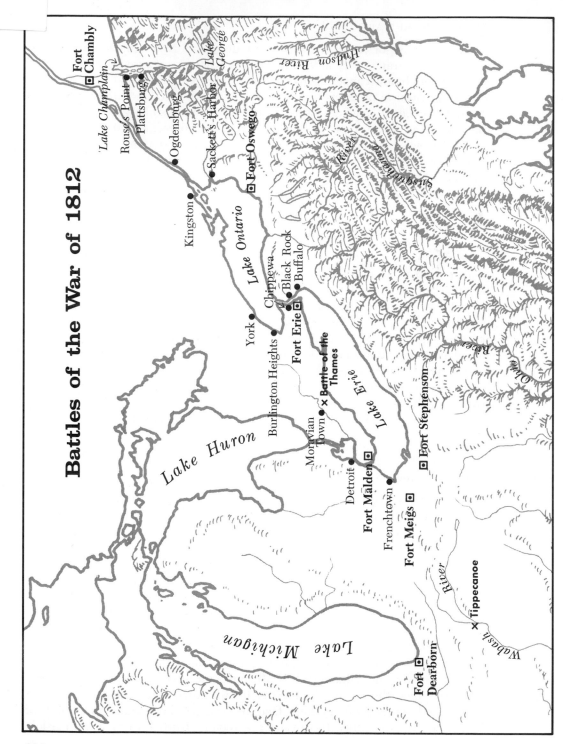

Battles of the War of 1812

Fort Chambly

Lake Champlain

Rouse's Point

Plattsburg

Ogdensburg

Sackett's Harbor

Fort Oswego

Kingston

Lake George

Hudson River

Susquehanna River

Lake Ontario

York

Burlington Heights

Chippewa

Black Rock

Buffalo

Fort Erie

Battle of the Thames

Lake Huron

Moravian Town

Lake Erie

Detroit

Fort Malden

Frenchtown

Fort Meigs

Fort Stephenson

Ohio River

Lake Michigan

Fort Dearborn

Tippecanoe

Wabash River

stating that he was too old for it. He also pointed out that he had insufficient provisions and that the British gunboats controlled Lake Erie. But Madison brushed aside these objections, and so Hull marched across Ohio at the head of 2,000 militia and Regulars. He occupied Detroit on July 5, but never did attack Fort Malden despite a series of bombastic proclamations announcing his intention to do so. In fact he suffered a paralysis of will which permitted the initiative to pass over to Gen. Isaac Brock's British-Indian force. Brock executed a series of clever moves which caused the panicky Hull to surrender his entire force on August 16. This was a shocking and humiliating defeat for Americans who were committed to a war for the vindication of the national honor. Hull was subsequently court-martialed in 1814, the court concluding that "the rolls of the army are no longer to be disgraced by having upon them the name of brigadier general Wm Hull."

The news got worse before it got better. In 1796 the government had established a fur-trading or factory system in the Northwest to help pacify the Indians. By 1812 the two key posts were at Michilimackinac and Chicago. On July 17 a band of British traders and Indians captured the first of these, and on August 15 Capt. Nathan Held was forced to surrender Fort Dearborn at the site of Chicago. While attempting to lead his garrison south along the sand dunes, Held was attacked by some 400 Potawatomie warriors. Thirty-five men, women, and children were clubbed down in the "Fort Dearborn Massacre," one of the most memorable if unpleasant episodes in the history of the Chicago area.

William Henry Harrison replaced Hull as commander of the Northwestern Army. The thirty-nine-year-old general was ordered to defend the frontier and retake Detroit. The first assignment was easier than the second. In fact, Harrison was forced to remain on the defensive, his principal bastions being Fort Wayne and Fort Meigs on the Maumee. An injudicious advance by one of Harrison's columns under Gen. Samuel Winchester on January 22 resulted in an American defeat, the River Raisin massacre, in which fifty American prisoners were scalped by the Indians. Harrison spent most of the summer of 1813 beating off attacks on Fort Meigs by British-Indian forces under a new antagonist, Gen. Henry Proctor.

Harrison's success was finally made possible by naval control of Lake Erie. Oliver Hazard Perry, a twenty-eight-year-old Rhode Islander, constructed a freshwater navy at Presque Isle on the eastern shore of the lake. Through British laxity he was able to sneak his homemade flotilla over the sandbar and sail it west to Put-In-Bay. Here, on September 10, Perry smashed the British lake squadron in a 3-hour battle made memorable not only by the young commander's military skill but also by his literary ability. "We have met the enemy and they are ours" has proved to be deathless prose.

This naval victory put General Proctor in an untenable position, since the Americans could bypass Fort Malden. On September 18 he announced to

Tecumseh his intention of retreating toward Niagara. The chief pleaded with him to stay and fight: "Father! You have got the arms and ammunition which our great father sent for his red children. If you have an idea of going away, give them to us, and you may go and welcome from us. Our lives are in the hands of the Great Spirit. We are determined to defend our lands, and if it be his will, we wish to leave our bones upon them." Proctor talked vaguely about laying his bones down too, but still insisted on retreating. Tecumseh finally got his promise to make a stand at the Thames River.

Harrison's army of 4,500 men was made up largely of Kentucky volunteers. These had been raised by Governor Isaac Shelby, a hero of King's Mountain in the Revolution, and by the War Hawk congressman Richard M. Johnson. At the end of September Harrison ferried his men across the lake and reoccupied Detroit. He then started after Proctor and the Indians. On October 5, 1813, he caught up with them 2 miles west of Moraviantown on the Thames. Colonel Johnson's mounted infantry were sent directly against the center of the British lines, on the theory that American backwoodsmen could carry muskets on horseback quite easily. The tactic succeeded, and the British were routed. The Indians had to be dislodged by hand-to-hand combat in the swamps bordering the river, and in this melee Tecumseh was killed. Tradition has it that the soldiers flayed the body of an Indian whom they believed to be Tecumseh, and took the strips of skin home for use as razorstrops.

Harrison's campaign had broken up the Indian confederacy and driven the British from Fort Malden. "The hero of the Thames" went back East where he was lionized as one of the country's few victorious generals. Since the northwestern phase of the war was now over, Harrison had plans to move east and fight along the St. Lawrence frontier. But the War Department thwarted these plans, and so he resigned from the Army in disgust. The vacant major general's commission was given to Andrew Jackson of Tennessee, the other western military hero of the war. And the scene of Jackson's exploits was the swamp and pine country of the Gulf Coast.

Louisiana and Florida

In 1804 Congress divided the Louisiana Purchase lands by a line running west from the Mississippi along the 33rd parallel. The area north of the line was organized as Louisiana Territory, while that to the south of it was called the Territory of Orleans. When Orleans became a state in 1812 it took the Louisiana name, the northern territory thereupon being retitled "Missouri." The polyglot population of Orleans seemed to pose a serious problem in assimilation. Thomas Jefferson, for one, did not believe that the 30,000 inhabitants were ready for self-government. While he was a philosophical democrat, the President sometimes dispensed with the "consent of the governed." Congress apparently agreed with him, for they gave him complete control of the administrative machinery by authorizing him to appoint the territory's governor, its lawmaking council, and its superior court judges. The Louisianans complained about this outside control, and with conscious irony called Jefferson's attention to the Declaration of Independence. Furthermore, there were demands that the laws be published in French, and that Governor William Claiborne take more advice from the Creole* leaders.

Most of these difficulties were ironed out, but many Eastern congressmen did not think that the territory should become part of the United States. In the debates on this subject, Josiah Quincy of Massachusetts said: "You have no authority to throw the rights and property of this people into a 'hotch-pot' with the wild men on the Missouri, or with the mixed, though more respectable, race of Anglo-Hispano-Gallo-Americans who bask on the sands, in the mouth of the Mississippi." But such objections were overcome, since the sugar and cotton plantations around New Orleans indicated that there was a solid economic foundation for statehood. On April 30, 1812, Louisiana was added to the Union.

Adjacent to Louisiana on the east was Spanish West Florida. Presidents Jefferson and Madison had both been looking for some pretext by which to gobble up this province, since the Gulf ports were considered desirable for economic reasons. The official line was that the region had been part of the Louisiana Purchase. Jefferson stated his view in a "Historical Memoir" of September 7, 1803, in which he argued that "France had formal and actual possession of the coast from Mobile to the bay of St. Bernard [Texas]." Since the United States had purchased Louisiana intact from France, it stood to reason that we too should have Mobile and the adjacent lands east to the Perdido River. But with amusing illogicality, Jefferson tried to negotiate a purchase of the Floridas from whomever would sell them: France or Spain. When these efforts fell flat, it appeared that only a manufactured revolution would free West Florida from the Spaniards' grip.

On September 23, 1810, some 100 American filibusters under Philemon Thomas captured the Spanish fort at Baton Rouge. They declared West Florida to be independent, but then applied to the United States for annexation. Within a few weeks President Madison proclaimed the area between Baton Rouge and the Perdido to be part of the United States, basing his action upon the Louisiana Purchase argument. The lands west of the Pearl River were incorporated into Louisiana, while those east of it to the Perdido were made part of the Mississippi Territory. American troops occupied all the region except for the grand prize, Mobile. This was held by a strong Spanish garrison, and Madison was unwilling to risk a war to seize it. After the War of 1812 broke out, General Wilkinson finally occupied the city in April of 1813.

Madison also sponsored an abortive plan to annex East Florida. George Mathews, a seventy-two-year-old brigadier general in the Georgia militia, was encouraged to invade the Spanish province with 200 self-styled

*"Creole" meant a white person of French or Spanish extraction.

"Florida patriots." Blatantly supported by an American army and naval force, the "patriots" moved south in March of 1812 and laid siege to St. Augustine. But there Mathews was recalled and repudiated by the ungrateful Madison, who was nearing war with England and did not want to be involved with Spain at the same time.

After war was declared, however, Madison thought he would occupy East Florida to prevent its use as a British base. Two thousand Tennessee volunteers were sent south in December for this purpose, but at Natchez they were ordered to disband and return home. Antiadministration congressmen had been able to block Madison's plan. The thwarted Tennesseans had a difficult 800-mile march back through the snow to Nashville, but their commander displayed such hardihood that he became known as "Old Hickory." Andrew Jackson entered the main road of American history with a nickname which did full justice to the man.

Jackson in the Southwest

Jackson was born on March 15, 1767, in the backwoods of South Carolina. His Scotch-Irish family were strong supporters of the Revolution, and Jackson's two brothers died as a result of war wounds. He himself received the first of many scars when he was struck across the hand and head with a sword after refusing to shine a British officer's boots. Following the war Andrew turned into a teen-age dandy who spent most of his time at the horse races. In 1788 he struck out across the mountains to try his luck at Nashville. There he was a lawyer, storekeeper, cotton planter, and land speculator. Soon he was holding a variety of political jobs as a protégé of the Blount faction. These included

Gen. Andrew Jackson in 1816.
Source: Yale University Library.

brief terms in the House (1796) and in the Senate (1798), the latter of which he resigned following the revelations of the Blount conspiracy. He then served in judicial posts over the next dozen years. In 1802 Jackson won the commission as major general of the state militia. This was a fitting position for a natural-born fighter who only needed a war to prove his abilities. Contemporary accounts describe the general as being a gaunt six-footer whose hawklike eyes reflected an unbreakable will.

When the war was declared Jackson supported it with great enthusiasm. He wrote that "Great Britain, by multiplied outrages on our rights . . . has made war the only alternative that could preserve the honour and dignity of the nation." The general was also willing to give the Indians and Spaniards a drubbing as well. When ordered to march on Florida, he wrote the Secretary of War that he and his men "will rejoice to place the American eagle on the ramparts of Mobile, Pensacola, and Fort St. Augustine." The canceling of these orders at Natchez meant that General Wilkinson obtained what glory there was in "placing the American eagle" on the walls at Mobile. Jackson could only lead his foot-weary troops back home.

But the government still needed "Old Hickory" and his Tennessee riflemen. The Creeks had to be broken up lest they cooperate with their traditional British allies in a sweep inland against the Mississippi lifeline. Tecumseh on a trip in 1812 had whipped up the young warriors with tales of the British victory at Detroit. The war faction of "Red Sticks" was led by William Weatherford, a nephew of the famed Alexander McGillivray. They struck at Fort Mims, some 40 miles north of Mobile, on August 30, 1813, and slaughtered all but a handful of the 550 people who had taken refuge there. This massacre sent shock waves along the frontier, and in Tennessee it resulted in the raising of an army of 2,500 men. Among the volunteers was Ensign Sam Houston, a future President of the Republic of Texas, and Private Davy Crockett, future folk hero. Andrew Jackson was hospitalized when the call went out, recovering from bullet wounds received in a fight with Jesse and Thomas Hart Benton. But in an amazing display of mind over matter he dragged himself from bed and led his troops south on October 9.

Jackson overcame multiple obstacles in winning the Creek War. The terrain was difficult, contractors did not come through with needed supplies, and the short-term enlistees wanted to go home. Yet he fought a series of successful battles with the enemy, the climactic one being at Horseshoe Bend on the Tallapoosa. There the Creeks had built a formidable log barricade across the neck of the peninsula. Jackson's men stormed this in a frontal assault, while his Cherokee auxiliaries swam the river and removed the enemy's canoes to prevent an escape. The result was a no-quarter slaughter in which 557 Creeks were killed. This battle of March 27, 1814, broke the back of the Creek nation and sent the surviving Red Sticks fleeing into East Florida. The victorious general moved on down to the junction of the Coosa and Tallapoosa Rivers, where he dictated the Treaty of Fort Jackson to the remaining chiefs (both friendly and hostile) on August 9. The Indians were forced to give up 22 million acres of land in Georgia and Alabama.

Having throttled the Creeks, Jackson now turned to deal with the contemptible Spaniards. Beating off a British naval attack against Mobile, he next marched on Pensacola to punish the Spaniards for having harbored the attackers. Jackson acted on his own authority; the fact that he did not have Washington's permission to invade foreign soil was a technicality which did not bother him in the least. A successful assault on November 7 led to the surrender and demolition of the forts guarding Pensacola Bay. This operation was simply a warmup for the big match against the British at New Orleans.

Battle of New Orleans

Jackson moved his troops west in a leisurely manner, never expecting the main British attack to be directed at New Orleans. Upon arriving at the city on December 2, however, he learned that this was in fact the enemy's intention. Nine thousand well-equipped troops, many of them "Wellington invincibles" from Europe, had left Jamaica for the Mississippi. Jackson scrambled to erect defenses across the swamps and bayous leading into the city, and threw together one of the most heterogeneous armies ever to fight under the American flag. The core of his 5,000-man force consisted of 800 Regulars and some 2,500 Tennessee Volunteers. Added to these troops were other contingents whose marching songs ranged from *Yankee Doodle* to *The Marseillaise*: a Creole militia battalion from New Orleans; a company of white collar and professional men known as Beale's Sharpshooters; sixty Choctaw Indians; Adair's Kentuckians; a battalion of free Negroes; and the Baratarian pirates under Jean and Dominque Laffite.

Jackson was criticized for his employment of these last two groups. Arming colored men was considered by some to be a dangerous practice, since the city had experienced a slave revolt in 1811. When questioned by his paymaster on this point, Jackson replied that "it is enough for you to receive my orders for the payment of the troops with the necessary muster rolls without inquiring whether the troops are white, black, or tea." As far as Laffite and his men were concerned, Jackson at first refused to accept the services of what he called the "lawless brigands." The brothers operated as smugglers and privateers out of Barataria Bay to the west of New Orleans. But they were excellent artillerists, and equally important, they were able to obtain large quantities of guns and ammunition. So the general reluctantly took them out of jail and put them in the lines, where they did outstanding work.

The British entered Lake Borgne from the east and landed within 9 miles of the city. From Maj. Gen. Sir Edward Pakenham on down through the ranks, they were confident of routing the Americans, whom they called

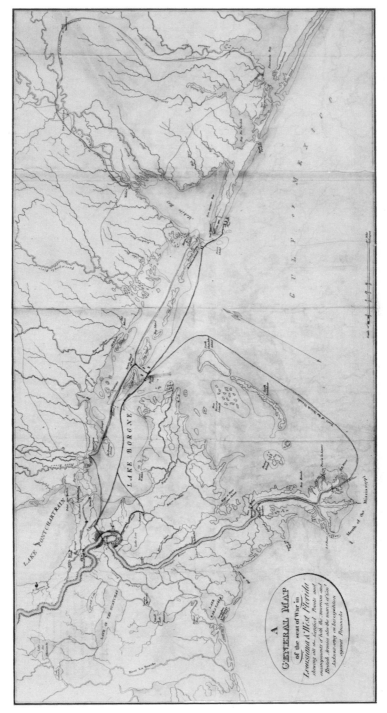

General map of the New Orleans Campaign. Source: Yale University Library.

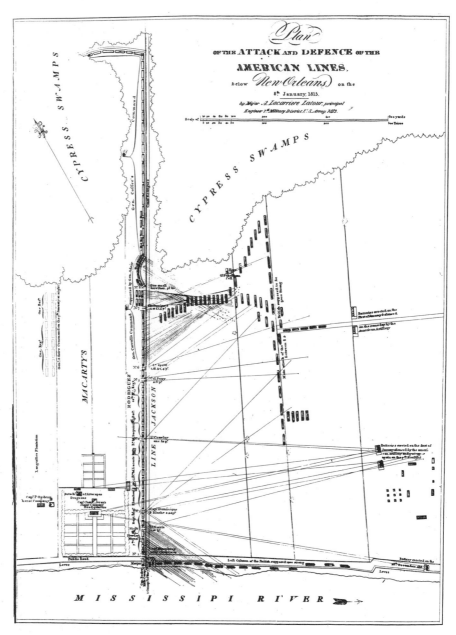

Plan of attack and defense at New Orleans. Source: Yale University Library.

"the dirty shirts." The backwoodsmen were dirty, but then cleanliness has never been necessary for good marksmanship. Jackson established his lines behind the Rodriguez Canal, which ran for about a mile across sugarcane fields from a cypress swamp on Jackson's left to the Mississippi River on his right. Behind the canal his men had built a log-and-mud parapet some 7 feet high, against which the British had to advance since they could not turn either flank. On January 8, 1815, they did advance across the cane stubble in the conventional massed columns. In their red-and-white uniforms they made a gorgeous picture— and a perfect target. Jackson's artillery did an effective job of decimating the British ranks, and only a handful of the enemy ever reached the canal. The British suffered over 2,000 casualties, including General Pakenham, before the remnants of their torn regiments pulled back. Jackson's losses totaled twenty-one men killed and wounded. David had slain Goliath.

The Battle of New Orleans was fought 2 weeks after the war had been formally ended by the Treaty of Ghent on December 24. Since ratifications had not been exchanged, it is quite possible that Britain would have tried to get territorial concessions in the south had Pakenham been victorious. And British control of the lower Mississippi would have changed the course of American history. As it was, the chief impact of Jackson's victory was psychological. The American people had been worn down by a frustrating war in which they had suffered many defeats. In August, the British army had taken Washington and burned the public buildings, President Madison fleeing just in time to escape capture. In September, Sir George Prevost's massive 15,000-man invasion force advancing down Lake Champlain had been turned back only by the seemingly providential victory of Thomas Macdonough's gunboats at Plattsburg Bay. In the midst of these alarms it was exhilarating to get news of a clear-cut victory. RISING GLORY OF THE AMERICAN REPUBLIC was the way the *Boston Patriot* headlined the battle. A Jackson biographer exulted to hear of the general "with his undisciplined yeomanry drive the pride of Europe before him." Since news of New Orleans and of the peace treaty arrived in Washington only 10 days apart, the public naturally identified the one with the other.

The country's new soldier-hero deserved credit for a major accomplishment. He had marshalled his troops well and had beaten off a well-trained and numerically superior enemy. He had welded together an army which embodied the democratic principle. His Anglo-Hispano-Gallo-Negro-Indian soldiers had been picked because of their fighting ability rather than their racial origins or social class. Much of the same philosophy would be apparent in Jackson's presidential administrations from 1828 to 1836. Yet during the crisis Jackson had clashed with the civilian authorities in Louisiana. His imposition of martial law in the city and his vigorous exercise of power were resented by all three branches of the state government. Nor was this the last time that

Andrew Jackson would be embroiled in controversies resulting from his head-strong behavior.

The battle also left a legacy of folklore. The chief legends were concerned with the alleged prowess of the Tennessee and Kentucky riflemen, both of whom became the subjects of popular anecdotes. One concerned an English officer on patrol who surrendered to a Tennessean because "I had no alternative; for I have been told these d—d *Yankee riflemen can pick a squirrel's eye out as far as they can see it.*" This is very close to a classic tale, "the Gone Coon," in which an animal surrenders upon learning that he is being stalked by a famous marksman. The Kentuckians, however, became the chief beneficiaries of the lore by means of a popular song entitled "The Hunters of Kentucky." The actor Noah Ludlow appeared on the New Orleans stage in 1822, costumed in buckskins and fur cap, and received tremendous ovations when he sang this song. A key stanza went:

> *But Jackson he was wide awake,*
> *And he was not scar'd at trifles,*
> *For well he knew what aim we take*
> *With our Kentucky rifles.*
> *So he led us down to Cypress swamp,*
> *The ground was low and mucky,*
> *There stood John Bull in martial pomp*
> *And here was old Kentucky.*
> *O Kentucky, the hunters of Kentucky!*
> *O Kentucky, the hunters of Kentucky!*

Some 2,000 Kentuckians under Generals Thomas and Adair had indeed been at New Orleans, but they played a minor part in the battle. To Jackson's dismay they had come without weapons, or as one contemporary historian put it, "so ill equipped with arms as to be incapable of rendering any considerable service." Furthermore, the artillery rather than the riflemen had been chiefly responsible for chewing up the English columns. But folklore does not have to be history, and so "the Kentuckian" became not only the principal hero of New Orleans but also the archetypal American backwoodsman.

End of the War

The Treaty of Ghent recognized the indecisive nature of the war. There were no territorial gains for either side, and the treaty was signed on the basis of *status quo ante bellum*. Nothing was said about maritime rights, the ostensible cause of the conflict. All that the Americans had proved was that they were willing to fight for such rights. The British for their part abandoned efforts to establish an Indian buffer state along the Great Lakes, thus clearing the way for American occupation of the Old Northwest. In the Southwest, the victory at New Orleans had made Louisiana and West Florida secure against foreign threats. In that area, however, the backwash of war had left one piece of unfinished business. This was the disposition of Spanish-held East Florida, which, said the *Niles' Register,* "will just as naturally come into our possession as the waters of the Mississippi seek the sea."

President James Monroe made unsuccessful attempts to purchase the territory, which had become a haven for escaped slaves and hostile Indians. When General Jackson took control of the Florida border in 1817 he decided to clean out this riffraff once and for all. Acting on what he thought was implicit approval from the President, he marched across the border in the spring of 1818 and seized both Pensacola and the fort at St. Marks further east. He killed a few Indians and threatened the Spanish Governor with dire consequences if he didn't police his province. He also arrested two British subjects, who bore the vaudevillian names of Armbrister and Arbuthnot, and executed them for inciting the Indians. All in all it was an exciting trip for the red-haired general and his Tennessee scalp hunters.

Jackson's foray caused a diplomatic uproar in Washington and Madrid, however, with the Spanish demanding that he be punished. Cabinet meetings in Washington debated the still-unresolved question of whether Jackson had indeed been authorized to cross the border. Later political enmities grew out of these meetings, since Henry Clay (publicly) and John C. Calhoun (privately) were both critical of Jackson's actions. But Secretary of State John Quincy Adams was able to capitalize on the situation by pointing out to Madrid that such episodes would recur unless Spain either policed the province or ceded it to the United States. The Spanish government eventually gave way under this pressure, and the result was the Adams-Onís Treaty of February 22, 1819. All of East Florida was ceded in exchange for trading privileges and American assumption of 5 million dollars worth of damage claims against Spain.

This treaty, ratified in 1821, also defined the Spanish-American border in the Southwest. The staircase boundary line ran from the Gulf up the Sabine River to the 32nd parallel, and on further north to the Red River; west along the Red to the 100th meridian; north again to the Arkansas, then west along that river to its source; then due north to the 42nd parallel, and along that line to the Pacific. American claims to Texas were thus officially abandoned. But lines on a piece of paper meant little to the frontiersmen of the Southwest. On the lands west of the Sabine they would in time demonstrate the truth of the old adage that possession is nine-tenths of the law.

Selected Readings   Harry L. Coles, *The War of 1812* (Chicago, 1965), is a good brief history. Bradford Perkins (ed.), *The Causes of the War of 1812* (New York, 1962), is a paperback collection of articles by leading authorities including Julius W. Pratt, George R. Taylor, and Norman K. Risjord. Pratt's book on *The Expansionists of 1812* (New York, 1925) and his article on "Western War Aims in the War of 1812," *Mississippi Valley Historical Review*, vol. 12 (June, 1925), are well worth reading.

Warren H. Goodman, "The Origins of the War of 1812: A Survey of Changing Interpretations," *Mississippi Valley Historical Review*, vol. 28 (September, 1941), is recommended. "The War Hawks and the War of 1812," *Indiana Magazine of History*, vol. 58 (June, 1964), is an enlightening discussion of the war Congress by several authorities. Robert B. McAfee, *History of the Late War in the Western Country* (Lexington, 1816), was written from original documents. Benson J. Lossing, *The Pictorial Field Book of the War of 1812* (New York, 1869), has many wood engravings of battle sites in the West.

Alec R. Gilpin, *The War of 1812 in the Old Northwest* (East Lansing, 1958), is a good military survey. Reginald Horsman, "British Indian Policy in the Northwest, 1807-1812," *Mississippi Valley Historical Review*, vol. 45 (June, 1958), details the relations between Tecumseh and the British Indian agents. Freeman Cleaves, *Old Tippecanoe: William Henry Harrison and His Times* (New York, 1939), and Glenn Tucker, *Tecumseh: Vision of Glory* (Indianapolis, 1956), are the recommended biographies. Carl F. Klinck (ed.), *Tecumseh: Fact and Fiction in Early Records* (New York, 1961), is an intriguing collection of primary documents.

Useful for the Southwest are Isaac J. Cox, *The West Florida Controversy, 1798-1813* (Baltimore, 1918), Rembert W. Patrick, *Florida Fiasco: Rampant Rebels on the Georgia-Florida Border, 1810-1815* (Athens, Ga., 1954), and Volume III of Alcée Fortier, *A History of Louisiana*, 4 vols. (New York, 1904). On the battle of New Orleans, Fortier is useful, but the classic account is by Arsene Lacarriere Latour, *Historical Memoir of the War in West Florida and Louisiana* (Philadelphia, 1816). Latour's extensive appendices contain many documents of the battle. Charles B. Brooks, *The Siege of New Orleans* (Seattle, 1961), is a popular treatment.

John Reid and John Henry Eaton, *The Life of Andrew Jackson* (Philadelphia, 1817), is a contemporary biography which has much on both the Creek War and New Orleans. Marquis James, *Andrew Jackson, the Border Captain* (New York, 1933), is the best modern biography, and covers the general's career up to 1824. Robert V. Remini, *Andrew Jackson* (New York, 1966), is a satisfactory short biography. John William Ward, *Andrew Jackson—Symbol of an Age* (New York, 1953), is an impressive analysis of the hero making that followed the battle of New Orleans. Thomas M. Marshall, *A History of the Western Boundary of the Louisiana Purchase, 1819-1841* (Berkeley, 1914), is helpful on the Adams-Onís treaty.

IX. To the Mississippi and Beyond

After the war, a jostling crowd of emigrants occupied much of the vacant land east of the Mississippi. Some of the more ambitious or adventurous crossed the great river and began planting new settlements all the way from Iowa to Arkansas. This folk migration cannot be described as either "little" or "moderate"; it must be called "great." The roads and rivers were jammed with westbound "movers" who appeared to be almost as numerous as the mosquitoes which swarmed around their campfires at night. "Old America seems to be breaking up and moving west," observed Morris Birkbeck in 1817. There was no doubt that the pioneers were creating a new cultural pattern as they laid the foundations for the granary of America in the Northwest and a cotton kingdom in the Southwest.

Migration to the Old Northwest   The country north of the Ohio is known to geographers as the central lowlands. Glaciers had at one time pushed down as far as the southern tip of Illinois and Indiana, leaving the land fairly level and blanketing it with rich black soil. In 1815, however, most of the region was covered with virgin forests—oak and elm in the south giving way to spruce and pine in Wisconsin and Michigan. The settler made war upon these forests, his principal weapon being the familiar light chopping ax. The trees were turned into firewood, used for log cabins, or fashioned into split-rail fences. The grand prairie of central and eastern Illinois had already been cleared of trees by nature, but settlers avoided this area until the 1840s because of a folk belief that land without trees was sterile. Early settlers also found that the cost of breaking and fencing prairie land was three times the cost of the land itself. So the major drama of settlement was played in the forest "clearings."

The advance guard on the northwestern frontier was the same half-hunter, half-farmer class which had led the way across the Appalachians. Landing on the north bank of the Ohio, the emigrant would lead his family up a river valley or an old Indian trail until he found a likely piece of land. A lean-to or the semblance of a log cabin would go up, an unfenced patch of corn would be planted, and the squatter would be in fact if not in law the "master of all he surveyed." He would eat what corn he could salvage from the squirrels and turkeys, but for the most part he lived off the land. Game animals, honey, nuts, and wild fruit were the staples of his diet. Turkey breasts were eaten as a substitute for bread. Despite its hardships and hazards, this life appealed to restless individuals who made up a substantial part of the floating western population. A good example of the type would be Abraham Lincoln's family.

Lincoln was born in a Kentucky log cabin in 1809. He was descended from people who had moved from Pennsylvania to Virginia to Kentucky, and his father Thomas Lincoln had the same wanderlust. When Abraham was seven the family migrated to the Indiana woods, and lived under primitive conditions in a "half-faced camp." Other removals took them west to Illinois, and by 1830 Abe had settled on the Sangamon River in that state. His was a typical backwoods youth, which meant a good deal of hard physical labor and practically no formal education. The new states of the Old Northwest paid lip service to education, but roads and canals came before schools. Lincoln picked up what learning he could from the Bible and other books which he borrowed from neighbors. As President, he became the best-known example of the self-made man, but there were many like him in the trans-Ohio country.

When civilization began to close in on him, the squatter would usually "break for the high timber." He would sell his "cabin rights" or "tomahawk improvements" to the next wave of settlers, those whom Frederick Jackskon Turner called the equipped farmers. These men were able to borrow money to make lasting improvements in the property. They rooted out the stumps, put up a split-rail fence to keep hogs out of the corn, and "remodeled" the log cabin by adding paper-covered windows and a puncheon* floor. These farmers might be bought out in turn by what contemporaries called the "men of capital." They would put in barns, build a frame house, improve the roads. They might invest in a gristmill or a sawmill, and perhaps attempt to promote a new town in the area. This cycle, with variations, repeated itself as the frontier advanced.

The people who participated in this mass migration were attracted by the myth of the valley, which represented the lands bordering the Ohio as a western paradise. The image was embodied in songs, travel books, pictorial art, and the sales talk of land speculators. One song promised:

> *Now move your family westward,*
> *Good health you will enjoy,*
> *And rise to wealth and honor*
> *In the state of El-anoy.*

---

*Puncheons were split logs with smoothly planed surfaces.

The land was extremely fertile, once the forest cover had been chopped away, but believing in the myth did not bring "wealth and honor" to all. There were thousands of men under fifty years of age who had moved five or six times and still owned no more than an ax and a gun. As for "Good health," the Northwest was a medical chamber of horrors. Cholera and bilious fever raged through the settlements, and the "milk sick" was also common. This disease, which carried away Lincoln's mother, was caused by a poisonous weed which the cows consumed. Malaria was then known as the ague, and it caused the afflicted to shake so "that the dishes rattled on the shelves." There were many kinds of "fevers," and Dr. William Daily in his *Indian Doctor's Practice of Medicine* classified them as continual, remitting, intermitting, tertian, simple and double, anticipating, postponing, and erratic. It was easier to get a disease than to find a suitable name for it.

Clouds of mosquitoes and flies came through open doors and windows, though only oversensitive travelers seemed to be bothered by them. William Oliver reported on the flies: "Molasses, sugar, preserved fruit, bread, everything on the table is loaded with them, and the very operation of fanning them off drives numbers of them into the molasses and other things of an adhesive nature. It is not safe to open your mouth." In such conditions it is no surprise that disease flourished. For cures the pioneer had to turn to quacks, whose prescriptions usually included bleeding, blistering, and large doses of calomel. There was great popular confidence in Indian medicine. "Herb and root doctors," both white and red, played a prominent role in many settlements.

Southerners, Yankees, and Germans

The health hazards, the back-breaking labor, and the economic disappointments did not deter thousands to whom "West" was a magic word. The migrant population that moved into the Midwest was quite diverse, but its three principal stocks were the Upland Southerners, the New England Yankees, and the Pennsylvania Germans. In the first of these groups were families like the Lincolns which had been "movers" for several generations. Of English, Scotch, and Scotch-Irish descent, they had settled in the Virginia-Carolina Piedmont, and had followed Daniel Boone into Kentucky. Since the groups tended to move along parallel geographic lines, the Uplanders settled principally in southern Ohio, Indiana, or Illinois, and went on into Missouri.

The Southerners brought cultural baggage along with their physical possessions. In the new environment they continued to prefer grits and gravy for breakfast, and admired a good hound dog as much as a fine horse. Their speech, which strongly influenced that of the lower Midwest, was Elizabethan English modified by various "Americanisms." They talked of "yourn" and "hisn," were "onsartin" or "sadful," and took good care of their "shootin'-irons" and "critters." While the bulk of the Uplanders had little property, there were slaveowners and would-be slaveowners among them. Many of those who opposed

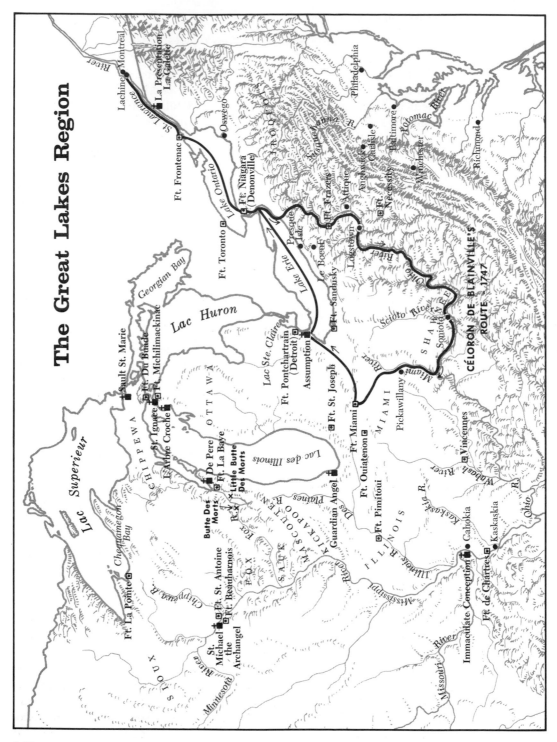

The Great Lakes Region

Lachine Montreal
La Présentation
La Galette
St. Lawrence River
Philadelphia

Ft. Frontenac
Oswego

Lake Ontario
Ft. Niagara (Denonville)
Ft. Toronto

Susquehanna R.
Carlisle
Aughwick
Baltimore
Potomac River
Winchester
Ft. Necessity
Richmond

IROQUOIS

Ft. Frazets
Venango
Presque Isle
Le Boeuf
Logstown
Ohio River

Lake Erie

Ft. Sandusky

Lac Ste. Claire
Ft. Pontchartrain (Detroit)
Assumption

Scioto River
Squaw POINTE
SHAWNEE

CÉLORON DE BLAINVILLE'S ROUTE — 1747

Georgian Bay

Lac Huron

Sault St. Marie
Ft. Du Brude
Ft. Michilimackinac
St. Ignace
L'Arbre Croche

OTTAWA

De Pere
Ft. La Baye
Little Butte Des Morts
Butte Des Morts
FOX RIVER

Ft. St. Joseph
Ft. Miami
MIAMI
Pickawillany
Miami River

Lac des Illinois

Guardian Angel
Des Plaines
KICKAPOO
MASCOUTEN
SAUK
FOX

Ft. Ouiatenon
Ft. Pimitoui
ILLINOIS

Vincennes
Wabash River
Kaskaskia River

Lac Superieur

Chequamegoh Bay
Chippewa R.

CHIPPEWA

Ft. La Pointe
Chippewa R.
Ft. St. Antoine
Ft. Beauharnois
St. Michael the Archangel

SIOUX

Minnesota River

Mississippi River

Missouri River

Illinois River

Immaculate Conception
Cahokia
Kaskaskia
Ft. de Chartres
Ohio

slavery could still be described as anti-Negro. Political candidates like Abraham Lincoln who campaigned in central and southern Illinois had to make clear that they did not believe that the races were equal.

The Southerners were a carefree lot, and were quite casual about such things as land titles. Thus they were in marked contrast to the Yankees, whom they suspected of being bluenosed busybodies. Contemporary reaction to New Englanders was based upon the stereotype of the Yankee peddler, a shrewd and angular sharper who sold wooden nutmegs and other gimcracks to unsuspecting housewives. The actual Yankee was honest, but he was a thrifty individual who was careful with both his land titles and his dollars. He also brought west the old Puritan regulating heritage that clashed with the Southern impulse to ignore regulations. Yet the two groups got along fairly well, and it was not unknown for a Yankee storekeeper to marry a belle from Old Kaintuck.

The large-scale New England migration came in the 1830s and 1840s when the "Merino mania" swept the East. The new textile mills were supplied by the lucky few who got into sheep ranching at the right moment. Those who sold their lands could either work in the mills or seek new opportunities in the West. The Yankees and York State men settled the upper panel of the Old Northwest: Michigan, northern Indiana and Illinois, eastern Wisconsin. The Germans, who came both from the Old Country and from Pennsylvania, were numerous around such towns as Indianapolis, Fort Wayne, Chicago, and Peoria. Like the Yankees they were hardworking and thrifty. Their farms were models of order and intensive tillage, with large barns for the cattle and ample smokehouses that bulged with a dozen kinds of sausage and cheese. To their neighbors the Germans appeared to be "old fashioned," but they too became part of the new blend of peoples that made up the Old Northwest.

English Travelers

The composite character that was formed in this great heartland was marked by optimism, self-reliance, and a strong sense of equality. Foreign travelers commented unfavorably upon the latter. Alexis de Tocqueville, who visited the country at the height of the Jacksonian period in 1832, framed the classic dictum that the Americans "love equality more than liberty." English visitors, of whom there was an oversupply, generally agreed with the comment of William Faux that "the traveler, who must necessarily often mix with the very dregs of society in this country, should be prepared with plain clothes, or the dress of a mechanic, a gentlemanly appearance only exciting unfriendly or curious feelings, which defeat his object and make his superiority painful." The travelers also disapproved of the universal love of money, the constant yawning and stretching, and the filthy habits (particularly tobacco chewing) of their hosts. Mrs. Anthony Trollope deplored the lack of theaters in Cincinnati, and was horrified by the excesses of the camp meetings. On the positive side, they appreciated the hospitality which they were always shown, and also commented favorably upon the huge dinners of venison, fowl, whiskey, and coffee, which were common.

Many of the Englishmen were clearly sensation mongers. Adlard Welby referred to Americans as "clothed savages," while others called them "semi-barbarians." Emphasis was placed upon the fighting and gouging matches in which all Americans supposedly indulged. Faux reported: "I saw a man this day with his face sadly disfigured. He had lost his nose, bitten off close down to its root, in a fight with a nose-loving neighbor." Welby reported as sober truth the stories he had been told of a famous "gouger" who kept as trophies the eyes which he had extracted during his combats. It is evident that the "stuffing" of inquisitive strangers was a favorite pastime in the new West.

The most noteworthy English reporters on the Old Northwest were actual settlers. Morris Birkbeck and his associate George Flower rode and walked from the east coast to Illinois in the spring of 1817. Fifty miles north of the Ohio River landing at Shawneetown, they established the "English Prairie," a colony to attract yeomen and artisans from their home country. Birkbeck wrote that "the land is rich natural meadow bounded by timbered land, within reach of two navigable rivers, and may be rendered immediately productive at a small expense." Settlers did come, and the town of New Albion soon boasted a gristmill, a brewery, and a Unitarian church. Birkbeck's writings included *Notes on a Journey in America from the Coast of Virginia to the Territory of Illinois*, which went through eleven editions in Philadelphia and London between 1817 and 1819. This book brought the Illinois prairies to public attention.

Paths of Settlement

Most settlers continued to avoid the prairie, however, and headed for choice timberlands along the rivers. The lower and middle Wabash was one of these preferred areas. Sales at the government land office in Vincennes increased by 425 percent in the year 1816. After Indian claims south of the Wabash-Maumee line were cleared by the New Purchase of 1818, more prospective "Hoosiers" squatted on the waiting lands. The upper Wabash was settled more slowly, since there were no roads from the Ohio. By the beginning of 1816 the territory was thought to have the 60,000 people required for statehood, and in December Congress approved Indiana's constitution and ushered it into the Union.

Illinois Territory also attracted war veterans, squatters, and cash buyers in such numbers that its 1815 population of 15,000 had grown to 40,000 within 3 years. Statehood was granted in 1818 on the safe assumption that the figure would continue to climb. The lower third of the state had been cleared of Indian title by Governor Harrison before the war, so the first rush of settlers was to this area by way of Shawneetown or Vincennes. The Kickapoo ceded their claim to lands south of the Illinois River in 1819, and squatters and speculators raced in to pick off the best wooded locations. Title was also cleared to 2 million acres between the Illinois and the Mississippi, which Congress in 1812 had set aside as a military tract for veterans' bounties. Speculators bought up many of the warrants, but settlement did get under way in 1818. The middle stretches of the Illinois were the borderland of settlement between Southerners and Yankees.

Western Illinois also had some choice locations. The "American Bottom" has nothing to do with anatomy, but denominates a strip of land which extended northward from the mouth of the Kaskaskia for about 90 miles along the Mississippi. The black soil, 10 feet deep, had produced 75 bushels of corn per acre for a hundred years since the first Frenchmen had begun cultivating it. Now it was the turn of lucky American purchasers to enjoy the same yields. In the northwestern corner of the state there was money to be made in a different kind of enterprise—lead mining. Indians and Frenchmen had scratched away at the surface deposits along the Fever River, but in 1822 Col. James Johnson got a government lease and brought in Negro slaves to open up the rich seams. By 1825 there were a thousand people in the "diggings," and Galena had become a boomtown resembling those found in the Far West later in the century.

In the northeastern corner of Illinois was Chicago, a windswept collection of shacks and wigwams with a population of fifty people in 1830. By 1835 the figure was up to 3,300, many of this number being speculators who were busy marking off city streets through the frogponds and hog wallows. Within a few more years Chicago was on its way to greatness, a model of rapid city building, after overcoming various deficiencies. One of these was the shortage of women, and the *Chicago Democrat* in 1836 promised that "all who emigrate West will not be subject to a long and tedious courtship, as we do things here by steam."

Settlers also began moving into Wisconsin, which was a part of Michigan Territory until 1836. The only settlements there were the fur-trading posts at either end of the old Marquette-Jolliet route: Green Bay at the mouth of the Fox River and Prairie du Chien at the mouth of the Wisconsin. In 1835 Green Bay acquired a government land office, and Yankee farmers began mingling with the French traders. "The Milwauky" became all the rage that same year, and speculators also started promoting the beautiful Four Lakes region to the west. The country north of the Wisconsin-Fox line remained unsettled for many years. Not until the late 1840s and 1850s did German and Norwegian emigrants begin hewing farms out of the unbroken pine forests.

Michigan in 1825 was still populated by mosquitoes, wolves, and Indians. Governor Lewis Cass made herculean efforts to overcome popular indifference to his thinly settled territory. Much adverse publicity had followed the Tiffin Report, issued in 1815 by the surveyor general of the Northwest, which declared that "not one acre out of a hundred would admit of cultivation." School geographies carried maps with the words "Interminable Swamp" across the interior of Michigan. But completion of the Erie Canal in 1825 brought a trickle of settlers that had become a torrent by1836. Lake steamers, the first of which was the *Walk-in-the-Water* of 1818, were carrying Yankee and York State emigrants from Buffalo to Detroit in only a day and a half by 1830. From Detroit, the movers could follow a stump-dotted road north to Saginaw Bay. Others went west along the Chicago Road, which ran just above the Indiana boundary line, and settled Michigan's southern tier of counties. Although the territory had ample population for statehood by 1835, admission to the Union was delayed until 1837 because of a boundary squabble with Ohio.

Role of the Federal Government

The footloose folk who wanted to try their luck in the Northwest traveled in a variety of conveyances over roads that were uniformly poor. The Ohio River was still a major route to the Promised Land, and it was dotted with flatboats, arks, and rafts come high water or low. But the decade of 1820 to 1830 was one of frantic roadbuilding activity by private turnpike companies, the states, and the federal government. The latter had sponsored such projects as early as 1796. In that year Congress had promised Ebenezer Zane three sections of land if he would cut a "highway" from opposite Wheeling to a point on the Ohio across from Limestone (later Maysville), Kentucky. Zane's Trace ran for 200 miles through towering forests. It got heavy use, and one traveler reported the road had ruts deep enough to bury a horse in. Yet the trace led to the founding of Zanesville, and brought prosperity to Chillicothe and other towns in southern Ohio.

The most grandiose federal project was the National or Cumberland Road, begun in 1811. It was financed partly by the proceeds from government land sales in Ohio, Indiana, and Illinois, and was started because of demands from those states. The "road of capitals" began at Cumberland on the Potomac and ran to Wheeling, Zanesville, Columbus (by 1833), Indianapolis, and Vandalia. There was a constant stream of traffic: stagecoaches, Conestoga wagons, buggies, carts of every conceivable shape and size, people on foot or on horseback. And as the people moved west, they encountered great herds of cattle, sheep, and hogs being driven east to Philadelphia or Baltimore. The roadbed was topped with crushed gravel and ran across cut stone bridges and culverts. Yet there were also deep gullies and gaping potholes, which remained unfilled because Congress had appropriated no money for maintenance. Inhabitants along the route who made money by pulling travelers out of the mud were said to have lavished great care on their mudholes during the dry season. But for all its shortcomings, the road served as a symbol of federal involvement in the West.

The national government assumed many other responsibilities on the northwestern frontier. It operated the land offices which registered and sold millions of acres. It ran Indian "factories" (official fur-trading posts) at a number of locations, and made many scores of treaties with the tribes which claimed land in the region. It established various army posts in northern Illinois and in Wisconsin to protect the settlers and to weaken the British influence on the Indians. Among the important posts established from 1816 to 1819 were Fort Armstrong at the mouth of the Rock River, Fort Crawford at Prairie du Chien, and Fort Snelling on the upper Mississippi at the site of Minneapolis-St. Paul.

Presidents Monroe, Adams, and Jackson all followed Jefferson's policy of removing the Indian tribes to reservations west of the Mississippi. The treaty agents often found themselves trying to catch up with the squatters, who advanced into unceded lands with as much consideration for Indian titles as a swarm of locusts. But once-proud tribes like the Potawatomie had become powerless. They were victims of the white man's vices, principally whiskey, and settlers regarded the tribesmen less as a threat than as a nuisance. Their most disconcerting hobby was staring at housewives through the cabin windows. Thus there was practically no opportunity for settlers of the Old Northwest to participate in the kind of "Indian War" that had made heroes of men like Harrison and Jackson. Fortunately for the thrill seekers, however, a Sauk Indian named Black Hawk was unwilling to give up his lands along the Rock River.

Black Hawk War

The Black Hawk "War," which barely qualifies for that title, is important for two reasons. It was the last Indian war of the Old Northwest, and several of the participants were later important in American history. The notables included Capt. Abraham Lincoln of the Illinois Mounted Volunteers, Col. Zachary Taylor of the Regular Army, and Lt. Jefferson Davis of the same service. These men were on the periphery of the war, and Lincoln later made fun of his role in it. Speaking before Congress in 1846, he remarked that "if General Cass went in advance of me picking huckleberries, I guess I surpassed him in charges on the wild onions. If he saw any live, fighting Indians, it was more than I did; but I had a good many bloody struggles with the mosquitoes."

In the fall of 1831 increasing harassment from squatters and pressure from the state government forced Black Hawk to move his village from Rock River across the Mississippi into Iowa. But a hard winter there brought him back to Illinois on April 5, 1832, at the head of some 1,000 men, women, and children. Black Hawk was at this time sixty-six years old, had fought against the Americans in the War of 1812, and had continued to make trips to Fort Malden since then. In fact, medicine men misled him into believing that the British would come to his aid in case of trouble. A younger chief, Keokuk, advised him against returning to Illinois, but the stubborn old warrior insisted upon "planting corn on the old grounds."

Bloodshed probably could have been avoided, but Governor John Reynolds needed an "Indian War" to help him politically. Volunteers were immediately called out to repel the "invasion," and the Regular Army was also alerted. Black Hawk fought several skirmishes with the whites, and then fled up the Rock River into Wisconsin. He managed to cross over to the north bank of the Wisconsin with his starving band, but the pursuing army finally trapped him as he tried to cross the Mississippi. In the Bad Axe Massacre some 300 Indians were mowed down in a crossfire from troops on one side and a gunboat on the other. Black Hawk himself survived to dictate an autobiography, and to be exhibited in the East as a living specimen of the "noble savage."

The war was a bloody lesson to the other tribes of the Old Northwest. The related Sauk-Fox tribes paid an immediate penalty for Black Hawk's ill-advised venture by having to cede a 50-mile-wide strip along the west bank of the Mississippi. The retreating red men usually left little but names behind them. In this case it was "Iowa," a Fox word meaning "this is the land." And so it proved to be for the lead miners at Dubuque and the farmers who settled the Black Hawk Purchase beginning in 1833. In the absence of territorial government before 1838, the Iowa squatters formed extralegal "claim clubs" to protect their landholdings. Intruders who insisted upon bidding against club members at auctions usually found themselves on the receiving end of kicks and blows which convinced them that they would be happier in another territory. The clubs not only protected members' claims, but also served as a vehicle for small-scale speculation by squatters who wished to sell their claims to latecomers. The clubs are another notable example of how individualistic frontiersmen banded together for their own protection (or self-interest) when the official government was far to the east.

Religion

There were a few other occasions on which frontiersmen could get together. The militia muster, ostensibly held to sharpen combat skills, was actually an occasion for drinking and politicking. The cabin raising brought neighbors together for feasting and dancing after the structure had been finished. Another popular social event was the camp meeting, a principal tool of the Protestant sects. These meetings proved their value during the Great Revival of 1800 to 1805, in which thousands repented of their sins and "came to Jesus." Much attention has been given to the more sensational aspects of these revivals, including the physical contortions or "jerks," the "holy laughter," and the promiscuous sexual behavior which presumably accompanied them. English visitors from

Charles Dickens to Mrs. Trollope were especially critical of these excesses. Yet the meetings should be viewed as social institutions, since they offered a momentary reprieve from boredom and isolation.

The Presbyterians had joined with the Methodists and Baptists in conducting some of the great revivals at the turn of the century, but they soon repudiated such spectacular methods. The price they paid was a slow growth for their frontier churches, and a schism which created the more evangelical Cumberland Presbyterians. The Presbyterians' intellectual approach did not appeal to frontiersmen, and their "aristocratic" associations were a distinct disadvantage in the backwoods. So the Methodists and Baptists became the principal sponsors of camp meetings, and the former in particular enjoyed great success with them during the pioneer period.

The Methodists also utilized circuit riders. The crusading zeal and physical hardihood of these saddlebag preachers was well known. On bitter cold days the folk expression was: "There's nothing out today but crows and Methodist preachers." They rode for six days out of seven, holding a cabin meeting whenever they could get enough people together. The itinerants were poorly educated men who "murdered the king's English," and in fact many of them were hostile to formal education. Yet they spoke the language of the frontier, and their reward was mounting membership totals.

Peter Cartwright was the best known of the Methodist preachers. His *Autobiography* catalogs the sins of which frontiersmen were guilty: cardplaying; dancing; horseracing; drunkenness; fiddling; blasphemy. Cartwright was a well-muscled Kentuckian who fought verbal battles with the devil and physical battles with the rowdies who attempted to break up his camp meetings. Contemporaries even credited him with having whipped the notorious bully Mike Fink, which Cartwright described as "a wonderful story which has no foundation in fact." One of his few defeats came when he ran for Congress against Abraham Lincoln in 1846. During a debate Cartwright asked those who wished to go to heaven to stand, and again those who did not wish to go to hell. He remarked that Lincoln had not risen on either occasion, whereupon Lincoln stood up and said: "I am going to Congress."

Cotton Frontier in the Old Southwest

Though the Old Southwest was settled at the same time as the North, the social and economic pattern was quite different. The Gulf states became a one-crop section whose fortunes rose and fell with the world price of "King Cotton." Negro slavery was legally and morally acceptable south of the Ohio, and the slaves were the base of a pyramidal social structure that was unique in frontier history. At the apex of the pyramid were the successful slaveowing planters who, though a numerical minority, set the style for the whole society. The familiar hunter-farmers and equipped farmers of other frontiers took part in the Southern migration, but since they yielded political leadership to the larger planters, they have been shadowy figures in historical writing. Whatever their social or economic position, the pioneers came principally from the lower South, thus creating a much more homogeneous society than that of the Old Northwest.

It is ironical that a "damned Yankee," Eli Whitney, should have contributed so much to the pattern of Southern development. His cotton gin, invented in 1793, consisted of a revolving cylinder with wire brushes which combed the seeds from the lint. Mechanization increased rather than decreased the demand for slaves, since more hands were needed for the greater acreage now made possible. Black soil and a sunny climate also made the production of Upland cotton quite profitable all the way from Tennessee to Texas. On the other hand, the old lands of Tidewater Virginia and the Carolinas had been exhausted by generations of use and abuse. Many tobacco planters sold out, and took their families and slaves to Alabama and Mississippi for a new start.

The land routes to the West were often no more than old Indian trails. Migrants could follow the Fall Line Road, the western portion of which was known as the Federal Road after the government took an interest in it in 1808. This ran from Richmond through Raleigh, Columbia, and Milledgeville to the Alabama River settlements. The Great Valley Road ran from Washington down to Knoxville, where a crude trail could be followed to Huntsville in northern Alabama. Some travelers preferred to take oceangoing vessels around to Mobile. From there (after 1820) they could take steamboats up the Tombigbee River into the center of the state. As on most frontiers, getting there was half the fight.

The most favored locations for cotton planting were the bottomlands along such rivers as the Tennessee, Tombigbee, Alabama, and Pearl. The first great rush into Alabama was to the Tennessee Valley where it dipped down into the northern part of the territory. Another desirable location was the Black Belt, a crescent of black soil some 50 miles wide which ran across south-central Alabama to the Mississippi line. Mississippi had its Bluff Hills, whose sunny slopes attracted many former Georgians and Tennesseans. The Flood Plains along the Mississippi itself were not planted until a levee system was built in the 1840s.

Most planters preferred to buy cleared or semicleared land from the yeomen farmers and squatters who had preceded them. A number of adjacent strips of such land would be purchased, and then planted about equally with cotton and corn. If the planter utilized his slave labor effectively and had a good first year's crop, he would be able to buy still more land and slaves. Within a few additional years he would be calling his plantation by a fancy name like "Rosewell" or "Naomi Hall," even though his house was still a log cabin. Rooms would be added at either end of the original structure, then a second story, then a portico with pseudo-Greek columns. The successful planter would by that time have acquired the title of "Judge" or "Colonel," though this did not necessarily mean that he had served on the court or in the army. Such men, typified by Jefferson Davis of Mississippi, formed the social and political aristocracy of the Old South.

The small farmers who sold their lands could move to the newer frontiers in Arkansas or Missouri. Those who chose to remain could make a comfortable living, though they did not become well-to-do. Many of them moved into the pine hills of northern Alabama, where they ran hogs and cattle or raised corn for the larger plantations. Others settled the lands bordering the Gulf, which were also suitable for cattle raising but were too wet for cotton. The upper levels of this small-farmer class were yeomen of the type familiar in the earlier Piedmont region of Virginia. At the lower levels were the "Crackers" or "hillbillies" who occupied the marginal and wornout lands. This group has received undue attention in most histories, usually in the form of horror stories about parasitic hookworms. These farmers did not man a frontier line in the conventional sense. There was instead a broken pattern of settlement along the favored river bottoms and upland locations.

Three-fourths of the whites did not own slaves, though most of them aspired to do so. The Negroes are the "invisible men" of the Southern frontier. Being a submerged and illiterate population, their exact contribution has been recorded in folklore rather than in history. But they were a substantial part of the pioneering population. Out of Alabama's 1820 total of 128,000 people, 21,780 were slaves, and the percentage kept rising as new cotton lands were opened up. Though the Negro helped to conquer the Southern forests, his presence in the frontier population became a subject of controversy. Opposition to the continued westward expansion of slavery helped sharpen the sectional differences which led to a civil war.

In 1802 Georgia had finally ceded the lands west of her present boundary to Congress, in exchange for a sweetener of $1,250,000. The western part of Mississippi Territory became a state in December of 1817. The eastern part, Alabama, was settled so swiftly that its population multiplied sixteen times between 1810 and 1820. News of the great fertility of the Tennessee River area attracted droves of speculators to the land office at Huntsville. Among them were human vultures who preyed on squatters by threatening to bid on their lands at auction unless they were bought off. The situation lent credence to the folk expression, "It's good to be shifty in a new country." But so many settlers came that Alabama was admitted to the Union in 1819. In both Alabama and Mississippi the typical governing unit was the county court, a legislative-judicial body through which the aristocracy maintained their power. Yet the two states adopted constitutions that were little different, with the exception of a clause permitting slavery, from those of Indiana and Illinois. All free whites could vote and be elected to the state legislature when they reached twenty-one.

Removal of the Civilized Tribes

The story of Indian removal in the Old Southwest is not for those with sensitive stomachs. The Civilized Tribes were ejected from their lands by a series of treaties which stand like tombstones along a road to oblivion. The men who effected these treaties clearly mirrored the social attitudes of their time. There was a double standard in the treatment of whites and Indians, and the precepts of Christianity and legal obligations which governed the relations of white men were considered to be irrelevant as far as Indians were concerned. Minority rights had to be sacrificed where necessary in the interests of "progress."

Even the revered President Jefferson shared such attitudes. He heartily approved of the Compact of 1802, by which the federal government promised Georgia that it would remove the Indians from that state as expeditiously as possible. Jefferson was not above utilizing the Indian trading stations for such purposes, by forcing the tribes to pay their debts at these stations in the form of land cessions. After George Troup became Governor in 1823, Georgia began badgering the federal government to remove the Creeks and Cherokees within her borders. The Creeks were the first to feel the toe of the boot. By the Washington Treaty of 1826, they reluctantly agreed to go to lands west of Arkansas, and for 2 years the removal process went on. Governor Troup also bellowed for the removal of the Cherokees, two-thirds of whom lived in northern Georgia. But this tribe proved to be a formidable antagonist.

The Cherokees had advanced far along the white man's road by the middle 20s. They had benefited enormously from the mission schools which several Protestant denominations had established among them. From these had emerged literate leaders who understood the workings of government and could parry the thrusts of the Georgians. The Cherokee Republic, formed in 1827, had a constitution patterned after that of the United States. The government included a bicameral legislature, a supreme court, and the other appurtenances of representative democracy. The *Cherokee Phoenix* was a newspaper printed in both English and Cherokee, the latter having an alphabet of 86 characters invented by the far-famed Sequoyah. And a number of Cherokees had even married white women.

All these signs of progress enraged the Georgians. The Cherokees were unfit to live in the state since they were savages who could never learn the white man's ways. The fact that they were doing so undermined the whole argument. In exasperation the state legislature passed a law in 1827 which permitted whites to settle on Cherokee lands regardless of treaties. Thus the tribe was placed in a position where the federal government was their only protection. The presidential election of 1828 made Andrew Jackson the Great White Father. Unfortunately, Jackson had been a Cherokee hater since his earliest days in Tennessee, despite the fact that warriors from the Cherokee Nation had served him well at Horseshoe Bend. He was just as determined as Georgia to rid the

South of redskins, and he backed up the state by having Congress pass the Indian Removal Act of 1830. This decreed that the Indians accept payment for their eastern land and leave for the Indian Territory.

The Cherokees fought a rearguard action in the courts to prevent removal. The great constitutional lawyer William Wirt argued two test cases before the Supreme Court. In *Cherokee Nation v. Georgia* (1831) he sought an injunction to restrain the state from enforcing its laws over the Indians and seizing their lands. But John Marshall in speaking for the Court held that the tribe was not a state of the Union nor a foreign nation. Since the tribesmen were not citizens, they could not bring a suit before the Court. In 1832 Wirt argued the case of *Worcester v. Georgia*, involving the conviction of a minister for living on Cherokee lands without a state license. This time Marshall maintained that "the laws of Georgia have no right to enter [the Cherokee Nation] but with the assent of the Cherokees themselves or in conformity with treaties and with acts of Congress." Georgia paid no attention whatsoever to this decision, and threatened to use force against United States troops to protect state interests. As for President Jackson, he is reported to have said: "John Marshall has made his decision, now let him enforce it."

These defeats shattered tribal unity and lead to the emergence of a treaty faction. In December of 1835 the leaders of this minority signed the Treaty of New Echota, which consented to the removal of all 15,000 Cherokees in 1838. So that year a federal army herded them west on the "Trail of Tears," along which some 4,000 died of disease and exposure. (A few hundred escaped to the North Carolina mountains, where their descendants live to this day.) Other tribes went through similar experiences, but since the Cherokees were the most advanced and literate, their case has always been of special interest.

The tribes were settled in the Indian Territory.* Beginning with President Monroe, it had been the intention of the government to move most of the Indians to lands lying west of Arkansas and Missouri. Secretary of War Lewis Cass instructed his commissioners in 1832 to locate the tribes "in districts sufficiently fertile, salubrious, and extensive." Thus there was no scheme to dump the Indians in the "Great American Desert," and the region between Arkansas' western border and the 100th meridian was considered to be both fertile and eminently habitable. Of course Cherokees and Choctaws who had been settled earlier in western Arkansas were pressured into moving once more, beyond the 95th meridian. The Cherokees got a 7-million-acre reservation in the northern part of the new territory, along with an "Outlet" to the 100th meridian which would enable them to reach buffalo country.

The Creeks, Choctaws, and Chickasaws were ousted from Alabama and Mississippi by treaties to which the words "fraudulent" and "disgraceful" seem to apply. Such at least was the case with the Treaty of Dancing Rabbit

*In 1866 the Indian Territory took the name Oklahoma, a Choctaw word meaning "red people."

Creek (1830), in which the Choctaws were beguiled into surrending 7½ million acres in western Alabama and eastern Mississippi. The Creeks and Chickasaws in Alabama signed removal treaties in 1832, and each followed its own "trail of tears" to the West. These tribes were settled on various tracts south to the Red River.

The Seminoles were a tribe of largely Creek derivation, which fought two wars against the United States. In 1817 to 1818 after battling with Andrew Jackson, they were promised a reservation in central Florida around Lake Okee-chobee. The region was fit only for alligators and water moccasins, but by the 1830s land-greedy Americans were claiming that it was too good for Indians. In the war of 1835 to 1842 a succession of generals, including Zachary Taylor, made futile efforts to dislodge the savages, who were superbly led by Osceola. As a matter of fact, the American army demonstrated that it had little aptitude for guerrilla warfare in swampy, semitropical country. The Seminoles were finally persuaded to go to Oklahoma in 1842, though several hundred of them remained in the Everglades. Their great-grandchildren officially ended the war against the United States in 1962.

Water Transportation

The Mississippi River linked the northwest and southwest frontiers of this period. Handpowered craft continued to be heavily used even after the intro-duction of the steamboat in 1811. The keelboat in particular was well adapted to the river trade, since it could carry up to 30 tons of freight on the downstream voyage. In addition, it could be handpoled back up from New Orleans to Pitts-burgh, a journey which took about 4 months. When the riverbed was unsuited to poling, the boatmen had to go ashore and pull the vessel up by hand, an opera-tion known as "cordelling." At other times the guide rope would be fastened to a tree and the men would haul the craft up to it by "warping."

These boatmen had an enormous capacity for physical punishment. Even after a dawn-to-dusk regimen of poling or warping, they were still capable of midnight revels. An old song preserves some of the flavor of their lives:

Dance, boatman, dance
Dance all night till broad daylight,
And go home with the gals in the morning.

They were generally a hard set, and had a well-deserved reputation for drinking and fighting. The "King of the Keelboatmen" was Mike Fink, born at Fort Pitt in 1770 and killed by a companion on the upper Missouri in 1823. In his prime Fink was acknowledged to be the champion "gouger" among the rivermen. He boasted that he was half horse and half alligator, also styling himself upon oc-casion as the "Snapping Turtle of the Ohio." He was renowned as a marksman who could shoot the tin cup from a companion's head. Fink became the subject for a cycle of frontier tall tales which made him the archetype of the Western boatman.

The romantic days of the keelboatmen were numbered, however, once steamboats became operative. Powered by steam-driven paddle wheels at the stern or side, these vessels were essentially glorified keelboats in design. They were long and flat, a fact concealed by the elaborate two- and three-story superstructures which became fashionable in later years. The new era dawned when Nicholas J. Roosevelt rode Robert Fulton's *New Orleans* down to that city from Cincinnati in the fall of 1811. Other patentees soon joined in the competition, and by the 1820s steamboats were traveling on all the important western rivers. The fastest of them made the trip from New Orleans to Louisville in 9 days. The decks and salons were crowded with passengers who paid $100 for a Pittsburgh-New Orleans ticket. "Hoosiers" and "Wolverines" mingled with Yankee peddlers and Georgia planters. As freight the boats carried pork, whiskey, and flour downstream; sugar, coffee, and cotton upstream. This trade meant prosperity for such cities as Pittsburgh, Louisville, Cincinnati, and St. Louis. It also was a powerful economic bond between the Old Northwest and the Old Southwest, and one that affected the sectional alignments before the Civil War.

Missouri and Arkansas

Steamboats also carried cargo and emigrants up the Missouri and Arkansas Rivers to settlements in those two territories. Americans had gone into Missouri when it was still Spanish soil. Small colonies of farmers took root at New Madrid and Cape Girardeau, and in the St. Genevieve district, which also attracted lead miners. Others took up tracts of land along the Missouri, leaving St. Louis to the old French families. In 1799 Daniel Boone, driven from his Kentucky home by lawsuits, had accepted the Spanish government's invitation to move across the Mississippi. He became a large landholder and a minor government official when he settled at St. Charles, northwest of St. Louis. By 1807 the old pioneer's sons were making salt at a spot upriver known thereafter as "Boone's Lick." The new town of Franklin, Missouri, sprang up near the Lick to become a famous outfitting center for the far-western trade. In the spring of 1819 the first steamboats made their appearance at this bustling outpost.

Thousands of Southern Uplanders followed Boone after the Louisiana Purchase. They settled along the Missouri to raise corn, wheat, and tobacco, while a few of the more adventurous tried the fur trade. By the time of Boone's death in 1820 these "wild men along the Missouri" were pounding at the doors of statehood. The region had been organized as Louisiana Territory in 1805, but in 1812 it had been renamed Missouri Territory, with William Clark as its "Governor and Superintendent of Indian Affairs." A great influx of emigrants after the war had brought the territory's population to 67,000 by 1820. Of this total, 10,000 were Negro slaves.

The crisis over slavery in Missouri was the first of many that led to Fort Sumter and Appomattox. The controversy started when a statehood enabling act was presented to Congress in February 1819. One result of this proposal was the division of Missouri, the region south of 36°30' to the Louisiana border being set up as Arkansas Territory. But an amendment by Representative James Tallmadge of New York to prohibit slavery in Missouri caused a postponement of the statehood bill. The game of political teeter-totter between the free and slave-holding sections had been an even match: Indiana (1816) and Mississippi (1817); Illinois (1818) and Alabama (1819). But if slavery were barred in Missouri, the North would add to its political weight and the South would find itself suspended on the loser's end of the board. The question of whether or not slavery should accompany the expanding western frontier caused a table-thumping, fist-waving debate in the Congress that took 2 years to settle.

Henry Clay took a leading role in piloting the Missouri Compromise through both houses of Congress. The nucleus of the settlement was a "marriage bill" by which Maine, a free state that had been detached from Massachusetts, was regarded as balancing the admission of Missouri as a slave state. An amendment by Senator Jesse Thomas of Illinois also became part of the compromise. This prohibited slavery in the Louisiana Purchase lands north of 36°30', with the exception of Missouri itself. Missouri was finally admitted under these provisions in August of 1821, after a further debate caused by a clause in its constitution which barred free Negroes from the state. But the question of slavery extension had become part of the national dialog, and had been inseparably attached to western expansion itself.

Arkansas Territory, like Missouri, was peopled primarily by those from the Southern Appalachians, Kentucky, and Tennessee. Typical of the migrants was William Lewis, who had been born in Virginia in 1801. His wife was born in Tennessee in 1805. They had six children born in Kentucky between 1825 and 1836. Their seventh child was born in Newton County, Arkansas, in 1838, and their other five children were born in the same area during the next 10 years. Families of this type went up the Arkansas or White Rivers and became squatters in the bottomlands. Sharp ridges between the river valleys retarded both trading and settlement within the territory itself. Yet the Arkansans were proud of their chosen land, boasting that potato hills were mistaken for Indian mounds and that the corn shot up so fast it killed hogs which got in the way. The citizens also claimed to be unmatched hunters, a tradition exemplified by T. B. Thorpe's story of the "Big Bear of Arkansas." Thorpe's hunter, Jim Doggett, described Arkansas as "the creation state, the finishing up country." He also told of having killed the "creation bear," which walked through fences and had a skin which made a bedspread so large that "it left several feet on each side to tuck up." With the aid of propaganda like this, Congress was ready to admit Arkansas as a state in June of 1836.

Thus American settlers in the years up to 1840 had spread over the interior between the Appalachians and the Mississippi, leaving only a few islands of wilderness behind them. They had created a new type of social pattern, and had brought a half dozen important states into the Union. In Arkansas, Missouri, and Iowa they had established a salient for further expansion into the Far West. And it was to the strange lands beyond the Missouri that the next generation of pioneers now turned.

Selected Readings   R. Carlyle Buley, *The Old Northwest, 1815-1840*, 2 vols. (Indianapolis, 1950), is an exhaustive study which incorporates much original research. Frederick Jackson Turner, *The Rise of the New West, 1819-1829* (New York, 1906), is an older and more limited discussion. Francis S. Philbrick, *The Rise of the West* (New York, 1965), is a lawyer's survey of the period from 1763 to 1840, and contains a critique of the Turner thesis. Frank R. Kramer, *Voices in the Valley* (Madison, Wis., 1964), has perceptive comments on the three principal migrant stocks and their way of life. Joseph Schafer, "The Yankee and Teuton in Wisconsin," *Wisconsin Magazine of History*, vol. 6 (1922-23), is a basic source. Walter Havighurst, *Wilderness for Sale* (New York, 1956), and John A. Caruso, *The Great Lakes Frontier* (Indianapolis, 1960), are good popular narratives. Ralph L. Rusk, *The Literature of the Middle Western Frontier*, 2 vols. (New York, 1925), is a somewhat dated bibliography.

Reuben G. Thwaites, *Early Western Travels, 1748-1846*, 32 vols. (Cleveland, 1904-1907), reprints important travel narratives including (vol. XI) those of William Faux and Adlard Welby. Charles Boewe, *Praire Albion* (Carbondale, Ill., 1961), is a skillful editing of the Birkbeck-Flower journals. Philip D. Jordan, *The National Road* (Indianapolis, 1948), is readable. Cyrenus Cole, *I Am a Man—The Indian Black Hawk* (Iowa City, 1938), should be supplemented by Donald Jackson (ed.), *Blackhawk, an Autobiography* (Urbana, 1955), which includes a summary of the war. The most thorough state histories are of World War I vintage: Logan Esarey, *A History of Indiana from Its Exploration to 1850* (Indianapolis, 1915); Theodore C. Pease, *The Frontier State* [Illinois] *1818-1848* (Springfield, Ill., 1918); and George N. Fuller, *Economic and Social Beginnings of Michigan* (Lansing, 1916). Allan G. Bogue, "The Iowa Claim Clubs: Symbol and Substance," *Mississippi Valley Historical Review*, vol. 45 (September, 1958), corrects many misconceptions.

William Warren Sweet's four-volume series on *Religion on the American Frontier: A Collection of Source Materials* includes vol. I, *The Baptists* (New York, 1931); vol. II, *The Presbyterians* (Chicago, 1936); vol. III, *The Congregationalists* (Chicago, 1939); and vol. IV, *The Methodists* (Chicago, 1946). Charles A. Johnson, "The Frontier Camp Meeting," *Mississippi Valley Historical Review*, vol. 37 (June, 1950), is a good introduction to the topic, which is more extensively treated in the same author's *The Frontier Camp Meeting* (Dallas, 1955). T. Scott Miyakawa, *Protestants and Pioneers* (Chicago, 1964), is a largely sociological analysis which concludes that, contrary to the Turner thesis, conformity rather than individualism was encouraged by the Protestant sects. Ray Billington, *The Protestant Crusade* (New York, 1953), is a good survey. Peter Cartwright, *Autobiography* (New York, 1857), is a primary account that is anecdotal and highly interesting.

Thomas P. Abernethy, *The South in the New Nation* (Chapel Hill, N.C., 1961), has an instructive chapter on the Great Migration. Everett Dick, *The Dixie Frontier, a Social History* (New York, 1948), is a wide-ranging survey. Frank L. Owsley, *Plain Folk of the Old South* (Baton Rouge, 1949), disputes many traditional ideas about the poverty and incapacity of the yeomen farmers. Avery Craven, *Soil Exhaustion as a Factor in the Agricultural History of Virginia and Maryland, 1606-1860* (Urbana, 1926), is a standard monograph.

Robert S. Cotterill, *The Southern Indians, the Story of the Five Civilized Tribes before Removal* (Norman, 1954), gives a good overall picture. Grace Woodward, *The Cherokee* (Norman, 1963), is a thorough discussion. Dale Van Every, *The Disinherited* (New York, 1966), is an impassioned indictment of the removals. Francis Paul Prucha, *American Indian Policy in the Formative Years* (Cambridge, 1962), is a monograph which has material on Jackson's removal policy. The same author's "Indian Removal and the Great American Desert," *Indiana Magazine of History*, vol. 59 (December, 1963), demonstrates that removal was not a scheme to dump Indians in the "desert." Archer B. Hulbert, *Waterways of Western Expansion* (Cleveland, 1904), and Leland Baldwin, *The Keelboat Age on Western Waters* (Pittsburgh, 1941), are classic accounts. Walter Blair and Franklin Meine, *Half-Horse, Half-Alligator: The Growth of the Mike Fink Legend* (Chicago, 1956), reprints many stories about the famous boatman. The "Dance, Boatman, Dance" song is printed in W. P. Strickland, *The Pioneer of the West* (New York, 1856).

Edwin C. McReynolds, *Missouri: A History of the Crossroads State* (Norman, 1962), is solid and factual. Glover Moore, *The Missouri Controversy, 1819-1821* (Lexington, 1953); an admirable discussion. W. Clement Eaton, *Henry Clay and the Art of American Politics* (Boston, 1957), is a good biography of the "Great Pacificator." Otto E. Rayburn, *Ozark Country* (New York, 1941), and James R. Masterson, *Tall Tales of Arkansaw* (Boston, 1943), blend history and folklore.

X. The Far Western Frontier

Beyond the Missouri, Nature confronted man with an unparalleled set of obstacles. There were treeless plains whose vast dimensions and featureless terrain were habitually compared with the ocean. Snow-topped mountains at 14,000 feet above sea level rose next to sandy deserts far below. No other frontier required such far-reaching changes in individual and social adaption. The pioneers, who appeared to be of Lilliputian scale on this enormous landscape, often paid with their lives for attempting to traverse or settle the region. Yet conquer it they did, and the settlement of the Great West is one of the epic chapters in American history.

The Plains Province   The first of the physiographic regions west of the Missouri was the Interior Plains. The eastern half of this province, known as the Prairie or Low Plains, generally received over 20 inches of rainfall per year. The prairie grass grew waist-high in places, and most of the land could be farmed in the same manner as that of the Mississippi Basin. The terrain was level, but there was no timber except for scattered stands of willows or cottonwood along the streams. Between the 98th and 100th meridian the Prairie gave way to the High Plains, which had short grass, a subhumid climate, and less than 20 inches of annual precipitation. The Plains tilt imperceptibly upward toward the mountains, rising from about 2,000 to 6,000 feet at the base of the Rockies. A few wide, shallow rivers flow eastward to join the Missouri or Mississippi. Typical of these is one which early French explorers called the Plat, their word for "flat." Dignified by the addition of a superfluous "te," the Platte Valley, which rises in Colorado and joins the Missouri in Nebraska, became an important avenue for western expansion.

157

The natural grasses of the Plains province supported large numbers of antelope, jackrabbits, and prairie dogs. The most important animal was the buffalo, a shaggy beast numbering between 4 and 12 million before the advent of the white man. The huge herds, sometimes 10 miles long, thundered across the plains until the 1870s when hunters caused their near-extinction. The buffalo were a four-legged food supply for the Indian tribes of the region, who were by consequence nomadic rather than sedentary.

The most powerful of the northern tribes were the Sioux, who called themselves Dakotas. They claimed territory from Minnesota (their original home) through South Dakota and Nebraska into Wyoming. Some of the great leaders of Indian history, including Red Cloud and Crazy Horse, belonged to one of the seven major tribes making up the Sioux Nation. Ideally the chief men of these divisions met in grand council once a year. But the governmental structure was quite fluid, being based upon small family hunting bands. The headman of each band secured his position through family background, achievement of dreams and visions, or success in war. Practically all the young men aspired to be warriors, since these were the heroes of a society in which warfare was constant. Valor was rewarded by membership in elite societies, often called the

Buffalo and covered wagons. Source: Title Insurance and Trust Company, Los Angeles.

Sioux village on the River Brule near Pine Ridge. From a photo taken by W. C. Graybill in 1891. Source: Library of Congress.

"Dog Soldiers," and by elaborate coup systems. "Counting coup" was to strike an enemy, a feat which entitled the warrior to wear an eagle feather in his hair. Scalps were also taken as a sign of victory.

The bands which made up the various Sioux tribes followed the buffalo on seasonal hunts, first on foot and then on horses when these became common in the eighteenth century. The buffalo's skin was turned into robes and moccasins, or it was scraped and dried by the squaws for use in the cone-shaped tepee, the characteristic shelter on the Plains. The meat was eaten raw or lightly cooked, with the brains, the tongue, and the gristle about the nostrils being particularly delectable. Gourmets enjoyed a soup which was made from the buffalo's tail. Portions of meat were often cut into thin strips which were dried in the sun to make "jerky," or were pulverized for "pemmican," both high-protein rations which were carried on war or hunting trips. The animal's hoofs and horns made scraping tools, the skull became a ceremonial headdress, and its intestines were used for water containers. In the absence of timber on the Plains, buffalo dung, known to American pioneers as "buffalo chips," was used for fuel. In fact, the Indians utilized the animal so thoroughly that only a few scraps were left for the dogs to fight over.

Among other nomadic tribes with a horse and buffalo culture were the Blackfeet of Montana, whose three principal divisions were the Blackfeet proper, the Piegans, and the Bloods. The Cheyenne of the Wyoming-Colorado border region were allies of the Arapaho, who also occupied the middle Plains. Further south were the Comanches and Kiowas, who roamed from western Oklahoma through western Texas. Both these tribes were celebrated traders as well as warriors, and the Kiowas became the most adept practitioners of sign language.

These Indians were all superb horsemen, the "finest light cavalry in the world" according to Gen. George Crook, and thus they were a considerable military threat when white men began crossing the plains. Wild horses were indigenous to the American continent, but became extinct in prehistoric times. The Spanish *conquistadores*, however, reintroduced them to the New World. The horse frontier moved northward with the Spanish colonial system, since the mission ranches maintained sizable herds. The Indians picked up strays or stole horses from these ranches in the late seventeenth century. The Pueblo Revolt of 1680 emptied New Mexico of Spaniards for a dozen years, and in this interim more horses were traded to the northern tribes.

The horse wrought revolutionary changes in the Indians' methods of hunting, transportation, and warfare. The buffalo could be chased down with greater chances of success. More baggage could be carried on the A-shaped travois, the trailing poles which carried the tepee and other baggage. The range of war parties was vastly increased, and horsemanship was widely admired as a warriors' attribute. Horses also became one of the principal forms of wealth, with only whiskey, tobacco, and guns being more highly valued. Among the Sioux, one horse would buy a shield, a warbonnet, or a wife.

A few tribes on the eastern Plains lived in permanent villages. The Mandans of the upper Missouri, and the Pawnees and Osages along the lower reaches of the river, raised corn and occupied earth or willow-frame houses. The Mandan lodges were round and beehive-shaped, being constructed of earth-covered logs with a floor dug down 3 or 4 feet below ground level. Several dozen people lived in these dwellings. The Mandans worshiped nature in various forms, but the epitome of religious expression was the Sun Dance, which was common to most Plains tribes. This was a bloody ritual in which skewers would be run through the flesh of the back and chest. The young men would shuffle back and forth, staring at the sun, until the skewers broke through the skin. These dances were regarded as an initiation into manhood as well as a test of religious faith.

Rocky Mountain Province

Running across North America in a southeasterly direction were the "Shining Mountains," the Stony Mountains, or as they eventually were called, the Rocky Mountains. The Northern Rockies of present-day Montana, Idaho, and Wyoming are a chaotic tangle of parallel ranges including the Lewis, the Wind River, and the Big Horn. South of these lies the Wyoming Basin, a plateau where South Pass and Bridger Pass could be used as gateways to the farther West. The Southern Rockies of Colorado include dozens of peaks (such as Pike's and Long's) which are over 14,000 feet high, and there are few passes through them. The continuation of the Rockies into New Mexico has retained its Spanish name of the Sangre de Cristo range.

This physiographic province is noted for its cold winters and heavy snows, which have been known to fall in July and August at the higher elevations. However, the dryness of the air makes the preservation of meat and animal skins more practicable than on the Low Plains. The mountain slopes were covered with pine and spruce forests which sheltered wolves, elk, deer, mountain lions, and bear. The latter included the *ursus horribilis* or grizzly bear, the most feared animal in the West, and large numbers of the more common brown and black bears. Westerners claimed that the way to tell the difference between grizzlies and browns was to climb a tree, and that if the bear came up after you he was a brown. The most important animal was the beaver, whose presence in large numbers along the Rocky Mountain streams brought American fur trappers into the region.

There were numerous Indian tribes in the mountains. In Idaho lived the Salish, who through the vagaries of sign language came to be called Flatheads. The fact that their heads were as round as anyone else's caused tourists endless disappointment. The Big Horn country along the Montana-Wyoming boundary was the home of the Crows or Absaroka, the most noted horse thieves in the West. Among this tribe it was common for middle-aged men to own thirty to sixty animals, and a warrior with only twenty horses was considered "poor." South and west of them lived peoples of the Shoshonean family. The Northern Shoshonis of Idaho and Wyoming are remembered because the "Bird Woman" Sacajawea was an interpreter for Lewis and Clark, and because Chief Washakie was remarkably friendly with the whites. In western Colorado lived the Utes, whom Kit Carson said were the best rifle shots of all. These mountain tribes were hunters rather than agriculturalists, and they lived in buffalo-skin tepees or willow-frame lodges.

Intermountain Province

The three principal areas of the Intermountain province are the Columbia Plateau, the Great Basin, and the Colorado Plateau. The first of these lies west of the Northern Rockies, in Idaho and Washington. A region of volcanic rock, it includes the drainage basins for the Columbia and Snake Rivers. The latter is aptly named, for it twists and turns through 600 miles of cliffs and plains on its way to join the Columbia. In this province lived some of the noblest and meanest Indians in God's creation. The former were Nez Percé, a dignified people who were friends of the whites until 1877. The latter were the Bannocks of southern Idaho, a treacherous type of "Digger" Indian.

South of the Columbia Plateau lies an ancient lake bed known as the Great Basin, which stretches for some 600 miles from Utah's Wasatch Mountains to the Sierra Nevada. It covers western Utah, Nevada, and parts of southern Oregon and eastern California. Actually the "Basin" is a land of high ranges, averaging 9,000 feet, which are separated by desert plains. There is little vegetation on the sandy floors of these deserts, and most of it is sagebrush or greasewood. The few rivers, of which the most important is the Humboldt, simply disappear into the thirsty ground at "sinks." All things considered, the basin is one of the most desolate and forbidding pieces of real estate in North America.

Nevertheless, Digger Indians lived in this area. The term derives from their habit of scrabbling in the soil for roots and insects. The Diggers had the lowest cultural level of any Indians in the country, living in virtual nakedness under rock shelters and scooped-out hollows in the dry riverbeds. Rats, snakes, insects, and an occasional rabbit were the staples of their diet. Grasshopper pie was considered to be a *pièce de résistance*. Specific tribes within this group included the Gosiutes of the Salt Lake region, the Paiutes and Washoe of Nevada, and the Yuma and Mojave who lived along the lower Colorado. All these tribes were harmless except for the Yuma and Mojave, who perpetrated several massacres that made travel through their country perilous at times for both Spaniards and Americans.

The Colorado Plateau is a land of mesas and canyons. Its river gorges, particularly the Grand Canyon in Arizona and the Black Canyon of the Gunnison in Colorado, are among the natural wonders of the world. Early explorers, however, found travel in this picturesque region to be extremely difficult. They spent fruitless days, like flies on a windowpane, attempting to find easy routes across the plateau or trails which would take them down the canyon walls to the precious river water below. The river system is centered on the great Colorado of the West and its tributaries, the chief of which are the Green, the Little Colorado, and the Gila.

Living along the Gila and Salt Rivers in southern Arizona were the closely related Pima and Papago tribes. They were agriculturalists who raised

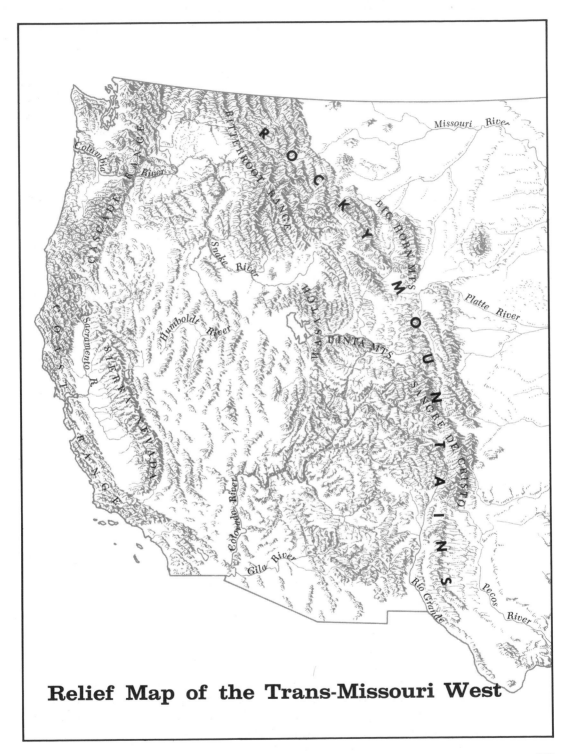

Relief Map of the Trans-Missouri West

beans, corn, and melons by means of extensive irrigation ditches. These canals, fully developed by 700 A.D., covered hundreds of miles around today's Phoenix. To the north and east lived a group of tribes which the Spanish labeled the Pueblo. They lived in stone houses or in "furnished apartments" built in tiers along the cliffs. Access to these dwellings was by means of ladders which were pulled up at night or in times of danger. They too raised corn and fruit in cultivated fields along the streams, and made pottery and blankets that were beautifully decorated. The Pueblo society included the Hopi of northeastern Arizona, the Zuñi of western New Mexico, and a variety of Keresan or Tano villages scattered along the Rio Grande and the upper reaches of the Pecos. The continued occupation of the pueblos down to the present day, the practice of peculiar customs like the Snake Dance, and the existence of old pueblo ruins have led to the intensive investigation of the Pueblo culture by archeologists and anthropologists.

Nomadic tribes of the Colorado Plateau region were the Navaho and Apache. The former ranged across northern New Mexico and southern Colorado. They were marauders during their earlier history, but at some time during the Spanish period the adoption of sheep and goat herding changed their pattern of living. They also developed an outstanding craft tradition in blankets and baskets. The Apaches were an Athapascan cultural-linguistic unit whose three major divisions were the San Carlos, the Chiricahua, and the Mescalero. They retained a warlike character right up to the surrender of Geronimo in 1886. They were perfectly adapted to the arid environment of southern New Mexico and Arizona, where they lived in caves or brush-covered wickiups. Tough and merciless, these raiders were enemies of the Pueblo tribes, the Spaniards, and the Americans in turn.

Pacific Coast Province

The Pacific Coast province is walled off from the east by two great mountain chains, the Cascades in the north and the Sierra Nevada in California. These mountains are heavily forested down into northern California, and the principal task of westward-moving settlers was to find passes through the 12,000-foot peaks which are common along both ranges. Travel was risky most of the year because of heavy snowfall. Nestled between these mountains and the smaller Coast Range adjacent to the ocean were desirable farming areas. The Willamette Valley of Oregon was bordered by lush meadows that proved to be ideal for wheat and cattle raising. In California the Sacramento and San Joaquin Valleys, though destitute of timber, were covered with a spontaneous growth of grass and clover. A mild climate and the wise use of irrigation would in time make this region a vast fruitbowl, with apples, peaches, and oranges among the leading crops. In the pioneer period the adjacent plains were crowded with wild horses, elk, antelope, bear, deer, geese, and ducks.

In Oregon and Washington the Chinook and other coastal tribes lived on salmon and harvested the abundant forests for their log canoes, plank houses, and totem poles. The long rainy winters permitted the evolution of elaborate ceremonials and complex political systems. In California were a variety of small tribal units which spoke a veritable Babel of tongues. From north to south the chief linguistic families were the Shastan, the Maidu, the Miwok, the Salinan, and the Chumash. Most of these Indians were a step above the Digger level, being "hunters and gatherers" who lived on acorns and fish. By and large they were a gentle, harmless people, and thus likely candidates for extermination by American intruders.

Exploration and settlement of the spacious trans-Missouri region thus involved adaption to great extremes of terrain and climate. The endless sky, the frightening deserts, the infinitely frigid mountain ranges were facts which required reorientation in men's physical lives and in their imaginations. Successive waves of pioneers underwent such adaptions even though they tried to hold on to their old folkways. Spearheading the advance into this terra incognita were intrepid young men who held Army commissions from the United States government.

Lewis and Clark

Thomas Jefferson had long been interested in exploration of the Far West for scientific and geographical purposes. While minister to Paris in 1786 he had met John Ledyard, a rugged ex-Marine from Connecticut, and had persuaded him to undertake a transcontinental walking tour that was to go east through Russia, down the Pacific Coast and then to the Missouri. Ledyard got as far as Siberia before he was stopped as a suspected spy and hustled back across the border. Then in 1792 Jefferson proposed that the American Philosophical Society send Andre Michaux, a French botanist, to find a Northwest Passage through the "Stony Mountains." This project collapsed when it was found that Michaux was a secret agent who was involved in the nefarious schemes of Citizen Genet. But after Jefferson became President in 1801 he was finally able to launch the momentous expedition.

Even before the Louisiana Purchase, Jefferson had been making plans to send a small party up the Missouri. On January 18, 1803, he had sent a secret message to Congress asking $2,500 for this purpose. England, France, and Spain were informed of the proposed journey, but not of its real purpose. As Jefferson stated this purpose in his message, it was for "extending the external commerce of the United States," a reference both to the inland fur trade and to the Pacific Coast trade in sea otter skins and china goods. The President was still interested in the scientific and "literary" aspects of the enterprise, but he could hardly expect to get funds from Congress for a mere daisy-picking excursion.

Even after the Louisiana Purchase, economic penetration was still a principal objective, as indicated by Jefferson's instructions to Meriwether Lewis: "The object of your mission is to explore the Missouri river, & such principal

Meriwether Lewis. Source: Independence   *William Clark. Source: Independence*
Historical National Park Collection.   *Historical National Park Collection.*

stream of it, as, by it's course & communication with the waters of the Pacific Ocean, may offer the most direct & practicable water communication across this continent, for the purposes of commerce." Embedded in these instructions is the ancient idea of a Northwest Passage. In Jefferson's conception there would be but one short portage between the headwaters of the Missouri and those of the Columbia; a "portage" which in fact turned out to be over 200 miles of the most rugged mountain country in North America. The scientific purposes were still important, and Lewis and Clark received elaborate instructions regarding observations of the Indian tribes, the terrain and climate, the animals and flowers. One added purpose, now that the route lay within United States territory, was to acquaint the Indian tribes with the American flag and inform them of the change of White Fathers. Here it should be noted that the Spanish authorities in North America did not concede that the purchase extended north of the Platte River. Nemesio Salcedo, commandant of the internal provinces of Mexico, wrote his government that he was going to "cut off the gigantic steps of our neighbors," and in fact he sent an army force to overtake "Captain Merry Weather Lewis." But the Spaniards never caught up with the fast-flying Americans, who had left St. Charles for the unknown wilderness on May 21, 1804.

The co-commanders of the "Corps of Volunteers for North-western Discovery" were ideally suited to the job at hand. Lt. William Clark was a tall

Virginian of thirty-three, who, like his older brother George, possessed an innate talent for frontier enterprise. He proved to be a capable mapmaker, riverman, and all-around engineer. Captain Lewis was twenty-nine, a six-footer who had been an officer with Anthony Wayne and had served as Jefferson's private secretary. He became the botanist and zoologist of the expedition, after having taken a cram course in natural science and geography at Philadelphia. The twenty-nine individuals who made up the rest of the Corps were Regular Army men and Kentucky hunters. Among them were Sgt. Patrick Gass, whose journal of the trip was the first to be published; John Colter, who was to become a famous mountain man and an explorer in his own right; and George Drouillard (anglicized as Drewyer), an outstanding interpreter and hunter who was later important in the fur trade. Also accompanying the expedition was the giant Negro slave York, whom Clark had inherited from his father. He was a source of wonder to the Indians, who thought that he had painted himself with charcoal as a symbol of bravery.

Hidatsa chief attempting to rub off York's "color." From an 1909 oil painting by Charles M. Russell. Source: Montana Historical Society, Helena.

The expedition made its way up the Missouri in a huge keelboat, and reached the Mandan villages near the great bend of the river at the end of October. Here they built a stockade, called Fort Mandan, and spent the winter of 1804-1805. Both leaders made copious notes on the Mandans, which became valuable for anthropological and historical purposes after the tribe was virtually wiped out by smallpox in 1837. The men built dugout canoes which were to be used for the trip further upriver. And a seventeen-year-old Shoshoni woman named Sacajawea was added to the party as an interpreter. Sacajawea was actually Mrs. Toussaint Charbonneau, the wife of a trader who had purchased her from Minataree captors 4 years before. She and her newborn son were permitted to go along partly for diplomatic purposes, since Lewis hoped to get horses from her people in the mountains.

On April 7 the expedition shoved off from Fort Mandan and again headed west through country that was alive with game. Lewis had his troubles with the grizzly bears, who chased him into the river on one occasion. The travelers made a time-consuming portage around the Great Falls in Montana. In July they reached the Three Forks of the Missouri, which they named the Jefferson, the Madison, and the Gallatin in honor of those officials. Here they did not find the Shoshoni, which caused Lewis to write in his journal: "If we do not find them, or some other nation who have horses, I fear the successful issue of our voyage will be very doubtful." But Sacajawea began to recognize the landmarks, and beyond Lemhi Pass the explorers found a band of the elusive tribesmen headed by none other than Sacajawea's brother.

Buying horses from the Shoshoni, Lewis and Clark traveled above the clouds along the Lolo Trail through the Bitterroot Range. After a tortuous 9-day trip the exhausted men finally got through the mountains to a Nez Percé village. Here they rested up for the final leg of their voyage down the Snake and Columbia Rivers to the coast. Subsisting on dog meat and dried salmon, they found that traveling by canoe through the shoals and chutes of these rivers was not one of the more restful parts of the journey. The Indians of the Columbia were sullen and treacherous, corrupted by years of contact with the white man. (British traders had been operating along the Oregon coast for 20 years.) But in November the party finally reached the Pacific. Fort Clatsop was built on a tributary of the Columbia, and here the men spent a sopping wet winter in 1805-1806.

On the return journey in the spring of 1806 the two leaders divided their party at the Bitterroots. Clark blazed a new trail over the mountains to the southeast and followed the Yellowstone River down to the Missouri. Lewis with three men headed north to explore the boundaries of the Louisiana Purchase. He scouted the banks of a river which he called Maria's, in honor of a girl friend named Maria Wood. This was home territory for the Blackfeet, the most dangerous Indians of the northern plains, and Lewis had the misfortune to run into a party of them. In the clash that followed, two of the Indians were killed,

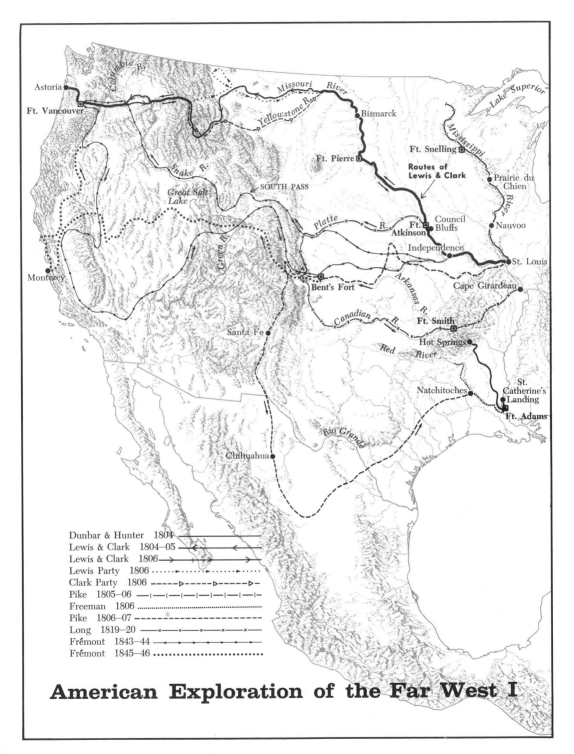

Astoria

Ft. Vancouver

Columbia R.

Snake R.

Yellowstone R.

Missouri River

Bismarck

Ft. Pierre

Mississippi R.

Ft. Snelling

**Routes of
Lewis & Clark**

Prairie du
Chien

Nauvoo

*Great Salt
Lake*

SOUTH PASS

Green R.

Platte   *R.*

Ft.
Atkinson

Council
Bluffs

Independence

St. Louis

Monterey

Bent's Fort

Arkansas R.

Cape Girardeau

Canadian   R.

Ft. Smith

Santa Fe

Red   *River*

Hot Springs

Rio Grande

Natchitoches

St.
Catherine's
Landing

Ft. Adams

Chihuahua

Dunbar & Hunter   1804
Lewis & Clark   1804–05
Lewis & Clark   1806
Lewis Party   1806
Clark Party   1806
Pike   1805–06
Freeman   1806
Pike   1806–07
Long   1819–20
Frémont   1843–44
Frémont   1845–46

American Exploration of the Far West I

an episode which was the first cause of prolonged Blackfoot hostility toward the Americans. Lewis rode full tilt down the river, and joined Clark below the Yellowstone on August 12. The reunited party floated rapidly down the Missouri and made a triumphal entry into St. Louis on September 23.

The Lewis and Clark expedition was a success. The explorers had traveled 6,000 miles in 28 months, and only one man (who died of appendicitis) had been lost. They had met Indians from eleven major tribes, and only Lewis's scrape with the Blackfeet had marred a perfect record in dealings with them. As the first Americans to cross the continent, they had given their nation a solid claim to the Oregon country. On the negative side, they had demolished the old idea of a Northwest Passage to the Pacific, at least as far as the Northern Rockies were concerned. They found the Northwest to be a treasury of beaver; as Lewis put it: "That portion of the Continent watered by the Missouri and all its branches from the Cheyenne upwards abound more in beaver and Common otter, than any other streams on earth." This welcome information would bring large numbers of American trappers to the area within a short period. The explorers had collected enough information and specimens of flora and fauna to keep scientists occupied for years. Lewis was the first to describe the grizzly bear, the prairie dog, the mountain goat, and numerous other birds and animals. The leaders were also liguistic pioneers who added several hundred words to the American language, including canvasback, ironwood, and snow-berries. Some of their geographical place-names, such as Council Bluffs and Milk River, have been retained. As a consequence of all this, the government's subsequent efforts at far-western exploration would seem anticlimactic in comparison with this first and greatest expedition of all.

Southwestern Exploration

Jefferson also convinced Congress to finance scientific and mapping expeditions up the Red and Arkansas Rivers on the southwestern borderland. William Dunbar of Natchez headed one of these parties in the fall of 1804. But learning of Spanish threats to seize Americans on the Red, he turned north to journey along the Ouachita instead. In the summer of 1806 another group under Thomas Freeman labored some 600 miles up the Red, only to be turned back beyond Natchitoches by a large Spanish cavalry patrol. Both these expeditions yielded valuable scientific information, but they had not accomplished their primary mission. This disappointing record was only slightly improved upon by Zebulon Montgomery Pike, who also searched in vain for the sources of the Red.

Lieutenant Pike's reputation in frontier history rests upon two expedi-tions. Both were ordered out not by Jefferson but by Gen. James Wilkinson, acting in his capacity as commander of the western army and Governor of Louisiana Territory. The President and the War Department were informed of the trips, however, and later gave them official approval. The first mission, under-

taken in 1805 to 1806, was for the purpose of locating the source of the Mississippi. Pike was at this time an ambitious twenty-six-year-old who had been on
frontier duty at Vincennes and Kaskaskia. Taking twenty enlisted men, he left
St. Louis by keelboat on August 9, 1805. He found British traders operating all
along the upper reaches of the river, enjoying profits of 1,000 percent and paying
no tariffs to the United States government. After lecturing the traders on their
sinful behavior, he pushed on to Leech Lake in Minnesota. This he identified
as the source of the Mississippi, although he was actually 25 miles from the
true source at Lake Itasca. Pike wintered in the region and returned to St.
Louis in April of 1806, having gathered some useful information about the
northern wilderness.

The lieutenant got little rest, for on July 15 Wilkinson had started
him on his way to the Rocky Mountains. The purposes of Pike's second expedition were to return fifty-one Osage captives to their homes in Missouri, hold
peace conferences with the Comanches, and map the Arkansas and Red Rivers.
The unstated purpose, judging from Pike's letters to Wilkinson, was to spy on
the Spaniards. This assignment was not simply Wilkinson's idea, for he had been
instructed by the Secretary of War to send out intelligence missions along the
Spanish border. But Pike suffered considerable embarrassment upon his return
because of charges that he was involved with Wilkinson in the contemporaneous
Aaron Burr conspiracy to invade Mexico. Pike was apparently innocent of any
connection with this plot, but the cloak and dagger nature of his activities
naturally aroused suspicion. Judged as a military reconnaissance, Pike's trip
was a success. Viewed as a scientific and mapping enterprise, it was enough of
a failure to justify the current description of its leader as the "Lost Pathfinder."

Pike's small and poorly equipped party of twenty-two men was not
one of the more promising to venture out onto the western plains. The young
commander described his soldiers as "a Dam'd Set of Rascels," and referred to
the Osages as a "faithless set of poltroons." Also accompanying Pike was the
enigmatic Dr. John H. Robinson, whose exact role is uncertain although he
appears to have been still another spy. The unlikely entourage traveled across
Kansas, after dropping off the Osage "poltroons," and visited pro-Spanish
Pawnees on the Republican River. The party then followed the Arkansas to
the site of Pueblo, Colorado, where Pike made an unsuccessful attempt to
climb the mountain peak which bears his name. It was now November and the
soldiers, all wearing thin cotton uniforms, suffered intensely from the subzero
cold. But Pike, displaying that capacity for determined self-punishment of
which American explorers were often capable, continued his search for the
elusive Red River. He went north to the headwaters of the Platte, explored the
Royal Gorge of the Arkansas, and finally on January 30 blundered across the
Rio Grande in Colorado's San Luis Valley. He built a log stockade on a small
tributary of the river, and awaited the Spaniards. Dr. Robinson had gone ahead
to Sante Fe (where he played a tricky game with the authorities), so Pike knew

that a patrol would soon be along to pick him up. When it did appear, on February 16, Pike wore an innocent face as he asked, "Is this not the Red River?"

Pike and his men were taken to Santa Fe, where the Governor interrogated him, confiscated his trunkful of papers, and then sent him down to Chihuahua for further questioning. The Spanish authorities decided not to make an issue of Pike's trespass, and he and several of his men were sent back to the United States by way of Texas, arriving at Natchitoches on July 1, 1807. It is said that Americans do not make good spies, but Pike stuffed the rifle barrels of his men with detailed notes on Mexican geography and military dispositions. Much of the information, made known when his *Journals* were published in 1810, helped draw American settlers to the Southwest. On the other hand, he also reported that "these vast plains of the western hemisphere may become in time as celebrated as the sandy deserts of Africa; for I saw in my route, in various places, tracts of many leagues where the wind had thrown up the sand in all the fanciful forms of the ocean's rolling waves, and on which not a speck of vegetable matter existed." This passage marks the origin of the Great American Desert concept, which dominated popular thinking about the Interior Plains until after the Civil War. Pike regarded this barrier as something of a blessing, since by keeping Americans penned up east of the Missouri it would tend to hold the Union together. Thus this expedition was important, even though Pike was a bumbling explorer who did not find the source of the Red River, missed the Comanches, and did not even climb "Pike's Peak."

Great American Desert

The idea of a Great American Desert was also perpetuated as a result of the Stephen H. Long expedition of 1820. Government exploration had been suspended during the War of 1812, but was resumed after the peace treaty. Major Long, a Dartmouth graduate and West Point mathematics instructor, began his postwar career by picking sites for Fort Smith in Arkansas and Fort Snelling in Minnesota. He also commanded the scientific contingent during the abortive Yellowstone Expedition of 1819. This operation, conducted by Col. Henry Atkinson, collapsed at Council Bluffs when the steamboats carrying the troops upriver broke down. Long and his scientists were sent instead to explore the headwaters of the Platte, the Arkansas, and (hopefully) the Red.

With a small party of nineteen men, Major Long left the Missouri on June 6, 1820. He followed the Platte to the Rockies, where he gave his name to one of the highest mountains in Colorado. Dr. Edwin James, the expedition's chronicler, finally succeeded in climbing Pike's Peak. After exploring the Royal Gorge, Long divided his party and sent one group down the Arkansas while he tried his luck at finding the Red. But he mistook the Canadian River as his objective, and followed it down to its junction with the Arkansas. Once again an American expedition had failed in its primary mission, and in fact, not until 1852 did a survey party under Capt. Randolph Marcy finally locate the source of this important river in the Texas Panhandle.

In the published report on his trip Long declared the region between the Missouri and the Rockies to be "wholly unfit for cultivation." Though Zebulon Pike was the real father of the idea, Long was the first to use the term "Great American Desert," and on his map the High Plains are so designated. Subsequent travelers such as Josiah Gregg and Thomas Farnham seconded this idea, and compared the Kansas-Oklahoma region to the Sahara. The maps in grammar school geographies used Long's "Desert" label. Long also sang Pike's refrain about the plains barrier being of benefit in that it would prevent an intolerable overextension of our political system. In point of fact, much of the land west of the 98th meridian was desert. It had insufficient rainfall to support to Eastern type of agriculture, and American technology was not yet equal to the challenge of semiarid land. Not until after the Civil War did the water-pump windmill and other technological innovations enable western farmers to push into the lands which Pike and Long had explored. It was perhaps fortunate, then, that settlers avoided the plains during this period and moved instead to California, Oregon, and east Texas.

John C. Frémont

There were various minor military expeditions in the 20s and 30s. Colonel Atkinson's Indian peace commission of 1825 went up the Missouri well beyond the mouth of the Yellowstone and contacted numerous tribes. Col. Henry Dodge led his Dragoons on several peacekeeping missions across the plains during this period. The most important one was a 1,600-mile march to the Rockies by way of the Platte and Arkansas Rivers in the summer of 1835. But these were not primarily exploratory expeditions, and none of them went beyond the Rockies. With the creation of the Army Corps of Topographical Engineers in 1838 (out of a smaller Topographical Bureau), it became possible to conduct major scientific and mapping expeditions. Col. John Abert was the commanding officer of this Corps, and his star performer was Lt. John Charles Frémont.

Frémont was a bright, handsome, dashing young man of twenty-nine when he undertook his first major expedition in 1842. He had previously served under the French scientist, J. N. Nicollet, in a survey of the Minnesota River in 1838. The experience had brought Frémont into contact with various Indian tribes, had taught him the essentials of topographical and scientific observation, and had stimulated his interest in wilderness exploration. But the most fateful event in his life came when he returned to Washington and won the love of Jessie Benton, sixteen-year-old daughter of Senator Thomas Hart Benton of Missouri. The Senator did not regard the penniless young man's attentions to his daughter with favor, but as often happens, the lovers paid no attention to parental admonitions. They eloped, and after the marriage the forgiving father decided that maybe he could make something out of his son-in-law after all.

Through Benton's influence, Lieutenant Frémont was put in charge of an expedition which was to describe the line of travel to Oregon and to fix the position of South Pass in Wyoming. Congress voted the money for this and Frémont's subsequent expeditions, which were supposedly under the direction of the War Department. But since Frémont took his orders from Senator Benton, the trips may be regarded as family enterprises. Frémont's 1842 party consisted of twenty-five men, including Charles Preuss as topographer and the mountain man Kit Carson as guide. Setting out from Choteau's Landing on June 10, Frémont followed the Platte River into Colorado. From St. Vrain's Fort he went north to Fort Laramie and followed the Sweetwater River to South Pass. From there the party went further north to explore the Wind River Mountains. They took the North Platte on the return trip and got back to the Kansas River on October 10.

As an exploratory effort the actual results of this trip were negligible. The route to South Pass was already well known, and Frémont had not ventured into the less familiar lands west of the Rockies. Yet his report was skillfully edited by Jessie and became popular reading fare. Congress was so impressed by it that they gave Frémont funds and a virtual carte blanche for a second expedition. The trip of 1843 to 1844 was another secret mission whose exact purpose was known to few besides Benton and Frémont. The inclusion of a howitzer cast doubt upon the "scientific" intent of the expedition, and Colonel Abert in fact sent Frémont a letter recalling him to Washington for an explanation. But the ever-watchful Jessie held this letter and wrote her husband to leave the Kansas River as quickly as possible. He departed, howitzer and all, on May 29.

The "Pathfinder's"* party of thirty-nine men again included Preuss as topographer, with Thomas Fitzpatrick and Kit Carson as principal guides. The men traveled to Bent's Fort on the Arkansas, moved north to South Pass, then turned west to explore the Salt Lake. Frémont followed the Snake River to Oregon, and there decided to explore the region to the south. He wandered across the "Great Basin," a name which he conferred, looking in vain for an outlet to the ocean—the Spaniards' mythical Rio Buenaventura. The desert took its toll of men and horses. So Frémont decided to cross the mountains into Mexican California instead of going east. Floundering through 10-foot snowdrifts and eating mule meat, the explorers arrived safely at John Sutter's fort on the Sacramento River early in March. On the return trip Frémont went south along the San Joaquin Valley, then turned east through Tehachapi Pass. He followed the "'Old Spanish Trail" for a way before moving north to visit Utah

*Frémont was given this title in 1856, when he was campaigning for President.

Lake, and from there he went through Colorado and across the plains to arrive in St. Louis on August 6, 1844.

This was the most important government expedition since Lewis and Clark. Frémont was a trained observer who made the first reasonably accurate survey of the region between South Pass and the Pacific. He revealed the true nature of the Great Basin, and in so doing destroyed the myth of the Rio Buenaventura. His descriptions of California as an agricultural paradise ("the deep-blue sky and sunny climate of Smyrna and Palermo") drew American settlers to that province. In fact, the *Report of the Exploring Expedition,* of which Congress had 10,000 copies printed, was packed with a good deal of useful information for prospective migrants. It also featured the individual heroics of Frémont and his mountaineers, particularly Carson, and these helped make the report a popular classic.

The mountain men who had accompanied and guided Frémont were familiar with most of the territory covered by the expedition. The search for untouched beaver-trapping grounds had taken men like Carson and Fitzpatrick into the remotest corners of the trans-Missouri West. But the trappers seldom committed their knowledge to paper. Only when explorers with scientific or technical training came into the region were their contributions to geographical knowledge made known to the general public. It then became evident that these men were the genuine pathfinders of the West.

Selected Readings Geography is described in N. M. Fenneman, *Physiography of the Western United States* (New York, 1931); Ralph H. Brown, *Historical Geography of the United States* (New York, 1948); and E. W. Gilbert, *The Exploration of Western America, 1800-1850: An Historical Geography* (New York, 1966), originally published in 1933.

Robert H. Lowie, *Indians of the Plains* (New York, 1954), an excellent introduction to the subject, has been published in paperback (New York, 1962). George E. Hyde, *Indians of the High Plains* (Norman, 1959), focuses on the period before 1800. Royal B. Hassrick and others, *The Sioux: Life and Customs of a Warrior Society* (Norman, 1964), is outstanding. George Bird Grinnell, *The Fighting Cheyennes* (New York, 1915) is one classic among many written by a leading student. John C. Ewers, *The Blackfeet: Raiders of the Northwestern Plains* (Norman, 1958), is good. Ernest Wallace and E. A. Hoebel, *The Comanches: Lords of the South Plains* (Norman, 1952), is now standard. Robert H. Lowie, *The Crow Indians* (New York, 1935), is for the general reader. Virginia C. Trenholm and Maurine Carley, *The Shoshoni: Sentinels of the Rockies* (Norman, 1964), is reliable. Francis Haines, *The Nez Perces: Tribesmen of the Columbia Plateau* (Norman, 1955), is the best book on a tribe about which too much has been written. Alfred H. Bowers, *Mandan Social and Ceremonial Organization* (Chicago, 1950), is primarily anthropological. Ruth M. Underhill, *The Navajos* (Norman, 1956), is outstanding. Erna Fergusson, *Dancing Gods: Indian Ceremonials of New Mexico and Arizona* (New York, 1931), is useful and well written. C. L. Sonnichsen, *The Mescalero Apaches* (Norman, 1959), is uneven in quality.

A. L. Kroeber, *Handbook of the Indians of California* (Washington, 1925), is useful, as is Robert F. Heizer and M. A. Whipple (eds.), *California Indians: A Source Book* (Berkeley, 1957), a collection of articles for the lay reader.

Among many books dealing with the horse, two of the most useful are Walker Wyman, *The Wild Horse of the West* (Caldwell, Idaho, 1945), and Frank G. Roe, *The Indian and the Horse* (Norman, 1955), the latter being polemical in tone. Robert West Howard, *The Horse in America* (New York, 1966), is for popular reading. Martin S. Garretson, *The American Bison* (New York, 1938), and Frank G. Roe, *The North American Buffalo* (Toronto, 1951) are both serious scientific studies, the latter being more thorough. E. Douglas Branch, *The Hunting of the Buffalo* (New York, 1929), is exceptionally well written. Stories about bears are collected in Edgar and Bessie Doak Haynes, *The Grizzly Bear* (Norman, 1966). William Philo Clark, *The Indian Sign Language* (Philadelphia, 1885), describes an interesting aspect of Plains culture.

A good starting point for study of Lewis and Clark is Ralph B. Guiness, "The Purpose of the Lewis and Clark Expedition," *Mississippi Valley Historical Review*, vol. 20 (June, 1933), which emphasizes the politico-commercial nature of the expedition. Also of general interest is Donald Jackson, "The Public Image of Lewis and Clark," *Pacific Northwest Quarterly*, vol. 57 (January, 1966). The classic collection is Reuben G. Thwaites (ed.), *The Original Journals of the Lewis and Clark Expedition*, 8 vols. (New York, 1904-05). Bernard DeVoto, *The Journals of Lewis and Clark* (Boston, 1953), is a one-volume condensation also available in paperback. Calvin Tomkins, *The Lewis and Clark Trail* (New York, 1965), is short and well illustrated. Donald Jackson has edited *The Letters of the Lewis and Clark Expedition* (Urbana, 1962). Richard Dillon, *Meriwether Lewis* (New York, 1965), is the best biography, though it puts Clark in the shadows. John Bakeless, *Lewis and Clark* (New York, 1947), is largely a narrative of the expedition rather than a biography.

W. Eugene Hollon, *The Lost Pathfinder: Zebulon Montgomery Pike* (Norman, 1949), is a well-rounded biography written in a too-sober style. Donald Jackson, "How Lost Was Zebulon Pike?," *American Heritage*, vol. 16(February, 1965), concludes that he was truly lost. Jackson has edited *The Journals of Zebulon Montgomery Pike*, 2 vols. (Norman, 1966), which replaces Elliot Coues (ed.), *The Expeditions of Zebulon Montgomery Pike*, 3 vols. (New York, 1895). The Long expedition was chronicled by Edwin James in *An Account of an Expedition from Pittsburgh to the Rocky Mountains*, reprinted in volumes 14 to 17 of Reuben G. Thwaites (ed.), *Early Western Travels*, 32 vols. (Cleveland, 1904-1906). Discussions of the Great American Desert are in Ralph C. Morris, "The Notion of a Great American Desert East of the Rockies," *Mississippi Valley Historical Review*, vol. 13 (September, 1926); W. Eugene Hollon, *The Great American Desert* (New York, 1966); Richard H. Dillon, "Stephen Long's Great American Desert," *Montana Magazine of History*, vol. 18 (Summer, 1968); and Part V of Walter Prescott Webb, *The Great Plains* (New York, 1931). Francis Paul Prucha, "Indian Removal and the Great American Desert," *Indiana Magazine of History*, vol. 59 (December, 1963), traces the evolution of the "desert" concept in maps.

William H. Goetzmann, *Army Exploration in the American West* (New Haven, 1959), is a useful introduction. Goetzmann's *Exploration and Empire* (New

York, 1966), also has much material on official expeditions. Allan Nevins, *Frémont: Pathmarker of the West* (New York, 1939), is laudatory, while Cardinal Goodwin, *John Charles Frémont* (Palo Alto, Calif., 1930), is critical. Charles Preuss, *Exploring with Frémont* (Norman, 1958), is a topographer's journal which throws much light on Frémont's operations. Allan Nevins (ed.), *Narratives of Exploration and Adventure* (New York, 1956), is a useful one-volume compilation of Frémont's reports.

XI. The Fur Trappers

The frontier fur trade was an international business with roots in New York, Montreal, and London. In its simplest form the business consisted of stripping the coats off of beaver, otter, or muskrat and making them into hats for gentlemen in London and Paris. In its broader aspects, however, the trade touched many vital economic and political interests. It was considered to be subject to government supervision because of its obvious relation to Indian affairs and to land policy. It had from its origins furnished a motive for exploration and political expansion, and many of the noted pathbreakers were fur men. In fact, the exploits of the trappers during the romantic era of the trade, between 1807 and 1840, have eclipsed the more sober accomplishments of the great merchants in their well-heated countinghouses. There is a certain justice in this, for the field men were the cutting edge of Anglo-American expansion toward the Pacific.

Spanish and British Fur Trade   St. Louis was named for Louis XV of France, but its cosmopolitan character is revealed by the fact that it was the center for first the Spanish and then the American fur trade. At the end of the French period the New Orleans firm of Maxtent, Laclede and Company had been granted an 8-year monopoly on trade with the Missouri Indians. This grant was confirmed by the Spanish when they took possession of Louisiana, so in 1764 Pierre Laclede Liguest went upriver to pick a site for the company's trading post. He chose a high limestone cliff safe from floods, and located at a position to dominate the strategic Missouri-Mississippi confluence.

Although St. Louis became a Spanish garrison town (in 1770), its residents were largely French. Families such as the Chouteaus and the Gratiots dominated the fur trade until well into the American period. They served both their own interests and those of the Spanish King as they extended the trading frontier further up the Missouri during the 1780s. They got as far as the Mandan villages in North Dakota before running into the stone wall of British competition.

The Hudson's Bay Company, chartered in 1670, was the king of British fur-trading companies. It operated not only in the Hudson's Bay region but also in the vast Canadian hinterland west to the Pacific. In 1783 a group of aggressive Montreal merchants founded the Northwest Company to compete with the older concern. The pushy spirit of their traders resulted in some significant exploratory work. Alexander Mackenzie, for example, became "the first man West" when he crossed the continent by way of the Saskatchewan Mountains in 1793. The cutthroat competition with the HBC forced the Nor'westers to go into both American and Spanish territory, where the superiority of their trading goods gave them a decided advantage. Operating out of Fort William on Lake Superior, they were particularly strong in the Great Lakes area, and westward through Iowa and Minnesota to the upper Missouri. American efforts to oust these unwelcome visitors was a drawn-out affair stretching from Anthony Wayne's campaign in 1794 to the Treaty of Ghent in 1815. The Spaniards, who were trading as far as the Mandan villages by 1790, also reacted by sending various expeditions up the Missouri to drive the interlopers off. These expeditions were uniform in their futility.

The British gave arms to the Sioux and Arikara tribes along the river, who repaid their benefactors by turning back a Spanish expedition under Jacques d'Eglise in 1791. The Englishmen also began to subvert the Osages along the lower river, and this was the final straw for the enraged Spaniards. To stop such incursions, Auguste Chouteau built Fort Carondelet among the Osages, incidentally initiating a profitable family trading relationship with that tribe. Another step was taken in 1794 with the organization of a "Company of Explorers of the Upper Missouri." This firm, made up of St. Louis merchants headed by a glib promoter named Jacques Clamorgan, was authorized to strengthen Spanish trading interests on the river. The company sent out three expeditions for this purpose, but none of them got as far as the Mandans. The makeshift nature of these operations is revealed by the third trip, in 1795. The two ranking "Spaniards" were Scotch-born James Mackay, a former trader for the Northwest Company, and a young Welshman named John Evans. The latter was seeking a lost tribe of Welsh Indians, supposed descendants of colonists brought to America in the twelfth century by a mythical "King Madoc." He was sent upriver from a base camp near the Platte, and did in fact reach the Mandans in the fall of 1796. Evans, who was instructed to write his records with fruit juice in case the ink ran out, found no Welsh-speaking Indians—only the Mandans and British traders. The latter listened intently while Evans, a Methodist, read a proclamation ordering them to leave "His Catholic Majesty's Dominions." The episode was a comic finale to Spanish efforts on the upper Missouri, and the British traders were still there when Lewis and Clark appeared in 1804.

Manuel Lisa

After the United States purchased Louisiana in 1803, St. Louis became the center for the American fur trade. The trappers who congregated there pushed upriver as soon as the change of flags had been formalized by a ceremony in the village itself. When Lewis and Clark were returning in the spring of 1806, they encountered Joseph Dickson and Forest Handcock west of the Mandan villages. The two adventurers persuaded John Colter to get his release from Lewis and join them, and the trio headed toward the mountains. Little information survives about this trip, or about several other trapping parties which Lewis and Clark encountered. All that is known is that men were drawn irresistibly to the Northern Rockies by the lure of the unknown and the desire for profits.

The man who first brought organization to the Missouri fur-trading business was "the black Spaniard," Manuel Lisa. A native of New Orleans but an early migrant to St. Louis, Lisa was regarded as an upstart and a troublemaker by the established French merchants. He built posts along the Missouri to keep the barrier tribes (Sioux and Arikara) happy, and took expeditions into the mountains to secure pelts directly from the more "primitive" Indians. His first effort, in the spring of 1807, involved two keelboats and a party of some fifty men. The former Lewis and Clark scouts George Drouillard and John Colter were hired for the trip, the latter as he descended the river from the Dickson-Handcock venture. By guile and bravado, Lisa got past the Arikara villages and went all the way up the Yellowstone to its juncture with the Big Horn. At this point he built Fort Manuel (sometimes called Fort Raymond in honor of Lisa's infant son), and wintered there in 1807-1808 while his scouts tramped over the countryside to bring Indians in for trading.

John Colter became the first of the mountain-man heroes as a result of his travels during this winter. He explored the Big Horn Valley, and went west on a circular tour through Jackson Hole and the Yellowstone Park region.* In the following summer he fought alongside a band of Flatheads and Crows against a Blackfoot war party. This episode, added to Lewis's encounter of 2 years before, heaped more coals on the fires of Blackfoot hatred for Americans. When Colter had the misfortune to be captured by these same Indians during the fall hunt, he faced a slow death by torture. But the savages were in a sportive mood, so they stripped him naked and gave him a running start of 100 yards on the spear-carrying warriors. Colter outdistanced all but one

---

*It is now agreed that Colter missed the main geyser area, and that the boiling springs and sulphur flows of "Colter's Hell" were east of the present national park.

pursuer, whom he managed to surprise and kill. He finally plunged into a stream and hid under a pile of driftwood until the Blackfeet went away. Some versions of "Colter's Run" have him hiding in a beaver lodge and never trapping beaver thereafter. But this tradition is belied by the fact that he remained active in the business until 1810.

Lisa meanwhile returned to St. Louis with the furs which he had been able to secure. The initial success enabled him to attract enough additional capital to form the Missouri Fur Company. Among his partners were such important men as Auguste and Pierre Chouteau, Andrew Henry, and William Clark. The company sent a veritable army of 200 men upriver in the spring of 1809. The hunters dared to trap in the Three Forks region despite warnings from Colter and others that they would be attacked by the Blackfeet. There were in fact several attacks, in one of which the accomplished George Drouillard was killed. Consequently Major Henry moved over the Continental Divide into present Idaho, where he built a fort on Henry's Fork of the Snake River. Here the trappers were safe from the terrible Blackfoot raiders, but they were also outside the prime beaver grounds. In fact, the losses of men and money between 1809 and 1811 so discouraged the partners that the company was reorganized in 1812. The war of that year also disrupted the fur trade, with Lisa using his great skills to keep tribes along the river loyal to the United States. He also continued to be the company's guiding spirit through subsequent reorganizations until his death in 1820.

John Jacob Astor

Another fur trader with continental aspirations was John Jacob Astor, a German butcher boy who came to New York as a steerage passenger in 1784. He arrived with $25 cash, and with seven flutes as his stock in trade. But Astor was more interested in beaver pelts than in music. A tireless worker and a hardheaded merchant, he had by 1800 become the leading factor or agent in the American fur trade. His ambitions were limitless, though they were touched with patriotism as well as self-interest. Combating the British companies in the far Northwest might lead to American political dominance there. The firm which Astor organized in 1808 bore the presumptuous title of the American Fur Company. It was to be the instrument through which he would create a vast fur-trade empire of international dimensions, to be named with characteristic modesty, "Astoria." The plan was to draw furs from the interior by way of the Columbia, and carry them to China in a fleet of ships.

This scheme involved the construction of a depot at the mouth of the Columbia. Therefore in 1810 Astor organized the Pacific Fur Company as a subsidiary of the parent concern, and sent expeditions by sea and by land to build the post. The *Tonquin* left New York in September with a full cargo of trading goods. The 6-month voyage around the Horn was marred by thunderous arguments between Astor's traders and the vessel's captain, appropriately named Thorn. But the ship finally reached the mouth of the Columbia in March of 1811. The trading goods were unloaded on the south bank of the river, where some of the men began building Fort Astoria. The irascible Captain Thorn sailed further up the coast to Vancouver Island, where he met his Waterloo. Hostile savages surprised him and massacred all the crew except for one wounded white man, who touched off the powder magazine and blew both the Indians and the *Tonquin* to kingdom come.

Meanwhile the "Overland Astorians" had left St. Louis by keelboat in March of 1811. They were led by Wilson P. Hunt, a young New Jersey store-keeper who was a novice at wilderness travel. Yet his party of sixty men, like most of Astor's outfits, was made up largely of experienced Canadians such as Ramsay Crooks and Donald McKenzie. When Hunt reached the Arikara villages along the North Dakota-South Dakota boundary, he decided to head across the plains rather than risk a Blackfoot attack upriver. On July 11 the Astorians led their packhorses into the unknown lands which lay hundreds of miles south of the Lewis and Clark trail. They skirted the northern edge of the Black Hills, and plodded through Wyoming to the Wind River Mountains. They climbed up and over these to the Green River, where they turned south. At Henry's Fork of the Snake the tenderfoot Hunt made a serious mistake. Ignoring the advice of local Indians, he abandoned the horses and attempted to go down the Snake by canoe. The craft were ripped apart by the churning rapids and whirlpools down-river, so the expedition had to make its way to the Columbia on foot and in small parties. On January 18, 1812, the first detachment under McKenzie finally limped into Astoria, with Hunt and his emaciated crew coming in a month later. For all its sufferings, this expedition, brought to life in Washington Irvings's classic *Astoria*, helped blaze the western portions of the future Oregon Trail.

Comparable exploratory work along the trail was done by an east-bound party which for want of a better name has been called "the Returning Astorians." Headed by Robert Stuart, the seven-man group left the Fort on June 29, 1812, carrying letters for Astor. The journey was marked by starvation, mad-ness, and the threat of cannibalism. In the Rocky Mountains their horses were stolen by Crow Indians, so the men went by foot around the southern end of the Wind River Range. Here they passed a grand opening through the Continental Divide: the famed South Pass. The pass, a sage-covered plain some 5 miles wide, proved to be a gateway through which wagons could be taken to Oregon. Stuart did not actually traverse the pass, however, and so not until Jed Smith's trip from the East in 1824 was its existence made known. The Astorians wintered in Wyoming, and then followed the Sweetwater and the Platte along what later became the eastern segment of the Oregon Trail. They arrived in St. Louis on April 12, 1813, having learned on their way downriver of the outbreak of the War of 1812.

Astor's plan to dominate the far-western fur trade was well conceived

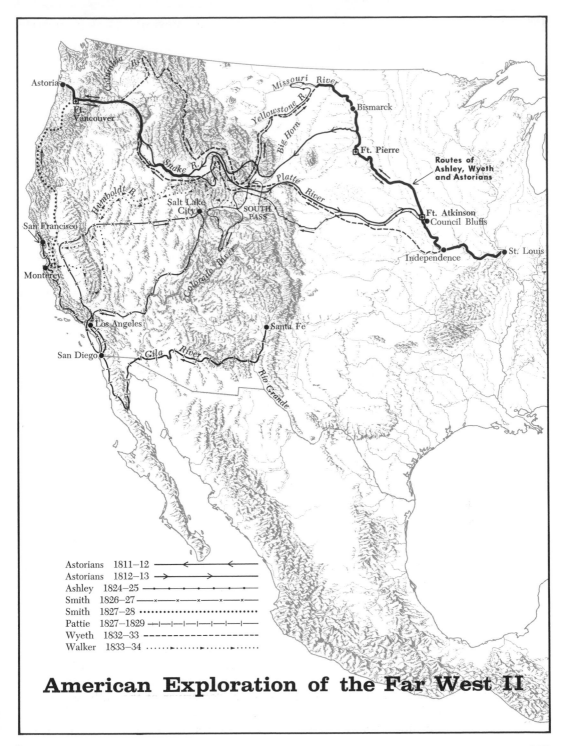

Astoria

Columbia R.

Ft. Vancouver

Snake R.

Missouri River

Yellowstone R.

Big Horn

Bismarck

Ft. Pierre

**Routes of
Wyeth
and Astorians**

Humboldt R.

San Francisco

Salt Lake City

SOUTH PASS

Platte River

Ft. Atkinson
Council Bluffs

Monterey

Colorado River

Independence

St. Louis

Los Angeles

Santa Fe

San Diego

Gila River

Rio Grande

Astorians 1811–12
Astorians 1812–13
Ashley 1824–25
Smith 1826–27
Smith 1827–28
Pattie 1827–1829
Wyeth 1832–33
Walker 1833–34

American Exploration of the Far West II

but poorly executed. The failure to build a series of forts between St. Louis and Astoria left that post at the mercy of the British navy when war was declared. In fact, the fort was sold to the Northwest Company (at a bargain price of $58,000) to prevent its capture by H.M.S. *Raccoon*. Also, better leaders might have been chosen for the field expeditions. Wilson P. Hunt was particularly negligent of his duties, and conditions at the fort deteriorated while he deliberately absented himself on trading missions. In any case, the collapse of the Astoria enterprise put the Oregon country and its beaver trade firmly in British hands.

      After the war, Astor devoted most of his attention and his enormous financial resources to the Great Lakes. His company's Northern Department, centered at Mackinac, had Ramsay Crooks and Robert Stuart as principal agents. But before Astor could monopolize the trade of the Lakes and the upper Mississippi, he had to destroy the government factory system. This was a chain of official fur-trading posts. Begun in 1796, the system was designed to keep the Indians happy by selling them trade goods at near cost. By 1817 there were nineteen factories in operation, including a number west of the Mississippi. But all these posts had trouble competing against the private traders. The latter had superior goods, usually of British manufacture, and they made liberal use of liquor. The red men became so elated after doses of "firewater" that they seldom noticed the low prices they were getting for their furs. Still, the factories were a brake on profiteering, and thus an irritant that had to be removed. The political influence of Astor and other traders, exerted principally through Senator Benton of Missouri, resulted in the demise of the government system. In the spring of 1822 Congress ended official trading with the tribes, and turned the whole business over to the tender mercies of the commercial traders. The only government supervision was a requirement that trading licenses, obtained from territorial governors or military post commanders, be restricted to citizens of the United States.

The Fur Trappers

That same year Astor moved into the Missouri trade by establishing a Western Department at St. Louis. But there he had to compete with other ambitious entrepreneurs who hoped to make a fortune from furs. Among these was Joshua Pilcher, who had succeeded Lisa as head of the old Missouri Fur Company and who had some 300 men in the field in 1822. There was also William H. Ashley, who joined with Andrew Henry to form one of the more creative trading outfits. On February 13, 1822, these partners placed an ad in the St. Louis *Missouri Gazette* addressed to "enterprising young men" who wished to work on the upper Missouri for from 1 to 3 years. Among the volunteers for this hazardous employment were such future luminaries of the mountain fur trade as James Bridger, Jedediah Smith, Thomas Fitzpatrick, and James Beckwourth.

The trappers were a more varied group than the popular stereotype would suggest. Most were uneducated, took Indian wives, and enjoyed a smoke and a drink. But others (like Jed Smith) were literate and straitlaced gentlemen who touched neither liquor nor Indian women. Half the trappers were native Americans, the rest were French-Canadians and mixed-bloods. Jim Beckwourth was a Virginia-born mulatto, described by Francis Parkman as "a mongrel of French, American and negro blood." Edward Rose was a "breed" of Cherokee, Negro, and white ancestry. The common denominators seem to have been physical courage of the ultimate degree, an instinctive intelligence about wilderness ways, and a sense of self-reliance bordering on the anarchic.

Insecurity was the price of the trappers' great freedom. Death grinned at them from behind every tree or clump of willows. A Blackfoot arrow, a charging grizzly bear, a boiling whirlpool were familiar hazards. Starvation was also a possibility, and the trapper had to know how to live off the land. Badgers,

The mountain man Joseph Walker and his squaw. From a painting by Alfred Jacob Miller. Source: Walters Art Gallery.

Moonlight camp scene. From a painting by Alfred Jacob Miller. Source: Walters Art Gallery.

mountain goats, and skunks were less than tasty, but they had to make do when buffalo was scarce. Sometimes no game at all could be found. Then the trapper tried to boil and eat buffalo hides or the soles of his moccasins.

The trappers went into the mountains during the prime hunting seasons, which were late fall and early spring. Their equipment was well adapted to the environment of peaks and plains. The "plains rifle," usually one made by Jacob Hawken of St. Louis, was a shortened version of the Kentucky rifle. The buckskin suit and the scalping knife were copied from the Indians. The iron traps, however, were superior to any Indian hunting device. These were placed at likely spots in the mountain streams, being baited with a glandular substance called castorum. When sprung, the trap pinned the beaver to the river bottom and drowned him. The mountain man worked his trap lines from canoes when possible, but in shallower streams he had to undergo a numbing foot bath by wading out and retrieving his catch. The skins were stretched on willow hoops for drying, and were then tied up in hundred-pound packs. The season's catch was taken out of the mountains by horse or in "bull boats" fashioned of buffalo hides. After grading and further processing at St. Louis or Montreal, most of the pelts were shipped to Europe.

While engaged in their business, the trappers were also of necessity explorers. Jed Smith wrote of his 1827 trip to California: "I of course expected to find Beaver which with us hunters is a primary object but I was also led on by the love of novelty common to all which is much increased by the pursuit of its gratification." Most of the mountain men were blessesd with photographic minds. As Capt. J. W. Gunnison said of Jim Bridger: "With a buffalo skin and a piece of charcoal he will map out any portion of this immense region, and delini-ate mountains, streams, and the circular valleys called 'holes' with wonderful accuracy." It is not surprising that the trappers were employed as guides after the decline of the fur trade. Vignettes of a few of the more noteworthy trapper-explorers follow:

Jim Bridger. An unlettered blacksmith's apprentice, Bridger answered Ashley's advertisement and became a full-fledged mountain man in short order. In the fall of 1824, while serving with an Ashley-Henry party, he was the first white man to see the Great Salt Lake. In 1830 he became one of the principals of the Rocky Mountain Fur Company, and led trapping brigades all over the country between the Canadian border and southern Colorado. In 1843, after the decline of the trade, he built Fort Bridger in Wyoming as a way station on the Oregon Trail. There he and his Indian wife, affectionately referred to as Dang-Yore-Hide, entertained travelers until Mormons forced the closing of the post. The visitors often asked the former mountain man naive questions about his experiences. The stories he told, though well known to most trappers, have come to be known collectively as "Old Jim Bridger's Lies." They constituted a body of tall tales featuring petrified birds, glass mountains, and alarm-clock canyons. By the time Bridger died at his farm near Kansas City in 1881, he was being referred to as the "Daniel Boone of the Rockies."

Kit Carson. Of typical Kentucky-Missouri stock, Carson ran away from his job as a saddler's apprentice in 1826 and joined a wagon train for Santa Fe. The short, bandy-legged youth had a pleasing personality, and was signed on as a trapper for Ewing Young's California expedition in 1829. Thereafter "Kit" ranged over much of the mountain west, participating in some of the most memorable Indian fights of the period. In 1834 he formed his own band of in-dependent trappers, the "Carson Men." After serving as a hunter for Bent's Fort on the Arkansas, he was hired as a guide by Lt. John Charles Frémont. Carson went on the first three of Frémont's far-western expeditions in the 1840s, and the resulting publicity made him a national celebrity. He was an officer in the Mexi-can War, and an Indian agent at Taos during the 1850s. As an Army general in the Civil War his principal assignment was subduing the Navahos. At his death in 1867 he was still in the Army, widely respected despite the fact that he had never learned to write anything more than his own signature.

Jedediah Strong Smith.   Born in New York state, Smith was a Puritan in both religion and temperament. He had little interest in women, whiskey, or tobacco, and was thus something of an oddity among mountaineers. His literary ability, revealed in letters and fragments of a journal, also mark him as being above average. Yet he could lead men, and had a hard self-discipline that saved him more than once. As one of the first "Ashley men," he had several close brushes with death. Going west in 1823, he came face to face with a grizzly bear which attempted to take off his head with one bite. After a companion sewed his scalp and ears back on, Smith resumed his journey and in March of 1824 made the first westward crossing of South Pass. In 1826 he rang up another "first" by making an overland trip to California. A second trip in 1827 was marred by a Mojave Indian attack in which half of Smith's men were wiped out. He traveled north from California to Oregon, where he survived another massacre, and eventually made his way back to base camp near Salt Lake. These trips made Smith the most accomplished explorer of the Far West. His phenomenal luck finally ran out in 1831, when he was killed by Comanches along the Cimarron River.

Thomas Fitzpatrick.   A native of Ireland, Fitzpatrick acquired a rudimentary education that enabled him to make use of his high intelligence. In 1823 he was one of Ashley's men who survived an Arikara attack on the upper Missouri. In 1824 he accompanied Jed Smith in making an effective discovery of South Pass. He continued to be a highly talented leader of trapping parties until 1830, when in partnership with Bridger and others he formed the Rocky Mountain Fur Company. In 1832 Fitzpatrick was chased by Blackfeet near Pierre's Hole in Wyoming, a desperate game of hide-and-seek that turned his hair snow white. About the same time his left hand was mutilated by an exploding rifle barrel, a common accident in the mountains, and he was henceforth known to the Indians as "Broken Hand." In 1841 he guided the first emigrant party (Bartleson-Bidwell) to California, and served in a similar capacity with Frémont's second expedition of 1843 to 1844. Then until his death in 1854 he was an Indian agent, responsible for all tribes between Fort Laramie and Bent's Fort. He was a principal negotiator of the great Fort Laramie Treaty of 1851.

William H. Ashley

Thus William H. Ashley gathered together some capable men for his trading effort. Ashley himself was a typical self-made man of the period, and had been a miner, land speculator, and merchant before becoming a trapper-trader. His first two expeditions were hit by bad luck. In 1822 a boat sent to supply Andrew Henry's field party on the Yellowstone was wrecked with all of the $10,000 cargo being lost. In 1823 his keelboats were attacked at the Arikara villages and fifteen men were killed. These setbacks cooled the partners' enthusiasm for the upper Missouri, and Ashley shifted his operations to the central Rockies. His introduction there of what he called the "rendavoze" changed the pattern of the mountain trade.

The chief advantage of the rendezvous system was that it was a cheaper and more dependable method of getting furs. Expensive forts did not have to be maintained, for the roving trappers simply brought their catch to some preselected location in June or July. White hunters were more reliable than the Indians, and they could do a more efficient job of trapping the streams. Ashley held the first rendezvous at Henry's Fork on the Green River in 1825. The manufactured goods which he brought out from St. Louis were exchanged for the trappers' "hairy bank notes." Ashley failed to bring any liquor to this rendezvous, a serious oversight which was corrected the next year. In fact, the annual meetings, sixteen of which were held up to 1840, were often bacchanals whose excesses shocked visiting missionaries. The shooting matches, horse races, and impromptu dances with the Indian maidens were sometimes interrupted by outburts of violence. Yet the sensational cavorting should not obscure the fact that the rendezvous introduced an economic arrangement which worked.

Competing Companies

Ashley's profits were so great that he was able to retire from business and go into politics. His successors carried his system more widely into the mountains, and indeed all the way to California. First in the line of descent was Smith, Jackson & Sublette, to whom Ashley sold his stock of merchandise in July of 1826. William L. Sublette handled business affairs, David E. Jackson was in charge of trapping, and Jed Smith concerned himself primarily with exploring for new beaver territory west of the Salt Lake. Smith's trips of 1826 and 1827 opened a route from the lake to California. The other two leaders also did their share of pathfinding: Sublette's party, for example, was the first to see the main geyser area of Yellowstone Park. The partners were so financially successful, despite Smith's troubles on the coast, that by 1830 they were ready to turn their business over to others.

The interests were sold in August to Thomas Fitzpatrick, Jim Bridger, and three others, who operated under the name of the Rocky Mountain Fur Company. The brigades of this company were responsible for exploring much of the country north to the Three Forks and west to the Salmon. They made known the sources of the Platte, Green, and Snake Rivers while fighting off Blackfoot warriors and competing trappers. The RMF partners lacked business experience, however, and soon found themselves in debt to their supplier. The financial difficulties caused the company to be dissolved at the summer rendezvous of 1834.

From this point on, the mountain trade was dominated by Astor's mammoth American Fur Company.

During the height of intercompany competition in 1832 and 1833, the RMF had to meet the challenge not only of Astor's men but of small independent organizations. Among these was Gantt and Blackwell, who came into the field in 1831 but lasted only a year. Then there was Nathaniel J. Wyeth, a Boston ice dealer who made two brave attempts to enter the business, in 1832 and in 1834. On the second of these ventures he built Fort Hall on the Snake River, but he was badly outclassed in competition with the giants and had to sell out to the Hudson's Bay Company. One independent operation that has been saved from obscurity by the pen of Washington Irving was that of Capt. Benjamin Louis Eulalie Bonneville.

Bonneville, born in Paris and educated at West Point, was granted a leave of absence from the Army to undertake a western journey. The trip was presumably to add to official knowledge of the area, but it was to be financed by trapping and trading. Alfred Seaton, a New York fur dealer, was the most important of several associates who backed the venture. Bonneville's party of 110 men left Fort Osage in Missouri on May 1, 1832. They had twenty wagons, the first wagon train to be taken through South Pass. On the Green River the men built a rough fortification, referred to by rival trappers as "Fort Nonsense" and "Bonneville's Folly." Bonneville himself did not do much exploring during his 3 years in the mountains, nor did he have any success with the trapping. He does shine in the reflected glory of others, however, for he sent Joseph Reddeford Walker on a trip that went along the Humboldt River and across the Sierras into California. Bonneville also prepared a reliable map which gave the War Department a clearer picture of the Rocky Mountain and Great Basin area. This map was based (without acknowledgment) partly upon an earlier one drawn by Jed Smith, and the captain's conceit in naming the Salt Lake as "Lake Bonneville" drew fire from many mountain veterans. On balance it does appear that the captain was a "history-made man." Without the assistance of Irving's *Adventures of Captain Bonneville* (1837), he would have been remembered simply as an ineffectual career man who enjoyed vacationing in the mountains.

American Fur Company

Meanwhile the American Fur Company moved with the slow but inexorable strength of a glacier, absorbing all competitors first on the Missouri and then in the Rockies. It even opened trade with the Blackfeet, through the good offices of a trapper named Berger who had lived among them for a time. In 1831 a band of Piegans was brought to the company's Fort Union at the mouth of the Yellowstone, and they agreed to the construction of a trading post on the Maria's River. The company also went after the mountain trade, with no scruples about the methods used. Their brigade leaders simply dogged the footsteps of

Bridger and the other RMF men to find the most productive beaver streams. Large quantities of liquor were sold to the Indians, despite a congressional law (July 9, 1832) prohibiting this practice. The usual recipe for trade whiskey was: 1 quart of alcohol; 1 pound of black chewing tobacco; 1 handful of red peppers; 1 bottle of ginger; 1 quart of black molasses; Missouri River water. This beverage, though revolting, was probably less harmful to the Indians than straight alcohol would have been.

John Jacob Astor retired in 1834. He sold his Western Department to Pratte, Chouteau and Company of St. Louis, although the organization was still referred to as the American Fur Company. Pierre Chouteau, Jr. was the dominant figure in the concern, and he continued to send caravans to the mountains until the end of the rendezvous system in 1840. The change in fashion from beaver to silk hats during the 30s resulted in a gradual decline of beaverskin prices. In addition, the beaver were being trapped out and were much harder to find in many areas. The American Fur Company and other outfits consequently started trading more and more in buffalo skins and robes. Since these were procured principally from Indians, the mountain men found themselves out of jobs. They became guides, farmers, ranchers, storekeepers, and in some cases (notably that of Thomas L. "Pegleg" Smith), horse rustlers.

Hudson's Bay Company

The American trapping parties not only engaged in dog-eat-dog competition with each other, they also tangled with the Hudson's Bay Company. Parliament in 1821 had ordered a merger of the Northwest Company and the HBC to end the virtual civil war that existed between them. This move created a monolithic organization that not only gathered more furs at cheaper prices, but was also strong enough to rebuff American efforts to trade in the far Northwest. In fact, the company's policy was to trap the Utah-Idaho-Oregon region so thoroughly that a "Fur Desert" would be created. This policy would serve political as well as economic objectives, since the American mountaineers were regarded as unofficial agents of national expansion. Sir George Simpson, Governor-General of the HBC, put the British case quite well when he wrote in 1826: "The greatest and best protection we can have from opposition is keeping the country closely hunted, as the first step that the American Government will take towards Colonization is through their Indian Traders and if the country becomes exhausted in Fur bearing animals they can have no inducement to proceed thither."

Dr. John McLoughlin was put in charge of this effort in 1824. Though noted for his integrity and humanity, the doctor was a hulking 6-foot-4-inch giant "such as I should not like to meet in a dark Night in one of the bye lanes in the neighbourhood of London." He did an effective job of expanding the British trade in all directions. His headquarters were at Fort Vancouver, built on the north bank of the Columbia opposite the site of today's Portland. The key man in the company's field operations was bullnecked Peter Skene Ogden, the *enfant terrible* of the British trapping fraternity. As head of the so-called Snake River Brigade between 1824 and 1830, he made six trips that were important for far-western exploration.

Ogden's first expedition, in 1824 to 1825, took him to the Bear Lake region of Utah. The brigade was within about 30 miles of the Salt Lake, which Ogden did not visit. While in the area he encountered a band of American trappers under Johnson Gardner. Gardner, waving a flag, roared that Ogden was trespassing on American soil. This *pronunciamento* overlooked the fact that both parties were actually in Mexican territory. To add insult to ignorance, Gardner enticed a number of the HBC men to bring their furs and join his outfit. But Ogden surmounted this challenge and went on to make more significant explorations in the following years. During the winter of 1828-1829 he discovered Humboldt River, first called the Mary's, along which wagons would one day travel to California. Then in 1829 to 1830 he went from the Columbia all the way down to the mouth of the Colorado, and came back through the great Central Valley of California. Although Ogden moved to another job in 1830, HBC parties continued to hunt along both the Sacramento and San Joaquin Rivers until 1843.

The Southwest

American trappers also penetrated the Spanish Southwest during the same period. Following news of Pike's expedition, adventurous traders attempted to open a St. Louis-Santa Fe trade. Robert McKnight and James Baird led a small party to Santa Fe in the spring of 1812. They were rewarded by being thrown into prison, where they remained until 1820. In 1817 Auguste P. Chouteau and Jules De Mun were trapping the headwaters of the Arkansas when they were arrested by Spanish troops. Their furs worth $30,000 were confiscated and they spent 48 days in the *calabozo* at Santa Fe, suffering the indignity of having to eat beans without salt, before being sent home. With the Mexican Revolution in 1821, however, the restrictive Spanish policy was overthrown. Sante Fe and Taos became favored resorts of American trappers, who came by the hundreds with or without Mexican passports. They drank the "Taos lightning," elbowed aside natives at the fandangos, and laughed at the government's regulations and at its puny military force. They also ranged to all points of the compass in search of pelts, and opened new trails between New Mexico and California.

Two of the more prominent trappers in this area were William Wolfskill and Ewing Young. In the spring of 1824 they led a party north to the San Juan and other tributaries of the Colorado, returning to Santa Fe with $10,000 worth of skins. By 1826 various independent bands were operating along Arizona's Gila River as far west as its juncture with the Colorado. And between 1827 and 1830 no less than four American trapping parties crossed from New Mexico to the California coast. The best known of these, in 1827, included Sylvester and James Ohio Pattie, the latter of whom published a *Narrative* of the trip in 1831. Ewing Young also braved the Mojave Desert in 1829 and worked his way up the San Joaquin Valley, encountering Peter Skene Ogden along the way. A record of this trip has been preserved in the autobiography of Kit Carson, then an apprentice mountaineer. In the winter of 1830-1831 another party led by Wolfskill and George Yount pioneered the Old Spanish Trail from Santa Fe to Los Angeles. This was no more than a pack trail, parts of which had been used by Spanish traders in earlier years. It crossed the Colorado and Green Rivers to the Sevier in southern Utah, followed the Virgin down to the Mojave Desert, then ran along the Mojave River and through Cajon Pass to San Gabriel Mission.

The infiltration of American trappers, along with merchants who were developing the St. Louis-Santa Fe trade during the 20s and 30s, represented in the long run a threat to the interests of the Mexican government. The same process was occurring in the provinces of Texas and California, yet few officials worried about the possible political consequences. In the free-and-easy atmosphere of New Mexico, the immediate benefits of American trade dispelled apprehensions about what might happen in the future. And after all, American activity in the Southwest had been of short duration compared with the long record of Spanish involvement there.

Selected Readings   The standard work on the subject is Hiram M. Chittenden, *The American Fur Trade of the Far West*, 2 vols. (New York, 1935). Paul C. Phillips, *The Fur Trade*, 2 vols. (Norman, 1961), emphasizes business and commercial affairs. Bernard DeVoto, *Across the Wide Missouri* (Boston, 1947), deals with the peak years of the mountain fur trade, 1832-1838.

The origins of St. Louis are described briefly in Richard C. Wade, *The Urban Frontier* (Chicago, 1959); for more detailed information consult J. F. McDermott, *The Early Histories of St. Louis* (St. Louis, 1952). Spanish fur trading on the Missouri is described in Abraham P. Nasatir (ed.), *Before Lewis and Clark: Documents Illustrating the History of the Missouri, 1785-1804*, 2 vols. (St. Louis, 1952). Information on John Evans is in David Williams, "John Evans' Strange Journey," *American Historical Review*, vol. 54 (January, April, 1949); Bernard DeVoto, *The Course of Empire* (Boston, 1952), has much on Evans and on other Spanish and American explorers prior to 1807. John S. Galbraith, *The Hudson's Bay Company as an Imperial Factor, 1821-1869* (Berkeley, 1957), is scholarly. Douglas Mackay, *The Honourable Company* (Indianapolis, 1936), is a satisfactory general history, while Edwin E. Rich, *The History of the Hudson's Bay Company, 1670-1870*, 2 vols. (London, 1958), is definitive. The story of "the company's" rival is well told in Marjorie W. Campbell, *The Northwest Company* (New York, 1957). See also Kenneth A. Spaulding (ed.), Alexander Ross, *Fur Traders of the Far West* (Norman, 1956). An edition of Alexander Mackenzie's journal is in Walter Sheppe (ed.), *First Man West* (Berkeley, 1962).

An indispensable biography is Richard E. Oglesby, *Manuel Lisa and the Opening of the Missouri Fur Trade* (Norman, 1963). The definitive Colter biography is Burton Harris, *John Colter* (New York, 1952). Kenneth W. Porter, *John Jacob Astor,*

Business Man, 2 vols. (Cambridge, 1931), is scholarly. John Upton Terrell, *Furs by Astor* (New York, 1963), is an informative and lively popular account. David Lavender, *Fist in the Wilderness* (Garden City, 1964), deals primarily with the Great Lakes but sheds light on the American Fur Company's Missouri operations. The classic account of the Astoria enterprise is Washington Irving's *Astoria,* originally published in 1836, of which the best modern edition has been edited by Edgeley W. Todd (Norman, 1964). The story of the returning Astorians is told in Robert Stuart's journal, which has been edited by Philip A. Rollins, *The Discovery of the Oregon Trail* (New York, 1935), an edition now superseded by Kenneth A. Spaulding (ed.), *On the Oregon Trail: Robert Stuart's Journal of Discovery* (Norman, 1953). Ora B. Peake, *A History of the United States Indian Factory System, 1795-1822* (Denver, 1954), is written in a wooden style but covers the major points of the government system. Francis Paul Prucha, *American Indian Policy in the Formative Years* (Cambridge, 1962), is quite detailed.

LeRoy R. Hafen (ed.), *The Mountain Men and the Fur Trade of the Far West,* 5 vols. (Glendale, 1965-1968), includes a brief summary of the trade and biographical sketches of rank-and-file mountain men. Stanley Vestal, *Mountain Men* (Boston, 1937), is a popular survey. A classic first-hand account is George F. Ruxton, *Life in the Far West,* first published in 1848 and most recently edited by LeRoy Hafen (Norman, 1950). Standard biographies of noted mountaineers are J. Cecil Alter, *James Bridger* (Salt Lake City, 1925); Edwin L. Sabin, *Kit Carson Days,* 2 vols. (New York, 1935); Dale L. Morgan, *Jedediah Smith and the Opening of the West* (Indianapolis, 1953); and LeRoy Hafen and W. J. Ghent, *Broken Hand, The Life Story of Thomas Fitzpatrick* (Denver, 1931). Further information on Smith is in Maurice S. Sullivan (ed.), *The Travels of Jedediah Smith* (Santa Ana, Calif., 1934); and in Harrison C. Dale (ed.), *The Ashley-Smith Explorations and the Discovery of a Central Route to the Pacific, 1822-1829* (Glendale, 1941). For Ashley, see Dale L. Morgan (ed.), *The West of William H. Ashley* (Denver, 1963), a monumental collection of letters and diaries.

Edgeley W. Todd (ed.), *The Adventures of Captain Bonneville* (Norman, 1961), is the best modern edition of Irving's classic. John E. Sunder, *The Fur Trade of the Upper Missouri, 1840-1865* (Norman, 1965), details a neglected subject. Gloria Griffen Cline, *Exploring the Great Basin* (Norman, 1963), has much information on Peter Skene Ogden's travels. Documentary information is in Edwin E. Rich (ed.), *Peter Skene Ogden's Snake Country Journals,* 2 vols. (London, 1950), and in Frederick Merk (ed.), *Fur Trade and Empire, George Simpson's Journal* (Cambridge, 1931). William Goetzmann, "The Mountain Man as Jacksonian Man," *American Quarterly,* vol. 15 (Fall, 1963), analyzes the careers of 446 trappers. William E. Holston, "The Diet of the Mountain Men," *California Historical Society Quarterly,* vol. 42 (December, 1963), describes the effects of an all-meat diet. Robert Glass Cleland, *This Reckless Breed of Men* (New York, 1952), is the foundation work on the Southwestern fur trade. LeRoy R. and Ann W. Hafen, *The Old Spanish Trail* (Glendale, 1954), is valuable.

XII. The Spanish Frontier

Early Spanish exploration in the present American Southwest was motivated by various economic and geographical fantasies. Fabulous empires, known under the names of Cíbola and Quivira, were believed to be located in the northern interior. There too would be found the Strait of Anián, a Spanish version of the Northwest Passage, and its tributary rivers including the Rio Buenaventura. Somewhere to the northwest, "on the right hand of the Indies," was the island of California, populated by Amazons under Queen Calafia. The magnetic pull of this "Northern Mystery" drew a succession of Spanish explorers from Mexico. The history of their activities is in part a story of the progressive destruction of the cherished myths one after another. Yet the spirit of the age was romantic rather than practical, and so the dreams were abandoned with great reluctance.

The Seven Cities and Quivira The successes of Hernando Cortes in central Mexico prompted others to believe that they could duplicate his feats by finding an "Otro Mexico." Even as Cortes himself continued to direct seaborne explorations of the Gulf of California, eager noblemen were petitioning Viceroy Antonio Mendoza for permission to undertake a land expedition in the same general direction. The return of Cabeza de Vaca had aroused great interest in the New Mexico region, and so Mendoza decided in 1538 to send out a preliminary reconnaissance which would check de Vaca's story. Father Marcos de Niza, a Franciscan known to subsequent history as "the Lying Monk," was placed in charge of the trip. Accompanying him as a guide was the Negro Estevanico, survivor of Cabeza de Vaca's journey, and a body of Christian Indians. Father Marcos intended to find the Seven Cities of Cíbola. The ancient Spanish legend told of seven bishops who had fled from Moorish invaders in the eleventh century. They had taken the church treasure with them to a region in the Atlantic

195

and had built "Seven Cities of the Antilles" whose streets were paved with gold and whose walls were studded with turquoise.

During the northward trip Estevanico went ahead of the main party, sending back encouraging messages, and finally reached the first of the Seven Cities. He was actually at Hawikuh, the principal Zuñi pueblo, located on today's Arizona-New Mexico border. But there the Negro's overbearing attitude and his demands for tribute aroused the Indians, and they killed him. Because of this episode, Father Marcos himself never reached "Cíbola," though he claimed that from a nearby hill he had seen its golden walls gleaming in the sun. This misrepresentation, passed on to Viceroy Mendoza when Marcos returned in the fall of 1539, led to the organization of the greatest Spanish *entrada* into the Southwest. The goals of the expedition were the Seven Cities and the equally wealthy kingdom of Quivira.

Coronado

Francisco Vasquez de Coronado was thirty years old, and the governor of Nueva Galicia province, when Mendoza chose him to lead the northern expedition in 1540. Contemporary accounts speak of Coronado as a courageous and soldierly individual, and yet one who was remarkably gentle for a *conquistador*. Many of the rootless aristocrats hanging around Mexico City were glad enough to sign up for the trip, since conquest of the Seven Cities would presumably yield unlimited riches. More important, they were willing to sink their own money into the expedition, which was privately financed although it had royal approval. Thus it was a lavishly equipped party which left Compostela in February of 1540 and followed the West Coast Corridor north: 250 spade-bearded noblemen in buckskins and armor breastplates, several hundred Indian allies, and some 1,500 animals. Coronado's eventual itinerary of Cíbola—Tiguex—the Buffalo Plains—and Quivira took him through parts of Arizona, New Mexico, Texas, Oklahoma, and Kansas.

At Cíbola the first of the Spaniards' dreams was shattered. The Zuñi village was not constructed of gold, as the suddenly unpopular Father Marcos had claimed, but was simply a little stone pueblo "all crumpled together." But Coronado remained optimistic. To search for the elusive golden cities he sent out a side expedition which visited the Hopi pueblos and the Grand Canyon in Arizona. The captain-general moved his main force to Tiguex, a group of pueblos located on the Rio Grande just north of modern Albuquerque. Spanish levies of food and clothing from these towns resulted in the Tiguex War of 1540 to 1541, the first of several that the Spaniards had to fight over the next few generations before the Pueblo Indians were tamed. After subduing the natives, Coronado decided to explore the "Buffalo Plains" to the east in search of the rumored kingdom of Quivira. An Indian slave named El Turco—"the Turk"—spoon-fed Coronado with lies about this kingdom. He maintained that Tatarrax, the Lord

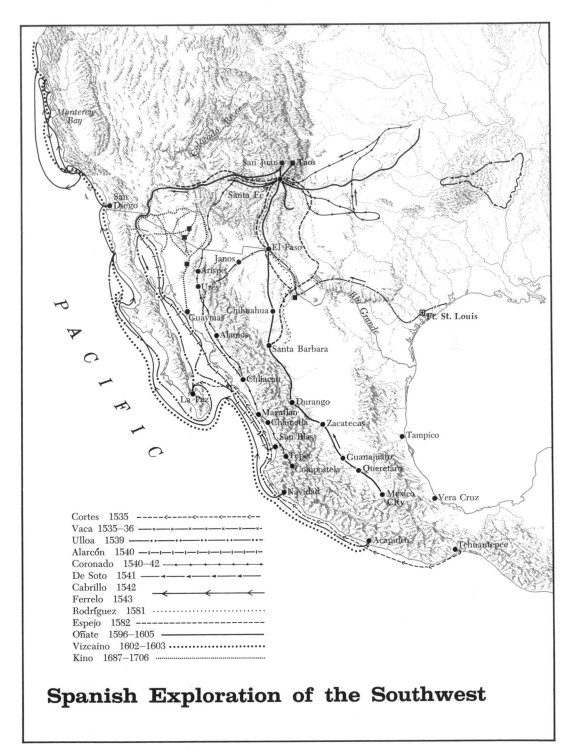

Monterey
Bay

San
Diego

San Juan ● Taos

Santa Fe

El Paso

Janos
Arispe
Ures

Guaymas

Chihuahua

Alamos

Santa Barbara

P A C I F I C

Culiacan

La Paz

Durango

Mazatlan
Chametla   Zacatecas
San Blas

Tepec   Guanajuato
Compostela   Queretaro

Navidad   Mexico
                City

Acapulco

Tampico

Ft. St. Louis

Colorado River

Rio Grande

Vera Cruz

Tehuantepec

Cortes   1535   – – – ‹– – – ‹– – – ‹– – –‹–
Vaca 1535–36   –x–x–x–x–x–x–x–x–x–
Ulloa 1539   ————••————••——
Alarcón 1540   –ı–ı–ı–ı–ı–ı–ı–ı–ı–
Coronado 1540–42   —•—•—•—•—•—•—
De Soto 1541   ——‹——‹——‹——‹——
Cabrillo 1542   ⟵———⟵———⟵———
Ferrelo 1543
Rodríguez 1581   ....
Espejo 1582   – – – – – – – – – – – – – –
Oñate 1596–1605   ————————————
Vizcaino 1602–1603   •••••••••••••••••••••••
Kino 1687–1706   ....

Spanish Exploration of the Southwest

of Quivira, took naps under a tree hung with golden bells. Another of his whoppers was that the Quivira River contained fish as big as horses. In the spring of 1541 the captain set out for this end-of-the-rainbow province, taking the loquacious El Turco along as a guide.

The Indians at Tiguex hoped that El Turco would be able to lead the Spaniards so far onto the plains that their horses would give out and they would die. Travel in the region had its dangers, and the plan might have succeeded if Coronado had been less alert. The Spaniards met wandering tribes of Indians, and of them Coronado remarked: "I went wherever they led me until we reached some plains as bare of landmarks as if we were surrounded by the sea." Among the few landmarks were distant cliffs which gave the appearance of stone fortifications, and hence the area was called the Llano Estacado or Stockaded Plains. At Palo Duro Canyon in the Texas Panhandle, Coronado sent the main part of his army back to Tiguex, while he rode north with thirty men to find Quivira. In August of 1541 he reached his goal, which turned out to be a village of Wichita Indians living along the Smoky Hill River in Kansas. The savages occupied grass lodges rather than palaces, and among their less endearing customs was that of carrying buffalo intestines around their necks from which they drank the stomach juices when thirsty. At this point, amidst the shambles of the Quivira dream, El Turco's deviousness was finally recognized, and he was put to death by the garrote.

Coronado returned to Mexico the next year, reaching Culiacan in June of 1542. Since he had found neither gold nor silver, there was some muttering against him in Mexico City and an official inquiry was later held. Overlooked was the fact that he had made notable contributions to a knowledge of North American geography, particularly in obtaining a fairly accurate idea of the width of the continent. He had demonstrated that Spaniards could negotiate the plains as well as the mountain and mesa country. This was not surprising, since the bare and arid landscape was much like that of Spain itself. But the government made little use of Coronado's information. His reports were buried in the archives, and for 40 years there were no further attempts to explore the Rio Grande region.

Coastal Exploration

Efforts were also made to penetrate the Northern Mystery by seaborne expeditions from the west coast of Mexico. The goals of these voyages were discovery of the Strait of Anián, the Amazon Island, or any of the rich cities that were supposed to lie in that direction. The ships, usually built on the west coast and based at Navidad or Acapulco, were leaky craft manned by conscripts and other unfortunate landlubbers. Thus the captains often had to contend with mutinies as well as with hurricanes, uncharted shoals, and strong contrary winds from the northwest. Yet the picture of Pacific Coast geography was gradually put together by these redoubtable mariners.

Since Cortes was the organizer of early expeditions into the Gulf of California, it is understandable why its waters are called the Sea of Cortes. In 1533 one of his ships, captained by Fortún Jimenez, sailed up the Gulf and discovered the peninsula of Baja California. The survivors of the trip, however, reported the peninsula to be an island—a belief not dispelled until the explorations of Father Kino in 1702. In 1539 one of Cortes's last projects was the dispatch of another coastwise expedition commanded by Francisco de Ulloa. The captain reached the mouth of the Colorado, sailed down the leeward side of the peninsula, and went up its western side as far north as Cedros Island. In his diary, Ulloa first applied the word "California" to the peninsula. The term was taken from a popular novel by Garci Ordoñez Montalvo, *Las Sergas de Esplándian* (1508), where it was used to describe a mythical kingdom "close to the terrestrial paradise." On this island, ruled by the giant queen Calafia, the Spaniards expected to find not only voluptuous Amazons but a landscape sprinkled with pearls and gold. "Their arms were of gold," reads the novel, "and so was the harness of the wild beasts they tamed to ride; for in the whole island there was no metal but gold."

Viceroy Mendoza succeeded Cortes as the sponsor of coastal exploration when the latter returned to Spain in 1540. Two ships commanded by Hernando de Alarcón were sent up to the head of the Gulf, where they were to cooperate with Coronado's land expedition. In August of 1540 Alarcón ascended the Rio Colorado as far as the Gila junction. He concluded that California was a peninsula instead of an island, but his musings made little impact on the Spanish mapmakers. Mendoza himself believed that the Strait of Anián was located further up the California coast. He therefore outfitted two small ships and placed them under the command of Juan Rodriguez Cabrillo, who sailed from Navidad on June 27, 1542.

Captain Cabrillo, whose name translates rather unheroically as "little goat," was a skilled and courageous navigator. In 4 months he sailed the coast to 41° N latitude, near the Eel River in California, on the way discovering San Diego Bay, the Channel Islands, and Drake's Bay. Santa Monica Bay he called Bahia de los Fumos ("Bay of Smokes"), a name with contemporary validity, because thousands of Indian campfires created an ominous pall in the mountain basin. Cabrillo died of an infection on San Miguel Island, but his lieutenant, Bartolomé Ferrelo, sailed north again—perhaps as far as Oregon—and eventually got back to Navidad on April 14, 1543.

Spanish officials had little incentive for following up on Cabrillo's discoveries until Sir Francis Drake made his appearance on the Pacific in 1579. After raiding Spanish treasure ships off Peru, the notorious seadog started back to England by way of California. He landed at Drake's Bay, north of the Golden

Gate, and spent a month repairing his vessel *The Golden Hind.* The captain maintained cordial relations with the Miwok Indians, and left with them a brass plate proclaiming "New Albion" to be part of the English empire. The depredations of Drake and other English freebooters led the government at Mexico City to plan steps for the protection of their northwestern coast. In addition, it was widely believed that Drake had found the Strait of Anián, and the Spaniards were accordingly anxious to find and occupy its Pacific entrance before the English returned.

The principal voyage in this program was made by Sebastian Vizcaino in 1602. Sailing from Acapulco on May 5 with three ships, he had a slow voyage and did not reach San Diego until November 12. Vizcaino would have made a good press agent, since he had a fondness for superlatives. San Diego harbor he described as "the best to be found in all the South Sea." His description of Monterey Bay was so glowing that later Spanish explorers could not recognize the place when they found it. There Vizcaino claimed to have seen black cattle, pelicanlike animals, and "civilized" Indians of the Aztec type. The captain displayed less imagination in choosing names for landmarks. He simply used the name of the saint for that particular day, and thus California has San Diego, Santa Catalina, and Santa Barbara. Vizcaino departed from the text by naming Monterey after the viceroy who had sent him north; and while he was off hunting elk, the friars named the Carmel River valley after their own religious order. The trip also yielded a comparatively accurate map of the California coast, which Vizcaino explored as far north as Cape Mendocino. Yet after his return, there was little further activity in Alta California until 1769. The resources of New Spain were being used instead to support an advance into New Mexico.

New Mexico

Drake's raid inspired renewed Spanish activity in New Mexico, since his supposed discovery of the Strait of Anián required an outpost against further English expansion. Since Coronado's time the mining and ranching frontier had slowly advanced toward the region. The discovery of silver mines at Zacatecas and San Luis Potosi had brought more colonists to the north, and by the end of the century the line of settlement ran through what is now Chihuahua province. From 1580 to 1581 there had been a brief "rediscovery" of New Mexico. Father Augustin Rodriguez and a dozen companions visited the pueblos as far north as Taos and as far west as Zuñi, seeking converts to the church. Two other Franciscans who accompanied Rodriguez chose to remain with him in New Mexico, and all three met death at the hands of the Pueblo Indians. Then in 1582 a merchant-adventurer named Antonio Espejo, accompanied by a friar and fourteen soldiers, led an independent expedition up the Rio Grande to Taos. Espejo also rode west into Arizona, seeking rumored silver mines. This time an Indian tale was grounded in truth, for he found these mines in the mountains north of modern Prescott. Espejo's report on the economic possibilities in Nuevo Mexico inspired a flurry of proposals by various noblemen eager to undertake the conquest of the province. But the Crown chose to ignore all these offers until 1597, when it finally approved the colonization project of Don Juan de Oñate.

Oñate, a wealthy mine owner from Zacatecas, got his expedition under way in February of 1598. As Governor, he had charge of 130 soldier-colonists, 10 Franciscan friars, and large number of servants and Indians. He also took 83 wagons and 7,000 head of livestock. The long train wound its way up the Rio Grande to a point 30 miles north of modern Sante Fe. There Oñate took possession of New Mexico "and all adjoining provinces" for God, for King, and for himself. The pueblo that he built here was named San Juan de los Caballeros.

San Juan had an unhappy history. The Governor spent much of his time suppressing the Indians, who were ready to contest the foreigners' occupation of their country. A revolt at Acoma in 1599 was put down by a ruthless assault against that mesa fortress. All the surviving male captives over twenty-five had one foot cut off, while the women and children were bound to personal service. The severity of Oñate's punishments later got him into serious trouble with the royal government. There was also much dissatisfaction among the colonists, many of whom were more interested in gold prospecting than in farming. These troubles were revealed when Oñate led an expedition eastward toward Quivira in 1601. Upon his return from this wild-goose chase he found that most of the colonists and friars had deserted the town and started back to Mexico. In an attempt to restore his prestige, the Governor undertook a trip to the South Sea in 1604. On this journey he reexplored the routes taken by Coronado and Espejo, and eventually reached the Gulf of California.* The expedition diarist, Father Escobar, dutifully recorded more Indian tales about the Northern Mystery. Among these was that of a tribe whose men were totally bald, another which slept under water, and still another which had ears long enough to shelter five or six persons. But neither these fables nor the rediscovery of a route to the South Sea did much to save Oñate. In August of 1607 he was forced to resign in disgrace, and was later tried for the crimes committed during his conquest.

In 1610 Santa Fe was founded as the new capital, its location being chosen primarily for reasons of defense. By 1630 the villa had a garrison of 250 men, and was the center of Spanish power in the Southwest. New Mexico itself became a missionary field for the Franciscans. This effort was supported by the Crown, despite bitter church-state conflicts in the province and the problems of supplying the missions over a rugged 1,500-mile trail from Mexico City. But the friars made slow progress in winning converts until the veneer of Spanish cul-

*On the return trip Oñate carved his name on the El Morro Inscription Rock, a famous landmark near Zuñi.

ture was suddenly ripped away by the Pueblo Revolt of 1680. The Indians, led by the medicine man Popé, resented the strict religious control as well as the personal services which they were required to render. Ironically, the rebels took clappers from mission bells and made them into spears for use against the Christians. The 2,500 Spaniards had to flee down the Rio Grande to El Paso del Norte, a nascent community of adobe huts strung alongside a mission which had been founded in 1660. Reconquest of the province by Don Diego de Vargas in 1692 made possible a solidification of Spanish control. Thereafter the ranchos were gradually reestablished on the upper tributaries of the Rio Grande. During the eighteenth century and down to the American period there was a slow growth of the Spanish population and of agricultural production, which was based primarily on sheep ranching and the raising of irrigated corn and beans.

The French Threat

In the eighteenth century the scene of Spanish frontier activity shifted to the east and southeast of Santa Fe. Texas was a region of fertile soil and benign climate which had attracted small parties of missionaries and traders since the middle of the seventeenth century. But both the New Mexico and Texas frontiers were exposed to two dangers: French traders and Indian marauders. The French threat was often more imagined than real, but it was sufficient to keep Spanish officials jittery. The first major shock was LaSalle's appearance at Matagorda Bay in 1685. News of this landing, gained from captured French privateers, gave it the dimensions of a full-scale invasion. A Spanish patrol finally located the ruins of LaSalle's "Fort St. Louis," as well as two sun-blackened Frenchmen living as slaves of the Indians, in the spring of 1689. This was an anticlimactic episode, but the possibility of further French incursions led to the planting of a mission at San Francisco de Tejas on the Neches River in northeastern Texas. The outpost, however, had to be abandoned in 1693 because of Indian hostility.

The Spanish advanced to another point on the Rio Grande in 1699 when they established the presidio of San Juan Bautista near Eagle Pass. To this post in 1704 came Louis de St. Denis, a young Frenchman sent across Texas by the Governor of Louisiana to open trade with the Spanish provinces. The brassy intruder faced a long prison term, but he talked his way out of the predicament and later married the presidio commander's granddaughter. In fact, St. Denis led a Spanish colonizing expedition east to the Nacogdoches region in the spring of 1716. His was one of a half dozen presidio-mission outposts established that year between the Neches and Red Rivers in an attempt to counter French expansionism.

Yet the French traders continued to enjoy much success among the Indians along the Red and Arkansas Rivers. Unlike the Spanish, they did not try to settle the tribesmen into fixed villages or harry them into becoming Christians. They were content to follow the nomads, exchanging brandy and guns for buffalo robes and horses. They also persisted in their attempt to open up trade with the Spanish provinces. The boldest effort of this type was made by the Mallet brothers, Paul and Pierre, in the spring of 1739. Starting from Illinois with a dozen companions and a pack train of trading goods, they went along the Platte River and then dropped down through southeastern Colorado and into Santa Fe. Though welcomed by the residents of the pueblo, their proposal to open a regular trade (French manufactured goods for Spanish silver) was officially disapproved, and they were ordered deported. The brothers then returned to French territory by way of the Canadian River. Yet a surreptitious trade was carried on for the next 20 years by bribing of officials. Santa Fe was too far from Mexico City for its residents to resist the temptation of foreign goods. Thus the French continued to press upon New Spain's northern borderlands until 1763. In that year all grounds of dispute were removed by the transfer of Louisiana to Spain, which thus became the sole colonial power in the Southwest.

Indian Barrier

The Indians were a more serious threat to the Spanish frontier than the French traders. In fact they proved to be an insuperable obstacle to an advance out onto the Plains. The Comanches and Apaches became implacable foes of the Spaniards during the eighteenth century, but other tribes were also troublesome. In the summer of 1720, for example, Capt. Pedro de Villasur rode up to the North Platte to demonstrate Spanish military prowess by punishing the Pawnees for their alleged friendship with the French. His force was routed by the Indians, who were said to have been trained in tactics by the French. In Texas, the traditional presidios and missions were ineffective without a thick population and a strong army to support them. Indeed, nowhere in America had missionary work been such a complete failure. Typical of the fate awaiting these outposts was that of the Apache mission established on the San Saba River in 1757. This overture to their enemies enraged the Comanches, who destroyed the mission within a year. To avenge the insult, a 500-man punitive expedition under Col. Diego Parilla was dispatched in the summer of 1759. It was flattened by the Comanches on the Red River.

A cold-eyed survey of the situation by the Marquis de Rubí in 1767 resulted in a contraction of the Texas frontier by hundreds of miles. San Antonio de Bexar, where a villa and mission had been built in 1718, was strengthened to become the key outpost north of the Rio Grande. The province of Nuevo Santander, embracing the coastal region stretching from Tampico to the San Antonio River, could be settled in the 1740s and 1750s only because it was safely outside the territory of the hostile tribes. But central and northern Texas remained the undisputed habitat of the Comanches. In their movement south this tribe pushed the Apaches into the mountains of New Mexico, where they in turn attacked the settlements along the Rio Grande. There the menacing dust cloud on the horizon sent the farmer and his family running for their thick-walled adobe ranchhouse, where they manned the loopholes with ancient muskets and prayed for God's help against the heathen foe.

Pimeria Alta

While brown-robed Franciscans labored along the Rio Grande, black-robed Jesuits were pushing their own mission frontier into northern Sonora and southern Arizona. In Spanish and Mexican times there was no province called "Arizona." The high lands of the Pima Indians, bounded on the north by the Gila and on the west by the Colorado, were referred to as Pimeria Alta. During the seventeenth century the Jesuits were responsible for developing the present provinces of Durango, Chihuahua, Sinaloa, Sonora, and Baja California. They advanced along the West Coast Corridor of Mexico, building a series of missions which became steppingstones to the northern wilderness. In this region they encountered a climate and terrain which were as much a test of physical stamina as of religious zeal. The deserts of upper Sonora and Arizona had blast-furnace temperatures, an overabundance of scorpions and sidewinders, and waterless trails to which the missionaries gave such names as El Camino del Diablo. Yet by 1700 the dedicated sons of Loyola had left their footprints on this vast cactus patch and had established the first mission in today's Arizona.

The most accomplished of the Jesuits working on this particular borderland was Father Eusebio Kino, who is remembered as an explorer, mapmaker, and historian. Born in Italy, educated in Germany, and taking his vows in Spain, Kino exemplified the cosmopolitan nature of the Catholic missionary effort in his era. Kino entered Pimeria Alta in 1687 when he founded the mother mission of Dolores, located about 120 miles south of present Tucson. There he worked tirelessly over the next dozen years to build a network of missions to the north and west. By 1700 he was convinced that the Pimas and Papagos of southern Arizona were ready for Christianity, and his efforts resulted in the founding of San Xavier del Bac. This adobe mission, 9 miles from Tucson, eventually became one of the finest specimens of Spanish colonial architecture. Within 2 years, two other missions (Tumacacori and Guevavi) were established on Arizona's Santa Cruz River. In 1701 and 1702 Kino undertook major exploratory trips to the Colorado and the Gulf of California. These journeys confirmed his belief that California was a peninsula, and it is so shown on the widely used map which he published in 1705.

After Kino's death among the Pimas in 1711, the Jesuit effort lagged. A succession of German-born missionaries attempted to hold the frontier line, but they faced the ever-present threat of Apache attack or a "converts" rebellion. It is not surprising that the missions in this region were usually built as fortresses, complete with military towers and defensive parapets. A presidio was built at Tubac in 1752, but the government was never able to safeguard the missionaries until it bought off the Apaches with subsidies in the 1790s. Hence the missions were in a precarious state at the time of the expulsion of the Jesuits in 1767. But the Arizona frontier seemed to attract unusually capable men, for Francisco Garcés became the resident father at San Xavier del Bac in 1768. This Franciscan undertook a number of expeditions that helped make known the approaches to California.

Alta California

The permanent settlement of Alta or Upper California in 1769 was undertaken for both negative and positive reasons. It was in part a reaction against the Russians, who were hunting sea otter on the Aleutian Islands and whose further progress down the coast would menace Spanish claims. Thus garrisons had to be established at two strategic locations: San Diego and Monterey. On the positive side, the colonization project was to extend the Spanish dominions and establish the Catholic faith by the usual mission method. The whole program was formulated and promoted by José de Gálvez, the energetic Visitador-General of New Spain. His field commanders were Don Gaspar de Portolá, the Governor of Lower California, and Junipero Serra, president of the Franciscan missions there.

The staging area was at Loreto on the peninsula, and there Galvez gathered 220 men who were sent north in four divisions, two by sea and two by land. The major overland party set out in May of 1769, reaching San Diego the next month. The sea expedition was so decimated by scurvy that the further trip from San Diego to Monterey had to be made by land. Portolá left San Diego on July 14 with sixty-seven walking skeletons. The record of this trip is preserved in the diary of Father Juan Crespi, surely one of the most observant of the Spanish padres. While the party rested to celebrate the jubilee of Our Lady of Los Angeles, he noted that the surrounding area "has all the requisites for a large settlement." The men lived on antelope, encountered huge bears (*brutos ferocísimos*), and affixed place-names to the new land. The sight of a Cañalino Indian making a canoe suggested Carpinteria, while the killing of a sea gull was honored by "Gaviota Pass." The party worked its way up the coast and struggled across the rugged Santa Lucia Mountains into the Salinas Valley. Portolá did not recognize Monterey Bay, being misled by Vizcaino's over-enthusiastic description of it. So he sent some of his men inland near the present Moss Landing, and they crossed the Coast Range and explored in the vicinity of Palo Alto. A scouting party led by Sergeant Ortega stumbled upon San Francisco Bay quite by accident. This "harbor of harbors" was obviously of great strategic value, so it too would have a presidio-mission settlement. But with supplies running low, Portolá had to retrace his steps. He got back to

San Diego in January of 1770, and the settlement of Monterey was delayed until June of that year.

Meanwhile Father Serra had established the first mission of the great California chain, San Diego de Alcalá, on July 16. Crippled by an infected foot, Serra nonetheless possessed great physical energy and a single-minded devotion to the missionary task. Relying more on hard work than on miracles, he was adept at begging needed supplies from Mexico City and at inspiring his colleagues. By the time of his death in 1784 he had founded nine missions and had baptized over 4,000 natives.

After the Portolá-Serra expedition, the job of occupying California went forward under great difficulties. The presidios and missions at San Diego and Monterey were hopeful gestures rather than impressive monuments to Spanish colonial power. The major problem was subsistence. Despite the favorable climate, crops were not raised successfully for many years. Cattle herds could not be brought from Mexico in the small ships that were California's chief means of supply. Hence an overland route from Sonora, a "Sonora-Monterey handclasp," was necessary to keep the fledgling province in business.

Part of the route had already been traversed by Father Garcés in his search for Indian converts. Garcés was exceptionally well qualified for missionary work; among other attributes he had a cast-iron stomach. As his colleague Pedro Font remarked: "He is just like an Indian himself . . . and though the food of the Indians is as nasty and disgusting as their dirty selves, the padre eats it with great gusto, and says that it is appetizing and very nice." In 1771 the Father had visited the river tribes and had then crossed the Colorado Desert to reach the foot of the San Jacinto Mountains. It was thus natural that he should serve as guide for the first official reconnaissance of the prospective route. Leading the party was Juan Bautista de Anza, a sturdy frontier captain from the presidio at Tubac. Departing from that post with forty soldiers on January 8, 1774, Anza and Garcés crossed the sun-tortured deserts and reached the brand-new mission of San Gabriel on March 22. The two men returned to Arizona, and the next year Anza led a full-scale colonizing expedition to San Francisco. The captain departed in October with 240 colonists (half of them children) and 200 head of livestock. Garcés accompanied this expedition as far as the Colorado River, where he embarked on an independent tour that took him from Needles around Soda Lake, then down the Mojave River and through Cajon Pass to San Gabriel. This so-called "Mojave Trail" was later the path of American mountain men and gold seekers. Anza successfully crossed the deserts, entered California by way of San Carlos Pass, and saw to it that his trail-worn emigrés were safely deposited at San Francisco.

Attempts to maintain this overland route were doomed. In 1780 two missions were founded on the west bank of the Colorado to serve as way stations on the California trail. They were without presidio protection, a fact betraying a dangerous ignorance of Spanish frontier history. In July of 1781 both stations were wiped out in a Yuma uprising, and Father Garcés was among the fifty Spaniards who were killed. After this there were no further attempts to open communication with California by land. The search for a more northerly route, from Sante Fe to Monterey, had been unsuccessfully undertaken by Fathers Escalante and Dominguez in 1776. During 6 months they traveled 1,500 miles from Santa Fe, and became the first white men to explore the Great Basin. They reached Utah Lake and descended the Green River, which they claimed was the Rio Buenaventura and the route to the Strait of Anián. But the western mountain barrier appeared to be too dangerous to cross in winter, so they returned to the New Mexican capital. Escalante's journal and a map drawn by Bernardo Miera y Pacheo became the foundation for further exploration toward Utah, but the land route to California remained closed.

The slender string of Spanish outposts between San Diego and San Francisco managed to survive despite the shaky supply system. The presidio and mission at Monterey were followed by others up and down the Coast. By 1782 the province could count four presidios (San Diego, Santa Barbara, Monterey, and San Francisco); two pueblos (San Jose and Los Angeles); and nine missions. The two pueblos were the despair of the padres, for the residents did little but gamble, strum the guitar, and make love to the Indian women. San Jose, founded in 1777, was a wide-open town, the Las Vegas of early California. Los Angeles was founded in 1781 by forty-four low-caste peons from Sinaloa. By 1800 it had a population of 315 sinful, fun-loving inhabitants.

The missions, however, continued to bear the major burden of colonization. The familiar rituals involved in converting and civilizing the primitives went on as they had for centuries. All neophytes were roused at sunrise for Mass. After breakfast the men were put to work tending the cattle and sheep, or to practicing such trades as tanning and masonry. The women were employed

The founding of Los Angeles. Source: From a model in the Los Angeles County Museum of Natural History.

at cooking, spinning, candlemaking, and other domestic tasks. Though in theory the natives were to be won to Christianity by persuasion, in practice it was thought necessary to discipline them by shackles, stocks, and stripes. Each mission had its *calabozo* for recalcitrant neophytes, who often fled to the Tulare marshes when they tired of civilization. Pursuit of these fugitives led to exploration of the Central Valley. Gabriel Moraga led troops up the San Joaquin as far as the latitude of San Francisco in 1806, and in 1808 he explored the Sacramento and Feather Rivers. But the Spaniards generally preferred the Coast. There in the sunset years of their colonial system they continued to establish the missions and private ranchos that are the most familiar institutions of early California.

Life in pastoral California appears in retrospect to have possessed an Arcadian grace and simplicity. There were rumblings of dissatisfaction over some of the mother country's policies, particularly trade restrictions and the exclusion of native sons from high office, but California was loyal to Spain. The Mexican Revolution of 1820 to 1821 caused little excitement in the province. But when Colonel Agustin de Iturbide proclaimed the independence of Mexico in February of 1821, California was ill-prepared for the change of government. The result was seen in the conspiracies and revolts that plagued the province for the next 25 years, and that left it too weak to defend itself against American infiltration.

The Santa Fe Trail

In fact, all the northern provinces were in danger. The Mexican Republic had little chance to prove itself in Texas, New Mexico, or California before the Anglo-Americans crowded in. The Spanish-speaking population, always small at best, was too thinly scattered over the vast Southwest for it to be more than a paper-thin barrier against the Yankees. One obvious soft spot in the perimeter was Santa Fe, whose residents had an addictive desire for American goods. The town, built of flat-topped adobe houses, appeared to the visiting Dr. Wislizenus to be "more like a prairie-dog village than a capital." In 1827 it had a population of some 5,000 Mexicans and Indians who made blankets, leather goods, and other products for sale in Mexico City. But the local demand for hardware and finished cotton could not be satisfied by the trickle of imports from Veracruz, and thus the door was opened to Missouri traders.

The Santa Fe trade had its origins in the earlier trips of the Mallet brothers, Zebulon M. Pike, and various French and American merchants. But the trade began in earnest in 1821, with the change of regimes at Mexico City. Capt. William Becknell, "Father of the Santa Fe Trail," left the Missouri River on September 1, 1821, with a pack train of goods that he intended to trade with the Indians. In the mountains he encountered Mexican soldiers who invited him to sell his wares in Santa Fe, which he did at considerable profit. From this time until 1846, with the exception of a brief period of tariff limitations in 1842 and 1843, the "commerce of the prairies" was carried on to the mutual satisfaction of American sellers and Mexican buyers.

The Santa Fe Trail ran for some 800 miles from its eastern terminus, which was first at Franklin and then at Independence in Missouri. The usual route was through Council Grove, across the Arkansas and Cimarron Rivers, and then into Santa Fe by way of Las Vegas. The Mountain Branch followed a longer, safer, and more northerly route along the Arkansas to Bent's Fort. From there the caravans went through Raton Pass to Santa Fe, or followed the Old Taos Trail by way of the Huerfano River and La Veta Pass. The mule-drawn Conestoga wagons and Pittsburgh wagons were organized into caravans which usually left in May of each year and reached Santa Fe within 2 to 3 months. The traders elected a "Captain of the Caravan," who had authority to direct the order of travel, pick campsites, and assign guard watches. Defense against Pawnee or Comanche raiders was an important consideration, since the United States government provided cavalry escorts at infrequent intervals. Hence the trains were organized in military fashion, with the wagons being formed into a hollow square at night. Yet the amount of blood shed on the Trail was often exaggerated. Josiah Gregg reported that less than a dozen men were killed along its course up to 1843.* The natural hazards were feared as much as the Indians, encompassing cloudbursts, prairie fires, desert mirages, and storms of baseball-size hailstones.

Upon arriving at the plaza in Santa Fe, the Americans were permitted to unload their cargoes of cottons and cutlery after greasing the palms of the customs inspectors. They then had to sell their goods; if unsuccessful in Santa Fe they had to go deeper into Mexico. On their return trip the merchants took back silver bullion, furs, and mules. The latter, referred to as Spanish Jacks and Jennies, made Missouri the center of a considerable mule-raising industry. While waiting for the transactions to be completed, the Americans enjoyed themselves in town. The immemorial fascination that Latin culture has held for puritanical Northerners was again in evidence. While the Americans felt a strong sense of superiority to the lazy natives, this did not deter them from acquiring a taste for El Paso brandy, dark-haired senoritas, and *chile con carne*.

The Santa Fe trade averaged about $130,000 a year. The silver bullion and milled dollars that were brought back to Missouri meant prosperity for that state, and profits of 10 to 40 percent for the individual merchants. In its broader aspects the trade turned American attention toward New Mexico, and revealed the ease with which that province might be conquered. The trail itself was like a huge spear pointing from the Missouri to the Rio Grande. So while the Santa Feans dozed under the azure skies, keeping alive the old colonial traditions in architecture, agriculture, and religion, the *norteamericanos* were envisioning a more active future for the mountain province. In the broad

*One of the casualties (in 1831) was Jedediah Smith, killed by Comanches.

sweep of frontier history the Mexican years appear to be little more than a picturesque prelude to American occupation.

Selected Readings   Herbert E. Bolton is the classic historian of the Spanish frontier. A useful selection of his most important articles is in John Francis Bannon (ed.), *Bolton and the Spanish Borderlands* (Norman, 1964). Bolton's *The Spanish Borderlands* (New Haven, 1921) is a short survey, his *Spanish Exploration in the Southwest, 1542-1706* (New York, 1916), is a collection of documents, and his *Coronado, Knight of Pueblo and Plains* (New York, 1950), is the standard biography. Documentary sources for Coronado are in George P. Hammond and Agapito Rey (eds.), *Narratives of the Coronado Expedition*, 2 vols. (Albuquerque, 1940). Carl O. Sauer, *The Road to Cíbola* (Berkeley, 1932), is good on geographical details. Charles Gibson, *Spain in America* (New York, 1966), is a first-rate survey of the colonial system, emphasizing Latin America.

       Donald C. Cutter, "Sources of the Name California," *Arizona and the West*, vol. 3 (Autumn, 1961), is informative. Henry Raupp Wagner, "Spanish Voyages to the Northwest Coast: The Voyage of Juan Rodriguez Cabrillo," *California Historical Society Quarterly*, vol. 7 (March, 1928), is a good introductory article, while his *Sir Francis Drake's Voyage around the World, Its Aims and Achievements* (San Francisco, 1926), is important. See also R. B. Haselden, "Is the Drake Plate of Brass Genuine?," *California Historical Society Quarterly*, vol. 16 (September, 1937), and Francis Farquhar and Walter Starr, "Drake in California: A Review of the Evidence and the Testimony of the Plate of Brass," *California Historical Society Quarterly*, vol. 36 (March, 1957).

       George P. Hammond, "The Search for the Fabulous in the Settlement of the Southwest," *Utah Historical Quarterly*, vol. 24 (January, 1956), is a good introduction to New Mexican history. Hubert Howe Bancroft, *History of Arizona and New Mexico, 1530-1888*, was recently reissued in a facsimile edition (Albuquerque, 1962) with forewords by Senators Clinton P. Anderson and Barry Goldwater. It remains a worthwhile source. Warren A. Beck, *New Mexico: A History in Four Centuries* (Norman, 1962), has rather scanty coverage of the first three centuries. George P. Hammond and Agapito Rey are editors of *Don Juan de Oñate, Colonizer of New Mexico*, 2 vols. (Albuquerque, 1953); documents. See also Herbert E. Bolton, "Father Escobar's Relation of the Oñate Expedition to California," *Catholic Historical Review*, vol. 5 (April, 1919). Much superbly written information about Santa Fe, the Pueblo Revolt, and El Paso is included in Paul Horgan, *The Great River: The Rio Grande in North American History*, rev. ed. (New York, 1960).

       Rupert N. Richardson, *Texas, the Lone Star State* (New York, 1943), is the best introduction. Volume 10 of Hubert H. Bancroft's *History of the Pacific States* [*The North Mexican States, 1581-1800*] (San Francisco, 1883), deals in part with Texas. Henry Folmer, *Franco-Spanish Rivalry in North America, 1542-1763* (Glendale, 1953), treats an important theme. Ross Phares, *Cavalier in the Wilderness* (Baton Rouge, 1952), is a biography of Louis St. Denis. Herbert E. Bolton's "French Intrusion into New Mexico, 1749-1752," was published in *The Pacific Ocean in History* (New York, 1917), and in the Bannon book cited above. Indian affairs in Texas and New Mexico are detailed in Ernest Wallace and E. A. Hoebel, *The Comanches: Lords of the South Plains* (Norman, 1952), and in Jack D. Forbes, *Apache, Navaho, and Spaniard* (Norman, 1960). Herbert E. Bolton published two biographies of Father Kino: *The Padre on Horseback* (San Francisco, 1932), and the much longer *Rim of Christendom* (New York, 1936).

Details about the occupation of California are ably presented in Robert Glass Cleland, *From Wilderness to Empire* (New York, 1944), and in Andrew Rolle, *California: A History* (New York, 1963). An older work that can be used with profit is Irving B. Richman, *California under Spain and Mexico, 1535-1847* (Boston, 1911). Douglas S. Watson, *The Spanish Occupation of California* (San Francisco, 1934), narrates the Portolá-Serra expedition. Crespi's diary of this expedition is included in Herbert E. Bolton, *Fray Juan Crespi, Missionary Explorer of the Pacific Coast* (Berkeley, 1927). Father Zephyrin Engelhardt, *The Missions and Missionaries of California*, 4 vols. (San Francisco, 1908-1915), is standard. Theodore Maynard, *The Long Road of Father Serra* (New York, 1954), is the best short biography.

Elliot Coues (ed.), *On the Trail of a Spanish Pioneer: The Diary and Itinerary of Francisco Garcés*, 2 vols. (New York, 1900), should be supplemented by Herbert E. Bolton, "The Early Explorations of Father Garcés on the Pacific Slope," in *The Pacific Ocean in History* (New York, 1917). Bolton edited *Anza's California Expeditions*, 5 vols. (Berkeley, 1930). See also Frederick Teggert (ed.), *The Anza Expedition of 1775-76: The Diary of Pedro Font* (Berkeley, 1913). Herbert E. Bolton, *Pageant in the Wilderness* (Salt Lake City, 1951), is the story of the Escalante expedition.

Robert L. Duffus, *The Santa Fe Trail* (New York, 1930), is the standard popular account. The 1844 edition of Josiah Gregg's *Commerce of the Prairies* is the classic first-hand narrative of the trail. It is available in Max L. Moorhead (ed.), *Josiah Gregg, Commerce of the Prairies,* (Norman, 1962) and in Archibald Hanna (ed.), *Commerce of the Prairies*, 2 vols. (Philadelphia, 1962). David Lavender, *Bent's Fort* (Garden City, 1954), is outstanding. Thomas J. Farnham's *Travels in the Great Western Prairies* (1834), which deals in part with the trail, is reprinted as volumes 28 and 29 of Reuben G. Thwaites, *Early Western Travels* (Cleveland, 1906). A reprinting of "Capt. Thomas Becknell's Journal of Two Expeditions from Boone's Lick to Sante Fe" appears in *Missouri Historical Review*, vol. 4 (January, 1910).

XIII. Americans in Texas

Texas has had a violent past. Its history crackles with gunfire, the cries of wounded or dying men, the thundering hoofbeats of contending armies. A three-cornered battle among Americans, Indians, and Mexicans for possession of the region bred a military tradition that is still very much alive. Furthermore, the dangers and opportunities of this particular frontier seemed to attract unusually obstreperous characters. They crossed the Sabine border legally or illegally, fought a revolution against the Mexican government, ran their own republic for 9 years, and then joined the Union during the expansionist mania of the 1840s. Though it reads at times like adventure fiction, the Texas chronicle is true despite occasional touches of exaggeration.

The Filibusters American spies and revolutionists had penetrated Texas long before it passed from Spanish to Mexican hands. Among the infiltrators was Philip Nolan, a personable Irishman who was a protégé of Gen. James Wilkinson. Beginning in 1790 he made several trips into the region west of Nacogdoches, ostensibly for horse trading. But Nolan spent unusual amounts of time making maps and collecting intelligence about military installations. In 1797 he obtained a Spanish passport through Wilkinson's influence with the Governor of Louisiana, and proceeded as far south as San Antonio. There his activities aroused the suspicion of the government, but Nolan managed to scuttle back across the border before he could be arrested.

In 1800 he was not so lucky. That fall he led twenty-eight men across the Sabine in what amounted to an armed reconnaissance of the province. This time the Spanish military responded with more alacrity. They caught up with the Americans near today's Waco, and Nolan was killed in the first fusillade. His ears were cut off and sent back to Mexico City, an inglorious if not uncommon conclusion to a filibustering career. The other Americans were sent to various prisons in Mexico.

Nolan's activities were apparently related to some of General Wilkinson's schemes. Exactly what these schemes were was a matter of conjecture in the Southwest. Andrew Ellicott, the government surveyor at Natchez, reported that Wilkinson planned to establish a new independent empire with Mexico City as its center. Wilkinson's subsequent involvement in the Aaron Burr conspiracy was more direct evidence of his designs on Texas. Burr, former Vice President of the United States, decided in 1806 to recoup his fortunes by a brilliant maneuver. He would provoke a war with Spain along the lower Mississippi, march a volunteer army into Mexico, and then become emperor of the newly liberated nation. Wilkinson was probably to create the necessary "incident" along the Sabine, and then command the invading army. Burr began gathering men and supplies at Blennerhassett Island on the Ohio. But after calculating the odds, Wilkinson decided to save his own skin and denounce Burr. He arranged a Neutral Ground treaty with the Spaniards (the neutral territory to be between the Sabine and the Arroyo Hondo) and then rushed back to New Orleans to repel Burr's invasion. Burr was arrested in Mississippi and returned to the East for trial. Despite President Jefferson's unseemly attempts to get him convicted of treason, he was discharged for lack of evidence. Wilkinson put on another splendid performance of outraged innocence at the trial, and managed to wriggle off the hook once again.

A more serious episode was the Gutierrez-Magee invasion of 1812. Jose Bernardo Gutierrez de Lara was a blacksmith and a revolutionary who escaped across the Sabine after the suppression of the Hidalgo uprising. In the United States he appealed for aid in "liberating" Texas. About 600 Mexicans and American volunteers joined his "Republican Army of the North." Some of these men were idealists like Gutierrez; most were hard-bitten adventurers who expected to get Texas land as part of the spoils of war. The army was commanded by Augustus Magee, a leathery West Point graduate who had just resigned his lieutenant's commission.

The invaders crossed the border in August and advanced as far south as La Bahiá [Goliad]. There Magee died of natural causes in February, 1813. Gutierrez marched on San Antonio, capturing it in April. He butchered the captured Spanish officers, an act which alienated the Americans and began the dissolution of his army. In addition, Gutierrez wanted Texas to remain part of Mexico after its liberation, while the Americans were thinking of an independent republic. They began drifting north, and by the end of the year the government forces had completely smashed the weakened revolutionary army.

A final filibustering effort was mounted in the summer of 1819 by James Long, a swashbuckling physician from Natchez. Again his army was made up largely of land-hungry adventurers. Crossing the Sabine on June 23, 1819, Dr. Long issued a proclamation declaring Texas an independent republic. More

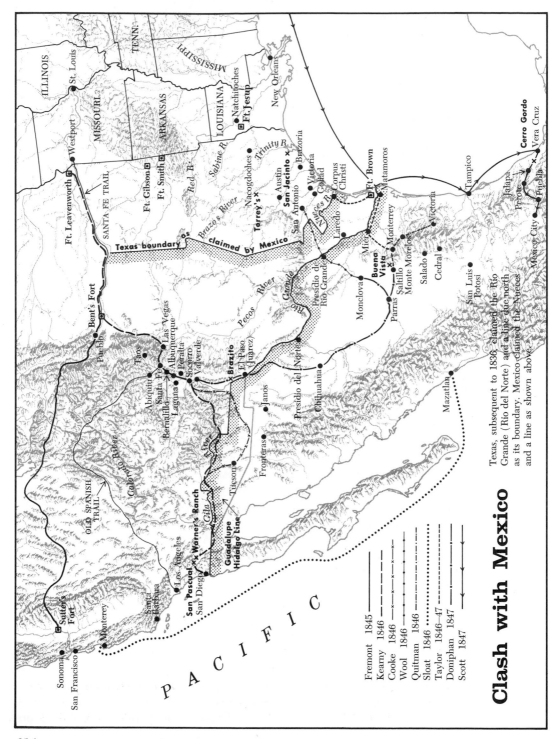

ILLINOIS
St. Louis
MISSOURI
Westport
Ft. Leavenworth
SANTA FE TRAIL
Bent's Fort
Pueblo
OLD SPANISH TRAIL
Colorado River
Los Angeles
Sonoma
San Francisco
Monterey
Santa Barbara
Sutter's Fort
San Pascual
San Diego
Warner's Ranch
Guadalupe Hidalgo Line
Gila River
Tucson
Fronteras
Janos
Taos
Abiquiu
Santa Fe
Bernalillo
Laguna
Albuquerque
Peralta
Socorro
Valverde
El Paso (Juárez)
Brazito
Las Vegas
Presidio del Norte
Chihuahua
Pecos River
Rio Grande River
Canada River
Mazatlan

TENN.
MISSISSIPPI
ARKANSAS
Ft. Gibson
Ft. Smith
Red R.
Sabine R.
LOUISIANA
Ft. Jesup
Natchitoches
New Orleans
Brazos River
Trinity R.
Nacogdoches
Torrey's
Austin
San Jacinto
San Antonio
Nueces R.
Laredo
Presidio de Rio Grande
Monclova

Texas boundary claimed by Mexico

Brazoria
Victoria
Goliad
Corpus Christi
Ft. Brown
Matamoros
Mier
Buena Vista
Monterey
Victoria
Monte Morelos
Saltillo
Parras
Salado
Cedral
San Luis Potosi
Tampico
Cerro Gordo
Vera Cruz
Jalapa
Perote
Puebla
Mexico City

PACIFIC

Texas, subsequent to 1836, claimed the Rio
Grande (Rio del Norte) and a line due north
as its boundary. Mexico claimed the Nueces
and a line as shown above.

Fremont 1845 ————
Kearny 1846 —·—·—
Cooke 1846 —×—×—
Wool 1846 —•—•—
Quitman 1846 —+—+—
Sloat 1846 ··········
Taylor 1846–47 ————
Doniphan 1847 ————
Scott 1847 ————→

Clash with Mexico

214

skilled in surgery than in military tactics, however, he made the mistake of breaking his force up into small detachments. These were run down and driven off by the royalist army. Long made a second attempt to invade Texas in 1821, but this time he was captured at La Bahiá. While pleading his case in Mexico City, he was killed under mysterious circumstances.

The Austins

Since Americans seemed to be more interested in Texas than its own citizens were, the Spanish government decided to permit some of them to enter as legal immigrants. Leading the way was Connecticut-born Moses Austin, who had become a Catholic and a Spanish subject upon moving from Virginia to Missouri in 1798. The Louisiana Purchase and the extension of American government had brought high taxes, militia duty, a rigid land system, and other dubious "benefits" which men like Austin had gone into Spanish territory to escape. In addition, his mining operations at St. Genevieve had not done well, and he was looking for an opportunity to do better somewhere else.

In 1820 Austin went to San Antonio and asked for permission to bring in 300 families who would grow cotton, sugar, and corn. The project was approved with the aid of the self-styled "Baron de Bastrop," an influential colonist whom Austin had known in the United States. But the return trip to Missouri was too much for Austin. He caught pneumonia and died in June of 1821. However, his son, Stephen F. Austin, had promised to carry out the colonization project.

Stephen Austin was a small, wiry individual with a rather sober personality. He liked to claim that he had been educated in the "School of Adversity." Actually he had received a fairly good education for that day and age, although this had not done much for his spelling. Austin took a fatherly interest in the colonists whom he brought to Texas, and he possessed the tact and patience to deal with Mexican officialdom. The revolution against Spain had of course upset the original contract, so Austin had to go to Mexico City in the spring of 1822 and nurse his father's colonization proposal through the Congress. He spent almost a year in the Capital, learning something of both the Spanish language and the Mexican character. The maddening procrastination of the officials was a severe trial then and later, but Austin managed to keep a lid on his impatience. The reward was that he was able to return to Texas in the spring of 1823 with a confirmation of his contract.

Austin's colony included the fairest part of the province, the coastal plain between the San Jacinto and Lavaca Rivers as far north as the Nacogdoches-San Antonio Road. The "Old Three Hundred," the first families introduced under the grant, settled along the Brazos and Colorado Rivers. Austin distributed land, organized defenses against threatening Karankawa and Waco Indians, and administered governmental affairs from the hamlet of San

Felipe de Austin.* He proved to be the greatest of the contractors or *empresarios* operating in Texas, and under subsequent contracts he brought in large numbers of Americans. All told, he authorized 1,540 grants to settlers, and the total population of his colony had reached 5,665 by the spring of 1831.

Empresarios

Other *empresarios* had been clamoring for the right to bring colonists to Texas. Hence the Mexican Congress passed a general colonization law in 1824. This delegated most power to the state governments, with only a few reservations. One of these was that foreigners were not to settle within 10 leagues (25 miles) of the coast. The state congress of Texas-Coahuila in turn passed a colonization law on March 24, 1825. This permitted *empresario* grants similar to Austin's. Each settler was entitled to 1 *labor* (177 acres) if he planned to engage in farming, or 24 *labors* (4,428 acres) if he planned to raise cattle. Human nature being what it is, practically all colonists classed themselves as stock raisers. The land was paid for by minimal fees over a 6-year period. The *empresario* himself would get 67,000 acres for each 200 families he settled within a 6-year period. He did not have title to the land distributed to colonists; titles were granted by the government. He merely had the right to settle families within the designated area of the grant, and then receive his reward in land.

Fifteen contracts were signed under the Texas-Coahuila colonization law by 1829. They were issued both to Americans (Green DeWitt; Haden Edwards) and to Mexicans (Martín DeLeon; Lorenzo de Zavala). These other *empresarios* were not as successful as Austin. None of the fifteen contracts was entirely fulfilled, and in several of the grants not a single family was settled. This alerted the Mexican government to the speculative nature of some of the enterprises. The American *empresarios*, including Austin, also faced some difficult problems, the most troublesome involving religion, slavery, and local government.

Catholicism, Slavery, and Local Government

Only Catholics could settle in Texas. In contrast to the United States, Mexico had an established church. The Constitution of 1824 reads: "The religion of the Mexican Nation is, and shall be perpetually, the Apostolic Roman Catholic. The Nation protects it by wise and just laws, and prohibits the exercise of any other." Austin was unhappy with the Church and its "Fryers," whom he described as "miserable drones." But he professed Catholicism as a formality and so did the other colonists, even though they were predominantly of Methodist or Baptist background. There were few active churches of any kind in Texas, and

*San Felipe de Austin on the Brazos River should not be confused with today's Austin, which is on the Colorado.

hence Sundays were spent breaking in mustangs rather than listening to sermons. But by 1834 the absence of public worship had become a problem. Under a rather ambiguous law of that year which apparently granted religious toleration, many of the Protestants organized churches in the northeastern part of the state, thus widening the cultural gap between themselves and the Mexicans.

Negro slavery gave Stephen F. Austin more headaches than any other problem. The Mexicans drew much of their political philosophy from the French Revolution, with its demands for "Liberty, Equality, Fraternity." In the Constitution of 1824, this idealism was translated into a prohibition on slavery. Slaves could not be bought or sold in Texas, and the children of those already there would become free at the age of fourteen. However the constitutional prohibition was evaded under the terms of a state law passed in May of 1828. This allowed immigrants to "liberate" their slaves and then make them indentured servants for life. The subterfuge was fairly effective, but Texas slaveowners never felt quite secure while they were under Mexican rule. There were periodic rumors of emancipation, and in 1830 it appeared that this step might be taken when the federal Congress prohibited the further introduction of slaves. So Austin had to jump into action and defend an institution about which he himself had serious doubts.

Austin also had his hands full with problems of local government, which he largely administered in his own grant up to 1827. Mexico had retained much of the Spanish political system, which was based upon a town council (*ayuntamiento*) elected by the people. These municipal governments were in turn grouped under a department political chief, and the chain of command ran back to the Texas-Coahuila state government at Saltillo. The long distances, the language barrier, the slow-motion reaction of Mexican officials guaranteed that the Anglo-American settlers would be unhappy. The lack of a system of courts was also objectionable to men raised in the Anglo-Saxon tradition. Austin worked hard to get an increased number of municipalities, a judicial system, and the publication of laws in both English and Spanish. He was partially successful in these efforts, but by the time the government got around to granting the requests, greater causes of dissension had arisen.

The Fredonian Rebellion

As if the inherent difficulties in Anglo-Mexican relations were not great enough, one of the *empresarios* turned out to be a rambunctious individual "with all the bark on." Haden Edwards, aided by his brother Benjamin, had received a contract in 1825 to settle 800 families in east Texas. Edwards did not understand the authority granted him in the contract. Upon his arrival at Nacogdoches he began to cancel and issue land titles, a power reserved to the state government. Much of the land in this area had been settled by old Spanish families, and Edwards threatened to confiscate these lands if the owners could not validate their titles. These actions caused an uproar which was heard all the way to Mexico City. The result was that the government abruptly canceled Edwards' contract and ordered him to leave Texas.

Edwards was short-tempered, a common enough trait in Texans of this period. So instead of leaving the region as ordered, he raised the banner of revolution. His Fredonian Republic aimed at "free and unmolested independence from the Sabine to the Rio Grande." Edwards' regulators never numbered more than thirty, though the self-styled "ring-tailed panthers" were a hard lot. In addition, a handful of Cherokees joined the movement, being disgruntled with Mexican vacillation over a land allotment for the tribe. The red and white flag which the republicans ran up at Nacogdoches on December 16, 1826, symbolized the equality of these races—a startling departure from the usual frontier attitude.

The insurrection was bound to fail, since Edwards could neither get aid from the United States nor from Austin's colony. Austin, in fact, saw his own position endangered by Edwards' rashness, and wrote him to follow a more temperate course. When the rebellion flared up, 250 of Austin's militia joined the Mexican troops sent to crush it. Edwards and his followers thereupon fled across the border.

The episode should have convinced the government that the majority of American immigrants were loyal and peaceful citizens. But in fact the officials began to take a closer look at the possible dangers of the current colonization policy. The record of what had happened in Florida and Louisiana was there for all to read. The efforts of President Jackson to buy Texas also betrayed American intentions. Under his instructions, Joel Poinsett had offered 5 million dollars for most of the province. When this offer was turned down, the new American minister, Anthony Butler, tried to bribe officials into accepting its sale.

Colonization Law of 1830

The dangers were quite apparent to Gen. Jose Mier y Terán, who made a thorough political and military survey of Texas in 1828 and 1829. The general found hundreds of American families settled without government consent. On the other hand, there were few Mexicans in the province, most of them clustered around San Antonio.* In his report he talked about "smouldering fires," and warned that "either the government occupies Texas *now*, or it is lost forever." Terán recommended countercolonization by Mexicans and Europeans to check American influence. Other recommendations were incorporated into what Texans regarded as the infamous colonization law of April 6, 1830.

Among provisions of the law was an increase in the number of troops for Texas. Garrisons manned by convict-soldiers were established at San Antonio, Goliad, Anahuac, and elsewhere. Further immigration from the United

*Of the 1834 population of 30,000, only one-tenth were Mexican.

States was prohibited. All foreigners had to obtain Mexican passports. The law recognized existing slavery, but forbade the further introduction of slaves. These provisions caused a hue and cry among the American settlers. Stephen Austin appealed for a removal of the ban on further immigration, his argument being that many colonists were still en route. The law was interpreted to permit the entry of these latecomers, but the military occupation of Texas was expedited.

The law undoubtedly discouraged many responsible settlers, but did not deter the more unruly. It was at this time that Texas began to acquire its reputation as a home of rascals. James Ohio Pattie, whose *Personal Narrative* was published in 1831, described the province as an "Elysium of rogues." Back in the States, "G.T.T." (Gone to Texas) was written on legal documents to describe those who had fled west in a hurry to escape debts or prosecution for other crimes. Residents of the older sections of the country liked to make Texans the butt of jokes which revolved around their propensity for breaking laws. For example: One man in trouble consulted a lawyer, who advised him to leave town before sundown. "Leave? Where'll I go? Ain't I in Texas now?"

Many of those who crossed the border after 1830 were of a type that would prove to be dangerous to the Mexican government. William Barret Travis was one of these. Travis was a high-strung, twenty-three-year-old lawyer from Alabama who came to Texas in 1831. Like many others, he had left home because of domestic difficulties, and in fact he was divorced in 1835. His head was filled with romantic notions about liberty, democracy, and other concepts that were subversive in the Mexican context. What made Travis and others like him so dangerous was that they were willing to die for these ideals.

Sam Houston made his first appearance in Texas at the end of 1832. Texas has a well-known reputation for attracting and nurturing men of outsized physical dimensions, and Houston always looked taller than his 6 feet 2 inches. During his strange career he was a citizen of four countries: the United States, the Cherokee Nation, Mexico, and the Republic of Texas. He had lived among the Cherokees in his native Tennessee, and subsequently spent much time looking after their interests. In fact, his first journey to Texas was undertaken at the request of his friend, President Jackson, to make a survey of Indian affairs there. Houston's aggressiveness was destined to make him a leader of the revolutionary movement after he became a permanent resident of Nacogdoches in 1835.

As part of the tightening-up process initiated by the law of 1830, the federal government sent customs collectors to the Gulf ports. As with the American Revolution, customs duties and inspectors are important in Texas history. The *empresario* contracts had exempted colonists from tariffs, hence the attempt to enforce their collection caused difficulties. This was especially the case at Anahuac, where the garrison was commanded by a renegade Kentuckian and bully named John Bradburn. His arrest of several Americans, including William B. Travis, triggered an insurrection in June of 1832 that eventually forced his resignation. The colonists' defiance might have provoked the wrath of the Mexican government, except that the government was at the time too busy fighting a much more serious revolution led by Antonio Lopez de Santa Anna. The Texans supported Santa Anna, since he was posing as a liberal and a champion of the federal Constitution. The maneuver paid off, since Santa Anna was victorious. He approved of the actions of his friends in Texas, so it was *Viva Santa Anna!*

Conventions of 1832 and 1833

To seek a redress of other grievances, the Texans resorted to a traditional frontier procedure: the holding of a convention. Delegates from the various districts met at San Felipe de Austin on October 1, 1832. They drew up resolutions asking for continued tariff exemptions, removal of the ban on American immigration, and separation of Texas from Coahuila. The petition was not delivered because of the turbulent political situation in Mexico, so a second convention was held in April of 1833. It reconfirmed the principles of the first meeting, and in addition drew up a state constitution. Stephen F. Austin took the petition to Mexico City to get Santa Anna's approval. The difficulties he encountered there caused him, "in a moment of irritation and impatience," to write an indiscreet letter to the San Antonio town council, urging them to form a separate state government even without approval from Mexico City. The government granted many of the Texan requests (though not separation from Coahuila), but when Austin started home in January his letter became known and he was hauled back to Mexico City and thrown into prison.

During a year's incarceration Austin became convinced that Santa Anna was destroying the federal system. The general was betraying the revolution, using the platform of liberalism to cover the creation of a dictatorship. Consequently when Austin was released and went back to Texas in 1835, his stated beliefs were that "war is our only resource. There is no other remedy but to defend our rights, our country, and ourselves by force of arms." Such pronouncements crystallized public opinion in opposition to Santa Anna. These sentiments had also been expressed in Austin's absence by the so-called "war party," a group of hotspurs which included W. B. Travis. Thus by the fall of 1835 the stage was set for armed resistance to Santa Anna's centralist ambitions.

The Revolution

The root cause of the Texas Revolution lay in the racial and political differences between governors and governed. The Mexicans had lived for three centuries under a paternalistic system which gave them little opportunity to develop political talent. The Constitution of 1824, which supposedly borrowed much from the United States Constitution, was actually a quite different kind of document. There was no bill of rights, no freedom-of-religion clause, and few restrictions on the central government. The Mexicans were not philosophically committed to either federalism or democracy. Even at that, the federalism which the constitution promised was being subverted by Santa Anna.

The whole situation caused "grumbling and growling" among the American settlers. This arose, as Austin put it, "from a principle which is common to all North Americans, a feeling which is the natural offspring of the unbounded republican liberty enjoyed by all classes in the United States; that is, jealousy of undue encroachments on personal rights, and a general repugnance to everything that wore even the semblance of a stretch of power." The political uncertainties were complicated by racial distrust. Most Anglo-Texans were disdainful of the Mexicans, whom they regarded as lazy and superstitious. They felt that if it came to a contest of arms, the Mexicans would run away at the first fire.

The Texans soon had their own Lexington and Concord. Fighting actually began at Gonzales on October 2, 1835, when the colonists attacked the Mexican garrison. Following another clash at Goliad, a loosely organized mob of volunteers descended on San Antonio. This "Army of the People" was headed by Austin, James Bowie, and James Fannin. An assault led by Uncle Ben Milam drove Gen. Martín Cós from the town on December 5. Cós agreed to withdraw back across the Rio Grande, thus leaving Texas free of Mexican troops. The

Survivors of the Texas Revolution. From a photo taken at Goliad in 1906. Source: University of Texas Library.

victory at San Antonio caused the Texans to become overconfident, and thus contributed indirectly to the debacles at Goliad and the Alamo.

Meanwhile a "consultation" was held at San Felipe de Austin to declare the cause for taking up arms. The conferees issued a statement on November 7 that they were fighting "in defense of the republican principles of the federal constitution of Mexico." Ironically, that Constitution had already been repealed by the rubber-stamp Congress on October 3. The logic of the situation called for complete independence, and within 4 months this had in fact become the revolution's objective. The consultation also formed a provisional government with a governor (Henry Smith), a council, and a commander-in-chief for the army (Sam Houston).

Unfortunately, Houston's army existed only on paper. He assembled a complete staff of officers—enough for twenty-six companies of infantry and cavalry—but there were no men to serve in the ranks. Furthermore, the council denied him control over the volunteer army at San Antonio, so he could act only in an advisory capacity. A bitter struggle between Governor Smith and the council resulted in a confused state of affairs at the seat of government and a chaotic situation in the field. In January Houston directed James Bowie (then at Goliad) to proceed to San Antonio and *dismantle the fortifications*. Governor Smith, on the other hand, sent W. B. Travis, now a colonel in the Texas Regular Army, to *reinforce the post*. Caught in this network of cross-purposes and conflicting authority, the Texas forces lurched toward disaster.

The Alamo

The Alamo was a deathtrap. The walls of the old San Antonio mission were crumbling, and though the mission complex had been used as a Spanish military garrison, it had not been built to withstand siege. Yet Bowie and Travis decided to make a stand there despite Houston's order that it be abandoned. In his diary Travis revealed that he had been reading the novels of Sir Walter Scott [*Ivanhoe*; *Rob Roy*] in which men die for chivalric ideals. Under this romantic inspiration Travis seemed bound and determined to die for an ideal himself. He was not a man to compromise; as he put it in his last letter, the choice was either "VICTORY OR DEATH."

James Bowie had been born in Kentucky in 1796. He had acquired a national reputation as a knife fighter, and the "Bowie knife" was a familiar accouterment in Texas. He and his brothers had made a living by rather dubious means: slave smuggling in Louisiana, the sale of fraudulent Spanish land grants in Arkansas; and James himself had "Gone to Texas" in 1828. He had married into a prominent Mexican family and had become a large-scale land speculator. His holdings in southern Texas, amounting to a million acres or more, gave him sufficient reason for wanting to stop the Mexican invasion at San Antonio.

The fall of the Alamo. Source: University of Texas Library.

General Santa Anna, professional soldier, admirer of Napoleon, and superb egotist, had announced as early as August of 1835 his intention of crushing the Texans. By the middle of February he had an army of some 6,000 men concentrated at Laredo. After a slow advance, his force reached San Antonio on February 23, 1836. Looking cross river toward the Alamo, the general was enraged to see flying above it a flag with the numerals "1824." This insult to his supreme authority would have to be avenged by blood.

Other volunteers had come into the Alamo before Santa Anna appeared. About half of the total force of 183 men were recent arrivals from Kentucky, Tennessee, and sixteen other states of the Union. Among them was David Crockett, the "Coonskin Congressman," who had come from west Tennessee with a dozen companions. Crocket (a Whig) decided to go to Texas after being defeated for reelection by the Jacksonian Democrats. Naturally he allied himself with the anti-Jackson group in the province, and was thus in opposition to Jackson's friend Sam Houston. It is quite possible that Bowie, Travis, and Crockett hoped to score a smashing victory against overwhelming odds, much as Jackson had done at New Orleans. They would in this way become the political as well as military heroes of Texas and thus rise to national prominence. This possibility does not mean that one should discount their devotion to liberty. These men were almost pure examples of the genus "American Democrat," and their opposition to a Mexican dictatorship would have been easy to predict.

The siege of the Alamo lasted for 13 days. The final assault was launched on the morning of March 6, being preceded by the playing of the ceremonial *deguello* ("throat-cutting"). During the operation, Santa Anna had absorbed an estimated 1,500 casualties, so his orders as regards the defenders were *"no hay prisoneros."* Bowie, sick from typhoid-pneumonia, was killed as he lay on his cot in the mission chapel. Crockett, contrary to legend, appears to have fallen in the early days of the siege. There are many stories about what occurred in the Alamo, but they belong to folklore rather than to history. There were several survivors, including Mrs. Dickenson, the wife of an artillery officer, and Travis's slave "Jim." Santa Anna permitted them to leave for the East, but their testimony about the battle was garbled and contradictory.

The Mexicans scored another victory on March 20 when Gen. Jóse Urrea, commanding the right wing of Santa Anna's army, forced the surrender of Colonel Fannin's men near Goliad. On the 27th these prisoners, about 350 in all, were executed by order of Santa Anna. The two military catastrophes sent the residents of Texas fleeing eastward in the "Runaway Scrape." But they also aroused one of the most primitive human motives: the desire for revenge. "Remember the Alamo" and "Remember Goliad" became slogans that turned all Texans into revolutionists.

Independence

Meanwhile the purpose of the war had changed from a defense of the federal Constitution to complete independence. This change had been formalized by a convention held at the village of Washington-on-the-Brazos. On March 2 the fifty-nine delegates approved a declaration of independence, which was modeled upon that written by Thomas Jefferson. The convention also drew up a constitution for the Republic of Texas. This document was based upon the United States Constitution and on those of several southwestern states. It set a 3-year term for the president, who could not immediately succeed himself, and provided for a congress and a judicial system. It also made slavery legal, and extended generous land grants (a *labor* and a *league*) to heads of family. Finally, the convention sent Stephen Austin to secure aid in the United States, and reconfirmed Sam Houston as commander of the army.

The "Old Chief" went to Gonzales, and then led his army on a 6-week retreat before Santa Anna's advancing legions. Although Austin eventually secured many volunteers in the States, Houston found it necessary to do battle with an army composed principally of Texans. In a parklike setting along San Jacinto Creek, a tributary of Galveston Bay, the "so-called General Houston" turned to face his contemptuous enemies. On the afternoon of April 21 he prepared his 900 troops for an assault on Santa Anna's 1,300. The Texans' four-piece band did not know any military tunes, so at the moment of attack they played a love song, "Will You Come to My Bower I Have Shaded for You." But Houston's grim-faced riflemen did not care for mood music: "Remember the Alamo" was on their lips. In an 18-minute battle 630 Mexicans were killed and 730 taken prisoner. Among the captives was Antonio Lopez de Santa Anna himself.

Houston managed to save Santa Anna's life. This was a monumental achievement in view of the passions aroused by the massacres at San Antonio and Goliad. In fact, one of the standard topics for Texas debating clubs in succeeding years was "Ought the Texian government to have put Santa Anna to death in 1836?" In exchange for his freedom, Santa Anna ordered his army to withdraw beyond the Rio Grande. He also promised to use his influence to secure Mexican recognition of Texan independence. Santa Anna later repudiated his pledge, but it was obvious that Mexico had lost effective control of her rebellious province.

Republic of Texas

The first election in the independent Republic of Texas made Sam Houston the president, and he took the oath of office on October 22, 1836. In the same general election the Texans voted overwhelmingly for annexation to the United States. But President Jackson, despite his friendship for Houston, walked around the issues of recognition and annexation on tiptoe. He felt that the initiative for these measures should come from Congress, and he wanted to save his successor, Martin Van Buren, from any embarrassment on the issue. Congress did go so far as to vote funds for sending a diplomatic representative to Texas. So on the last day of his term, March 3, 1837, Jackson extended recognition by appointing a chargé d'affaires to the Republic. A proposal for annexation, formally presented in 1837, got nowhere. In the Congress such proposals were drowned in a torrent of petitions from the northeastern states, who objected to the admission of more slave territory. The result was that annexation remained a dead issue for several years.

Life in the Republic possessed many of the classic features of frontier social history. Settlers poured in after the war, attracted by government offers of free land. As Houston put it: "You may escape the small pox, but you can never escape the contagion of land loving." Most of the newcomers were from states of the Old Southwest, though a sizable German migration in the 1840s settled New Braunfels and other towns in the San Antonio region. The typical Texan was deficient in book knowledge, but he was a neighborly individual who enjoyed square dances and horse racing in his spare time. He lived in a simple wooden cabin, and his diet of corn "dodgers," fried beef, and black coffee was guaranteed to put curls in anyone's hair. His life had few comforts, "a heaven for men and dogs but a hell for women and oxen." The three basic products which sustained him were cotton, corn, and cattle. Since most settlers had raised all three in their previous homes, the only innovations were in cattle herding, where the techniques of the Mexican *vaqueros* were adopted.

Executive Mansion Houston 1837-38
Republic of Texas
Sam Houston, President

The Executive Mansion of the Republic of Texas in 1837-38. Source: University of Texas Library.

The individualism of the Texans was epitomized by Sam Houston. The Old Chief was a prodigious drinker, a compulsive handshaker, and a vigorous orator. The informality of his dress was remarkable even in the wide-open atmosphere of the Republic. He frequently wore a sombrero, Indian breeches, and a Mexican blanket. He even delivered his second inaugural address wearing a buckskin hunting shirt.

The continuing threat from Indians and Mexicans made the Texans a military people. The habit of wearing Bowie knives and pistols persisted for many years, and these weapons were also used to settle personal quarrels. The narratives of the Republic are dotted with accounts of beatings, canings, shootings, and other acts of violence. Francis Sheridan wrote to a friend in England, doubtless with some Texan-like exaggeration, that "it is considered unsafe to walk through the streets of the principal Towns without being armed. The Bowie knife is the weapon most in vogue."

The government of the Republic seemed able to operate despite an awesome shortage of funds. It maintained a small army and navy, dispatched diplomatic representatives, and established local government. Its three presidents, Houston (two terms), Mirabeau Lamar, and Anson Jones, were concerned primarily with frontier defense. Mexico continued to threaten the infant government, though this was not a one-way street. Governor Lamar, in particular, was expansionist-minded. In 1841 he raised and equipped an army to occupy Santa Fe, claiming the Rio Grande as a boundary. This ended disastrously with the surrender and imprisonment of the whole contingent. The next year another expedition against Mier in nothern Mexico was also a catastrophe, and indeed a Mexican army swept north and occupied San Antonio. These clashes did nothing to improve international relations. Joseph Eve in 1842 spoke for most Texans when he described the Mexicans as "a feble, dastardly, superstitious priest ridden race of mongrels, composed of Spanish Indian and negro blood." Many of the old scores would be settled during the Mexican War in 1846.

Admission to the Union

Texas has never been sure whether it belonged to the "South" or the "West." Part of the difficulty has to do with the Negro slaves, who by 1847 constituted 27 percent of the total population. The question of slavery was therefore linked with that of annexation. Houston's policy was that of a good poker player, and American officials were never sure what his hand was. He cultivated relations with England and France, accepting their diplomatic representatives and raising the specter of Texas becoming a British colony. England, of course, desired an independent source of raw cotton and another market for her manufactured goods. The fly in the soup was that England, home of the worldwide antislavery movement, wished to see Texas organized on the basis of free labor. She delayed recognition of the Republic until 1840 in hopes of getting abolition accepted there.

These developments alarmed Southern slaveholders, and the resulting controversy made annexation an issue in the 1844 election. The Whig nominee, Henry Clay, opposed annexation on the grounds that it might bring on a war with Mexico. Democrat James K. Polk favored it, and his party's platform included a statement that "the reoccupation of Oregon and the reannexation of Texas are great American measures." Polk's victory, an expression of the expansionist urge of the period, meant that Texas would at last be added to the Union.

The outgoing President, John Tyler, wanted the credit for bringing the Lone Star Republic into the fold. In 1844 Tyler and Secretary of State Calhoun had drawn up a treaty of annexation. They had stressed the supposed British plot to seize Texas, and Calhoun in particular had insisted that there was a plan to destroy the Southern slave system. As Senator Benton remarked, it "was a cry of wolf where there was no wolf," and the treaty was soundly defeated. But Tyler did not give up. Knowing that he could not get the necessary two-thirds vote in the Senate, he proposed that Texas be admitted instead by joint resolution of Congress, a method requiring only a simple majority. The treaty slid through both houses by narrow margins, and Tyler signed it on March 1, 1845. On October 13 the voters of Texas approved the terms of annexation and a proposed state constitution. The Congress again passed the treaty, and when President James K. Polk signed it on December 29, 1845, Texas became a state.

Selected Readings   Rupert N. Richardson, *Texas: The Lone Star State* (New York, 1958), remains the best general history. Much valuable reference material is in Walter P. Webb (ed.), *The Handbook of Texas*, 2 vols. (Austin, 1952). Harris G. Warren, *The Sword Was Their Passport* (Baton Rouge, 1943), is a commendable study of the filibusters. Much on the same subject is in Hodding Carter, *Doomed Road of Empire: The Spanish Trail of Conquest* (New York, 1963). Eugene C. Barker, *The Life of Stephen F. Austin* (Nashville, 1925), is indispensable. The same author's *Mexico and Texas, 1821-1835* (Dallas, 1925) is a classic set of lectures. Samuel H. Lowrie, *Culture Conflict in Texas, 1821-1835* (New York, 1932), is quite informative.

William C. Binkley, *The Texas Revolution* (Baton Rouge, 1952), is a basic interpretive work. Watson Parker, "Influences from the United States on the Mexican Constitution of 1824," *Arizona and the West*, vol. 4 (Summer, 1964), contributes to an understanding of the Mexican background. Wilfred H. Callcott, *Santa Anna* (Norman, 1936), is a well-written biography, while Carlos E. Castañeda (trans.), *The Mexican Side of the Texas Revolution* (Dallas, 1928), contains reports by Generals Santa Anna, Urrea, and others. The Alamo has been the subject of much popularly written but still carefully researched history. Lon Tinkle, *13 Days to Glory* (New York, 1958), and Walter Lord, *A Time to Stand* (New York, 1961), are examples. The most scholarly study of the siege was the uncopyrighted doctoral dissertation of Amelia Williams, "A Critical Study of the Siege of the Alamo," parts of which were published in volumes 36 and 37 of the *Southwestern Historical Quarterly* (April, 1933-April, 1934). Sidelights on the defenders may be found in Frank X. Tolbert, *An Informal History of Texas* (New York, 1961). J. Frank Dobie, "James Bowie," in *American West*, vol. 2 (Spring, 1965), is a no-holds-barred article. James A. Shackford, *David Crockett: The Man and the Legend* (Chapel Hill, N.C., 1956), contains an excellent discussion of Crockett's role in Texas, and includes Madame Candelaria's testimony about his death early in the siege. Joseph Leach, *The Typical Texan: Biography of an American Myth* (Dallas, 1952), interprets Crockett and Houston from the viewpoint of literature and social history. John Q. Anderson (ed.), *Tales of Frontier Texas, 1830-1860* (Dallas, 1966), also has much on heroes. Marquis James, *The Raven: A Biography of Sam Houston* (Indianapolis, 1929), is standard. Llerena Friend, *Sam Houston, The Great Designer* (Austin, 1954), is detailed and scholarly. Amelia W. Williams and Eugene C. Barker are editors of *The Writings of Sam Houston*, 8 vols. (Austin, 1938-1943). Frank X. Tolbert, *The Day of San Jacinto* (New York, 1959), is uncritical.

For political affairs in the Republic see Stanley Siegel, *A Political History of the Texas Republic* (Austin, 1956), and Joseph W. Schmitz, *Texas Statecraft* (San Antonio, 1945). Social history is the subject of William R. Hogan, *The Texas Republic* (Norman, 1946), and Joseph W. Schmitz, *Texas Culture in the Days of the Republic* (San Antonio, 1960), the latter being overly concise. W. Eugene Hollon and Ruth Lapham Butler (eds.), *William Bollaert's Texas* (Norman, 1956), is the diary of an

Englishman, and gives a good picture of social life in the Republic from 1841 to 1844. Noel Loomis, *The Texan-Santa Fe Pioneers* (Norman, 1958), is the well-written story of a disaster. An entire issue of *American West*, vol. 5 (May, 1968), is devoted to "The Republic of Texas."

Justin H. Smith, *The Annexation of Texas* (New York, 1911), is ponderous. Frederick Merk, "A Safety Valve Thesis and Texan Annexation," *Mississippi Valley Historical Review*, vol. 49 (December, 1962), deals with slavery. The same author's *Manifest Destiny and Mission in American History* (New York, 1963) also sheds light on annexation. George L. Rives, *The United States and Mexico, 1821-1848*, 2 vols. (New York, 1913), is a thorough political history.

XIV. The Trail to Oregon

What was the natural western boundary of the United States? Thomas Jefferson and Thomas Hart Benton, both champion expansionists, thought that it would be the Rocky Mountains. They were confident that Americans would settle the Pacific Coast, but felt that the distances were so great that political incorporation into the Union was unlikely. Rather, they foresaw an independent maritime republic having commercial ties with Asia rather than the Atlantic coast. So on the crest of the mountains, Senator Benton told Congress in 1825, "the statue of the fabled god, Terminus, should be raised . . . never to be thrown down." But both men underestimated the propulsive force of the great folk migration which had carried Americans over the Appalachians and beyond the Mississippi. The quest for cheap land and a better way of life was to take thousands of farmers across the Great American Desert, past the "terminus" of the Rocky Mountains, and into the virginal coastal valleys of Oregon and California. Dressed in drab homespuns, their faces yellowed by jaundice, the emigrants hardly looked the part of empire builders. But they did in fact give the United States a republican empire embracing 1,300 miles of Pacific coastline from Puget Sound to San Diego Bay.

International Rivalry in Oregon In 1765 Maj. Robert Rogers asked Parliament to finance a trans-Mississippi expedition that would find the "Ouragon." This mythical river was another version of the Northwest Passage. The word was given further currency by Jonathan Carver, an employee of Rogers, in his *Travels in the Interior Parts of North America* (1778). Though mentioned in Jedidiah Morse's *American Gazeteer* (1797), it did not become fixed in geographical nomenclature until the 1820s. Then it referred not only to the present state but also to Washington, Idaho, and parts of Montana and Wyoming.

Possession of the Oregon country was the prize in a game of diplomatic musical chairs. England, the United States, Spain, and Russia were the original contestants, but the latter two were eliminated rather early. So the traditional Anglo-Saxon rivals prepared for another struggle that might have to be decided by war. The claims of both countries were based upon land and sea explorations. The English Captain James Cook had cruised the Oregon coast as far south as 44° in 1778, looking for a western entrance to the Northwest Passage. During the next 20 years other English merchantmen were trading for sea otter skins with the Indians. Capt. George Vancouver sailed from San Diego to Alaska in 1792, making maps as he went. Then in the spring of 1793 Alexander Mackenzie of the Northwest Company crossed the Canadian Rockies and came out on what he thought was the Columbia (though it was actually the Fraser River in today's British Columbia). Thus by the time of Astor's ill-fated trading venture, the British were claiming with considerable inaccuracy that the Americans "have no pretensions by Discovery either by Water or Land, the right in both cases clearly belonging to Great Britain by the discoveries of Cook, Vancouver, and Mackenzie."

Actually, American traders from Boston had been operating along the Oregon coast as early as 1788. Yankee gimcracks were traded off to the glassy-eyed natives in exchange for the infinitely more valuable sea otter skins. The pelts were taken to China by way of the Hawaiian Islands, and the skippers would return to New England with cargoes of silk, tea, and chinaware. One result of this trade was that New England commercial interests would strongly support political efforts at acquisition of Oregon. As Senator Robert Winthrop of Massachusetts told Congress in 1844: "I cannot forget that the American claim to Oregon, so far as it rests upon discovery, dates back to Massachusetts adventure and Boston enterprise." After England became embroiled in the Napoleonic Wars during the 1790s, these Yankees dominated the Northwest trade. In fact, the Indians came to call all white men "Bostons." One of the Bostons was Capt. Robert Gray. In May of 1792 he managed to get across the sandbar at the mouth of a magnificent river, which he named in honor of his ship as the Columbia. Gray's feat meant added points for America in the imperial contest.

The Lewis and Clark expedition in 1805 also buttressed the American claim. This first land journey to the Columbia had the further effect of convincing the American people that they had a right to the disputed region. The fur-trading post at Fort Astoria was also a victory, for Astor's men beat a British expedition to the site by a few months. Even seizure of the post during the War of 1812 did not erase American claims. The Treaty of Ghent called for the restoration of wartime conquests, so Astoria was grudgingly returned to the United States. This act constituted British recognition of American tenure on the south bank of the Columbia.

In the absence of any clear-cut verdict as to who was entitled to

Oregon, England and the United States agreed to "let the future decide." A treaty of joint occupation was signed on October 20, 1818, and was to run for 10 years. It permitted citizens of both countries to live and trade in the area. The heart of the controversy was the territory between the Columbia and the 49th parallel: most of today's state of Washington. England was willing to concede the south bank of the Columbia to the Americans, who despite much propaganda about "54-40 or Fight" were always willing to settle for a westward extension of the 49th parallel border. But the stakes of the game—land, furs, and national prestige—were too high, and stubborn men seem to have been chosen as negotiators on both sides. So the boundary was not defined for many years.

Spain withdrew from the competition in 1819 as a result of the Adams-Onís treaty. This placed the American-Spanish border along the 42nd parallel, the present California-Oregon state line. American claims to 50-40 were henceforth based upon the ceded Spanish rights to that northern latitude. Russia too backed out after being challenged by both the United States and England. Her claims to territory extending as far south as the 51st parallel were surrendered in treaties with the two countries signed in 1824 and 1825. Thus by 1825 the Anglo-American contest centered on the region between the 42nd parallel on the south and 54°40′ on the north.

England was dominant in the area until the 1840s. The Hudson's Bay Company was a private concern, but it maintained close contacts with the government and represented imperial interests. Old-timers wisecracked that HBC stood for "Here Before Christ." The Company's Fort Vancouver, described by American visitors as "the New York of the Pacific," was the most famous trading post in the West. The central stockade, with its storehouses and residential quarters, was surrounded by farms and orchards. Dr. John McLoughlin encouraged his employees to raise wheat, fruit, cattle, and hogs, thus establishing an agricultural base for the fur trade. The doctor also built a system of forts eastward along the Columbia and into the interior of Oregon and Washington. These outposts were essential instruments of the Company's "Fur Desert" policy: keeping the Americans at arm's length by ruthless trapping of the approaches to Oregon. The tactic succeeded, and England consequently maintained a firm grasp on the Northwest.

American Propagandists

Though their statements had all the ferocity of a mouse challenging a lion, some Americans promoted our claims to Oregon during the decades of British dominance. Representative John Floyd of Virginia had a strong interest in the West. He was the son of a noted Kentucky pioneer, and his cousin (Charles Floyd) had been with Lewis and Clark. So in January of 1821 he asked the Congress to finance a fur-trading house at the mouth of the Columbia. Twelve months later he urged the creation of a Territory of Oregon. But Congress remained indifferent to such proposals. The distances involved seemed too great. It was pointed out that a representative from Oregon would be able to spend only 2 weeks a year at Washington; the rest of his time would be spent in traveling. Even Senator Benton, who favored the military occupation of Oregon, felt in 1825 that the Rocky Mountains would be our "natural" boundary. In the face of such a limp response it was clear that the government was unprepared to back up its grand claims to the Columbia.

One propagandist, however, kept needling Congress during these years. He was Hall Jackson Kelley, a nervous and nearsighted schoolteacher from Boston. Kelley had never seen a prairie dog or a buffalo, but he had a wide-ranging imagination and he believed everything he read. The most important book in his library was Nicholas Biddle's 1814 edition of the Lewis and Clark *Journals*. From these Kelley derived the vision of a prosperous American commonwealth on the Columbia. Beginning in 1824 he pushed his views on annexation in letters and petitions to Congress and the newspapers. Many contemporaries thought he was mad, and like most dreamers, he has fared badly at the hands of historians. In 1830 he did form an emigration society that was to "transplant New England in Oregon." Despite its mouth-filling title (The American Society for Encouraging the Settlement of Oregon Territory) and its impressive membership list (about 500 persons), the enterprise never got beyond the talking stage. Kelley was a classic example of the "impractical" schoolteacher, so he was important as a publicist rather than as a pioneer. His writings did much to familiarize Americans with both the name and the region which were the subjects of his voluminous production.

Nathaniel J. Wyeth

Nathaniel J. Wyeth was another of the unlikely cast of characters who had roles in the Oregon epic. He was a successful Boston ice dealer, an occupation seemingly unrelated to fur trading on the Columbia. Yet Wyeth's scheme was really a duplication of Astor's, that is, a trading post at the mouth of the river to be supplied by sea. An added feature was a plan to ship dried salmon back to the States. Wyeth underestimated both the power of the Hudson's Bay Company and the difficulties of actually getting to Oregon. Yet with that innocent self-confidence which marked Americans of this period, he organized a Pacific Trading Company and enlisted twenty-one greenhorns to go west with him.

When Wyeth reached St. Louis in the spring of 1832, he was fortunate in being able to join the year's fur-trading caravan. William Sublette, the crusty mountain man who piloted the train, had taken wagons as far as the Wind River in 1830. This feat had caused the St. Louis *Beacon* to exult that "the ease with which they did it, and could have gone on to the mouth of the Columbia, shows the folly and nonsense of those '*scientific*' characters who talk of the Rocky

Mountains as the barrier which is to stop the westward march of the American people." This was a premature conclusion, for wagons did not go all the way to the Columbia until the migrations of the 1840s. Sublette told Wyeth to leave his vehicles in St. Louis, and the joint expedition traveled together as far as Pierre's Hole, where Wyeth joined a Rocky Mountain Fur Company brigade for the further trip up the Snake River and into Oregon. Upon arriving at Fort Vancouver, he learned that his supply ship had been wrecked at sea. All Wyeth could do was turn around and start back home again. But significantly, two of his men remained in the Willamette Valley, thus becoming the first permanent American settlers in Oregon.

Wyeth made another attempt to establish his fur and salmon business in 1834. On the way west he built a depot for his goods on the Snake River in southeastern Idaho, and Fort Hall subsequently became a stopping point on the Oregon Trail. Wyeth's major post was at the mouth of the Willamette, but his prospects were never bright. The HBC toyed with him as a child plays with an insect, and then it squashed him under foot by cutting prices. He was forced to sell all his interests to the company, including Fort Hall, and returned to Boston as a sadder but wiser iceman.

The Missionaries

Accompanying Wyeth on this second trip was Jason Lee, a powerful, black-bearded Methodist preacher. Lee was the first of several important missionaries who helped prepare Oregon for American occupation. They were also to leave a Puritan imprint upon society in the future state. In the fall of 1831 four Oregon Indians had accompanied some traders down to St. Louis. William Walker, a Christianized Wyandot, heard of the visit and made up a story that they had come to learn the white man's religion. The tale was printed in the Methodist *Christian Advocate*, accompanied by a fanciful illustration depicting the deformed heads of Flathead children. The presumed appeal for religious instruc-

Jason Lee. Source: Oregon Historical Society.

tions tugged at the heartstrings of congregations in the East, and contributions for a Flathead mission poured in to the offices of the *Advocate*. Lee and his nephew Daniel volunteered to take on the job of instructing these Indians.

Lee did not establish his mission among the Flatheads, however. After seeing some specimens of the tribe at Pierre's Hole, he decided to go 500 miles further west from their country to the Willamette Since only a couple dozen Indians still lived in the valley, it is clear that Lee intended to minister to clean-cut American farmers rather than hopelessly degenerate savages. In fact, Lee's mission, built about 60 miles up from the mouth of the river, was the Trojan Horse of the English-American contest for Oregon. It became the nucleus for a sizable American colony that sprang up over the next dozen years.

Meanwhile the Presbyterians and Congregationalists, acting through their American Board of Foreign Missions, had also become interested in Oregon. The Reverend Samuel Parker and Dr. Marcus Whitman made an exploratory trip in the summer of 1835, accompanying the trapper caravan as usual. At rendezvous in Wyoming the missioners came face to face with some of the rawness of Western life. Whitman pried an embedded arrowhead out of Jim Bridger's back (the anesthetic being forty-rod whiskey), while Parker saw Kit Carson kill the camp bully in a fight over an Indian squaw. Parker went on to Fort Vancouver to scout for mission locations, while Whitman returned to New York State and hurriedly prepared to take out the expedition of 1836.

Marcus Whitman and his shapely blond wife, Narcissa, were both dedicated missioners. He was a medical doctor, however, not an ordained minister, and hence had to persuade a regular missionary to join him in Oregon. Mr. and Mrs. Henry Spalding agreed to go. Spalding had earlier been a rejected suitor of Narcissa Whitman, which made for a rather sticky social situation on the trail. Yet the expedition got under way in the spring of 1836, the missionaries going along with Thomas Fitzpatrick and the fur-trader caravan of that year.

The Whitmans and Spaldings experienced most of the trials and tribulations of later emigrant trains. There were clouds of mosquitoes, and when Indians were around there were lice. River crossings were especially exasperating, for the people had to go over on horses or in bullboats. The wagons were taken across on rafts, or were floated over after the boxes were covered with waterproofed skins to make a type of barge. The wagons themselves were a constant headache, since axletrees or tongues might break; and when the wooden wheels shrank, the iron tires would fall off. Then the metal would have to be reforged and refitted to the wheel. Despite such difficulties, Whitman managed to take his wagon (whittled down to a two-wheel cart) as far as Fort Boise in western Idaho.

Like those who followed them, the missioners cooked their bacon, beans, and buffalo meat over fires made with the dried buffalo "chips." Fresh meat from game animals was a necessity along the trail, since the supplies brought from Independence often went bad. As a later traveler (Alonzo Delano) wrote: "We discovered that we had been imposed upon . . . in the purchase of our bacon, for it began to exhibit more signs of life than we had bargained for. It became necessary to scrape and smoke it, in order to get rid of its tendency to walk in insect form." Thirst was also a problem along the waterless stretches of the trail. A buffalo's stomach was sometimes drained off for drinking. John Townsend, a Philadelphia scientist who accompanied Wyeth and Lee in 1834, found himself drinking buffalo blood: "I plunged my head into the reeking ventricles, and drank until forced to stop for breath. I felt somewhat ashamed of assimilating myself so nearly to the brutes." Indians were a nuisance but not a menace during the migrations of the next decade, but one always felt anxious when they were around. It was never wise to wander off alone or to be caught without firearms.

The Whitmans planted their mission among the Cayuse Indians at Waiilatpu, 22 miles from the Hudson's Bay Company's Fort Walla Walla. The Spaldings went on to Lapwai Creek (near present Lewiston) in Idaho. These regions were never attractive to American settlers, virtually all of whom headed for the Willamette Valley. It is thus ironical that the missioners who took their commitment to the Indians most seriously were less important in the actual settlement of Oregon than Jason Lee, who practically ignored the red men. Lee went back to the United States in 1838 on a fundraising tour. He took two Chinook Indians with him, and they were a sensation in the East even though their heads were pointed rather than flattened. Lee returned to Oregon by ship in 1839, bringing fifty-one men and women settlers with him. They included teachers, ministers, a doctor, and a number of skilled artisans. This "Great Reinforcement" began to balance the scales somewhat in the disputed area.

The Catholics were also active in the Northwest, and it seems that the four Indians who had appeared at St. Louis in 1831 were really seeking Catholic missionaries. Father Francois Blanchet reached Oregon from Canada in 1838, and started missions at Walla Walla, Colville, and elsewhere. The priests enjoyed greater success with the Indians than the Protestants, probably because the principles of Catholicism were made more understandable to the Indians. The best-known Catholic in the region was the Jesuit Pierre DeSmet. In the 1840's he established a half dozen missions in Idaho and western Montana, north of the main route to Oregon. He subsequently made a number of important exploratory trips in the northern Rockies.

The Oregon Trail

In 1836 President Jackson had sent Lt. William A. Slacum to Oregon as a spy. Slacum did his job well, gathering information on the British posts and urging the American settlers to petition for admission to the United States. Slacum's official report was presented to Congress in 1837. It emphasized military aspects of the Oregon question, and dwelt at some length on the value of Puget Sound.

Senator Lewis Linn of Missouri consequently introduced a bill calling for the military occupation of the Columbia. The bill did not pass, but Congress went so far as to appoint an Indian subagent for Oregon.

The agent was Dr. Elijah White, a Methodist minister who had spent three unhappy years in Oregon as an assistant to Jason Lee. In 1842 White promoted and organized the first sizable wagon train to take the Oregon Trail. In 1841 a smaller contingent of twenty-four men and women had left the California-bound Bartleson-Bidwell party at Soda Springs, and had gone on to Oregon. But Dr. White had no less than 107 bona fide pioneers in his train, together with eighteen wagons and assorted cattle and dogs. The "jumping-off" place was Independence, Missouri, the westernmost settlement on the main American frontier. From here it was 2,000 miles to the Willamette, representing a trip of from 4 to 6 months.

The wagons normally went north from Independence to the south bank of the Platte River, whose valley they followed to Fort Laramie. At this famous adobe-walled trading post, 642 miles out from Independence, the more fearful or comfort-loving emigrants turned back toward civilization. They had had enough of dust, rainstorms, and sickness. The go-getters went west along the aptly named Sweetwater River and crossed the Continental Divide at South Pass, 7,500 feet above sea level. From here the migrants could take a long southern dip to Fort Bridger, or they could continue in a northwesterly direction by the Sublette Cutoff. Both these trails converged north of Bear Lake and then ran on to Fort Hall. From the fort the trail swung along the Snake River, past Fort Boise, and on to the Columbia by way of the Blue Mountains. The worst part of the trail was the 60-mile stretch between the Dalles and the Willamette. The settlers had to grope their way over the Cascade Mountains, lowering wagons by means of cables in several places. Or they could risk everything by shooting a series of terrifying rapids on rafts. Some of them lost the gamble and their lives just short of the Promised Land.

Courage and endurance were among the heroic qualities called forth by travel to Oregon. But less admirable traits were also in evidence. The psychological strains of travel in a strange land, together with the anxiety about disease, or one's cattle, or the Indians, led to short tempers. Most of the emigrant trains were torn by factionalism. Francis Parkman, who encountered one such train in 1846, observed that "It was easy to see that fear and dissension prevailed among them . . . many were murmuring against the leader they had chosen, and wished to depose him; and this discontent was fomented by some ambitious spirits, who had hopes of succeeding in his place." The 1842 caravan was afflicted with this divisiveness. Dr. White was unfortunately a pompous little man who seemed to be puffed up with his own importance. So his leadership was successfully challenged by young Lansford Hastings, who was elected train captain. In his *Emigrant's Guide to Oregon and California* (1845), Hastings described the familiar phenomenon: "We had proceeded only a few days

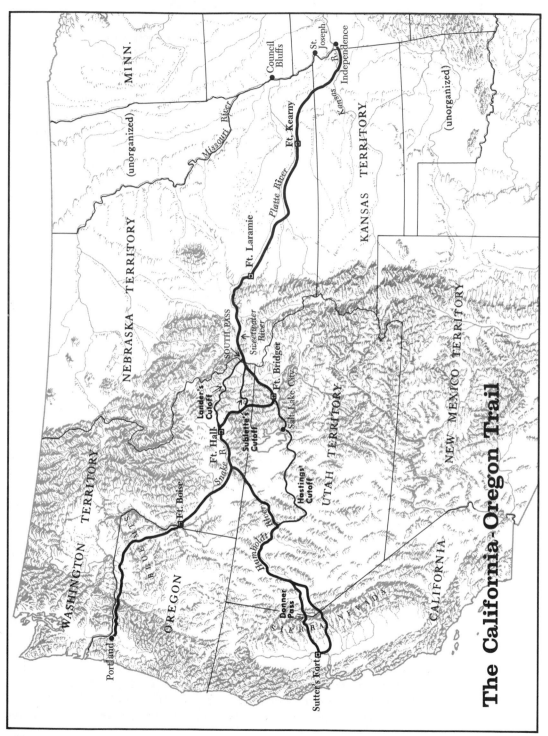

The California-Oregon Trail

travel, from our native land of order and security, when the 'American character' was fully exhibited. All appeared to be determined to govern, but not to be governed. Here we were, without law, without order, and without restraint; in a state of nature, amid the confused, revolving, fragments of elementary society!" The typical emigrant train was thus an assemblage of individualists without discipline. It appears that stability of location was necessary before the usual processes of frontier self-government could function effectively.

The Key Year 1843

Divisions also occurred in the caravan of 1843, a pivotal year in Oregon history. This was the largest train yet, an estimated 1,000 people in all. Most of these were fairly successful farmers rather than ne'er-do-wells, since it required a substantial investment of from $700 to $1,500 in oxen, wagons, and food to make the months-long trip to the Coast. The emigrants elected their train captain by lining up behind the candidates as in a game of "snap-the-whip." Peter Burnett, a future governor of California, won the election although he had a typically short term. He resigned when he could not heal the breach between those who wished to travel more rapidly and those who had large numbers of livestock. These latter formed a separate "cow column" which traveled at a slower pace. Its captain was Jesse Applegate, who later wrote a famous narrative of the trip. He included a description of how the wagons formed a circular stockade at sunset: "In about an hour, five thousand animals are close up to the encampment, and the teamsters are busy selecting their teams and driving them inside the 'corral' to be yoked. The corral is a circle one hundred yards deep, formed with wagons connected strongly with each other; the wagon in the rear being connected with the wagon in front by its tongue and ox-chains. It is a strong barrier that the vicious ox cannot break, and in case of an attack of the Sioux would be no contemptible entrenchment." The wagons used were not the Conestogas of the Santa Fe trade, but ordinary farm wagons fitted with canvas tops.

Accompanying this '43 train was Marcus Whitman. The previous year Elijah White had delivered to him a sealed letter from the American Board, ordering the closing of all but one of the Oregon missions. Whitman made a frantic wintertime journey back East by way of New Mexico, and persuaded the board to rescind the order. This feat, admirable in itself, somehow became linked with American acquisition of Oregon. The legend was embalmed in books bearing such titles as *How Marcus Whitman Saved Oregon*. But Whitman's advice was especially helpful when the emigrants passed into the region beyond Fort Hall.

The government was also represented on the Oregon Trail this year, in the person of John Charles Frémont. The doughty captain was leading his mountaineers on another exploring expedition whose purpose was to "examine the broad region south of the Columbia River, lying between the Rocky Mountains and the Pacific Ocean." Frémont went all the way to Fort Vancouver before turning south into the Great Basin. His observations were embodied in a published report which referred to "an easy carriage road across our continent from the Western States to the Oregon." Such favorable statements helped stimulate further migration to the Northwest.

But it was the plain American farmer with his enormous brood of children who won Oregon for the United States. What Congressman Andrew Kennedy of Indiana described as the "American multiplication table" was involved. "Go to the West and see a young man with his mate of eighteen; after the lapse of thirty years, visit him again and instead of two, you will find twenty two. This is what I call the American multiplication table." These farmers, the bulk of whom came from the Mississippi Valley, took the trail to Oregon for various reasons. Economics was certainly involved: a depression had hit the valley following the Panic of 1837, and prices for farm crops were down. In contrast, the Willamette was said to be incredibly fertile, and a man could grow bumper crops of wheat in the perpetual spring weather. Furthermore, in 1841 Senator Linn's bill to give every settler 640 acres of free land in Oregon passed the Senate, and though it failed in the House it naturally drew more attention to the coastal area. For others a simple curiosity about the West, or a sense of adventure, were a sufficient motive. Some may even have gone with the patriotic intention of making Oregon American territory, though this motive was usually not remembered until 30 or 40 years after the event.

Many of the travelers learned about Oregon through letters from relatives or friends who had already gone west. This correspondence (often printed in local newspapers) was supplemented by literary influences. A number of books about the Oregon country had been published. The most influential of these were the Lewis and Clark *Journals* and Washington Irving's *Astoria* (1836). Another source of information was John K. Townsend's *Narrative* (1839). Townsend, the naturalist who had accompanied the Wyeth-Lee expedition in 1834, wrote particularly good descriptions of the geography along the trail route. The Reverend Samuel Parker had also written up his trip in *Journal of An Exploring Tour Beyond the Rocky Mountains* (1838), and information from church sources was also obtained from articles in the *Christian Advocate*. Extracts from these and other publications were read and discussed by the prospective emigrants.

So 1843 was the beginning of large-scale migration along the Overland Trail. Some 1,400 settlers infected with the "Oregon Fever" came over the route in 1844, and 3,000 in 1845. By the end of that year the total population of Oregon had reached 6,000. Practically all of this number had settled on the Willamette; only thirty Americans lived north of the Columbia. Yet Dr. McLoughlin and the Hudson's Bay people could see that the time of reckoning was not far off.

Self-government

The Oregon settlers were in a no-man's-land as far as their property and legal rights were concerned. Under the joint occupation agreement (renewed in 1827) neither England nor the United States had political authority in the area. As they had instinctively done on earlier frontiers, the settlers improvised their own governmental system. A move in this direction had been made as early as 1841, but the all-powerful Hudson's Bay Company had frowned on the effort and it had died. By the spring of 1843, however, the Americans were sufficiently numerous so that they could institute a provisional government. Discussions were initiated at the "wolf meetings," which were held primarily to plan a *defensive and destructive* WAR" against predatory animals. Bounties were set at 50 cents for a small wolf, $3 for a large wolf, and $5 for a panther. (Characteristically, Indians received half as much as whites.) A resolution favoring the establishment of civil government was also adopted at the March 6 meeting.

In July the frame of government was approved. Based largely on the laws of Iowa Territory, it included a plural executive (three-man committee), a prohibition on slavery, and individual "subscription" in place of taxation. Frontier influence was apparent in the legalization of marriage for males at age sixteen and females at fourteen. The amateurish features of the system had to be revised the next year. The plural executive was changed to a single governor, and taxes were instituted. Other major changes were made before territorial status was finally achieved in 1848. The provisional government was an admirable example of the kind of spontaneous search for law and order found in the Watauga Association, the Nashborough Compact, and similar frontier documents.

Annexation

The influx of "patriotic pioneers" moved President Polk to pursue a settlement of the boundary question. In his inaugural address on March 4, 1845, the president had announced that "our title to the country of the Oregon is 'clear and unquestionable,' and already are our people preparing to perfect that title by occupying it with their wives and children." Just what boundary Polk was claiming for the United States was not clear. The Democratic platform in 1844 had called for the "re-occupation of Oregon," and the party's campaign slogan had been an equally imprecise "Texas and Oregon." In July, however, Polk clarified his position by offering Britain a division line at the 49th parallel.

The British minister at Washington immediately rejected the offer. In response, Polk took a hard line, reasserting America's claim to all of Oregon up to 54°40'. Our inheritance of Spanish rights to this area and the opposition to further European colonization enunciated in the Monroe Doctrine were the bases of Polk's position. At his request Congress on April 23, 1846, passed a resolution terminating the joint-occupation agreement. At this time the 54-40 or Fight slogan gained currency among the more bellicose Democrats. The all-Oregon movement was centered in the states of the Old Northwest (particularly Illinois and Indiana) and in Missouri. But in June England offered a compromise at the 49th parallel. The transfer of the Hudson's Bay Company's headquarters to Vancouver Island in 1845 made it possible for the British government to yield its Columbia River claim gracefully. Polk accepted the offer, since war had been declared on Mexico in May and he did not wish to tangle with the British Navy at the same time. The Senate apparently agreed with him, for it voted acceptance of the treaty on June 15, 1846.

The "ultras" from the Northwest stormed at Polk's "betrayal." Senator Benton, though he accepted the compromise, was moved to remark: "Oh! mountain that was delivered of a mouse, thy name shall henceforth be fifty-four forty!" Yet of the two major interests supporting Oregon annexation, the agrarian-pioneer of the Northwest and the maritime-commercial of New England, the latter was satisfied so long as Puget Sound was included in the compromise. Nor did Polk seem anxious to fight for the rather dubious claim to the northernmost line. Like the Eastern Whigs, he was interested in harbors, and when England gave up the Sound his goals in the Oregon country had been achieved.

A bill to organize territorial government for Oregon became snarled in the slavery controversy. John C. Calhoun and his fellow slaveholders demanded elimination of the antislavery clause in the provisional government. They were unsuccessful, but the fight delayed passage of the measure until August of 1848. Much popular sympathy for the Oregonians had followed the Whitman Massacre of November 29, 1847. Marcus and Narcissa Whitman along with eleven men at the Waiilatpu mission were hacked to pieces by the Cayuse, who blamed them for a devastating measles epidemic. So national expansionism triumphed over Southern obstructionism, and Oregon was on the road to becoming the thirty-third state of the Union.

Selected Readings   General regional histories valuable for insights into Oregon acquisition are Oscar O. Winther, *The Great Northwest* (New York, 1947); Dorothy O. Johanssen and Charles M. Gates, *Empire on the Columbia* (New York, 1957); and Earl Pomeroy, *The Pacific Slope* (New York, 1965). Norman Graebner, *Empire on the Pacific* (New York, 1955), maintains that commercial interests were more important than pioneering in winning Oregon: "Any interpretation of westward extension beyond Texas is meaningless unless defined in terms of commerce and harbors." This theory is challenged by William H. Goetzmann, *When the Eagle Screamed: The Romantic Horizon in American Diplomacy, 1800-1860* (New York, 1966). The traditional view may be found in the articles of a leading student, Frederick Merk. See especially "The Oregon Pioneers and the Boundary," *American Historical Review*, vol. 29 (July, 1924), and "The Genesis of the Oregon Question," *Mississippi Valley*

Historical Review, vol. 36 (March, 1950). These and other articles are brought together in Merk's *The Oregon Question: Essays in Anglo-American Diplomacy and Politics* (Cambridge, 1967). Melville C. Jacobs, *Winning Oregon* (Caldwell, Idaho, 1938), though in need of revision in places, is still a good short monograph on the expansionist movement.

The activities of the Hudson's Bay Company may be followed in John S. Galbraith, *The Hudson's Bay Company* (Cambridge, 1957), and in the McLoughlin biography by Richard K. Montgomery, *The White-Headed Eagle* (New York, 1935). A standard biography is Fred W. Powell, *Hall Jackson Kelley—Prophet of Oregon* (Portland, 1917), while the same author's *Hall J. Kelley on Oregon* (Princeton, 1932) is a collection of writings. Nathaniel J. Wyeth's story is told in John B. Wyeth, *Oregon*, and reprinted in volume 21 of Reuben G. Thwaites, *Early Western Travels* (Cleveland, 1905).

A good starting point for study of the missionary effort is Nard Jones, *The Great Command* (Boston, 1959), a popular biography of Marcus Whitman. A more extensive treatment is Clifford M. Drury, *Marcus Whitman, M.D.* (Caldwell, Idaho, 1937). See also Cornelius J. Brosman, *Jason Lee, Prophet of the New Oregon* (New York, 1932). John Upton Terrell gives a satisfactory overview of the Catholic effort in *Black Robe: The Life of Pierre-Jean DeSmet* (Garden City, N.Y., 1964). Information on the missionaries may also be found in David Lavender, *Westward Vision: The Story of the Oregon Trail* (New York, 1963), the last fourth of which is specifically concerned with the trail.

A classic primary source is Francis Parkman's *The California and Oregon Trail*, originally published in 1849 and now available in numerous editions. Bernard DeVoto, *The Year of Decision: 1846* (Boston, 1943), has superb chapters on the Oregon Trail. Jay Monaghan, *The Overland Trail* (Indianapolis, 1947), is well written, while James C. Bell, *Opening a Highway to the Pacific, 1838-1846* (New York, 1921), is scholarly but skimpy. Irene D. Paden, *The Wake of the Prairie Schooner* (New York, 1943), is part history and part personal narrative about both California and Oregon emigrant routes. Frederica B. Coons, *The Trail to Oregon* (Portland, 1954), is a brief, lightly written account based on primary sources. Lansford W. Hastings, *The Emigrant's Guide to Oregon and California*, has been published in a facsimile edition (Princeton, 1932). Frank C. Robertson, *Fort Hall* (New York, 1963), is good popular history. Jesse Applegate, "A Day with the Cow Column," was originally published in the *Overland Monthly*, vol. 1 (August, 1868). Oliver W. Nixon, *How Marcus Whitman Saved Oregon* (Chicago, 1895), advances the legend. John K. Townsend's *Narrative of a Journey across the Rocky Mountains to the Columbia River* was reprinted in volume 21 of Reuben G. Thwaites, *Early Western Travels* (Cleveland, 1905).

Details of annexation are in the books by Merk and Graebner cited above and in J. S. Reeves, *American Diplomacy under Tyler and Polk* (Baltimore, 1907), which is a classic. Edwin A. Miles, "Fifty-four Forty or Fight—An American Political Legend," *Mississippi Valley Historical Review*, vol. 44 (September, 1957), demolishes the legend. Peter H. Burnett, *Recollections and Opinions of an Old Pioneer* (New York, 1880), is informative on the provisional government.

XV. The California Frontier

California was the ultimate frontier. Its clover-clad valleys, abundant game, and sunny climate seemed to promise a happy ending for the whole westward movement. Yet since the province clearly belonged to a foreign nation, it entered the American consciousness at a much later date than did neighboring Oregon. The frontiersmen and the national political leaders were only mildly interested in California, the latter principally because of San Francisco Bay. But Yankee infiltration, together with the obvious feebleness of Mexico's political control, made the outcome self-evident. Americans had been drifting into the region since the early years of the century. In letters and books the more literate of them spoke highly of the climate and the economic possibilities, while describing the native Spaniards as yahoos. This kind of publicity brought the province within the scope of American territorial ambition.

Yankees by Sea   The sea otter and China trade brought the first Americans to Alta California. Beginning in 1795 the New England traders found good hunting along the Coast, particularly in the Santa Barbara Channel Islands. They began to put in at San Diego or San Francisco to take on wood and water. A small-scale trade, manufactured items for fresh food, was carried on at these ports. Such trading was illegal, but since officials often participated the law was unenforceable. In fact, the presidio *comandantes* were parties to the considerable smuggling that was conducted at such points as Santa Cruz and San Pedro.

Occasionally the Yankee traders bumped into a conscientious official who had not absorbed the easy-going habits of California. When Capt. William Shaler touched at San Diego in 1803, the presidio commandant attempted to arrest his second mate and two sailors for smuggling. Shaler rescued his men at gunpoint and then fought an artillery duel with the batteries at the mouth of the harbor. It is not surprising that when Shaler published a description of California in Philadelphia's *American Register* (in 1808), he spoke enthusiastically of the climate but called the Spaniards degraded.

The sea otter trade flourished until the outbreak of the War of 1812 made it dangerous for Boston ships to sail the high seas. After the peace treaty the fur trade was resumed, but its boom days were gone. By 1820 overhunting had made otter rather scarce. But in the 1820s American contacts with California were maintained by whalers and hide and tallow traders. On their way back to New England from the Pacific, the whaling ships would put in at San Francisco or Monterey for repairs and supplies. The crews reported favorably on these ports when they got home. More important were the hide traders, who appeared after Mexican rule had been established.

Vast herds of cattle, most of them belonging to the missions, roamed the California valleys. They were a source of meat, the jawbreaking slabs of *carne asada* that has long been a staple of the Mexican diet. A few of the hides were worked up into rawhide, but the padres utilized only a small percentage of their herds in this way. So there was a ready supply when the hide trade officially began in 1822. The Englishmen Hugh McCulloch and William Hartnell got the first contract with the missions, but Americans soon elbowed their way into the trade. William A. Gale appeared in California in 1822 also, and became a resident merchant for the Boston firm of Bryant & Sturgis. Other Yankee merchants who came during the 20s and 30s included Thomas O. Larkin in Monterey, Alfred Robinson in Santa Barbara, Abel Stearns in Los Angeles, and John J. Warner in the San Diego area. These men became Mexican citizens, learned the language, and many of them married native women.

After "secularization" of the missions in 1834, most of the hide business went through private ranchos. The hides sold for $2 each. They were scraped, tied in bundles, and then dumped on the beach. The Yankee sailors or "droghers" had the unenviable job of loading them into longboats and rowing out to the trading vessel. Theoretically all foreign traders stopped at the white-walled customhouse in Monterey and paid duties on their cargoes of furniture, iron, and other manufactured goods. In practice there was always much smuggling, bribery, and employment of subterfuges to avoid payment of full duties. It is interesting to note that among the goods sold to the Californians were New England boots and shoes made from California hides. The price markup on this footgear represented profits of 300 percent for the traders.

The hide business (and the allied trade in tallow for candles) prospered until 1838. Thereafter a scarcity of hides and the increasingly restrictive policy of the provincial government caused it to decline. But it had made the region familiar to people on the east coast. Richard Henry Dana had dropped out of Harvard and shipped as a common seaman aboard a hide trader in 1836. His book *Two Years Before the Mast*, published in 1840, dealt principally with California. Dana spent much time ashore in San Diego and Santa Barbara, so he was able to observe the California way of life at close range. His descriptions of the climate appealed to many Easterners, who then as now dream of snow-free winters.

Yankees by Land

American merchants like Thomas Larkin or Alfred Robinson were welcomed because they dealt in manufactured goods which the Mexican economy itself could not supply. But beginning in 1826 a more dangerous type of American started to appear in California. He was the mountain man: hard as nails, skilled in riflery, and about as sensitive to Mexican political rights as a grizzly bear. Mexican officials had hoped that the deserts and mountains to the east would shield the province against such intrusions. Imagine their dismay when on November 26, 1826, Jedediah Smith and seventeen of his fur trappers appeared at San Gabriel mission. The Governor for one knew he would now have the unpleasant task of taking the wolf by the ears.

Smith had left his base camp near Salt Lake 3 months before. His search for new beaver streams took him along what later became a southern branch of the California Trail: Utah Lake—the Sevier River—the Virgin—the Colorado—and the Mojave. This trailbreaking by the first Americans to enter

Jedediah Smith arrives at San Gabriel Mission. Source: From a model in the Los Angeles County Museum of Natural History.

California from overland was a feat of which they could be justly proud. The dog-tired mountaineers rested at San Gabriel, patching their tattered shirts with missionmade cloth and quaffing liberal amounts of *aguardiente.*

Governor José Maria Echeandía did not share posterity's admiration for Smith's exploit. In fact he ordered the intruders to leave pronto and to take the route by which they had come. Smith did leave on January 18 (1827), but after traversing Cajon Pass he swung northward and went up the unknown San Joaquin Valley. He left most of his men to trap in the upper tributaries of the valley, while he and two companions struggled across the Sierra Nevada at some point unknown. There was too much snow in the mountains and not enough water on the Nevada-Utah deserts. But Smith made it back to his camp at Bear Lake on July 3. On the 12th he wrote a letter to William Clark, now based in St. Louis as Superintendent of Indian Affairs, describing the trip. This letter appeared in a St. Louis newspaper and was eventually published in France, thus making Smith an international celebrity. The young mountaineer spent only 10 days in camp before again leaving for California with eighteen men. While crossing the Colorado on rafts, the trappers were attacked by Mojave Indians who killed ten of the party. Smith and the survivors stumbled across the desert and once again presented themselves at San Gabriel.

There were no welcome mats out for Smith this time. In fact, when he went north he was jailed, first at San Jose and then at Monterey. The Governor was persuaded to free him through the intercession of several hide traders who happened to be in the capital and who posted the necessary bail. After his lucky deliverance, Smith went north into Oregon for further trapping. On the Umpqua River his party was attacked by Indians and only Smith and two other men escaped. They sought refuge at Fort Vancouver, and from there made their way back to Salt Lake. Smith's two trips to California were feats of physical endurance that entitle him to a place in the pantheon of frontier heroes.

Other American trappers turned up in California the next year, 1828. They were the party of Sylvester and James Ohio Pattie, father and son, who had walked across the desert from the Colorado River to San Diego. The Patties were Kentuckians who had drifted down to Santa Fe in 1824. They engaged in fur trading, and the father also ran the Santa Rita copper mines for a while. Their adventures with grizzly bears, Apaches, and beautiful Mexican maidens, recorded in James Pattie's *Personal Narrative* (1831), strain the credulity of modern readers. James evidently depicted himself in a much more heroic role than the facts warranted. But there is sugar amidst the salt, and a number of his statements can be verified by other sources. Mexican documents confirm that the Patties appeared at San Diego in the spring of 1828.

Governor Echeandía, having just gotten rid of the obnoxious Smith for the second time, was sick and tired of American trespassers. So he threw the Patties and their six companions into jail. The father died as a result of his confinement. James was kept behind bars for several months, and much of the

Personal Narrative is taken up with an exaggerated account of the cruelty of Mexican bureaucrats. The brash young man finally managed to spring himself when a smallpox epidemic hit the province. He happened to have a supply of vaccine, used for the Indians working at the Santa Rita mine, and he agreed to vaccinate residents and mission Indians in exchange for his freedom. The wanderer returned to the United States by way of Mexico in 1830, and in Cincinnati he told his quasi-factual story to an entranced publisher.

Other American trappers based at Santa Fe or Taos were only a step behind the Patties in penetrating California. They made various improvements in the Patties' Gila River route and the more familiar "Old Spanish Trail." Such men as Ewing Young and William Wolfskill traveled west with large and well-armed parties which made the Mexican authorities think twice about attempting to arrest them. Young trapped along the San Joaquin Valley in 1829 and 1830. When he was near Los Angeles on the return trip, the Mexicans planned to arrest his men by getting them drunk. But in their inebriated condition, one James Higgins shot and killed James Lawrence. "Such conduct frightened the Mexicans," reports Kit Carson, "and they departed in all haste, fearing that if men without provocation would shoot one another, it would require but little to cause them to murder them."

In 1833 Joseph Walker explored the central route into California by way of the Humboldt River Valley. Walker was one of Captain Bonneville's men, and his trip was an outgrowth of the captain's rather enigmatic fur-trading venture. Bonneville sent Walker out from the Green River rendezvous with sixty men and with instructions to locate fresh beaver streams west of the Salt Lake. This was one of the more picturesque trapper-explorer parties. Walker was a rawboned Virginian, widely admired for both his character and leadership. In his party was Zenas Leonard, serving as clerk and journalkeeper, and George Nidever, who remained in California to become a legendary bear hunter. Nidever was possibly the trapper whom Leonard remembered as having a powerful gun named "Knock-Him-Stiff."

These men pioneered a large part of the future California Trail. This ran beside the Humbolt, a thin ribbon of water along which, as Zenas Leonard put it, "you may travel for many days without finding a stick large enough to make a walking cane." They passed Walker Lake and made an arduous crossing of the Sierra Nevada, probably in the area of today's Yosemite National Park. On November 21 they reached the coast some 40 miles below San Francisco. A symbolic meeting of American sailors and mountain men occurred at this point when the hide trader *Lagoda* hove into view. "Captain Baggshaw strongly insisted on us going on board and partaking of the ship's fare, stating that he had a few casks of untapped Coneac. This was an invitation that none of us had the least desire to refuse, and accordingly forty five of us went on board the *Lagoda*, leaving the remainder to take care of the camp &c."

Walker followed a more southerly route on his return trip in April of 1834. He went by way of the Kern River, and then discovered Walker Pass through the mountains. Six of his trappers stayed behind in California. They became part of the American community there, but were clearly a more dangerous and volatile group than the merchants. This was proven when Juan Alvarado overthrew the California government in 1836. His success was due to the assistance of a group of former sailors and mountain men headed by Isaac Graham of Tennessee.

There were Englishmen, Frenchmen, and various other foreigners besides Americans living in California during this period. Among them was John Augustus Sutter, a German-Swiss adventurer who arrived in 1839. An ex-shopkeeper, he represented himself as a heroic military officer. This pose so impressed the Mexican authorities that they permitted him to claim land and erect a fort far inland. Indeed, Sutter wanted to be as far away from the government as possible, for his proposed "New Helvetia" was to be a feudal principality. Sutter's Fort on the Sacramento had by 1842 become an imposing structure equipped with artillery. Here the self-styled "Captain" supervised a large number of employees engaged in ranching and farming, while he played the gracious host in the manner of Swiss hotelkeepers. As far as American contacts with California were concerned, he regarded himself as the friend and champion of overland emigrants. It became customary for these newcomers to head for Sutter's Fort where they could be sure of a welcome reception.

Overland Emigration

Overland emigration to California became significant beginning in 1841. Many of the same motives affecting migration to Oregon were also evident in the case of the southern province. Indeed, migrants heading for one region often switched in midjourney and chose the other. Health seeking perhaps directed more people to California. Residents of the Mississippi Valley commonly suffered from the ague (malaria), and the sunnier climate of California was said to cure that affliction. In addition to economic and patriotic considerations, many enthusiastic literary influences helped arouse interest in California. Washington Irving in *Adventures of Captain Bonneville* (1837) had described Joe Walker's trip in grandiloquent terms: "They came down upon the plains of New California, a fertile region extending along the coast, with magnificent forests, verdant savannas, and prairies that look like stately parks." California has always inspired such euphoric descriptions, much to the disgust of Oregonians who point out that it has "four months grass and eight months drought."

The mountain men who had been to the province helped to publicize its virtues by word of mouth. Antoine Robidoux was a talkative trapper who returned to Missouri in 1840. Some of his tales, such as those of men living to be 250 years old in the benign climate, were discounted. But the more believable aspects of his reports helped encourage the formation of a Western

Emigration Society in Platte County. Counterpropaganda by worried merchants caused the Society to dwindle in numbers, but a party was organized to take the trail from Independence in the spring of '41.

This Bartleson-Bidwell party consisted at the outset of some sixty-nine men and women. It was guided as far as Soda Springs by the trapper Thomas Fitzpatrick. At that point thirty-three persons headed south and west toward California, having been given a few imprecise suggestions concerning mountains, deserts, and rivers. Their nominal leader was John Bartleson, but the former schoolteacher John Bidwell was the man to whom all listened. The little group blundered across the desolate country north of Salt Lake, abandoning their wagons but eventually reaching the Humboldt River. By the time they crossed the crest of the Sierra Nevada in the Stanislaus River region, the last of their oxen was being consumed for food. John Bidwell was happy to get the windpipe of a coyote for supper one night. On October 30 they reached the San Joaquin Valley, the first company of emigrants to enter California from overland. The individuals scattered throughout the province and took various jobs, Bidwell going to work for Captain Sutter.

Another group of Americans, the Workman-Rowland party, also came to California in 1841. William Workman and John Rowland were both respected merchants in Santa Fe. But in 1841 they fell under suspicion because of the reports of an invasion from Texas. So with twenty-five others they packed up and moved west by way of the Old Spanish Trail to Los Angeles. Many of these emigrants stayed on the Coast, and the two leaders became prominent ranchers in Southern California.

Joseph Chiles, a veteran of the Bartleson-Bidwell trip, returned to Missouri in 1842. In the spring of 1843 he became the guide for a California-bound wagon train. Much of the way west his group traveled with the great Oregon migration of that year, and eighteen of these wagons switched their destination and joined Chiles. In addition, he encountered Joseph Walker near Fort Laramie and employed the former mountain man as his lieutenant. At Fort Hall, Chiles split the party up because of a shortage of food. He and thirteen young men explored a new route into California by way of the Mount Shasta area in the northeastern corner of the state. Walker with the other twenty-five emigrants followed his route of '34, that is, down the Humboldt and then south toward Walker Pass. In the vicinity of Owens Lake he had to abandon his wagons as the mules were exhausted. On December 3 the little band plodded across the pass. Another week's journey took them to the Coast Range, where they celebrated Christmas by stuffing themselves with roast venison.

Despite the heroics of Chiles and Walker, a central route by which wagons could be taken into California had not yet been established. In 1844, however, Elisha Stevens got twenty-three people and half a dozen wagons through the mountains by way of Truckee Pass. Stevens was elected train captain at the "jump-off" point in Council Bluffs, Iowa. A taciturn carpenter, he is a good example of the noteworthy roles that "common men" often play in frontier history. A relatively uneventful journey brought the pioneers to the Humboldt Sink by October 1. They decided to chance a direct westward crossing of the mountains from here. Passing over the Forty Mile Desert, they began the long climb upward and, by means of block and tackle, managed to take their wagons across what was later to be called Donner Pass. This became a commonly used route in 1845 and subsequently.

Several hundred persons came over what could now be called the "California Trail" in 1845. On a map the western third of the trail began to look like a frayed rope end, for there were a number of cutoffs. Some of these short-cuts proved to be disastrous for those who took them. The most notorious example was the Hastings Cutoff. Lansford Hastings was a glib and ambitious young man who had gone to Oregon in 1843, moved to California, and then returned to the States in '44. Early in 1845 he published *The Emigrant's Guide to Oregon and California*. This was basically a real-estate advertising brochure. It drew such an extravagantly colored picture of California that it was known in Oregon as "the book of lies." Hastings advised emigrants to leave the main Oregon Trail 200 miles east of Fort Hall, and then go by way of Fort Bridger, the south end of Salt Lake, and a "short" desert crossing to the Humboldt. The major flaw in the advice was that Hastings had never seen this route!

Nonetheless, in 1846 eighty wagons took the cutoff, guided by the great author himself. West of the lake they found a dreadful sand and salt desert some 80 miles wide, the crossing of which killed off most of the livestock. Upon reaching the Humboldt, it was found that the "cutoff" was actually 125 miles *longer* than the usual route by way of Fort Hall. The tail end of the group that tried this shortcut was the Donner party, comprising twenty-three wagons and eighty-seven people. Because of their difficulties in crossing the salt desert they were late in reaching the mountains, and were trapped there by an early snowfall. So they had to spend the winer of 1846-1847 in the area of today's Donner Pass and Donner Lake. The forty-seven survivors who were brought out in the spring related what has become one of the prime horror stories of frontier history. It is doubtful if the term "heroic" applies to this party, for their demoralization and inability to police their own ranks led to thievery and cannibalism during that desperate winter.

Anglo Attitudes

The great interest in California apparent in 1845 had been generated in part by a barrage of books, articles, and letters. These all praised the climate, while deploring the Mexican people and the provincial government. The Mexicans themselves were quite aware of these attitudes. As subprefect Francisco Guerrero wrote to General Castro: "Friend, the idea these gentlemen have formed for themselves is, that God made the world and them also, therefore what there is in the world belongs to them as sons of God." The theme of White Protestant superiority was expressed by Americans of varying occupations and intellects. Richard Henry Dana, the Boston Brahmin, had remarked rather mildly that the native Californians "lacked industry, frugality, and enterprise." The professional traveler Thomas J. Farnham, in his *Travels in the Californias* (1844), had described them in much more forceful terms as "a miserable people," who "sleep and smoke, and hum some tune of Castilian laziness, while surrounding nature is thus inviting them to the noblest and richest rewards of honourable toil." The mountain man James Clyman viewed them as "a proud Lazy indolent people doing nothing but ride after herds from place to place without any appearant object." And Commodore Charles Wilkes, who made an exhaustive survey of the province on behalf of the U.S. Navy in 1841, wrote that "although I was prepared for anarchy and confusion, I was surprised when I found a total absence of all government in California, and even its forms and ceremonies thrown aside."

Statements like these indicated a belief that Yankees would make better use of California than its present owners. Such views were also held by many of the resident merchants. They actively promoted the immigration of their former countrymen with the object of either annexation or the creation of an American protectorate. Alfred Robinson, for example, hoped that "the American population will be sufficiently numerous to play the Texas game." The key figure among the merchants was Thomas O. Larkin of Monterey. He had moved to California from Boston in 1832, and had made himself *persona grata* to the Mexican authorities. Larkin was appointed American consul in 1843, and it is clear that from this date he was working to bring California into the Union by peaceful means. His letters to the *New York Herald* and other papers were public efforts toward his goal. After he was appointed a secret agent in April of 1846 his reports to the President were a confidential effort toward the same end.

U.S. Government Policy

The United States government had earlier manifested an interest in California for military and commercial reasons. In 1835 President Jackson offered Mexico $500,000 for San Francisco Bay, acknowledged to be the finest harbor on the Pacific. The offer was not accepted, but President John Tyler in 1842 instructed Waddy Thompson to renew the proposal. This negotiation collapsed as a result of the Jones episode of that same year. Commodore Thomas ap Catesby Jones, U.S. Navy, was one of those minor figures of history who appear in the right place at the wrong time. Hearing a rumor of war between the United States and Mexico, he sailed north from Peru and seized Monterey on October 19. Information that the rumor was false reached the commodore within 2 days, and he hauled down the American flag with profuse apologies

Monterey, California, as it appeared in 1845. From a sketch by Lt. Joseph W. Revere, U.S.N. Source: Los Angeles County Museum of Natural History.

all around. The residents of Monterey treated the episode rather lightly, and in fact they held a ball for the visitors. As Thomas Larkin put it: "The officers spent their time ashore hunting wild deer or dancing with tame Dears, both being plentiful in and around Monterey." On the other hand, this exposure of American ambitions brought scowls in Mexico City.

The national government's policy on California was shaped by a paranoid fear of Anglo-French designs against that fair province. The Frenchman Eugéne de Mofras had been snooping around on the Coast in 1840, and his frank proposal of a French protectorate disturbed Washington. Yet the British were much more to be feared. There were numerous references in the press to British plans for taking over California as payment for debts owed by Mexico. The activities of the Royal Navy in the Pacific were viewed with alarm. Larkin wrote letters warning of the aggressiveness of the Hudson's Bay Company, which he called the "Colossus of the North." Actually the British government was supremely indifferent to California, being unwilling to risk war with the United States over it. But President Polk had no way of knowing this, and governments act on the basis of what they *think* is true. So when Polk took office in 1845 he was determined to advance American claims in the area as a counter to the British threat.

The President did not favor seizure or invasion of the province. Rather, he dispatched John Slidell to Mexico City with instructions to offer Mexico up to 40 million dollars for California and New Mexico. No Mexican government, however, could entertain such proposals and expect to remain in office. So the Herrera regime refused to receive Slidell, and he returned to Washington. Polk thereupon instructed secret agent Larkin to soften up the Californians, that is, gently lead them into a revolution which would result in annexation to the United States. Larkin made substantial progress toward this goal with such local leaders as Jose Castro and Mariano Vallejo. As he wrote on April 23 (1846): "Some of the great ones here are preparing for the coming change . . . the pear is ripe for falling." But before the "pear" could fall naturally, it was plucked off the tree by the Bear Flag revolutionists.

Frémont Returns

John Charles Frémont had left St. Louis in the spring of 1845 on the third of his far-western expeditions. Though billed as a "scientific" trip, it may be viewed as an early type of CIA operation. The captain was evidently instructed to infiltrate California and take advantage of any opportunity that might offer itself, whether a local uprising or war with Mexico. The "scientists" were sixty-two well-armed mountain men, including Kit Carson and Joe Walker, all of whom were dog loyal to Frémont. The "Pathfinder" went west by way of the Arkansas, Salt Lake, and the Humboldt Valley. With fifteen of his dangerous-looking companions he crossed the Sierra Nevada at Truckee Pass, sending Walker and the others around by the southern route through Walker Pass. In February he presented himself to Jose Castro, *comandante* at Monterey. The general was not overjoyed to see him.

Frémont was given permission to remain in California as long as he stayed clear of the Coast. But whenever a line was drawn, Frémont just had to cross it. He moved into the Salinas Valley with his entire force, and so General Castro ordered him to leave the province at once. Frémont responded by raising the American flag atop the local Hawk's or Gavilan Peak. For 3 days the two commanders engaged in a long-distance glaring match, with Castro the victor. Having proved the inviolable right of American scientists to camp anywhere they chose, Frémont packed up and moved with provocative slowness toward the Oregon country.

Lt. Archibald Gillespie of the Marine Corps, posing as a merchant, rode north from Monterey and overtook Frémont in the Klamath Lake area. He delivered a verbal message from President Polk and a packet of letters from Senator Benton. Whatever their contents, and a long historical debate has raged over the question, the effect of these messages was to send Frémont back-tracking down to the Sacramento Valley. From his camp at Marysville Buttes he offered inflammatory advice to the American-born settlers in the Sacramento-Sonoma-Napa area. It seems doubtful that Frémont was following Polk's policy, since the President had hoped for a peaceful movement by the native Californians themselves. But rumors of war with Mexico and exaggerated reports of atrocities committed against Americans soon led these settlers into undertaking an armed revolution.

The Bear Flag Revolution

The Bear Party was an amalgam of sailors, hunters, and ne'er-do-wells. The few responsible men in the movement may be counted on the fingers of one hand. The established merchants had nothing to do with the Bear Flag revolt, and indeed Thomas Larkin was notably critical of the whole operation as a needless display of bravado. But on June 10, 1846, these settlers launched their revolution. They seized and imprisoned a number of Mexicans, most of whom (like Mariano Vallejo) were pro-American. On June 15, the rebels ran up a cotton flag in the plaza at Sonoma. It bore the legend "California Republic," and the figure of what was supposed to be a grizzly bear. A carpenter named William B. Ide drew up a surprisingly felicitous proclamation announcing an end to "Military Despotism" and the beginning of a government which would encourage industry, virtue, and literature, among other things. The Republic thus created was to exist for all of 3½ weeks.

Captain Frémont, having watched the amateurs act out their little drama, decided it was time for a professional performer to come on stage. He announced that he was taking charge of the revolution, and who could gainsay the son-in-law of Senator Benton? With his combined force of mountain men and Bear Flaggers he marched toward Monterey. Arriving there on July 19, he found that a United States Navy squadron under Commodore John D. Sloat had already occupied the town following news of the outbreak of war with Mexico in May. The short-lived California Republic thus came to an end. Most of the Bear Flaggers enlisted under Frémont in the California Battalion, organized by Commodore Robert F. Stockton (Sloat's successor) to help him conquer all of the province.

Mexican War Operations

"Pacification" of California should have been easy. The mountain man James Clyman observed in 1846 that "the Military and all parts of the government are weak imbecile and poorly organized and still less respected." Thomas Farnham had found the presidio at San Francisco in a state of decay, manned only by wild dogs and vultures. The last Mexican Governor of California, Manuel Micheltorena, had been expelled following his defeat at Cahuenga Pass in February of 1845. Thus even before the outbreak of war, Mexico was no longer in control of the distant province. The native Californians themselves seemed to be a negligible military threat, but as it turned out, they had a few surprises for the Yankees.

The American operations started off well. The Navy ferried Frémont and his seasick mountain men down to San Diego, while Stockton landed near Los Angeles. Both towns were occupied with only a few defiant shots having been fired. Stockton sent Kit Carson east with dispatches announcing the bloodless conquest, and on August 17 he installed Frémont as governor of the newly annexed province. Both he and Frémont then returned to northern California. At the end of September, however, the commodore received shocking news of a revolt in Los Angeles. The ungrateful Californians, annoyed by the imposition of martial law, had actually risen up and forced the surrender of the tiny garrison commanded by Lieutenant Gillespie.

Stockton planned to repeat his previous maneuver. But "Governor" Frémont violated his orders to proceed to San Diego and chose to land at Monterey instead. So Stockton found himself in San Diego at the end of November with insufficient men to put down the Los Angeles revolt. Meanwhile part of the "Army of the West" under Brig. Gen. Stephen Watts Kearny was marching toward the Coast from Santa Fe. Meeting Carson with news of the glorious victory in California, Kearny sent most of his dragoons back to Santa Fe and continued on with a hundred men. On December 6 his tired troopers clashed with Californian horsemen at the hamlet of San Pascual, 40 miles northeast of San Diego. This battle came close to being an American defeat, with almost a third of Kearny's men being killed by the enemy lancers. Furthermore, the general was besieged, and had to send Carson and two others through the Californian lines at night to call on Stockton for aid. Stockton's sailors and marines arrived in the nick of time, and the united force proceeded to San Diego.

Stockton and Kearny, the former technically in command, marched north and after a brief skirmish recaptured Los Angeles on January 10, 1847. Frémont meanwhile had finally arrived in the area and had signed, independently of his superiors, the Treaty of Cahuenga with the rebels. Stockton approved this agreement, since after all it had been arranged by his own appointee as civil governor. But Frémont and Kearny were soon embroiled in a bitter dispute over who had authority in California. Kearny was a tight-lipped professional who had little use for flamboyant publicity seekers. After orders arrived in February making him military and civil governor, he deposed Frémont and took him back to Washington for a court-martial. Frémont was found guilty of mutiny and disobedience, but was permitted to resign from the Army. It must be said of Frémont that when offered an opportunity to make a mistake, he usually took it. In deferring to the Navy (Stockton) rather than the Army, he made the wrong choice. Frémont claimed in his *Memoirs* that he had won California for the United States. It appears rather that the United States won California in spite of Frémont.

Selected Readings   Hubert Howe Bancroft's *History of California*, 7 vols. (San Francisco, 1884-1890), is the grandfather of state histories. Shorter and more recent works include John Caughey, *California*, 2d ed. (New York, 1953); Robert G. Cleland, *From Wilderness to Empire: A History of California*, 2d ed. (New York, 1959); Andrew Rolle, *California: A History* (New York, 1963); and Walton Bean, *California: An Interpretive History* (New York, 1968).

Adele Ogden, *The California Sea Otter Trade, 1784-1848* (Berkeley, 1941), is informative. Donald M. Brown (ed.), *China Trade Days in California* (Berkeley, 1947), is the journal of a trader during the 1830s. William Shaler's articles have been reprinted as *Journal of a Voyage between China and the North-Western Coast of America, Made in 1804* (Claremont, 1935). Richard Henry Dana's *Two Years Before the Mast*, originally published in 1840, is available in many reprintings. John H. Kemble has edited a two-volume edition with valuable biographical information (Los Angeles, 1964).

Jedediah Smith's California adventures are detailed in Dale L. Morgan's *Jedediah Smith and the Opening of the West* (Indianapolis, 1953). A more popularized version of the same subject is Alson J. Smith, *Men Against the Mountains* (New York, 1965). James Ohio Pattie's *Personal Narrative* is available in several modern editions, the most recent (Philadelphia, 1961) with an introduction by William H. Goetzmann. Stanton A. Coblentz, *The Swallowing Wilderness, the Life of a Frontiersman: James Ohio Pattie* (New York, 1961), is based on the *Narrative*. Joseph J. Hill of the Bancroft Library wrote several outstanding articles on the trade in this area: "New Light on Pattie and the Southwestern Fur Trade," *Southwestern Historical Quarterly*, vol. 26 (April, 1923), and "Ewing Young in the Fur Trade of the American Southwest," *Oregon Historical Quarterly*, vol. 24 (March, 1923). The classic study of New Mexico-California contacts is Robert G. Cleland, *This Reckless Breed of Men* (New York,

1950). Kit Carson's *Autobiography* has been reprinted several times, most recently in paperback (Lincoln, Neb., 1966). For Joseph Walker see Douglas S. Watson, *West Wind: The Life of Joseph Reddeford Walker* (Los Angeles, 1932), and John C. Ewers (ed.), *The Adventures of Zenas Leonard, Fur Trader* (Norman, 1959), an annotated reprinting of Leonard's original 1839 *Narrative*. William H. Ellison's *The Life and Adventures of George Nidever* (Berkeley, 1937) is also interesting. James P. Zollinger, *Sutter: The Man and His Empire* (New York, 1939), can be supplemented by Oscar Lewis, *Sutter's Fort: Gateway to the Gold Fields* (New York, 1966), and Richard Dillon, *Fool's Gold: A Biography of John A. Sutter* (New York, 1967).

The indispensable book on the overland emigration is George R. Stewart, *The California Trail: An Epic with Many Heroes* (New York, 1962), which is expertly written and based on numerous overland journals. An older but still valuable work on the same subject is Jay Monaghan, *The Overland Trail* (New York, 1947). John Bidwell, *Journey to California* (San Francisco, 1937), is the reprint of a primary document. Lansford Hastings' *Emigrant's Guide* was published in a facsimile edition (Princeton, 1932). John E. Bauer, "The Health-Seekers in the Westward Movement, 1830-1900," *Mississippi Valley Historical Review*, vol. 46 (June, 1959), discusses California and Oregon. For the Donner party see Charles F. McGlashan, *History of the Donner Party: A Tragedy of the Sierra*, rev. ed., (Stanford, 1966). This book, originally published in 1879, is based on interviews with survivors. George R. Stewart, *Ordeal by Hunger*, 2d ed. (Boston, 1960), is the best historical reconstruction of the episode. Dale Morgan (ed.), *Overland in 1846: Diaries and Letters of the California-Oregon Trail*, 2 vols. (Georgetown, Calif., 1963) is a useful sourcebook. Robert G. Cleland, *The Early Sentiment for the Annexation of California* (Austin, 1914), is an excellent short analysis. John Hawgood, "The Pattern of Yankee Infiltration in Mexican Alta California," *Pacific Historical Review*, vol. 27 (February, 1958), expertly analyzes "maritime" and "pioneering" interests. The same author has edited *First and Last Consul* (San Marino, Calif., 1962), a selection of Thomas Larkin's letters. Reuben L. Underwood, *From Cowhide to Golden Fleece* (Stanford, 1939), is a Larkin biography, while George P. Hammond (ed.), *The Larkin Papers*, 16 vols. (Berkeley, 1951-1964), should be consulted for detail. U.S. government policy is covered in Jesse L. Reeves, *American Diplomacy under Tyler and Polk* (Baltimore, 1907); in Norman Graebner, *Empire on the Pacific* (New York, 1955); and in Thomas A. Bailey, *A Diplomatic History of the American People*, 5th ed. (New York, 1955).

Frémont's activities in California during 1846 have been the subject of a lively debate. A good survey of the problem is Charles T. Duncan, "Fremont in California: Hero or Mountebank?," *Nebraska History*, vol. 29 (March, 1948). Allan Nevins, *Fremont: Pathmarker of the West* (New York, 1939), takes a favorable view of the captain, as do Frederick Dellenbaugh in *Frémont and '49* (New York, 1914) and William Brandon in *The Man and the Mountain* (New York, 1955). Highly critical of him are Bernard DeVoto in *Year of Decision: 1846* (Boston, 1943) and Dwight Clarke in *Stephen Watts Kearny: Soldier of the West* (Norman, 1961). Frémont's role in the Bear Flag revolt is also part of the voluminous literature on that subject. See George Tays, "Fremont Had No Secret Instructions," *Pacific Historical Review*, vol. 9 (June, 1940); John Hawgood, "John C. Fremont and the Bear Flag Revolution: A Reappraisal," *Southern California Quarterly*, vol. 44 (June, 1962); Werner H. Marti, *Messenger of Destiny: The California Adventures of Archibald H. Gillespie* (San Francisco, 1960);

and Fred B. Rogers, *William Brown Ide, Bear Flagger* (San Francisco, 1962). Issues of the *California Historical Society Quarterly* between 1922 and 1930 reprint many primary documents concerning the Bear Flag movement.

Mexican War operations in California are covered briefly in Otis A. Singletary, *The Mexican War* (Chicago, 1960), and more extensively in Justin Smith, *The War with Mexico*, 2 vols. (New York, 1919). See also Dwight Clarke's *Stephen Watts Kearny* and Arthur Woodward, *Lances at San Pascual* (San Francisco, 1948).

XVI. The War of Manifest Destiny

The explanation of the Mexican War lies in the low opinion which Americans, especially those in the West, had of their darker-skinned neighbors. Various political grievances might be mentioned as causes of the conflict. These include Mexico's refusal to recognize the annexation of Texas; American demands for a Rio Grande boundary; Mexico's inability to pay the damage claims of American citizens; or President Polk's inordinate desire to annex California. But massed behind these immediate issues were racial and cultural antagonisms of long standing. American-born settlers and traders from Texas to California had become accustomed to deriding the "greasers," while the latter in turn had unkind words for the "gringos." Spokesmen for Anglo-Saxon expansionism justified the war by doctrines akin to that of "the white man's burden." But their rhetoric has not stood the test of time, and like it or not, the United States has commonly been regarded as the aggressor in an unjust war of conquest.

"Manifest Destiny"   The phrase "Manifest Destinty" covers a baker's dozen of ideas, all of them serving to justify occupation of Mexican territory. In addition to the overarching belief in racial superiority, the most important concepts were those of geographic predestination, the democratic mission, and divine favor. To many statesmen the logic of North American geography seemed to call for annexation of adjacent territories. Such "natural" boundaries were elastic; they tended to expand as the population moved west. As early as 1789, Jedidiah Morse in his *American Geography* was predicting that "we cannot but anticipate the period, as not far distant, when the AMERICAN EMPIRE will comprehend millions of souls, west of the Mississippi." In the early years of the century Thomas Jefferson and others had moved the "natural" boundary to the Rocky Mountains, and by 1846 it had inevitably reached the Pacific Ocean. In Texas, the Rio Grande rather than the Nueces seemed to be the predestined border between the United States and Mexico.

Americans were a superpeople, whose great fecundity (Representative Kennedy's multiplication table) made further territorial acquisitions necessary. Contemplation of such expansion inspired normally earthbound politicians to sublime flights of rhetoric. At the New Jersey Democratic convention in 1844, a Major Davezac proclaimed: "Make way, I say, for the young American Buffalo—he has not yet got land enough. . . . We will give him Oregon for his summer shade, and the region of Texas for his winter pasture." Opponents of the war, on the other hand, attempted to deflate such grand pretensions. Abraham Lincoln, for one, quoted the farmer who said: "I ain't greedy, I just want the land that jines mine."

In addition, America had a God-sanctioned mission to spread democracy to backward peoples. Westward expansion was linked to the growth of political liberty. This country—as the model republic—would give Mexicans, Cubans, and others an opportunity to discard their despotic systems in favor of American-style democracy. Conversely, expansion of our system would weaken the influence of decadent Europe on this continent. The introduction of a soap and water civilization and Anglo-Saxon political institutions was usually seen as part of a divine plan. Although the war was not a Protestant crusade (Polk sent Catholic emissaries to assure the Mexicans that there would be no interference with their religion), it was made clear throughout that He was on our side.

Though the ideas comprising Manifest Destiny had been in circulation for many years, the specific phrase itself was first used by John L. O'Sullivan in 1845. O'Sullivan, a romantic and exuberant son of Ireland, edited a New York magazine called the *Democratic Review*. In the July issue he wrote of "the fulfillment of our manifest destiny to overspread the continent alloted by Providence for the free development of our yearly multiplying millions." Later in the year the phrase reappeared in O'Sullivan's editorials for the *New York Morning News*, and it was then picked up by Congressmen and other public speakers. The advocates of expansion now had a neat phrase which summed up the imperial vision.

Causes of the War

The ideology of Manifest Destiny was not a cause of the Mexican War but rather a justification for it. There were plenty of down-to-earth reasons why the war broke out when it did. First of all, American citizens had claims against Mexico for property seized or destroyed during the periodic revolutions. An international arbitration commission had been formed in 1839, and it had awarded Americans 2 million dollars. Mexico made three payments (out of thirty-six), and then confessed its inability to continue them because of an empty treasury. Polk indicated a willingness to accept land as indemnity for the unpaid balance, but the Mexican regimes were consistently hostile to such suggestions.

Secondly, the United States inherited the Texan claim to the Rio Grande boundary. The 1845 treaty of annexation required that "Questions of boundaries with foreign nations are to be adjusted by the United States." The Texas claim had been based upon the rather dubious agreement sweated out of the captured General Santa Anna in 1836. The land between the Nueces and the Rio Grande was barren and unoccupied, but Polk decided to claim the Rio Grande border as far west as El Paso. The Mexican view was that the Nueces had always been the southern limit of Texas, even during the Spanish period. Movement of American troops into the disputed area would therefore be regarded as an act of war.

A third issue, and as far as Mexico was concerned the most important, was the annexation of Texas. As soon as President Tyler signed the treaty in March of 1845, Mexico broke off diplomatic relations and recalled her minister from Washington. The treaty was viewed as proving beyond a doubt that the United States had masterminded the seizure of the province. If they got away with it this time, what was to prevent them from repeating the tactic in other Mexican provinces? So the Mexican government once again declared its intention to reconquer Texas—all the way back to the Sabine. Such declarations made it quite unlikely that peace negotiations would be successful.

A fourth possible cause stems from Polk's desire for California. That this was a cause has always been the Whig view; as Senator Robert Winthrop remarked: "had there been no California there would have been no Mexican War." This charge is hard to prove, since Polk made no public statements about territorial ambitions there. His instructions to Thomas Larkin indicate a great interest in acquiring Cailfornia, but by means of a peaceful takeover rather than by war. Perhaps it would be most accurate to say that once war had been declared on other issues, Polk was determined to annex California (and New Mexico as well) as indemnity for American blood and treasure.

Whig spokesmen also advanced the "conspiracy thesis" about the war. This postulated that a sinister plot by slaveholders to annex Texas was now entering its second stage with the conquest of even more Mexican territory. Massachusetts was the home of this thesis, and abolitionist leaders were its chief proponents. The Quaker abolitionist Benjamin Lundy may be credited with originating the idea, for in 1837 he issued pamphlets denouncing the Texas Revolution as a slaveholders' plot. Representative John Quincy Adams popularized the thesis in Congress during the early 40s, and so it was readymade for application to the Mexican War. Charles Sumner propounded it in public speeches, and James Russell Lowell (speaking through his principal character in the *Biglow Papers*) advanced it in literary circles. But with so many other possibilities, who needs a conspiracy? Southern slaveholders were divided over the Mexican War, and John C. Calhoun, for one, was opposed to it. The con-

Cartoon of James K. Polk as a "War President." Source: Library of Congress.

spiracy thesis was always a sickly child, and it now lies in the graveyard of historical theories under a tombstone reading "requiescat in pacem."

The Nation Faces War

Throughout 1845 Polk was still hopeful of solving the differences with Mexico by negotiation. In November John Slidell was dispatched to Mexico City as an envoy empowered to discuss the three key issues of claims, the Texas boundary, and the possible purchase of California. But Slidell was unable to open negotiations, being rebuffed on a technicality, and returned to Washington. Polk thereupon decided that he would have to prod Mexico into war. In July Gen. Zachary Taylor had been sent to Corpus Christi at the mouth of the Nueces with 4,000 men. On January 13, 1846, the President ordered him to move south to the Rio Grande. The red flag was being waved before the Mexican bull.

The military faction ruling Mexico, headed by Gen. Mariano Paredes, was little different from the other political gangs which had governed that unhappy Republic since independence. It welcomed war in the firm belief that its forces could crush the cowardly gringos. The army had been trained by European officers, and the cavalry in particular was highly regarded. The resplendent uniforms of the troops, red and green pompons, sashes, and epaulettes, should have been enough to overawe even the most die-hard Yankees. The Mexicans had the advantage of shorter lines of supply and familiarity with the land. Believing that he held all the aces, President Paredes ordered Gen. Mariano Arista to initiate hostilities on the Rio Grande.

General Taylor had taken up position across from Matamoros. He threw up a rough fortification called Fort Brown, and sent out the usual reconnaissance patrols. On April 25 one of these patrols was attacked and captured by Mexican cavalry on the north bank of the river. This was the break for which Polk had been waiting. Disgusted by the failure of the Slidell mission, he had already proposed to his cabinet on May 9 that a declaration of war be made. But he could now draw up a war message which branded Mexico as the aggressor: "But now, after reiterated menaces, Mexico has passed the boundary of the United States, has invaded our territory and shed American blood upon American soil." This message, delivered on May 11, 1846, took only 2 days to pass through a dazed Congress. The legislators voted (174 to 14 in the House and 40 to 2 in the Senate) to appropriate 10 million dollars for the war and to raise an army of 50,000 volunteers.

The congressional vote did not indicate the considerable opposition to the war among Whigs, abolitionists, intellectuals, and dissident Democrats. The abolitionists in Massachusetts and Ohio were particularly vehement in their denunciations of the conflict. Whig and abolitionist newspapers called it "the President's War" and "an Executive Contrivance." Many of the Whigs, along with such intellectuals as Ralph Waldo Emerson and Henry David Thoreau, had doubts about the morality of our cause. They saw it as unjustified aggression against a weaker neighbor. Ten months after the conflict began, a new Whig Congressman from Illinois got up in the House and introduced his "spot resolutions." Abraham Lincoln called upon Polk to show the exact spot on American soil where American blood had been shed. This proposal earned Lincoln the nickname of "Spotty," and contributed to his defeat for reelection in a state where the war was popular.

Opposition to the war seems to have been a matter of conscience or partisan politics rather than of sectional alignments. But it is clear that the Northeastern states took a cool attitude, while the West was enthusiastic. The Mississippi Valley supplied the bulk of the army volunteers, with Tennessee and Missouri exceeding their allotments several times over.* The cotton South

*The Mississippi Valley and Texas furnished 49,000 volunteers compared to 13,000 from the original Thirteen States.

was divided on the issue. The leaders of the older South Atlantic states, such as John C. Calhoun of South Carolina and Alexander Stephens of Georgia, balked at supporting a war which threatened to strengthen the federal power and to precipitate a sectional controversy over slavery. The newer Southwestern states, on the other hand, seem to have been true believers in the expansionist ideology of the period. Like their cousins further up the valley, they swarmed to the recruiting offices, expecting to "revel in the halls of the Montezumas" within a month of enlisting. The prevailing impression was that war with Mexico would be all fun and games. As the New Orleans *Commercial Bulletin* put it: "Mexico has a feeble and degraded soldiery, who would be scattered like chaff by the first volley from the Anglo-Saxon rifle, the first charge of the Anglo-Saxon bayonet." So the amazing energies of the frontier people were now to be channeled into war.

Who is James K. Polk?

James K. Polk is honored for having added vast territories to the United States, over 1 million square miles in fact. Despite this accomplishment, he usually ranks no higher than Number Ten on the rating scale of Presidents. Undoubtedly his personality has much to do with this, for contemporaries regarded him as "cold and reserved." He never took a drink, never cracked a joke, and never even chopped down a cherry tree. A precise, humorless man, he lacked the colorful attributes of his political mentor Andrew Jackson. Despite the difference in their personalities, Polk was known in his adopted state of Tennessee as "Young Hickory," and he had been a party-line Jacksonian Democrat since

Drilling raw recruits. From John Frost, Pictorial History of the Mexican War *(1849). Source: Huntington Library.*

1824. After serving as governor of the state, he had by the time of the Democratic convention in 1844 become the first "dark horse" presidential candidate. "Who is James K. Polk?" asked the Whigs in mock surprise, pretending they had never heard of a man who had served 4 years as Speaker of the U.S. House of Representatives. Their own candidate, Henry Clay, tried to stay on both sides of the Texas-annexation issue, but he suffered a defeat when New York State tipped the election to Polk. The majority of the American people were bent on territorial expansion, and Polk's Oregon-plus-Texas platform won their votes.

Polk's general plan was to occupy Mexico's northern provinces immediately in the hope of a quick victory. The President needed a "small" war. He was quite aware of the fact that all the generals of the Regular Army were Whigs. Success in the field would automatically make them presidential candidates, so he had to finish off the Mexicans before towering reputations could be established. The President's increasingly bitter fulminations against both Zachary Taylor and Winfield Scott as the war dragged on through 1847 register the failure of his plans.

Taylor to Monterrey

Taylor won two victories along the Rio Grande even before war had been officially declared. On May 8 his blue-clad Regulars drove Arista's larger force from the meadow battlefield at Palo Alto, 18 miles northeast of Matamoros. The next day the two armies collided in the dry lagoon of Resaca de la Palma. Again the Americans were victorious, inflicting 1,200 casualties on the stampeding Mexicans while losing only 150 men themselves. Taylor's "Flying Artillery," officered by young West Pointers, proved to be decisive at Palo Alto, The brass six-pounders could be wheeled about with great speed, and their accurate fire shredded the Mexican lines. On the other hand, the enemy's shot traveled at bowling-ball speed, and the Americans were usually able to dance out of the way. At the battle of the Resaca it was the Americans' aggressiveness and skill with the bayonet that won the day. These victories seemed to confirm the generally held belief in the superiority of Anglo-Saxon arms and armies.

Taylor occupied Matamoros, and in the first week of June began his advance toward Monterrey. By mid-September he reached that strategic city, his 3,000 Regulars having been augmented en route by some 3,000 untrained volunteers from the States. On the 20th he began his assault, and 3 days of bitter house-by-house combat were required before the defenders gave up. Taylor agreed to a 2-month armistice, and permitted the Mexican forces to withdraw to the south. Polk was horrified upon learning of this unauthorized armistice, and immediately sent Taylor orders to cancel it. The general did so reluctantly, and one notices from this point on an increasing hostility between the two men. In November Taylor moved his army down to Saltillo, and began planning further operations.

Kearny's "Army of the West"

In 1846, Polk dispatched an army to occupy New Mexico, the gateway to California. Col. (shortly Brigadier General) Stephen Watts Kearny was at Fort Leavenworth with one of the Army's crack regiments, the First Dragoons. He was ordered to take this unit along with the First Missouri Mounted Volunteers and invade first New Mexico and then California. Kearny was a capable officer with many years' experience on the frontier, so he knew how to organize his little army of 1,600 men. The Missourians were typical of the farmboy volunteers who flocked to the recruiting offices and signed up for 1-year hitches when war was declared. They were at first sight an unimpressive lot, without recognizable uniforms and sadly lacking in discipline. Orders were either obeyed or ignored on the basis of *vox populi*. Officers were voted in and out of their exalted ranks as the spirit moved. Yet these frontiersmen were, in the words of the English traveler George Ruxton, "as full of fight as a gamecock," and they called themselves without too much exaggeration "the ring-tailed roarers." Their commanding colonel (by election) was Alexander Doniphan, a huge lawyer from Liberty, Missouri. He was to lead them on a march of 3,500 miles through northern Mexico, one of the best conducted military expeditions in United States history.

On June 27, 1846, Kearny started his combined force out from Fort Leavenworth. A relentless march along the route of the Santa Fe Trail brought him to the passes east of the mountain capital by mid-August. The question at this point was: Would Governor Manuel Armijo order his provincial troops to defend these passes? To find out, Kearny sent the trader James Magoffin into Santa Fe. Magoffin was a jovial soul well known to the leading New Mexicans for his champagne parties. He had held private conversations with Polk, who probably commissioned him to act as a confidential agent. Governor Armijo would have made an ideal villain for a Hollywood "western." Described by Ruxton as "a mountain of fat," he decorated the walls of his office with dried human ears. He had more than his share of human weaknesses, most of them requiring large sums of money, so Magoffin undoubtedly played upon his cupidity. At any rate, Kearny marched his army into Santa Fe on August 18 without encountering any opposition from the fast-retreating fat man.

Kearny next followed another part of his orders by annexing New Mexico to the United States and forming a government for the new territory. With the assistance of Doniphan and several other Missouri lawyer-soldiers, he drew up a constitution known as the Kearny Code. This gave the New Mexicans such startlingly new rights as civil and religious liberty, and caused some complaints from Washington on the grounds that only Congress could dispense such liberties. But the code remained on the books, and has continued to be a fundamental part of New Mexico's law ever since. Kearny showed less wisdom in picking officers for the new government. He installed the "American

Party" of Taos and Santa Fe merchants (Ceran St. Vrain; Charles and William Bent) in these positions, thus failing to conciliate the older Mexican families. This mistake led directly to the Taos Revolt of January, 1847, in which Governor Charles Bent and twenty other Americans were killed.

On September 25 Kearny left for California with 300 Dragoons. His route was "a leap in the dark of a thousand miles"; down the Rio Grande, west along the Gila to the Colorado, and across the sahara between Yuma and San Diego. Near Socorro, Kearny met Kit Carson carrying dispatches of the Stockton-Frémont conquest of California. This news caused him to send 200 of the troopers back to Santa Fe. He also ordered the unhappy Carson (who had not seen his family in Taos for 18 months) to guide him to California. The little column headed west, its progress reported by Lt. William H. Emory of the Engineers, who wrote the first accurate account of the Southwest. His story of fatigue and hunger is relieved by scientific observations on barrel cactus, horned frogs, and tarantulas. Some of Emory's most perceptive comments concern the Apaches, a band of whom were encountered on the Gila: "The Mexican dress and saddles predominated, showing where they had chiefly made up their wardrobe. One had a jacket made of a Henry Clay flag, which aroused un-pleasant sensations, for the acquisition, no doubt, cost one of our countrymen his life." The force began to change from cavalry to infantry as horses and mules gave up the ghost. But Kearny reached California in December, being accorded a hostile reception by Andrés Pico's lancers at San Pascual. After driving off the enemy with Stockton's assistance, he went on to take part in the final pacification of California and the related imbroglio with John Charles Frémont.

Kearny had been ordered to locate a wagon road between Santa Fe and California. But time did not permit him to do so, and hence the job was left to Lt. Col. Philip St. George Cooke and the Mormon Battalion, who followed in 6 weeks. This battalion, 500 strong, had been enlisted at Council Bluffs in Iowa. President Polk permitted the Mormons to join the federal army principally out of fear that they might aid the Mexicans. As he told his diary on June 3, "the main object of taking them into service would be to conciliate them, and prevent them from assuming a hostile attitude toward the U.S. after their arrival in California." At Santa Fe, Colonel Cooke took charge of the "Saints" and then led them on a detour of some 475 miles south of Kearny's route, going through Tucson and parts of the future Gadsden Purchase area. The Battalion fought only two "battles": the first against a rampaging herd of wild bulls in Arizona; the second against ferocious dogs in Los Angeles. But their route was used by some 50,000 argonauts going to the goldfields, and it also became the path of the Southern Pacific Railroad.

Colonel Doniphan and his frontiersmen left Santa Fe in December of 1846, headed for Chihuahua. They occupied El Paso after a sharp fight against a larger Mexican force, and then in February continued across the deserts toward their objective. Again a frontal assault drove the larger enemy force from its positions, and the Missourians occupied Chihuahua on March 2, 1847. The next month Doniphan began a long march to join Taylor at Monterrey, and from there the "ring-tailed roarers" were eventually sent back to St. Louis. Though not of great military significance, the march was a testimonial to the physical hardihood of the frontier farmers who made up "Doniphan's Thousand."

"Old Rough and Ready"

Taylor remained camped at Saltillo during the fading months of 1846. He faced the usual problems of an army of occupation. The Regulars who made up the core of his army were contemptuous of the volunteers who had joined him since the Rio Grande battles. The letters of such future Civil War generals as George McClellan and George Meade harp upon the shortcomings of these citizen-soldiers. They were immoral, lacked discipline, and made a rumpled appearance. Tiring of a steady diet of dried beans, they helped themselves to the Mexicans' cattle, which they pretended was "slow venison." They also assaulted civilians in the occupied towns, and deserted when the going got rough. The Texas Rangers were even more of a problem for the Regulars. These bearded, buckskin-clad horsemen were valuable scouts and fierce fighters, but they were in Taylor's words "a lawless set." The Texans sat around their campfires all night drinking buckets of whiskey and dancing the "double shuffle" or the "Arkansas hoe-down." It was common knowledge that they never took prisoners, and that they were out to settle old scores dating back to the Alamo and Goliad. After the battle of Monterrey, most of the Rangers' enlistments were up, so Taylor was happy to let them depart.

Zachary Taylor did not make a good picture-book soldier. A stocky, leathery-faced individual, he was the most inelegantly dressed officer the United States Army ever saw. His usual uniform was an old straw hat and a linen smock covering checked shirt and blue trousers. He spoke in a slow Louisiana drawl which apparently reflected equally deliberate mental processes. As Gen. William Worth remarked: "I doubt whether an idea strategic or of any description had had the rudeness to invade the mind or imagination of our chief." But Taylor had the confidence of the rank and file, a valuable trait in citizen armies, and he was also blessed with good luck.

The general's victories at Palo Alto, Resaca de la Palma, and Monterrey made him a popular hero back in the United States. Color prints of his battles sold well, and idealized portraits of him appeared everywhere—even on cups and plates. He inspired songs and dances, such as "the Old Rough and Ready Quick Step." The Whig party, of course, took note of Taylor's renown, and under the guidance of old pro Thurlow Weed began building him up as a presidential candidate. Polk was aware of this ominous development, writing in his diary on November 21 that "Taylor is evidently a weak man and has been made giddy with the idea of the Presidency. . . . I am now satisfied that he is a narrow minded, bigotted partisan, without resources and wholly unqualified for the command he holds." Heaven knows no fury like a woman scorned, or like James K. Polk when menaced by a political rival.

The President had to find some way of slowing down Taylor's spiraling popularity. The original plan of forcing Mexico to surrender by seizing her northern provinces was evidently not succeeding. By mid-October of 1846, Polk and his Cabinet had concluded that an invasion of Mexico's heartland by way of the east coast port of Veracruz was the only way to end the war. Since both Taylor and Scott were Whigs, Polk hoped to create a new rank of lieutenant general and put Senator Thomas Hart Benton in charge of this invasion. But Congress refused to act on this wild proposal, so Polk reluctantly gave the command to Scott.

"Old Zac," however, still had one more surprise for the President. By mid-February many of his best troops had gone to join Scott, leaving him with about 5,000 men. At the same time, General Santa Anna, that old foe of the Americans, was advancing north with some 15,000 troops. On February 22, 1847, the two armies clashed at Buena Vista Ranch just south of Saltillo. In the bloody battle Taylor's volunteers proved their mettle and hurled back the Mexican advance time after time. Technically the battle was a draw; back in the United States it was hailed as another resounding victory. The exasperated Polk, however, refused to give Taylor any credit. He attributed the Mexican repulse to the "bravery and intrepidity of the men."

Scott Captures Mexico City

Winfield Scott appeared to be a much more likely presidential candidate than did Zachary Taylor. Six feet four inches tall, attired in gorgeous uniforms, he had the politician's insatiable love of applause. Yet he was also an outstanding field commander, and military historians describe his Mexico City campaign as "brilliant." This campaign in fact won the war, but Scott never really received full credit. The American mind vaguely recalls him as a 300-pound general who commanded the Army on the outbreak of the Civil War until he was replaced by more important men.

Scott landed at Veracruz on March 9, 1847, with an army of 10,000 men. It took him 6 months to fight his way through the mountain passes between the coast and the Capital. The climactic battle took place at Chapultepec Heights in Mexico City on September 13. The fighting army then became an army of occupation, while the State Department's chief clerk tried to negotiate a satisfactory peace treaty. This individual's name, sounding like some character in a Charles Dickens novel, was Nicholas P. Trist. An eccentric person, Trist was nonetheless industrious and had a command of Spanish. At first he and General Scott did not get on well together. Both were soon writing letters to Polk, each complaining about the other's "arrogance" and "meddling." The President had to make some choice in their rivalry, so on October 6 he issued orders recalling Trist.

The erstwhile commissioner decided to ignore these orders and to remain in Mexico City. For one thing, he and the general had become fast friends (Scott's gift of some guava jelly did the trick!), and for another, the negotiations were at a delicate stage which made it a "now or never" situation. So he wrote his superior a sixty-five page letter explaining this decision. The apoplectic President delivered the final judgment upon his peace commissioner: "an impudent and unqualified scoundrel."*

Treaty of Guadalupe Hidalgo

Yet Trist continued his negotiations, and on February 2, 1848, met with the Mexican commissioners in a suburb to sign the Treaty of Guadalupe Hidalgo. The key features of this document were agreement upon the Rio Grande border in Texas and the cession of both New Mexico and California. The United States agreed to pay 15 million dollars for the annexed territory, and to assume all of the outstanding American claims—now amounting to over 3 million dollars. By this treaty the United States acquired 522,256 square miles of Mexico's northern territory, and rounded out the nation's continental boundaries.

Polk was more or less handcuffed to Trist's treaty, for he was under great presssure from both the Whigs and the general public to end the war. At the same time an aggressive faction in his own party wanted to take all of Mexico. Democratic newspapers along the Northeastern coast from Boston to Baltimore were the principal advocates of total annexation. "Regeneration" of the backward Mexicans was the doctrine which justified such a step. As O'Sullivan pointed out in his *Democratic Review*: "The Mexican race now see, in the fate of the aborigines of the north, their own inevitable destiny. They must amalgamate and be lost, in the superior vigor of the Anglo-Saxon race, or they must utterly perish."

Certain Southern Democrats, notably Secretary of the Treasury Robert Walker from Mississippi, also supported total annexation. But the idea was not peculiarly Southern. Indeed, proslavery Democrats headed by Calhoun joined the Whigs in opposing the whole idea. Fear that annexation would weaken the slavery system was one reason for their opposition. The greatest problem was that the great bulk of the Mexican people were colored: Indian, Negro, mulatto, mestizo. The Southerners' racial views made them unwilling to accept such people to full and equal citizenship. Polk himself would have preferred to take more territory, perhaps to the Sierra Madre Mountains. But further delay might be fatal to peace and might split the Democratic party. So he sent the treaty to the Senate, where it was approved on March 10 by a vote of 38 to 14.

*Trist was fired, and was not paid for his expenses until 1870.

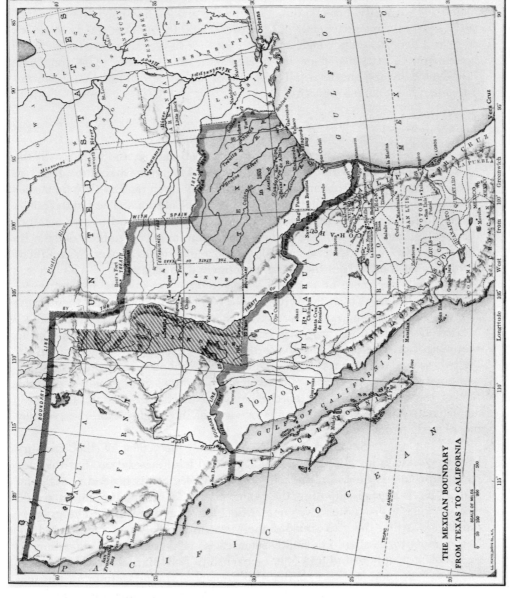

Map showing Adams-Onis treaty line (1819) and Guadalupe Hidalgo treaty line (1848). Source: Huntington Library.

The Mexican War was important both for the individuals involved and for subsequent national history. It made Zachary Taylor President of the United States in 1848, and helped advance the political careers of numerous other participants. Even Brig. Gen. Franklin Pierce, who had fainted at the sight of blood, managed to be elected President partly on the basis of his military record. Furthermore, Mexico was a training ground for Civil War generals. Capt. Robert E. Lee and Lt. Ulysses S. Grant were only two of the more noteworthy officers who served south of the Rio Grande.

The war also opened the door to that House of Horrors: slavery expansion. Polk unwittingly precipitated a sectional controversy over the issue in August of 1846, when he proposed an appropriation of 2 million dollars for diplomatic purposes. David Wilmot, an antislavery Democrat from Pennsylvania, attached to this bill his famous proviso: "That as an express and fundamental condition to the acquisition of any territory from the Republic of Mexico by the United States, by virtue of any treaty which may be negotiated between them, and to the use by the Executive of the moneys herein appropriated, neither slavery nor involuntary servitude shall ever exist in any part of said territory, except for crime, whereof the party shall first be duly convicted." The bill did not pass, but as many Southerners had feared, the disposition of conquered Mexican territory raised passions that led to Fort Sumter and the war between the North and South.

But President Polk is the key figure in the whole period. Judged from the standpoint of results, his administration was one of the greatest in American history. While criticized then and subsequently for taking land by war, no one has suggested that California or the Southwest be returned to Mexico. He pursued his expansionist program with the resolute determination befitting a staunch Presbyterian. It seems likely that James K. Polk would have made America a continental nation with or without God's help.

Gadsden Purchase

There was one final step in the program of aggressive expansion. Joint surveys of the treaty line from El Paso to California were based on J. D. Disturnell's "Map of the United Mexican States" (1847), which proved to be inaccurate. Consequently the two principal officials signed the Bartlett-Condé agreement, which was disadvantageous to the United States since it put the most practicable route for a transcontinental railroad in Mexican territory. Southern railroad interests demanded rectification of this mistake, so the expansionist-minded Franklin Pierce sent James Gadsden of South Carolina to purchase the needed land. In the Gadsden Treaty of December 30, 1853, Santa Anna sold nearly 30,000 square miles in southern New Mexico and Arizona for 10 million dollars. In time a railroad (the Southern Pacific) was built through the purchased area, and Arizona barely escaped being named "Gadsonia."

Selected Readings   Albert K. Weinberg, *Manifest Destiny* (Baltimore, 1935), is an exhaustive analysis of the idea. Frederick Merk, *Manifest Destiny and Mission in American History* (New York, 1963), revises some of Weinberg's conclusions. Julius W. Pratt, "The Ideology of American Expansion," in Avery Craven (ed.), *Essays in Honor of William E. Dodd* (Chicago, 1935), is an excellent short analysis. Articles discussing expansion are collected in Ramon Ruiz (ed.), *The Mexican War: Was It Manifest Destiny?* (New York, 1963), a paperback pamphlet.

Justin H. Smith, *The War with Mexico*, 2 vols. (New York, 1919), is still the standard history, and blames Mexico for the conflict. Otis Singletary, *The Mexican War* (Chicago, 1960), is the best short account. Good one-volume works, both strong on biography, are Alfred H. Bill, *Rehearsal for Conflict* (New York, 1947), and Robert S. Henry, *The Story of the Mexican War* (New York, 1950). Bernard DeVoto's *The Year of Decision, 1846* (Boston, 1943) is indispensable. Diplomatic aspects of the conflict are covered in the two older works, Jesse S. Reeves, *American Diplomacy under Tyler and Polk* (Baltimore, 1907), and George L. Rives, *The United States and Mexico, 1821-1848*, 2 vols. (New York, 1913). The "conspiracy thesis" is demolished by Chauncey W. Boucher, "In Re That Aggressive Slavocracy," *Mississippi Valley Historical Review*, vol. 8 (June, 1921). Peter T. Harstad and Richard W. Resh, "The Causes of the Mexican War: A Note on Changing Interpretations," *Arizona and the West*, vol. 6 (Winter, 1964), is a brief compilation of sources.

Eugene I. McCormac, *James K. Polk, a Political Biography* (Berkeley, 1922), must now be supplemented by Charles G. Sellers, *James K. Polk, Continentalist, 1843-1846* (Princeton, 1966), a detailed study. Joseph McCoy, *Polk and the Presidency* (Austin, 1960), is a good short analysis from a political scientist's point of view. The biographies should be balanced by Richard R. Stenberg, "The Failure of Polk's Mexican War Intrigue of 1845," *Pacific Historical Review*, vol. 4 (March, 1935), which depicts Polk as a master of deviousness. See also Glenn W. Price, *Origins of the War with Mexico: The Polk-Stockton Intrigue* (Austin, Texas, 1967), which maintains that Polk manufactured the war. Milo M. Quaife (ed), *The Diary of James K. Polk*, 4 vols. (Chicago 1910), is a basic source; more selective is Allan Nevins (ed.), *Polk: The Diary of a President* (New York, 1929).

For the "Army of the West" see Dwight L. Clarke, *Stephen Watts Kearny: Soldier of the West* (Norman, 1961) and Bernard DeVoto's *Year of Decision*. Howard R. Lamar, *The Far Southwest: A Territorial History* (New Haven, 1966), takes up the Kearny Code. William E. Connelley (ed.), *Doniphan's Expedition* (Topeka, 1907), is a useful collection of documents. William H. Emory's *Notes of a Military Reconnaissance* was originally issued in 1848; a modern reprint has been edited by Ross Calvin under the title of *Lieutenant Emory Reports* (Albuquerque, 1951). Cooke's *Journal of the March of the Mormon Battalion, 1846-1847* is reprinted in Ralph P. Bieber (ed.), *Exploring Southwestern Trails* (Glendale, Calif., 1938). Bieber's article on "The Southwestern Trails to California in 1849," *Mississippi Valley Historical Review*, vol. 12 (December, 1925) indicated the extent to which subsequent travelers utilized Cooke's wagon road.

Recommended biographies are Holman Hamilton, *Zachary Taylor, Soldier of the Republic* (New York, 1942); Brainerd Dyer, *Zachary Taylor* (Baton Rouge, 1946); and Charles W. Elliott, *Winfield Scott: The Soldier and the Man* (New York, 1937). John Q. Anderson, "Soldier Lore of the War with Mexico," *Western Humanities*

Review, vol. 11 (Autumn, 1957), is excellent. See also John P. Bloom, " 'Johnny Gringo' in Northern Mexico," *Arizona and the West*, vol. 4 (Autumn, 1962). Walter P. Webb's *The Texas Rangers* (Boston, 1935) has a chapter on the Mexican War. Samuel E. Chamberlain, *My Confession* (New York, 1956), is a fascinating account by an enlisted man, and is even partly true. David Lavender, *Climax at Buena Vista* (Philadelphia, 1966), is a concise account of Taylor's battles.

For peace making see George L. Rives, *The United States and Mexico*, and Louis M. Sears, "Nicholas P. Trist, a Diplomat with Ideals," *Mississippi Valley Historical Review*, vol. 11 (June, 1924). The All-of-Mexico movement is dissected by John D. P. Fuller in "The Slavery Question and the Movement To Acquire Mexico, 1846-1848," *Mississippi Valley Historical Review*, vol. 21 (June, 1934), in the same author's *The Movement for the Acquisition of All Mexico* (Baltimore, 1936), and in Frederick Merk's *Manifest Destiny and Mission*. Paul N. Garber, *The Gadsden Treaty* (Baltimore, 1923), is standard, but see also Odie B. Faulk, *Too Far North, Too Far South: The Controversial Boundary Survey and the Gadsden Purchase* (Los Angeles, 1967), and Louis B. Schmidt, "Manifest Opportunity and the Gadsden Purchase," *Arizona and the West*, vol. 3 (Autumn, 1961).

XVII. The Mormons Advance

The Mormons break all the textbook rules for frontier history. Instead of the helter-skelter individualism of other pioneers, this religious group moved and colonized within a framework of social and political discipline rivaling that of the earlier Puritans. In politics, church and state were one; in economics, "private property" was really church property; and in social custom the sanctity of monogamous marriage was discarded for polygamy. These various departures from American tradition brought hatred and persecution by the community at large. But that very discipline and religious zeal which made the Mormons anathema to their neighbors enabled them to master the deserts in Utah. As successful through unorthodox pioneers, they deserve a separate place in the frontier chronicle.

Joseph Smith Mormonism was not a "frontier religion." It originated in the East, in New York state, and its adherents were New Englanders rather than frontiersmen. The Church of Jesus Christ of Latter-Day Saints was created by Joseph Smith of Palmyra, a town in upstate New York. Smith had started his career as a treasure hunter, claiming he could find buried money by use of magic stones and divining rods. In 1823 he experienced a vision in which the angel Moroni informed him that the true word of God was recorded on certain golden plates which were buried in a nearby hill. The Prophet found these plates and translated their hieroglyphics with the aid of magic spectacles or peepstones, causing scoffers to dub him "Peepstone Joe." But the translated document, published early in 1830 as the Book of Mormon, became the foundation of a new church.

      The Book of Mormon is essentially a history of two warring tribes who had migrated to this continent from Israel. They are the peace-loving Nephites and the blood-thirsty Lamanites, the former being progenitors of the

276

Mormons, and the latter, ancestors of the American Indians. The Nephites were eventually destroyed, but before this occurred their prophets Mormon and Moroni managed to inscribe the story of the true faith on the golden plates. The Book itself is heavily laced with quotations from the Bible, and the loose way in which quotes and paraphrases were made caused orthodox Christians to disapprove of it. The religious superstructure which was built upon this Book of Mormon borrowed from contemporary evangelical movements, and additions were made in the form of revelations by Smith. Its perfectionist, millenarian, and communitarian ideals were similar to those of the Shakers, Campbellites, and other sects which flourished in New York's "burnt-over district." But the Mormon Prophet made all the difference, for he had more magnetism than the ministers in the other camps.

Joseph Smith was tall, handsome, and blue-eyed. An imaginative and gregarious person, he had exceptional ability to convince even the most dubious that he was the Prophet of God on earth. While enemies described him as "shiftless" and "cunning," he continued to draw converts. His church grew despite defections, community hostility, and financial problems. Early in 1831 he moved from Palmyra to Kirtland in northeastern Ohio, the first of several moves in a westerly direction. That fall a branch of the church was also established at Independence, Missouri.

The Mormons were eventually driven from both of these locations. In Kirtland, Smith's financial difficulties caused the exodus. Denied a state bank charter, he went ahead anyway and founded what he called an "anti-bank company." This institution collapsed following the Panic of 1837, so Joseph and his top associates fled from the resulting lawsuits. Meanwhile, the Mormons in Missouri had been kicked around the state like a football. The Mormons' industry, their clannishness, and their holier-than-thou attitude always seemed to raise the hackles of neighboring "Gentiles." In Missouri they were under the added handicap of being Yankees and nonslaveholders in a largely Southern and slaveholding state. The result was mob attacks which drove them out of Independence in the fall of 1833.

Most of the refugees moved north into Clay County, where they founded the town of Far West. The Prophet joined them in 1838, but the reunited church continued to fare badly at the hands of armed mobs. To protect themselves, a secret society known variously as the Destroying Angels or the Danites was formed. This society was a natural response to the external threat, but it was also used to club down dissent within the church. The baleful eyes of such hard cases as Porter Rockwell and Bill Hickman, staring out from old photographs, reflect the undoubted fanaticism of early Mormonism. But even the Danites were no match for the swarming Missourians. Several pitched battles in the fall of 1838 left two dozen Mormon dead, and made it necessary for the church to pull up stakes once again. This time they briefly reversed the normal pattern by moving east, into Illinois.

The town of Nauvoo on the Mississippi became the new Mormon refuge. Joseph Smith controlled a powerful block of votes in a state where Democrats and Whigs were in hair-trigger balance. He used this leverage to get a charter from the legislature creating what amounted to a state within a state. The Mormons had their own laws, courts, and officials. Most worrisome to the Gentile neighbors was the fact that they also had their own militia, the 2,000-man Nauvoo Legion. But the strongest objections concerned the practice of polygamy. This custom was the result of another of the Prophet's "revelations" (additionally buttressed by references to the Old Testament). The doctrine was made known only to the inner circle, who practiced it more or less secretly. In fact it was not publicly proclaimed as a church policy until 1852. But polygamy was made known by the published letters of apostates from the church.

There were many Mormon baiters in the neighboring towns of Carthage and Warsaw. A press in Warsaw turned out such tracts as William Harris's *Mormonism Portrayed: Its Errors and Absurdities Exposed* (1841) and Joseph Jackson's *Adventures and Experiences Disclosing the Depths of Mormon Villainy* (1844). These play up the "arrogance" and "impudence" of the "empty pretender" Smith and his cohorts. The Illinoisans, alarmed by the Saints' growing economic power, responded as might be expected to this propaganda. Joseph Smith did not help the situation at all. He began to think of himself not only as King of the Kingdom of God but also as an occupant of the lesser office of President of the United States, and in 1844 he actually declared himself to be a presidential candidate. The enraged non-Mormon populace demanded nothing less than the head of "Holy Joe" and the expulsion of his followers.

In an attempt to avert an all-out attack on Nauvoo, Smith and his brother Hyrum surrendered themselves to the authorities at Carthage. But a mob of militiamen stormed the jail on the evening of June 27 (1844) and murdered both men. Enemies thought that the Prophet's death would shatter the church beyond repair. But the Mormons seemed to thrive on persecution. Like the Quakers, they were happiest when being hounded. They continued to survive after Smith's murder, and rallied behind a new leader.

Brigham Young to the West

Brigham Young succeeded Smith as Prophet, Seer, and Revelator. He did so only after a power struggle within the hierarchy. This maneuvering cost the church some members, since the losers (including Joseph Smith's son) took their followers and departed. But Young was undoubtedly best qualified to hold the flock together. Indeed he was a much more practical leader than Smith had been. Uneducated but possessed of shrewd intelligence, this former carpenter was also tremendously energetic and had great organizing ability. Surprisingly enough, the "Lion of the Lord" was not especially large in stature, being 5 feet

10 inches tall and compactly built. But to the faithful he was a man-mountain of strength.

Young needed every ounce of his energy to save the church from annihilation. The Illinois farmers were threatening a mass attack that would level Nauvoo to the ground. By the winter of 1846 the danger had become so great that Young decided to move out at once, even in zero temperatures. And where would they go but to the Great West? In February flatboats began taking the first contingents across the Mississippi to Iowa. By fall Nauvoo had been evacuated, the last parties fighting gun battles with emboldened Gentile scavengers. The destitute bands of Mormons, comprising 10,000 to 11,000 people, were strung out across Iowa all spring and summer. Some eventually reached Winter Quarters, a temporary way station located on the west bank of the Missouri near today's city of Omaha. This was technically Indian land and thus forbidden to white settlers, but Brigham Young wrangled permission to remain there temporarily.

It was at Winter Quarters, in the summer of 1846, that the Prophet received President Polk's request for 500 army volunteers. The church was in desperate need of cash to finance the trek further west, and what better source than an army payroll? In addition, California was being considered as a possible site for the new Zion, and the young men would go there at government expense. After alternate coaxing and roaring, Young got the Mormon battalion organized for service in a Gentile army.

The people in Winter Quarters and in the other camps across Iowa suffered terribly from poor shelter, insufficient food, and epidemic diseases. Hence the survivors were anxious to leave for the Promised Land, wherever that

Brigham Young at about forty-five years of age. Source: Utah State Historical Society

might be. Texas, California, British Columbia, and the Great Basin were all possibilities. Brigham Young consulted Lansford Hastings' *Guide*, Frémont's *Reports*, and other literary sources while he organized a "Pioneer Band" that would select the location. This carefully picked group of 143 men (there were also three women and two children) left the Missouri in mid-April of 1847. They traveled west by way of the so-called "Mormon Trail." Except for the first 200 miles across western Iowa, this was identical with the Oregon Trail. The Mormons generally followed the north bank of the Platte to avoid Missouri wagon trains on the more heavily traveled south bank, and this was true of the Pioneer Band.

Beyond South Pass, Brigham Young encountered Jim Bridger. The former mountain man did not seem too optimistic about the agricultural possibilities of the Salt Lake Valley; Mormon tradition maintains that he offered a thousand dollars for the first bushel of corn grown there. Young also made contact with Sam Brannan, who had taken a Mormon contingent to San Francisco by ship in 1846. Brannan tried to convince the Prophet to lead the flock to California. But Young had by now become opposed to settling on the Coast, since he felt that there would be too many Gentiles there. The Mormons must be completely isolated if they were to avoid a repetition of Nauvoo. This thought was undoubtedly in the Prophet's mind as he looked out over the Salt Lake Valley from the summit of the Wasatch Mountains on July 24 and said "This is the Place."

The Great Basin Frontier

The Pioneer Band immediately went to work plowing the ground for a potato crop, digging irrigation ditches, and constructing log cabins and a fort on the site of Salt Lake City. Meanwhile the "first emigration" had also left the Missouri. This company was made up of 1,553 people, 556 wagons, oxen, sheep, and exactly 716 chickens. Details of starting times, guard mounts, and the methods of corralling wagons were all set down in instructions from Brigham Young. Like others that followed it in subsequent years, the train was organized into companies according to the biblical tens, fifties, and hundreds. This careful discipline and organization sets the Mormons apart from other Western emigrants. Even the Saints bickered and quarreled in the heat of a Nebraska summer, but the train's cohesiveness was not destroyed. They reached the valley at the end of September with few fatalities, although many of the 716 chickens wound up in stewpots before journey's end.

The colonists found that the Salt Lake Valley was almost more than they had bargained for. This was indisputably desert country, with rainfall of only 8 to 15 inches per year. It was a land of violent winds, of subzero winters, and of unfriendly fauna including rattlesnakes and crop-devouring insects. To men and women of New England origins the lack of trees was disheartening;

Mormon homesteaders in the Salt Lake Valley. From a photo taken in the late 1860s by Andrew Joseph Russell. Source: Huntington Library.

the visual backdrop was desert red and brown rather than Vermont green. It obviously would require more than faith to force a living from the gravelly soil.

The keys to Mormon success were irrigation farming and group co-operation. The Pioneer Band saw at once that the streams flowing out of the Wasatch Range would have to be dammed up and diverted into irrigation ditches if the Israelites were to survive. This was thus the first and the continuing job of work in the community. By 1852 approximately 1,000 miles of ditches had been constructed, and they spelled the difference between life and death. The Mormon contribution to modern irrigation techniques thus derived from a very compelling motive: self-preservation.

Successful irrigation was in turn made possible by the church's communitarian system. There was no landgrabbing or water monopoly on the classic frontier pattern. Water, timber, and land belonged to the community rather than to individuals. The distribution of these resources was accordingly determined by church authorities. Theirs was the doctrine of stewardship, by which the church regulated property rights for the benefit of the whole Kingdom of God. This economic planning meant first that the irrigation ditches got dug, and second that the water was made available to all. The church apportioned house lots and farming land on the same basis, that is, according to need.

This system represented total rule by the church, more specifically by Brigham Young as president, aided and advised by the Council of the Twelve Apostles. Decisions on both religious and secular matters went from here to the bishops and then to the church membership. As one official put it: "The Lord spoke to Brigham, Brigham to the Bishops, and the Bishops to the people." When the church hierarchy decided that the city should be divided into 10-acre blocks, and that the streets should be a supersized 120 feet wide, this is how they were laid out. Such authoritarianism would have caused riots among other American frontiersmen, but to the Mormons it was simply God speaking through his prophet on earth.

Despite the efficiency with which they tackled the wilderness, the Mormons had their "starving time." The winter of 1847-1848 was relatively mild, but since they were still experimenting with the new agriculture, the pioneers had to live on thistles and sego lily roots. Then the spring wheat in 1848 was attacked by clouds of crickets. Fortunately sea gulls came in from Salt Lake to feed on the insects, saving at least part of the crop. This was recorded as a divine "Providence," similar to those of the seventeenth century Puritans. The winter of 1848-1849 was also a desperate one because of the reduced crop and an increased population. Brigham Young had brought out another of his carefully organized trains that summer, this one totaling 2,500 people. The result was again a starving time, with various stories of how grain sacks were miraculously filled by the Lord.

The California gold rush also seemed to have some kind of providential significance, for the hordes of Gentile gold seekers brought economic prosperity to the Mormons. Between 10,000 and 15,000 argonauts stopped at Salt Lake City in 1849 and again in 1850. They spent money, lots of it, for supplies, fresh livestock, and the repair of wagons. In their impatience to get to the Coast, many traders disposed of their clothing, tools, and other goods at half price. The result was a tremendous boost for the whole Mormon economy. It meant not only survival but expanded programs of colonization and immigration.

Mormon Expansion

The Mormons were a colonizing people. Within 10 years of the founding of Salt Lake City, ninety-six other settlements had been established throughout the West. The earliest of these, such as Provo, Parowan, and St. George, were planted close to Jed Smith's old fur-trading route to California. Utah's "Dixie" region was an alkali desert; as the Mormon song "St. George" puts it: "Mesquite! Soap-root! Prickly-pears and briars!" Those who were "elected" to these colonizing missions sometimes found it hard to leave their original homes. But the reluctant ones were usually persuaded that they were helping to build God's kingdom on earth.

One goal of colonization was economic self-sufficiency for the Mormon enterprise. If they were to be free from Gentile domination, the Saints would have to produce their own sugar, cotton, iron, and other imported products. So the church used its tithes to support manufacturing efforts, most of them unsuccessful. Sugar beets grown in the saline soil proved to be inedible.

Technical problems connected with iron smelting could not be solved. But towns were founded in connection with these various schemes: Parowan, for example, being established in 1850 to support the iron industry.

The towns were built on the model of Salt Lake City, and they resembled in many respects the "nucleated villages" of New England. That is, the people were concentrated around the church and fort, going to outlying fields for farming. Although forts were always the first structure to be built, Mormon history is remarkably free of Indian wars. The church believed that the descendants of the Lamanites were capable of redemption, so it followed a friendly policy toward the neighboring Shoshones and Utes. There were skirmishes in the early years, but as one elder put it, "we shoot the Indians with tobacco and bread rather than with powder and lead." In fact, Mormon friendship with the Indians was one reason for rising Gentile hostility during the 1850s. It was thought that Brigham Young was somehow conniving with the savages to no good purpose.

Mormon communities were established as far north as Idaho, but most of them were built to the south and west. A settlement was planted at Nevada's Carson Valley in 1849, and the sale of supplies to miners and migrants netted handsome profits. Brigham Young's ambitious expansionist program also involved a "Mormon Corridor" to the sea with outlets at San Pedro and San Diego. The route was to be used to bring both merchandise and immigrants to Salt Lake City. In 1851 the church purchased the Rancho del San Bernardino in California as an important outpost along this corridor. The 500 settlers there were instructed to raise cotton, sugar, olives, and other tropical products, again with economic independence in mind. It is also ironic, in view of the subsequent history of that desert Babylon, that the Mormans built a little post at Las Vegas, Nevada, in 1855.

Income from the gold seekers also enabled the church to bring more converts to Utah. Then, as now, the Latter-Day Saints maintained a vigorous missionary program both in the East and overseas. The year 1850 saw the formation of a Perpetual Emigrating Company to assist these immigrants financially. All the Mormons still remaining in Iowa were brought out by 1852. The foreign immigrants were overwhelmingly of British origin. Of 22,000 converts who sailed from Liverpool in the years up to 1855, some 19,500 were from England. There were 2,000 from the Scandinavian countries and only a few hundred from other European nations. Practically all these people were of working-class origin, with laborers predominating.

The Saints' Character

Historians quite naturally compare the Mormons with the Puritans, since both fled to a wilderness Zion in order to escape persecution. There are also certain similarities in personal traits, what with a premium on industry, frugality, and temperance. But Mormonism was a much more optimistic faith than Calvinism, since salvation was a matter of free will. In addition, the spirit of Jacksonian democracy had seeped into the very bone and marrow of individual Mormons. Both church doctrine and the exigencies of frontier living worked toward a kind of equalitarianism that was foreign to the Massachusetts Saints. The Mormons were really neither Puritans nor frontiersmen, but a unique blend of the two.

The church officially demanded abstinence of its members. The Saints were to stay away from coffee, whiskey, and Spanish cigars. Mormon journals reveal that these prohibitions were often ignored. Excessive drinking and the use of vulgar language are noted from time to time. The settlers made beer and whiskey out of local crops, their specialty being a rum called "Valley Tan" which was concocted from molasses and green tea. Unlike the Puritans, they believed in singing, dancing, and theatrical performances. "Man is that he might have joy," says the Book of Mormon. Though much of the music had a religious purpose, there is a body of secular folksong dealing with the pioneering experience.

Mormons also had an earthy sense of humor, and ribald jokes were told even about Brigham Young. Joseph Smith's claim that Brigham could "eat more eggs and beget more children than any man in the State of Illinois" seemed to be borne out by facts. The Lion of the Lord had twenty-seven wives and an estimated fifty-seven children. Legend states that he slept in a great bed with five wives on each side, and that he struck a gong when he wished to turn over. One poor woman failed to hear the signal and was permanently lamed when she did not shift with the others.

Government by Theocracy

In Mormonland the leaders of the church and of the government were one and the same. This situation continued for many years after Utah had technically become part of the United States territorial system. When the Mormons first settled at Salt Lake they were on Mexican soil. The Treaty of Guadalupe Hidalgo in 1848 put them back in the United States; as one elder (Sam Brannan) remarked as he stepped ashore in San Francisco, "there's that damn flag again." Actually the Saints considered themselves to be American citizens, and had always planned on forming another state of the Union. But there were certain dangers in federal rule, as they had found out in Missouri and Illinois when the national government had been either unwilling or unable to protect them against mobs. To avoid a repetition of such disasters, the church formed a provisional "State of Deseret" with Brigham Young as governor. A convention at Salt Lake City in March of 1849 drew up a proposed constitution that was little different from that of other states. The boundaries, however, were of truly Western dimensions. They included 265,000 square miles (compared with Utah's present 84,476) that reached east to the Rocky Mountains, south to the Mexican border, west to the Sierra Nevada, and north into Wyoming, Idaho, and Oregon. The Mormon strategy was to gain statehood immediately and thus avoid the carpet-bag government of the territorial stage.

But Congress chose to make Utah a territory (in 1850), considerably reducing its boundaries in the process. Brigham Young was made Governor, so the church continued to rule even though Gentiles were appointed as federal judges and as territorial secretary. These non-Mormon officials fought bitter battles with the church for control of the territorial government. Since their juries were made up of Mormons, the judges found it practically impossible to get any convictions. They saw that the power of Brigham Young reached all the way down to the grass roots. The county governments, for example, took directions from the church, with bishops managing local civil affairs. Brigham Young was in the habit of issuing political directives as President of the Church rather than as Governor of the Territory.

A set of particularly virulent anti-Mormon judges was appointed in 1855. Their struggles with the church hierarchy set off a chain reaction which led to the "Utah War." Shortly after this quarrel broke out, the Mormons underwent a religious revival, and some of the extremist churchmen made violent threats against the Gentiles. This emotional fervor finally was translated into violence. The best-known episode at the time was the Mountain Meadows Massacre of September 11, 1857. This occurred 300 miles south of Salt Lake City when the Fancher wagon train from Missouri was attacked and wiped out by Indians and Mormons disguised as Indians. The attack took place after the Mormons had promised safe conduct through Utah. Only a few children below speaking age were spared; the 120 adults were all killed. A Danite leader named John D. Lee was executed for the crime in 1877, but the responsibility of Brigham Young has been much debated. It must be said that the Missourians were not entirely blameless, since they named their oxen "Brigham" and offered other provocative insults. Yet the episode seared deeply into the Mormon conscience. One tradition maintains that the Devil periodically comes up out of the ground and smokes his pipe at the site.

The "Utah War"

Even before the carnage at Mountain Meadows, President James Buchanan had decided to reassert federal authority in Utah. He ordered an army of 2,500 men to the territory in May of 1857. The President was responding to a public opinion that was becoming increasingly hostile to the Saints. These sentiments had been whipped up not only by the reports of the anti-Mormon judges but by what Brigham Young called "hireling priests and howling editors." The usual targets of the newspapers were polygamy and the Danites. The *New York Tribune* of January 6 wrapped it all up by calling the Mormons "ecstatico-religious, tyrannico-politic, and poly-uxorial loafers." It is true that the Saints had revealed an

almost fanatic determination to expel federal representatives, whom they regarded as parasites. There was no assurance of constitutional guarantees in Utah,
and church law took precedence over federal law. On the other hand, Buchanan
did not take time to investigate the situation or even to inform Brigham Young
that a new governor was being sent to replace him. Instead the President rushed
out an armed force that was to punish the Mormons for their rebellious behavior.
The result was an expensive and inept campaign that accomplished little.

The Army crawled slowly to Fort Bridger, there to spend the winter
of 1857-1858. It had been harassed all the way from South Pass by Maj. Lot
Smith's "Mormon Raiders," who burned wagon trains, ran off livestock, and
caused constant midnight alarms. The Mormons, conditioned by their experiences in Missouri and Illinois, believed that the Army was coming to destroy
their church. Brigham Young therefore called in all the faithful to help defend
Zion against the United States invaders. One result of this call was that the outposts at Carson Valley, San Bernardino, and elsewhere were vacated, never to
be reoccupied by the Mormons. The Prophet also decided that if the Army
reached Salt Lake that fall he would follow a "burn and flee" policy. Fortunately
the Army's enforced pause at Fort Bridger gave the federal administration a
chance to reconsider its actions. By spring it had decided, partly on the basis of
congressional criticism, that punishment of the Mormons might not be wise.

Thomas L. Kane, a self-appointed champion of the Mormons, acted
as a go-between. He persuaded the new federal governor, Alfred Cumming, to
go unescorted into Salt Lake City and confer with the Saints. The result was that
the Mormons accepted the administration's demands, and permitted Cumming
to replace Young in the governorship. However, the church continued to operate
its shadow government for many years. Brigham Young remained the most
powerful man in the territory until his death in 1877.

The "Utah War" caused a permanent contraction of the Kingdom of
God and temporarily disrupted an interesting experiment in immigration technique. This was the hand-cart brigade, initiated in 1856 as a money-saving device. Foreign converts were brought as far as Iowa City on the railroad. There
they transferred possessions and minimal food supplies to two-wheeled carts
which were then pushed and pulled the 1,300 miles to Salt Lake City. Brigham
Young continued these brigades despite the dangers which became apparent
the very first year of operation. In 1856 five companies totaling 1,900 people left
Iowa. The last two of these got a late start, were trapped by early snows, and
lost 200 dead in the Wyoming mountains. But cart brigades went west in 1857,
1859, and 1860, with some 3,000 immigrants walking the whole toilsome trail.

Utah continued to grow in population, but statehood was delayed
until 1896 principally because of popular opposition to polygamy. Congressional
efforts to bring the Mormons into line with national custom finally bore fruit in
the Edmunds Act of 1882. This set fines and imprisonment for the practice of
polygamy. The Mormon church itself accepted the verdict, for in 1890 President

Wilford Woodruff issued a manifesto declaring that polygamy was no longer an essential doctrine. Even in the 1960s, however, dissident sects continued the practice.

Mormonism remained a suspect religion to most Americans well into the twentieth century. Magazine articles and book-length exposés of sin in Salt Lake City constitute almost a distinct genre of American literature. In Zane Grey's novel *Riders of the Purple Sage* (1912), which has been read by millions, Mormons are the villains. But to the frontier historian the Saints are significant because of their unique cooperative system and their impressive conquest of the desert environment. By the pragmatic standards of the frontiersmen themselves, a system is judged by how well it works.

Selected Readings   There is a tremendous amount of historical writing on the Mormons, much of it published in the last 15 years. Since Joseph Smith created the religion, an essential book is Fawn M. Brodie, *No Man Knows My History, the Life of Joseph Smith* (New York, 1945), a brilliant biography written in a sceptical spirit. Useful general surveys of Mormonism include Thomas F. O'Dea, *The Mormons* (Chicago, 1957), by a Catholic sociologist; Nels Anderson, *Desert Saints* (Chicago, 1942), also written from a sociological standpoint; and for the official church point of view, Brigham H. Roberts, *A Comprehensive History of the Church of Jesus Christ of Latter-Day Saints,* 6 vols. (Salt Lake City, 1930).

Morris R. Werner's *Brigham Young* (New York, 1925) remains the standard biography. It may be supplemented by a valuable primary source, John A. Widtsoe (ed.), *Discourses of Brigham Young* (Salt Lake City, 1954). Robert B. Flanders, *Nauvoo: Kingdom on the Mississippi* (Urbana, 1965), does not relate the Nauvoo experience to general Mormon history. Wallace Stegner, *The Gathering of Zion: The Story of the Mormon Trail* (New York, 1964), is Western history at its best. Primary documents dealing with the migration are in William Mulder and A. R. Mortensen, *Among the Mormons: Human Accounts by Contemporary Observers* (New York, 1958). Also valuable is Juanita Brooks (ed.), *On the Mormon Frontier: The Diary of Hosea Stout, 1844-1861,* 2 vols. (Salt Lake City, 1965).

Details of Utah settlement are in Hubert Howe Bancroft, *History of Utah, 1540-1886* (San Francisco, 1889); Dale L. Morgan, *The Great Salt Lake* (Indianapolis, 1947); and Ray B. West, *Kingdom of the Saints* (New York, 1957). Charles H. Brough, *Irrigation in Utah* (Baltimore, 1898), remains valuable. Leonard J. Arrington, *Great Basin Kingdom: An Economic History of the Latter-Day Saints, 1830-1890* (Cambridge, 1958) is now definitive in its field. Milton R. Hunter, *Brigham Young the Colonizer* (Salt Lake City, 1940), relates the expansion outward from Salt Lake. The same author's article on "The Mormon Corridor," *Pacific Historical Review,* vol. 8 (June, 1939), is excellent.

William Mulder, *Homeward to Zion: The Mormon Migration from Scandinavia* (Minneapolis, 1957), and Philip A. M. Taylor, *Expectations Westward: The Mormons and the Emigration of Their British Converts in the Nineteenth Century* (Ithaca, 1966), deal with the two main immigrant groups. Austin and Alta Fife, *Saints of Sage and Saddle* (Bloomington, Ind., 1956), is a classic on Mormon folklore.

James B. Allen, "Ecclesiastical Influence on Local Government in the Territory of Utah," *Arizona and the West,* vol. 8 (Spring, 1966), is revealing. Juanita Brooks, a Mormon, has written the standard account of *The Mountain Meadows Massacre* (Norman, 1962). See also her *John Doyle Lee: Zealot, Pioneer Builder, Scapegoat* (Glendale, Calif., 1961). Norman Furniss, *The Mormon Conflict, 1850-1859* (New Haven, 1960), is a superb analysis of the "Utah War" and is now available in paperback. LeRoy R. and Ann W. Hafen, *Handcarts to Zion* (Glendale, Calif., 1960), is a complete printing of documents. Thomas G. Alexander and James B. Allen (eds.), "The Mormons in the Mountain West: A Selective Bibliography," *Arizona and the West,* vol. 9 (Winter, 1967), emphasizes recent scholarship.

XVIII. The Rise of the "West"

The study of American political and economic history in the decades from 1820 to the Civil War almost requires trifocal glasses. One must watch the North, the South, or the new West as each defined and then defended its own sectional interest. Though Negro slavery was one of the underlying issues, it was kept pretty much out of the spotlight until 1846. Most of the noise was about tariffs, federally financed "internal improvements," and public land policies. The people of the West* quickly learned to vote on the basis of sectional self-interest as well as by political party or class lines. Wooed by both North and South, the West had by the mid-40s come to see eye to eye with the Northeastern states on most of the key economic issues. The ultimate result was the creation of a sectional alliance above the Mason-Dixon line, one that went to war against the South in 1861 as a united "North." But for a number of years following the Panic of 1819, it looked as if the dividing line might be a vertical one splitting East from West.

The West in the Panic of 1819   Panics are easier to describe than to understand or predict. For 4 years following the Treaty of Ghent, the West enjoyed economic prosperity along with the rest of the nation. A good market for farm products in war-ravaged Europe sent prices for cattle, grain, and cotton spiraling upward. Much of this income went into land speculation, which had been made easy by the credit provisions written into national land laws since 1800. The settler-speculator claimed 320 acres instead of 160, blithely putting himself

*In the 20s and 30s the "West" comprised the states of the Old Northwest together with Kentucky, Tennessee, and Missouri. From the mid-40s and through the 50s the last three were generally classed as "Southern" because of their slavery systems.

289

out on a limb that would be sawed off in case of hard times. The usual dangers of inflation and speculation were compounded by an unstable banking structure. By 1818 there were 392 private banks* in the country. They bore such picturesque names as the Owl Creek Bank and the Saddlebag Bank, but practically all of them had inadequate specie reserves to back up their paper issues. They were popular in the West, since they made enormous extensions of credit to farmers.

The only financial institution capable of curtailing the overextension of credit was the Second Bank of the United States. Chartered in 1816 as a semi-public corporation, it was run by Eastern bankers from the main branch at Philadelphia. In 1819, after Langdon Cheves became director, the Bank began moving to restrict credit. It cut down its own loans, and demanded that the state banks redeem their notes in specie. Since few of them could do so, they collapsed in a cloud of worthless paper. Soon states such as Indiana, Illinois, and Tennessee were left without any private banking facilities at all. Farm prices started buckling at about the same time, since Europe was catching up with its own demand. By the end of 1819 crops were rotting in the fields, and "safe" currency had gone out of circulation. In trans-Appalachia the "B.U.S." was blamed for blowing down the house of cards. It was henceforth the "Monster," out to destroy the workingman and farmer. According to Senator Benton, all the cities of the West were "mortaged to this money power. . . . They are in the jaws of the Monster. A lump of butter in the mouth of a dog—one gulp, one swallow, and all is gone!"

Whatever its causes, the panic played havoc with the land system. For the individual farmer who still owed money on his acres, it meant a court judgment and dispossession. For the United States government it meant a sickening decline in land sales, from 5,110,000 acres in 1819 to 781,000 acres in 1821. Like children with a cut finger going to Mother, the farmers asked their state legislatures and the national Congress for stay laws and other debtor relief. Congress responded with the Land Act of 1820. The minimum price was lowered from $1.64 to $1.25 an acre, and the minimum unit from 160 to 80 acres. But the credit feature was abolished, as experience had proved that farmers usually filed on more land than they could pay for. Congress also offered the Relief Act of 1821. This extended the time of payment, or permitted the purchaser to return part of his lands to the government and retain the remaining portion. This act was extended year by year until 1832.

The Sectional Lineup

The disastrous depression made the Western farmer and crossroads merchant more politically conscious. They voted for candidates who attacked the monster

*These were called "state banks," a rather misleading term, for though they had charters from state legislatures they were run by private investors.

Bank and who urged more debtor-relief laws. In national politics these dis-
contented people would soon rally behind Andrew Jackson. But in March of
1824 the more conservatively inclined Henry Clay of Kentucky attempted to win
the West's support for his own "American Plan."

Speaker Clay's basic proposal was for a partnership of Northeast and
West. New England's manufacturing system had gotten off to a good start during
the war. The rising banker-manufacturer group was in consequence strongly
protectionist. It demanded tariffs to shield its "infant industries" against lower-
priced British imports. The West was an agricultural section, a land of family
farms averaging about 200 acres each. Although there was some manufacturing
at Cleveland and Cincinnati, its chief products were corn, wheat, cattle, and
hogs. Clay's argument was that these goods had to be sold in the "home market."
The export market in Europe was too unstable, as the panic had just shown,
hence the West must sell to the Northeast. As more manufacturing cities arose
in Massachusetts and Connecticut, there would be an increasing demand for
Western pork and wheat. But the creation of this market was dependent in turn
upon tariff protection for the manufacturers. Clay's argument was so convincing
that the West voted for the protective tariffs in 1824, 1828, and 1832.

Clay's proposal for federally financed internal improvements also
found favor in the West, which desperately needed canals and turnpikes to carry
its crops to the East. While New York was wealthy enough so that it could build
its own Erie Canal, the Western states did not have the money for such projects.
"Uncle Sam had to do it" was the basic Western position right up to the Civil
War period. The Northeast in general agreed, for it wanted to speed its shoes,
hardware, and textiles out to the Western markets.

Having struck responsive chords with his tariff and internal improvements proposals, Clay should have marched triumphantly to the Presidency on
the consolidated votes of Northeast and West. Alas! it was never to be. The
American Plan also called for support of the U.S. Bank, but that had become a
dirty word west of the Appalachians. Besides this, Clay spoke up for high-
priced public lands. This was agreeable to the leaders of the Northeast, who
feared that their labor supply would be drained away if land were easily available. But the bedrock position of the West throughout its history had been for
low-priced public lands. As far as the states of the upper Mississipipi Valley were
concerned, Clay zigged when he should have zagged on this issue.

Nor did Clay's plan win him many popularity contests in the South,
which as a section voted "no" on all four of the major issues. The South bitterly
opposed the protective tariffs of 1824, 1828, 1832. It argued that these were unconstitutional, since Congress could set tariffs only for revenue purposes. But its
basic objection rested on economic grounds. The South was a free-trade section.
Approximately two-thirds of its cotton crop went to England, which sent manufactured goods in return. Tariffs on these imports penalized the cotton planters
in order to benefit Yankee manufacturers. No wonder the South threatened nulli-

fication of these tariffs, or that South Carolina actually attempted to do so in 1832.

Southern statesmen were against federally financed internal improvements, again on constitutional grounds. Except for military roads, they followed the Jeffersonian strict-constructionist doctrine which left such improvements to the states. The leaders opposed the Bank for both constitutional and economic reasons, since many Southerners wanted to start their own banks. And after 1830 the section was increasingly inclined to a policy of high-priced public lands. The extension of its own frontier was blocked by the Ozark Plateau and the federal Indian Territory, so the Northwest stood to gain more by a liberal land policy. And after 1854 when slavery became a burning sectional issue, one finds the leaders reasoning that free land equaled free soil, and thus they opposed "homestead" proposals. However, the South seemed willing to bargain with the West on the land issue if it could get the tariffs whittled down in return.

Jackson and the Bank

All these sectional issues were juggled around during Andrew Jackson's Presidency. The "Hero of New Orleans" has traditionally been regarded as the champion of the West. He expressed pure frontier attitudes on several issues, notably the removal of the Indians from the Old Southwest. At his inaugural reception in 1829, hordes of unwashed backwoodsmen surged through the White House trying to shake hands with Old Hickory. They lapped up the bowlfuls of punch, broke furniture, shattered windows, and gave each other bloody noses during impromptu fistfights. This spectacle seemed to epitomize the strong frontier influence in Jacksonianism.

But neither the voting pattern in 1828 nor Jackson's policies in office seemed to be that clear-cut. True, the Western and Southern farmers voted for him, but so did the workingmen and the protectionists in Pennsylvania and New York. The vote was more by class lines than by sections, with Jackson's party being a farmer-laborer-small capitalist coalition. As President he favored a "judicious" tariff, whatever that meant. But apparently neither the 1828 "Tariff of Abominations" nor the slightly lower 1832 levies were considered to be "injudicious." The Southerners had hoped that Jackson would befriend them by urging a downward revision of these schedules. In this hope they were sorely disappointed.

On neither internal improvements nor land policy does Jackson appear to have been an ardent spokesman of the pioneer West. In 1830 he vetoed the Maysville Turnpike Bill, which would have appropriated federal funds for a road through Kentucky. He based the veto on constitutional grounds, but it is worth remembering that Kentucky was the home state of his archrival Henry Clay. In land policy Jackson generally favored lowered prices and settlement of the unoccupied lands by "independent farmers." But this did not mean that he spoke for the typical squatter. A case in point is the break between him and Representative David Crockett over the latter's land bill.

The Vacant Land Bill had been introduced in the House of Representatives in 1828. It would relinquish all vacant federal land in Tennessee to the state, which would then sell it to the highest bidders. Crockett proposed instead to give the land directly to the squatters of west Tennessee. This position brought him into conflict with the landed gentry and with the Jackson-Polk machine, which planned to sell the land at higher prices than the poor could afford to pay. After the bill's defeat in 1829 the embittered Crockett switched over to the Whigs, remarking that "I have not got a Coller Round my neck marked 'My Dog'—with the name of Andrew Jackson on it." Jackson was actually a well-to-do planter who owned slaves, cotton lands, and an impressive estate in "the Hermitage." His views on economic matters were usually those of a typical border conservative. If one wants a purer example of the pioneer democrat, he would have to pick David Crockett.

The Bank Veto

On the bank issue, though, Jackson spoke in terms that delighted Westerners all up and down the social scale. "King Andrew," as the Whigs dubbed him, was out to slay the dragon. The President had not been hostile to the B.U.S. before 1828; in fact he had once owned shares in its Nashville branch. But many of his supporters wanted the Bank destroyed, albeit for different and conflicting reasons. There was the party's "paper money wing" of Western and Southern speculators who objected to the Bank's control over credit expansion. Allied to these were the rising capitalists, East and West, who wanted to start big banks of their own and resented Philadelphia's monopoly. Then there were the "hard money men," the left wing of the Jackson coalition. These were farmers and workers who had been pauperized by being paid with depreciated banknotes of various kinds. Rightly or wrongly they blamed their troubles on the B.U.S., demanding its dissolution and the payment of all wages in gold or silver. Listening to their chorus, Jackson became convinced that the Bank's death would bring an end to speculation and other economic evils. The reasoning was as logical as that of a dog biting its own tail, for the Bank was the one stabilizing agency in the national financial system. But politics does not obey the rules of logic.

The President vetoed the Bank recharter bill on July 10, 1832. He covered all bases: un-American (too many British stockholders); unconstitutional (nothing in the document about semiprivate corporations); and undemocratic (run by a clique of "paper aristocrats"). The anti-Bank men howled with glee over the demise of their enemy. On the other hand the Bank's director Nicholas Biddle, known in the Democratic press as "Old Nick the Regulator," joined with Henry Clay in attempting to save the institution. Biddle proved his political ineptitude by having 30,000 copies of the veto message printed and distributed to show why Jackson rated an "F" for economic analysis. But the plan back-fired, for the public was convinced that Jackson's argument was sound. The presidential election that fall turned largely on the Bank issue, and Jackson's resounding triumph over Clay (219 electoral votes to 49) meant that the veto would stand.

Speculation and Panic

Jackson took the government funds from the B.U.S. and put them into private banks. It just happened that the directors of these favored or "pet" banks were staunch Jacksonian Democrats. While the President's removal of the deposits may have been good politics, it was bad economics. The fires of speculation were stoked up once again, and the boom-bust pattern of 1819 was repeated. The West became a mushroom field of local banks, which numbered 329 in 1830 and 788 in 1837. They extended loans for every conceivable purpose, and practically begged people to become borrowers. Again much of the credit was used for land speculation. The National Land Office recorded sales of 2 million acres in 1831 and of 20 million acres in 1836. "Paper towns" went up all over the Western map. Anybody who was anybody speculated; even the reverend clergy rubbed shoulders with sharpers and professional land agents at the government auctions.

Jackson also contributed to the speculative orgy by releasing surplus federal funds to the states. Incredible as it may seem to modern readers, the United States government actually had a Treasury surplus (36 million dollars) instead of a debt in the mid-30s. This had been built up by land sales, the high tariffs, and Jackson's refusal to spend federal funds for internal improvements. The Northeast and the Whigs favored "Distribution" or refund of this money to the states according to population. The West and the Democrats had generally wanted to reduce government income by cutting land prices. By 1836, however, the West's frantic desire for internal improvements had made it anxious to get hold of funds immediately. Pressured by his friends in the West and South, Jackson signed a Distribution Bill on June 3, 1836.

The West then embarked on what were usually called "Mammoth Internal Improvement Programs" for the building of canals, railways, and turn-pikes. Although the states made phenomenal progress, many of the projects were poorly planned and inadequately financed. Every little hamlet wanted a steamboat landing or a canal, and politicians found it hard to resist anyone's request. The result was a topheavy financial structure that would topple at the slightest breeze.

President Jackson saw the dangers of the unchecked speculation toward the conclusion of his second term. On July 16, 1836, he issued a Specie Circular which ordered that only gold and silver be accepted for government land. This belated effort to check bank credit only contributed to an already dangerous situation. Specie began to disappear from circulation. Finally the New York banks suspended specie payments on May 10, 1837, and this precipitated another slam-bang panic. Other contributory causes were a series of poor crops in 1835 to 1837 which weakened farmers' purchasing power, and a financial crisis in England which forced British creditors to call in their American loans.

Election of "Old Tippecanoe"

The depression did not really hit the West until 1839, but then crop prices began to tumble. Banks had already folded up, the internal improvement projects lay half finished, and now men fled to the cities in an attempt to get work. The Democratic administration was saddled with the depression, always a bad situation for any political party. President Martin Van Buren attempted to hold the Jacksonian coalition together, but the stresses and strains were too great. And in the presidential campaign of 1840 the Whigs turned the Democrats' own guns against them by employing what might be called the rugged-old-hero technique.

The election of William Henry Harrison was a case of "triumphant humbuggery." The Whigs utilized public relations techniques to sell "Old Tippecanoe" as a thoroughgoing democrat. An unfortunate remark by a Democratic editor that Harrison should stay in his log cabin drinking hard cider was turned to good account in what has been known ever since as the Log Cabin and Hard Cider campaign. These and other symbols associated with the West were effectively exploited. As Virginia's Democratic "Committee on Humbugs" reported: "the Whigs have raised in this state seventeen log cabins ornamented by two stuffed bear skins, one living bear, together with coon skins, brooms, gourds, and cider barrels innumerable." Whig publicists pointed out that the homespun Harrison drank cider while the effete Van Buren sipped imported wine and used "Double Extract of Queen Victoria" on his whiskers. The campaign song "Tyler and Tippecanoe" boasted (to the tune of "Rosin the Bow"):

> *Again and again fill your glasses*
> *Bid Martin Van Buren adieu*
> *We'll now please ourselves and our lasses*
> *And we'll vote for old Tippecanoe.*

Harrison's decisive election victory, while it was effected by salesmanship, was also an assertion of the West's new-found identity and power.

Land Policy: Preemption to Homestead

Actually the Whigs were the rich man's party. Right down the line from Henry Clay to Abraham Lincoln they favored high land prices and distribution. Lincoln believed that high prices would discourage speculators and protect the small farmer, but such views were not general in his own section. The Democratic alternatives of graduation, donation, and preemption, most ably advocated by Senator Benton, were more enthusiastically received.

Benton had introduced a graduation bill in the Senate as early as 1824. The idea was to reduce the price of unsold public lands until they reached 50 cents an acre. Those still unsold would then be given to the states (donation) and eventually to the people. The Whigs and the conservative North Atlantic states blocked this and subsequent bills during the next 30 years. Finally in 1854 a graduation bill did become law. Ironically, it benefited speculators who gobbled up much "swamp" land that was actually quite valuable.

The West had more success with preemption. Recognition of the rights of squatters had long been one of the section's loudest demands. By the Intrusion Act of 1807, squatters were technically trespassers on the public domain and were subject to 6 months' imprisonment if convicted. This law was unenforceable, as Congress realized in 1830 when it passed the first of several temporary preemption laws. These were renewed at 2-year intervals, but by 1840 the frontiersmen were demanding a permanent statute. Senator Benton's "log cabin bill" of that year was backed by the Democrats, who were partially motivated by a desire to reveal the falsity of the Whigs' claim to being friends of the West. Sure enough, Whigs solidly opposed the bill, and it was allowed to die in the House of Representatives.

Yet a permanent preemption law was passed in 1841, and surprisingly enough its sponsor was that same Henry Clay who had once referred to squatters as "lawless rabble." The death of the sixty-eight-year-old Harrison before a year in office and the accession of the strict constructionist John Tyler to the Presidency forced Clay to change his tactics. He had to make his pet bill a combined preemption-distribution measure. But to satisfy Tyler and the Southerners the distribution of funds was to cease if tariffs went over the 20-percent level. Since tariffs did go above that level in 1842, the distribution feature of the bill quickly became a "dead letter." But preemption was now on the books, the frontier interests having won their goal almost by accident.

The preemption bill helped to democratize the public land system. The squatter could now get first crack at his 160 acres before it was auctioned off. He still had to buy the land at the current minimum price of $1.25 an acre, but the speculators would not automatically appropriate the fruits of his labor as had happened so often before. Congress had finally recognized that the small farmers, or "Cabin Boys" as Jackson called them, should be encouraged. Since they were not a likely source of revenue, it is clear that the basic purpose of the legislation was settlement rather than sales.

There was a kin relationship between the concepts of preemption and of absolutely free homesteads. The evolution of popular thinking on this subject finally culminated in the passage of a Homestead Act in 1862 after several earlier legislative failures. The Western farmers were of course the largest bloc supporting free 160-acre homesteads. From the mid-40s on, they were joined by Eastern workingmen who believed that free land would mean higher wages and better conditions for themselves. Under the leadership of George Henry Evans, a New York trade unionist, they supported a Land Reform movement which aimed at passage of appropriate legislation. Horace Greeley, the Whig newspaper editor who had attacked the preemption bill, was converted in 1846 to this doctrine of "land for the landless." His *New York Tribune* editorials in support of the principle are variants of the "safety valve theory" about western expansion.

It is interesting that the Eastern banker-manufacturer group also switched its support to low-priced public lands. This was in part due to the great influx of foreign immigrants, especially Irishmen fleeing the potato famines of the early 40s. The reservoir of cheap labor erased all the old anxieties about the loss of factory workers to the West. In addition, it became increasingly apparent that the West rather than the South was to be the prime market for industrial products. Greeley put it quite well when he wrote in 1849: "Every smoke that rises in [the] Great West marks a new customer to the counting rooms and warehouses of New York." Land policy thus became another building block in the legislative bridge between Northeast and West.

After 1854 the South opposed homestead. To that section the whole idea had become associated with "free soil." The Democratic President James Buchanan, who listened to his Southern advisers, vetoed a homestead bill in 1860. On the other hand, the Republican party, with its strong base in the Northwest, adopted the principle between 1858 and 1860. Abraham Lincoln adhered to his party's platform, and abandoned his earlier commitment to high-priced public lands. With the Southerners out of the Union, it was possible for him to sign the Homestead Act on May 20, 1862. It specified that a settler be given title to 160 acres if he lived on it for 5 years and made certain improvements. In theory at least, the old Jeffersonian idea of a freehold republic in the West could now be realized.

Slavery and Expansion

Land policy was important to the West, but in national politics after 1846 it took a back seat to slavery. No other issue was so important as this in determining sectional positions. The Northwest and the Southwest were joined by the great natural entity of the Mississippi Valley. But slavery drew a horizontal line across the river and into the lands beyond. To the north of the line was a society based on equality, enterprise, and constant competition. To the south of it was one based on a static paternalism and the denial of opportunity to the bonded class. It was not that the Northwesterners desired to root out slavery in the Old South, though the handful of abolitionists did want to do so, but rather that the system threatened to expand into the trans-Missouri region. Such a prospect was intolerable to the free white farmers, who regarded these lands as reserved for themselves.

Slavery and westward expansion had first been joined in unholy matrimony during 1820. The Missouri Compromise of that year had drawn the 36°30′ line as the northern limit of the slave system. In the time-honored tradition of American politics, each section had gotten half a loaf. The compromise was the basis of sectional peace for a quarter of a century. To be sure, there were fanatical extremists who attacked slavery on moral grounds. William Lloyd Garrison began publishing his *Liberator* in 1831, and he publicly burned the Constitution since it legalized slavery. James G. Birney founded the American Anti-Slavery Society in 1833, and urged gradual emancipation. By 1844 Birney had achieved enough respectability to run as a presidential candidate of the Liberty party. Though it gained only a laughable 7,000 votes, this splinter party took enough New York votes from Clay to put James K. Polk in the White House. After this, the leaders in both major parties stopped laughing at the "lunatic fringe."

President Polk seemed rather obtuse in failing to see any connection between slavery and territorial expansion. When David Wilmot introduced his proviso to bar slavery in the newly acquired Mexican lands, the baffled President proclaimed that there was no relation between the two. The Southern leaders were more astute, and they clearly saw the challenge implicit in Wilmot's bill. From here on, they argued that the citizens of a state had the constitutional right to take slaves into federal territories, and that Congress could not prohibit them from so doing.

Slavery expansion was an issue in the 1848 election. Martin Van Buren was the candidate of a Free Soil party whose platform was based on the Wilmot Proviso and a litany of "Free Soil, Free Labor, Free Speech, and Free Men." He drew an impressive 291,000 votes, although the Whig candidate Zachary Taylor won the three-cornered race from him and Democrat Lewis Cass. Taylor possessed the inestimable advantage of having taken no stand on any important issue. Since he was a slaveholder from Louisiana, the South expected him to defend its "peculiar institution." But Old Rough and Ready had his own ideas on the subject. It turned out that Taylor's concept of the national welfare bulked larger than the interests of his own section or class.

Compromise of 1850

This became apparent when California applied for statehood with a no-slavery constitution at the end of 1849. Taylor had encouraged immediate application as a means of bypassing the territorial stage and its inevitable brannigan over slavery. The radical Southerners were infuriated by this move to block them from a wealthy and populous region. John C. Calhoun in his greatest speech (March 4, 1850) reviewed the declining power of the South and predicted its secession unless Northern persecution ceased. But the blunt Taylor had spent his life boxing the ears of unruly soldiers, and he was not going to take any backtalk from slave-owning Senators. The President's determination to force the statehood bill through Congress made for an ominous situation there during the early months of 1850.

The "Great Pacificator" Henry Clay worked out a series of proposals known collectively as the Compromise of 1850. California was to be admitted as a free state; Texas was to surrender its claims to New Mexico in return for congressional payment of her debt; the slave trade (though not slavery) was abolished in the District of Columbia; Congress was to frame a more effective fugitive slave law; Utah and New Mexico territories were to be organized with no mention of slavery. Implicit in this last provision was the idea of "popular sovereignty," under which the residents of a territory would eventually vote upon the issue. It took Senator Stephen A. Douglas of Illinois and compromise-minded Democrats from all sections to get the bills passed. Taylor declared his firm opposition to the package, but his death from a stomach disorder on July 9 removed him from the scene. Vice President Millard Fillmore was a seasoned politician who understood the mechanics of compromise. He signed the various proposals in mid-September, effecting what seemed to be a sectional truce on the slavery controversy.

Kansas-Nebraska Act

Unfortunately, Senator Douglas soon broke the truce which he had been instrumental in arranging. His bill to organize Kansas and Nebraska territories, which became law in May of 1854, was one of the most momentous in American history. It reopened the whole controversy over slavery in the territories, split the Democrats along sectional lines, created a new Republican party, and whipped up mutual fear and distrust on both sides of the Mason-Dixon line. Douglas of course did not envision this result. His bill seemed to offer a perfect solution to the whole problem. This was the principle of "popular sovereignty," or to use the less elegant but more accurate term, "squatter sovereignty." Here was the democratic method of deciding the issue. Kansas would undoubtedly be settled by Missourians who would vote to become a slave state. Nebraska would be settled from Iowa and Illinois, and would choose to be a free state. Thus each section would get a slice of the pie. The Senator also expected to get something for himself, namely, a railroad terminus in Chicago, where he had extensive real estate investments. Kansas was closed to travel and emigration since much of it was federal Indian reservation. The Indian barrier had to be removed and the two territories organized quickly if Douglas's Chicago-San Francisco rail route was to be chosen over the New Orleans-San Diego alternative. It might also be pointed out that the Democratic party was suffering from "tired blood," and Douglas thought he would help revive it by introducing some fresh issues. His firecracker, though, turned out to be a stick of dynamite.

The violent opposition to the bill stemmed from its repeal of the Missouri Compromise and the sacred 36°30′ line. This threatened the security of farmers in the Old Northwest. Yankees, Germans, and even many Southern Uplanders from the section knew they could not compete with slave labor. Abraham Lincoln, who left his law practice and reentered politics as a result of this bill, spoke for many when he said that "slave states are places for poor white people to move FROM; and not to remove TO." Democrats left their party in droves. Thomas Hart Benton remarked of the 5-foot Douglas: "That part of his body, Sir, which men wish to kick, is too near the ground." These "anti-Nebraska" Democrats joined with former Whigs like Lincoln and with ex-Free Soilers to create a new Republican party. The Republicans' organizing principle was opposition to the westward extension of slavery. This was the basic plank in the rather barebones platform upon which John Charles Frémont campaigned for President in 1856.

The Kansas War

Squatter sovereignty did not work in Kansas. Indeed, enough blood was spilled so that the Civil War may be said to have begun there 5 years before Fort Sumter. Proslavery squatters from Missouri crowded across the border of "their Kansas" within a month of the bill's passage, and founded towns at Leavenworth and Atchison. Shortly thereafter antislavery New Englanders settled Lawrence, Manhattan, and Topeka. Many of these, totaling 600 in the summer of 1854, were sponsored by the Emigrant Aid Company of Massachusetts. The company started out as a commercial enterprise, but it soon acquired political overtones. The director Eli Thayer described the migrants as "pioneers of freedom." Actually the bulk of the Kansas settlers were from Ohio, Illinois, and Iowa rather than New England. But to the Missourians everyone from north of the Ohio was a "black and poisonous abolitionist."

In the spring of 1855 elections were held for a territorial legislature. Bands of Missouri "Regulators," armed to the teeth with horse pistols and Bowie knives, poured into Kansas to make certain that it voted for slavery. At the polls they cast ballots for their absent brothers, uncles, and cousins. Hence there were four times as many votes (6,000) as there were registered voters (1,500)! Naturally the new legislature passed laws legalizing slavery and prescribing heavy penalties for those who even spoke against the institution. The free-state men responded by holding a convention at Topeka in October and forming their own government. In a situation resembling that of Tennessee in the 1780s, the territory had two constitutions, two governors, and two legislatures.

On May 21, 1856, a small army of Missouri "Border Ruffians" sacked the town of Lawrence. In retaliation Old John Brown and his sons murdered five proslavery men in the Potawatomie Massacre. Brown was undoubtedly a fanatic, but he had originally come to Kansas for economic reasons and not to fight slavery. In fact, much of the bushwhacking and cabin burning during the next 2 years resulted from arguments over land claims rather than slavery. But it was a "newspaper war," and reporters treated every skirmish as evidence that there was a crusade for democracy on the plains.

In Washington both the Pierce and the Buchanan administrations attempted to appease the South. Buchanan was determined to admit Kansas under the proslavery Lecompton constitution of 1857, but the territory's free-state majority rejected this document in a referendum. The Missourians and free-staters continued their debates with Sharps rifles, and the federal army seemed unable to stop the raiding. Men famous in later frontier history were involved in these contests. James Butler "Wild Bill" Hickok was a gunman in Jim Lane's free-state band, and young William F. Cody saw his father stabbed when delivering a speech against slavery. The unsettled situation continued until the Colorado gold strikes in 1858 diverted attention from politics. When Kansas finally did become a state in 1861, her constitution excluded slavery.

The Civil War

The election of Abraham Lincoln in 1860 amounted to formal ratification of the Northeast-Northwest pact. The Republican platform incorporated many of the old cross-sectional measures such as tariffs and internal improvements, along with the relatively newer proposal for homestead. Both sections shared the same general antipathy for slavery. Lincoln's solid victory margin in the Northwest is explained by the influx of free-soil settlers during the 1850s. These were New Englanders and Germans for the most part, both of whom had strong antislavery traditions.

In addition to political and ideological bonds, the two sections had also been drawn closer together economically by the pattern of railroad construction. Thirty-one thousand miles of railway had been built in the United States by 1861. Of this total, 22,000 miles lay north of the Maryland border and the Ohio River. The Baltimore & Ohio had reached the river at Wheeling by 1852, and the Pennsylvania had run its line from Philadelphia to Pittsburgh by 1854. Two railways, the New York Central and the Erie, ran from New York City to Lake Erie by the mid-50s. There they connected with a maze of independent lines running to all points of the compass in Ohio, Michigan, Indiana, and Illinois. These East-West links between the seaboard and the interior represented a sectional marriage as well as a triumph of technology over nature. In the quarter century before 1850, the competition between the Erie Canal barges and the river steamers from the South had come out about even. But now Western trade was directed over the Appalachians instead of down the Mississippi to New Orleans. The South built its railroads much more slowly, and in a disconnected pattern that put it in a poor competitive position as far as the Northwest's trade was concerned. The penalty was a growing commercial isolation that supplemented and reinforced the section's political alienation.

So the election of the "black abolitionist" Lincoln was followed by secession and war. In the West the Civil War involved only a few pockets of conflict. The Kansas-Missouri feud was continued, with much of the fighting on that borderland being done by guerrilla bands. Such freebooters as Jim Lane and Charles Jennison led their "Jayhawkers" on raids into Missouri, where they took the property and lives of Unionists as well as Southern sympathizers. After the Confederate Army was driven from Missouri in 1862, the Southern effort too was conducted by irregular bands. The most notorious of these was led by William Clarke Quantrill. His recruiting slogan of "Join Quantrill and rob the banks" attracted hard-eyed young men like Frank and Jesse James. The most celebrated of the band's many atrocities was the Lawrence Massacre of August 21, 1863. One hundred and fifty men were killed as the raiders settled old scores with the "abolitionist" town. The slaughter on both sides must be viewed against the whole violent history of the area before the war began.

Jesse James at seventeen. A guerrilla fighter equipped with three guns. Source: William Tilghman Collection, Division of Manuscripts, University of Oklahoma Library.

Elsewhere in the trans-Missouri region the most important Confederate operation was Gen. Henry H. Sibley's invasion of New Mexico in 1861 and 1862. The plan was to seize the Rio Grande Valley, march across Arizona, and join with Southern sympathizers in Los Angeles to bring California with its gold mines into the Confederate orbit. Sibley and his Texans did capture Santa Fe. But then Gen. Edward Canby's Union Regulars and the Colorado Volunteers turned him back at the battle of Glorieta Pass on March 28, 1862. Sibley's ignominious retreat marked the effective end of any real Confederate threats to the Southwest, though not of further schemes for its conquest. One plan was to invade the region from Mexico, using disguised miners to capture the Union forts and establish a Confederate territorial government. In view of the strong federal garrison which had been assigned to New Mexico, the author of such a project must have been harebrained indeed. His name was Lansford W. Hastings.

Selected Readings   Frederick Jackson Turner, *The Rise of the New West, 1819-1829* (New York, 1906) and *The United States, 1830-1850* (New York, 1935) are still basic on sectionalism. Marcus Cunliffe, *The Nation Takes Shape, 1789-1837* (Chicago, 1959), has a brief discussion of sectionalism. Samuel Rezneck, "The Depression of 1819-1822, a Social History," *American Historical Review,* vol. 34 (October, 1933), is useful. Clay's "American Plan" is outlined in Clement Eaton, *Henry Clay and the Art of American Politics* (Boston, 1957). Charles S. Sydnor, *The Development of Southern Sectionalism, 1819-1848* (Baton Rouge, 1948), is excellent.

Thomas P. Abernethy, *From Frontier to Plantation in Tennessee* (Chapel Hill, N.C., 1932), emphasizes Jackson's aristocratic leanings. For the Jackson-Crockett split over the Land Bill, see James A. Shackford, *David Crockett, the Man and the Legend* (Chapel Hill, N.C., 1956). Bray Hammond's article on "Jackson, Biddle, and the Bank of the United States," *Journal of Economic History,* vol. 17 (May, 1947), is an excellent introduction to the Bank war. Hammond's *Banks and Politics in America from the Revolution to the Civil War* (Princeton, 1957) is outstanding. Arthur M. Schlesinger, Jr.'s *The Age of Jackson* (New York, 1945) broke new paths in political history, but it fumbles on economic matters and overpraises Jackson. A pamphlet edited by George R. Taylor, *Jackson Versus Biddle — the Struggle over the Second Bank of the United States* (New York, 1949), is a useful collection of articles. See also Thomas P. Govan, *Nicholas Biddle, Nationalist and Public Banker* (Chicago, 1959).

Reginald McGrane, *The Panic of 1837* (Chicago, 1924), is standard. Samuel Rezneck, "The Social History of an American Depression, 1837-1843," *American Historical Review,* vol. 40 (July, 1935), is helpful. Paul W. Gates, "The Role of the Land Speculator in Western Development," *Pennsylvania Magazine of History and Biography,* vol. 66 (July, 1942), has much on the Panic of 1837. Robert G. Gunderson, *The Log Cabin Campaign* (Lexington, 1957), is standard on the 1840 election; see also Freeman Cleves, *Old Tippecanoe: William Henry Harrison and His Times* (New York, 1939). Roy M. Robbins, *Our Landed Heritage* (Princeton, 1942), has the best analysis of preemption and homestead. William N. Chambers, *Old Bullion Benton, Senator from the New West* (Boston, 1956), is useful on this subject. Helene S. Zahler, *Eastern Workingmen and National Land Policy, 1829-1862* (New York, 1941), is of interest.

Among the better books on the rise of the antislavery movement are Gilbert H. Barnes, *The Anti-Slavery Impulse, 1830-1844* (New York, 1933); Dwight L. Dumond, *Antislavery: The Crusade for Freedom in America* (Ann Arbor, 1961); John L. Thomas, *The Liberator: William Lloyd Garrison* (Boston, 1963); and Betty Fladeland, *James Gillespie Birney: Slaveholder to Abolitionist* (Ithaca, N.Y., 1955). Holman Hamilton, *Prologue to Conflict: The Crisis and Compromise of 1850* (Lexington, 1964), is indispensable. Roy F. Nichols, "The Kansas Nebraska Act: A Century of Historiography," *Mississippi Valley Historical Review*, vol. 43 (September, 1956), reviews the literature. Frank H. Hodder, "The Railroad Background of the Kansas-Nebraska Act;" *Mississippi Valley Historical Review*, vol. 12 (June 1925), called attention to Douglas's motives. James C. Malin, *The Nebraska Question, 1852-1854* (Lawrence, 1953), emphasizes frontier influences. Ruhl J. Bartlett, *John C. Frémont and the Republican Party* (Columbus, 1930), discusses political results of the Kansas-Nebraska Act. Eugene H. Berwanger, *The Frontier Against Slavery* (Urbana, Ill., 1967), demonstrates that anti-Negro prejudice shaped Western views of slavery extension. William F. Zornow, *Kansas: A History of the Jayhawk State* (Norman, 1957), has concise coverage of the "war" there. Alice Nichols, *Bleeding Kansas* (New York, 1954), is a popular work. James C. Malin, *John Brown and the Legend of Fifty Six* (Philadelphia, 1942), is a superb and massive analysis. Samuel A. Johnson, *The Battle Cry of Freedom* (Lawrence, 1954), is a scholarly study of the Emigrant Aid Company.

General aspects of the Civil War are covered in Allan Nevins, *The Ordeal of the Union*, 2 vols. (New York, 1947), and in Avery Craven, *The Coming of the Civil War* (Chicago, 1957). See also Benjamin P. Thomas, *Abraham Lincoln: A Biography* (New York, 1952). Robert G. Athearn, "West of Appomattox: Civil War beyond the Great River," *Montana Magazine of History*, vol. 11 (April, 1962), is a general summary, while the whole volume is devoted to articles on the war in the West. Also of general usefulness is Charles D. Sacconaghi, "A Bibliographical Note on the Civil War in the West," *Arizona and the West*, vol. 8 (Winter, 1966). Jay Monaghan, *Civil War on the Western Border, 1854-1865* (Boston, 1955), is a competent narrative of the Kansas-Missouri conflicts. William E. Connelley, *Quantrill and the Border Wars* (Cedar Rapids, 1910), set out to make a villain of Quantrill; more objective is Albert Castel, *William Clarke Quantrill: His Life and Times* (New York, 1961). William C. Whitford, *Colorado Volunteers in the Civil War: The New Mexico Campaign in 1862* (Denver, 1906) is still basic, while Robert L. Kerby, *The Confederate Invasion of New Mexico and Arizona* (Los Angeles, 1958), is concise. William J. Hunsaker's "Lansford W. Hastings' Project for the Invasion and Conquest of Arizona and New Mexico for the Southern Confederacy" is in *Arizona Historical Review*, vol. 4 (July, 1931).

XIX. Far Western Mining Frontiers

If the Far West was short on certain important resources, notably water and timber, it still possessed more than enough land and minerals. The land attracted the farmer, while gold and silver lured the miner. There were mineral "strikes," "rushes," and "bonanzas" from 1849 until almost the end of the century. California in 1849, Nevada and Colorado in 1859, Montana in 1862, and South Dakota in 1875 mark the rather erratic progress of the mining frontier, which often reversed the orthodox pattern by advancing from west to east. Eager prospectors tramped all over the mountainous West, leaving little of it unexplored and coincidentally accelerating settlement. Mining stimulated the economic and political development of several Western states, created important cities, and made a few individuals richer than Croesus.

The California Gold Rush The story begins in California on January 24, 1848. The principal character is James Marshall, a carpenter whom Captain Sutter had hired to build a sawmill at Coloma on the American River. While inspecting the bed of the millrace, Marshall found two pieces of gold. The discovery was reported to Sutter, and the two men tried to keep it a secret. But wagging tongues soon made the news known in San Francisco and Monterey. By May and June the repeated cry of "Gold from the American River!" had set off a local rush in that direction. Farmers, soldiers, and artisans earning $7 a month left to make $200 a day at placer mining. The Rev. Walter Colton, a Navy chaplain serving as alcalde of Monterey, reported that "our servants have run, one after another, till we are almost in despair. . . . A general of the United States Army, the commander of a man-of-war, and the Alcalde of Monterey, in a smoking kitchen, grinding coffee, toasting a herring, and peeling onions! These gold mines are going to upset all the domestic arrangements of society, turning the head to the tail, and the tail to the head."

News of the gold strikes reached the East that fall, and President Polk reported on them in his farewell message to Congress on December 5. The result was a mass migration of argonauts or "Forty-Niners." Some 4,000 to 5,000 men reached California by early 1849, and between 40,000 and 50,000 had arrived there by the end of that year. They represented all strata of society and every imaginable type of character. There were Mexican War veterans, farmers, gamblers, college dropouts, unhappy husbands, and sturdy New Englanders. Despite the diversity of background, the migrants were all motivated by the hope of quick wealth. While children dreamed of sugar plums, grown men counted bags of gold dust in their sleep. The result was a population explosion of nigh incredible proportions over the next few years. If statistics do not lie, the state had a population (excluding Indians) of 14,000 in 1848, and of 250,000 in 1852.

The gold seekers followed three major routes to California. One was by ship around Cape Horn, an uncomfortable journey of 19,000 miles which normally took 6 months. A shorter sea route went by way of the Isthmus of Panama. The recently organized United States Mail Steamship Company took passengers from New York to Chagres on the east coast of Panama. Pack mules were used for the trip across the isthmus to the west coast port of "Panama City." Here the travelers waited and wilted in the tropical heat until a ship of the Pacific Mail Steamship Company could pick them up. While the perils of this route have been exaggerated, there was danger from yellow fever, cholera, and other diseases. The chief drawback was the instability of the sailing schedules, for the crews jumped ship in San Francisco and joined in the race to the diggings. Since both sea routes were expensive, the bulk of the argonauts went by the overland trails.

The old California Trail by way of the Platte and Humboldt Valleys was the most heavily used route to the mines. Emigrants from the lower Mississippi Valley went across Texas by various trails to El Paso. There they could follow the route of Colonel Cooke's Mormon Battalion through Tucson, General Kearny's Gila River trail, or the Old Spanish Trail still further north. All these avenues could be followed by the discarded sofas, tables, and armchairs of inexperienced travelers. As diarist Milus Gay wrote of his trip across the Forty Mile desert west of the Humboldt Sink: "Continuing across the desert got across to Carsonville on Carson River about 4pm 12 or 15 miles of the latter part of the Journey being sandy was very hard on our cattle the distance across is perhaps about 40 miles—such destruction of property as I saw across the Desert I have never seen—I think I passed the carcasses of 1200 head of cattle and horses and a great many waggons—Harnesses—cooking utensils—tools—water casks &c at a moderate estimate the amount I would think the property cost in the U.S. $50,000."

A typical guide to the California gold fields. Source: Huntington Library.

Mining Operations

Upon arrival the gold diggers headed for the Mother Lode, a strip of mining country running for 120 miles from Sutter's Fort south to Mariposa. Here in the western foothills of the Sierra Nevada was one of the richest and most accessible gold regions in the world. Mining was rather easy in the first few years, and men could pry nuggets from the rocks with their knives, a practice known as "crevicing." Many of the surface pockets could be emptied by pick and shovel. The simplest hand method was to "wash out" the gold by swirling the shoveled earth around in a pan. The gold flakes would remain in the bottom while the sand and clay were washed over the edge. Also in use was the "cradle," a wooden trough on rockers with cleats nailed across the bottom. The miner shoveled his "pay dirt" into the trough, which he then rocked with one hand while ladling in water with the other. The cleats caught most of the gold, while the lighter mud and gravel were washed out at the open end. Often two or three men worked these devices. The "long tom" and the sluice were stationary troughs, also equipped with cleats, which were capable of handling much

Miners in the California Mother Lode using pans and "rockers." From an old daguerreotype. Source: Los Angeles County Museum of Natural History.

greater volumes of water including fully diverted streams. Both required any-where from three to twenty men for their operation, depending on the length.

The discovery of gold was all a matter of chance. As "Dame Shirley" (Mrs. Louise Clappe) wrote: "Gold mining is Nature's great lottery scheme." As with any lottery, few of the participants held winning tickets. One man might be industrious, and yet lose everything but his shirt after several months' hard work, while another would make thousands of dollars in a few hours.

There were tests which the shrewd prospector could apply. The color of a cliff or outcrop was the best clue to the presence of minerals. California mining folklore is filled with stories of how rich claims were discovered. Some-times it is a matter of "hunter's luck"—wild shots fired at game will chip off a gold-bearing rock. "Boob's luck" is also featured, with a greenhorn being directed to some unlikely spot and inevitably striking it rich. A Swede in Eldorado County hit a $5,000 pocket after being told to dig under a certain live oak tree. Animals are often involved, and the traditional straying mule is usually found by a rich outcrop. Old-time prospectors are said to have examined the teeth of horses and mules for gold particles. Squirrels, rats, and gophers are supposed to store nuggets in their holes, and the Gopher Mine at Kelsey is named for this manner of discovery. There are also the familiar tales of last-chance mines. The destitute prospector "brings her in" with his very last round of blasting powder, as was reputedly the case with the Empire Mine at Grass Valley. The dubious nature of these explanations reflects the fact that there was no infallible method of finding the precious deposits.

California Society

Once arrived at "the diggings," the would-be millionaire attacked the earth with all the vigor appropriate to his financial expectations. He lived in a canvas tent or in a crude shack, and ate little but beans, bacon, and "flapjacks." It was a masculine society, to the extent of 92 percent, and the miners' diaries reflect their loneliness ("Saturday night and no place to go a courting—God bless the ladies") as do their songs ("Oh Susannah, don't you cry for me"). "Painted ladies" made their appearance in 1850 and after, but as usual only those men with high incomes and low morals could afford their company for very long. The range of recreational pursuits in the camps is revealed by their names: Whiskey Diggings, Brandy City, and Delirium Tremens. The methods of social control are similarly reflected in such names as Hangtown and Git-up-and-Git.

The mining population was thoroughly cosmopolitan. Australians, Hawaiians, Frenchmen, Irishmen, Chileans, Chinese, and Mexicans turned up in large numbers. The last three groups were targets of considerable hostility, and they were frequently driven from their claims by mobs. The Mexicans were most numerous in the southern part of the Mother Lode, with the camp at Sonora being their principal gathering point. They were good miners and they minded their own business, although they too had their bad men. In the first 2 months of 1853 a mad-dog brigand terrorized Amador and Calaveras Counties. His first name was Joaquin, and his last name may have been Murieta. He and his band killed two dozen people, most of them Chinese, before a company of state rangers shot him down. The actual Joaquin bears little relationship to the Robin Hood outlaw described by John Rollin Ridge, a San Francisco newspaperman who launched the legend.

The Americans, who constituted about 80 percent of the population, were no better and no worse than their fellows back East. The argonaut was different from the usual pioneer, since he had come not to build a home but to make his pile and then clear out. Of course the basic American character branched out into all kinds of wild offshoots in response to the new social and physical environment. Men who in the East had never used a cuss word became experts in profanity. The quiet bookkeeper turned into an extrovert drinker and gambler. The great reshuffling of social arrangements made California the most democratic society on earth. Men who had been sailors, Army privates, or day laborers hired physicians and ex-professors to saw wood or drive ox teams. This practical equality of all members of the community left its imprint on the state's history.

Law and Order

The generality of miners were honest and hard working. But murderers, sluice robbers, and rowdies appeared on all mining frontiers. That men with a "past" were drawn to California was indicated in a popular song:

> *Oh, what was your name in the States?*
> *Was it Thompson, or Johnson or Bates?*
> *Did you murder your wife*
> *and fly for your life?*
> *Say, what was your name in the States?*

In the absence of courts and laws, the mining camps had to frame their own rules for the protection of mining claims and the punishment of crime. California technically had a military government prior to statehood, but the army was stretched so thin that its authority existed in name only.

The basic property unit was the "claim." Since mining land actually belonged to the government, mining laws were basically squatters' agreements. The claim belonged to the man who discovered it, and it could be retained as long as it was actively worked. Usually 5 days' absence resulted in forfeiture. The size of the claim, arguments between rival claimants, and other such matters were decided by miners' committees, whose area of governance was known as a "district." The regulations adopted by these committees were later written into California law, and were exported to the other mining regions of the West.

When the United States government framed its own mining laws in the acts of 1866 and 1872, it could do no better than recognize these local customs. The 1872 act consolidated all the local mining codes into one federal law.

Such crimes as murder, robbery, and horse stealing were also judged by the miners' own courts or "popular tribunals." Suspected offenders were tried before open meetings of all the miners, who declared their verdicts by voice vote. Since there were no jails, those found guilty were sentenced to banishment, whipping, or death. Of all the camps in the Mother Lode, every other one had its "hanging tree," which subsequently became the pride of the local Chamber of Commerce. Where miners' courts proved ineffective, secret vigilance committees arose. These were especially active in California, including San Francisco in 1851 and 1856. The vigilante groups have been defended and deplored over the years by various writers. On the one hand they provided rough and ready justice for the guilty. On the other hand there was no system of appeals, and there were cases of mob law in which men were executed without the benefit of a fair trial. What can be said is that miners' courts and vigilantes were a natural development on a frontier without formal agencies of law and order.

The flush times of California mining continued through 1852, when over 81 million dollars worth of gold was taken out. Thereafter a more scientific type of operation involving heavy machinery became common. Hydraulic mining, which makes use of high-pressure hoses to loosen gold-bearing dirt from hillsides, originated in California. Tunneling into solid-rock veins or lodes, technically known as "quartz mining," also became important in the mid-50s. These methods required heavy capital investments and considerable technical knowledge, so they were not attractive to the pioneer type of miner with his get-rich-quick philosophy. When Eastern corporations and capital began to dominate mining in the state, these "Old Californians" could either work for wages or take the trail to Nevada, Colorado, or wherever new strikes seemed to promise "regular '49 times."

Gold influenced California's history more than any other single factor. The state's commercial development was speeded up, and its population expanded by leaps and bounds. San Francisco became the Coast's great metropolis, and the gateway cities of Sacramento and Stockton also boomed. Many who came to dig took one look at the mining camps and decided to become ranchers, hotelkeepers, or tradesmen. Those four famous Sacramento merchants—Leland Stanford, Collis Huntington, Mark Hopkins, and Charles Crocker—came during the gold rush period and laid the foundations for immense fortunes.

The most immediate benefit of the gold rush was statehood. It was obvious by mid-1849 that California was already much too wealthy and populous for mere territorial status. Thus President Taylor was basically correct, though hardly tactful, in his rigid insistence upon adoption of the statehood bill. The military governor, Gen. Bennett Riley, called for a convention to meet at Monterey in September of 1849. The forty-eight delegates drew up a constitution (printed in both English and Spanish) which barred slavery, dueling, and divorce. They also set the eastern boundary of the state along its present line. A referendum that fall voted approval of the constitution, and also elected a governor (Peter H. Burnett) and a legislature. California thus had a working government well before Millard Fillmore signed the statehood bill in September of 1850.

Colorado's "Fifty-Niners"

California was the most important mining region in the Far West, but there were promising strikes at other locations. Colorado's first boom turned out to be a flash in the pan. The early prospectors, and indeed the whole movement to Colorado, followed the normal east-to-west pattern. William Green Russell had prospected both in his native Georgia and in California. With a party of Georgians and Cherokees he spent the summer of 1858 panning the little streams which flowed toward the South Platte River. On Cherry Creek he found a few deposits, though nothing to get excited about. But samples of this gold were carried back to Missouri by an imaginative trader named John Cantrell, whose Munchhausen-like tales set off a race for the Rockies. The Panic of 1857 had made men anxious to find quick wealth, and the merchants of Missouri and Kansas were all too eager to sell them supplies.

Fifty thousand men left the Missouri frontier for Colorado (then part of Kansas Territory) in 1859. They went along the Platte River, by way of the Arkansas and Bent's Fort, or if they were unwise, by a waterless and Indian-infested middle route along the Smoky Hill River. They painted "Pike's Peak or Bust" on their wagons, a slightly inaccurate slogan since the diggings at Denver City were 60 miles north of the peak. But the amounts of placer gold were disappointingly small, and soon dejected bands of "Fifty-Niners" were trudging back East, this time with the slogan "Pike's Peak be Damned" on the wagons.

A few promising strikes were made to the west of Denver. A Georgian named John H. Gregory found gold-bearing quartz at Gregory Gulch near today's Black Hawk and Central City. An Old Californian, George A. Jackson, also found placer deposits at Idaho Springs. Other prospectors began moving into the canyons to the west and south of these locations, working at 8,000 to 10,000 feet above sea level. There was, in fact, a broad belt of mining country lying along the Continental Divide from Boulder County in the north to the San Juan Mountains in the south. Unfortunately for the Fifty-Niners this was in veins or lodes, which meant "quartz mining" and expensive machinery.

Colorado's population, which numbered 34,000 in the 1860 census, shrank steadily during the decade. The Civil War, serious Indian troubles, and perhaps the relative proximity of Missouri all helped to discourage population growth. After the war, a farming frontier began to take shape, and agriculture

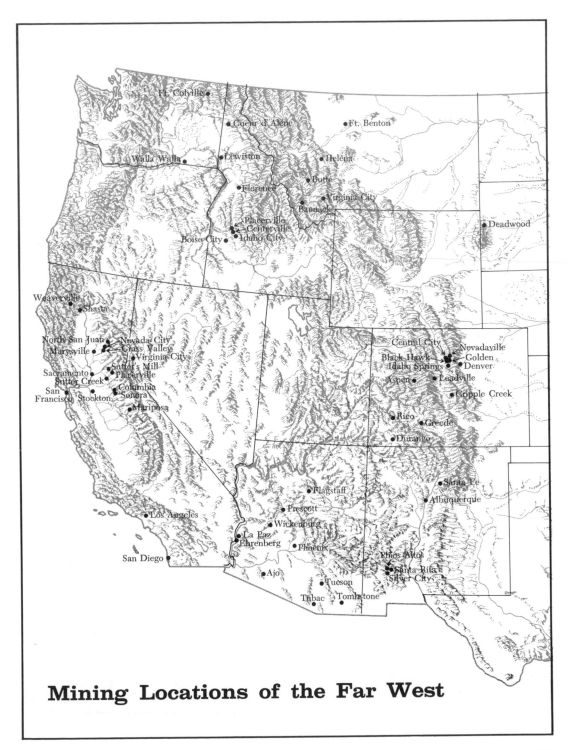

Mining Locations of the Far West

returned more income to the territory than did gold or silver. Not until the late 70s, and after statehood (1876), did Colorado realize her full potential in mining development. Then she was blessed with a succession of great silver strikes at Leadville (1878), Aspen (1880), and Creede (1891).

Nevada Bonanza

In 1859 the Comstock Lode was discovered in the Washoe mining district of western Nevada. This mixed silver and gold deposit was located on the wind-swept slopes of Mount Davidson, part of the Virginia Range east of the Sierra Nevada. Two Irishmen named Patrick McLaughlin and Peter O'Riley discovered an outcrop of gold and what they called "blue stuff," which was actually silver. When the assays made this fact known, thousands of Californians raced east-ward across the Sierra Nevada. The shanty town of Virginia City blossomed at the site of the strike, which was named for one Henry Comstock. "Old Pancake" has been a target for virtually all writers since he was not the actual discoverer of the lode but had merely bluffed his way into a partnership with McLaughlin and O'Riley. But surely any man who can outtalk two Irishmen deserves a place in history!

Ten thousand men rushed to the new bonanza in 1859 and 1860. They were the usual motley crowd of speculators, placer miners, gamblers, lawyers, and saloonkeepers. There were also substantial numbers of foreigners, particularly Chinese, Germans, Irishmen, and Cornishmen, the last of whom had a long

A famous mining town: Virginia City, Nevada. Source: Bancroft Library.

tradition of mine work. The play-for-pay girls, bearing inimitable names like "Bulldog Kate" and "Hog-eyed Mary," were there. So were famous badmen like Sam Brown, Sugarfoot Mike, Farmer Pease, and Pock-Marked Jake. Virginia City soon had the normal ratio of saloons to churches: 150 to 3. The English visitor Charles Dilke reported that "through every open door the diggers can be seen tossing the whiskey down their throats with a scowl of resolve, as though they were committing suicide—which, indeed, except in the point of speed, is probably the case." Yet "culture" was not lacking; interested citizens raised funds for a library, and four theaters in town played Shakespearean tragedy as well as minstrel shows.

Virginia City was not really representative of mining towns in the West, for it had a certain unique flavor. The town's characters come alive in the pages of its many newspapers, the most famous of which was the *Territorial Enterprise*. The star reporters were Mark Twain and Dan DeQuille (the pen name of William Wright). They specialized in hoaxes, humor, and verbal insult. Twain's best spoof was on "The Petrified Man," while DeQuille wrote about the inventor of a cooling suit who froze to death in Death Valley when his machinery jammed. Twain's *Roughing It* (1872) and DeQuille's *The Big Bonanza* (1876) are both basic sources for Nevada history. Twain's individualism, his robust humor, and his love of democracy well represent the kind of people among whom he lived in the Virginia City years from 1862 to 1864.

California quartz miners came to Washoe and contributed to important technological advances in tunneling and ore refining. George Hearst was one of these, and he began accumulating one of California's most impressive personal fortunes. But Virginia City's economic progress was very uneven, partly due to the technical problems of deep mining, and in the late 60s it appeared as if the town's days were numbered. Then another strike in 1873, called the Big Bonanza, brought the town back to life. It yielded 135 million dollars in gold and silver by 1880, and created a new crop of supermillionaires (John Mackay, James Fair, James Flood, and William O'Brien) known as the "Kings of the Comstock." With the profits, these men built ornate mansions on San Francisco's Nob Hill, and bought seats in the United States Senate as well as titled European sons-in-law for their daughters.

The Comstock Lode, including the Big Bonanza, yielded about 300 million dollars in silver and gold between 1860 and 1880. Most of this capital flowed into San Francisco and central California, making Nevada a colonial appendage of its giant neighbor. Still Nevada was given statehood with unseemly haste. In 1864 the territory had only 20,000 people, but Abraham Lincoln was facing a difficult reelection campaign and he needed all the electoral votes he could get. So in October the statehood bill was run through Congress over Democratic objections, and Nevadans dutifully voted for Old Abe in the general election.

Northwestern Mines

Idaho and western Montana also figured in the mining picture after 1860. The Idaho strikes followed a north-to-south pattern. In the summer of 1860, Capt. E. D. Pierce's party prospected the tangled wilderness along the Clearwater River, a tributary of the Snake. Their discoveries led to a rush into that area and the founding of Orofino and Pierce City. In 1861 there was another frenzied stampede to the Salmon River country. Thirty thousand men poured into that region during 1862, with Florence being the major town. There were "yonder-siders" from California, greenhorns from Missouri, together with deserters from both Civil War armies and more than the usual number of badmen. Orofino was one of the most dangerous towns in the country, and its citizens expected a "dead man for breakfast" every day. As the surface placers were cleaned out in the Clearwater and Salmon areas, the mining frontier moved down to the Boise Basin of southern Idaho. From 1863 to 1870 such towns as Idaho City and Boise City became the center of the most productive and heavily populated part of the territory. When the placers began to give out there, the Chinese moved in and reworked the old claims.

Montana's boom years ran from 1862 through 1868. The three key strikes were at Bannack City in 1862, at Alder Gulch (Virgina City) in 1863, and at Last Chance Gulch (Helena) in 1864. John White made the first discoveries in the Bannack area at Grasshopper Creek. Prospectors found Alder Gulch while retreating from an Indian war party. Within 2 years the gulch had yielded 20 million dollars of gold dust, and the town of Virginia City had a population of 10,000. The town's sheriff was Henry Plummer, who used his office to organize one of the most ruthless criminal gangs in the West. A network of spies kept Plummer and his cohorts informed of all gold shipments, so they were ready and waiting when the stages were dispatched. This was a classic case of the need for vigilante justice in the mining camps. Several lionhearted miners formed a secret society, with rituals and passwords, to bring the outlaws to the end of a rope. During a 6-week period in 1864, the vigilantes captured, tried, and executed twenty-two members of the gang, including Sheriff Plummer himself.

Both Idaho and Montana were handicapped by their physical isolation. The first Missouri River steamboat had reached Fort Benton in 1859, but service was irregular and it was still 200 miles by freight wagon from the fort to the mines. The Idaho mines were reached mainly from the Columbia, and the western part of the Mullan Road, which led to the mines, was in bad condition. Transportation within both territories was expensive and fraught with difficulties. The winters were long and hard in that high and open country. The Indians of Idaho were the gentle Nez Percé, but those in Montana were both mean and tough. Despite these problems, mining did open the way for later expansion of farming and ranching. It also was an impetus for territorial organization, for Idaho in 1863 and for Montana in 1864.

The Black Hills

One of the last great mining rushes was into lands guaranteed to the Sioux Indians for "as long as the sun shall set." For many years the red men had been going to the Black Hills of South Dakota to cut lodgepoles and to harvest wild fruit. In the Fort Laramie Treaty of 1868 the federal government had established a Sioux Reservation west of the Missouri River that included the Hills. This treaty was worth no more and no less than others which had been signed over several generations of frontier history. It would be broken at the convenience of the white man.

The government itself precipitated the rush into the area. To prove once and for all that the rumors of gold were unfounded, it sent an army expedition to the Black Hills in the summer of 1874. Gen. George Armstrong Custer commanded the force of 1,200 soldiers, which was accompanied by civilian miners, scientists, and newspaper reporters. Custer was the type to squeeze maximum publicity from any venture in which he had a hand, and so when a few nuggets of gold were found at a spot called French Creek, he trumpeted the news that gold could be found "from the grass roots down." This was also the theme of the reporter's stories, and the result was another of the famous rushes. By the summer of 1875 there were from 600 to 800 men prospecting in the Black Hills. Legally they were all trespassers, and the Army caught and ejected as many as it could. But any reading of frontier history would have indicated how impossible their task was.

In 1875 the government made two attempts to buy the Black Hills, but the angry Sioux chiefs refused both offers. All pretense of legality was then abandoned, and the government declared the area open to any prospector who cared to risk his hair by going into it. Thus the traditional pattern of the earlier mining rushes was repeated. The Black Hills were less productive than other parts of the United States, but there were shallow placer claims from the future site of Custer City on the south to Deadwood Gulch in the north.

Deadwood sprang to life early in 1876. It reached its peak in 1877, when some 12,000 people lived in the general area. The town was built up on the steep sides of a narrow gulch, with many of the houses being so frail that a man had to be careful about leaning against the walls. Many of the residents were veterans of earlier rushes, and they flooded in by wagon and by pack-horse, or on the stages of the Cheyenne and Black Hills Express Line. Among those who organized prospecting parties in Cheyenne was "Wild Bill" Hickok. He rode into Deadwood accompanied by "Calamity Jane" Cannary, who is said to have followed him "as a dog follows its master." Thus arose one of America's most enduring romantic legends, one which overlooks the fact that Hickock was happily married when he left Cheyenne. Wild Bill made a few sporadic attempts to locate mining claims, but he spent most of his time playing poker in the numerous saloons. On August 2, 1876, he held the "dead man's hand" of aces and eights. At that moment Jack McCall shot him through the back of the head, an unchivalrous method but one immeasurably safer than a face-to-face encounter.

The Homestake Mine at Lead, 4 miles from Deadwood, proved to be the most profitable in the region, and indeed it is still producing today. The enormous lode was discovered in 1876 by Moses Manuel, who had drifted all over the West before trying Deadwood. The ubiquitous George Hearst bought the property from Manuel, and his mine soon dominated gold production in the Black Hills. The whole region was a dangerous one because of hornet-mad Indians and white outlaws. The bandits so infested the roads around the diggings that stage holdups were almost a ho-hum affair. The miners' invasion of the Indian lands led indirectly to the Sioux War of 1876, in which General Custer's candle was snuffed out. Otherwise the general pattern was typical of mining rushes to other areas.

The Southwest

Mining development in Arizona and New Mexico was hampered by severe transportation difficulties, the extreme danger from Indians, and one of the harshest physical environments in the country. The result was that up to 1880 both areas ranked at the bottom of states and territories producing gold and silver. Prior to the Civil War, some gold mining had been done in New Mexico near the old Santa Rita copper mines. But these diggings had to be abandoned in 1861 under pressure from the Apaches. On Arizona's Gila River, a boomlet had been started in 1858 by the discovery of placer gold some 20 miles east of Yuma. Other strikes were shortly made up the Colorado at Ehrenburg and La Paz, and during the early 60s both gold and silver placers were found in the interior at Prescott and Wickenburg. The departure of federal army units to the East when war began adversely affected these operations. Arizona lost population during the war, and the Apaches made a prospector's life expectancy lower here than in any other part of the West.

Gen. George Crook's campaigns in the early 70s made some progress in blunting the Indian threat, although large parts of Arizona were still unsafe. Thus when prospector Ed Schieffelin proposed to explore southeastern Arizona, the Army predicted he would find only his own tombstone. As luck would have it, Schieffelin in 1877 discovered a rich silver lode at what became Tombstone, Arizona. The rush there in 1878 to 1879 repeated the older pattern of '49. By the end of 1881 the town had a population of some 10,000, and such mines as the Lucky Cuss and the Contention were yielding silver bullion that would total 25 million dollars by 1884. The city marshal was Wyatt Earp, who with his mustachioed brothers ran a gambling house as a sideline. Every red-blooded American boy knows about the Earp-Clanton gunfight at the O.K. Corral on October 26, 1881. Wyatt Earp cleaned up on the "cowboys" in this one, but he decided that despite it fine climate Arizona was rather unhealthy for him. He moved around elsewhere in the West, and eventually settled in Los Angeles where he died with his boots off at the age of eighty-one.

New Mexico enjoyed a silver boom in the late 70s centered at the aptly named Silver City. Arizona turned more and more to copper, and by the mid-80s it had several well-capitalized mines run by such organizations as Phelps-Dodge and Company. Like the mining developments in Colorado and Montana during the same period, these mines followed an industrial, rather than a frontier pattern: viz., heavy capital investments, advanced machinery, wage labor. As such, they are outside the scope of frontier history. The strike at Cripple Creek, Colorado, in 1893 hardly belongs to the pioneer period when the miners enjoyed such conveniences as telephones and electric lights!

Mining and the American Character

Mining activity spurred the development and settlement of the Far West. Of equal interest is what the mining frontiers reveal about the American character. That "M-factor" of movement and migration which has always distinguished the Americans is quite apparent in this occupation. Prospectors like Moses Manuel and Ed Schieffelin had wandered all over the West looking for the One Big Strike before they finally made it. Thousands of other less successful and hence nameless men jumped about like grasshoppers from California to Nevada to Idaho. The restlessness and optimism that still seem to be American traits were found in extreme form among the floating population of the mining camps.

The speculative nature of mining reveals a gambling mentality. Not only the prospectors themselves but those who "grubstaked" the searchers or bought mining stocks were indulging in the great national pastime of the 1800s. This fever was revealed in the games of chance like poker, faro, or monte which were the chief recreations in the camps. One played in Nature's great lottery all day out at the gulch, and then bet against the saloonkeeper at night. It was "all hail" the winner and "tough luck" for the losers in either place.

Finally, the swift and ruthless exploitation of the mineral resources is indicative of American psychology. It was almost a requirement of mining towns that they be as ugly as sin. Virginia City, Nevada, did have ornate mansions and brick buildings, but it was an exception. The representative town was a collection of ramshackle structures running along a single street, with a pile of tailings at one end and eroded gullies at the other. No one cared to invest in permanent buildings because the deposits might suddenly play out. The idea was to move in, clean out the easily mined lodes, and having made one's pile, move to San Francisco for a life of oysters and champagne. Unless the region had ores that could be profitably extracted with more sophisticated machinery, the population fled leaving a "ghost town" and a ruined landscape. Perhaps these towns, whether "restored" or not, tell more about the nation's attitude toward its natural resources than one cares to know.

Selected Readings   Two basic surveys are William S. Greever, *The Bonanza West: The Story of the Western Mining Rushes, 1848-1900* (Norman, 1963), and Rodman W. Paul, *Mining Frontiers of the Far West, 1848-1880* (New York, 1963), the former being strong on social history and the latter on technological developments. Carl I. Wheat, *Books of the California Gold Rush* (Berkeley, 1949), is a good introduction to the subject. John W. Caughey, *Gold Is the Cornerstone* (Berkeley, 1948), is a standard work. Marshall's story is in George F. Parson, *The Life and Adventures of James W. Marshall* (San Francisco, 1935), though this should be supplemented by the diary of one of his workmen, Henry W. Bigler, edited by Erwin G. Gudde, *Bigler's Chronicle of the West* (Berkeley, 1962). Three standard accounts of sea transportation are Raymond A. Rydell, *Cape Horn to the Pacific* (Berkeley, 1952); John H. Kemble, *The Panama Route, 1848-1869* (Berkeley, 1943); and Oscar Lewis, *Sea Routes to the Gold Fields* (New York, 1949). Land routes are described in Archer B. Hulbert, *The Forty Niners* (Boston, 1931), which is a composite of various journals; Ralph P. Bieber (ed.), *Southern Trails to California in 1849* (Glendale, Calif., 1937); and W. Turrentine Jackson, *Wagon Roads West* (Berkeley, 1952). George R. Stewart, *The California Trail* (New York, 1962), also treats of '49.

Carl I. Wheat edited the letters of Mrs. Louise A. K. S. Clappe under the title of *The Shirley Letters from the California Mines, 1851-1852* (New York, 1949). Another classic is Bayard Taylor's *Eldorado, or, Adventures in the Path of Empire,* originally published in 1850, but also reprinted (New York, 1949). Walker D. Wyman (ed.), *California Emigrant Letters* (New York, 1952), is valuable. Wayland D. Hand, "California Miners' Folklore," *California Folklore Quarterly,* vol. 1 (January, 1942), is interesting, as is Richard E. Lingenfelter and Richard A. Dwyer (eds.), *The Songs of the Gold Rush* (Berkeley, 1964). Elisabeth Margo, *Taming the Forty-Niner* (New York, 1955), is a delightful social history. John Rollin Ridge, *The Life and Adventures of Joaquin Murieta* (1854), has been reprinted (Norman, 1955). The best short analysis of the legend is Remi Nadeau, "Joaquin — Hero, Villain or Myth?", *Westways,* vol. 55 (January, 1963); see also Joseph H. Jackson, *Bad Company* (New York, 1949).

Charles H. Shinn's classic book, *Mining Camps: A Study in American Frontier Government,* originally issued in 1885, has had modern reprintings in hardback (New York, 1948) and in paper (New York, 1965). See also William H. Ellison, *A Self-Governing Dominion: California, 1849-1860* (Berkeley, 1950). For vigilantes consult Hubert H. Bancroft, *Popular Tribunals,* 2 vols. (San Francisco, 1887); John W. Caughey, *Their Majesties the Mob* (Chicago, 1960), principally documents; and Alan Valentine, *Vigilante Justice* (New York, 1956), which deals with San Francisco.

For Colorado see Percy S. Fritz, *Colorado: The Centennial State* (New York, 1941); LeRoy S. Hafen (ed.), *Colorado Gold Rush: Contemporary Letters and Reports, 1858-1859* (Glendale, Calif., 1941); Muriel S. Wolle, *Stampede to Timberline: The Ghost Towns and Mining Camps of Colorado* (Boulder, Colo., 1949); and George F. Willison, *Here They Dug the Gold* (New York, 1931). Richard G. Lillard, *Desert Challenge: An Interpretation of Nevada* (New York, 1942), and Gilman M. Ostrander, *Nevada, the Great Rotten Borough* (New York, 1966), are both informative. For detailed history see Effie M. Mack, *Nevada: A History of the State from the Earliest Times through the Civil War* (Glendale, Calif., 1936), and Grant H. Smith, *History of the Comstock Lode* (Reno, 1943), written by a lawyer who grew up in

Virginia City during its bonanza period. Paul Fatout, *Mark Twain in Virginia City* (Bloomington, Ind., 1964), is recommended. Mark Twain's *Roughing It* has had a modern reprinting (New York, 1953) as has Dan DeQuille's *Big Bonanza* (New York, 1947).

Merrill D. Beal and Merle W. Wells, *History of Idaho*, 3 vols. (New York, 1959), is excellent. Merrill G. Burlingame, *The Montana Frontier* (Helena, 1942), and Joseph Kinsey Howard, *Montana: High, Wide, and Handsome* (New Haven, 1943), have material on mining. Granville Stuart, *Forty Years on the Frontier*, 2 vols. (Cleveland, 1925), is a basic primary source, as is Thomas J. Dimsdale ,*The Vigilantes of Montana* (1866), recently reprinted (Norman, 1953). Donald M. Jackson, *Custer's Gold* (New Haven, 1966), recounts the 1874 expedition. Watson Parker, *Gold in the Black Hills* (Norman, 1966), covers 1874 to 1879. Duncan Aikman, *Calamity Jane and the Lady Wildcats* (New York, 1929), holds up well; while Joseph G. Rosa, *They Called Him Wild Bill* (Norman, 1964), is the definitive biography. Howard R. Lamar, *Dakota Territory, 1861-1899* (New Haven, 1956), has a chapter on the Black Hills. Agnes W. Spring, *The Cheyenne and Black Hills Stage and Express Routes* (Glendale, Calif., 1949) is useful.

Warren A. Beck, *New Mexico: A History in Four Centuries* (Norman, 1962), has a short chapter on mining. Rufus K. Wyllys, *Arizona: The History of a Frontier State* (Phoenix, 1950), touches on mining, as does Frank C. Lockwood, *Pioneer Days in Arizona* (New York, 1932). John Myers Myers, *The Last Chance: Tombstone's Early Years* (New York, 1950), is good, while Walter Noble Burns, *Tombstone* (Garden City, N.Y., 1927), is to be avoided. Wyatt Earp still awaits a reliable biographer; a start was made by Ed Bartholomew, *Wyatt Earp; 1879 to 1882, the Man and the Myth* (Toyahvale, Texas, 1964), which is hard reading. George W. Pierson, "The M-Factor in American History," *American Quarterly,* vol. 14 (Summer, 1962), while not concerned with historical aspects is nevertheless relevant to mining frontiers.

XX. Roads and Rails

Movement is the basic theme of frontier history. People, mail, and freight were taken west on wagons, steamboats, stagecoaches, and railroads. This traffic went through, around, or over such obstacles as deserts, mountains, and angry Indian tribes. Transportation in the trans-Missouri region was a risky and expensive business, one which private enterprise was seldom capable of undertaking by itself. So the federal government had to play Santa Claus, dispensing lucrative contracts to freighters and stage companies, granting land to the railways, and employing the Army to build roads and trails. With this aid, the various transportation lines moved into the West, pulling civilization along behind them.

The Mail Problem Mail service to the Pacific Coast was one of the most acute of the transcontinental transportation problems. News from home, even if it were an unfaithful maiden's "Dear John" letter, was the one insatiable demand of those in the West. The distances were so great that federal subsidies were required. Under government contracts for monthly mail delivery signed in 1847, the United States Mail Steamship Company and the Pacific Mail Steamship Company began a cross-Panama service in 1849. This was a slow route and an expensive one, what with postal rates averaging 50 cents an ounce. After completion of a railroad across the isthmus in 1855, the companies managed to shave down the New York-San Francisco delivery time to 3 weeks. The steamers continued to be important for both mail and passenger traffic up to the completion of the transcontinental railroad in 1869. But Westerners sent petitions to Congress demanding a more direct overland service.

Sporadic attempts to provide such service had been made from both ends of the line. In 1850, Samuel H. Woodson was awarded a contract of $19,000 per year to carry monthly mail by pack train along the Platte River route from

Map of the principal routes to the West. From Captain Randolph B. Marcy, The Prairie Traveler (1859). Source: Huntington Library.

Independence to Salt Lake City. A year later George Chorpenning got a contract of $14,000 a year for the Salt Lake-Sacramento route. The story of both these pioneer operations is one of travail without end. Chorpenning in particular had trouble with the Indians—his partner being killed in a Ute attack—and with deep snows in the Sierra Nevada. In fact, during the winter he had to send his horsemen along the Mormon Corridor, with the San Francisco mail being delivered to Los Angeles and then taken north by ship.

A single-line stagecoach service was started in 1857, though it followed a rather peculiar San Antonio-San Diego route. In 1854 James Birch had formed the California Stage Company, a highly successful line which soon had a near monopoly within the state. His contract with the Post Office Department called for twice-a-month mail. Almost as an afterthought, passengers were also carried. Since mules were used to draw the coaches, Birch's line fully deserved its satirical nickname of the "Jackass Mail." The service was fairly reliable, but within 2 years the government had established a full-fledged stage line from St. Louis to San Francisco.

The Overland Mail Company was formed in 1857 as an amalgamation of four express companies: Adams, American, National, and Wells Fargo. It was also known to contemporaries as the "Butterfield Overland Mail" in deference to its first president, John Butterfield of American Express. This possessive title should not cloud the fact that Wells, Fargo & Company was the dominant power among the four. Begun in 1852 as a banking and express concern, it had in 5 years branched out into a multitude of stage and mail operations as well. The relationship between it and the Overland Mail Company was in the nature of an interlocking directorate. Four of the company's ten directors were from Wells Fargo, whose power was demonstrated when it demanded and got the removal of John Butterfield as president in 1860.

Butterfield, however, should be given credit for his organizational ability. A former stage driver himself, he understood all the problems involved in setting up a 2,800-mile cross-country mail route. The Overland Mail Company was the successful bidder for the government mail contract, which was awarded on March 3, 1857. Congress had given Postmaster General Aaron Brown authority to choose the contractor. Brown was from Tennessee, and was passionately devoted to a southern route for the new line. So when Butterfield promised to go by way of El Paso and Yuma, he got the nod. Nor was it surprising that one of the company's two eastern terminals was in Memphis, Tennessee.

The contract called for semiweekly service between St. Louis and San Francisco. The mail was to be delivered within 25 days, which turned out to be a rather accurate estimate of the running time. The federal subsidy amounted to $600,000 a year over a 6-year period. Butterfield began building 141 stage stations spaced at 10- to 50-mile intervals along what was called the "Ox-Bow" or the "Horse-Shoe" route. The two lines from St. Louis and Memphis converged at Fort Smith, Arkansas, and then the route was by way of El Paso, Fort Yuma,

No. 1.] [Sep. 16th, 1858.

OVERLAND MAIL COMPANY.

THROUGH TIME SCHEDULE BETWEEN

ST. LOUIS, MO., MEMPHIS, TENN. } & SAN FRANCISCO, CAL.

GOING WEST.

LEAVE.	DAYS.	Hour.	Distance, Place to Place.	Time allowed.	Av'ge Miles per Hour.
			Miles.	No. Hours	
St. Louis, Mo., & Memphis, Tenn. }	Every Monday & Thursday,	8.00 A.M			
P. R. R. Terminus, "	" Monday & Thursday,	6.00 P.M	160	10	16
Springfield, "	" Wednesday & Saturday	7.45 A.M	143	37¾	$3\frac{7}{9}$
Fayetteville, "	" Thursday & Sunday,	10.15 A.M	100	26½	$3\frac{7}{9}$
Fort Smith, Ark.	" Friday & Monday,	3.30 A.M	65	17¼	$3\frac{7}{9}$
Sherman, Texas	" Sunday & Wednesday,	12.30 A.M	205	45	4½
Fort Belknap. "	" Monday & Thursday,	9.00 A.M	146½	32½	4½
Fort Chadbourn, "	" Tuesday & Friday,	3.15 P.M	136	30¼	4½
Pecos River, (Em. Crossing.)	" Thursday & Sunday,	3.45 A.M	165	36½	4½
El Paso,	" Saturday & Tuesday,	11.00 A.M	248½	55¼	4½
Soldier's Farewell	" Sunday & Wednesday,	8.30 P.M	150	33½	4½
Tucson, Arizona	" Tuesday & Friday,	1.30 P.M	184½	41	4½
Gila River,* "	" Wednesday & Saturday	9.00 P.M	141	31½	4½
Fort Yuma, Cal.	" Friday & Monday,	3.00 A.M	135	30	4½
San Bernardino "	" Saturday & Tuesday,	11.00 P.M	200	44	4½
Ft. Tejon, (Via Los Angelos.)	" Monday & Thursday,	7.30 A.M	150	32½	4½
Visalia, "	" Tuesday & Friday,	11.30 A.M	127	28	4½
Firebaugh's Ferry, "	" Wednesday & Saturday	5.30 A.M	82	18	4½
(Arrive) San Francisco,	" Thursday & Sunday,	8.30 A.M	163	27	6

GOING EAST.

LEAVE.	DAYS.	Hour.	Distance, Place to Place.	Time allowed.	Av'ge Miles per Hour.
San Francisco, Cal.	Every Monday & Thursday,	8.00 A.M	Miles.	No. Hours	
Firebaugh's Ferry, "	" Tuesday & Friday,	11.00 A.M	163	27	6
Visalia, "	" Wednesday & Saturday,	5.00 A.M	82	18	4½
Ft. Tejon, (Via Los Angelos to)	" Thursday & Sunday,	9.00 A.M	127	28	4½
San Bernardino, "	" Friday & Monday,	5.30 P.M	150	32½	4½
Fort Yuma, "	" Sunday & Wednesday,	1.30 P.M	200	44	4½
Gila River,* Arizona	" Monday & Thursday,	7.30 P.M	135	30	4½
Tucson, "	" Wednesday & Saturday	3.00 A.M	141	31½	4½
Soldier's Farewell,	" Thursday & Sunday,	8.00 P.M	184½	41	4½
El Paso, Tex.	" Saturday & Tuesday,	5.30 A.M	150	33½	4½
Pecos River, (Em. Crossing.)	" Monday & Thursday	12.45 P.M	248½	55¼	4½
Fort Chadbourn, "	" Wednesday & Saturday	1.15 A.M	165	36½	4½
Fort Belknap, "	" Thursday & Sunday,	7.30 A.M	136	30¼	4½
Sherman, "	" Friday & Monday,	4.00 P.M	146½	32½	4½
Fort Smith, Ark.	" Sunday & Wednesday,	1.00 P.M	205	45	4½
Fayetteville, Mo.	" Monday, & Thursday,	6.15 A.M	65	17¼	$3\frac{7}{9}$
Springfield, "	" Tuesday & Friday,	8.45 A.M	100	26½	$3\frac{7}{9}$
P. R. R. Terminus, "	" Wednesday & Saturday	10.30 P.M	143	37¾	$3\frac{7}{9}$
(Arrive) St. Louis, Mo., & Memphis, Tenn. }	" Thursday & Sunday,		160	10	16

This Schedule may not be exact—Superintendents, Agents, Station-men, Conductors, Drivers and all employees are particularly directed to use every possible exertion to get the Stages through in quick time, even though they may be ahead of this time.

If they are behind this time, it will be necessary to urge the animals on to the highest speed that they can be driven without injury.

Remember that no allowance is made in the time for ferries, changing teams, &c. It is therefore necessary that each driver increase his speed over the average per hour enough to gain the necessary time for meals, changing teams, crossing ferries, &c.

Every person in the Company's employ will always bear in mind that each minute of time is of importance. If each driver on the route loses fifteen (15) minutes, it would make a total loss of time, on the entire route, of twenty-five (25) hours, or, more than one day. If each one loses ten (10) minutes it would make a total loss of sixteen and one half (16½) hours, or, the best part of a day.

On the contrary, if each driver gains that amount of time, it leaves a margin of time against accidents and extra delays.

All hands will see the great necessity of promptness and dispatch: every minute of time is valuable as the Company are under heavy forfeit if the mail is behind time.

Conductors must note the hour and date of departure from Stations, the causes of delay, if any, and all particulars. They must also report the same fully to their respective Superintendents.

* The Station referred to on Gila River, is 40 miles west of Maricopa Wells.

JOHN BUTTERFIELD.
Pres't.

Original timetable of the "Butterfield" Overland Stage. Source: Huntington Library.

Los Angeles, and the San Joaquin Valley to San Francisco. The stages began rolling on September 16, 1858.

Two hundred and fifty Concord coaches made by the famous Abbott-Downing Company of New Hampshire were used. The mail was placed under the driver's seat, or in a leather "boot" at the rear of the carriage. Nine passengers, who paid $200 for a through ticket, could be stuffed inside the coach. They had the dubious privilege of being bounced like yo-yos between the hard seats and the roof. Stage travel was not for the sensitive, the physically delicate, or the discriminating diner. At station stops the cry of "come and get it or we'll throw it to the hogs!" indicated the approximate tastiness of the dollar-a-plate meals, which featured ancient bacon and blackened bread. The stations themselves bore little resemblance to the carefully manicured establishments in Hollywood films. In Arizona and New Mexico especially, they were simply adobe huts lacking all comforts except shade.

While it appeared at a somewhat later date (1877), the following list of travel suggestions printed by the *Omaha Herald* had relevance for all stagecoach passengers:

> The best seat inside a stage is the one next to the driver. Even if you have a tendency to seasickness when riding backwards, you'll get over it and will get less jolts and jostling. Don't let any sly elph trade you his midseat.
>
> In cold weather don't ride with tight fitting boots, shoes or gloves. When the driver asks you to get off and walk, do so without grumb-

The Rock Creek (Nebraska) stage station in 1861. On the right, a Concord stage. The man on the left has been identified as David C. McCanles, who was killed at the station by "Wild Bill" Hickok. Source: California State Library.

ling. He won't request it unless absolutely necessary. If the team runs away — sit still and take your chances. If you jump; nine out of ten times you will get hurt.

In very cold weather abstain entirely from liquor when on the road; because you will freeze twice as quickly when under the influence.

Don't growl at the food received at the station; stage companies generally provide the best they can get. Don't keep the stage waiting. Don't smoke a strong pipe inside the coach — spit on the leeward side. If you have anything to drink in a bottle pass it around. Procure your stimulants before starting as 'ranch' (stage depot) whiskey is not 'nectar.'

Don't swear or lop over neighbors when sleeping. Take small change to pay expenses. Never shoot on the road as the noise might frighten the horses. Don't discuss politics or religion. Don't point out where murders have been committed if there are women passengers.

Don't lag at the wash basin. Don't grease your hair because travel is dusty. Don't imagine for a moment that you are going on a picnic. Expect annoyances, discomfort, and some hardship.

The Overland Mail Company did a good job. As the volume of mail and short-haul passenger traffic built up, money flowed into the company's coffers. Nonetheless, in the North there was much criticism of the Butterfield route, the main argument being that the central route by way of South Pass was a shorter and much more logical one. It was the coming of the Civil War which forced an abandonment of the southern route. Because Confederate guerrillas began attacking the stage stations and running off stock, Congress moved the whole operation northward in March of 1861.

Even before the war, an attempt to publicize the advantages of the South Pass route was made by the firm of Russell, Majors & Waddell. Their consequent ruination revealed the perils of private transportation efforts when unsupported by Uncle Sam's largesse, and proved the truth of Andrew Carnegie's dictum that "pioneering don't pay."

Russell, Majors & Waddell

William H. Russell, Alexander Majors, and William B. Waddell were representative frontier businessmen. The volatile and temperamental Russell was the most active of the three, often to the discomfiture of his more stolid partners. Their firm began as a freighting outfit. On March 27, 1855, a 2-year contract with the government for hauling military supplies west of the Missouri River gave them a virtual monopoly on that business. They dominated freighting on the plains for about 5 years, the peak being reached in 1858 when they had 4,000 men and 3,500 wagons in service.

Wagon freighting may have been a prosaic business, but it was among the top dozen in the nation as measured by capital invested. In 1860 this amounted to 5½ million dollars for wages, equipment, and stock. It was a business which flourished from 1840 until the transcontinental railroad was completed in 1869. The freighter supplied the scattered army posts, the Indian agencies, and the mining camps with food and manufactured goods. Such towns as Denver, Salt Lake City, and Helena were kept alive by the freighters. And the business was also vitally important in the economic development of the Missouri Valley.

The Missouri River landings at Atchison, St. Joseph, and Council Bluffs were the major shipping points. Ox-drawn Murphy wagons packed with manufactured goods, groceries, liquor, and mining equipment headed out along the Platte for the Kansas military outposts, or followed the old Santa Fe Trail toward Fort Union and other points in New Mexico. The "bullwhackers" who drove these ox teams ranked low in the frontier social scale; if stage drivers were the aristocracy, teamsters were the proletariat. What sensible man would plod along under a broiling sun, cracking a 30-foot whip over the heads of lumbering animals? One can be sure that the ox drivers had frequent recourse to swear words, despite that incredible pledge that Alexander Majors required of his employees: "While I am in the employ of A. Majors, I agree not to use profane language, not to get drunk, not to gamble, not to treat animals cruelly, and not to do anything else that is incompatible with the conduct of a gentleman."

Russell, Majors & Waddell prospered until the Mormon War of 1857 to 1858. Two of their wagon trains were destroyed by Lot Smith's raiders, and the government never reimbursed the firm for its losses. As a result, the partners' credit was seriously impaired. But it was Russell's unwise plunge into the express business that brought bankruptcy. He was convinced that the Colorado gold rush was a heaven-sent opportunity for a profitable stage line. So on April 18, 1859, the first stages of his Leavenworth and Pike's Peak Express Company left for Denver City. At first Russell attempted to run a new line across central Kansas, but within 2 months the route was shifted north to the more familiar Platte River route. Unfortunately the country was not yet sufficiently developed to support a stage line, and so the L. & P.P. lost money from the day of its formation. Russell also added to his liabilities by buying up the contract of the J. M. Hockaday Company for mail service between the Missouri and Salt Lake City.

Majors and Waddell were soon sucked into the whirlpool. On October 28, 1859, Russell, Majors & Waddell took over the bankrupt stage line, reorganizing it as a new company called the Central Overland California and Pike's Peak Express. They intended to carry mail, passengers, and freight all the way from Leavenworth to Placerville, California. The firm's name was against it, and so were the financial odds. In addition, Russell's attempt to publicize this central route by means of a "pony express" amounted to a kiss of death for Russell, Majors & Waddell.

The Pony Express was basically an advertising device. It was intended to give the C.O.C. & P.P. what Russell called a "worldwide reputation," and thus lead to a government mail contract over the central route. In pursuance of this ambitious objective, Russell built 153 stations between St. Joseph, Missouri, and Sacramento, California, generally following the line of the old California Trail. They were stocked with the best ponies money could buy, and 120 young riders (orphans preferred) were hired to carry the mail. The company promised to deliver letters in 10 days on a weekly schedule. Rates were initially $5 an ounce, though later were reduced to $1 per half ounce. Service commenced at both ends of the line on April 3, 1860.

The field operations of the Pony Express make a more interesting story than its unhappy financial history. The riders, who included such representative figures as William F. Cody and Pony Bob Haslam, seemed to epitomize the spirit of the Old West. Unlike the stagecoachmen, they rode all by themselves, little specks of humanity in the enormous panorama of mountain and sky. The riders carried the mail in a thin leather pouch called a *mochila*, which was slit in the middle so it could be slipped off and on saddle horns in a few seconds. Each rider traveled from 35 to 75 miles on a run, using three horses. To add spice to the job, they were occasionally chased by Indians.

The Pony Express was an anachronism even at its inception. The Pacific Telegraph Company, aided by government subsidies, was building its line across the plains all during 1861. When it connected with the California-based Overland Telegraph Company at Salt Lake City on October 24, the Pony Express was given the coup de grace. Russell, Majors & Waddell did get favorable publicity from their brainchild, but not the coveted mail contract. The government threw them a little bone in May (1860) by annulling George Chorpenning's contract for mail delivery between Salt Lake City and San Francisco, but this was an inadequate award. The whole situation is rather ironic in view of the fact that Congress did shift the mail service to the central route after the Civil War began. The Overland Mail Company, which was the only serious contender for the new contract since Russell, Majors & Waddell had been on the financial skids since 1859, signed the contract on March 2, 1861. It provided for a daily mail service along the central route, a semiweekly Pony Express, and a grand subsidy of 1 million dollars per year. William B. Dinsmore, as president of the Overland Mail Company, signed a subcontract with William H. Russell which permitted the C.O.C. & P.P. to handle the service between Missouri and Salt Lake City. The Overland Mail Company (and of course Wells Fargo) had a strong voice in the operation and management of the Pony Express until its termination.

Ben Holladay

The C.O.C. & P.P. was too far gone by mid-1861 for even the Overland Mail contract to make much difference. The Pony Express did not cause the firm's bankruptcy, for it had been bankrupt ever since 1859. It was heavily indebted

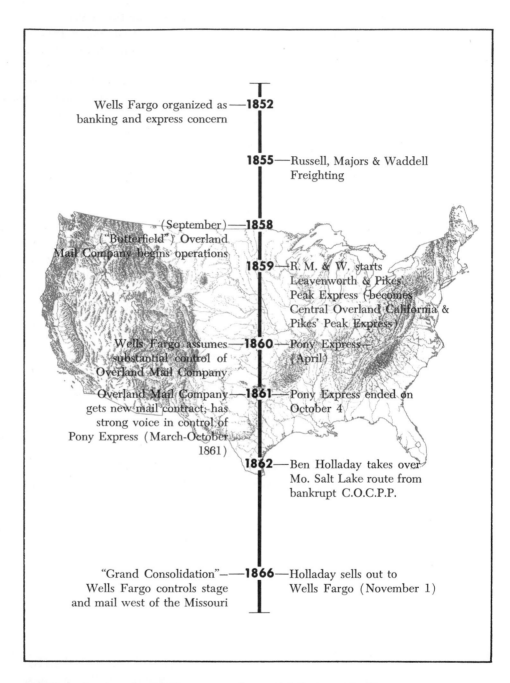

Wells Fargo organized as —**1852**
banking and express concern

1855—Russell, Majors & Waddell
Freighting

(September)—**1858**
("Butterfield") Overland
Mail Company begins operations

1859—R. M. & W. starts
Leavenworth & Pikes'
Peak Express (becomes
Central Overland California &
Pikes' Peak Express)

Wells Fargo assumes—**1860**—Pony Express—
substantial control of (April)
Overland Mail Company

Overland Mail Company—**1861**—Pony Express ended on
gets new mail contract; has October 4
strong voice in control of
Pony Express (March-October
1861)

1862—Ben Holladay takes over
Mo. Salt Lake route from
bankrupt C.O.C.P.P.

"Grand Consolidation"—**1866**—Holladay sells out to
Wells Fargo controls stage Wells Fargo (November 1)
and mail west of the Missouri

Timeline showing the development and eventual fusion of Wells, Fargo & Company and Russell, Majors & Waddell.

to one Benjamin Holladay for about $200,000. Finally, in March of 1862 Holladay took over the company and the Missouri-Salt Lake mail contract along with it. Exit Mr. Russell, Mr. Majors, and Mr. Waddell, all of whom ended their careers wearing rags.

Ben Holladay was a dynamic, irascible frontiersman with a steel-trap mind. Like Alexander Majors, he had started out as a supply contractor and freighter in the rough-and-tumble Southwest. He moved quickly to revamp his newly acquired stage line, renaming it the Overland Stage Company, and putting it on a more direct route to Denver and Salt Lake City by way of the South Platte and Bridger Pass. Soon he was running stages from the Mormon capital up to Virginia City, Montana, Walla Walla, and other points of the "Inland Empire." By 1866 this wily "Napoleon of the West" had 3,145 miles in his stage network.

Holladay was shrewd enough to realize that the advent of the transcontinental railroad would shrink his profits to the vanishing point. So in a "grand consolidation" of November 1, 1866, he sold out to Wells, Fargo & Company, who from that date forward controlled all major express and stagecoach operations west of the Missouri. Stagecoaching continued in the West until 1900. Much of the business was to areas not served by any railroad, such as Dead-

A Concord stage in restored condition. Source: Los Angeles County Museum of Natural History.

wood in the late 70s. It was a business, but a romantic one, and the sight of those swaying Concord coaches was not easily forgotten.

Steamboats on the River

The slogan "waterways in the East; wagonways in the West" was not wholly applicable. Although the nature of the terrain made canals unsuitable in the West, the larger rivers continued to carry heavy steamboat traffic until the 1870s. The Arkansas, the Red River of the South, and the Missouri were the major arteries. Since military supplies for the interior forts were a principal cargo, it is not surprising that steamboat navigation reached its peak in the Civil War years. On the Missouri the boats had reached the head of navigation near Fort Benton, Montana Territory, in 1859. Their arrival was followed shortly by the gold rush to Virginia City and Helena, with a consequent boom in traffic. Forty-three boats docked at the fort in 1867, unloading 15,000 tons of supplies and about 10,000 passengers. This was literally the high-water mark of upriver transport. Thereafter the westward extension of railroads to such points as Bismarck and Sioux City cut into the river business.

Steamboat operations were also significant on the Texas Gulf rivers, on California's Sacramento waterway, and in the Pacific Northwest. Service on the Columbia River had by 1860 become a monopoly of the Oregon Steam Navigation Company, a giant operation with assets of 5 million dollars. It served the Willamette River towns as well as those along the Columbia east to the Dalles River. With the assistance af railroad portages, it even sent boats as far as Lewiston, Idaho, thus hastening the settlement of the interior mountain regions.

Federal Transport Activities

The United States government had a large hand in the survey and construction of trans-Mississippi "wagonways." The Army and the Interior Department were the two agencies involved, the former building roads that were more local than continental in character. In the mid-50s the military paid particular attention to the shortening and improvement of the Kansas-Nebraska segment of the California Trail, the objective being quicker supply of frontier forts. Another consequential project (1858 to 1860) was the Mullan Road, which ran for 600 miles from Fort Benton to Fort Walla Walla. Surveyed by Lt. John Mullan, this military road saw heavy travel by miners going to the Montana and Idaho gold strikes. All told, the Army Topographical Engineers built thirty-four separate roads in the Far West during the decade 1850 to 1860, at a cost of 1 million dollars.

Emphasis on the military aspects of road projects was necessary to overcome the strict-constructionist views of Congressmen from the Old South.

Among those accepting the "national defense" argument was Jefferson Davis, Secretary of War between 1853 and 1857. He was particularly interested in making the frontier Army more effective, and this meant improved supply networks. Roadbuilding was only part of his program. Another project (1855 to 1858) was the unsuccessful attempt to drill artesian wells in the Llano Estacado. Davis also initiated an experiment in the use of Arabian camels to supply frontier garrisons. In the spring of 1856 a herd of the unattractive animals was brought to Texas, and the next year Lt. Edward F. Beale took a brigade of them along on a wagon-road survey to Los Angeles. They hardly contributed to the dignity of the United States Army, and the Indians in New Mexico thought that Beale was bringing a circus to town. Civilian teamsters refused to work with the dromedaries, and the herd was eventually turned loose to take care of itself. Some of these animals were rounded up and sold at San Antonio in 1866, and local chronicles record the sighting of camels in Arizona and Nevada as late as 1907.

The Transcontinental Railroad

Exotic though they were, stagecoaches and camels hardly bear comparison with the steam locomotive in their impact upon far-western transportation. On the eve of the Civil War, the western fringes of the nation's railroad network were fairly close to the frontier. The established methods of construction and finance were utilized to keep the lines inching along toward the Missouri River. By 1860 there were 1,814 miles of track in the trans-Mississippi area, most of it in Iowa and Missouri. In 1859 the Hannibal and St. Joseph became the first railroad to reach the "Big Muddy." Building continued during the war, and by 1865 there were 3,270 miles in use. In that same year the Missouri Pacific finally completed its line between St. Louis and Kansas City. The Missouri Pacific had first been named the Pacific Railroad, and most of the other companies in the region had either "Western" or "Pacific" in their titles. It was clear that they intended to go all the way across the continent.

There were three prophets who preached the gospel of a transcontinental railway. First in line was Asa Whitney, a New York merchant who had made a fortune in the China trade. Whitney was so obsessed with the idea of a Pacific railroad that he spent all his money promoting it—and finished his days as a milkman in Washington, D.C. In January of 1845 he presented the first of several memorials to Congress, proposing to build a line from Lake Michigan to the Pacific in return for a grant of land 60 miles wide along the route. Naturally Whitney's argument emphasized the necessity of such a railroad for greater trade with Asia. He also claimed it was indispensable for agricultural settlement of the trans-Mississippi region, since the settlers there had no way of getting their crops to market. Whitney's project was much too ambitious for the government at that time, but the debates over it influenced both Thomas Hart Benton and William Gilpin.

Senator Benton had long believed in the glorious future of the West, as regards both commercial and agricultural development, and his speeches were dotted with references to "an American road to India." In 1849 he introduced a bill for a Central National Road to be built from St. Louis to the west coast, and to be financed with the income from land sales. It was to be both a railway and, playing it safe, a wagon road. Gilpin was one of Benton's associates, and he too lectured Congress and citizen groups on the need for a transcontinental rail line. A newspaper editor and later the first Territorial Governor of Colorado, he argued that the completion of the National Railway was part of our historical destiny. "Diplomacy and war have brought to us the completion of our territory and peace," he told the citizens of Independence in 1849. "From this we advance to the RESULTS. These results are, for the present, the imperial expansion of our Republic to the other ocean, fraternity with Asia, and the construction across the centre of our territory, from ocean to ocean, of a great iron pathway, specially national to us, international to the northern continents of America, Asia, and Europe."

With all this ecstatic praise of the iron pathway, one wonders why construction had not started in the mid-50s. Sectional rivalry and financing were the two major problems, the Scylla and Charybdis which wrecked all transcontinental railroad proposals in the prewar decade. Whichever region got the eastern terminus of the road would enjoy tremendous economic advantages. So politicians from Chicago, St. Louis, Memphis, New Orleans, and other likely spots all jockeyed for position, with the result that they canceled each other out. In an attempt to shift the decision from politics to science, the Congress passed a Pacific Railroad Survey Act in 1853. This appropriated $150,000 (subsequently increased) to find "the most practical and economical route for a railroad from the Mississippi to the Pacific Ocean." The four routes chosen for survey were those which had the most political support. Ironically enough, the first transcontinental railroad was built up the Platte River Valley, a route not included in the survey.

The Northern Trail between the 47th and 49th parallels from St. Paul along the upper Missouri to Puget Sound was surveyed by a party under Isaac I. Stevens, Governor of Washington Territory. A second party under Lt. John Gunnison looked over the extremely rugged 38th parallel route from the Arkansas River to Salt Lake. Lt. Amiel Whipple was enthusiastic about the 35th parallel line which he explored from Fort Smith, Arkansas through Albuquerque to Los Angeles. Finally, the Southern Trail ran along the 32nd parallel from Fulton, Arkansas, through central Texas and southern Arizona to San Diego. This was the route favored by Secretary of War Davis, and he ordered its further exploration. Lt. J. G. Parke worked eastward from Fort Yuma to El Paso, while Lt. John Pope surveyed the Texas segment. The upshot of the survey was that all routes were practical; the engineers had failed to give the politicians any way out of the sectional maze.

The outbreak of the Civil War ended the sectional deadlock and made a central route the inevitable choice. This left only the funding problem to be solved. Such forward-looking senators as Benton, Douglas, and Clay had earlier found an answer in their various land-subsidy proposals. Douglas actually set the precedent when he pushed his Illinois Central bill through Congress in 1850. Under its terms the government granted the railroad alternate sections of land along the route, parcels which eventually totaled over 2½ million acres. This aid enabled the Illinois Central to complete its main line from Chicago to Cairo in 1856. It also ushered in an era of land disposition which lasted until 1871, and which saw the Congress giving away more than 130 million acres to numerous Western railroads.

President Lincoln also embraced the land-grant principle, and it was written into the Pacific Railroad Act of July 1, 1862. The bill chartered the Union Pacific and the Central Pacific companies to build a transcontinental line. They were given a 400-foot right-of-way and ten alternate sections of land for each mile of track laid. When this proved an insufficient inducement, the allotment was increased to twenty alternate sections by a subsequent bill of 1864. But land subsidies were not enough, and the original bill also made provision for loans. Government bonds were to be issued to the companies as work progressed. The sums were geared to the nature of the terrain: $16,000 per mile on the flatlands, $32,000 in the foothills, and $48,000 in the mountains. These bonds were not gifts but loans, on which principal and interest were to be repaid in 30 years. Most of them were in fact repaid in the "final settlement" of 1898. But during the 60s they could be turned into cash which was used to finance construction.

The Railway Builder's Frontier

Men, money, and materials were taken up in the war effort, so it was the middle of 1865 before the two companies really swung into action. Dr. Thomas Durant was the most active executive of the Union Pacific, and he cast about for a chief engineer to locate the route west from Omaha. Grenville M. Dodge was only thirty-five years old when Durant signed him on, but he was already a battle-scarred major general in the Union Army. He excelled as a surveyor and organizer, while command of an Indian campaign in 1865 had made him familiar with the country west to Utah. During 1866 and 1867 Dodge laid out the route along the North and South Platte Rivers, through Lone Tree Pass, and across the Wyoming Basin and the Wasatch Range to Salt Lake. Still, many responsible men found it hard to take the project seriously. Gen. William Tecumseh Sherman remarked that "when the orators spoke so confidently of the determination to build two thousand miles of railway across the plains, mountains, and desert, devoid of timber, with no population, but on the contrary raided by the bold and bloody Sioux and Cheyennes . . . I was disposed to treat it jocularly."

Corrine, Utah, a typical log-and-tent railroad construction town. From a photo by Andrew Joseph Russell. Source: Yale University Library.

Twenty-man squads of surveyors went ahead to mark the locations for cuts, grades, and river crossings. They bore the brunt of Indian attacks, though the red men also harried track crews. Railroad building in Nebraska was a dangerous business, and many scalps were lost. Few were as lucky as young William Thompson, who not only survived a scalping but retrieved his hair when it fell from the warrior's belt.* The Army was supposed to protect the crews, but the situation was that of one soldier trying to surround three Indians. Nevertheless, by the end of 1866, some 260 miles of track had been laid, and the U.P. was at North Platte, Nebraska. The work gangs, made up principally of Irishmen and war veterans, turned that town into the first "Hell on Wheels." These log and tent cities offered drinking, gambling, fist fighting, and other recreation on a 24-hour-a-day basis; but as soon as the railhead was moved further west, they usually reverted to the owls and prairie dogs. Julesburg (reached early in 1867) was reputed to be the "wickedest city," but Cheyenne (1868) certainly rivaled it for the title.

While the Union Pacific was building toward the Rocky Mountains, the Central Pacific was blasting tunnels and cuts through the granite walls of the Sierra Nevada. This company had been organized in 1861, even before the congressional charter. It was started by Theodore D. Judah, a civil engineer whose obsession with the Pacific railroad earned him the nickname of "crazy Judah." He published pamphlets and visited Congress, but made little headway until he interested the "Big Four" of Sacramento businessmen in his project. The most able of the group was Collis P. Huntington, a hard-driving Connecticut Yankee who had already built up a small fortune as a hardware merchant. His partner was "Uncle Mark" Hopkins, a sad-faced accountant known for his shrewd judgment. Leland Stanford was a rather shaggy-looking grocer, whose ability to deliver bland speeches made him governor of the state (in 1861) and a logical choice for president of the line. The fourth member of the quartet was

*Thompson's scalp is now on display at the Omaha Public Library.

Charles Crocker, a ham-fisted dry goods merchant who bossed the construction work.

Judah broke with the Big Four in 1863, a classic case of the engineer versus the businessman. He went East that fall in an attempt to get enough capital to buy them out, but he caught yellow fever while crossing Panama and died in New York City. One of Judah's complaints had been the Central Pacific's award of exclusive construction contracts to Charles Crocker Company (later the Contract and Finance Company). This company was made up of the four associates, who were clearly not averse to scratching their own backs. The Union Pacific had a similar relationship with the Credit Mobilier, theoretically a separate company but one actually composed of U.P. stockholders who paid themselves magnificent prices for supplying the railroad. Organized by Oakes Ames, this company's operations were exposed in 1873 and became one of the major financial scandals in American history.

In justice to the Big Four it should be pointed out that the difficulties were very great. They had to borrow money to the hilt, and this in the face of the banking fraternity's belief that they would never complete the project. So Huntington pressed Congress for a doubled land grant, which was effected in the 1864 bill. He was also successful in persuading Lincoln that the Sierra Nevada Mountains began only 7 miles east of Sacramento, thus acquiring subsidy bonds of $48,000 per mile instead of $16,000. The technical and supply problems were almost as great as the financial ones. Rails and other equipment had to be shipped from the East by way of Cape Horn. Judah had picked the route to be followed through the mountains, but Crocker and the others had had no experience in railroad building. So the work went on at the proverbial snail's pace, with only 30 miles of track being laid in 1866. By 1867 there were 6,000 Chinese in the C.P.'s labor gangs. "Crocker's pets" weighed all of 110 pounds each, but they proved to be indefatigible workers and were more reliable than the Irishmen. The engineers used nitroglycerin to blast tunnels through the mountains, and the Chinese wheeled the rocks away in one-horse carts. By the summer of 1867 track had been laid through the 7,000-foot Donner Pass, 105 miles east of Sacramento.

In 1866 Congress revised the original charter and gave the Central Pacific permission to build eastward from the California line until it met the Union Pacific. So there was a race in 1868 to lay more track and thus harvest added government bonds. Indeed the two roads were planning to pass each other, and both graded a line between Ogden and Promontory in Utah. The Irishmen and the Chinese did not love each other, and they took turns setting off blasts which buried the other company's work gangs. Congress finally put an end to the nonsense and ordered the lines to join north of the Salt Lake at Promontory Point. There on May 10, 1869, special trains from San Francisco and Omaha brought officials from both ends of the continent to watch Leland Stanford and Thomas Durant drive the "Golden Spike." A gaping crowd of soldiers,

Central Pacific's first locomotive was the "Gov. Stanford," named in honor of Leland Stanford, California governor and first president of the railroad. Built in the East and shipped around Cape Horn, the picturesque woodburner was assembled at Sacramento, where the first trip was made November 10, 1863. Source: Southern Pacific.

Chinese, Mormons, Indians, and Irishmen watched the impressive ceremony. Completion of the "great iron pathway" was certainly an epochal event in the nation's history.

Both lines were in many respects jerry-built, with flimsy bridges, narrow embankments, and poorly laid track. Grenville Dodge spent the whole year after the linkup at Promontory trying to bring the Union Pacific up to standard. The roads had been built over fantastic distances, totaling 1,775 miles, across extremely difficult terrain. They spearheaded and promoted settlement of the Great Plains. And while other lines were soon run across the country, the central route retained its preeminence and the historic glory of being "first."

Other Transcontinental Lines

Four other transcontinental railroads were completed by 1893. They were the Northern Pacific (1883), the Great Northern (1893), the Santa Fe (1883), and the Southern Pacific-Texas Pacific system (1882). The Northern Pacific was chartered by Congress on July 2, 1864. It was to build from Lake Superior to Puget Sound. While it received no loans, it did get an exceptionally generous land grant of twenty alternate sections in the states and forty alternate sections in the territories. This eventually added up to 40 million acres, the largest grant to any single railroad. But the project languished until Jay Cooke, the Philadelphia financial wizard, took control in 1869. Five hundred miles of rail were laid from Minnesota to Bismarck, in Dakota Territory, by 1873. By that year, however, construction costs and excessive dividends had brought Jay Cooke to the end of his rope. When his investment company declared itself bankrupt on September 17, the declaration triggered another of those terrifying American panics. Railroad building was suspended all through the Great West, and many companies never recovered. Eventually Henry Villard, a German-born journalist turned capitalist, secured control of the line in 1881. In 2 years he pushed construction of the Northern Pacific until it was joined with his Oregon Central Railroad running into Portland, thus completing another transcontinental link.

The Great Northern was built through the land of high passes and heavy snows from Duluth to Seattle. James J. Hill, a one-eyed Canadian immigrant, occupies a high place in railroad history. His careful construction and conservative financial policies make quite a contrast to men like Jay Cooke. Hill took control of the bankrupt St. Paul and Pacific in 1878. He thereby acquired the St. Paul's 3-million-acre federal land grant within Minnesota, although west of the Red River Valley the Great Northern was a "landless" road. Hill built slowly across North Dakota and Montana, attracting foreign immigrants and adding feeder lines to increase freight revenue. By 1887 he had reached Great Falls, and in 1893 the line was completed to Seattle.

On the southern routes, the Atchison, Topeka & Santa Fe received federal grants for part of its line. Created by Cyrus K. Holliday in 1859, the railroad got a 3-million-acre grant in 1863 on condition that it build to the Colorado border. This point was reached in 1872, and the Santa Fe reaped not only the federal subsidy but much of the traffic from the booming Kansas "cow towns." In 1878 it defeated the local Denver and Rio Grande in a "war" for possession of Raton Pass, and was thus able to build on to Albuquerque with a branch line to Santa Fe itself. In 1880 the Santa Fe merged with the Atlantic & Pacific, a land-grant railroad which because of financial troubles had reached only as far as Vinita, Indian Territory. The Santa Fe subsequently built east to this point, and west from Albuquerque to Needles on the Colorado River. An agreement with the Southern Pacific in 1883 gave the Santa Fe trackage rights through California to San Francisco.

Finally, the Southern Pacific was organized by the Big Four to monopolize traffic in California. It completed its line to Yuma by 1877. At this point Collis Huntington decided to build eastward through the Yuma Indian Reservation even without government permission. At the same time, Thomas A. Scott's Texas & Pacific was racing west from Shreveport in order to gain a federal land grant across New Mexico and Arizona. But financial problems caused Scott to

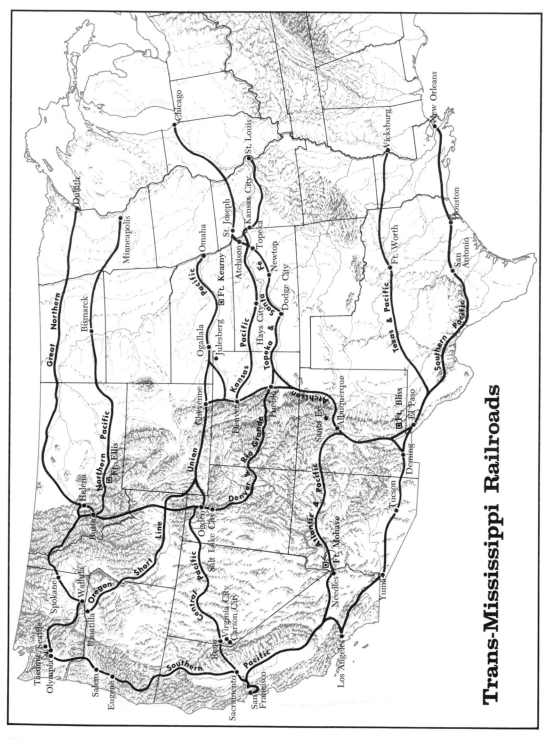

Trans-Mississippi Railroads

sell out to Jay Gould, who then made an agreement with Huntington to join the Southern Pacific at El Paso. This junction was made in 1882, thus completing another cross-country railway.

Other railroads of less than continental dimensions also received substantial land grants. The Kansas Pacific, for example, completed its line from Kansas City to Denver in 1870 with the aid of a federal grant and loans. The same was true of the so-called "Granger" lines which blanketed the upper Midwest in the 60s and 70s. The largest of these lines were based in Chicago, and included the Milwaukee & St. Paul, the North Western, the Rock Island, and the Burlington & Quincy. They all received substantial state as well as federal aid. Nine different states granted about 48 million acres of land to various railroads. This made a grand total of some 180 million acres from both federal and state sources combined, not to mention county and town subsidies of various kinds. The size and disposition of these grants were the causes of much political conflict in the postwar generation.

Antirailroad Sentiment

Congress had indicated its doubts about the land grants by terminating them in 1871. Among the Western farmers there were demands that the lands already granted be returned to the people. In theory the farmers should have been grateful to the roads, since having land without transportation was like owning one shoe. In practice there were loud complaints about abuses. Some of the roads held their lands off the market for a speculative rise in prices or to escape taxation. When they did sell, it was at prohibitive prices which averaged $5 an acre compared with the government minimum of $2.50 an acre. Freight rates were levied on the principle of "all that the traffic will bear." While land already occupied under the Preemption Act of 1841 or the Homestead Act of 1862 was exempted from railroad claims, the companies found ways of leaning on the homesteader until he cried "Uncle" and moved out. It was apparent to some that there was a basic incompatibility between railroad subsidies and the homestead principle.

On a formal level the homesteaders' opposition to the railroad companies took the form of new political parties. The National Grange of the Patrons of Husbandry was formed by Oliver H. Kelley in 1867 as a social organization. But in the mid-70s it turned to political action by organizing Anti-Monopoly parties which demanded regulation of railroad abuses. Unsuccessful in these efforts, the Anti-Monopolists fused with the Greenback Party and eventually became part of the Populist movement. At its Omaha Convention in 1892 the Populist party expressed the ultimate degree of antirailroad sentiment by calling for government ownership of the roads and reclamation of all the unused landholdings.

A more spontaneous expression of the farmers' attitude was seen in the sympathy accorded those who robbed trains. The first such robbery was carried off by the Reno brothers in southern Indiana on October 6, 1866. But the most noted practitioners were in the West. Sam Bass was a Texas cowboy who got tired of punching cows for $30 a month. So in 1877 he rode north to Nebraska with several companions and held up a Union Pacific express train, taking off $65,000 in gold. He spent this money freely among the appreciative squatters back home, until the Texas Rangers gunned him down the next year. Frank and Jesse James hold top rank among train robbers. Their first job was a Rock Island express which was deliberately wrecked near Council Bluffs, Iowa, on July 20, 1873. A succession of other holdups over the next 8 years gave the James boys a reputation as the greatest outlaws in American history. The only line in a three-state area that was spared from Jesse's depredations was the Hannibal and St. Joseph, which had taken the precaution of giving his mother a lifetime pass. The robberies were accompanied by the gratuitous murder of conductors and passengers, but an impressive body of folksongs and tales made Jesse James a Robin Hood hero who "took from the rich and gave to the poor." This lore was rooted in the popular belief that the railroads were fleecing the farmer, and that turnabout was fair play.

The question of whether the government was too generous to the railroads is still debated by historians. As far as the government was concerned the land grants were a bargain, for the railroads were required to carry government mail and freight at 50 percent of the commercial rate. As for the settlers, many of them lost lands to the railroad companies or suffered various kinds of economic injustice at their hands. Still the lines had to be built to facilitate westward expansion, and private capital was incapable of doing the job. So the characteristic American form of a publicly subsidized private corporation was the logical answer. When the drawbacks were subtracted from the benefits, the result was still a net gain for the West.

Selected Readings   Oscar O. Winther, *The Transportation Frontier, 1865-1900* (New York, 1964), is a top-rated survey of the whole subject. LeRoy R. Hafen, *The Overland Mail 1849-1869* (Cleveland, 1926), is the classic study. Roscoe and Margaret Conkling, *The Butterfield Overland Mail*, 3 vols. (Glendale, Calif., 1947), is detailed. John H. Kemble, "The Panama Route to the Pacific Coast, 1848-1869," *Pacific Historical Review*, vol. 7 (March, 1938), is basic. Oscar O. Winther, *Express and Stagecoach Days in California* (Stanford, 1936), covers the early mail contracts. W. Turrentine Jackson, "A New Look at Wells Fargo, Stagecoaches and the Pony Express," *California Historical Society Quarterly*, vol. 45 (December, 1966), is an important article on the relationship between Wells Fargo and the Overland Mail Company. Alvin F. Harlow, *Old Waybills* (New York, 1934), and Edward Hungerford, *Wells Fargo, Advancing the American Frontier* (New York, 1949), are for popular consumption. Waterman L. Ormsby, *The Butterfield Overland Mail* (San Marino, Calif., 1942), is a rather disappointing account of the first westbound stage trip. *The Omaha*

Herald list of tips for stage travelers is printed in J. L. Humphreys, *The Lost Towns and Roads of America* (New York, 1961).

The basic work on Russell, Majors & Waddell is Raymond W. and Mary L. Settle, *Empire on Wheels* (Stanford, 1949); their later *War Drums and Wagon Wheels* (San Francisco, 1966) adds little. Alexander Majors told fragments of the story in *Seventy Years on the Frontier* (Chicago, 1893). Henry P. Walker, *The Wagonmasters: High Plains Freighting from the Earliest Days of the Santa Fe Trail to 1880* (Norman, 1966), is a comprehensive treatment. The Settles have also described the Pony Express in *Saddles and Spurs* (Harrisburg, Pa., 1955), but the best work on the subject is Roy S. Bloss, *Pony Express — the Great Gamble* (Berkeley, 1959), a well-illustrated and thoroughly researched volume. Don Russell, *The Lives and Legends of Buffalo Bill* (Norman, 1960), has much on the same subject. Ben Holladay has had two biographers: J. V. Frederick, *Ben Holladay: the Stagecoach King* (Glendale, 1940), sober and scholarly; and Ellis Lucia, *The Saga of Ben Holladay* (New York, 1959), journalistic.

William E. Lass, *A History of Steamboating on the Upper Missouri River* (Lincoln, Neb., 1962), updates some of the material in Hiram M. Chittenden's *History of Early Steamboat Navigation on the Missouri River*, 2 vols. (New York, 1903). Also useful are Louis C. Hunter, *Steamboats on the Western Rivers* (Cambridge, 1949), and Randall V. Mills, *Stern-Wheelers up Columbia* (Palo Alto, 1947). The two basic authorities on federal road building are W. Turrentine Jackson, *Wagon Roads West* (Berkeley, 1952), and William H. Goetzmann, *Army Exploration in the American West, 1803-1863* (New Haven, 1959), both of whom reject "romantic" history. The camel experiment is described in Lewis B. Lesley (ed.), *Uncle Sam's Camels* (Cambridge, 1929), a collection of documents.

John F. Stover, *American Railroads* (Chicago, 1961), is a short survey with chapters on the West. For detail see Robert E. Riegel's excellent *The Story of the Western Railroads* (New York, 1926), also available in paperback (Lincoln, Neb., 1964). Margaret L. Brown, "Asa Whitney and His Pacific Railroad Publicity Campaign," *Mississippi Valley Historical Review*, vol. 20 (September, 1933), is informative. Much material on the "road to India" theme of Benton and Gilpin is found in Henry Nash Smith, *Virgin Land* (Cambridge, 1950). George L. Albright, *Official Explorations for Pacific Railroads* (Berkeley, 1921), deals with the survey, as does Chapter VIII of William Goetzmann's *Army Exploration in the American West*. The Illinois Central and subsequent land grants are treated competently in Roy M. Robbins, *Our Landed Heritage* (Princeton, 1942). An influential article is Robert S. Henry, "The Railroad Land Grant Legend in American History Texts," *Mississippi Valley Historical Review*, vol. 32 (September, 1945), written by a railroad executive. This should be read in conjunction with the statements of various authorities collected under the title of "Comments on the Railroad Land Grant Legend" in vol. 32 (March, 1946).

For the building of the Union Pacific see Wesley S. Griswold, *A Work of Giants* (New York, 1962), and John D. Galloway, *The First Transcontinental Railroad: Central Pacific; Union Pacific* (New York, 1950), both of which are strong on biography, anecdotes, and engineering. Wallace D. Farnham, "Grenville Dodge and the Union Pacific: A Study of Historical Legends," *Journal of American History*, vol. 51 (March, 1965), shows that Dodge had little to do with the physical construction of the line. Stanley P. Hirshson, *Grenville M. Dodge: Soldier, Politician, Railroad Pioneer* (Bloomington, Ind., 1967), is an outstanding biography. Oscar Lewis, *The Big Four* (New York, 1938), is well written. Edwin L. Sabin, *Building the Pacific Railway* (Philadelphia, 1919), was written by an eyewitness to the Promontory Point ceremony.

James B. Hedges, *Henry Villard and the Railways of the Northwest* (New Haven, 1930), is a fine biography. Stewart H. Holbrook, *James J. Hill: A Great Life in Brief* (New York, 1955), reads well. Lawrence L. Waters, *Steel Trails to Santa Fe* (Lawrence, Kan., 1950), is the best of several books on this line. Robert G. Athearn, *Rebel of the Rockies: A History of the Denver and Rio Grande Western Railroad* (New Haven, 1962), is a model of railroad history. Stuart Daggett, *Chapters on the History of the Southern Pacific* (New York, 1922), and S. G. Reed, *A History of Texas Railroads* (Houston, 1941) cover aspects of the southernmost route.

Farmer opposition to the railroads is examined in Fred A. Shannon, *The Farmer's Last Frontier* (New York, 1945); Solon J. Buck, *The Granger Movement* (Cambridge, 1913); the same author's *The Agrarian Crusade* (New Haven, 1921); and John D. Hicks, *The Populist Revolt* (Minneapolis, 1931). Wayne Gard's *Sam Bass* (Boston, 1936) is a classic. William Anderson Settle, Jr., *Jesse James Was His Name* (Columbia, Mo., 1966), is the first and only scholarly study of this outlaw, and examines both folklore and history.

XXI. The Last Indian Wars

The history of Indian-white relations has a certain somber uniformity. A treaty is made with the white man's government, usually by a few chiefs who do not and cannot speak for the whole tribe. The treaty is violated by advancing miners or homesteaders, and when the Indians resist these encroachments, they are crushed by the Army. The exploitation of the tribesmen by corrupt government agents can cause the fighting, and almost always follows it. The late nineteenth century generation of Americans condoned and praised the exploits of its Indian-fighting Army, and the wars on the plains have always been the most spectacular features of frontier history. To a modern generation, these wars appear to be not epics but tragedies.

The "Permanent" Indian Country   From the administration of President Monroe until 1848 it was assumed that there would be a "Permanent Indian Country." This was generally conceived to be located west of Arkansas, Missouri, and Iowa to the Rocky Mountains, and north of the Red River. The concept was embodied in congressional legislation, particularly the act of 1834 which defined the limits of this "permanent" territory and which created a separate Indian Department with its own commissioner and subagents. Whites were supposedly barred from the reserved area unless they had a license. During the 30s and 40s the government maintained a line of forts along the borderland. Fort Kearny was built on the Platte in 1849 to guard the Oregon Trail, while the same year the old fur-trading post at Fort Laramie became an army garrison. In addition, two regiments of mounted riflemen, part of a frontier army which numbered 7,700 men by 1855, were assigned to police duty along the trail. But by 1848 it had become evident that Indians had too much land for their own good, and that to protect them most of it should be taken away.

Various developments doomed the "permanent" policy. With the settlement of the Pacific Coast, the overland trails saw an increasing amount of traffic. The Platte River route in particular lay in the middle of Indian country. Then there was the irresistible advance of the white population. Missouri had been cleared of Indians by 1832, and Iowa was pretty well freed of them by 1846. This brought the line of settlement right up to Kansas and Nebraska. Indeed, Brigham Young established his "Winter Quarters" on federal Indian lands in Nebraska itself. Thus to government officials it seemed apparent that the protection of these settlers and of the Platte River corridor required a new policy.

That policy, formulated in the years between 1848 and 1854, called for grouping of the Indians into two great colonies. There would be one in the north (now the Dakotas) and one in the south (now Oklahoma). This segregation would clear the central route to the Pacific, and would presumably safeguard the Indians by removing them from contact with settlers. The first step in the process was the great Fort Laramie Treaty of September, 1851. Chiefs of the Sioux, Cheyenne, Arapaho, and a half dozen other Plains tribes were called together by Thomas Fitzpatrick, agent for the Upper Platte district. Under terms of the treaty the tribes were to receive an annuity of $50,000 per year for 50 years as payment for transit rights by settlers. (Congress later amended this to 10 years, but actually paid annuities to the Indians for 15 years.) Definite territorial limits were assigned to each tribe, a strange concept to nomadic hunters. This was also an ominous precedent, although the Indians did not realize it at the time. Once the government had established the general principle of setting aside definite reservations, it could whittle them down in subsequent treaties with individual tribes. A treaty similar to that of Fort Laramie was made with the Comanches and Kiowas at Fort Atkinson (Kansas) in 1853.

By 1854 there were strong demands for removal of the red men from Kansas and Nebraska. As early as 1849, William Gilpin had complained that "savages ejected from the older States, have been bought up and planted as a wall along the western frontier and across the line of progress. These are metaphysically called foreign nations." Unfortunately for the poor savages, they always seemed to be standing "across the line of progress." Senator Douglas's desire to organize the Nebraska country into territories was of course the primary motive for extinguishing the Indian titles there. Such tribes as the Omaha, Kickapoo, and Delaware were bullied into accepting land elsewhere. Since Kansas and southern Nebraska were originally parts of the Permanent Indian Country, it was clear by 1854 that the words "permanent" and "Indian" no longer applied to that region.

This year also marked the outbreak of the Great Sioux War, which lasted off and on until 1890. Like Mrs. O'Leary's animal that started the Chicago fire in 1871, the killing of an emigrant's cow by Minneconju Sioux near Fort Laramie on August 17 also had serious consequences. Lt. John Grattan of the 6th Infantry, a fresh-minted West Pointer, had declared that with thirty men he

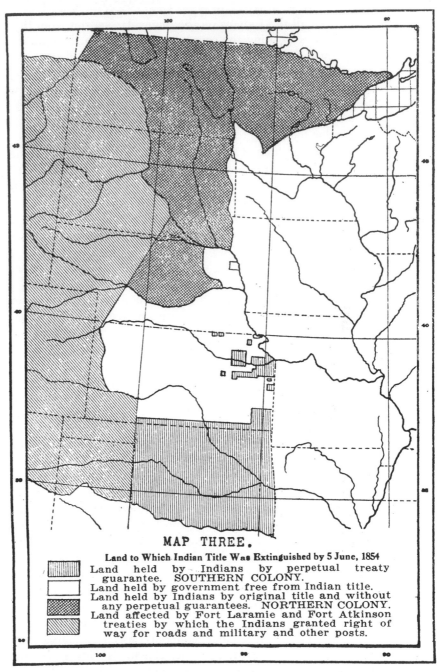

MAP THREE.

Land to Which Indian Title Was Extinguished by 5 June, 1854

Land held by Indians by perpetual treaty guarantee. SOUTHERN COLONY.

Land held by government free from Indian title.

Land held by Indians by original title and without any perpetual guarantees. NORTHERN COLONY.

Land affected by Fort Laramie and Fort Atkinson treaties by which the Indians granted right of way for roads and military and other posts.

Map showing area to which Indian title had been extinguished by June 5, 1854. From James C. Malin Indian Policy and Westward Expansion *(1921). Source: Huntington Library.*

could rout all the Indians on the plains. He set out from the fort with twenty-nine soldiers to bring the cow killer back for punishment. A misunderstanding occurred at the Sioux camp, and the overconfident lieutenant and his entire detail were wiped out.

Following this episode, Col. William S. Harney led several sweeps through the Sioux country above the Platte in 1855 and 1856. He fought one major engagement at Ash Hollow in Nebraska, and issued warnings to other bands that they were to stay north of the river. The troops were too widely scattered to act as much of a brake on the Indians, and travel along the Oregon Trail now became a game of chance. Bands of young warriors attacked emigrants, stagecoaches, and ranches. After all, the emigrants killed off the buffalo as they went through the country, and they brought such diseases as smallpox and cholera along with them. In the Sioux and Cheyenne villages, the "White-eyes" were now added to the list of approved targets.

The Civil War

The Indian problem reached monumental dimensions during the Civil War, when most of the federal troops were pulled back East. The Army was left in the position of a lone firefighter trying to stamp out a dozen conflagrations at once. The five Civilized Tribes settled in the Indian Territory were one source of concern. Their geographical position more or less forced them to become Confederate allies. The Cherokees were badly split on the question of remaining neutral or joining the South. But there were many slaveholders in the tribe, and they pressured head chief John Ross into signing a treaty with the Confederates in November of 1861. Thousands of the Unionist faction thereupon packed up and fled north. Stand Watie's Cherokee brigade served with the Confederate Army in several battles, as did units from the other tribes. In consequence, all of them suffered after the war, when they were forced to relinquish the western portions of their lands as punishment for "disloyalty."

The first major outbreak during the war occurred to the east, in the Santee Sioux Reservation along the Minnesota River. The corrupt practices of Indian traders and the encroachments of white farmers were two familiar causes of the bloodshed. The "blanket" faction of young warriors initiated hostilities in August of 1861, soon drawing the "farmer" faction after them. Eight hundred Indians under Chief Little Crow attacked along 200 miles of frontier, with the town of New Ulm being the first to go up in flames. Seven hundred settlers are thought to have been killed in the uprising. By October the Army had restored order. Among the subsequent ceremonies was the hanging of thirty-eight Indians from a single scaffold the day after Christmas. However, most of the offending Sioux were removed to a reservation in far-western Nebraska.

On the central plains, Sioux and Cheyenne raiders swept across the North Platte-Sweetwater route at will. These tribes had been aroused earlier when the Fifty-Niners had swarmed through the buffalo country on their way to Colorado, and thus some of the prospectors ended up in lonely graves along the Smoky Hill Trail. After the Civil War broke out, the red men attacked the stages of Ben Holladay's Overland Mail Company, forcing him to shift to a more southerly route. Isolated farmers and ranchers also had to fight or flee. The government had attempted to avoid such developments by buying Indian lands. In a treaty signed at Fort Wise, Colorado Territory, in 1861, the Southern Cheyenne and the Arapaho had agreed to accept a small reservation where Sand Creek flows into the Arkansas. However, the country was so desolate and short on game that not even a wolf could make a living on it, and so the tribesmen continued to roam across the plains as they had always done. Any white man who happened to be in their path had to be extremely careful. Indians were like the proverbial women; one could never be sure what they were going to do next.

In the spring of 1864, Governor John Evans of Colorado ordered the roving Indians to report to Fort Lyon or suffer the consequences. By fall some 500 Cheyenne and Arapaho under Chief Black Kettle were camped at Sand Creek. They flew an American flag as evidence of their peaceful disposition. But vengeful Colorado militia troops commanded by Col. John M. Chivington were marching toward the hapless tribesmen. The colonel was a 6-foot-6-inch former Methodist preacher who evidently believed in the mosaic law of tooth for tooth. With the tacit approval of the Army commander at Fort Lyon, the Coloradans surrounded Black Kettle's camp and attacked it on November 29. Two hundred men, women, and children were killed, many of them being horribly mutilated. The victors returned to Denver with 100 scalps, and basked in the applause of their fellow citizens. The *Rocky Mountain News* wrote: "Among the brilliant feats of arms in Indian warfare, the recent campaign of our Colorado Volunteers will stand in history, with few rivals, and none to exceed it in final results." Back East the Sand Creek affair drew demands for a congressional investigation. After collecting testimony, the committee charged Chivington with a "foul and dastardly massacre." The episode is still regarded as one of the more controversial in frontier history. To the Indians it was a case of white-man treachery and the survivors took what revenge they could.

The Frontier Army

The end of the Civil War in the East did not mean peace in the West. In every year from 1866 to 1890 the Army's Inspector General reported that there had been at least one encounter with Indians. These ranged from full-dress battles down to isolated attacks on parties of woodchoppers or haycutters. There were various reasons why the pot was kept boiling. The Army favored a tough policy, with such generals as Sherman and Sheridan even recommending extermination of the redskins. In this view they were largely supported by the frontier population. The Topeka *Weekly Leader* in 1867 expressed the racial hatreds of the

General Custer and his aides meeting four Indians before the drawn up horsemen on both sides. From a painting by Charles Schreyvogel, 1903. Source: Library of Congress.

day when it characterized the Indians as "a set of miserable, dirty, lousy, blanketed, thieving, lying, sneaking, murdering, graceless, faithless, gut-eating skunks° as the Lord ever permitted to infest the earth, and whose immediate and final extermination all men, except Indian agents and traders, should pray for."

Humanitarians and pacifists made slow headway against such traditional attitudes. Another of the barriers to any "peace policy" was the division of responsibility and consequent rivalry between the Interior Department and the War Department. The Indian Bureau had been transferred to Interior in 1849, and the result was a bizarre situation. The United States government used its Army to fight the Indians, while at the same time its Indian Bureau offered food, weapons, and sanctuary to the marauding bands. "The Indian is in the position of a willful boy, with a powerful but henpecked father, and an indulgent, weak mother," wrote Col. Richard I. Dodge. When coaxing and presents failed to keep the Indians in line, the Army was called on for the dirty work. The military commanders had many unkind things to say about the civilian agency. When

°"Skunk" entered the language in the seventeenth century, and is derived from an Indian word.

George Armstrong Custer faced a hostile party of Cheyenne in western Kansas one day in 1867, he noted that "each one was supplied with either a breech-loading rifle or revolver, sometimes with both—the latter obtained through the wise foresight and strong love of fair play which prevails in the Indian Department."

So the "peacetime" Army was called upon to pacify the West. The officer corps was in general well-trained and highly competent, though heavy drinking ruined some careers. Most of the officers had held higher ranks in the Civil War. Custer, for example, had been a major general of Volunteers but became a lieutenant colonel in the shrunken postwar Army. About half the enlisted soldiers were American-born, and the rest came from Ireland, Germany, England, and a half dozen other European nations. Negro troopers, called "buffalo soldiers" by the Indians because of their woolly hair, were enlisted in two separate regiments under white officers. The Army had a high desertion rate, since pay was poor and there were no recreational opportunities at the dusty frontier forts. Punishments included being tied up by the thumbs, being spread-eagled on a wagon wheel, or having to carry 30-pound logs around the parade ground. Most of the glory attached to the cavalry, and to such dashing cavaliers as Custer and Ranald MacKenzie. Yet the Indians had great respect for the "walk-a-heaps" of the infantry.

Accompanying most military expeditions were civilian scouts. Men like Jim Bridger, Buffalo Bill Cody, and "California Joe" Milner served as the Army's eyes and ears. Friendly Indians, notably Pawnees and Crows, were also used on the central plains. These men understood the nature of Indian warfare, which was marked by ambush, infiltration, feints, decoying, and many of the other maneuvers of classical guerrilla warfare. The Indians seldom made direct frontal assults. Nor, except in a few cases, did they persist in an action when casualties became heavy. Accounts of Indian losses are usually exaggerated in both Army and civilian reports.* If all these figures were totaled up, they would exceed by three times the estimated number of Indians on the plains.

Unfortunately, some officers never lived long enough to learn that Indian fighting was different from the carefully diagramed exercises in their West Point manuals. The losers were generally young, inexperienced, and ambitious. One famous example is found in the annals of the Red Cloud War of 1865 to 1867. This conflict erupted when the Army tried to build a wagon road along the Bozeman Trail. The trail, also called the Powder River Road, was a shortcut through central Wyoming to the Virginia City mines. It ran from the North Platte along the east side of the Big Horn Mountains, then cut across the headwaters of the Yellowstone and went through Bozeman Pass. This was the heart of Sioux buffalo-hunting country, but despite warnings from the Oglala chief Red Cloud, the government decided to improve and protect the road.

*A typical example: Cheyenne warriors later told George Bird Grinnell that nine of their number had been killed at the Beecher's Island fight [see page 354]: the Army commander's report claimed thirty-two.

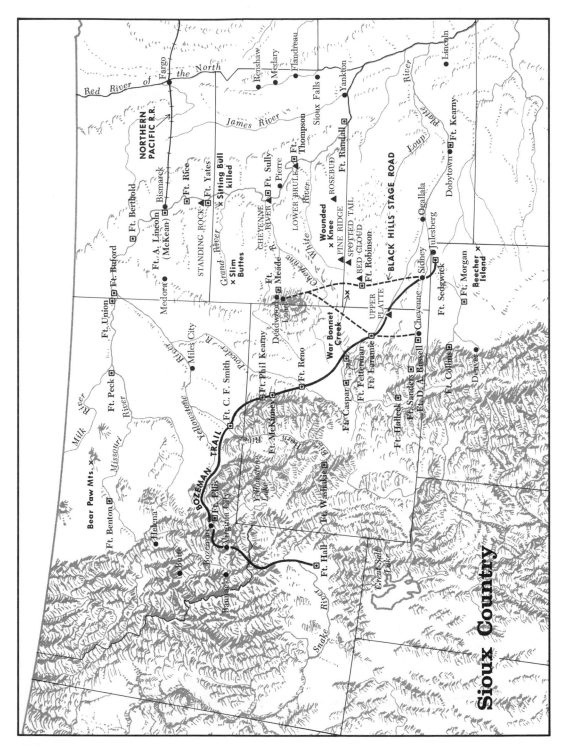

Sioux Country

Col. Henry B. Carrington executed his orders in 1866 and 1867, and built Forts Reno, Phil Kearny, and C. F. Smith along the route. Red Cloud's Sioux and their Cheyenne allies kept all these outposts under virtual siege. Supply wagons and woodchopping crews were shot up when they dared to venture out. On December 21, 1866, Capt. William J. Fetterman took eighty-one men and left Fort Kearny to relieve one of these besieged wood details. He was heard to declare that he would "ride through the whole Sioux Nation." In hilly terrain perfectly suited to surprise, the Sioux employed their favorite device of a decoy party. When Fetterman charged after these decoys, his contingent was surrounded and wiped out to the last man.

The "Fetterman Massacre" and renewed pressure from pacifists brought a new government policy. A Peace Commission composed of four civilians and three generals was formed in 1866 to find solutions to the "Indian problem." The commissioners agreed to the abandonment of the forts along the Bozeman Trail. This was part of a package offered to the Sioux at Fort Laramie in 1868. The treaty signed that spring guaranteed them a huge reservation west of the Missouri River in today's South Dakota. They were also given hunting rights in the Big Horn-Powder River country, which was described in the treaty as "unceded Indian territory."

Peace Council at Fort Laramie, 1868. Source: U. S. Signal Corps–National Archives.

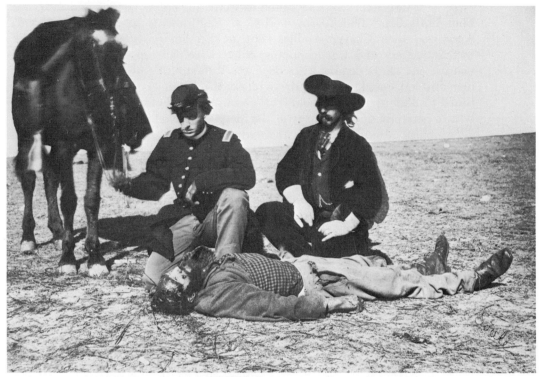

Scalped buffalo hunter near Fort Dodge, Kansas. From a photo taken by W. W. Soule.
Source: Los Angeles County Museum of Natural History.

The building of the Union Pacific across Nebraska and the Kansas Pacific across Kansas brought more Indian troubles in 1867. The Sioux and Cheyenne raided the survey and track-laying crews, and sometimes tore up the rails. Gen. Winfield Scott Hancock was ordered to sweep the railroad routes clear of these marauders. But the wily red men always managed to slip away. When the Indians did choose to fight, it was usually where they had numerical superiority. Couriers and small scouting patrols were their favorite targets. During September of 1868, a patrol of fifty scouts under Maj. George A. Forsyth was trapped by Sioux and Cheyenne at Beecher's Island on the Arikaree Fork of the Republican River in Colorado. The odds there were about 10 to 1 in favor of the Indians. The scouts, however, had new Spencer seven-shot repeating rifles, and these weapons saved them from annihilation.

The white man's technology gave him an edge in warfare. Such world-famous weapons as the Colt revolver and the Winchester rifle are justifiably identified with the subjugation of the Indians. Samuel Colt began producing "six-shooters" about 1838. They were used by Texas Rangers against the Comanches from the early 40s on, and then became known all across the Plains country as the best weapon devised for close-range combat against mounted warriors. The Winchester Model 1866 was a redesigned version of the earlier Henry rifle. A lever-action repeater, it had a bright brass frame which caused it to be known as the "yellow boy." This gun and the improved '73 model were used by such plainsmen as Buffalo Bill Cody. However, the Army generally was issued older muskets, and cavalrymen carried Springfield carbines.

War on the Southern Plains

The southern plains below the Platte River had been relatively quiet, but by the fall of 1867 the situation seemed to call for a new treaty. Four major tribes were called to a powwow at Medicine Lodge Creek in Kansas. The treaty signed there in October guaranteed safe passage for whites across the southern plains, ceded more Indian lands, and granted tribal annuities of $25,000 per year for 15 years. Provision for the distribution of farm implements indicated that one hopeful purpose of the treaty was to start the tribes on the road to civilization. In addition, the Comanches and Kiowas accepted a reservation in western Indian Territory, between the Red and Washita Rivers. The luckless Arapaho and Southern Cheyenne were assigned 3 million bone-dry acres further north, between the Cimarron and the Arkansas.

The Medicine Lodge Treaty did not stop the raiding. During the summer and fall of 1868, Cheyenne and Kiowa bands hit the Smoky Hill Trail in Kansas. They returned south with scalps, prisoners, pictures, watches, bedding, and other memorabilia of their exploits. The exasperated General Sheridan, who then held the Western command, decided that a winter campaign would be the only way to punish the savages. A three-pronged attack into Oklahoma was designed to crush any Indians who were off their reservation. The main force was the 7th Cavalry Regiment, commanded by Lieutenant Colonel Custer. The "Boy General" is one of the most talked-about figures in Western history. No one who knew that he had finished Number Thirty-four in his West Point class of thirty-four could have guessed that he would rise so rapidly. Impetuous and egotistical, Custer clearly belonged to the "brass-band and bugle school." Still, he was well-suited to Indian fighting. Floundering through deep snows, his command reached a large Cheyenne village on the Washita River, and attacked at dawn on November 27. Custer claimed in his report that 103 "warriors" were killed, including that same chief Black Kettle who had survived Sand Creek. Humanitarians and Custer critics, who were numerous, claimed that his figures were padded and included many women and children. But "Yellow Hair" was praised by the frontier people, and the Battle of the Washita gave the 7th Cavalry an enviable reputation.

One of Custer's rivals for glory was Col. Ranald Mackenzie of the 4th Cavalry. His principal field of operations were the lonely plains of west Texas. The enemies here were the Comanches and Kiowas, both of whom had carried on a running war with the Texans for more than a generation. There were light-ning attacks on ranches and stage lines, in some of which white women were abducted to become Indian squaws. The most famous example of this kind was Cynthia Ann Parker, captured in 1836, whose son Quanah became a well-known Comanche war chief. Mackenzie was ordered to break the power of these raid-ers, and he hung on like a bulldog until the job was finished.

Both of these southern tribes were angered not only by the intrusion of the white man's ranches and transportation lines, but by the slaughter of the buffalo. There was a direct relationship between the buffalo and the Indians' independence; when one was gone so was the other. In fact, traditions in most of the Plains tribes held that their race would disappear when there were no more buffalo. The Army fully realized the relationship, and General Sheridan encouraged the eradication of the herds ("the Indians' commissary") so that the tribesmen would be forced into farming.

At first the animals were killed to feed the railroad construction crews. William F. Cody became known as "Buffalo Bill" when he was employed as a hunter by the Kansas Pacific. In 8 months between October, 1867, and May, 1868, he killed 4,280 buffalo. Soon "sportsmen" were going out onto the plains to pop away at the animals, leaving the carcasses to rot. Then in 1869 a new tan-ning process was devised which made buffalo skins usable in shoes and saddles. Hunting was systematized, and parties of professional "hide men" began that great shoot-out which resulted in the near extermination of all 7 million buffalo by 1883.

The Indians hated the buffalo hunters. But stopping them was like a bare-handed man trying to grab a porcupine. The hunters used heavy .50 caliber Sharps rifles which had killing power at distances approaching 1 mile. The classic encounter occurred on June 27, 1874, when Quanah Parker's Comanches attacked at Abode Walls, a sod-house hunting camp on the Canadian River in Texas. Six hundred Indians were unable to dislodge twenty-six well-armed hunt-ers. Billy Dixon and W. B. "Bat" Masterson were prominent in the defense, the former shooting a warrior from his horse at a distance later found to be 1,538 yards.

During 1870 and 1871 raids continued in the Texas Panhandle area. Leader of several of these was Satanta, a big and boisterous Kiowa whose brag-ging often got him into trouble. At Fort Sill in the summer of 1871 he boasted of having killed some teamsters, with the result that he was arrested with two other chiefs and sentenced to prison. But peace-policy advocates objected to the action, and so 2 years later he was freed. As the Indian agent at Fort Sill remarked with apt imagery: "the effect on the Kiowas of the release of Satanta—a daring and treacherous chief—was like a dark rolling cloud on the western horizon."

Satanta had a leading role in the last great conflict of the southern plains, the Red River War of 1874. Over 3,000 troops were put in the field that summer to smash the prairie raiders, who had killed sixty settlers in Texas and

The Kiowa chief Satanta. From a photo taken at Fort Sill by W. W. Soule. Source: Los Angeles County Museum of Natural History.

Colorado. Fourteen pitched battles were fought with Comanche and Kiowa bands during the campaign. In September, MacKenzie finally penetrated Palo Duro Canyon, the Comanche stronghold in the Texas Panhandle. His victory there over Quanah Parker's band forced the tribesmen to go back to their reservation. By the middle of 1875 Indian resistance had been broken, and the way was opened for settlement of the Panhandle and the Staked Plains.

Grant's Peace Policy

While the soldiers were slugging it out with the Indians on the plains, President Ulysses S. Grant was trying to institute a more humane policy. Emphasis was placed upon education of the tribesmen and careful management of Indian-agency appropriations. After taking office in 1869, the President also began filling positions in the Indian Bureau with men recommended by various churches.

Since the first two agency positions went to Quakers, this has sometimes been called the "Quaker Policy." Church participation in the management of Indian affairs was tried until 1877, when it was gradually discontinued. Unfortunately, Indian agencies were a source of profit, so carpetbag politicians got the choice assignments. This had been true before the Quaker Policy was tried, and it remained so during and after that policy. To be sure, there were a number of honest and dedicated agents, but the general quality was low. The agent could divert most or all of the supplies intended for the Indians to private contractors, and pocket the money himself. He could "pad" the agency requisitions, or report double the number of Indians on the reservation, and sell the surplus items. In one case, elastic garters were sent out to a tribe which had never even heard of stockings! Even at that the goods were of poor quality: pistols burst in the Indians' hands; blankets became unglued at the first rainfall; the beef and bread rations were often green with age. Frequently adding to the difficulty were Indian traders, who hovered about the reservations and sold "firewater" to the tribesmen.

Corruption in the Indian agencies was only another reason why the signing of treaties never guaranteed peace on the frontier. The pressure of miners and homesteaders on the remaining Indian lands meant that treaties were being violated even at the moment the chiefs were putting their marks on the paper. And the nomadic tribes would not stay on the assigned reservations. They wanted to lead the carefree life as they had done from time out of mind. Sophisticated Easterners saw something romantic in this impulse, a suggestion of Adam in the Garden of Eden. To frontier folk, Indians off the reservation were about as picturesque as lions and tigers let out of the zoo.

The Sioux War of 1876

All of these root causes were involved in the Sioux War of 1876. The rush of miners into the Black Hills during the summer of 1875 demonstrated the inability of the federal government to restrain its own citizens. At the same time, Indian agents began reporting that young men were leaving the Spotted Tail and Red Cloud reservations to join the nontreaty Sioux in the Big Horn Mountains. The most influential of these "blanket Indians" were Sitting Bull and Crazy Horse. The former was a medicine man who enjoyed great prestige among the tribesmen by virtue of his dreams and visions. Crazy Horse was a war chief, regarded by military authorities as the finest cavalry tactician the Indian race ever produced. Worried officials of the Indian Bureau sent out runners with an ultimatum ordering these truants to return to their reservations by February 1, 1876. They were warned that the Army would be called in to punish them unless the ultimatum was obeyed.

The absentees were not given sufficient time to obey the order. But Sitting Bull and his followers among the Hunkpapa Sioux would not have obeyed it even if they had had all the time in the world. The Army was fully aware of this fact, and it planned a three-pronged offensive to trap and defeat the offenders in the Big Horn country. Gen. George Crook was to advance north from Fort Fetterman on the Platte, Col. John Gibbon was to move southeast from Fort Ellis in Montana, while Gen. Alfred Terry was to march west from Fort Abraham Lincoln in Dakota Territory. The plans went awry when Crook was defeated in a sharp battle with Crazy Horse at Montana's Rosebud Creek on June 17. This loss prevented Crook from joining with Terry, and had serious consequences for the fight on the Little Big Horn.

In the meantime, Terry's "Dakota Column" had advanced up the Yellowstone. At the mouth of the Rosebud he sent Lt. Col. Custer and twelve troops of the 7th Cavalry to block any southward retreat of the Indians from the Little Big Horn Valley. But when Custer saw a big travois trail leading west toward the valley, he decided to follow it. Custer's famous "luck" deserted him on June 25 when he found the Indian village and attacked. He committed a cardinal error by failing to gather sufficient intelligence about the numbers and disposition of the enemy. Estimates of the total number of Indians, who were principally Sioux and Cheyenne, range from 2,500 to 10,000. Custer's own battalion of 231 men was wiped out when warriors led by Crazy Horse and Gall overran his position on "Custer Hill." One horse, bearing the Indian name "Comanche," was the only living symbol of the United States Army after the battle.

"Custer's Last Stand" shocked and humiliated the nation. In Philadelphia the Centennial Convention was displaying steam engines, dynamos, and other triumphs of our industrial civilization. Yet a primitive people had decimated one of the country's elite military units. Public opinion called for chastisement of the "red barbarians." Army regiments were funneled into the northern plains, and they battered any Indian villages they found. Crazy Horse had to surrender, and was killed "while attempting to escape" from an Army fort in 1877. Sitting Bull fled across the Canadian border, and did not return to the United States until 1881. Thus by 1877 the great fighting days of the Sioux Nation were over.

The Modoc, Nez Percé, and Ute Wars

The decade of the 70s also saw the taming of other, smaller tribes. The Modocs lived in the Tule Lake region along the California-Oregon border. One band of the tribe was led by a particularly obstreperous subchief known to the whites as Captain Jack. He was a gangster type who attempted to extort food and money from the settlers, and they demanded his removal from the area. In 1872, an Army force under Gen. E. R. S. Canby was handed the messy job of prying the Modocs loose from their refuge in the lava beds. For the numbers involved, this was probably the most expensive Indian war in Army history. Canby was killed during a "peace conference," one of the few cases of red-man treachery. One thousand troops suffered over one hundred casualties before Captain Jack and his lieutenants were captured and hanged. The remnants of the tribe were hustled off to "malaria country" in southeastern Oklahoma.

The Nez Percé had been friendly with the Americans ever since their first meeting with Lewis and Clark. That explosive advance of the frontier had brought large numbers of white men into the Wallowa Valley of eastern Oregon during the 60s. The Indian Bureau therefore insisted that Chief Joseph and his people settle on the Lapwai reservation in Idaho. Just as the move was about to begin, young braves attacked the nearby settlers and Joseph decided to flee into Canada. For 4 months in the summer of 1877 he led his band on a flight covering 1,500 miles, fighting running battles with several Army columns that had been sent to stop him. On the way, he passed through the Yellowstone Lake region, which had been designated as a national park by President Grant in 1872. Some of the tourists got more sight-seeing thrills than they wanted. Two visitors from Helena were killed, and several others were wounded in encounters with the young braves. Chief Joseph pushed on into north central Montana. Here in October he surrendered to Gen. Nelson A. Miles, making a much-admired speech declaring that "from where the sun now stands I will fight no more forever." Thus the Nez Percé too were carted off to Indian Territory.

The Utes were booted out of western Colorado in 1879 after they dared to bite the hand that fed them. In 1873 the noose had tightened when the northern branch of the tribe had agreed to settle on the White River reservation. Nathan Meeker became agent at White River in 1878; an unfortunate choice as it turned out. Described as "a man of Puritan stamp," he tried to change his wards into white men much too quickly. It had always proved impossible to turn a warrior into a ploughman overnight, but Meeker must not have grasped this fact. The resentful red men suddenly slaughtered Meeker and took to the war path as of old. They were inevitably crushed by federal troops, and then deported to a desolate reservation in Utah.

The "Extermination Policy" in Arizona and New Mexico

The mountain and desert country of Arizona and New Mexico was the scene of almost continual warfare until 1886. The Navahos had been dangerous until 1864, when Col. Kit Carson invaded their Canyon de Chelly stronghold in Arizona and then forced them onto the Bosque Redondo reservation in New Mexico. Thereafter the Apaches were the scourge of the Southwestern frontier.

These small, wiry tribesmen were true professionals. They understood that the object of warfare was to kill the enemy, whether Mexican or Anglo, and they were proficient at the job. A master of concealment and surprise, the Apache seemed to walk on cat feet. He knew how to subsist on field mice and cactus pulp, and he could ride 70 miles a day where the cavalry could only do

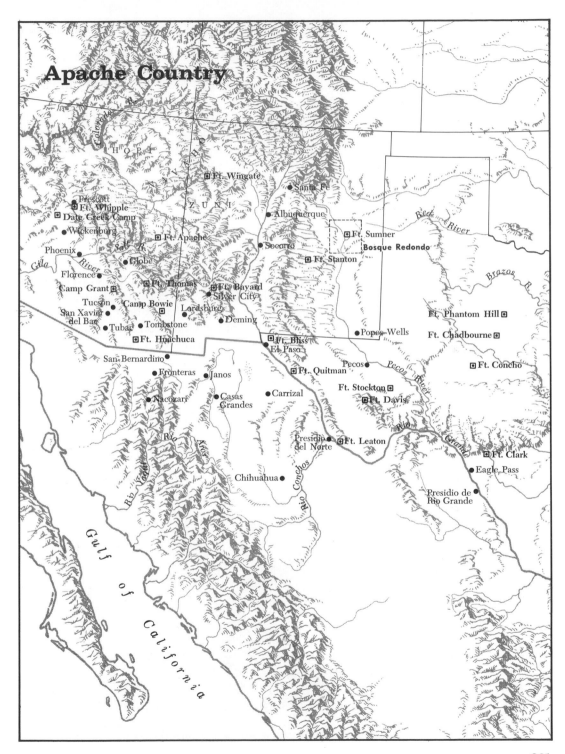

Apache Country

Colorado R.

HOPI

NAVAJO

ZUNI

Ft. Wingate

Santa Fe

Prescott
Ft. Whipple
Date Creek Camp
Wickenburg

Albuquerque

Ft. Apache

Ft. Sumner
Bosque Redondo

Red River

Phoenix
Salt R.
Globe
Florence
Camp Grant
Tucson
Camp Bowie
San Xavier
del Bac
Tubac
Tombstone
Ft. Huachuca

Gila River

Socorro
Ft. Stanton

Ft. Thomas
Ft. Bayard
Silver City
Lordsburg
Deming

Brazos R.

Ft. Phantom Hill

Ft. Chadbourne

Popes Wells

San Bernardino

Fronteras
Janos

Nacozari
Casas
Grandes

Carrizal

Ft. Bliss
El Paso

Ft. Quitman

Pecos

Pecos River

Ft. Stockton

Ft. Davis

Ft. Concho

Rio

Rio Yaqui

Presidio
del Norte
Ft. Leaton

Rio Grande

Ft. Clark

Eagle Pass

Chihuahua

Rio Conchos

Presidio de
Rio Grande

Gulf of California

361

25. When the Army guarded waterholes, the Apache traveled for days with water carried in an animal bladder. The almost perfect matching of man to land enabled great war leaders like Cochise, Victorio, and Geronimo to run circles around the United States Army.

Cochise took the warparth in 1861 after a too-clever second lieutenant tried to take him prisoner by trickery. He escaped, and launched a war against the United States which lasted until 1872. The Army reciprocated, following an extermination policy in the late 60s. General Ord, commanding the Department of California, wrote in September of 1869 that "I encouraged the troops to capture and root out the Apache by every means, and to hunt them as they would wild animals." Despite these efforts the Indian menace grew worse; it is no exaggeration to say that by 1870 the whites lived on the reservation and the Apaches occupied the country. For a time in 1871 it seemed as if a new day might be dawning when Vincent Colyer and Gen. George Crook both arrived in Arizona. Colyer was a Quaker, who had been sent out as a federal Indian Commissioner to try and make peace with the Apaches. Crook, a veteran of Indian campaigns in Oregon and Idaho, shared the frontiersman's scepticism about the peace policy and about Colyer, whom he called "Vincent the Good." So while Colyer patted the Apaches on the head, Crook readied the Army for a hard campaign. The

Gen. George Crook and Apache Scouts. Source: U. S. Signal Corps—National Archives.

Quaker commissioner distributed annuities and set up several reservations, most of them poorly located. In fact, much of the subsequent trouble stemmed from the Indian Bureau's insistence upon concentrating the Chiricahuas and Mimbrenos at the San Carlos reservation on the Gila, an unhealthy spot for mountain Indians. The breakdown of the peace policy is revealed by the fact that fifty-four separate Apache attacks occurred in Arizona between September, 1871 and September of 1872.

The blond-whiskered Crook was called upon to round up the hostiles. He saw that the usual cavalry methods would have to be discarded. Pack trains and Apache scouts were the principal tools which he used. Pack trains could be taken into terrain where cavalry horses could not survive. In employing scouts, who were trained by the noted guide Al Sieber, he made use of one of the oldest practices in Indian warfare. Until his reassignment to the Department of the Platte in 1875, he won a reputation for efficiency and fairness in a very trying situation.

Crook returned to the Department of Arizona in 1882 and was thus involved in the "Geronimo War." He followed the renegade chief into Mexico in 1883, and forced him to surrender. Two years later the wily Mimbreno left the reservation again to raid on both sides of the Rio Grande. A trail of plundered ranches and mutilated bodies marked his progress through Arizona and New Mexico. Finally in 1886 young Lt. Charles Gatewood persuaded the old warrior to surrender. He and his band were shipped to Florida for safekeeping. And Crook's Apache scouts were rewarded for their long years of service by being packed off to Florida also.

Wounded Knee

One final episode brought the Indian wars to a close in 1890, the same year in which the Bureau of the Census declared that the frontier itself no longer existed. The Ghost Dance movement, which began among a destitute band of Paiutes in western Nevada, had many similarities to other messianic movements which seem to spring up among oppressed people. Its prophet was Wovoka, also known as Big Rumbling Belly. He was the ward of a white ranching family, who had given him the Christian name of Jack Wilson. After the Ghost Dance was performed, the dead were supposed to come back to life, the buffalo would return, and the earth would open up and swallow the white man. The hypnotic effect of the songs used in the dances, and the addition of a belief that the so-called "Ghost shirts" would ward off bullets, made this initially peaceful movement a potentially dangerous one.

The Ghost Dance craze swept over practically every western tribe. But it had most impact upon the Sioux, and such honored chiefs as Red Cloud and Sitting Bull believed in it. The Army had its hands full trying to prevent any violent outbreaks. On December 29 an attempt to disarm some Ghost Dancers gathered at Wounded Knee Creek on the Pine Ridge reservation in South Dakota resulted in a pitched battle. The troopers of the 7th Cavalry opened up with Hotchkiss guns which tore the Indians apart. There were 153 known dead among the Sioux, while others undoubtedly died away from the field. Twenty-five soldiers were killed. Wounded Knee was the biggest news story since the Custer disaster, but it made a sad finale to the story of the Indian wars in America.

Shifting Government Policy

The two decades from 1870 to 1890 saw many changes in Indian policy. A congressional law of March 3, 1871, ended the custom of regarding Indian tribes as sovereign nations. Henceforth they were to be treated as wards of the government, and "treaties" now became "agreements." The change permitted the House of Representatives to share in the negotiations with various tribes. This move was followed by a concerted effort to break down tribal unity. By destroying the power of chiefs, it was thought that the red men could be civilized much more quickly.

On the reservations the attempt to make the inmates "walk the white man's road" did not go well. The once-proud buffalo hunters became beggarly and apathetic. Their physical deterioration and psychological confusion were evidence of profound "cultural shock." Several agricultural-mechanical training schools were opened on the reservations, the emphasis on education being an outgrowth of Grant's peace policy. Some institutions were also established in the East, with the Carlisle Indian School in Pennsylvania (1879) being the most famous of this kind. Unfortunately, graduates of the Eastern schools became "misfits" when they returned to their tribes.

Various volunteer organizations were formed for humanitarian purposes, and they had an influence on government policy. The most effective of these was the Indian Rights Association (1882), which maintained a representative in Washington. Nor may one overlook the impact of Helen Hunt Jackson's *A Century of Dishonor* (1881). As the title indicates, the book was a scorching denunciation of the government's treatment of the Indians. It is in many respects a propaganda tract rather than a rational analysis. But the abuses which it described, including numerous violations of treaties, led to a congressional investigation of the whole situation.

The culmination of the Indian-rights movement was the Dawes Individual Allotment Act of 1887. The Democratic President, Grover Cleveland, and Senator Henry L. Dawes of Massachusetts sought to protect the individual Indian by assigning him generally a 160-acre homestead. The federal government was to hold this plot in trust for 25 years, so the Indian would not lose it to unscrupulous whites. The law also provided that the Indians would become United States citizens upon receiving their land allotment.

While Cleveland, Dawes, and the Indian-rights people were well-intentioned, the act had the effect of releasing millions of additional acres to white settlers. After the individual Indians received their plots, the remaining lands were subdivided by the government and settled under the Homestead Act. By 1906, some 75 million acres released under the Dawes Act had been appropriated by whites. The most sensational episode in this great barbecue was the rush into Oklahoma on April 22, 1889. Almost 2 million acres were claimed by "boomers" and "sooners" within a few hours' time.

The allotment policy was ended with the Indian Reorganization Act of 1934. This legislation also reversed the policy of breaking down tribal unity, and attempted to encourage the maintenance of ancient traditions. The "New Deal for the Indian" reflected a romantic view, one that has alternated over the years with the more tough-minded approach. The fluctuations in policy indicate that white America has not found any satisfactory solution for the problems of this particular minority. The Indian continues to be part of America's "unfinished business."

Selected Readings   William Brandon, *The American Heritage Book of Indians* (New York, 1961), is short and well written, as is William T. Hagan, *American Indians* (Chicago, 1961). For individual tribes see bibliography for Chapter X. James C. Malin, *Indian Policy and Westward Expansion* (Lawrence, Kan., 1921), is a basic monograph which examines the period up to 1854. The U.S. National Park Service has written *Soldier and Brave: Indian and Military Affairs in the Trans-Mississippi West* (New York, 1963), which includes an excellent historical summary and a guide to fort locations. Ralph K. Andrist, *The Long Death: The Last Days of the Plains Indian* (New York, 1964), is a satisfactory popular narrative. Paul I. Wellman, *Death on the Prairie* (New York, 1934), is also popular. John Tebbel, *A Compact History of the Indian Wars* (New York, 1966), is so-so. B. W. Allred (ed.), *Great Western Indian Fights* (Garden City, N. Y., 1960), is a useful collection of articles by members of the Potomac Corral of the "Westerners."

LeRoy R. Hafen and Francis M. Young, *Fort Laramie and the Pageant of the West, 1834-1890* (Glendale, 1938), describes the Grattan affair and Harney's campaigns. Charles M. Oehler, *The Great Sioux Uprising* (New York, 1959), is a competent work on the Minnesota outbreak of 1862. Stan Hoig, *The Sand Creek Massacre* (Norman, 1961), is a concise and careful study. On this subject see also Donald J. Berthrong, *The Southern Cheyennes* (Norman, 1963), and William H. Leckie, *The Military Conquest of the Southern Plains* (Norman, 1963). Col. Richard I. Dodge, *The Plains of the Great West* (New York, 1959), records the War-Interior squabbles. Robert G. Athearn, *William Tecumseh Sherman and the Settlement of the West* (Norman, 1956), deals with the overall military picture. For detailed studies of the enlisted soldier see Don Rickey, Jr., *Forty Miles a Day on Beans and Hay* (Norman, 1963), and William H. Leckie, *The Buffalo Soldiers* (Norman, 1967). The war along the Bozeman Trail is expertly analyzed in James C. Olson, *Red Cloud and the Sioux Problem* (Lincoln, 1965). Dee Brown, *Fort Phil Kearny: An American Saga* (New York, 1962), examines the Fetterman Massacre. Margaret I. Carrington, *Ab-sa-Ra-Ka, Land of Massacre* (Philadelphia, 1878), is a contemporary defense of

Colonel Carrington. For the full background see Grace R. Hebard and E. R. Brinin-stool, *The Bozeman Trail*, 2 vols. (Cleveland, 1922). On the Beecher's Island affair consult George Bird Grinnell, *The Fighting Cheyennes* (New York, 1915). Charles E. Chapel, *Guns of the Old West* (New York, 1961), combines history with a discussion of firearms.

Douglas C. Jones, *The Treaty of Medicine Lodge* (Norman, 1966), is a collection and analysis of newspaper reporters' stories. Carl C. Rister, *Border Command, General Phil Sheridan in the West* (Norman, 1944), is informative. George A. Custer's *My Life on the Plains*, originally published in 1874, has been reprinted with an introduction by Edgar I. Stewart (Norman, 1962). It contains material on the Washita affair. The best biography is Jay Monaghan, *Custer* (Boston, 1959). Edward S. Wallace, "Border Warrior," *American Heritage*, vol. 9 (June, 1958), compares Custer unfavorably with Mackenzie. Capt. Robert G. Carter, *On the Border with Mackenzie* (New York, 1961), is a complete account of the Indian wars on the Texas frontier in the 70s. See also two classics: Rupert N. Richardson, *The Comanche Barrier to South Plains Settlement* (Glendale, 1933), and Wilbur S. Nye, *Carbine and Lance, the Story of Old Fort Sill* (Norman, 1937). The extermination of the buffalo is a subject which has attracted popular writers: E. Douglas Branch, *Hunting the Buffalo* (New York, 1929); Mari Sandoz, *The Buffalo Hunters* (New York, 1954); Wayne Gard, *The Great Buffalo Hunt* (New York, 1959); the last is recommended.

Grant's "peace policy" is analyzed in Loring B. Priest, *Uncle Sam's Stepchildren: The Reformation of United States Indian Policy, 1865-1887* (New Brunswick, N.J., 1942). Henry E. Fritz, *The Movement for Indian Assimilation, 1860-1890* (Philadelphia, 1963), stresses the role of the churches. The Sioux War of 1876 is most ably explained in Edgar I. Stewart, *Custer's Luck* (Norman, 1955). Stanley Vestal, *Sitting Bull, Champion of the Sioux* (Boston, 1932), and Mari Sandoz, *Crazy Horse* (New York, 1942), are standard biographies. Robert M. Utley, *Custer and the Great Controversy* (Los Angeles, 1962), is a good analysis of the legend. Kent L. Steckmesser, *The Western Hero in History and Legend* (Norman, 1965), attempts an evaluation of Custer. W. A. Graham (ed.), *The Custer Myth: A Source Book of Custeriana* (Harrisburg, Pa., 1953), reprints relevant documents on the "Last Stand."

Keith A. Murray, *The Modocs and Their War* (Norman, 1959), is standard. Considering their role in history, too many books have been written about the Nez Percé. Recent works which cross all the *t*'s and dot all the *i*'s are Alvin M. Josephy, Jr., *The Nez Percé Indians and the Opening of the Northwest* (New Haven, 1965), and Mark H. Brown, *The Flight of the Nez Percé* (New York, 1966). Marshall Sprague, *Massacre: The Tragedy at White River* (Boston, 1957), recounts the Ute uprising.

Paul I. Wellman, *Death on the Desert* (New York, 1933), is a popular account of the Apache wars, while Dan L. Thrapp, *The Conquest of Apacheria* (Norman, 1967), is scholarly. John G. Bourke, *On the Border with Crook* (New York, 1891), is a biography which lauds Crook's "great services" and "noble character." See also Martin F. Schmitt (ed.), *General George Crook, His Autobiography* (Norman, 1946), which covers the period up to 1876. Dan L. Thrapp, *Al Sieber, Chief of Scouts* (Norman, 1964), deals with the Apache Scouts. Robert M. Utley, "The Bascom Affair: A Reconstruction," *Arizona and the West*, vol. 3 (Spring, 1961), recounts the attempt to seize Cochise. Britton Davis, *The Truth about Geronimo* (New Haven, 1929), is a classic reminiscence; see also John Bigelow, Jr., *On the Bloody Trail of Geronimo* (Los Angeles, 1958). Frank C. Lockwood, *The Apache Indians* (New York, 1938), is reliable. Edward H. Spicer, *Cycles of Conquest* (Tucson, 1962), is a monumental study of the southwestern tribes from 1588 to 1960.

Robert M. Utley, *The Last Days of the Sioux Nation* (New Haven, 1963), is a superb analysis of the Ghost Dance episode. Paul D. Bailey, *Wovoka, the Indian Messiah* (Los Angeles, 1957), is a good biography. Helen Hunt Jackson's *A Century of Dishonor* has been reprinted in a paperback edition (New York, 1965) with an introduction by Andrew F. Rolle. William A. Brophy and Sophie D. Aberle (eds.), *The Indian, America's Unfinished Business* (Norman, 1966), is a collection of articles dealing with recent federal policy. Robert M. Utley, *Frontiersmen in Blue: The United States Army and the Indian, 1848-1865* (New York, 1967), is detailed and well written.

XXII. The Great Plains Frontier

One of the ten tested plots for Western fiction and films is that of Cattleman versus Homesteader. The historical basis for their conflict rests upon the westward advance of the farmers' frontier as it met the northward advance of the cattle frontier. Both groups claimed public land on the Great Plains, that treeless and windswept expanse which stretched from the 98th meridian to the Rocky Mountains and from Texas to Montana. Both faced serious problems because of the natural hazards in the region, which, until the Civil War, had been called the "Great American Desert." However, Yankee ingenuity produced such technological marvels as barbed wire and windmills which enabled both sets of pioneers to advance onto this last frontier. The great historical movement begun at Jamestown in 1607 played its final scenes in Abilene and Dodge City.

Texas Origins of the Cattle Business   The cattlemen were first to exploit the new frontier. Pasturing of cattle on the open range had proved to be a profitable business in parts of the Far West even before the Civil War. In the 1850s, former mountain men had bought wornout and footsore animals from Oregon emigrants and had fattened them up in the valleys of Wyoming's Green River for later sale. The 1859 gold rush to Colorado brought John W. Iliff into the cattle business there. He began running herds of several thousand head along the South Platte River, the beef being sold to the miners at premium prices. Montana also developed a local cattle industry as a consequence of the gold strikes at Virginia City and Helena in the early 60s. The business reached its fullest development in the years from 1867 to 1885, with the state of Texas being the Queen Mother of the "cattle kingdom."

The Spanish had brought herds of cattle to Mexico in the sixteenth century. The animals moved north with the advance of the mining and ranching frontier. After the founding of Laredo on the north bank of the Rio Grande in 1755, the brush country between there and the Nueces Valley became the domain of cattle and horse herds. A favorable climate and sufficient grass meant that the animals multiplied by geometric progression. By 1865, there were an estimated 4 million "longhorns" in southern Texas. These steers were lean, muscular, wild-eyed, and mean-tempered. A man who found himself afoot among them had to run for dear life. Still they made tough but tasty beefsteaks. And since they could survive blizzards, drought, "Spanish fever," and long trail drives, they were better suited to the plains environment than Eastern-bred "barnyard stock."

During the 50s there had been sporadic attempts to market the longhorns in New Orleans and in the North. There were trail drives to Shreveport and to Galveston, with the steers being shipped by boat down the Red River or across the Gulf of Mexico to New Orleans. A few herds were taken to St. Louis and other points in Missouri, and in 1856 a drive went to Chicago. After gold was discovered in California, the miners there consumed much of the local beef supply. So some courageous Texans took their lives in their hands and made several drives across New Mexico and Arizona to the Coast, realizing a narrow profit despite losses from drought and Indians. Cattle trailing did not become big business, however, until the postwar period.

In 1866, cattle selling for $3 to $4 a head in Texas were worth $30 to $40 in Kansas City. It didn't take a B.A. degree to figure out that if one could walk the beef to Kansas he would make money. Unfortunately, all sorts of hazards were wrapped around that word "if"; in fact, the 1866 drive was a catastrophe. The Texas cattlemen, many of them returned Confederate veterans, rounded up herds totaling about 200,000 animals. They drove from San Antonio north through the Indian Territory, following what was called the Shawnee Trail or the Sedalia Trail, since the target was Sedalia on the Missouri Pacific Railroad. Border bandits made tremendous inroads on the herds or demanded "protection money" for safe passage, and Indians ran off sizable numbers of animals. In addition, the irate farmers of Kansas and Missouri imposed "shotgun quarantine" on the Texas herds. These longhorns often carried ticks which spread the Spanish fever among Northern dairy cattle, which had no resistance to the disease. From this point on, quarantine laws prohibiting the introduction of Texas animals during the summer months became a familiar feature of the cattle frontier.

To avoid some of the difficulties encountered in '66, the railroad loading point would have to be located further west. One of the first to realize this fact was a young Illinois livestock dealer named Joseph G. McCoy. He went to the railroad companies with hat in hand, and asked them to promise favorable rates for shipping cattle to Chicago. The Kansas Pacific agreed to guarantee low rates to the Missouri River, while the Hannibal & St. Joseph made a similar promise for the Missouri-to-Chicago section. As his loading point, McCoy chose

Cowboy drinking from a spring. Source: Erwin F. Smith—Library of Congress.

Abilene, which in his words was "a small dead place . . . of about one dozen log huts." The town's lone saloonkeeper had to supplement his income by selling prairie dogs to tourists. McCoy soon had the place jumping. In 2 months during the summer of 1867 he built barns, loading pens, offices, and a hotel called the Drover's Cottage. He also dispatched publicity agents to invite Texans to bring their herds to Abilene. They came, and the word "cow town" entered the American language.

The Trail Drive

The trail drive was one of the basic institutions of the open-range cattle business. The "dogies"* were rounded up in the spring, marked with the owner's brand, then herded north. The most important man in the drive was the trail boss or "ramrod." He picked the route, assigned guard watches, and was wholly responsible for delivering the cattle to the owner at the railroad loading point. Next in importance was the cook, whose meals could make the trip a pleasure or a nightmare. In the 70s and 80s a chuck wagon accompanied the drive. It was loaded

---

*A "dogie" originally meant an anemic calf, "one that has lost its mammy and whose pappy has run off with another cow."

with beans, corn meal, molasses, and coffee, which supplemented the basic fare of beef and wild game. The herding crew itself was composed of drovers or "cow boys."

The cowboys tended to be young men, capable of absorbing extreme physical punishment. It was not unusual for them to remain in the saddle for 36 hours at a stretch. For risking life and limb in stampedes, blizzards, and Indian attacks, they were paid $15 to $20 a month plus board. Mexicans and Negroes, small numbers of whom also worked as trail hands, were usually paid a few dollars less. Yet there was no shortage of volunteers. If a man ever loved his job, it was the cowboy. Few of them would admit this, though, for around strangers they were about as talkative as a cigar-store Indian.

There had been "cattle hunters" and trail drives in American frontier history as early as the seventeenth century, and some of the practices on the Great Plains were derived from this earlier experience. On the other hand, much

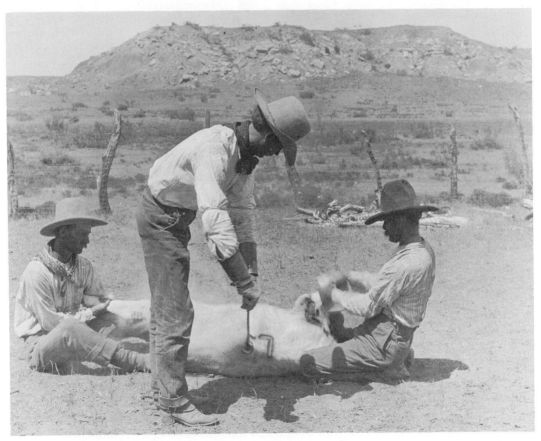

Burning a brand on a calf. Source: Erwin F. Smith–Library of Congress.

Cook getting breakfast at the chuck wagon. Source: Erwin F. Smith–Library of Congress.

of the equipment, terminology, and technique of the American cowboy was borrowed from the Mexican *vaquero.* As the old cowpuncher James Cook put it: "Their instructors in the art of cowboy work were Mexicans." The big-horned saddle, the rawhide rope, the spurs were all part of the inheritance. Of course the pupils changed many of the Spanish words into Texas English: *la reata* became "lariat"; *Chaparejos* became "chaps"; and *estampida* became "stampede." And the cowboy's costume of Stetson hat, bandanna, vest, and high-heeled boots, though picturesque enough, tended to be less elaborate than that of the *vaquero.* The Texans learned their lessons well, and in turn became instructors to their brethren on the northern ranges in Wyoming and Montana.

The hoof-marked trail running from San Antonio to Abilene was named for Jesse Chisholm, a Scotch-Cherokee trader who had worked the territory between the North Canadian and the Arkansas. The Chisholm Trail crossed not only these two rivers but also the Red, the Washita, and the Cimarron.

When any of them went over their banks it meant "big swimming," as the cowboys put it. In addition, stampedes were always a serious threat on the drive, and they could start as quick as a cat's wink. Thunder and lightning were the most common causes, but a barking dog, a snapping twig, or the click of a revolver hammer could set off a sudden rush. The cowboys then had to ride hell-bent-for-leather in an attempt to get the herd "milling" and under control. To quiet the cattle, the cowboys sang to them. A common tune was the wordless "Texas Lullaby." Other well-known songs, most of them filled with sadness and self-pity, included "I Ride an Old Paint," "Git Along Little Dogies," and "The Dying Cowboy." In the 70s the Indians were another menace to the herds. They demanded fees of 10 cents a head, under a provision of the Indian Act of 1834

Cowboys "belly up" to the bar in Old Tascosa, Texas Panhandle. Source: Erwin F. Smith–Library of Congress.

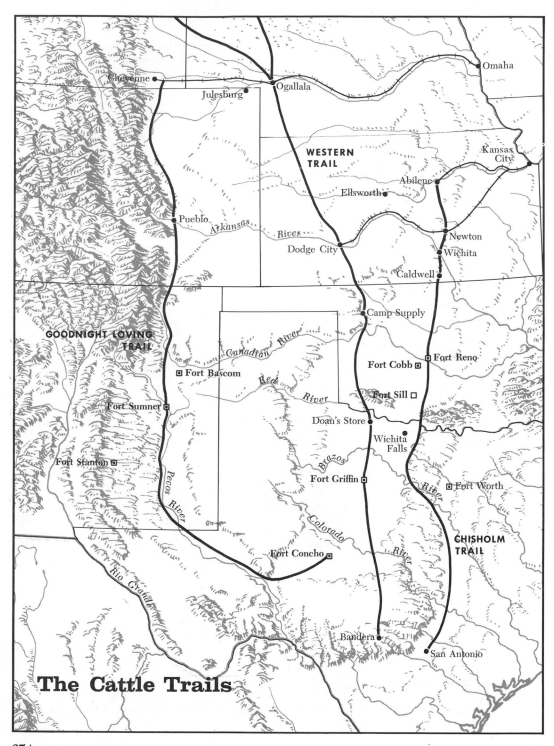

The Cattle Trails

Cheyenne

Julesburg

Ogallala

Omaha

WESTERN
TRAIL

Kansas
City

Abilene

Ellsworth

Pueblo

Arkansas   River

Newton

Dodge City

Wichita

Caldwell

Camp Supply

GOODNIGHT LOVING
TRAIL

Canadian   River

Fort Cobb

Fort Reno

Fort Bascom

Red   River

Fort Sill

Fort Sumner

Doan's Store

Wichita
Falls

Fort Stanton

Brazos

Fort Griffin

Fort Worth

Pecos   River

Colorado

River

CHISHOLM
TRAIL

Fort Concho

River

Rio Grande

Bandera

San Antonio

which required a tribe's consent before cattle could cross their land. And some tribesmen, notably the Comanches, enjoyed shooting arrows into both cows and cowboys.

Abilene

In the year 1867, about 35,000 cattle reached the Kansas Pacific at Abilene. In 1870 the figure was 300,000, and in 1871 it was 600,000. These statistics reveal the wisdom of McCoy's site selection, and measure the growth of Abilene itself. The town was not only a place of business but also the scene of entertainment. After 2 or 3 months on the trail, the cowboy was ready for a good time. Following a haircut, a shave, and perhaps the purchase of a new suit of clothes, he went out on the town. "I'm a wolf, and it's my night to howl," was the usual announcement. Abilene had such saloons as the Alamo, the Bull's Head, and the Old Fruit which offered the visitor all the drinking and gambling he could take—which was considerable. Contrary to the usual impression, "mixed drinks" were available in the saloons, as well as fine liqueurs and brandies. Entertainment, usually a piano player or a singer, was also offered in many establishments. If dancehall girls were part of the operation, the cowboy paid the price of two drinks to whirl her around the floor. He clomped about in boots and spurs, doing a jig that would win no prizes for grace or elegance. Tiring of the saloon, the cowboy could resort to the houses of prostitution in "McCoy's Addition" south of the railroad tracks. Women in this profession were referred to by such euphemisms as nymphs du prairie, scarlet ladies, painted cats, and calico queens. The income from taxes on these various enterprises was important to any cow town.

Abilene also heard the sound of gunfire when inebriated cowboys pulled their Colt revolvers and blazed away at windows, at lamps, and at each other. Quarrels were to be settled with guns or knives; fistfighting was beneath contempt. The average cowboy was not a skilled gunman, but some mighty dangerous gunfighters did work part-time as cowboys. John Wesley Hardin came up the trail in 1871, the same year that the city council had hired Wild Bill Hickok as marshal to enforce its "no-firearms" ordinance. Hickok patrolled the dusty streets with a shotgun on his arm, always kept his back to the wall, and in the words of cowboy Pascal Brown, "stood there and rolled his head from side to side looking at everything and everybody from under his eyebrows—just like a mad old bull." Some Texas gamblers urged Hardin to kill the obnoxious marshal, but the two men had a talk over champagne bottles and arranged a truce. Later in the year, Wild Bill killed one of the gamblers, Phil Coe, in a classic gun battle.

Farmers were more of a threat to the Texas cattle interests than Marshal Hickok. Theodore C. Henry became the leader of the "anti-cattle" element, which demanded "herd laws" under which farmers could collect damages for trampling of crops. They also wanted a quarantine law to keep Texas cattle out of the area during summer and fall. The Dickinson County Farmers' Protective Association pushed its crusade to make Abilene a wheat-farming center. The campaign reached its climax in 1872, when Henry sent a manifesto informing the Texans that they were no longer welcome in Abilene. The cattlemen took the suggestion, and moved their business elsewhere.

Other Cattle Towns

Beginning in 1872, Ellsworth on the Kansas Pacific and Wichita on the Santa Fe became the principal cattle markets. Both were wide-open towns on the model of Abilene. They competed with each other for the drovers' business, and sent agents down the trail. Wichita employed Abel H. "Shanghai" Pierce, whose voice could be heard half a mile away, as its drumbeater. The Kansas towns also had competition from Ogallalla, Nebraska, located 300 miles north of Ellsworth on the Union Pacific. Many cattlemen were willing to go the greater distance in hopes of higher prices for their beef. And then in southwestern Kansas there was Dodge City, which had been reached by the Santa Fe in 1872.

       This town grew up near a military post established by Gen. Grenville M. Dodge in 1864. It became the headquarters and outfitting center for buffalo hunters, whose business prospered until 1875. The cattle trade caught on slowly

James Butler "Wild Bill" Hickok as he appeared in the early 1870s. Source: Kansas State Historical Society, Topeka.

Dodge House, a famous hostelry in Dodge City, Kansas, 1874. Source: Kansas State Historical Society, Topeka.

and only 318 head were shipped in 1874. In fact, Dodge City never approached Abilene or Wichita as a shipping point. Most of the herds arriving there were trailed on up to Nebraska or beyond. But as farmers and their quarantine laws advanced west, more trail herds were routed through the town. The drives followed the Western or Dodge Trail, which went by way of Fort Griffin and Doan's Crossing of the Red River. The "Gomorrah of the Plains" had a population of buffalo hunters, soldiers, cowboys, and professional gunslingers who did not always get along with each other. The result was a succession of new graves on the town's famous Boot Hill. Wyatt Earp, Bat Masterson, and Bill Tilghman were among those who served as law officers. When the Santa Fe conductor asked a cowboy where he was going and got the answer "To Hell," he had to reply: "That will be fifty cents and get off at Dodge City."

The Texas longhorns which were driven north did not all go east on the railway cars. On the contrary, 60 percent of them were driven further north. They were sold to military posts or to the Indian reservations for beef rations. They were also used to stock the ranges in Kansas, Nebraska, Colorado, Wyoming, Montana, and Dakota. When prices were down, as they were after the Panic of 1873, the cattle were pastured until the market improved. These became the nucleus for ranching in the northern states and territories. Some of the Texans themselves chose to remain "north of 36." Colorado received the first large herds from Texas, and by 1869 there were 1 million cattle in that territory.

General view of Dodge City, 1879. Source: Kansas State Historical Society, Topeka.

Most of these came north by way of the Goodnight Trail, sometimes called the Goodnight-Loving Trail, which had been pioneered by Charles Goodnight in 1866. This ran west from Fort Concho to the Pecos River, then north through eastern New Mexico and Colorado as far as the Cheyenne area. Because Comanches and Kiowas infested this area, it was in its early years the most dangerous of the famous trails. Wyoming and Montana received increasing numbers of steers in the 70s. Also, cattle taken by covered-wagon pioneers to Oregon and Washington had multiplied so fast that thousands of them were driven back to Montana and Wyoming by way of the "Northern Trail" in the same decade.

Customs and Laws

Land, water, and cattle were the three basic properties involved in open-range ranching. The land was "public domain," but the cattlemen felt free to make use of it without getting Uncle Sam's permission. The rancher claimed a piece of land along a stream, and his "range right" ran back to the nearest divide. This right was similar to a squatters' claim; it had no standing in formal law. Western states and territories did pass laws protecting these rights to a certain extent by setting penalties for those who drove cattle from their "accustomed range." But these range rights rested ultimately upon six-gun law. If the cattleman found his range invaded by competitors, he sent his cowboys to drive them off by force.

The amount of land that could legally be claimed under the federal laws was grossly inadequate for the needs of ranchers. They could file for 160 acres under the Homestead Act. By two amendments to that law, the Timber Culture Act of 1873 and the Desert Land Act of 1878, they could acquire an additional 800 acres after meeting various requirements. The total of 960 acres was enough to start a tiny stock ranch, but for optimum operation the rancher needed 2,000 to 50,000 acres. Thus he was almost forced to lie and to have his cowboys enter homestead claims which they then signed over to him. Indeed, it was often a condition of employment that the cowboy do this. As early as 1875 the Commissioner of the General Land Office had proposed enlarging land units to accommodate Western settlers. Maj. John Wesley Powell, director of a federal survey in the Rocky Mountain region, filed a report in 1878 recommending a homestead unit of at least 2,568 acres in semiarid regions. But proposals for larger claims were regarded in the East as evidence of the greed of the "bovine kings."

Water was also acquired on a first-come-first-served basis. East of the 98th meridian the old English common-law doctrine of riparian rights had been retained. Under this doctrine all owners have equal rights to the use of a stream. In the West the "doctrine of appropriation," based to some extent upon Spanish-Mexican precedents, denied equality of use. It granted special privileges to the first-comer, with continuance of the privilege being dependent upon beneficial use. This custom resembled those by which miners regulated their "claims." Possession of the water source in effect meant control of all surrounding land to the next divide. In the semiarid West, "water" and "life" were synonymous.

The ownership of cattle was established by branding and the round-up. Every man who claimed a herd was expected to mark his animals in some distinctive way. Ranches named the Circle G, the Diamond S, and so forth reveal

Wyatt Earp. Source: Mercaldo Archives, New York.

the configuration of the brands. Sometimes additional markings were made; the jingle bob used by John S. Chisum of New Mexico was a slit which left the lower half of the ear flapping. The branding was normally done during roundups held in the spring and fall. The local ranchers would drive their herds to some preselected spot, which then became a scene of unimagined confusion. Since newborn calves followed their mothers, it was possible to identify and brand animals accordingly. Ownership of "mavericks," unbranded stray cows or orphaned calves, was also determined. In the interim between roundups, cowboys did "line riding" to turn back the neighbor's herds.

Even with branding, the ownership of cattle was a thorny problem. Rustling was one of the commonest crimes in the West, and some famous names in frontier history are connected with this ancient occupation in one way or another. Billy the Kid, for example, stole cattle in the Texas Panhandle during 1880 and sold them in New Mexico or Arizona to buyers who didn't ask a lot of questions. The rustlers could blot out brands or alter them with a little doodad called a "running iron." It is a standing joke in Western states that the patriarch of a wealthy ranching family had entered the territory with nothing more than a horse and a running iron. Or the cows of some ranchers always seemed to have twins or triplets, and the neighbors then had to warn them that their herd had better stop multiplying so fast.

Stockmen's associations were formed to protect the rights and property of the members. They organized roundups, registered cattle brands, and hired detectives to hunt down rustlers. Frontier individualism gave way to group effort in response to this need for protection. The effectiveness of these organizations varied from one state to another. Where mining and agricultural interests predominated, as in Montana, the association was less effective. Where the economy was primarily dependent upon stockraising, as in Wyoming, they enjoyed considerable power. In fact, the Wyoming Stock Growers' Association almost proved the truth of Lord Acton's dictum that "absolute power corrupts absolutely."

By a territorial law of 1884 the association secured control of all livestock affairs in Wyoming. The big cattlemen who dominated the organization used this authority to harass potential competitors among the small ranchers and homesteaders. Cattle were seized from "rustlers" without due process of law, on the principle of "guilty until proved innocent," and cowboys suspected of being rustlers were blacklisted. The farmer-ranchers fought back and by 1892 the situation was critical. Johnson County, which was as large as the state of Ohio, became the scene of a range war when the big cattle companies brought in Texas gunhands to clean out the "rustlers." President Grover Cleveland subsequently had to order out federal troops to save the besieged cattlemen and Texans from an enraged army of nesters and cowboys. It seems that the association made the mistake of attempting to use frontier or vigilante methods when Wyoming, in the second year of statehood, was no longer a frontier.

End of the Beef Bonanza

By 1879, cattle raising had become one of the hottest business investments in the country. Eastern and English capitalists formed huge "land and cattle" companies. The Swan Company of Wyoming was nominally capitalized at 2½ million dollars by 1883, and it owned so many cattle (an estimated 120,000 head) that the wagon bosses had to consult guidebooks to keep track of all the company brands. Northern cattlemen stopped importing Texas longhorns, and instead brought in Hereford and Durham bulls from Iowa to "breed up" their herds. Livestock journals reported profits of 50 percent annually. James Brisbin's *Beef Bonanza: or, How to Get Rich on the Plains* (1881) was a good example of the unrealistic publicity concerning the cattle business. Simply by multiplying numbers, Brisbin proved how John Doe could make a fortune. The difficulties were overlooked, and nothing was said about the wide fluctuations in cattle prices, or the diseases that could destroy an entire herd. For every John Chisum or Richard King who became a "cattle baron," there were five others who lost their shirts, and most of the big trail operators died broke.

The chief danger was overstocking of the ranges. Since the land was free to all, no one had authority to say when the saturation point had been reached. The increased use of barbed wire after its introduction in 1874 also reduced the amount of grazing land. One Colorado company had an estimated 1 million acres enclosed with wire. By 1885, cattle raising was ceasing to be a frontier industry. The Chisholm Trail was virtually closed, and traffic on the Western Trail was tapering off. Then two catastrophic winters in 1885-1886 and 1886-1887 brought the open-range period to an end.

Unusually severe blizzards and low temperatures in '85-'86 caused considerable losses among most stockmen. The barroom expression "Cheer up boys, whatever happens the tally books won't freeze," was hardly reassuring. The summer of 1886 was hot and dry, which meant that there was little grass and so the animals approached the winter in poor condition. In January of 1887 the Great Plains were hit by the greatest blizzard that the ranges had ever experienced, one that was not to be rivaled until 1949. Ranchers considered themselves fortunate when 35 or 40 percent of their herd survived. With 30-foot snowdrifts and temperatures at 50 below zero, the ranchers could only huddle in their cabins while the cattle froze to death. The spring revealed thousands of carcasses stacked up in the draws and along the barbed wire fences. It was a sight which old-time cowmen would never forget.

The range-cattle industry declined sharply after 1887, although it lingered on in some areas for another decade. The fair-weather ranchmen and the big Eastern companies, which had lost the most heavily, pulled out of the business. Where Wyoming had had 9 million head of cattle in 1886, it had 3 million in 1895. There was a shift from an open-range to a ranch basis, with barbed wire boundaries and careful control of the herds to prevent overgrazing. The cowboy spent much of his time building fences and cutting hay for winter fodder, a sad fate for the knight of the plains!

There was nothing inherently romantic about being a herder of cows. It was dirty, exhausting work. Riding "drag" at the dusty tail end of a trail herd was an example of the unpleasant duties involved. "Cow boy" was printed with quotation marks, and was synonymous with "ruffian" as late as the mid-1880s. But fiction writers rescued the cowboy from commonality. Prentiss Ingraham published a dime novel entitled *Buck Taylor, King of the Cowboys* in 1887, and this launched the literary legend. Owen Wister's bestseller *The Virginian* (1902) featured a cowboy hero who did not herd a single animal during the story. Zane Grey, Clarence Mulford, and a dozen other novelists created similarly idealized heroes. This mythical cowboy has been popular for several generations now, and in the world at large he is the best-known frontier character.

Sheepmen

Sheep ranching was competitive with cattle raising in several of the Plains states after the Civil War. The industry had been firmly rooted in California and New Mexico since the Spanish period, but in the 1870s sheepmen expanded into Colorado, Wyoming, Montana, and a few other states. Great eastbound trail drives, covering 1,500 to 2,500 miles, were organized to take the animals to feedlots and loading points in Nebraska and North Dakota. The business contributed greatly to the economic development of the Far West.

This expansion brought inevitable clashes with the cattlemen, who claimed that sheep cropped the grass so closely that they ruined pastureland for years. Cowboys attacked "snoozers" and drove their flocks over the cliffs. The Graham-Tewksbury feud in Arizona's Tonto Basin (1887) is really not a classic sheepman-cattleman war. Arizona had begun to receive large numbers of Texas cattle after the completion of the Southern Pacific line in 1881, and both families were engaged in cattle ranching. Then the Tewksburys attempted to bring sheep into the basin, and this move along with old personal feuds started the six-guns barking. In the long run, however, prices of mutton and wool were more stable than those of beef, and so sheep ranching enjoyed a steady growth and even attracted a number of former cattlemen. By the end of the century the Western states (including Texas) were raising more sheep than cattle.

The Farmer's Frontier

Ultimately the cowboy also lost his battle with the homesteader, whom he referred to by such ungenerous appellations as "sodbuster," "nester," and "hoeman." By 1865 the farmers' frontier lay along the 96th meridian in eastern Kansas and Nebraska. Its further extension onto the Great Plains was in part a result of the momentum created by several generations of westward movement, and in part the consequence of a massive advertising campaign. The federal government, the railroad companies, state immigration bureaus, private land companies, all beat the drums. They described the prairie-plains frontier as the greatest opportunity since the Garden of Eden.

There were certain imperfections in this picture of an Earthly Paradise. The railroad pamphlets said of the Platte region that "the traveler beholds, stretching away to the distant horizon, a flowering meadow of great fertility, clothed in grasses and watered by numerous streams, the margins of which are skirted by timber." The farmer on the plains looked in vain for these "numerous streams," and he found that his most serious problem was the lack of water. West of the 98th meridian in particular, the rainfall was normally below the 20 inches per year needed to grow the usual cereal crops. The polite word for such country is "subhumid"; the unvarnished term is "semiarid." Irrigation was impractical in all but a few areas because of the low velocity of the rivers and the rapid evaporation caused by prairie winds. In a cycle of dry years the settler might see the mirage of a farm home blown away in a cloud of dust.

Yet the Western publicists destroyed these geographical facts in their verbal barrages. They invented the slogan "Rain Follows the Plow." As farmers turned the sod face down, rainfall would automatically increase. There was a grain of truth in the slogan. Scientists have found that air above plowed land becomes less stable, so that thundershowers are more likely to occur. But the practice still cannot bring rainfall to adequate levels in a dry spell. Furthermore, people wanted to believe in the "myth of the Garden," and so they followed it into the West. In some respects the settlement of the Great Plains is a triumph of imagination over reality. Immigrants from Europe and from the Mississippi Valley states pushed up the Platte Valley, north and west of Omaha. They believed that they would enjoy the high crop yields promised by the railroad land agents and newspaper editors, and their faith is reflected in town names like Utopia, Happyland, Pleasant Hill.

The federal government also promoted settlement by legislating the "Great American Desert" out of existence. Passage of the Homestead Act in 1862 evidenced a belief that the farmer would settle the remaining West in 160-acre plots. The land was free, the law simply requiring 5 years' residence and the erection of a cabin. So millions of farmers—including liberal numbers of Germans, Scandinavians, and Irishmen along with the native Americans—came west on the various railroads. With a free homestead, and a good market for wheat both here and abroad, how could they lose?

Starving to Death on a Government Claim

As so often happens, dream and reality were miles apart. The Plains were deficient in other resources besides water, most notably timber. Until he had made enough money to import lumber for a frame house, the homesteader had to utilize local materials. Sometimes he carved a dugout in the side of a hill, with a stretched cowhide for a door. More often he took a spade and cut 3-foot blocks of earth, stacking them up to make a "sod house." The only wood used was a few poles for a door frame and for roof supports. These structures were all right until the spring rains, at which time the roof might fall in. As the song of the "Lane County Bachelor" puts it:

> *My house is constructed of natural soil*
> *The walls are erected according to Hoyle;*
> *The roof has no pitch but is level and plain*
> *And I never get wet till it happens to rain.*

The dirt floors attracted fleas, and bedbugs and rattlesnakes were likely to emerge from the walls. Yet the sod house was cool in summer, was fireproof, and lasted for 6 or 7 years. This was long enough for the settler to find out whether he could make a go of it or not.

The shortage of wood meant that the farmer also had to use native materials for fuel. Cow or buffalo chips were used in the 70s, and cornstalks and prairie grass were also burned. Montgomery Ward began advertising patented stoves for the burning of hay and grass in this period. The lack of trees meant that there was little shelter from the fierce summer heat. Nor could

"Independence on the Plains"—a pioneer woman gathering buffalo chips. Source: Kansas State Historical Society, Topeka.

Sod house in Custer County, Nebraska, about 1889. Source: Nebraska State Historical Society.

one build split-rail fences to keep cows and hogs out of the cornfields and the vegetable patch.

The homesteader also found that the boosters had not informed him about blizzards, drought, prairie fires, or grasshoppers. The grasshoppers came in 1874, a devouring carpet moving all the way from Texas to Dakota. They consumed the wheat, munched on lace curtains and leather harnesses, and found their way into water buckets and teakettles, making it necessary to strain all beverages. A 3-foot drift of the insects stopped a Union Pacific train at Kearny, Nebraska—a tall tale until one considers the lightness of the early loco-motives and the slipperiness of the rails. Most of the Plains became what would in modern parlance be called a "disaster area." Farmers heavily in debt or living on narrow financial margins were driven from the land. Food was short in some locations, and starvation was a possibility for quite a few families. The whole situation was summed up by the Lane County Bachelor:

> *Hoorah for Lane County the land of the free*
> *The home of the grasshopper, bedbug, and flea*
> *I'll sing loud her praises and boast of her fame*
> *While starving to death on my government claim.*

On the other hand, it is possible to exaggerate the sufferings of the sod-house settlers. Such writers as Hamlin Garland in *Main Traveled Roads* and Mari Sandoz in *Old Jules* have painted a bleak picture of loneliness and poverty that is not wholly accurate. The farmers certainly experienced hardship, a con-dition of any frontier. And women especially missed their friends and relatives "back East." But the farmers gathered to celebrate the usual holidays, and the

Fourth of July in particular was a great occasion in frontier days. Settlers would come in for miles around for a big dance and a parade, while their children were allowed to set off firecrackers. There were huge meals of buffalo meat, venison, and barbecued ox. The traditional speeches were preceded by toasts drunk to "George Washington," "Spartan Mothers of the American Revolution," "Nebraska," or "Our Friends Crossing the Plains." The dinner was followed by sack races, fat mens' races, and greased-pole climbs.

Other customs included taffy pulls, hayrack or bobsled parties, and quilting bees. Marriages were always followed by a shivaree, at which friends gathered at the house of the newlyweds to bang on tin pans or cow bells until "treats" were offered. Churches were established fairly quickly on the Plains frontier, and they were the center of much community activity. The "church social," with ice cream and strawberries as the bill of fare, was important. There were literary or debating societies which pondered such questions as "British Colonial Policy" or "Manifest Destiny." Spelling contests were judged in accord with that unimpeachable authority, the McGuffey Reader. There was also much singing and dancing. The large number of gospels, such as "Bringing in the Sheaves," were varied by secular songs like "Puttin' On the Agony" and "Little Old Sod Shanty." Since dancing was considered to be improper by many churches, the dances were called "play parties" and were accompanied by song only. "Old Joe Clark," "Skip to My Lou," and "Buffalo Gals" were standard tunes at these affairs.

Wire and Windmills

People continued moving west despite the hazards. In Kansas and Nebraska they crossed the deadline of the 98th meridian, and by 1880 had begun farming the short-grass country in the western third of those states. In Dakota the lands east of the Missouri were filled during a boom which lasted from 1868 to 1885, with only a brief slowdown following the Panic of 1873. Several developments made this expansion possible. First, there was a cycle of unusually wet years, which lasted generally until the late 80s and convinced the doubters that rain did "follow the plow." Second, the railroads continued their advance across the Plains, and they kept on advertising the land within their grants. Third, the invention of an effective barbed wire made crop farming possible over a much wider area. Fourth, the introduction of windmills resulted in a partial solution of the perennial water problem.

Inexpensive fencing was always one of the farmer's basic requirements. He had to keep his own animals out of the wheatfield and fruit orchard. If he was on the edge of cattle country, he had to stop the range herds from trampling his crops. In the absence of wood for split-rail fences, various substitutes were tried. Earth embankments were constructed by some farmers, but the osage-orange hedge was the most popular alternative, since it was "horse-high, bull-strong, and pig-tight." However, when Glidden's Patent Steel Barb Wire Fence went into production in 1874, the professional hedge grower became another victim of technological progress.

Joseph F. Glidden of DeKalb, Illinois, perfected the wire, although others had similar patents and there were years of court litigation. Sales skyrocketed as soon as production began. Ten thousand pounds of barbed wire were made and sold in 1874; the figure for 1880 was 80,500,000. The wire had far-reaching effects for both cattlemen and farmers on the Great Plains. Most cattle ranchers were opposed to its introduction, but they soon divided among themselves. There were the free-grass men and the fenced-range men. Fence-cutting wars in Texas and Wyoming followed attempts to enclose the public domain. But the major conflict was between the cattleman and the homesteader. The nester with his plows, hoes, and Sunday schools had never been an attractive figure to the rancher. But barbed wire was the ultimate *casus belli.*

Probably the most publicized clash was one which occurred on the Platte Valley in central Nebraska. Isom P. "Print" Olive was a Confederate veteran who moved his cattle operations from Texas to Custer County, Nebraska, in 1877. He ordered his men to cut the wire fences erected by homesteaders Mitchell and Ketchum, whose crops were then trampled by the longhorns. The two "sodbusters" killed some of Olive's cattle and sold the meat in town. Olive unsuccessfully laid siege to the farmers' home, but later abducted the two men and executed them with a "necktie party." Olive was sentenced to life imprisonment for the crime. Fence cutting, trampling of crops, shooting of steers, are episodes reported in Western newspapers all through the 70s and 80s.

The windmill was an old European device which was adopted and adapted for use on the Great Plains. Wells had to be dug or drilled to great depths, 200 feet or more, and the constant wind supplied the power to raise this water to the surface. The transcontinental railroads ordered the first of the improved American-made machines, and the more affluent cattle ranchers also began erecting them in the 70s. The farmer followed in the rancher's footsteps, but since he was seldom able to afford a factorymade mill, he had to construct his own. Some of these homemade machines, built with grocery crates and baling wire, would have done justice to the contemporary author Jules Verne. But they brought water into the farm home, kept the garden blooming, and in short, enabled the farmer to stay on the right side of that thin line separating survival from disaster.

Land-law Nightmares

Barbed wire and windmills helped the homesteader to overcome natural obstacles, but some of the land laws represented a man-made hazard. The Homestead Act was supposed to be the foundation of a great democratic land system on the Great Plains. Historians of gloomy disposition have pointed out how the act failed in this regard, and they have declared it dead and buried on numerous occasions. They have shown that only one-sixth of the public domain went to homesteaders, and that only about one-third of the homestead entries between 1862 and 1890 were ever made final. They also emphasize the fact that 160-acre units were unsuited to the Plains, that the act was subverted by unwise amendments, and that land speculation and monopolization continued after 1862. Students of more optimistic temperament, on the other hand, have said that the interment was premature. They maintain that the 160-acre allotment was feasible east of the 100th meridian, given the technology of that period, and that plenty of land was available under the act until the late 70s. At present, reconsideration of the record of entries is in fact restoring the Homestead Law's original reputation as a great and constructive measure, one that made possible a high percentage of owner-operated farms on the Great Plains.

It is true that large blocks of the public domain passed into the hands of railroads, land speculators, and state governments. The railroads got 181 million acres from federal and state sources. Most of the 140 million acres distributed under the Morrill Land Grant Act (or "Agricultural College Act") of 1862 went to speculators. This was an important bill in the history of American higher education. Congress utilized Henry Clay's old "distribution" idea to encourage training in scientific agriculture. The states received 30,000 acres of land scrip for each of their senators and representatives, a method which created something of an imbalance in the distribution. New York acquired almost 1 million acres, much of it prime timber or farming land in Wisconsin, while Kansas got only 90,000 acres. The states usually sold these lands to speculators, who then resold them to homesteaders willing and able to pay $5 to $10 an acre. Another 200 million acres were sold direct to speculators by the Land Office and, prior to the Dawes Act of 1887, by Indians. The result of all these transactions varied from state to state; in Kansas it meant that 40 percent of the public domain was withdrawn from homestead entry. The farmers' complaints about grants and speculations were translated into political action when good land became scarce after about 1880.

Yet much of the speculation was carried on by that "small homesteader" who was presumably being victimized by land monopolization. As early as 1860, Horace Greeley had remarked about his visit to Kansas that "the speculators in broadcloth are not one whit more rapacious or pernicious than the speculators in rags, while the latter are forty times more numerous." Many of the farmers filed claims under the Homestead Act or the Preemption Act with the intention of selling rather than settling them. This was made easy by a commutation clause in the Homestead Act, a provision that after 6 months the claimant could gain full title by paying the government $1.25 an acre in cash. This permitted a more rapid turnover which was of benefit to speculators both large and small. It was also well known that cattlemen and speculators employed "dummy entrymen" to file claims for them. The Land Office had insufficient personnel to check every fraud or misrepresentation. The officials could seldom determine that a cabin described as being "twelve by fourteen" referred to inches rather than feet.

All the lamentations about the land laws are more justifiable as regards the two major amendments to the Homestead Act. The Timber Culture Act of 1873 was a forlorn attempt to encourage the planting of "green belts" across the Plains. It was thought that trees would reduce the winds, increase precipitation, and attract desirable settlers. The homesteader could claim 160 acres if he planted 40 of them (reduced to 10 acres in 1878) with trees. After 10 years he would gain final title if the trees were still alive, which was not often the case. The law, which remained on the books until 1891, permitted some farmers to expand their holdings, and did result in limited forestation at places in Kansas, Nebraska, and Dakota. But Congress could not change the semiarid geography of the Plains by legislation alone.

The same truth was apparent in the Desert Land Act of 1877. This law applied in eleven Western states and territories, with the exception of a thin strip along the coast of California, Oregon, and Washington which got so much rain that not even a confirmed pessimist could call it "desert." A settler could claim one section, 640 acres, if he irrigated it within 3 years after filing

A house "Twelve by Fourteen."
Source: Huntington Library.

the papers. He had to pay 25 cents an acre initially, and an additional $1 an acre upon being given title. The law was framed with the best intentions, principally that of encouraging farm making in the semiarid and arid regions beyond the 98th meridian. It failed to do so, and instead became an instrument for fraud and land monopoly.

Cattle ranchers rather than farmers were the chief beneficiaries of the Desert Land Act. They dumped a bucket of water on the claim or plowed a furrow through it to meet the "irrigation" requirement. Cowboys were employed to make desert-land entries as well as homestead and preemption claims, thus enabling the cattleman to pyramid his holdings. When Thomas Donaldson published an exhaustive study of the public domain in 1883, he concluded that "the desert-land act has become an aid to land-grabbing. It should be repealed or a larger area given under it. It is useless for actual settlement, for poor men cannot irrigate it by means of expensive ditches and men of means could not afford to construct ditches for so small an area." The failure of the law is indicated by the fact that of 9 million acres claimed under it, final patents were issued on only 2.5 million acres.

Later Expansion

Despite the buffeting he took from nature and from his own government, the farmer-homesteader remained the eternal optimist. In 1878 and 1879 western Kansas and Nebraska were being settled. By 1880, the farmers' frontier was beyond the 100th meridian, supposedly proving that corn, wheat, and barley could be grown in semiarid lands. But in 1879 and again in 1880 there was a break in the unusual cycle of rainfall. Severe drought caused crop failures all through the central plains. Many discouraged and destitute farmers left, but then increased rainfall in 1883 caused a new wave of optimism and further settlement. By 1887 the prospects seemed so rosy that pioneer farmers were spilling over into eastern Colorado, the heart of Pike's and Long's Great American Desert. Maj. John Wesley Powell's warning that this region was suited only for grazing or irrigation farming was pooh-poohed. Newspaper editors reassured the settlers that the Colorado plains were in a "rain belt." But then searing drought in 1889 and again in 1890 revealed the region's true characteristics, brought the boom to an end, and ruined thousands of homesteaders.

The "bonanza farms" established after 1875 in the Red River Valley of North Dakota and Minnesota attracted farmers to the northern plains. These farms were also a look into the future, since they were large units operated on business principles. Officers of the Northern Pacific Railroad hired Oliver Dalrymple to demonstrate that bumper wheat crops could be produced by using scientific methods and the latest machinery. Dalrymple got 25 bushels per acre, and the resulting profits attracted Eastern capital. Elsewhere in eastern Dakota the usual type of pioneer operations were carried on. Between 1880 and

1890 the population of the territory increased about 3¾ times, and the number of farms increased by 5½ times. The "Dakota Boom" in both wheat and land came to an end in 1889 with that same terrible drought that paralyzed the rest of the Plains region.

The Dakotans were practically slavering when they thought about the lands of the Sioux Reservation, which comprised some 22 million acres between the Missouri River and the Black Hills. In February of 1890, some sections of the Indian lands were thrown open for settlement, and hundreds of homesteaders drove across the icebound river to locate farms and townsites. The "land rush" was not a new phenomenon in the history of the trans-Mississippi West. In 1843 the lands of the Sac and Fox Indians in central and southern Iowa were opened at midnight on April 30. At a signal from the Army, homesteaders rushed pell-mell across the boundary line and within a few hours had staked out almost every inch of ground. The most famous rushes were those into Oklahoma.

Squatters had begun infiltrating Oklahoma from Kansas in the 1870s. Railroad companies encouraged much of this illegal entry, since they found the Indians to be poor customers and they needed to build up their revenues by means of white settlement. Then on February 15, 1879, a part-Cherokee lawyer named Elias Boudinot published a newspaper article proclaiming that there were 14 million acres of government land available for homesteading in the territory. This kind of propaganda was music to the ears of David L. Payne, a 6-foot-4-inch adventurer who had at one time been assistant doorkeeper of the U.S. House of Representatives. Payne became the leader of the Kansas "boomers," and in 1879 he organized them into what was called the Oklahoma Colony. Between 1880 and 1884 squads of these would-be colonists repeatedly slipped past the federal troops and tried to settle in the 2-million-acre tract of central Oklahoma known as "the District." Each time the Army found them, burned their shacks, and drove them back into Kansas. Payne died in 1884, but others took over the leadership and continued to demand permanent settlement of the unoccupied Indian lands.

Congress finally agreed to open the District to settlement under the Homestead Law. The official time of the opening was set at 12:00 noon on April 22, 1889. By that hour at least 15,000 boomers had arrived at the boundary line along the Cherokee Outlet. The cavalry patrolled the line to keep out "moonlighters" or "sooners" who tried to cross before the appointed time. When the signal gun was fired, the crowd raced into the area like a pack of beagles following a trail. Within a few hours it was all over, with almost all of the 2 million acres having been claimed. Guthrie and Oklahoma City, which had previously been railway stations on the Santa Fe, were suddenly tent cities with thousands of inhabitants. There was something gloriously and characteristically American about this wild scramble for a share in what everyone imagined was a new Horn of Plenty.

There were other runs into Oklahoma over the next few years as more Indian lands were released under the Dawes Act. In 1891 settlers raced into the former Potawatomie, Iowa, and Shawnee lands east of the District. In 1892 some 25,000 homesteaders carved up the Cheyenne and Arapaho lands to the west. And the biggest rush of all, involving 100,000 settlers, occurred when the Cherokee Outlet was opened on September 16, 1893. This settlement inevitably brought political organization. Oklahoma became a territory in 1890, and was advanced to statehood in 1907.

Postfrontier Farming

The basic problem facing the farmer on the Great Plains was a shortage of water. Two possible solutions to the problem were irrigation and "dry farming." Irrigation was never practical on the Plains frontier, as distinguished from the Great Basin or Pacific Coast provinces. A few small projects were carried on along the Platte and Arkansas Rivers. Generally, though, the rivers in the region were not suited to this operation, and there was insufficient ground water to support extensive projects. Nor, as the Donaldson report made clear, could the average farmer finance irrigation ditches. The federal government finally entered the picture in 1894, when Congress passed the Carey Act. This act provided for donations of up to 1 million acres of land to arid states if the tracts were irrigated. None of the states involved was in a financial position to take advantage of the law. Despite subsequent government assistance and encouragement, the amount of land under irrigation in the West has remained relatively small to this day.

Dry farming gave the farmer some partial success. This type of farming was first tried in Utah about 1863, but it was not widely practiced until the twentieth century. The method features deep initial plowing (12 to 14 inches) to bring subsurface water up to the plant roots by capillary action. Frequent harrowing is necessary to break up the soil and retard evaporation. Big machines, extensive acreage, and rapid work are required. When the farmer could put all these elements together, he was able to make a decent living in semiarid country. Coupled with this method was the introduction of types of wheat that needed little water; these were mostly Russian imports from the Crimean region.

Mechanization also made it possible to bring larger areas under cultivation. Machines for both planting and harvesting gradually made the farmer more efficient. Steel plows that could turn over the prairie sod more easily were developed in the 70s. The spring-tooth harrow, the grain drill, and the hayloader were all developed in the same decade. And the threshing machine, which separated the wheat from the chaff in one-fourth the time it took by the ancient hand-winnowing method, became a familiar sight on the Plains during the 80s.

The appearance of these machines was a threat as well as a blessing, for in the long run fewer numbers of farmers would be needed. The frontier farmer, that stock figure of American history since colonial times, had by 1890 passed the zenith of his prestige and economic power. Unfavorable prices for wheat, the high cost of machinery, and the rise of cities all contributed to his decline. One final outcry at the loss of influence and importance was the Populist movement of the 90s. But during the frontier years the pioneer farmer had contributed the bulk of the trans-Mississippi population, which rose from 6,877,000 in 1870 to 16,775,000 in 1890. All things considered, he was fully justified in singing that prideful yet plaintive song, "The Farmer Is the Man That Feeds 'Em All."

Selected Readings Though emphasizing the northern ranges, Ernest S. Osgood's *The Day of the Cattleman* (Minneapolis, 1929) is an excellent survey, available in paperback (Chicago, 1957). Edward E. Dale, *The Range Cattle Industry* (Norman, 1930), and Louis Pelzer, *The Cattlemen's Frontier* (Glendale, 1936), are also useful. Most of J. Frank Dobie's books deal with Texas ranching; *The Longhorns* (New York, 1941) is the classic analysis of the basic stock animal. Joseph G. McCoy told the story of Abilene in *Historical Sketches of the Cattle Trade* (Kansas City, 1874), reprinted in a Xerox edition (Ann Arbor, 1966). There is a vast amount of literature on cowboys. The best place to start would be Joe B. Frantz and Julian E. Choate, Jr., *The American Cowboy: The Myth and the Reality* (Norman, 1955). Phillip A. Rollins, *The Cowboy* (New York, 1922), is more detailed. Philip Durham and Everett L. Jones, *The Negro Cowboys* (New York, 1965), is an excellent piece of scholarship. John A. Lomax collected *Cowboy Songs* (New York, 1938). Of first-hand accounts, Andy Adams, *The Log of a Cowboy* (Boston, 1903), and James H. Cook, *Fifty Years on the Old Frontier* (Norman, 1957), are recommended. J. Marvin Hunter, *Trail Drivers of Texas* (Nashville, 1925), is also a collection of reminiscences. Ramon Adams, *Western Words* (Norman, 1944), is a useful tool.

Wayne Gard, *The Chisholm Trail* (Norman, 1954), is a classic on the most famous of the trails. Harry Sinclair Drago, *Great American Cattle Trails* (New York, 1965), is a popular work marred by some factual errors. Events in Abilene are chronicled in Stuart Henry, *Conquering Our Great American Plains* (New York, 1930), a book which caused an uproar because of its antiromantic views. Floyd B. Streeter, *Prairie Trails and Cow Towns* (Boston, 1936), is informative. Robert R. Dykstra, *The Cattle Towns* (New York, 1968), is a well-documented analysis and is strong on sociology. Nyle H. Miller and Joseph W. Snell, *Why the West Was Wild* (Topeka, 1963), is a definitive work, based on newspaper accounts, of sheriffs and gunfighters in Kansas. Joseph G. Rosa, *They Called Him Wild Bill* (Norman, 1964), traces Hickok's Abilene career. Robert M. Wright, *Dodge City, the Cowboy Capital* (Topeka, 1913), and Stanley Vestal, *Queen of the Cowtowns: Dodge City* (New York, 1952), are standard. For ranching on the northern ranges see Harold E. Briggs, *Frontiers of the Northwest* (New York, 1940); Merrill G. Burlingame, *The Montana Frontier* (Helena, 1942); and T. A. Larson, *History of Wyoming* (Lincoln, 1965).

On laws and customs see relevant chapters in Walter P. Webb, *The Great Plains* (Boston, 1931). Wayne Gard, *Frontier Justice* (Norman, 1949), is also useful.

Helena H. Smith, *War on Powder River* (New York, 1966), is a well-researched history of the Johnson County War. It may be supplemented by A. S. Mercer, *The Banditti of the Plains* (Norman, 1954), the reprinting of a primary source. Business aspects of the range industry are well described in Lewis Atherton, *The Cattle Kings* (Bloomington, Ind., 1961). Gene M. Gressley, *Bankers and Cattlemen* (New York, 1966), which details Eastern investment, is uneven in quality. Charles W. Towne and Edward N. Wentworth, *Shepherd's Empire* (Norman, 1945), is the best book on sheep ranching.

Gilbert C. Fite, *The Farmers' Frontier, 1865-1900* (New York, 1966), is a good compact history. Part III of Henry Nash Smith, *Virgin Land* (Cambridge, 1950), entitled the "Garden of the World," has many valuable insights on Plains farming. Everett Dick, *The Sod-House Frontier, 1854-1900* (New York, 1937), is the standard social history. Howard Ruede, *Sod-House Days: Letters from a Kansas Homesteader* (New York, 1937), and John Ise, *Sod and Stubble* (New York, 1926), are first-hand accounts. Carl L. Wittke, *We Who Built America* (New York, 1939), treats foreign immigration to the West. Louise Pound, "Old Nebraska Folk Customs," *Nebraska History*, vol. 28 (January, 1947), is a revealing article. Henry D. and Frances T. McCallum, *The Wire That Fenced the West* (Norman, 1965), updates the material in Chapter 7 of Walter Webb's *The Great Plains*. Donald F. Danker, "Nebraska's Homemade Windmills," *The American West*, vol. 3 (Winter, 1966), is well illustrated. Two studies of "Print" Olive's career are Mari Sandoz, *The Cattlemen* (New York, 1958), and Richard Crabb, *Empire on the Platte* (New York, 1967). Clifford P. Westermeier, *Trailing the Cowboy* (Caldwell, Idaho, 1955), rounds up contemporary newspaper articles on cowboy-homesteader troubles.

Paul W. Gates, "The Homestead Law in an Incongruous Land System," *American Historical Review*, vol. 41 (July, 1936), is the classic critique. This article and others by specialists are collected in Vernon R. Carstensen (ed.), *The Public Lands: Studies in the History of the Public Domain* (Madison, 1963). Fred A. Shannon, *The Farmers' Last Frontier* (New York, 1945), attacks various myths about the operation of the land laws, while Roy M. Robbins in *Our Landed Heritage* (Princeton, 1942) records their exploitation. Thomas LeDuc's article on "State Disposal of the Agricultural College Land Scrip" is reprinted in Carstensen's *Public Lands*. For a more optimistic view of the Homestead Law see Gilbert Fite's *The Farmers' Frontier*. Paul W. Gates, *Fifty Million Acres: Conflicts over Kansas Land Policy, 1854-1890* (Ithaca, N.Y., 1954), is a fine study of a key state. Hiram M. Drache, *The Day of the Bonanza* (Fargo, N. Dak., 1964), is the history of the Red River farms. Wallace Stegner, *Beyond the Hundredth Meridian: John Wesley Powell and the Second Opening of the West* (Boston, 1954), is useful.

Roscoe L. Lokken, *Iowa Public Land Disposal* (Iowa City, 1942), has some material on the land rush in that state. Carl C. Rister, *Land Hunger: David L. Payne and the Oklahoma Boomers* (Norman, 1942), recommended. W. Eugene Hollon, "Rushing for Land: Oklahoma, 1889," *American West*, vol. 3 (Fall, 1966), is an excellent short analysis. For details consult Roy Gittinger, *The Formation of the State of Oklahoma, 1803-1906* (Norman, 1939). John A. Widstoe, *Dry Farming* (New York, 1911), describes the dry-farming method.

XXIII. The West since 1890

In 1890 the American frontier came to an end. No less an authority than the Superintendent of the Census declared in a bulletin for that year that "up to and including 1880 the country had a frontier of settlement, but at present the unsettled area has been so broken into by isolated bodies of settlement that there can hardly be said to be a frontier line." Historians are fond of pointing out that the westward movement continued after the cutoff date. In 1894 there were 600 million acres available for homesteading, and more land was entered under the Homestead Act between 1898 and 1917 than between 1868 and 1897. But these were mostly marginal lands, suitable for grazing perhaps but not for general farming. The homesteader with pioneering in his blood had to go into the Canadian West if he wanted the same opportunities his father had known, and over 1¼ million Americans did just that. Still, some of the problems of the frontier period remained after 1890, and the institutions that were formed during the westward movement have been important in the contemporary or trans-Missouri West.

From Territory to State   Four Western territories were still knocking on the doors of statehood after 1890. America's territorial system had been established by the Northwest Ordinance of 1787, and modified somewhat by the Wisconsin Organic Act of 1836. In the post-Civil War period the system was neither a great success nor a spectacular failure; it was simply there. The major difficulty was that since the executive and judicial officers of the territory were appointed by Congress, they owed nothing to the people whom they governed. Political patronage was the distinguishing feature of the system, and this usually meant economic exploitation by the carpetbaggers. Naturally the quality of officials varied greatly. The complaint that Arizona was a "tarrying post for every political tramp for many years," is typical of comments from every territory. There were the inevitable clashes between the federal governor and the locally elected legislature. The New Mexico assmbly went so far as to print a governor's message with a preface referring to the "false, erroneous, absurd, and ill-sounding ideas contained therein."

The problems were similar to those of any colonial or quasi-colonial system. It is not surprising to find Westerners making occasional reference to George the Third when complaining about outside control. One finds them drawing up state constitutions containing long clauses which prevent the granting of favors to corporations and railroads. "Home rule" was the desired objective, and so the territories tried to gain statehood as quickly as possible.

Rivalry between the two national political parties caused a delay in statehood for many territories. After Colorado joined the Union in 1876, her three delegates voted for the Republican Rutherford B. Hayes, so Democrats blocked other statehood bills for more than a decade. But the Fiftieth Congress finally bowed to the inevitable. In 1889 it passed the "Omnibus Bill" which admitted North and South Dakota, Montana, and Washington. In 1890 Benjamin Harrison approved the admission of two other lightly populated territories, Idaho and Wyoming, since they were both expected to vote Republican. Wyoming's constitution supports Frederick Jackson Turner's contention that "the West is a rich museum of political forms and experimentation. . . ." The document included a provision for female suffrage, an experiment that some observers thought would be disastrous.

In the postfrontier period, the four remaining territories all became states: Utah in 1896; Oklahoma in 1907; and Arizona and New Mexico in 1912. The long delay in the admission of Arizona and New Mexico, which had been territories since 1850, is explained in part by the usual congressional maneuvering and in part by the mulishness of the residents. Both areas grew slowly because of their isolation and their semiarid environment. In 1880 Arizona had only 40,441 inhabitants, although New Mexico had a more substantial 111,000. Both had at first been included in the original Omnibus Bill of 1888, but the Republicans turned thumbs down on their admission at that time.

In 1904 a single-state or "jointure" proposal was made. This caused an uproar among the Arizonans, who feared domination by the Spanish-speaking New Mexicans. Arizona was largely Anglo-American and Indian, although it did have a Mexican minority. New Mexico was fundamentally Spanish in its culture, and there was a strong Catholic influence. This "foreignness" disturbed many Anglo-Saxons, including Senator Albert Beveridge, who happened to be chairman of the Senate Committee on Territories. Beveridge was quite conscious of the "white man's burden," and he did not feel that the Spanish-speaking New Mexicans were ready for citizenship. He opposed separate statehood for that territory, and was in a position to pigeonhole admission bills. The Arizonans themselves rejected jointure in a popular referendum in 1906.

In 1910 the enabling act for the two states finally passed the Congress. New Mexico adopted a conservative state constitution, but Arizona's constitution reflected contemporary progressive ideas. These included provisions for female suffrage and for the recall of judges. President William Howard Taft, a former judge, refused to sign the bill until this latter clause was deleted. The Arizona legislature acquiesced in the change, but after Taft signed the admission proclamation the Arizonans reinserted the offending provision. The Westerners seemed to have that maverick disposition typical of frontiersmen long after the frontier was gone.

From Exploitation to Conservation

The importance of the federal government in the trans-Missouri West may be seen in other areas besides the territorial system. After 1890 the historic policy of land exploitation began to turn toward conservation and reclamation. Before this date Congress had assisted and encouraged private citizens to occupy the public domain. The Timber and Stone Act of 1878 was a measure which revealed the traditional attitude. The law applied to lands in Nevada, California, Oregon, and Washington that were "unfit for cultivation." A citizen could buy 160 acres for $2.50 per acre—a virtual giveaway considering the real value of the land. Lumbermen and quarry operators employed dummy entrymen and acquired millions of acres under the law until it was repealed in 1908. It was this kind of heedless exploitation that aroused a small group of conservationists to press for action that would save some of the virgin land.

"National Parks" and "National Forests" were created as a result of the conservationists' appeals. Yellowstone National Park had been established on March 1, 1872, years before there was any conservationist movement. A group of visiting outdoorsmen had simply decided that the geysers and other "natural wonders" there should be protected from commercial exploitation. Yellowstone set a precedent for later parks. John Muir, the famous naturalist and publicist, spearheaded a movement that resulted in the creation of Yosemite National Park in 1890. As the recreational value of these areas was recognized, other parks such as Glacier (1910), Rocky Mountain (1915), and Grand Teton (1929) were added.

The Forest Reserve Act of March 3, 1891, was slipped through Congress before its opponents ever knew it was there. President Harrison's Secretary of the Interior, John W. Noble, tacked on a "rider" to a public-lands bill which declared that the President "may reserve timber . . . as public reservations." Under this law, Presidents Benjamin Harrison, Grover Cleveland, and Theodore Roosevelt set aside 132 million acres which now comprise the greater part of the national forests in the West. In 1907 a group of Western Senators managed to get the Reserve Act repealed. But the day before he signed this bill, Roosevelt created 16 million acres of new forests in the Northwestern states, enraging quite a few private enterprisers in the region.

Roosevelt is particularly identified with the modern conservation movement. He had been a rancher in Dakota during the 1880s, and he remained an enthusiastic hunter and camper all his life, believing that the outdoors developed "manliness." Roosevelt was also influenced by Gifford Pinchot, whom he appointed as chief of the Bureau of Forestry (now the U.S. Forest Service). Pinchot, described as being "tree mad," had studied forestry in Europe after graduating from Yale. He believed in scientific management and selective cutting of the remaining forest lands, a position which brought him into conflict with men like Muir who wished to preserve an untouched wilderness. But Pinchot did contribute to the formulation of a comprehensive federal conservation policy.

Roosevelt was also a strong advocate of reclamation programs. Actually the guidelines for such a program had been laid down years earlier by Maj. John Wesley Powell. Powell was one of four great government survey leaders who mapped and measured the West during the 60s and 70s. The others were Clarence King, Ferdinand V. Hayden, and Lt. George M. Wheeler, all of whom were as competent as Powell but who received less popular attention. In his *Report on the Lands of the Arid Regions of the United States,* published in 1878, Powell urged an intelligent land-classification system. He described a program for irrigation districts and dams that was almost a blueprint for Roosevelt and his conservationists.

The Newlands Act of 1902 established a United States Reclamation Service and declared that money from land sales in the sixteen Western states was to be used for the construction of irrigation works. The federal government has undertaken many reclamation projects in the years since 1902, with varied results. The Shoshone Dam near Cody, Wyoming, and Boulder Dam (renamed Hoover Dam) on the Colorado are examples of the greatest of these projects. Construction of the latter, for example, made possible the reclamation of the Imperial Valley in California. One of the most ambitious efforts of all came in the 1950s with an attempt to tame the Missouri River. Although billions of dollars were spent by the Interior Department and the Army Corps of Engineers, this particular project has had dubious results.

Reclamation and irrigation mean dams, and the construction of dams has always brought howls from the devotees of "wilderness." One finds the irrigationists, the hydropower engineers, the lumbermen, and the grazing and mining interests doing battle with the Sierra Club and the Wilderness Society over disposition of the remaining undeveloped areas. Hetch-Hetchy, Echo Park, Glen Canyon are some of the more famous episodes in the continuing preservation-versus-utilization struggle. "Conservation" has been a popular issue ever since 1900, and being against it now is like opposing motherhood. The growing political power of the preservationists was demonstrated by the passage of a National Wilderness Preservation Act on September 3, 1964. A broad, policy-setting measure, it gave legal protection to some 50 million acres of wilderness. This represents only about 2 percent of the nation's land area, perhaps enough to give modern Americans some idea of the type of continent that their forefathers knew.

Trends in the West

People have continued to migrate west, attracted in part by the myth of the frontier past. Population growth has been spectacular in several states, particularly California and Arizona. California's 1940 population of 6,907,000 had swelled to 15,717,000 in 1960, and the state seemed destined to move past New York and into first place. The city of Phoenix, Arizona, had 156,000 people in 1945; in 1965 the figure was 520,000. Much of this growth has been at the expense of the Plains states. Rural depopulation has become a serious problem for Kansas, Nebraska, and the Dakotas. The exodus of farmers, who now constitute no more than 7 percent of the national population, has been speeded by mechanization. The use of laborsaving machinery, which began in the last decades of the nineteenth century, has increased by leaps and bounds ever since World War I. The result has been consolidation and corporate farming. A traveler on the Great Plains today may go for miles without seeing a man, a dog, or a farmhouse. The old 160-acre homestead unit does seem anachronistic indeed in a region where farms now average 1,500 acres.

Another traditional frontier occupation, the mining of gold and silver, has also declined steadily. On the other hand, the "mining" of oil, essentially a postfrontier business, has been especially important in Oklahoma, Texas, and California. States without extensive petroleum resources have tried to attract industries, particularly those which are related to national defense, like electronics. Many have also made a vigorous attempt to attract tourists, an industry of no small importance. Still, the long-range results of industrial growth are less than might be expected. With a few noted exceptions like Denver or Phoenix, the trans-Missouri West has not produced great metropolitan centers. While the region has become "urbanized," this description does not mean the same thing as it does in the East, that is, numerous cities with more than 50,000 people. The industrial and urban growth of the West has been and will continue to be limited for various reasons. It suffers from high freight rates, an absence of navigable rivers, and most important of all, a shortage of water. When the historian Walter Prescott Webb went so far as to describe all the country from the Missouri to the center of California and Oregon as a "desert," he was assailed

by Western newspaper editors who told him to take off his glasses and his
Ph.D. because he was in for a fight. While the West is becoming more like the
East in many respects, the stark facts of geography will always limit its industrial
potential.

One other fact of immense significance in the contemporary West has
been the presence of the federal government. In some cases, as with military
installations or defense plants, this presence is welcomed since it means larger
local payrolls. But Indian reservations, national forests, and other federal
reserves of various kinds are seen to be of dubious value, since they cut the
state's tax base. The federal government owns 47.7 percent of the land in the
eleven westernmost states. The percentages are staggering in some individual
cases, as for example 87.4 percent of Nevada and 64.4 percent of Utah. Much
of the land is worthless to the state; in Nevada the federal property is used for
bombing and gunnery ranges. On the other hand, much of the Indian and forest
reserves are valuable, and the states naturally would like to pry them loose for
exploitation. It appears that the pressure for utilization of these national properties will increase, particularly in the Rocky Mountain states.

An American Myth

The westward movement has been the greatest of our national myths. This myth
or fable has been the subject of a great body of popular literature. Novels,
plays, dime novels, movies, and television dramas have been based upon the
history of the West, principally the trans-Missouri region, but their purpose is
not the accurate exposition of history. They serve the imagination, and they
convey romantic rather than realistic concepts about the frontier experience.

It so happened that the romantic movement in literature coincided
with the westward movement in history. When James Fenimore Cooper began
publishing his Leatherstocking novels in 1823 with *The Pioneers*, he added the
frontier to the list of subjects that were suitable for romantic literary interpretation. His principal character, a buckskin-clad hunter who resembled Daniel
Boone, was such an attractive model that subsequent authors created quite
similar heroes. Cooper's major theme also influenced the tradition, emphasizing
as it did the melancholy implications of pioneering. That is, the pioneer's success
means the coming of civilization (usually symbolized by a woman character) and
the end of the freedom associated with frontier situations.

In the post-Civil War period the dime novels, five-and-ten-cent
thrillers written primarily for young boys, became the vehicle for the myth. The
plots were often diluted versions of Cooper's, while the characters were contemporary or near-contemporary individuals like Kit Carson, Wild Bill Hickok,
and Buffalo Bill Cody. The illustrated covers bore such titles as *Buffalo Bill's
Boys in Blue*; or *The Brimstone Band's Blot-Out* and *Wild Bill the Pistol Dead*

Shot; or *Dagger Don's Double.* Prentiss Ingraham, Edward S. Ellis, and Ned Buntline [E. Z. C. Judson] turned out dozens of these novels with assembly-line efficiency. When asked about his literary method, Ingraham replied: "Bang, bang! And another redskin bit the dust!" The stories tell us much about the postwar generation and particularly its views on racial matters.

One must not overlook the contribution which William F. Cody made to the myth. Cody had acquired a considerable reputation as a buffalo hunter and scout by 1872, and in that year he went East at the urging of Ned Buntline to appear in a play called "The Scouts of the Prairie." Cody was not one of the more modest men in American history, and he found that he enjoyed posturing before the footlights. It was an easy step from the stage to the Wild West Show, which Cody produced beginning in 1883. This was a distinctively American type of entertainment. It featured pony races, steer roping, Indian dances, and a reenactment of "The Attack on the Deadwood Stage." The cowboys' share of the program set a pattern for the rodeo, a type of roping and riding contest which is still popular in the United States. The sharpshooting of Annie Oakley was also a top attraction. Up until 1910 the show was an enormous success both here and in Europe, where Cody made tours in 1887 and again in 1889. The West became associated with drama and pageantry as a result of the performances.

The literary evolution of the "western" continued after the decline of the dime novel in the 1890s. Owen Wister's *The Virginian* (1902), which has sold over 1.6 million hardbound copies, set a pattern for hundreds of novels which were to be written over the next several decades. The Virginian lived by a chivalric "code" which among other things made it necessary for him to meet the villain in a face-to-face gunfight. Square-jawed heroes and beautiful Eastern schoolmarms were familiar characters in the novels of Zane Grey and Max Brand (Frederick Faust), the two most widely read Western authors to follow Wister. Although Grey died in 1939 and Brand in 1944, their works continue to be reprinted. They are popular because they give body and form to the myth.

The rise of the western novel was paralleled by development of the western movie. Edwin S. Porter produced *The Great Train Robbery* in 1903, and from this point on, the western has had a special place in American life. It would be impossible to overestimate the importance of these films on our views of frontier history. It is doubtful if college courses on the westward movement would be so numerous had not the western become so popular. Three generations of Americans have been enthralled by the heroics of William S. Hart, Tom Mix, Gary Cooper, John Wayne, and other Hollywood demigods. The stories in which these stars have appeared may purport to be based on history, but they are basically fairy tales in which the "good guys" invariably defeat the "bad guys." Indeed, history has been as putty in the hands of the

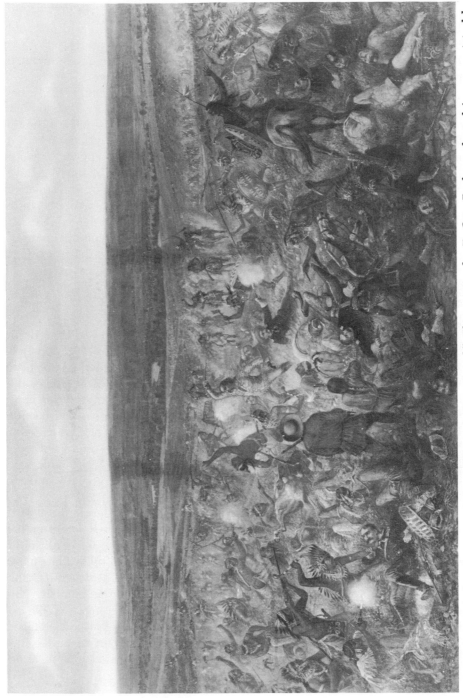

One of America's best-known paintings, "Custer's Last Stand." This version by F. Otto Becker, adapted from an original by Cassilly Adams, was used in beer advertisements. Custer's use of a sword is one of the historical inaccuracies in the painting. Source: Anheuser-Busch, Inc.

motion picture producer. He works and shapes it until it meets the needs of a ticket-buying mass audience. The result is a body of myths comparable to those of the ancient Greek world.

Television has added a further dimension to the myth. The proliferation of westerns on the new medium in the mid-1950s caused a severe depression in the market for both western novels and run-of-the-mill western movies. Many of the TV series have exploited actual historical figures, notably Wild Bill Hickok, Wyatt Earp, and Daniel Boone. The longest-running series has been *Gunsmoke*, featuring Sheriff Matt Dillon of Dodge City. Tourists continually ask for information about this individual, and the Kansas Historical Society must regretfully advise that "no police officer of this name ever served in early Dodge City." Thus does the line between history and fable become blurred in the popular mind.

The West itself has been quite willing to perpetuate the legend of its own past, although this was not always the case. In the early years of this century, many towns seemed ready to forget their wild and wicked period. But since Easterners were fascinated by the "Old West," the Westerners also began to glorify the long-ago days and even to manufacture a woolly past where necessary. So there are Covered Wagon Days, Frontier Days, Pioneer's Days, and similar celebrations. Prescott, Fort Worth, Cheyenne, and Dodge City sponsor the more prominent of these events.

Political leaders have also employed and furthered the myth at times. President John F. Kennedy was calling upon the old dream when he titled his legislative program the "New Frontier." The slogan suggested that he was trying to utilize the pioneering spirit to meet contemporary problems. President Lyndon B. Johnson, a native of Texas, has declared that "the Frontier in America is neither dead nor dormant—it lives as a source of our national vigor." The symbolism of the frontier does seem to have great appeal, and there is little question but that it remains a molding force in our civilization.

Mr. Turner and his Thesis

Historians as well as novelists and television producers have contributed to the interpretation of our frontier past. By far the most influential of the scholarly interpreters has been Frederick Jackson Turner (1861-1932). In fact, the American Historical Association voted Turner and Francis Parkman the two most significant historians of America. For some of his followers, Turner's thesis ranked just below the Bible and the Constitution as a sacred text. Nowadays, however, the true believer is in the position of the youth who claimed that his gun was the same one which "Grandpap" had carried through the Revolution. A traveler observed that since it had a new stock, barrel, and flintlock it must be a new gun, but the youth still insisted that it was "the same old gun 'Grandpap' carried through the Revolution."

The future professor was born in Portage, Wisconsin, a town located on the old French-Indian fur-trading route between the Great Lakes and the Mississippi Valley. A few mournful Indians still lived in the vicinity, and Turner grew up listening to stories and traditions of the frontier days. After graduating from the University of Wisconsin, he went to Johns Hopkins University in Baltimore, to study for a Ph.D. degree. Here he was a student of Herbert Baxter Adams, foremost exponent of the "germ theory." This emphasized the inheritance of institutions from Europe, particularly from medieval Germany, and left little room for environmental influences. In an essay on "The Germanic Origin of New England Towns," Adams declared that "the tree of English liberty certainly roots in German soil," and that "town institutions were propagated in New England by old English and Germanic ideas, brought over by Pilgrims and Puritans, and as ready to take root in the free soil of America as would Egyptian grain which had been drying in a mummy-case for thousands of years." Such views pleased many, including Theodore Roosevelt, who were admirers of Anglo-Germanic culture. But Turner thought they ignored the frontier experience.

Upon returning to Wisconsin as an instructor, Turner set out to revise the germ theory. A voracious reader, he studied population statistics and economic theory as well as political history. In view of the fact that his thesis emphasized the uniqueness of America, it is interesting that Turner borrowed much from French and Italian scholars. He was particularly indebted to Achille Loria, who had pointed to the effect of free land upon a nation's economic growth. By 1893 the various ideas had coalesced into a definite theory about American history. This theory was presented in a short paper entitled "The Significance of the Frontier in American History," which Turner read before the Chicago meeting of the American Historical Association.

Turner's thesis sentence was that "the existence of an area of free land,* its continuous recession, and the advance of American settlement westward, explain American development." Thus the man-land relationship was the key to history, and geography had an important role in determining national institutions. Turner's definition of the unoccupied-land area or "frontier" was two-sided, since the word meant both a place and a process. The frontier as *place* was never sharply defined; Turner simply called it "the mere edge of settlement" or "the outskirts of civilization." The frontier as *process* referred to the "perennial rebirth" of society in each new area. There was an evolution from primitive simplicity back up to urban complexity—a process measured by the repeated appearance of the same occupational types in succession: fur traders, cattlemen, miners, pioneer farmers, equipped farmers. This concept of the evolution of society from simple to complex forms clearly owed much to the contemporary influence of Darwinian science.

*By "free" Turner meant land that was unoccupied rather than land that was free of price tags.

Turner attributed quite a bit to the frontier environment-experience. Its influence was seen in the areas of nationalism, democracy, and the American character. He regarded the frontier as an agency for Americanization. Turner used the word "crucible" rather than "melting pot" (which did not become common until 1908), but the idea was the same. "In the crucible of the frontier the immigrants were Americanized, liberated, fused into a mixed race, English in neither nationality nor characteristics." Most of his supporting references were to the Scotch-Irish and Germans of the Old West frontier. In legislation, the frontier areas always worked to strengthen the national power. Turner cited as evidence the Louisiana Purchase and the demands for federally financed internal improvements. In its social and economic makeup the West was neither "North" nor "South," but a composite and hence national section.

Turner was not the first to equate the frontier with democracy. E. L. Godkin, editor of *The Nation*, had suggested the mutual dependence of the two in an essay published in 1865. But Turner made the most forceful statement of the relationship. Many of his memorable passages occur in works other than the frontier essay. In a commencement address of 1914 he stated that "American democracy was born of no theorist's dream; it was not carried in the *Susan Constant* to Virginia, nor in the *Mayflower* to Plymouth. It came out of the American forest, and it gained new strength each time it touched a new frontier." Critics have worked this passage over on numerous occasions, their basic position being that American democracy owes more to Milton, Locke, and Blackstone than to the frontier.

The democracy theme was also emphasized in the 1893 essay. The individualism or self-reliance attributed to frontiersmen worked toward social and political democracy. This assertion was supported by references to voting patterns and to the frontier origins of great American democrats. It was *western* New York which forced an extension of the suffrage in 1821. Such revered leaders as Thomas Jefferson, Andrew Jackson, and Abraham Lincoln were all raised near the edge of settlement. Turner especially stressed the rise of equalitarian doctrines associated with the election of his namesake, Jackson, whom he seems to have regarded as the Moses of democracy. One other idea which was suggested rather than elaborated at length was that of the safety valve. The frontier was a "gate of escape" from the oppressions of a closed society, and its existence helped to nurture democracy.

Finally, the essay was a classic statement about the American character. "To the frontier the American intellect owes its striking characteristics." Among these traits were individualism, practicality, materialism, and optimism. The "myth" of frontier individualism has been dissected by several writers, and other critics were to claim that these were the traits of all Americans and not just frontiersmen. Implicit in Turner's analysis was the assumption that America and Europe were at opposite ends of a scale, and that the further west one went the more "American" he became.

Turner's paper did not cause many ripples when it was first presented. But the author developed his theme further, as in an 1896 article for the *Atlantic Monthly*, and within a decade the "frontier thesis" was well known in the historical profession and among educated readers. The thesis really had all the elements for a classic document, since it seemed to express popular beliefs about the westering experience. Theodore Roosevelt wrote Turner that "I think you have struck some first class ideas, and have put into definite shape a good deal of thought which has been floating around rather loosely." This was Turner's real genius and real achievement: he brought all these half-conscious and unformed ideas together in one bold and coherent statement.

The subsequent history of the thesis is a record of the changing circumstances and moods of the American people. Up to the Great Depression of the 1930s it was regarded as the gospel truth. But in 1933 an explanation of our history based upon the agricultural frontier seemed irrelevant to an industrial civilization. One of the most poignant documents in that year was Louis M. Hacker's article on "Sections—or Classes?," published in *The Nation*. This accused Turner of "fabricating" a tradition in which there was a basic disregard of class antagonisms, which according to Hacker was now the most important problem in the nation. Throughout the 40s other critics also assailed what they usually called the "hypothesis." Most of these were brilliant young scholars who lived in east coast cities, who had had little contact with the West, and who emphasized the English heritage as the major component of American civilization.

Determining the truth of the Turner thesis is about as easy as measuring the density of fog. Much of the criticism has been in the nature of hairsplitting, such as faulting Turner for his imprecise definition of "frontier." It is difficult to see anything wrong with multiple meanings, and in American usage the word has always been loosely defined. Scholars like Fred A. Shannon who attacked the "safety valve" idea were, in effect, using a howitzer on a mosquito. Turner's "gate of escape" was offered more as a suggestion than as an assertion. Shannon did demonstrate that the Eastern wage earner could not afford to move directly west, but then Turner had never made such a claim. Recent scholarship has suggested that the frontier was in the nature of a sociopsychological safety valve; if people *believed* that the West was a gate of escape they would be less inclined to political radicalism.

Critics have been more on target when they fired at Turner's claims for nationalism and democracy. It is apparent, from the tenacity with which Germans, Scandinavians, and some other groups held on to their native languages and traditions, that the frontier was not as much of a melting pot as Turner thought. Or rather, that the Americanization process worked much more slowly than he had assumed. As far as the frontier and democracy equation is concerned, Utah and New Mexico form embarrassing exceptions. The Mormons and the Spanish-speaking New Mexicans both had paternalistic systems, and although the frontier modified their institutions to some extent, it did not make them Turner-style democrats. There is also a debate, still unresolved, over the extent to which democracy was carried into the West from the East by means of state constitutions, representative assemblies, and the like. And finally, there is the logical difficulty that if free land is responsible for democracy, one must explain the persistence of democracy after 1890. David Potter has theorized that science and technology might be the real cause of our success.

The concept of the frontiersman's individualism has been undermined somewhat, since there are numerous instances of group effort. On the earlier frontiers, there were community cabin raisings and husking bees. In the trans-Missouri West there were stockmen's associations, miners' courts, and claims clubs. Yet the theory of the relationship between the frontier and democracy seems to be the most firmly anchored of all. The narratives of European travelers in the West tend to buttress the thesis on this point. And studies by Merle Curti and his associates in Wisconsin have lent support to Turner's contentions. However, more research still needs to be done on this problem.

Other critics have emphasized the irrelevance of the thesis to our increasingly urbanized world. There is nothing in the essay pertinent to urbanism, to labor, to racial minorities. By its focus on internal migration it has tended to promote isolationism in an increasingly interdependent world. Even at its best, Turner's conclusions apply to the Midwest and not to other frontiers. It may be seen that practically every sentence and implication of the essay has come in for minute and usually unfriendly microscopy.

Recent analyses of the thesis have focused upon the metaphorical nature of Turner's statement. The "rebirth" of society on successive frontiers is one of these metaphors; the crucible concept is another. Metaphors are not subject to the rules of logic, since they are a type of poetic language. The argument is that Turner was so entranced by his metaphors that they blinded him to the facts. He became a "prisoner of the agrarian tradition." The thesis thus tells us more about American assumptions and beliefs than about the actual frontier. Like the story of Jonah and the Whale, it must be judged more as a statement of faith than as a record of truth.

It does seem that the West has been a state of mind as well as a fact of history. The very word is associated with ideas or emotions suggesting youth, opportunity, freedom. Since Americans are still a mobile people, "the West" appeals to a certain restlessness in the heart of each of us. It is true that in an urban civilization the world of the actual frontier seems ever more distant in both time and relevance. But the myth of the West is so much a part of our historical consciousness that it will never die. Like the purple sage on the deserts, it blossoms year after year.

Selected Readings   Earl Pomeroy, *The Territories and the United States, 1861-1890* (Philadelphia, 1947), is a basic monograph. Frederic L. Paxson's *History of the American Frontier* (Boston, 1924) has a classic chapter on the admission of the "Omnibus" states. For more detail see Howard R. Lamar, *Dakota Territory, 1861-1889* (New Haven, 1956). Lamar's article on "The Reluctant Admission: The Struggle To Admit Arizona and New Mexico to the Union," is printed in Robert G. Ferris (ed.), *The American West: An Appraisal* (Santa Fe, 1963). For more extensive analysis see Lamar's *The Far Southwest, 1846-1912: A Territorial History* (New Haven, 1966).

Roy M. Robbins, *Our Landed Heritage* (Princeton, 1942), details the changes in land policy and the rise of conservation. Roderick Nash, *Wilderness and the American Mind* (New Haven, 1967), is an excellent analysis of the conservation movement. Leo Marx, *The Machine in the Garden: Technology and the Pastoral Ideal* (New York, 1964), is also written from the point of view of intellectual history. Stewart Udall, *The Quiet Crisis* (New York, 1963), has much on national forest policy. John Ise, *Our National Park Policy: A Critical History* (Baltimore, 1961), and Michael Frome, *Whose Woods These Are: The Story of the National Forests* (Garden City, N.Y., 1962), are technical studies. Part III of William H. Goetzmann, *Exploration and Empire* (New York, 1966), deals with the great surveys.

On the contemporary West, Neil Morgan, *Westward Tilt: The American West Today* (New York, 1963), is a well-written account of the major developments. Robert G. Athearn, *High Country Empire* (Lincoln, Nebr., 1960), and W. Eugene Hollon, *The Southwest: Old and New* (New York, 1961), may be read together for a rounded picture of the whole central region. Earl Pomeroy, *The Pacific Slope* (New York, 1965), carries the story down to the mid-60s. Walter Prescott Webb's article on "The American West: Perpetual Mirage," appeared in *Harper's Magazine*, vol. 214 (May, 1957). In *An Honest Preface* (Boston, 1959), Webb describes the reaction of Westerners to his essay.

Henry Nash Smith, *Virgin Land* (Cambridge, 1950), analyzes both Cooper and the dime novels. Lucy L. Hazard, *The Frontier in American Literature* (New York, 1927), is best on the earlier frontiers. James K. Folsom, *The American Western Novel* (New Haven, 1966), is a scholarly analysis. Kent L. Steckmesser, *The Western Hero in History and Legend* (Norman, 1965), examines how novelists and dime novelists interpreted individual heroes. Don Russell, *The Lives and Legends of Buffalo Bill* (Norman, 1960), is definitive. Mody C. Boatright, "The American Rodeo," *American Quarterly*, vol. 16 (Summer, 1964), is of interest. George N. Fenin and William K. Everson, *The Western: from Silents to Cinerama* (New York, 1962), is a well-illustrated survey.

Turner's essay is printed in his *The Frontier in American History* (New York, 1920). It has been reprinted in paperback collections, which also include articles attacking or defending his thesis: George Rogers Taylor (ed.), *The Turner Thesis* (Boston, 1956); Ray Allen Billington (ed), *The Frontier Thesis: Valid Interpretation of American History?* (New York, 1966); and Richard Hofstadter and Seymour Lipset (eds.), *Turner and the Sociology of the Frontier* (New York, 1968). The Taylor collection includes Louis Hacker's *Nation* article and George W. Pierson's "The Frontier and American Institutions," one of the most trenchant critiques of the thesis. The Billington collection has one of Fred A. Shannon's articles attacking the "safety valve" idea, and David Potter's exposition of the role of abundance. O. L. Burnette, Jr. (ed.), *Wisconsin Witness to Frederick Jackson Turner* (Madison, 1961), is also a convenient collection of articles, most of them dated in the 1920s and 1930s. H. B. Adams' article, "The

Germanic Origin of New England Towns," was printed in the *Johns Hopkins Studies in Historical and Political Science*, vol. 2 (Baltimore, 1882).

Ray Allen Billington, *America's Frontier Heritage* (New York, 1966), examines the contemporary relevance of the Turner thesis, and includes an extensive bibliography on the "history of a theory." Most of the critical articles are in specialized periodicals. For a helpful guide through the maze see Walter Rundell's fine descriptive bibliography, "Interpretations of the American West," *Arizona and the West*, vol. 3 (Spring, Summer, 1961). Lee Benson, *Turner and Beard* (Glencoe, Ill., 1960), examines the influence of Loria upon Turner. William Coleman, "Science and Symbol in the Turner Hypothesis," *American Historical Review*, vol. 72 (October ,1966), is an outstanding article which examines the impact of Darwinism upon Turner. Jack D. Forbes, "Frontiers in American History," *Journal of the West*, vol. 1 (Summer, 1962), explores definitions of "frontier." Everett Lee, "The Turner Thesis Re-examined," *American Quarterly*, vol. 13 (Spring, 1961), and George M. Pierson, "The M-Factor in American History," *American Quarterly*, vol. 14 (Summer, 1962), both suggest that migration was more important that "pioneering." Merle Curti and others, *The Making of An American Community* (Stanford, 1959), tested the thesis by an intensive sociological study of Trempealeau County, Wisconsin. "In sum, our study, both in its quantitative and qualitative aspects, lends support to what we believe are the main implications of Turner's thesis about the frontier and democracy, so far as Trempealeau County is concerned." A required book for serious students.

Recent volumes which include critiques of the thesis from the point of view of economics, religion, history, and literature include David Potter, *People of Plenty* (Chicago, 1954); T. Scott Miyakawa, *Protestants and Pioneers* (Chicago, 1964); Francis S. Philbrick, *The Rise of the West* (New York, 1966); and Henry Smith's *Virgin Land*. David W. Noble, *Historians against History: The Frontier Thesis and the National Covenant in American Historical Writing* (Minneapolis, 1966) maintains that Turner and other prominent historians have presented an oversimplified view of our past. A good short analysis of the ups and downs of the Turner thesis is Earl Pomeroy, "The Changing West," in John Higham (ed.), *The Reconstruction of American History* (New York, 1962). See also W. N. Davis, Jr., "Will the West Survive as a Field in American History?," *Mississippi Valley Historical Review*, vol. 50 (March, 1964).

Index